Mies in Berlin

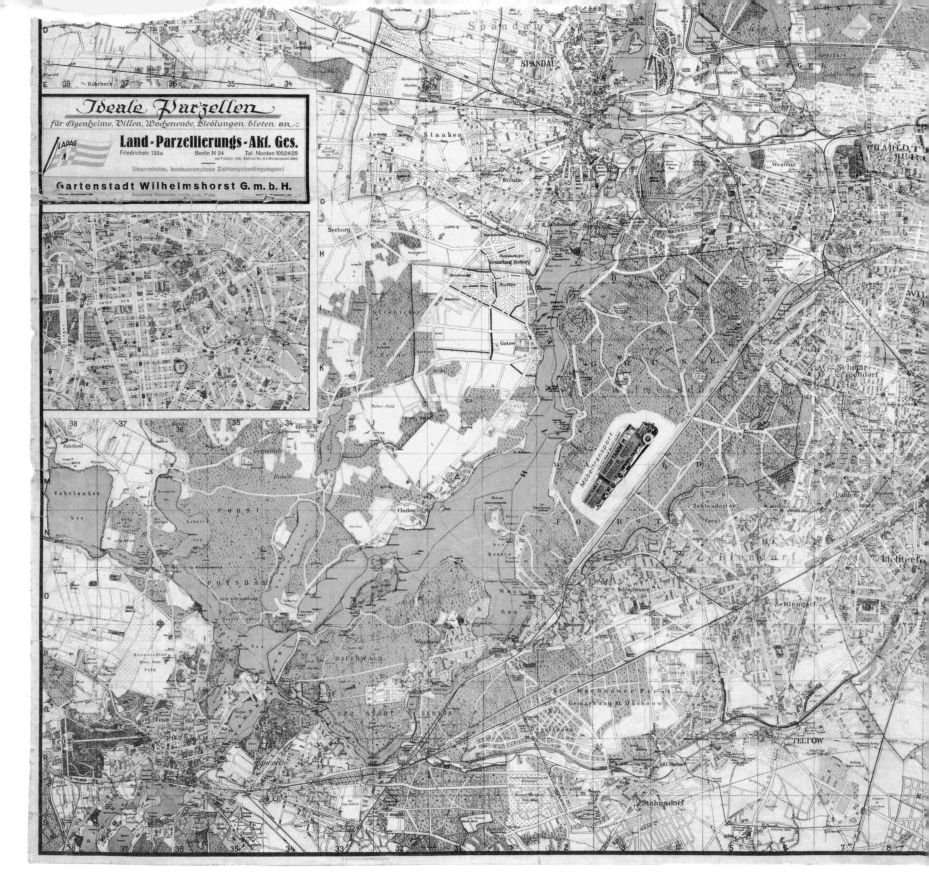

MIES IN BERLIN

TERENCE RILEY

BARRY BERGDOLL

With essays by

VITTORIO MAGNAGO LAMPUGNANI, DETLEF MERTINS,

WOLF TEGETHOFF, FRITZ NEUMEYER, JAN MARUHN,

ANDRES LEPIK, WALLIS MILLER, ROSEMARIE HAAG BLETTER,

AND JEAN-LOUIS COHEN

And with **l.m.v.d.r.,** *a Project by* THOMAS RUFF

The Museum of Modern Art, New York

Distributed by Harry N. Abrams, Inc., New York

Published in conjunction with the exhibition *Mies in Berlin*, at The Museum of Modern Art, New York,
June 21–September 11, 2001, organized by Terence Riley, Chief Curator, Department of Architecture and Design,
and Barry Bergdoll, Professor, Department of Art History, Columbia University, New York

The exhibition travels to the Staatliche Museen Zu Berlin–Preussischer Kulturbesitz, Berlin,
December 14, 2001–March 10, 2002; and the Fundación La Caixa, Barcelona, July 30–September 29, 2002

This exhibition is made possible by UBS PaineWebber and the Getty Grant Program

Generous support is also provided by the Lily Auchincloss Foundation, Inc.,
Peter Norton, Norton Family Foundation, Tishman Speyer Properties, and Knoll, Inc.

Additional funding is provided by Elise Jaffe and Jeffrey Brown, Mrs. Frances Lewis,
Sarah Peter, and The Government of The Federal Republic of Germany

Produced by the Department of Publications, The Museum of Modern Art, New York

Edited by David Frankel
Design by Antony Drobinski, Emsworth Design, Inc., with Gina Rossi
Production by Marc Sapir
Printed by Stamperia Valdonega, S.R.L., Verona
Bound by Legatoria Zanardi, Padua

The essays in this book by Vittorio Magnago Lampugnani, Andres Lepik, Jan Maruhn, and Fritz Neumeyer, and
the plate-section text by Lars Scharnholz, were translated from the German by Russell Stockman. The essay by
Jean-Louis Cohen was translated from the French by Jeanine Herman

This book is typeset in Walbaum, originally designed by Justus Erich Walbaum, and in Venus Medium and Bold
Extended, from the Bauer type foundry. The papers are 135 gsm Gardapat and 150 gsm Phoenix Imperial

Published by The Museum of Modern Art,
11 West 53 Street, New York, New York 10019

Clothbound edition distributed in the United States and Canada by Harry N. Abrams, Inc., New York
Clothbound edition distributed outside the United States and Canada by Thames & Hudson Ltd, London

Library of Congress Control Number: 2001088553
ISBN: 0-87070-018-9 (clothbound, MoMA/Thames & Hudson)
ISBN: 0-8109-6216-0 (clothbound, Abrams)
ISBN: 0-87070-019-7 (paperbound, MoMA)

Printed in Italy

Cover: Thomas Ruff. d.p.b. 02. 1999. Chromogenic color photograph, 51³⁄₁₆ x 6'4¼" (130 x 195 cm). Courtesy
Zwirner & Wirth, David Zwirner, Inc. Foldout, outer panel: Karl Friedrich Schinkel. *Ansicht der Linden mit Blick
auf Museum, Dom, und Schloss* (Perspective view of the museum from Unter den Linden with the cathedral and
the palace). 1823. Pencil on paper, 21⅞ x 43⁵⁄₁₆" (55 x 110 cm). Staatliche Museen zu Berlin. Kupferstichkabinet.
Sammlung der Zeichnungen und Druckgraphik (Schinkel-Archiv). Inner panel: *Berlin nebst Potsdam. Beilage
zum Berliner Adressbuch 1930* (Berlin and neighboring Potsdam. Insert to the Berlin directory 1930).
Printed color map. Berlin: August Scherl Press, 1930. Landesarchiv, Berlin

Contents

Director's Foreword

The work of Ludwig Mies van der Rohe was first featured at The Museum of Modern Art in 1932, in the landmark "International Style" exhibition curated by Philip Johnson and Henry-Russell Hitchcock. That exhibition presented Mies as one of the leading lights of a transnational movement in modern architecture, one with deep roots in the European avant-garde. In 1947, Mies's work appeared again at the Museum, although in this instance he was presented not as a peer among many but as the leading figure in the effort to come to terms with modernism as the official means of architectural expression in the postwar world.

In 1968, Mies made an unprecedented gift to the Museum: his entire archive of some 20,000 drawings and other papers. Bringing his relationship to the Museum full circle, the gift immeasurably enhanced our holdings in the key documents of modern architecture, but also placed a unique responsibility upon the Department of Architecture and Design. Since the 1986 exhibition of Mies's entire career, organized by Arthur Drexler on the occasion of the centennial of the architect's birth, the Department has labored to present an ongoing series of smaller exhibitions looking at various aspects of Mies's work in detail. In addition, a twenty-five-volume catalogue was published of the drawings in the Archive, giving scholars wide access to the Museum's holdings for the first time. And Franz Schulze,

in cooperation with the Museum, produced an in-depth biography that has become the standard reference on the architect's life.

In organizing *Mies in Berlin*, Terence Riley and Barry Bergdoll have added a new dimension to The Museum of Modern Art's relationship with Mies and his work. More than a generation after his death, the exhibition and book take a critical look at the architect's work in Europe—in and of itself. In his own lifetime, Mies did not make this distinction between his European and his American work, and as an active practitioner of the "building art" (as he referred to architecture), he should not have been expected simultaneously to be his own historian. Nevertheless, current scholarship has demonstrated that recognizing the cultural and physical roots of his European work is vitally important in fully understanding the breadth of his accomplishment. If Mies's work is to have relevance to a new generation of architects, that relevance will come not from periodic studies of his well-known masterworks but from a deep appreciation of the ways in which he was able to connect architecture to the most profound currents of the culture in which he conceived it.

—*Glenn D. Lowry*
Director, The Museum of Modern Art

Preface

Ludwig Mies van der Rohe was fifty-two years old when he set out to start his career anew in the United States, in the summer of 1938. Former director of the Bauhaus, active participant in associations, exhibitions, and publications of the Berlin avant-garde in the 1920s, he had seen his built work and theoretical projects featured in surveys of contemporary architecture not only in Europe but in the United States, in The Museum of Modern Art's first exhibition of architecture, the 1932 "International Style" show. Yet in the first book-length monograph on Mies, which accompanied the 1947 retrospective exhibition of his work at the same museum, Philip Johnson's preface opened with the claim, "Of all the great modern architects Mies van der Rohe is the least known."

In 1947, now over sixty, Mies and his long-time champion Johnson were able to present an impressive portfolio of current projects in Chicago. They also began the work of crafting a seamless history for an architect who, like so many of his compatriots, had experienced a rupture and estrangement every bit as dramatic as the new beginnings prophesied in the artistic manifestos of the years after World War I. For the next two decades—until Mies's death, in 1969—the work of crafting a design vocabulary for post–World War II America and the interpretation of the architect's three decades of practice in Berlin would remain inextricably linked. Mies's fascination with America, first announced in the early 1920s in dramatic skyscraper projects that would have fundamentally altered the image of the German capital with beacons of a new, secular culture, came to be seen retroactively as but the first steps toward the triumph of International Style clarity on the shores of Lake Michigan and in the stone-cliff cavern of Park Avenue.

Historians and critics of architecture and art have in recent years undertaken a critical analysis, even a deconstruction, of the heroic narratives of the modern movement, posing new questions and opening up new possibilities for both an intellectual and a creative engagement with architectural modernism's diverse production. These critical studies challenge us to engage afresh with the legacy of the many émigrés who began new career trajectories in America after National Socialism dispersed the creative impulses and personnel of the cosmopolitan art scene of Weimar Berlin. Yet as late as 1986, the centennial year of Mies's birth, his Berlin and Chicago productions were again treated as the seamless creation of a detached master architect, in Arthur Drexler's retrospective of Mies's work at this Museum. Drexler's exploration was little troubled by the tumultuous political, economic, and social upheavals that divided and characterized the two periods. The time admittedly was not ripe; at the height of architectural postmodernism, and of popular enthusiasm for the type of flip cliché that Tom Wolfe took up with gusto in *From Bauhaus to Our House* (1982), that retrospective found a chilly critical reception.

In 2001, fifteen years later, the situation has radically changed. A diverse and creative engagement with Mies's work is everywhere in evidence. Since the re-creation of the German Pavilion, Barcelona, in 1986, fervently discordant and original interpretations of the building have reopened the possibility of thinking about the physical experience and the ambiguous contingencies of that icon, frozen until then in black and white photography and in a rigidly canonical interpretation of its significance in the history of modern architecture. A creative reengagement with Mies's studies of transparency, as well as questions about architecture in relationship to nature, technology, and human consciousness, echo in the work of two generations of architects who have come to prominence since 1986, in everything from Herzog and de Meuron's Napanook winery in Napa, California, to Rem Koolhaas's Maison à Bordeaux, to Jesse Reiser and Nanako Umemoto's proposal for an ambitious rethinking of the American subdivision now under study in Bridgehampton, Long Island. These examples and many others convinced us of the timeliness of a fresh look at Mies's early work, even as a parallel exhibition organized by the Canadian Centre for Architecture, Montreal, and curated by Phyllis Lambert, was setting out to reappraise the architect's North American career after 1938. Together the two exhibitions reexamine both Mies's work in its original context and what it has to offer to the ongoing critical reevaluation of the legacy of modernism.

Mies in Berlin begins with the simplest of questions, namely, What would happen if we looked forward into Mies's career, rather than backward and retrospectively? How would we think about the architect—and about the works of both his apprentice years before World War I and his nearly two decades of practice after the war from his apartment/architectural studio at Am Karlsbad 24—if we forgot for a moment that in 1938 he left Berlin for Chicago? The aim of this exhibition and book is to situate Mies in a series of overlapping contexts that defined his architectural ambitions and practices from the moment of his *first* emigration, from the provincial city in which he was born— Aachen, in the old Prussian Rhineland—to Berlin, which was then emerging not only as the capital of imperial Germany but as a metropolis, one of the great new cities of exchange, ideas, images, and of course capital. To tell the story of Mies's ambitions to be a great architect in Berlin, we decided to restore him to the physical and cultural landscape that shaped his career, and that he ultimately proposed shaping in turn. In both the dense and vibrant urban center of Berlin and the great work of landscape and garden art that was the landscape of Potsdam, developed since the eighteenth century as an extraordinary dialogue between architecture and nature, Mies developed ideas about houses, office and commercial buildings, and

monuments that simultaneously reflected and engaged the cultural and architectural traditions of the Prussian capital.

But the landscape of Berlin is to be understood not simply as a set of physical givens, or of buildings by such past masters as Karl Friedrich Schinkel. It was also a place of contemporary models and discourses. Mies worked for Bruno Paul and then Peter Behrens, both of whom were addressing the development of a complete domestic environment for modern times, including in the architect's purview the design of furnishings and of the garden, viewed as a complementary space to the interior. Mies would also have been exposed to vehement debates over the very nature of the city as a place of economic exchange, of information, of altering patterns of the private and public spheres. He would have heard arguments over public housing, and over the possibility of a memorial in a time of political turmoil. These issues are the background and the subject matter of his work.

The challenge for *Mies in Berlin* was to avoid the kind of editing that Mies himself practiced on his German career when he eliminated nearly a dozen built and unbuilt works from the active record, favoring a handful of manifesto projects done for competition and exhibition and a small group of built works from the late 1920s and early '30s. This exhibition and book are the results of three years of research, during which a Columbia University seminar at The Museum of Modern Art (made possible by a generous grant from the Getty Trust) and numerous trips to Germany, Spain, Poland, and to the Mies van der Rohe Archive at the Library of Congress all played their parts in a comprehensive look at all of Mies's production—not only his famous projects but the buildings he later deemphasized or ignored, such as the neo-Biedermeier Werner House of 1912–13 and the Schinkelesque addition to a Potsdam private school of 1924. Seeing the two groups of projects together has yielded new insights into both.

The essays that compose this book were conceived as the first attempt at a synthesis of Mies's German career, intended not so much to offer a definitive new account—although we believe this survey to be more complete than any previous one—as to open new territory for discussion and interpretation. After an introduction by Terence Riley on the historiographical paradox of launching such an invitation to new thinking about Mies from The Museum of Modern Art, which has contributed more than any other institution to the image of the architect that has survived to this day, four major essays are organized in complementary pairs, reflecting the dualistic reasoning apparent in many of Mies's own notes on architecture. A first pair looks at the contexts of Berlin and Potsdam, the urban and suburban landscapes of Mies's thought and work. Vittorio Magnago Lampugnani situates Mies in relation to the pressing debates of his time over the urban form of Berlin, in terms not only of concrete proposals for the physical revamping and expansion of the city but of the very nature of the modern metropolis. Barry Bergdoll looks afresh at Mies's domestic work, analyzing the relationship of the architect's house designs both to the legacy of German Romantic ideas about landscape, nature, and consciousness and to early-twentieth-century German ideas on the reform of the garden. Mies's interest in the reform garden, a virtually unknown aspect of his thought, is of interest in its own right, but it serves here to open up a far-reaching line of research into the relationships between interior and exterior space in Mies's architecture.

The second pair of essays couples a provocative reading of Mies's response and contribution to Berlin's artistic avant-gardes in the 1920s with a discussion of his deep relationship to the architectural past. Detlef Mertins, whose 1990 conference and publication *The Presence of Mies* marked a new application of fresh critical interests and methods to the architect, looks at issues of transparency, spatial experimentation, and organic analogies in Mies's work, revealing its relationship to experiments as diverse as Expressionist painting and abstract film. His essay is followed by Wolf Tegethoff's exploration of Mies's response to the Berlin building tradition, with its inherently conservative tectonic and social demands. After a plate section including not only visual documentation but explanatory texts on Mies's German projects, a series of shorter essays by both established and younger scholars of Mies and of German modernism present recent discoveries that expand our knowledge of the architect's career, or offer new perspectives from which to explore his work. The book closes with an essay by Jean-Louis Cohen on what America was to Mies before he saw it—that is to say, what American modernism, architecture, urbanism, and culture meant to Mies as he moved forward on the path of his own work, confronting the challenges of modernization, of technology, of philosophical alienation, through architecture.

Mies's notion of the exhibition as a place in which to broach new ideas, and to try to capture and provoke its public with a visible portrait of a world in the throes of evolution and change, set the background for our own ambitions here. We hope that *Mies in Berlin*, as both exhibition and book, will offer new insights and questions about the architect's significance, both historically and in our own new century, that might fruitfully be developed in the ongoing critical appraisal of the legacy of architectural modernism.

—*Barry Bergdoll and Terence Riley*

Making History: Mies van der Rohe and The Museum of Modern Art

TERENCE RILEY

The Museum of Modern Art played a near exclusive role in shaping popular and critical understanding of Ludwig Mies van der Rohe's architecture for sixty years, from the 1932 "International Style" exhibition to the 1986 posthumous retrospective honoring the centennial of his birth. The authoritative role assumed by the museum, a virtual monopoly by mutual consent, is inversely proportional to Mies's diffidence about appearing as a salesman for his own architecture. Furthermore, Mies's reputation for being aloof and inaccessible might account for the fact that in 1947 there were very few writings *by* him and even fewer *about* him.[1]

A survey of the publications that followed the 1947 retrospective of the architect's work at the Museum, ten years after Mies's emigration to the United States, affirms the success of both Mies, the designer of the exhibition, and Philip Johnson, the author of the exhibition's publication,[2] in their respective tasks. The exhibition itself was widely covered in the media, from professional journals such as *Architectural Record* and *Architectural Forum* to general-circulation magazines such as *The New Yorker* and *Town and Country*. A smaller revolution might be seen in the exhibition design: its distinctive minimalist character and overscaled photomurals were frequently imitated in later exhibitions at the Museum, as well as at other museums around the world. The most enduring of all the Mies histories, Johnson's 1947 book is the principal source of virtually all of what might be called the common knowledge of Mies's life, work, and beliefs. Not the least of its contributions to the professional and public awareness of Mies is Johnson's quotation of the architect's "personal motto: less is more"[3]—words that have passed into near universal use.

If the book has assumed an outsized authority in the architect's bibliography, its uniqueness must be underscored. Until that time, not a single book, in any language, had been devoted to the architect's then four decades of work. Published in three editions and translated into both Spanish and German, Johnson's book has been in print nearly continuously for over a half a century.[4] Inasmuch, the seminal exhibition of 1947 serves as the lens through which this essay looks at the evolution of MoMA's representation of the architect, and at the nature of that representation in light of research available today.

Johnson's and Mies's efforts were complementary but not necessarily equivalent to one another. Whereas Johnson's book aspired to a traditional art-historical narrative, Mies's "text"—though not a text in the traditional sense—had its own message. The design can be "read" to discern his intentions: his attention to detail is famous and his experience as an exhibition designer was extensive. In 1928 he had put his thoughts about exhibitions into writing, declaring that they "must be demonstrations of leading forces" and "bring about a revolution in our thinking."[5] A wall label in the exhibition confirms his role: "This exhibition, the first comprehensive retrospective showing of the work of Mies van der Rohe, is also the architect's latest design. He is responsible for the nature of the display, its plan, the appearance of the room in which you stand."[6] Notwithstanding, there were logistical limitations on the material that could be shown; the vast majority of Mies's drawings were still in Germany, and were less accessible to the Museum than various kinds of photographic material—negatives, studio photographs, and copy prints.[7] But Mies used this material to great advantage, and perhaps to better effect than the drawings themselves would have had. Some of the images were greatly enlarged, recalling the scale of his oversized renderings of the 1920s.

Ada Louise Huxtable, who was a curatorial assistant on the exhibition (and later the architecture critic for the *New York Times*), commented at the time, "Using a new approach to the display of architecture, the photographs shown will be very large (the largest 20' x 14') and so arranged that they can be viewed from a distance to give the effect of actual buildings."[8]

As a whole, Herbert Matter's photographs of Mies's installation (frontispiece) show a remarkable resemblance to the collage perspectives of Mies's project for a Museum for a Small City (1942), which were included in the exhibition (fig. 1).[9] Within the existing gallery space, an area of roughly seventy by seventy feet, Mies designed a configuration of four freestanding partitions arranged in a pinwheel fashion (fig. 2). To one side of each of these partitions he attached a large photomural, edge to edge and floor to ceiling, so that it appeared to float in space, like the images of Picasso's *Guernica* (1937) in the Museum for a Small City collages. Mies also used groupings of the furniture he had designed for the German Pavilion, Barcelona (1928–29), and the Tugendhat House, Brno (1928–30), to further delineate the space, much as he had in the projects on display.[10]

Mies's intentions are well captured in photographs of the installation, particularly those by the American designer Charles Eames. In one photo Mies's furniture in the gallery appears before the photomurals of the Tugendhat House and the Friedrichstrasse Skyscraper Project (1921), so that the furniture in the gallery is superimposed over that in the Tugendhat photomural,

and over the visitors passing between. The perspectival spaces of the photomurals meld with that of Eames's photograph (fig. 3).

While Johnson's essay is divided into four chronological segments, Mies's design reflected no chronological or thematic narrative. The viewer would have had to glean any such references from the project titles, and from the abbreviated project descriptions discreetly placed next to the projects. The title of the exhibition—simply *Mies van der Rohe*—had no bracketing dates or other modifiers, and there were no extensive wall texts. As much as Johnson's essay was to be read, Mies's

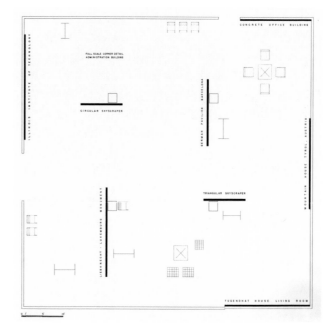

1 (bottom). Ludwig Mies van der Rohe. Museum for a Small City Project. 1942. Collage of cut-and-pasted reproductions and photographs on illustration board, 30 x 40" (76.2 x 101.6 cm). The Museum of Modern Art, New York. Mies van der Rohe Archive. Gift of the architect

2 (left). *Mies van der Rohe*, The Museum of Modern Art, New York. 1947. Curated by Philip Johnson, designed by Mies. Plan of exhibition. The Lily Auchincloss Study Center for Architecture and Design, The Museum of Modern Art, New York

installation design was a visual experience. The photography and perspective renderings favored an eye-level view; there were no axonometric drawings and only four plans and elevations. Also, with two entrances, Mies's pinwheel plan for the gallery had no particular direction to its circulation.

The earliest work Mies chose for the exhibition was the Kröller-Müller Villa Project (1912–13), the show's sole example of his dozen or so more "traditional" projects from before or soon after World War I. The most recent was his ongoing work for the Illinois Institute of Technology (IIT), in Chicago. Framed by these were two dozen projects, evenly divided between those completed

3. Installation view of *Mies van der Rohe*. The Museum of Modern Art, New York. 1947. Curated by Philip Johnson, designed by Mies. Photograph: Charles Eames. The Lily Auchincloss Study Center for Architecture and Design, The Museum of Modern Art, New York

before and after Mies's emigration, even though the former represented thirty years of work and the latter ten.

While this might indicate that the architect favored his newer work, the placement of the projects was subtler. All four of the freestanding photomurals and three others affixed to the outer walls represented European works.[11] Balancing this dominance were five models of American projects designed in the decade since Mies had emigrated, interspersed within the pinwheel plan: the Resor House, the Farnsworth House, the Drive-In Restaurant, the Group of Court-Houses, and the Library and Administration Building for IIT. A full-scale mock-up of the corner detail planned for the Library and Administration Building was also included.

The less historical dimension introduced by the lack of a chronological narrative in Mies's exhibition

design was reinforced by his use of new photographic prints of his work, in standard formats. The effective "newness" of all the material in the exhibition is evident in the installation photographs; no wear and tear distinguished the older projects from the newest.[12] The four principal photomurals, on the freestanding partitions, featured two unbuilt projects from the first half of the 1920s—the Friedrichstrasse Skyscraper Project of 1921 and the Glass Skyscraper Project of 1922— and two later, realized projects: the Monument to the November Revolution (1926) and the German Pavilion for the 1929 International Exposition in Barcelona. Three more projects were also distinguished by the photomural presentation, although they were hung less prominently, on the gallery's outer walls: the Concrete Office Building Project (1923), the Tugendhat House, and the Mountain House Studies (c. 1934)—one of Mies's designs for a house for himself, this one on a site in the Alps (1933).

As mentioned, the exhibition had two entrances. Opposite one entrance, two-thirds of the way across the gallery, the partition with the Friedrichstrasse Skyscraper photomural, seen in the Eames photograph in fig. 3, loomed before the visitor. This prominent display seems to confirm that, twenty-five years later, Mies continued to cherish this groundbreaking work, despite his younger critics' resistance to what they considered its residual Expressionism. The other entrance was in practice the principal entrance, and was marked by the exhibition's title, so that Mies's selection facing it—placed on the opposite side of the room, and framed by the freestanding partitions—held one of the most important places in the exhibition. Of all the messages that might be discerned from Mies's installation design, the central position, evident in Matter's photograph, of his unbuilt and relatively unheralded Mountain House is the least expected.

Part of Mies's task in organizing the exhibition, of course, was to exclude certain works, if only through limitations of space. Of this kind of editing, little can be said that isn't speculative, but some of his exclusions are notable, even curious. Whereas Johnson, in his essay, devotes considerable attention to Mies's role in planning the Weissenhof Housing Colony Master Plan in Stuttgart (1925–27) and designing the most prominently located

apartment house there, Mies omitted both from the exhibition. In fact he showed few large-scale works other than the skyscraper designs. The Urban Design Proposal for Alexanderplatz, Berlin (1929), the office buildings for Berlin and Stuttgart, the Reichsbank competition for Berlin (1933), the Administration Building for the Verseidag Silk Weaving Mills, Krefeld (1937–38)—all illustrated in Johnson's book—were not in the exhibition.

Mies's exclusion of his work prior to World War I (with the exception of the Kröller-Müller Villa) and his more traditional projects up until 1924 reflects a more systematic revision of his career. Between the end of the war and the mid-1920s, Mies turned away from the overt neoclassical influence of his former employer Peter Behrens, seeking to express the fundamental cultural shift created in the wake of the collapse of the German Empire. Not only did he radically reorient his architecture during these years, he took a new name (conjoining his mother's name with his father's to become Ludwig Miës van der Rohe) and adopted a new life as a socially unconventional bachelor-artist, distancing himself from his wife and children, and eventually settling into a permanent estrangement from them.[13] In that same period he directed an assistant to discard his more traditional architectural drawings to make room in the atelier.[14] In other words, he seems to have wedded the transformations he was going through to a negation of his past work and life.[15]

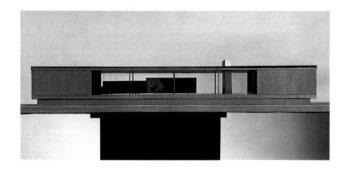

Mies's radical personal and professional transformation of the first half of the 1920s was not the first time that he had reappraised his earlier work. His designs for his first four residential commissions, the Riehl, Perls, Kröller-Müller, and Werner houses, show

that between 1907 and 1913 he was equally attracted to a stripped-down vernacular style and to the more classical approach evident in the work of his renowned employer Behrens. The enthusiastic reviews of the Riehl House would certainly have been an encouragement to the then twenty-year-old architect to pursue the former. However, two versions of the Perls House—the first with a steeply pitched roof like those of the Riehl and Werner houses, the second with a lower profile, more pronounced cornice, and more classical window and door openings—would indicate that Mies was not confirmed in his thinking at the time.[16]

The resolution of these conflicting impulses appears to have been the Kröller-Müller Villa Project. In the coming years Mies would try to have this design exhibited,[17] and would have it illustrated—along with the second scheme for the Perls House—in the books accompanying both the 1932 "International Style" exhibition and the 1947 retrospective. Meanwhile he refrained from publishing his more frankly vernacular works after 1911. In this decision he greatly influenced public and professional perception of his earliest European work, which came to be known in the 1920s as traditional yet reflecting, not the essentially local and less lofty influences of the vernacular, but broad classical themes in the manner of the nineteenth-century architect Karl Friedrich Schinkel. Indeed, as Mies reoriented his practice in those years, his rejection of the vernacular appears as outright disdain. Often, the "context" buildings that he included around his models and other renderings of his visionary projects of the 1920s seem to be dark and misshapen caricatures of traditional German vernacular structures.

Meanwhile some of Mies's inclusions in the 1947 show need further mention as well, specifically the Resor House Project and the Group of Court-Houses, of the

4 (left). Ludwig Mies van der Rohe. Resor House Project. 1937–38. Model of revised version, c. 1947: wood, plastic, paper, glass, copper, and paint, 5¾ x 48⅜ x 28⅛" (14.6 x 122.8 x 71.4 cm) The Museum of Modern Art, New York. Mies van der Rohe Archive. Special Purchase Fund

5 (below). Ludwig Mies van der Rohe. Resor House Project (detail). 1937–38. Photocollage of revised version, c. 1947: pencil and photograph on illustration board, 30 x 40" (76.2 x 101.6 cm). The Museum of Modern Art, New York. Mies van der Rohe Archive. Gift of the architect

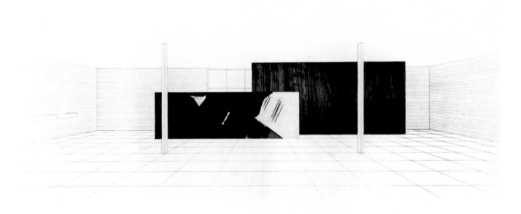

6. Ludwig Mies van der Rohe.
Court-House Project (detail). After
1938. Photocollage: pencil, wood
veneer, and cut-out reproduction
on illustration board, 30 x 40"
(76.2 x 101.6 cm). Delineator:
George Danforth. The Museum
of Modern Art, New York.
Mies van der Rohe Archive.
Gift of the architect

late 1930s. The design of the Resor House shown in the exhibition was significantly reworked from the design of 1938. The original design presented to the client is now little known, despite its status as Mies's first project for an American site. That same year the client decided not to build the house, and does not appear to have commissioned its redesign. The model and collage perspectives that Mies produced for the 1947 exhibition were an idealization of the actual project, with much of the actual Wyoming site eliminated. Johnson's description in the book reflects the original design of the house as "stretching across a river and resting on two stone bases."[18] In the reworked design, though, the house appears not at all like a bridge but rests solidly on a plinth (fig. 4). Furthermore, the new collage, which includes a postcard-perfect view of the Teton Range looming beyond the glass facade (fig. 5), replaced an earlier collage that featured the actual view from the site, with scattered camplike structures in the foreground.

Mies's installation also included three collage perspectives of interior views (fig. 6). These images hung on the wall behind the model for the Group of Court-Houses, which a wall label referred to as "the furthest development of Mies's 'court-house' scheme of 1931."[19] This rather modest arrangement had an enormous effect on the perception of Mies's work, introducing the term "court-house" into what is now near universal usage in the lexicon of modern architecture and generating entire books devoted to the study of this typology. The relationship between the model, which had been

produced as part of a student exercise at IIT, and the collages deserves scrutiny, however; none of the collages portrays any of the spaces in the model. Two of them correspond to a group of projects for Margarete Hubbe in Magdeburg in 1934–35,[20] while the third reflects a type of studio problem that Mies regularly assigned to his students at the Bauhaus and at IIT, where he taught in 1930–33 and 1938–58 respectively. George Danforth, one of Mies's students and later his successor as head of the Department of Architecture at IIT, confirms that all of the court-house material in the exhibition was made by himself and other students at the school.[21]

Mies's reworking of older designs, and his production of new collages from historical material, have caused confusion in interpretations by Johnson and by Mies's other chroniclers. Yet his actions are far from unique. Less interested in historiography than critical presentation, architects have refined older work for new exhibition and publication since Palladio's *I Quattri Libri*, in 1570. Even so, fully understanding these works means understanding what was *not* being represented: in the case of the Resor House, the real rather than the ideal landscape, in the case of the court-house, the longer history of its development through the work of Mies's students at the Bauhaus and IIT.

Mies's presentation of his work should be judged not as a historical account but as a project in itself. Like many of his best projects, it was collagelike in appearance— a product of studied excisions and additions that must be looked at both as a whole and in part. Inasmuch as the design had no linear narrative, it had no beginning and no end: Mies unsurprisingly focused on the evolving nature of his work, rather than on an accounting or summation.

Johnson, on the other hand, aspired to the authoritative narrative of traditional art history. I will not reprise his account in full here, but will summarize the points that have most influenced our perception of Mies, and particularly our understanding of his European work.

The first of Johnson's chapters covers Mies's earliest years, his professional formation, and his career until he was thirty-four. Johnson's account of Mies's childhood is notable in that, brief as it was, it was the first of any length to appear in print. Its influence can be seen in many other publications, all of which virtually repeat the outlines of Johnson's version.

Johnson's opening paragraph lays a foundation for his later interpretations of Mies's work of the 1940s. The architect's birthplace of Aachen is deemed significant: it was "the first capital of the Holy Roman Empire, had been the center of Western culture during the Early Middle Ages, and the Cathedral School, which Mies attended, had been founded by Charlemagne in the ninth century." Accordingly, for Johnson, Mies's childhood years bestowed upon him a specific heritage: a "medieval concept of order expressed in the writings of St. Augustine and St. Thomas Aquinas," which "influenced his architectural philosophy fully as much as modern principles of functionalism and structural clarity."[22] The book further outlines Mies's background as the son of a stonecutter and later as an apprentice tradesman, before moving into a more elaborate account of his first years in Berlin.

Here the text becomes more critical, as Johnson turns to the time Mies spent working for Behrens. Johnson positions the earliest of Mies's projects illustrated in the book, the Perls House, opposite his employer's Schröder House, both from 1911 (figs. 7, 8). Through Behrens, Johnson links Mies to Schinkel: "Mies at the age of twenty-five had become as accomplished

a designer in the Schinkel tradition as his teacher [Behrens]."[23] In fact Johnson—like Paul Westheim twenty years earlier, in the first published essay devoted to Mies's work[24]—interprets all of the prewar projects illustrated in terms of Schinkel's "romantic" classicism, rather than of his own initial reference to any medieval concept of order.

Johnson's efforts to present Mies's early work faced at best lukewarm endorsement from Mies. In the case of the Riehl House, with its more vernacular, less Schinkelesque profile, Mies apparently expressed outright disapproval: Johnson writes in the book's foreword, "Mies considers the Riehl House too uncharacteristic to publish."[25] Mies's first design for the Perls House, which was among those discarded in the mid-1920s, would no doubt also have been "too uncharacteristic" for Johnson's book. Copies of the drawings filed with the Zehlendorf building department show that it, too, had a steeply pitched roof reminiscent of Heinrich Tessenow's neovernacular buildings at Hellerau (figs. 9, 10). Indeed, the lower roofline and many of the other more classical elements of the Perls House were sketched over the finished drawings at the building department in Mies's own hand, suggesting that those elements were added late in the process.

Johnson closes his history of Mies's early career with the flat-roofed, Schinkelesque Kempner House (1919), of which he observes, "This was Mies's last Romantic design."[26] He seems to have been aware that this was incorrect,[27] but it was a position that Mies endorsed, at least tacitly, as it served to draw a polemical line between his work of the teens and his work of

7 (far left). Ludwig Mies van der Rohe. Perls House, Berlin. 1911–12

8. Peter Behrens. Schröder House, Hagen (now demolished). 1907–9

9. Ludwig Mies van der Rohe. Perls House, Berlin, 1911–12. Elevation: architectural print, 18⅛ x 30⁵⁄₁₆" (46 x 77 cm). Bezirksamt Zehlendorf von Berlin

10. Heinrich Tessenow. Bildungsanstalt für rhythmische Gymnastik/Dalcroze-Institut (Institute for rhythmic gymnastics/ Dalcroze institute), Hellerau. 1910. Perspective

the 1920s. Johnson's second chapter, which covers the years 1919–25, diverges from the first in several aspects, the most important of which is the historical method: where the first chapter follows what might be called a "vertical" line of thinking, the second is "horizontal" in framework, its references being contemporary and much broader than architecture alone. The text cites the positive influence of De Stijl, Russian Constructivism, Suprematism, and Dadaism—and the negative influence of Expressionism—in the fields of architecture, film, painting, and sculpture, as well as Mies's role in promoting them through his directing and financing of the avant-garde journal *G*.[28]

The illustrations for this chapter are devoted exclusively to five startlingly original projects that Mies designed between 1921 and 1924: the Friedrichstrasse Skyscraper, the Glass Skyscraper, the Concrete Country House, the Concrete Office Building, and the Brick Country House. Johnson's estimation is unambiguous: "Mies's position as a pioneer rests on these five projects."[29] The fact of Mies's watershed moment is beyond question, although Johnson goes farther in defining it than previous accounts had done—including his own of 1932.[30]

To justify his characterization of the five projects, Johnson needed not only to create a starting point for Mies's period of innovation—the Kempner House of 1919, purportedly the last "Romantic" design—but an endpoint as well. The opening paragraph of the third chapter did just that: "By 1925 the Weimar Republic was no longer revolutionary; hopes for a new and better world had dimmed. The period of experimental architectural projects was drawing to a close and for the first time since the war buildings were actually under construction."[31]

While the division of the 1920s into "visionary/ experimental" and "realistic/activist" shines a brilliant

light on the now canonical quintet from 1921–24, it has the reciprocal effect of isolating the subsequent work from any theoretical or ideological underpinning. The idea that the Barcelona pavilion was generated after a period of experimentation had drawn to a close limits our understanding of its theoretical achievement. The distinction between built and unbuilt, which is part and parcel of Johnson's demarcation (though it was not reflected in Mies's exhibition design), also separates the earlier projects from those that represent their

intellectual development. The Wolf House (1925–27) and the Monument to the November Revolution, for example, which flow across the mid-decade, experiment boldly with an architectonic language of shifting planes, interlocking masses, and spatial flows suggested in Mies's Brick Country House.

While Johnson's text creates a breach between the earlier and later work of the 1920s, it also suggests an underlying unity to Mies's work of the 1930s. Of those years he writes, "From 1931 to 1938 Mies developed a series of projects for court-houses in which the flow of space is confined within a single rectangle formed by the outside walls and the house conjoined."[32] Johnson's account deserves scrutiny, as it has not only been repeated in virtually every subsequent history of the architect's career but has spawned a whole bibliography of interpretations, the most popular of which sees the "court-house" as evidence of Mies's increasing withdrawal from his former public roles as a publisher, teacher, and critical leader of the profession under the mounting pressure of political crises.

The origins of the term "court-house," however, are not absolutely clear. English-speaking readers in 1947 might have presumed that the hyphenated term was German in origin, since both Huxtable's exhibition label and Johnson's text set it off with quotation marks. Yet the term appears in none of Mies's published writings before the 1947 exhibition.

A statement in a letter Mies wrote fifteen years after the exhibition both confirms and expands on Johnson's account: "I made these projects at the Bauhaus and during the years 1931 to 1938."[33] It isn't clear that Mies had explained to Johnson that his work on the court-house concept during the 1930s was nearly exclusively in the context of his teaching. Only one major court-house project, for Margarete Hubbe, emerged out of his practice; and most of the court-house drawings illustrated in Johnson's book were actually related to the Gericke and Hubbe houses (1932 and 1934–35), or else were made by Mies's IIT students, who reworked not only Mies's own designs for the Hubbe project but, most likely, designs by his former Bauhaus students, copies of which were circulated in the IIT studios. Not that the term "court-house" or its German equivalent, "*Hofhaus*," appears in any Bauhaus document—it does not—but it may well be that the genesis of the court-house neologism can be found in another term that was used there: *Flachbau mit Wohnhof*, literally, low construction with living court.[34] While Johnson expands the idea of a court-house scheme to include virtually all of Mies's work of the 1930s, it is clear that the studies Mies undertook to subdivide the Hubbe site in 1934 are the only instance outside of his teaching in which he designed residential structures wholly enclosed within a walled precinct. [35]

While the court-house continues to be thought of as Mies's archetypal project of the 1930s, if any project were to symbolize the effect of the political upheaval of that time on Mies's outlook, it would be the Mountain House, thought to be designed for a site in the Alps, where the architect had spent summer vacations and to which he decamped for a few months in 1933 with his collaborator and companion Lilly Reich and a few students after the closing of the Bauhaus by the Nazis. Of the several schemes that Mies generated as part of this exercise, the version that was included in Johnson's book and exhibition is the most elaborated.[36] In this scheme, an L-shaped structure wraps two sides of an open court. The approach to the house is on the opposite side from the court; the outside corner of the structure would have faced the visitor. While the facade facing the court is rendered in sheets of glass, the facade facing the approach is rendered in rough stonework, battered like an archaic fortification. A massive oak tree is part of the composition, standing like an immovable sentry before the entrance to the fragile glass house within. Whether consciously conceived as such or not, the Mountain House serves as an apt metaphor for the besieged architect, deprived of public commissions, in the cultural climate of Nazi Germany.

Johnson encapsulates the rise of National Socialism in a closing paragraph. "With the Nazis hostile to everything he represented, Mies began to look toward the more hospitable climate of America. He left Germany in the summer of 1937, and in 1944 he became an American citizen."[37] The narrative then segues into chapter 4, covering the years 1937–47 and discussing the first new projects for IIT.

Johnson's account of the master-planning phase for IIT includes illustrations of the earliest "ideal" studies, intermediate studies, and the final scheme of 1940, which laid out roughly twenty proposed buildings in a grid extending from one end of the campus to the other. Johnson devotes a large section of this chapter to the buildings for IIT that had been completed in 1947—the Minerals and Metals Research Building and the Alumni Hall—as well as the Chemistry Building, which was under construction, and the proposed Library and Administration Building. He continues his narrative with relatively brief descriptions of the Resor House, and with three commissions then still in design: the Farnsworth House, the Drive-In Restaurant, and the Promontory Apartments in Chicago. In addition to these commissions, Johnson includes an account of three self-initiated projects: a design for a plastic molded chair, the Museum for a Small City, and the Project for a Concert Hall, which Johnson singles out as Mies's "most astounding new creation."[38] In the book's closing paragraph, Johnson takes a stance more proactive than objectively historical, claiming that the latter three projects, "like all of [Mies's] American work, [are] exerting an even greater influence today than did his famous five projects of the early twenties."[39]

It should be clear by now that Mies's exhibition design and Johnson's essay intersected on some issues and differed on others, due to, not least of all, the nature of their respective roles and media. Indeed, as attested to in the design, Mies's attitude toward his own work (like that of many artists) was distinctly ahistorical, cast in a permanent present tense. The collagelike way in which he moved his projects in and out of a self-created pattern is evidence that he considered these projects first as ideas, and only second as objects or events bound in time and space. This attitude reappears in Ludwig Hilberseimer's monograph on Mies, of 1956: Hilberseimer, who taught with Mies at the Bauhaus and later at IIT, presented the work much as Mies had in 1947, intermingling projects by type, without any reference to chronology. Nor did he even mention in his text the fact that the architect was born in Germany and had emigrated, under dire circumstances, to the United States—a fact noted only in the biographical notes, on the book's last page, alongside the photograph credits.[40]

Simply by virtue of the fact that Johnson's text presents Mies's work chronologically, it is a document significantly different from the exhibition design. While Johnson maintains that Mies's earlier work is less dated than that of any of his contemporaries,[41] each of the book's four chapters refers to specific events—the architect's nineteenth-century birth, World War I, the state of the Weimar Republic in the mid-1920s, the rise of National Socialism in the 1930s—that inevitably cast a greater historical distance over Mies's European work than does Mies's own account.

Also, where Mies gave pride of place, in the form of the four freestanding photomurals, to the Friedrichstrasse Skyscraper, the Glass Skyscraper, the Monument to the November Revolution, and the German Pavilion in Barcelona—in other words, to works that span the 1920s—the central event of Johnson's narrative is his construction of an epiphanic transformation represented in the five canonical projects. While there is no disputing the importance of these projects, the creation of a uniquely visionary phase in Mies's career does more to cast Mies as a heroic artist in the Romantic tradition than to account for his architectural development. To make the five projects central is to force Mies's work into a "before" and an "after," leaving unsaid the possibility of continuities through the teens, 1920s, and 1930s. Mies himself, of course, had critically rejected his early vernacular interests and all but a few representative works from before World War I. In including them in the book, however, Johnson was not so much contesting Mies's decision as satisfying his own historical sensibility and, more important, heightening the drama of Mies's subsequent conversion.

From a contemporary perspective, Johnson's chronicle in this regard needs less correction than fleshing out. A revision of Mies's history need neither devalue the importance of the five projects nor overvalue the works preceding them. The latter, however, do need to be seen as more than prologue, and to be appreciated for their own merits. Whatever their stylistic differences, many of the projects from the teens are excellent in their conception and clarify Mies's development. The Riehl House, for example, may be traditionally vernacular in its appearance, but its positioning atop a prominent retaining wall is the first of many instances throughout Mies's career in which he used a podium to raise a structure above the ground plane. Similarly, the siting of the Urbig House (1915–17), with its extended rear terrace and its switchback stair leading into the landscape, clearly prefigures the basic compositional elements of the Tugendhat House and many others. The sketches for the first House for the Architect in Werder (1914) provide an equally introspective harbinger of the interlocking interior volumes and enclosed exterior spaces that would later characterize the German Pavilion in Barcelona and projects of the 1930s and later. In details, too, important continuities can be discerned: the vaunted "negative corner" of the proposed IIT

Library and Administration Building is clearly prefigured in the detailing of the Urbig House (figs. 11, 12).

While Johnson's account of Mies's career in Europe creates dramatic highs and lows, it also insinuates a line of thought in which Mies's work is referred to decreasingly in terms of German architectural and cultural influences and increasingly in more abstract and "universal" terms. Mies's first built work, the Riehl House, is described as an example of "the then popular traditional eighteenth-century style."[42] The architect's subsequent work from before World War I is then discussed in more expansive terms—the broader, though still specifically contextual, traditions of neoclassicism,

 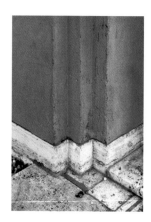

as well as transnational influences such as that of the Dutch architect H. P. Berlage. Through Behrens, Mies's work is connected not only to Schinkel but to the extranational forces of industrialization.

In his account of the canonical five projects, Johnson relates Mies's work of the early 1920s to native cultural influences only in mentioning what he sees as the unfortunate relationship of the Friedrichstrasse Skyscraper to Expressionism. He is portraying Mies's architecture as increasingly abstract and internationally oriented, and Expressionism is presumably too subjective and, perhaps, too German for him to consider it as valid a point of reference as the formal rationalism of Constructivism or De Stijl. As his narrative continues through the 1920s and '30s, he makes no further comparisons between Mies's work and any other contemporary architecture or cultural referent, except to establish his subject's ascendancy over even the foremost

modern architects—Le Corbusier, Walter Gropius, J. J. P. Oud, and Frank Lloyd Wright—with whom he had previously grouped Mies as a peer in the "International Style" exhibition of 1932.

Mies's work of the 1940s is presented in ever more abstract terms, both physically and metaphysically. In describing the Farnsworth House (1949–50; fig. 13), he notes that the steel-framed glass volume raised up on steel columns is "a radical departure from [Mies's] last European domestic projects, the earth-hugging courthouses."[43] He illustrates his description of the IIT campus with models showing Mies's use, unprecedented in his German work, of "idealized" abstract planning models

with no particular site (fig. 14). Perhaps most important, Johnson also perceives an important development in Mies's work: the use of the twenty-four-by-twenty-four-foot universal grid that controlled the urban design of IIT, the structural system of its buildings, and even the partitioning of the interior spaces (fig. 15).

In one of the book's most important sections, Johnson compares the IIT design to the Gothic cloisters of Oxford, and describes the buildings as "units of a large design, the subtle beauty of which will merge only when the whole is completed."[44] He extends the comparison in his description of the Library and Administration Building, which he calls "possibly Mies's greatest single design": the building is conceived in steel "just as a medieval design is conceived in terms of stone vaults and buttresses," and the "structural elements are revealed as are those of a Gothic cathedral."[45] These remarks bring the narrative full circle, echoing the

11. Ludwig Mies van der Rohe. Library and Administration Building Project, Illinois Institute of Technology, Chicago. 1942–43. Perspective view of corner: pencil on illustration board, 63 x 53" (160 x 134.6 cm). The Museum of Modern Art, New York. Mies van der Rohe Archive. Gift of the architect

12. Ludwig Mies van der Rohe. Urbig House, Potsdam-Neubabelsberg. 1915–17. Corner detail. Photograph: Kay Fingerle, 2000

13. Ludwig Mies van der Rohe. Farnsworth House, Plano, Illinois. 1949–50

first few lines of the book, where Johnson invokes Mies's childhood heritage—a "medieval concept of order expressed in the writings of St. Augustine and St. Thomas Aquinas."[46]

In this respect, Johnson's bracketing of Mies's entire career by a rubric of Thomist philosophical perspective was more prediction than history. While Mies

beginning of that conflict between subjective space and a wholly rational order that has since come to mark Mies's work."[47] He picks up this thought again in describing the Reichsbank proposal and the Verseidag Administration Building, the architect's later projects in Germany: "Dry and competent, these designs seem not to have been done by the architect of the Barcelona

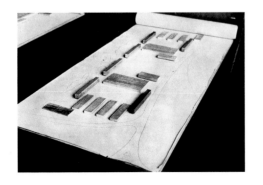

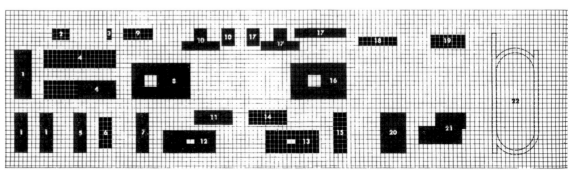

14. Ludwig Mies van der Rohe. Illinois Institute of Technology, Chicago. 1939–41. Photograph of model of theoretical campus plan. Chicago Historical Society

15. Ludwig Mies van der Rohe. Illinois Institute of Technology, Chicago. 1939–1941. Photograph of plan of campus master plan, final scheme. The Museum of Modern Art, New York. Mies van der Rohe Archive. Gift of the architect

had taken to quoting the writings of Aquinas and Augustine in the later 1920s, it is difficult to interpret his works of that time from the same philosophical perspective that Johnson adopts with regard to IIT. The more explicit expression of order and structure in the Library and Administration Building was indeed a new direction in Mies's work, and Johnson was prescient enough to see that it would be the hallmark of his American career.

The characterization of Mies's architectural career in terms of ever-increasing abstraction—from the "popular traditional" style of the Riehl House to the metaphysical Neoplatonism of the IIT Library and Administration Building—was first questioned by Arthur Drexler, who succeeded Johnson as the head of this Museum's Department of Architecture and Design in 1956. In many ways Drexler tended to reiterate the canonical history of Mies provided by Johnson. His monograph of 1960, however, demonstrates his growing reappraisal of important aspects of Johnson's text. Thirteen years after the 1947 retrospective, when Mies's American achievements were less novel, Drexler was more inclined not only to see distinctions between Mies's European and American work but also to judge them on their own terms. Of the German Pavilion in Barcelona Drexler writes, "[Within] its discipline is the

Pavilion or the court house projects. But with them Mies was quietly preparing a new foundation for his work."[48] In Drexler's view this "new foundation" would be fully explored in America: "The history of Mies's architecture in the United States has involved the gradual exclusion of everything that has seemed to him subjective and conditional.…His American work is a contest in which an imaginary absolute triumphs over reality."[49]

As important as it is, Drexler's view has not significantly altered the impressions created and codified by the 1947 book, in which Mies's German work was cast as prologue to his unfolding American career. This attitude is evident, for example, in the ongoing tendency to see the Friedrichstrasse Skyscraper as the precedent for Mies's American skyscrapers, a view apparent in Huxtable's label copy for a proposed Promontory Apartments exhibit in the 1947 show: "Compare the purity and structural directness of this building with the glass and concrete project of 1922 [sic]. Few artists are so consistent in their approach to design over a period of twenty-five years."[50]

Eventually Drexler's search for the subjective might have led him to question what had become conventional wisdom: Mies's stature as an international or universal architect, to the exclusion of national and local references. Shaping Mies in increasingly abstract terms, Johnson had referred to Thomistic universalism—perhaps the "imaginary absolute" to which Drexler refers. In the 1920s, however, even as Mies was considering the implications of Aquinas's writing, he was also maintaining that architecture was a product of specific conditional factors: "Each culture arises out of the landscape and its economic givens. Only in this connection can one even understand the term culture." He continues, "Transformations within cultures ... change the living conditions of a particular people, and this in turn leads to a change of formal expression."[51] Mies's linkage of the forms of architecture with the landscape and the historical and economic givens of a people would strongly suggest that he saw a limit to the notion of a global architecture, whether in terms of Thomist universalism or of an international cultural framework. In fact his understanding of the concept of culture was a principal reason for his reluctance to emigrate from Germany, even after his ability to secure commissions was severely limited. In this he was not unique among his peers: the novelist Thomas Mann, traveling abroad in 1933, remarked, "I am much too good a German, far too closely linked with the cultural traditions and the language of my country, for the thought of an exile lasting years, if not a lifetime, not to have a grave, a fateful significance for me."[52]

In any case, it is as important to look to more subjective interpretations of Mies's European work as to abstract ones. In presenting the Friedrichstrasse Skyscraper, for example, the publications of The Museum of Modern Art have generally emphasized its "international" qualities: its structural, economic, and technological rationalism, as well as its abstract aesthetic. In 1947, however, the one problem with this design, for Johnson, was that it was "rather Expressionistic in its oblique angles"—an echo of his writings from the "International Style" exhibition.[53] This supposed "defect" connected the design to a cultural context that was too "subjective and conditional," too historically laden, for Johnson's vision of an internationalized architecture. Yet the Expressionist character of the Friedrichstrasse project, rising phoenixlike above the ashes of Wilhelmine Berlin, is precisely what allows us to see it not only as a striking structural solution but as

a manifesto of what the architect remembered as "the grand and rich times in the twenties, which contributed so much to our western culture."[54]

Johnson's characterization of Mies's American work as physically and metaphysically abstract need not be considered incorrect. However, it may well be argued that this heightened sense of abstraction is a consequence of what Mann characterized as cultural exile rather than an innate and singular tendency in the architect's work. The Farnsworth House, as Johnson notes, is radically different from the architect's "earth-hugging" European houses. In many of the latter, indeed, including the Mountain House, it is almost impossible to separate the project from its landscape. The Farnsworth House, on the other hand, displays a tentative relationship to its site. Raised on columns to avoid flooding from the adjacent Fox River, the structure appears to float above the earth, touching it no more than required. Here the terrace is less an earthen podium than a suspended platform, apparently defying the earth's gravity. A shimmering apparition, the Farnsworth House seems metaphorically and literally transportable. Not only does it transcend its own landscape, it seems to be part of a larger, more abstract universe rather than a complete form in itself. In its construction, spatial qualities, and transparent skin, the house appears as a basic unit that might be multiplied to create, say, the 860 Lake Shore Drive Apartments in Chicago (1948–51; fig. 16).

By comparison, the Concrete Country House and Concrete Office Building projects from the early 1920s share structural and material affinities but retain important typological distinctions defined by their respective physical landscapes, the cultural dynamics of the time, and the history of both. Like most of Mies's German domestic designs, the Country House was an expression of the refined social and architectural culture of the archipelago of suburban districts around Potsdam, the country seat of the Hohenzollern dynasty. The cultural axis between Potsdam and metropolitan Berlin had been familiar to European architects since the time of Schinkel, whose monuments defined that axis as much as Palladio's had the axis between Venice and the surrounding Veneto district. Mies's projected

16. Ludwig Mies van der Rohe. 860 and 880 Lake Shore Drive Apartments, Chicago. 1948–51. A northeast corner living room showing the shoreline view to the north. Interior perspective view, collage: ink, pencil, watercolor, and gelatin silver photograph on illustration board, 28 x 36¼" (71.1 x 92.1 cm). The Museum of Modern Art, New York. Mies van der Rohe Archive. Gift of the architect

17 (below). Le Corbusier. Structural study, Maison Dom-ino. 1914–15. Fondation Le Corbusier, Paris

18 (right). Karl Friedrich Schinkel. Roman Bath and Court Gardener's House at Schloss Charlottenhof, Sanssouci, Potsdam. 1829–33. Perspective view. From Schinkel, *Sammlung Architektonischer Entwürfe* (1819–40)

house represented one half of the twentieth-century version of this classical duality—the suburban place of repose that balanced the frenetic life of the metropolis. The Concrete Office Building, while sharing the material and structural logic of the Country House, reflects its own contextual roots in Berlin's historic architecture and urban patterns. Its formal entry and raised first level reflect the sort of neoclassical urban strategies that any student of Schinkel's would recognize. The strip-window clerestories at the street and attic levels are "negative" versions of classical elements that defined all of Berlin's representative architecture: the stylobate and the cornice. Equally distinctive is the fact that the building is read as an independent block set within the fabric of the city, which, again, reflects the tendency in urban Berlin to set significant structures off from their surroundings. Unlike Le Corbusier's Maison Dom-ino (1914–15; fig. 17), where the structural language is reduced to verticals and horizontals, Mies's office block retains the expression of traditional trabeated construction in the beams that span the grid of columns, as in Schinkel's simplified neo-Tuscan Court

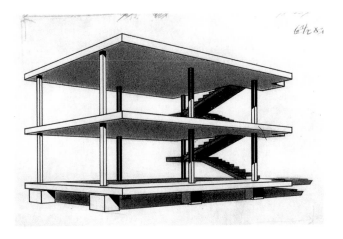

Gardener's House (1829–33; fig. 18), with their butt ends clearly visible on the exterior of the building.

The classic dualism so evident in Mies's projects had also been reiterated in the work of Behrens, whose work was clearly divided between his innovative industrial projects for the electrical conglomerate AEG and his more traditional work for suburban residences. Behrens's position puts both Mies's residential and

his urban projects in sharper focus, particularly in the five projects of 1921–24, even though the radical cultural changes of the 1920s might have been expected to lessen rather than intensify this aspect of his work. Both the urban projects (with their emphasis on technological and programmatic innovations) and the houses (with their Virgilian calm and bourgeois comforts) suggest an ongoing—though increasingly tense— dualism between the industrial city and the aestheticized domestic realm. This dualism is closer to the writings of Walter Benjamin than to the fundamental unity of Aquinas.

Any revision of the accepted history of Mies's architecture would involve the dismantling of an "imaginary absolute" that came to dominate any and all competing views of both his American work and, retroactively, his European work. Recent interest in Mies, as evidenced in the work of architects such as Herzog and de Meuron and Rem Koolhaas and in the writings of a new generation of critics such as K. Michael Hays and Detlef Mertins, demonstrates that a generation after his death, his legacy lies not in a presumed universalism but in the realm of the subjective and the conditional.

l.m.v.d.r.

A PROJECT BY THOMAS RUFF (1999–2001)

Page   a   d.p.b. 03, 04, 05. Each 1999
                11$\frac{7}{16}$ x 8$\frac{7}{16}$" (29 x 21.5 cm)
                d.p.b. 02. 1999
                51$\frac{3}{16}$ x 6'4$\frac{3}{4}$" (130 x 195 cm)

       b   w.h.s. 02. 2000
                51$\frac{3}{16}$ x 66$\frac{15}{16}$" (130 x 170 cm)
                a.s.b. 01. 2001
                51$\frac{3}{16}$ x 64$\frac{15}{16}$" (130 x 165 cm)

       c   h.t.b. 01. 1999
                6'1$\frac{3}{16}$" x 7'8$\frac{1}{2}$" (185 x 235 cm)

       d   h.l.k. 01. 2000
                51$\frac{3}{16}$" x 6'1$\frac{3}{16}$" (130 x 185 cm)

       e   h.e.k. 02. 2000
                51$\frac{3}{16}$" x 7'10$\frac{1}{2}$" (130 x 240 cm)

       f   h.w.b. 03. 2001
                51$\frac{3}{16}$ x 68$\frac{1}{8}$" (130 x 173 cm)
                h.p.b. 01. 2000
                51$\frac{3}{16}$ x 64$\frac{15}{16}$" (130 x 165 cm)

       g   h.r.p. 01. 2001
                51$\frac{3}{16}$ x 68$\frac{1}{8}$" (130 x 173 cm)

       h   h.u.p. 01. 2000
                51$\frac{3}{16}$ x 64$\frac{15}{16}$" (130 x 165 cm)

All images are chromogenic color photographs.
Courtesy Zwirner & Wirth, David Zwirner, Inc.

AFRIKANISCHE STRASSE
BERLIN-WEDDING

Essays

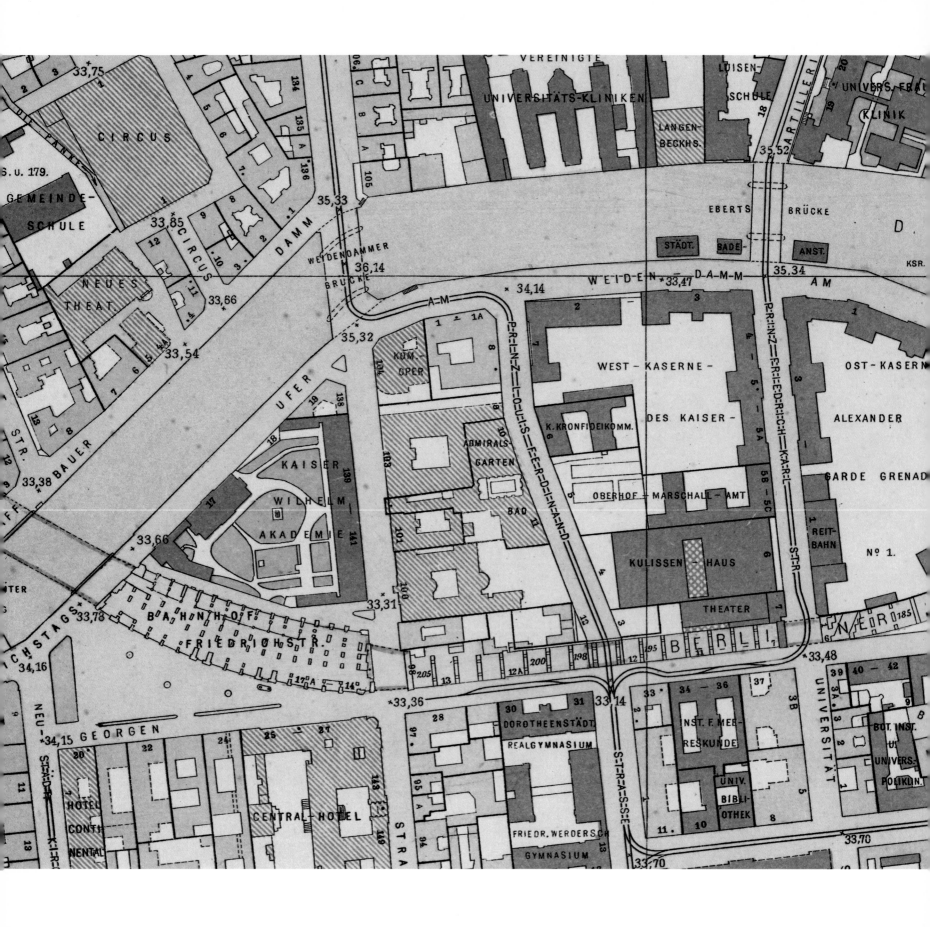

Berlin Modernism and the Architecture of the Metropolis

VITTORIO MAGNAGO LAMPUGNANI

In the late Wilhelmine era and during the Weimar Republic, German architects worked out a series of remarkable ideas for the design of the modern metropolis, and particularly for Berlin. The startling proposals of Ludwig Mies van der Rohe were one element in this concentrated body of thought on urban planning, an attempt to reimagine the city in terms of the new populations and technologies that would increasingly condition its needs. This essay will describe some of the various projects and proposals that emerged and interacted in Germany during the first third of the twentieth century. It is a story in which Mies himself will slip in and out of view; but it aims to suggest a crucial intellectual and practical context for his work.

Monumental Architecture for the Capital of the Reich: the "Gross-Berlin" Competition

In the second half of the nineteenth century, Berlin expanded rapidly. In 1819 it had numbered a mere 200,000 inhabitants, but by 1877 it had passed the million mark, and by the start of the twentieth century, Berlin and the towns around it had a population of 3.8 million. It was therefore startling but by no means far-fetched that the "Gross-Berlin" competition, announced by the city and its neighboring towns in 1908, was conceived for a city of at least 5 million. The competition was an attempt to come up with an "overall plan for the development of Greater Berlin," "a unified, grandiose solution both for the demands of traffic and those of beauty, public health, and economy."[1] Implicit in the announcement was a desire to give Berlin, as the capital of a latecomer among the world powers, a suitably imperial scope, with new public buildings and squares.

The competition essentially called for three things: the proposal of development guidelines in the roughly

2,000 square kilometers of the metropolitan region; a sample plan for a typical inner-city district; and suggestions for individual building projects. It was expected that these would include ways to improve working-class living conditions, create urban green space, and confront increasing traffic problems in the inner city. Reorganization of the railway network was seen as key to bringing urban development under control.

Twenty-seven designs were submitted—a low number, doubtless because of the ambition and complexity of the competition's demands. Complete familiarity with the city was essential if its problems were to be resolved, and the jury, which announced no decision until 1910, awarded prizes only to Berlin architects. Hermann Jansen—who happened to have collected the material for the competition's invitational brochure—won one of the two first prizes announced, for a design called "In the Limits of Possibility" (fig. 1). Jansen modestly limited himself to cautious adjustments of the city's existing fabric, concentrating on the planning of functional yet livable and aesthetically refined new housing districts and examining both public rail transportation and the private use of streets. With touching faith in progress, he asserted that "children as well as automobiles must be able to race about; preventing them from doing so would constitute a denial of their urges that would revenge itself."[2] The new metropolis that he conjured up, though hospitable to the automobile, was no less attuned to the needs of pedestrians than Camillo Sitte had insisted it be some years before.[3]

The second first prize went to Joseph Brix and Felix Genzmer, whose submission bore the rubric "Think Ahead" (fig. 2). Brix and Genzmer proposed an underground rail line directly under Königsplatz, connecting the Lehrter Bahnhof with the Potsdam and

described as a "work of peace and progress" thus mutated into a "huge monument to the defensive power of the Reich," a demonstration, through urban design, of Germany's new claim to world power.[4] The architectural idiom was a uniformity borrowed from classicism: "In the design of technical traffic as in the design of monumental buildings, the entire city of Berlin must form a *unified whole*, one that on the one hand embodies the modern metropolis and on the other represents the capital of the German empire."[5]

The project submitted by the firm of Havestadt & Contag, the traffic engineer Otto Blum, and the architect Bruno Schmitz, under the optimistic title "Where There's a Will There's a Way," earned fourth prize. The conception was even more monumental, but here the desire was less for an imperial capital than for a grandiose showplace of metropolitan culture. Once again, railway lines were concentrated and linked to

Anhalt train terminals. Königsplatz itself they restyled as a "forum of the Reich," with massive colonnades. But this, like other of their suggestions, was simply an eclectic borrowing—neither adequately motivated nor architecturally convincing—from the cities that Berlin seemed determined to emulate.

The third prize was awarded to "*Et in terra pax*," a design by the architect Bruno Möhring, the economist Rudolf Eberstadt, and the traffic engineer Richard Petersen (fig. 3). This plan placed a new opera house at the edge of the Tiergarten, with a square in front of it flanked by the ministry of justice and the ministry of the interior. The team also restructured Königsplatz, giving the lie to their motto of peace on earth: across from the Reichstag they placed a gigantic ministry of war, and the north side of the square was to contain the headquarters of the army's general staff, the naval office of the Reich, and the colonial office. What they

1. Hermann Jansen. Project for Tempelhofer Feld. 1910. Bird's-eye view: lithograph, 21 x 28¾" (53.5 x 73 cm). Berlinische Galerie, Berlin

2. Joseph Brix and Felix Genzmer. Project for Alexanderplatz-Königskolonade from "*Denk an künftig*" (Think ahead), entry in the Gross-Berlin competition. 1910. Perspective view: tempera on canvas, 35⅜ x 55 5⁄16" (90 x 140.5 cm). Plansammlung der Technische Universität Berlin

3. Bruno Möhring, Rudolf Eberstadt, Richard Petersen. Master plan for central Berlin, from "*Et in terra pax*," entry in the Gross-Berlin competition. 1910. Published in *Berliner Architekturwelt* 13 (1911)

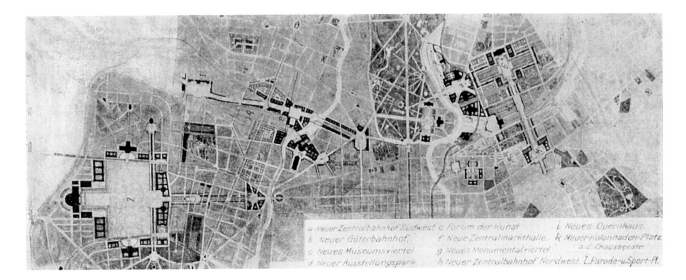

a. Neuer Zentralbahnhof Südwest. e. Forum der Kunst   i. Neues Opernhaus.
b. Neuer Güterbahnhof.   f. Neue Zentralmarkthalle. k. Neuer Kolonnaden-Platz
c. Neues Museumsviertel   g. Neues Monumentalviertel   a. d. Chausspestr.
d. Neuer Ausstellungspark.   h. Neuer Zentralbahnhof Nordwest. l. Parade-u.Sport-Pl.

4. Havestadt & Contag, Otto Blum, Bruno Schmitz. Master plan of central Berlin from "*Wo ein Wille, da ein Weg*" (Where there's a will there's a way), entry in the Gross-Berlin competition. 1910. Published in *Berliner Architektur-welt* 13 (1941)

5. Havestadt & Contag, Otto Blum, Bruno Schmitz. Project for Leipziger Platz and Potsdamer Platz from "*Wo ein Wille, da ein Weg*" (Where there's a will there's a way), entry in the Gross-Berlin competition. 1910. Perspective view: graphite and charcoal on paper, 22 ¹⁵⁄₁₆ x 62⅝" (58.2 x 159 cm). Plansammlung der Technische Universität, Berlin

new terminals in the north and south; once again, imposing new public complexes were created in the inner-city spaces thus liberated. These were to include a new central market hall before the main north station, a "forum of art" on the Spree River, and a monumental quarter farther north, with an allée accented by twin towers and a square dominated by a gigantic domed structure (fig. 4). Next to the south station a commercial quarter was envisioned, centering on Potsdamer Platz, which was to be dominated by a skyscraper. On the Fischerinsel, an island in the Spree, there was to be a "forum of labor," with an imposing municipal library, and on the Tempelhof field, a parade ground.

The two large charcoal perspective drawings (fig. 5) in which Schmitz presented this ambitious project shed light on his architectural bent and the tradition to which it belonged: the project was representative of Berlin, in that it was close to contemporary works by Alfred Messel and Ludwig Hoffmann, but it also showed influences from Paris's École des Beaux Arts and the American City Beautiful movement. From the latter, especially, it borrowed not only the urban concept of clustered public buildings and spaces but also a unifying neoclassical style, although in Schmitz's vision that style is romantically colored and emotional.

Indifference and Monotony: From Metropolitan Life to Metropolitan Architecture

The participants in the Gross-Berlin competition may have differed in their ideologies and in their abilities, but from Jansen to Schmitz they repeatedly sought uniformity in the cityscape, both as a whole and in individual neighborhoods. The notion played a major role in all German architectural thinking in the early twentieth century. It was not only a matter of building style; it also had to do with technological, functional, social, and political issues.

Writing in 1887, the sociologist Ferdinand Tönnies had already pointed out the relationship between lifestyles and urban forms.[6] His distinction between the small city and the metropolis in this regard was taken up by the sociologist and philosopher Georg Simmel, who developed it further in his lecture "*Die Großstädte und das Geistesleben*" (Metropolises and mental life), delivered in 1903.[7] In the village or small town Simmel found a relaxed rhythm, an adherence to group values, and the possibility of orienting oneself emotionally within a clearly structured community. In the metropolis, on the other hand, he saw an increasingly rapid pace, an almost unlimited individual freedom, a "heightened sensitivity" stemming from the multiplicity of impressions to which one was exposed, and a reliance on intellect as the only means of finding one's way in an anonymous society with uncertain contours. Exposed to a flood of stimuli, big-city dwellers developed an apathy, an indifference, a kind of uniform mask behind which to hide their feelings. For Simmel, the conflict between the individual and society, between singularity and homogeneity, which he held to be the problem of "modern life" *tout court*, seemed to manifest itself in the very architecture of the metropolis, where public buildings especially symbolized a "spirit of anonymity against which the individual personality could scarcely hold its own."[8] The physical appearance of the modern metropolis, then, was characterized by the impersonal and the superindividual.

If building forms were to reflect the society that produced them, however, then a metropolitan architecture that would mirror this particular society and its strengths should not resist uniformity but should actually embrace it. This is precisely what the architecture critic Karl Scheffler proposed in his essay "*Ein Weg zum Stil*" (A way to style), published in 1903, the same year as Simmel's lecture. Unlike Simmel, Scheffler did not see the cause of uniformity as "the pressures of society, of the historical legacy, of external culture and mechanics of life."[9] The cause was simply democracy, which fostered universal needs and therefore gave rise to universal floor plans: "Town houses are now built on speculation. A person lives in twenty different dwellings in his brief lifetime, and in principle all of them should be laid out as similarly as possible, so that he does not have to suffer any change in his routine. More and more, distinctions between floor plans are being erased. Indeed the ideal in urban building is a perfectly uniform floor plan for apartments with the same rent."[10] The functional conformity between interior and exterior also resulted in identical facades. Scheffler saw this not as an evil but as a welcome challenge: "The goal of a new urban architecture must be uniformity, the integration of entire blocks of dwellings.

From society's need for uniform floor plans comes the artistic demand to reduce all buildings of the same type—the rent being the key element—to a unified form."[11]

Scheffler refined these notions in his chief work, *Die Architektur der Großstadt* (The architecture of the metropolis), published in 1913. Ten years after "*Ein Weg zum Stil*," the Berlin theoretician was no longer so sure that the road from a democratic society to a uniform city ran in a straight line; it seemed rather to lead between the Scylla of vulgar eclecticism and the Charybdis of commercial formlessness. Since the masses could not be trusted to impose limits on themselves voluntarily, small groups of cultivated people had to step forward as the interpreters of democracy. They needed to ensure that the masses recognize the "force of convention," accepting the typical architectural pattern that is "the first requirement of a style."[12] In the metropolis, this meant "consistent uniformity of facades and identical architectural treatment of entire blocks of buildings, which create a beautiful line and give a strict rhythm to the big-city street."[13] Further, "The street wall becomes a single facade, whole quarters exhibit an architectural restfulness, and out of this noble uniformity a representative monumental style will later develop that will truly deserve the name 'modern.'"[14] This monumental style was to renew metropolitan architecture, lending it authenticity, dignity, and beauty. "It stands to reason that a consistently imposed uniformity can only enrich the overall appearance of a city. A metropolis in which apartment-house districts are made up of huge building blocks, with each block treated like a single, freestanding house—into such a city the dominant rhythm that we so sorely miss in our present nondescript diversity will necessarily return."[15]

Scheffler was doubtless the most convinced and convincing apologist for the uniformity to which the majority of Germany's early-twentieth-century progressive architects subscribed, but the issue spread well beyond the borders of the German Reich. As early as 1894, Hendrik Petrus Berlage had argued for an undecorated, simplified residential architecture as best suited to the demands of modern big-city life. In his book *L'Esthétique de la rue* (1901), Gustave Kahn had hoped that entire city blocks, all erected by the same builder, might be uniform in design. Seven years later, Emil Magne called for a "*suprême simplicité*" in urban architecture, corresponding to the simplicity of modern science. In a lecture at the London Town Planning Conference in 1910, the American architect and planner Daniel Hudson Burnham explained the relationship between a democratic society and a uniform city architecture. And in the same year, Otto Wagner declared at a conference in New York that "it is our democratic system, in which the community is hounded by the demand for inexpensive and hygienic housing and by the forced frugality of our way of living, that produces uniformity in our apartment houses."[16]

In the Wake of the Gross-Berlin Competition: The Mächler Plan (1908–20)

None of the Gross-Berlin competition proposals was realized, but they were exhibited in 1910 at the *Allgemeine Städtebau-Ausstellung* (Universal urban design exhibition) in Berlin. As a result, they influenced the period's international urban design at least as much as they had profited from it. During the debates leading up to the competition, Martin Mächler shaped a plan that he would rework in 1917 and again in 1919 (fig. 6). His goal was political and ambitious: "As a world metropolis," Berlin ought to represent, as Max Berg would put it, nothing less than "the German Empire's relationship to the rest of the world."[17] Mächler proposed grouping all ministries and foreign embassies, then scattered throughout the city, around or near Königsplatz (or, later, the "Platz der Republik," as the square was called under the postwar Weimar Republic). He envisioned a huge exposition park that would express "the excellence of the German *Volk* in its work in relationship to the world."[18] The Anhalt and Potsdam terminals were to be replaced by a new train station near Tempelhof, linked by subway to a central station to be built on the site of the Lehrter Bahnhof. In the interests of traffic flow, Mächler recommended extending Jägerstrasse through the Ministergärten. Most important, however, he pictured a broad north-south axis that would not only link the city's northern and southern districts but serve the symbolic function of boldly cutting across the

existing "absolutist" east-west axis. Mächler also eliminated the Siegesallee, with its thirty-two commemorative statues, or "stations of national pride,"[19] and the Siegessäule, the Victory Column monument.

This plan too was never realized, less because of its content than owing to the precarious economic—and political, and social, and ideological—situation of

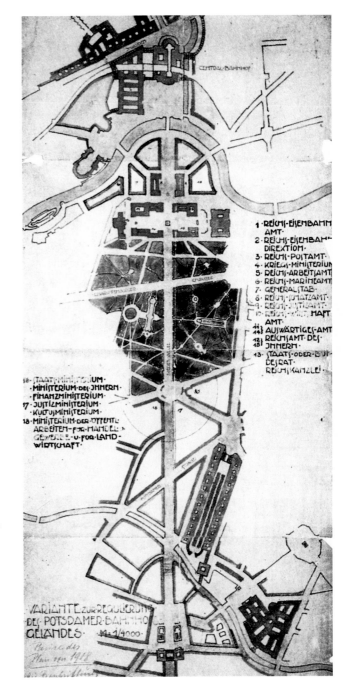

6. Martin Mächler. Project for North-South Axis, Berlin. 1908. Plan: diazotype with watercolor, 35⅛ x 16⅛" (90 x 41 cm). Plansammlung der Technische Universität, Berlin

Germany during and after World War I. The notion of a north-south axis, however, filling a serious and long-standing gap in the city's network of traffic arteries, lived on. Erwin Gutkind, for example, argued for the creation of a major north-south axis in a discussion of the competition for an addition to the Reichstag in 1929, and the idea would achieve its sinister apotheosis some years later in the planning of Albert Speer.

The Third Dimension in Urban Design, or the "Germanization" of the Skyscraper

Mies must have been aware of these debates, but only began to participate directly in them after World War I, when they increasingly addressed the issue of the skyscraper as a building type for Berlin. The question had already been posed;[20] for the Gross-Berlin competition of 1908, in fact, Schmitz's team had proposed their monumental skyscraper on Potsdamer Platz. The precedents repeatedly invoked were Chicago and New York—but they needed to be "Germanized."

In 1912, an opinion poll of politicians, business-people, and architects on the subject of the skyscraper, conducted by the Berlin newspaper *Morgenpost*, was documented in the brochure *"Berlins dritte Dimension"* (fig. 7). Here Peter Behrens strongly advocated the view that structures like those of North American cities were equally right for Berlin. Underscoring the skyscraper's aesthetic and symbolic potential, Behrens endorsed the "realization of a uniform character and stylistic idea in an entire city."[21] In 1913, Otto Rappold published a study investigating the technological and functional aspects of the new building type, using the example of American skyscrapers.[22] That same year, the Dresden architect and watercolorist K. Paul Andrae drew the first leaves of his series *Das grössere Berlin* (1913–16; fig. 8), a sequence of studies of skyscrapers and monumental buildings that he furnished with titles borrowed from music, such as "Allegro tanto" or "Andante maestoso." In no. VIII in the series he conjured a massive skyscraper city that in many respects anticipated Hugh Ferriss's visions of New York in *The Metropolis of Tomorrow*.[23] Andrae's skyscraper studies, originally conceived for an imperial Berlin, the capital of the German Reich, were exhibited in 1919, of all years, in

the *Ausstellung für unbekannte Architekten* (Exhibition of unknown architects), where they were misinterpreted as a guide to a "freer and stronger future."[24]

The real skyscraper debate began in Germany only in 1920. (It was anticipated by Paul Wittig's 1918 study *Über die ausnahmsweise Zulassung einzelner Turmhäuser in Berlin*, which advocated the construction of skyscrapers "solely for the purpose of improving urban beauty in metropolises, and accordingly in Berlin,"[25] and presented Wittig's own designs as examples.) The nation's first competition for a skyscraper was announced in Danzig in May of that year, and the architect responsible for the invitation delivered the lecture "Skyscrapers as a Means of Relieving the Housing Crisis."[26] Berg would develop this argument, as odd as it was successful, in two highly regarded essays later in the same year,[27] provoking a flood of further comment but also a number of more or less concrete designs for tall buildings.

Between 1920 and 1921, Möhring created designs for some twenty *Turmhäuser*—the German name for what was presumed would be a properly Germanic reinterpretation of the skyscraper—at carefully chosen sites in Berlin (fig. 9). With these he hoped to avoid both the uncontrolled concentrations of skyscrapers that had occurred in Chicago and New York and the

7. Kurt Szafranski. Cover, *Berlins dritte Dimension*. Brochure published by the *Berliner Morgenpost*, 1912. Staatsbibliothek Berlin

8. K. Paul Andrae. *Das grössere Berlin* VIII. 1913. Reprinted in *Wasmuths Monatshefte für Baukunst*, November–December 1923, p. 382

single tower through which the cityscape would "gain interest, to be sure, but still not take on the definite appearance of a modern city."[28] Otto Kohtz too began working up skyscraper designs for Berlin in 1920, hoping to create "with well placed and harmoniously designed skyscrapers a few architectural highlights in Berlin's humdrum yet restless sea of buildings," giving "the eye a focus and direction."[29] Like Möhring, he selected a few particularly visible sites for his projects, even venturing to place one on Königsplatz; during the war, he had wanted to build a *Siegeshalle* (Victory hall) here, but since victory had failed to materialize he made do with a *Reichshaus*, which would help to promote "welfare, health, morality, law, strength, spirit, and beauty" (figs. 10, 11).[30]

Kohtz's geometric "city crown" was to rise to a height of 200 meters (c. 656 feet) above a plot 130 meters (c. 426 feet) by 130 meters square. Like a

stepped pyramid, it would become smaller as it rose. Inside, an immense cruciform foyer was to bathe in a mystical light filtering through the colored glass of the tracery facade. In his own curious way, Kohtz took up Berg's proposal for easing the housing crisis; by collecting into his building all the state offices strewn about Berlin, he believed he could free up some 2,000 apartments previously commandeered for office space. He also saw the huge building site as a massive job-creation program, helping to reduce unemployment.[31] In 1921 Kohtz drew a second, more ponderous version of the same building, which Le Corbusier published with undisguised scorn in *L'Esprit nouveau* as an example of everything that was bad in contemporary German architecture.[32] Up into the 1940s, by which time Speer's plans for his *Grosse Halle* had banished the *Reichshaus* beyond recall, Kohtz never gave up the idea of building his monumental structure on the city's most prominent site.

9. Bruno Möhring. Project for high-rise office building at Askanischer Platz, Berlin. 1920. Perspective view from the Anhalter station. Published in *Stadtbaukunst alter und neuer Zeit* 22 (1920), p. 135

10. Otto Kohtz. Reichshaus am Königsplatz Project. 1920. Perspective: ink on dark vellum, 18⅞ x 28¾" (48 x 73 cm). Plansammlung der Technische Universität Berlin

11. Otto Kohtz. Reichshaus am Königsplatz Project. 1921. Elevation: ink on tracing paper, 7½ x 7⅟₁₆" (19 x 18 cm). Plansammlung der Technische Universität Berlin

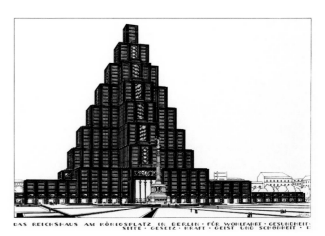

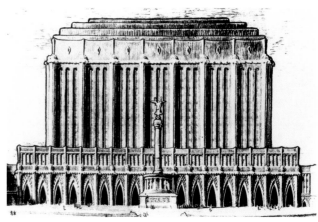

Several other designs for Berlin skyscrapers were produced in 1920, among them German Bestelmeyer's ten-story ring-shaped building for the Reichsschuldenverwaltung (State debt administration) on Oranienstrasse (rejected by the city building authority), Joseph Reuters's idiosyncratic, typically idealized skyscraper for Charlottenburg, and Hans Kraffert's American-style office tower on Blücherplatz. None of them was built, but that same year the Preussische Bauakademie (Prussian building academy) commissioned Möhring to investigate the possibility of developing a triangular site between the Spree, Friedrichstrasse, and the Friedrichstrasse railway station (frontispiece). His proposal of a twenty-two-story semicircular skyscraper was approved. Moreover, the committee established to explore the financing for such a project came to a positive conclusion. Accordingly, a corporation was formed. Having acquired the problematic but extraordinarily attractive property, in 1921 it announced a sensational competition for an office tower.

The Competition for the Friedrichstrasse Skyscraper, 1921

The sponsor, which called itself, appropriately enough, the Turmhaus-Aktiengesellschaft (Skyscraper corporation), invited only members of the Bund Deutscher Architekten (League of German architects) to participate in the competition, and gave them a brief six weeks to submit the required sketches. Even so, the project was appealing to Berlin's virtually unemployed architects, and over 140 works were submitted. Although well-known personalities like Hans Poelzig, Hans Scharoun, Hugo Häring, and Mies presented designs, the jury, made up of the conservative architects Bestelmeyer, Hermann Billing, Brix, and Heinrich Straumer, in addition to Ludwig Hoffmann, the city's building commissioner, awarded the prizes to more conservative designs, with one exception: the proposal by Hans and Wassili Luckhardt and Franz Hoffmann won second prize, and its authors were invited to develop it further. Like the other prize-winning designs, however, the proposal came to nothing owing to the indifference of the Turmhaus-Aktiengesellschaft, which had staged the competition, it now became

12. Hans Scharoun. Final entry, Friedrichstrasse Skyscraper competition. 1921. Published in *Frühlicht*, 1922

known, solely for publicity: in the spring of 1921, the corporation had already secretly contracted with Möhring, Kohtz, and Kraffert for the design it actually intended to build. Even so, the whole undertaking ultimately collapsed owing to the dilatory handling of building permits and subsequent financing difficulties.

The competition may have been a sham, but it did spur the development of new, more specific architectural ideas for tall structures. The variety of these ideas was astonishing: Poelzig's ponderous, late-Expressionist, three-sided plan, Häring's gigantic organlike tower, Scharoun's complex "cathedral of consumption" (fig. 12), Hans Soeder's prismatic composition, and especially Mies's pure, sharp-edged "crystal" provided basic solutions to the problem of the tall building. An autonomous tradition, though not necessarily "Germanic," was established. Individual features of these buildings would become the basic topoi of modernism in architecture, and some of them would stamp the visionary city created, and executed in an ingenious model, by Erich Kettelhut for Fritz Lang's film *Metropolis* (1926). A year after the Friedrichstrasse competition, German designers were able to enter an international competition for Chicago, the city that had witnessed the skyscraper's birth. None of the Europeans who participated in the competition for the Chicago Tribune Tower walked off with the coveted contract, but the exercise did give them a chance to present to an international public their reworked high-rises, freed of eclectic encumbrances, as European responses to the challenge of the American skyscraper.

A Glass Tower as Urban Building Block

The brochure detailing the results of the Friedrichstrasse skyscraper competition—printed in no small part as an alibi, and as a sop to the participating architects—omitted what was perhaps the most remarkable of the designs submitted: that by Mies. This was hardly surprising, for in his proposal, presented under the title "*Wabe*" (Honeycomb), the thirty-five-year-old architect had ignored almost all of the competition specifications. Leaving no significant open space on the triangular lot, the proposal placed a sharp-edged, prismlike tower twenty stories tall, without any setbacks, at each of the site's three corners. These three towers were linked by short corridors to a central, cylindrical service element housing stairways, elevators, and service rooms. On each of the site's three sides, then, two acute-angled prism-shaped buildings seemed to stand next to each other, separated by a deep vertical incision. In addition, each of these outer sides was divided into two separate surfaces angled slightly inward (fig. 13). The supporting structure was nowhere visible, but can be assumed to have been a steel skeleton with cantilevered floor slabs; the sheathing was entirely of glass.

For Mies, the competition was an opportunity to place a radical, programmatic design for a specific site before the public. The floor plan he provided was schematic, as he intended all floors to be identical, but he did supply a stunningly abstract view and three charcoal perspectives (not all of them in time for the deadline) that deliberately exaggerated the reflecting quality of the glass. Two of these drawings he collaged into photographs of the existing setting. Clearly he had adopted an enthusiasm for glass as a building material from the poet Paul Scheerbart, and had also assimilated

other Expressionist ideas having to do with crystals; it is telling that when he published his design, in 1922, it was in Bruno Taut's Expressionist journal *Frühlicht*. For that publication he wrote,

Only skyscrapers under construction reveal the bold constructive thoughts, and then the impression of the high-reaching steel skeletons is overpowering. With the raising of the walls, this impression is completely destroyed; the constructive thought, the necessary basis for artistic form-giving, is annihilated and frequently smothered by a meaningless and trivial jumble of forms. At very best one remains impressed by the sheer magnitude, and yet these buildings could have been more than just manifestations of our technical skill. This would mean, however, that one would have to give up the attempt to solve a new task with traditional forms; rather one should attempt to give form to the new task out of the nature of this task.[33]

Mies's text, far from any Scheerbartian exaltation, takes up a notion that Scheffler had developed in *Die Architektur der Großstadt* nine years earlier, that of the unfinished building as Ur-form for a new aesthetic of the metropolis.[34] On second glance, in fact, the

13. Ludwig Mies van der Rohe. Friedrichstrasse Skyscraper Project, entry in the Friedrichstrasse skyscraper competition. 1921. Photograph of lost photocollage. Bauhaus-Archiv Berlin

"Honeycomb" design reveals itself as more than a virtuoso experiment with a wholly new, radically purist architectural object; that object is at one and the same time an urban building block. In this respect it is comparable to the building that Burnham had erected in 1901 in New York, also on a triangular site, between Broadway and Fifth Avenue: the Fuller or Flatiron Building, as Burnham's sensational skyscraper soon came to be called. With its prismlike shape and restrained stone facade, that building presented itself as a heroic monolith, but also as the first structure in an outscaled city of the future for which it established not the exception but the rule. In the same way, Mies's glass tower conjured up a new, visionary city of glass giants, but for the time being made do with the existing one. An independent and somewhat anomalous block, it would have meshed with the existing urban fabric in only a limited way; yet thanks to its mirroring glass facades, its relationship to the surrounding structures was novel and intimate. Its extraordinary height and tremendous mass would have exploded Berlin's established scale, but its bulk was to be largely dematerialized by the reflecting glass, compensating for its enormity and softening the rupture it would have constituted. The Friedrichstrasse Skyscraper Project can thus be considered a viable element of the sort of metropolitan architecture anticipated by both Simmel and Scheffler: a block "treated like a single, freestanding house," its architecture anonymous, indifferent, and uniform.

Another Glass Tower as Urban Building Block

Only a few months later, Mies continued his experiments with basic sculptural forms and the ambiguous play of reflections by designing a second glass skyscraper. This time there was not even a competition, however dubious, as an incentive, and the building site was an irregular pentagon at the intersection of two broad streets. Here the architect envisioned a thirty-story tower, on an amoeba-shaped plan comprising two segments with numerous curves—or, more precisely, subtly angled panels. The segments were to be separated by two deep, curved notches that led to two entrances, which led in turn into an irregularly shaped foyer containing a doorman's box and two round shafts for stairways, elevators,

and service rooms. The bearing structure—once again visible only in a sketch, not in the plan—is a steel skeleton, and the curving, cantilevered floor slabs are sheathed, just as in the Friedrichstrasse Skyscraper, in a uniformly transparent glass skin.

Mies built a large model of this second glass tower, and again produced spectacular photomontages to show it in its intended setting. Even more than in the earlier proposal, the programmatic character of the building—and the exaggeration that implies—were fully apparent. The spaces were barely usable; the floor slabs could never have been made as thin as those suggested in the elegant model; the glass sheath would never in reality have been so transparent; and in 1922, no mechanical plant would have been able to heat such a structure in winter and cool it in summer. Functional and technological problems were not the architect's primary concern; he was mainly interested in the form, which he conceived of as suggested by the qualities and possibilities of his materials:

My experiments with a glass model helped me along the way and I soon recognized that by employing glass, it is not an effect of light and shadow one wants to achieve but a rich interplay of light reflections. . . . At first glance the contour of the ground plan appears arbitrary, but in reality it is the result of many experiments on the glass model. The curves were determined by the need to illuminate the interior, the effect of the building mass in the urban context, and finally the play of the desired light reflection. Ground plan contours in which the curves were calculated from the point of view of light and shadow revealed themselves on the model . . . as totally unsuitable.

The only fixed points in the ground plan are the stairs and the elevator shafts. All other subdivisions of the ground plan are to be adapted to the respective needs and executed in glass.[35]

The architect's assurances that his procedure was purely deductive must be taken with a grain of salt: they reflect his deliberate departure from the still prevailing intuitive, mystical approach of architectural Expressionism. Behind the seemingly rational arguments lurk the artistic influences that helped to give the Glass Skyscraper Project its free, rounded outline: the biomorphic architectural fantasies of Hermann Finsterlin, the smooth, swelling curves of Hans Arp, and even the organlike forms of Häring, with whom Mies had shared an office since the end of 1921.

If this second glass tower, in the interests of its sculptural aesthetic, ignored all practical considerations of construction, use, and maintenance even more drastically than the first one, it nonetheless constituted an urban building block, as its precursor did. This is above all apparent in the suppleness with which its plan was adapted to the complex conditions and shape of its site. (In one stretch it even abandoned its freely curving form and briefly followed the lot's straight boundary, as if it wanted to tie itself firmly to the site, if only for a few yards.) The view, again emphatically abstract, that opposes dark low structures to the building's soaring glass surface (plate 59), and the two photocollages placing the model in a fictitious setting of Berlin apartment blocks that almost might have been borrowed from Poelzig's village set for the film *The Golem* (plate 55), unmistakably demonstrate that this architectural sculpture in glass was destined for a metropolitan location. Unlike the first glass tower—and in contradiction of the architect's accompanying description—it engaged in a dialogue with its older surroundings not by mirroring them but through its own transparency. Yet once again it is thanks to such dialogue that the structure, though a break with what had come before, represents a continuity in the city's modernization.

An Element of the Uniform Metropolis: The Concrete Office Building, 1923

Mies also published his second glass tower in *Frühlicht* in 1922. That same year, his model of it was exhibited at the *Grosse Berliner Kunstausstellung*, where he also showed a photocollage that included an imposing perspective drawing of his first glass skyscraper project from 1921. A view of the second skyscraper reduced to twenty-one stories would serve as the frontispiece in the third issue of the avant-garde journal *G* (*Gestaltung*).

In the first issue of *G*—which began publishing in 1923, edited by Hans Richter, El Lissitzky, and the young Werner Graeff (formerly a Bauhaus student)—Mies had published an aggressive declaration of principles: "Any aesthetic speculation, any doctrine, and any formalism: we reject. Building art is the spatially apprehended will of the epoch. Alive. Changing. New. Not the yesterday, not the tomorrow, only the today is formable.

Only this building creates. Create form out of the nature of the task with the means of our own time. *That is our work*." This brief text, virtually a manifesto, was illustrated by a perspective drawing of an office building, identified as such in a large-type caption and described as follows: "The office building is a building of work, of organization, of clarity, of economy. Bright wide workrooms, uncluttered, undivided, only articulated according to the organism of the firm. The greatest effect with the least expenditure of means." This programmatic statement then became more precise: "The materials are concrete, iron, glass. Ferroconcrete buildings are essentially skeleton structures. Neither pastry [stucco] nor tank turrets. Supporting girder construction with a nonsupporting wall. That means skin and bone structures." Finally came a brief description: "The most practical distribution of the work stations determined room depth; it is sixteen meters. A double-shafted frame of eight-meter span-width with four-meter-long lateral cantilever brackets on either side was established as the most economical construction principle. The beam distance is five meters. This post-and-beam system supports the ceiling panel, which, angled vertically upward at the end of the cantilever arms, becomes exterior skin and and serves as back wall of the shelving, which was moved to the exterior walls in order to keep the interior uncluttered. Above the two-meter-high shelving is a continuous band of fenestration reaching to the ceiling."[36]

Although Mies's description of the Concrete Office Building Project once again suggests a purely utilitarian structure, its form determined by its function and method of construction, a glance at the illustration—a much-reduced reproduction of a nearly ten-foot-long perspective drawing—shows otherwise. In the middle of a nineteenth-century city, only sketchily suggested but clearly meant to represent a somber Mietskasernen-Berlin, rises an eight-story flat-roofed structure. It is extremely deep, and although its length is not precisely recognizable, this, too, is doubtless impressive. Its massive bulk is broken by uninterrupted horizontal bands of parapet wall, above which ribbons of window glass, also continuous and with only the thinnest of mullions, are set slightly back. Each of the seven upper stories projects almost imperceptibly beyond the one below, so that the building resembles a trapezoidal solid, growing wider toward the top. The bottom parapet wall is broken to form a wide entryway, through which an imposing flight of stairs leads up past five massive concrete pillars and into the building's interior.

This visionary design exists principally in the form of the one gigantic charcoal drawing that was exhibited with the design for the Concrete Country House Project at the *Grosse Berliner Kunstausstellung* of 1923, and then was published several times. It owes a great deal to a building designed and built nineteen years earlier: Frank Lloyd Wright's Larkin Building, in Buffalo, New York, the canonical example of a large, uniformly conceived office building with shelving against the outer wall. But Mies made out of his introverted model an extroverted new creation. In 1912, Behrens had warned, "Essentially, it is inconceivable why a structure at the service of serious, determined labor should not behave in a way that reflects that earnestness—why the function of such a building, which is characterized by such major requirements as maximum illumination of interior spaces, the possibility of changing their sizes and shapes at any time, unimpeded access between them, and full exploitation of available floor space for working stations, should not be adopted as an artistic motif."[37] Mies accomplished what Behrens was imagining here: he took the function of an office building as an artistic motif, and exaggerated it. The immense structure looms up out of the humus of the historical city. The beams of the ceiling slabs, and the supports with their widened tops, are visible—contrary to all laws of reflection—behind the windows. With a dignity more classical than modern, the open steps lead into this gigantic house of "serious, determined labor"— into spaces in which those who performed such labor would have been unable to look out at the street, thanks to the enclosing parapets, which were over six feet tall. The motif, clearly, was not so much work itself as the celebration of it, not the function but its dramatic setting, not a specific construction method but its architectonic glorification.

But there was more going on here. After the triangular and curved glass skyscraper projects, the Concrete Office Building was the third programmatic project of urban design that Mies worked out in the early 1920s. It was fundamentally different from its two precursors, for in the "new city" those were the possible exceptions, this the possible rule. In the drawing, the huge new structure stands in the old Berlin like some alien architectural body, but its dimensions adapt accommodatingly into the existing urban scheme. The new design does not presume to reform that pattern. In a city of closed, blocklike buildings, the Concrete Office Building would have been no more than a novel exemplary block. It realized not only beliefs of the radical, constructivist, and functionalist architectural avant-garde—with which Mies had allied himself relatively late, and with some misgivings—but also, and more important, the visions of basic, unadorned, uniform, and forthright blocks imagined by early-twentieth-century German architectural thinkers, especially Scheffler. Walter Curt Behrendt too had advocated such structures, describing them in detail in his 1911 dissertation, *Die einheitliche Blockfront als Raumelement im Städtebau*;[38] Mies's office block was an early and impressive demonstration of what one of them might look like.

Ludwig Hilberseimer: Metropolis Theories

In 1923, the same year in which Mies drew his Concrete Office Building, the Berlin architect and architectural theorist Ludwig Hilberseimer, a friend and colleague of Mies's, published his first sweeping reflections on the metropolis as a special architectural concern. In his essay "*Vom städtebaulichen Problem der Großstadt*" (On the urban planning problem of the metropolis), Hilberseimer identified the metropolis as a unique urban type, "a creation of modern times," and "the obvious and logical consequence of the industrialization of the world."

Through the most extreme concentration and the most extensive organization, an excess of intensity and energy is created. Since production is no longer content with meeting its own needs, it becomes pressed into overproduction, to the detriment of its neighbors—concentrating more on stimulating demands than on satisfying them. So the metropolis appears primarily as a creation of omnipotent big capital, an expression of capital's vast power and anonymity, a city type with unique socioeconomic and mass-psychological features, allowing for both the greatest isolation and the densest crowding of its inhabitants. The hectic pace of a life rhythm accelerated a thousandfold suppresses everything specific and individual. In certain features all metropolises are so similar that it is possible to speak of the internationality of their physiognomy.[39]

On the basis of this analysis, which owes something to Tönnies and Simmel, Hilberseimer develops maxims on the architecture of his megacity:

The map of the metropolis is generally based on an artificial, geometric system, and there is essentially nothing objectionable about such a plan, though its overuse in the nineteenth century has discredited it. It was often employed without reason, solely for convenience and for want of ideas and imagination, without regard for terrain, without elevated viewpoints, without any sense of architectonics. Nevertheless, a city layout based on geometry is in accord with the basic principles of all architecture, of which the straight line and right angle have always been the noblest elements. Does not the straight street that can be perceived in its entirety correspond more fully to our modern sensibility and desire for order than the one with arbitrary curves?[40]

Le Corbusier's book *Urbanisme*, which expresses similar ideas and preferences, would not appear until two years later.[41] The modern commitment to the orthogonal layout was not the only thing Hilberseimer anticipated in this essay; he also predicted that the issue of traffic would become "the alpha and omega of the entire city organism," and called for the sort of "distinct separation according to function" that, under the concept of "zoning," would mark the *Charte d'Athènes* (Athens charter) of 1933.[42]

The next year, in the crucial essay "*Großstadtarchitektur*," Hilberseimer re-presented these conclu-

sions—sometimes word for word—but also developed them further. Not content with a self-contained theory, he listed concrete formal characteristics of metropolitan architecture: massive cubic solids in which projections, setbacks, and indentations develop organically out of the structure itself, lending it rhythm; and broad smooth wall surfaces, with regularly placed windows providing visual interest. To Hilberseimer the coidentity of structure and form is hereby an "indispensable assumption." For

the necessity of shaping an often gigantic, heterogenous mass of material according to a formal law equally valid for each of its elements imposes a reduction of architectural forms to the most basic, most essential, and most universal. A limitation to the shapes of geometric solids—the basic elements of all architecture. . . . Shaping huge masses according to a universal law, suppressing diversity, is what Nietzsche took to be the very definition of style. The universal, the law itself, is honored and brought to the fore; the exception, conversely, is set aside. Nuance is erased. Mass becomes the master, chaos is forced to take on form, logically, unambiguously, mathematics, law.[43]

Here Hilberseimer finally formulates the central themes of his architectural theory. His two most important books, *Großstadtbauten* (1925) and *Großstadtarchitektur* (1927), would present them once again, in synopses of increasing complexity.[44]

Two Urban Models: The Residential City and the High-Rise City

In December 1923, when the journal *Bauwelt* announced a competition for solutions to the housing problem, Hilberseimer submitted four schematic drawings demonstrating a system of satellite cities (fig. 14). In this scheme, a working city (Type A) is ringed by residential cities (Type B; fig. 15). Each Type B city can accommodate 125,000 inhabitants and is linked by train to the economic, administrative, industrial, and cultural center A. Each is laid out as a precise rectangle consisting of seventy-eight blocks, themselves also rectangular and considerably elongated. Each block is divided into three sections by two connecting walks. Its long sides, running north-south, flank residential streets, while the short north and south ends contain shops facing an east-west commercial street. At the ends of these

14. Ludwig Hilberseimer. Diagram of a system of satellite cities (*Trabantenstadt*). From Hilberseimer, *Großstadtbauten* (Hannover: Aposs-Verlag, 1925), p. 11, fig. 4

15. Ludwig Hilberseimer. Plan of a residential satellite city (*Wohnstadt*). 1923. From Hilberseimer, *Großstadtarchitektur* (Stuttgart: Verlag Julius Hoffmann, 1927), p. 33, fig. 51

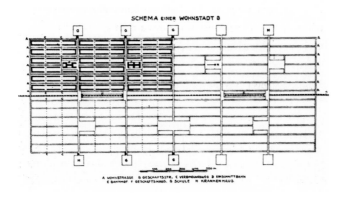

16. Ludwig Hilberseimer.
Apartment house blocks,
residential satellite city (*Wohn-stadt*). 1923. Perspective view.
From Hilberseimer, *Großstadtar-chitektur* (Stuttgart: Verlag Julius
Hoffmann, 1927), p. 33, fig. 53

17. Ludwig Hilberseimer.
Apartment house block. 1923.
Perspective. From Hilberseimer,
Großstadtbauten (Hannover:
Aposs-Verlag, 1925), p. 15, fig. 8

commercial streets, a little beyond the city boundary, are schools and hospitals, aligned with the street axes to serve as *points de vue* (fig. 16). Eight ten-story commercial buildings are disposed regularly in the urban grid, each facing an east-west street and set back half a block to preserve the symmetry. Along the city's north-south center axis runs a sunken rail line with two stations a kilometer (⅝ of a mile) apart.

Hilberseimer's residential block, the basic element of his ideal city, was derived from the traditional Berlin apartment block, of which it was a "corrected" version in terms of hygiene, function, efficiency, and aesthetics. The blocks are five stories tall on the long side and their windowed facades with simple loggias are regularly interrupted by slightly projecting stairwell towers (fig. 17). At either end they are abutted by two-story structures facing the commercial street, again with regular rows of windows above and display windows at the

sidewalk level. The height of these flat-roofed structures ensures sunlight and circulation for all of the apartments, about whose arrangement and layout nothing is said. Hilberseimer's satellite-city concept is ultimately no more than a modernist interpretation of Ebenezer Howard's garden city system; in fact he cites Letchworth and Welwyn Garden City as examples. But everything that in the English garden city is picturesque has given way to rationalistic efficiency.

In the fall of 1924, Hilberseimer visited Le Corbusier and saw the architect's drawings for the *ville contemporaine*, created two years previously (fig. 18). Under the influence of that urban-planning utopia, Hilberseimer next developed his own ideal design for a metropolis: the high-rise city (figs. 19–21). If his residential city of 1923 was based on the English garden-city model, his high-rise city of 1924 is a more efficient and rational reinterpretation of the contemporary American

18. Le Corbusier. Project for a Contemporary City of Three Million (*Ville contemporaine*). Aerial perspective in the form of a diorama prepared for the Salon d'Automne, Paris, of 1922, 16 meters (c. 52'6") long (lost)

19. Ludwig Hilberseimer. Project for a High-Rise City (*Hochhausstadt*), east-west street. 1924. Perspective view: ink and watercolor on paper, 38 x 58¼" (96.5 x 148 cm). The Art Institute of Chicago, Hilberseimer Collection

20. Ludwig Hilberseimer. Project for a High-Rise City (*Hochhausstadt*). 1924. Schematic plans and diagrams. From Hilberseimer, *Großstadtarchitektur* (Stuttgart: Verlag Julius Hoffmann, 1927), p. 17, fig. 22

21. Ludwig Hilberseimer. Project for a High-Rise City (*Hochhausstadt*), north-south street. 1924. Perspective view: ink and watercolor on paper, 38¼ x 55" (97 x 140 cm). The Art Institute of Chicago. Hilberseimer Collection. Gift of George E. Danforth

metropolis. In an early essay, Hilberseimer had already praised that prototype as the incarnation of the modern city, at the same time criticizing it for its lack of planning and resulting chaotic nature.[45] He now set out to compensate for its deficiencies without sacrificing its merits. He adopted the American city's orthogonal street plan (as he had in his residential, Type B city), giving its blocks his preferred shape of the elongated rectangle. He also adopted the architectural type of the high-rise, though modifying it in accordance with functional and hygienic considerations. But above all he concentrated on the problem of traffic, and his proposed solution was to stack one city on top of another: the city of work below, the city of housing above. Everyone would live directly above their workplace, so that their daily commute would be a brief elevator ride, reducing street traffic.

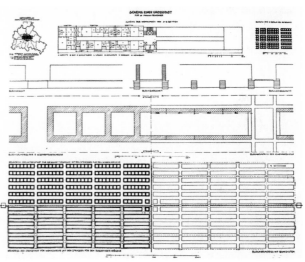

As published in journals and books,[46] Hilberseimer's design is presented in only three illustrations: a pieced-together ground plan in various scales, with schematic cross-sections and views; a partial perspective looking down an east-west street; and another perspective of a north-south street. The plan, a black-and-white drawing, demonstrates that this urban concept could accommodate 4 million people, the population of greater Berlin at the time, on less than 6,000 hectares (about twenty-three square miles)—less than the area of central Berlin, which in the mid 1920s housed only 2 million people, many of them inadequately. The two large perspectives, tinted in tones of grayish brown and overwhelmingly sober, show the structure and architecture of Hilberseimer's high-rise city, both based on logic,

efficiency, geometry, repetition, and uniformity. Slender fifteen-story residential slabs accommodate shops in the tall floors at their bases. Their facades bear monotonously regular rows of windows. These structures stand on shorter, weightier five-story buildings, simplified—and banalized—offshoots of the Concrete Office Building that Mies had drawn two years earlier. The towers are narrower than the buildings that form their bases, creating wide pedestrian sidewalks, connected by footbridges, at the junction of the two. The ground is far below, where a few automobiles can be seen in the immense streets. Still farther down, on four underground levels, subway and train tracks run at right angles to the streets. The distance of 600 meters (about 650 yards) between subway stops determines the length of the blocks.

The role Hilberseimer envisioned for his utopian design was strangely ambivalent. In *Großstadtbauten* he speaks enigmatically of some future problem that will require solution. In *Großstadtarchitektur* he presents his high-rise city as an abstraction allowing him to suggest solutions to specific problems. In his book *Entfaltung einer Planungsidee*, published in 1963, he looks back with genuine horror at his drawings from nearly forty years before: "Taken as a whole, the design for this high-rise city was wrong from the start. The result was more like a necropolis than a metropolis, a sterile landscape of asphalt and cement, inhuman in every respect."[47] This retrospective self-criticism was generous but unjustified: Hilberseimer was not attempting to provide views of some fictional ideal city, but simply schemata. This is why the drawings so closely resemble near-contemporary pictures by Heinrich Maria Davringhausen, Georg Grosz, and Anton Räderscheidt: in their mechanical repetition, their pitiless monotony, and their anonymity, they capture the deeper essence of the modern metropolis (fig. 22).

In this respect Hilberseimer's analysis of existing reality merged with realistic projections. Perhaps he meant to start from the point that Scheffler, with penetrating foresight, had arrived at ten years before, when, behind the hoardings around the apartment blocks under construction in Berlin, he discovered the seed of his new *Architektur der Großstadt*:

This uniformity is a result of demands that are beginning to take on the force of convention everywhere. Since big-city dwellers have already grown accustomed to certain floor plans, since they expect to be able to find their way around however often they move, and since the pressure of this demand leads in the same direction as the fact that mathematical calculations of how best to exploit a given building parcel come to the same conclusions with regard to floor plans, specific floor plans evolve. And in this case the typical is the first prerequisite of a style.

It thus turns out that the task of the architect of apartment houses is not so much erecting handsome, independent structures that stand out as particularly elegant from the long rows of apartment house facades, but rather—to put it baldly—deliberately creating living quarters for the masses. What is wanted is not the particular but the typical, not the exceptional but the universally

22. Heinrich Maria Davringhausen. *Der Schieber* (The profiteer; detail). 1920–21. Oil on canvas, 47 x 47" (120 x 120 cm). Kunstmuseum Düsseldorf im Ehrenhof

valid. And this is what happens when one follows the seemingly instinctive desire for uniformity to its logical conclusion.[48]

The City Model Is Modified (Wohlfahrtsstadt, 1926) and Put to Use (Berlin-City, 1928)

Hilberseimer returned to programmatic metropolitan design in 1928, producing a suggestion for the development of Berlin on which he would work for the next two years (fig. 23). For his redesign of the city center he took up the north-south-oriented rows from his high-rise city of 1924, but now he envisioned that the structures would be used only for stores and offices. This, then, was a sample fragment of what he had earlier called the Type A city, the counterpart of the residential Type B city envisioned in his 1923 satellite system. The slablike buildings are a modest eight stories tall; the first two floors of each are reserved for public and semipublic uses, and edge a large atrium that takes up the entire interior space of the block. Below them are underground parking and storerooms, above them offices stacked one above the other. At the building's tops are partially covered and landscaped roof terraces. For the orthogonal streets, Hilberseimer worked up two variants: a conventional one and one with three levels, separating foot and automobile traffic and providing lanes without intersections for cars.

The design, produced with no specific incentive and no real sponsor, puts Hilberseimer's earlier

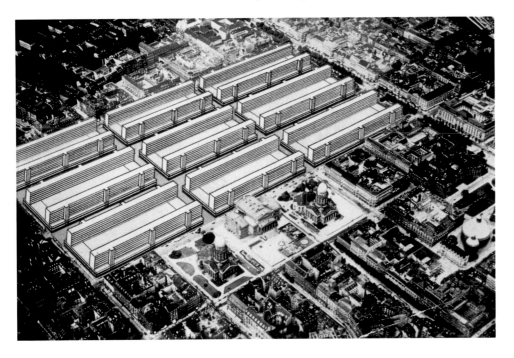

23. Ludwig Hilberseimer. Friedrichstadt development project, Berlin. 1928. Bird's-eye view of office and commercial buildings: photocollage, 6¾ x 9¾" (17 x 25 cm). The Art Institute of Chicago, Hilberseimer Collection

abstract utopias into a long-overdue confrontation with a complex reality, to which they adapt with obvious reluctance. Hilberseimer adopts the existing geometric parcels and scale of the historical city, and matches the heights of the buildings to their structural, social, and cultural context, their uses to economic necessities. But the monumental complex of the Gendarmenmarkt—in which two cathedrals and Karl Friedrich Schinkel's Schauspielhaus theater would have immediately bordered the new development—is treated as nonchalantly as if it were an ordinary Berlin block; and the juxtaposition of the modernistic city to

the elegant boulevard Unter den Linden could not be more abrupt.

The same arrogant rigor characterizes Hilberseimer's approximately simultaneous design for Berlin's historical core, between Alexanderplatz, the Lustgarten, and the Museuminsel. Only the northern part of the area escapes unchanged; otherwise, the historical fabric is forced to give way to an "orderly" grouping of high-rise, H-shaped slabs, and to a regular, landscaped row complex. As in the Voisin plan that Le Corbusier had worked out for Paris a few years earlier, modernism here simply erases the city's architectural memory in order to adapt it, crudely and arrogantly, to the "new spirit." This, too, Scheffler had foreseen and lightheartedly approved of.

In 1927, in his essay "*Die Wohnung als Gebrauchsgegenstand*" (The dwelling as utilitarian object),[49] Hilberseimer had rehabilitated the single-family dwelling surrounded by a garden, which he had previously condemned as chiefly responsible for the chaos of cities. Now, though, he was concerned to accommodate families in sparsely built-up suburbs, reserving inner-city housing for single people and childless couples. This new hypothesis led him to produce studies of new dwelling types, among them a house with a balcony, a two-story row house, and a one-story single-family house. In the latter, the living rooms lie near the street while the bedrooms are oriented to the garden. This design takes up some of Häring's notions and lends itself both to multiples in rows and to repetition in a kind of carpet development. With these studies Hilberseimer turned his own approach on its head: having begun with overall designs for a residential city and a high-rise city, only subsequently adding apartment floor-plans, he now proceeded from the single dwelling and multiples of it to an urban layout. Here his structures were much smaller, and green space, the importance of which he had meanwhile come to recognize, played a central role. After glorifying the metropolis, he now celebrated the suburban housing estate (fig. 24).

That Hilberseimer granted both of these a right to exist at the same time, and was intrigued with the possibility of designing them, is apparent from the model of Wohlfahrtsstadt that he created in 1926 for the *Ausstellung der freien Wohlfahrtspflege* (Private welfare

exhibition) in Düsseldorf and then Stuttgart (fig. 25). The center is made of giant fourteen-story cruciform- and H-shaped high-rises. As one moves outward, the density of this schematic toy city is reduced, step by step, until one reaches the tiny cubic single-family dwellings that ring its cheerless periphery in disciplined rows.

The Founding of the Circle

Early 1924 saw the retirement of Berlin's talented but conservative building commissioner, Ludwig Hoffmann, who had determined the city's building policies with a strong hand during a long tenure in office. Immediately afterward, several young architects joined together to promote their professional and cultural interests. The impetus came from Bruno Taut, who had nursed the idea of forming another group of architects ever since the dissolution of the lodgelike Expressionist *Gläserne Kette* (Crystal Chain) group in 1920. Some of his earlier colleagues were happy to join the new association: Scharoun, Hans and Wassili Luckhardt, Max Taut, and later Carl Krayl and Walter Gropius.

The *Zehnerring* (Circle of ten), or *Zwölferring* (Circle of twelve), as the group called itself depending on the current number of its members, was nevertheless quite different from the Crystal Chain. The earlier association had mainly fostered an exchange of ideas; the new one actively worked to further its professional interests. Beyond a commitment to the new architecture, these interests could not be reduced to any unified doctrine. Theoretical debate was avoided wherever possible—quite deliberately, for there was such diver-

sity of opinion within the alliance that it could easily have fallen apart.

Oddly enough, the first Circle of Ten numbered only nine: Otto Bartning, Behrens, Häring, Erich Mendelsohn, Mies, Poelzig, Walter Schilbach, and Bruno and Max Taut. They regularly met in Mies's and Häring's Berlin office. The group was soon expanded into the Circle of Twelve, which issued a press release presenting the Berlin building authorities with four demands for reform: greater creative freedom for the

individual architects, an end to political favoritism in the review of new designs, swifter approval of plans, and the appointment of qualified judges in competitions.

Within the Bund Deutscher Architekten, the Circle of Twelve was seen as a conspiratorial and rebellious subgroup, but the younger men emerged victorious. Their most urgent concern was acceded to in 1926: following an interim arrangement, their candidate, Martin Wagner, was named Hoffmann's successor as building commissioner. That same year the group was expanded beyond Berlin's boundaries and renamed the *Ring* (Circle). Its members now were Bartning, Behrendt, Behrens, Richard Döcker, Gropius, Häring, Otto Haesler, Hilberseimer, Arthur Korn, Krayl, Hans and Wassili

24. Ludwig Hilberseimer. Mixed-height housing development (*Mischbebauung*). c. 1930. Perspective view from balcony of single unit: ink on paper, 14½ x 20" (36.9 x 50.6 cm). The Art Institute of Chicago. Hilberseimer Collection

25. Ludwig Hilberseimer. *Wohlfahrtsstadt* (Welfare city). Model for *Ausstellung der freien Wohlfahrtspflege* (Private welfare exhibition), Düsseldorf and Stuttgart, 1926–27

Luckhardt, Ernst May, Mendelsohn, Adolf Meyer, Mies, Bernhard Pankok, Poelzig, Adolf Rading, Scharoun, Schilbach, Karl Schneider, Soeder, Bruno and Max Taut, Heinrich Tessenow, and Wagner.

The common goal of these architects was to promote the international modern movement. To that end they organized themselves as a society without leaders and without union status. Häring was named secretary; members committed themselves to mutual professional support. Among other things, the secretary was expected to take a position on "building problems of the present" as well as on "state and bureaucratic building policy and the building industry."[50] In 1926, the *Bauwelt* began to include a monthly insert edited by Häring and Hilberseimer and publishing buildings and designs by their colleagues. The Staatliches Bauhaus in Dessau was selected to serve as a repository and archive for important information. The association also organized exhibitions, sponsored instructional and documentary films, and supported publications, among them Bruno Taut's polemical *Bauen: Der neue Wohnbau*, which appeared in 1927 with a sarcastic dedication to the "beloved building police."[51]

The Deutscher Werkbund exhibition *Die Wohnung* (The dwelling), presented in Stuttgart in 1927, represented for the Circle both a triumph and a trap. Of the alliance's twenty-seven members, twenty-one participated in the exhibition. But conflicts between Mies and Döcker and especially between Mies and Häring, culminating in Mies's withdrawal from the Circle in August 1927, soon revealed that the only recently solidified front was crumbling.

In 1928 the Circle attached itself to the Congrès International d'Architecture Moderne (CIAM). There, too, immediate disagreements were evident, leading to the historic argument between Häring and Le Corbusier about organicism versus rationalism. In 1933 the Circle, already fragmented internally, was disbanded under the political pressure of National Socialism.

A Side Trip to the Provinces: The Weissenhof Housing Colony Master Plan, Stuttgart, 1927

In the early summer of 1925, the directors of the Deutscher Werkbund appointed Mies and Behrendt artistic advisors for an exhibition planned for 1926 in Stuttgart. Its theme was to be *Die Wohnung*, and a model development of modern housing was to be built as part of it. Days later the industrialist Peter Bruckmann (cofounder of the Deutscher Werkbund) and the mayor of Stuttgart, Karl Lautenschlager, submitted a memorandum on the exhibition. "The drive toward efficiency in every aspect of our lives," they wrote,

has not ignored the question of housing, and the economic conditions of our time forbid extravagance and force us to achieve maximum results with minimum expenditure. This means using materials and technologies in the construction of apartments, and in the housing industry in general, that reduce costs as well as simplifying housekeeping and improving living conditions as a whole. Consistent encouragement of such efforts will also mean improvement in big-city housing, a better way of life in general, and accordingly a stronger national economy.[52]

By about this time, a site on the Weissenhof, a hill on the outskirts of Stuttgart, had been selected. The south-facing slope was as yet undeveloped, seemed ideal for a housing project, and belonged to the city. The Stuttgart Stadterweiterungsamt (City expansion office) drew up a preliminary plan calling for twenty-nine single-family houses and a fourteen-unit apartment house here, and the building committee of Stuttgart's city council approved the construction of forty dwellings within the framework of the exhibition.

A preliminary list of architects was quickly made up.[53] In addition to Stuttgart natives Döcker, Richard Herre, Hugo Keuerleber, Adolf Gustav Schneck, and Paul Bonatz, it included Behrens, Tessenow, Bruno Taut, Gropius, Hilberseimer, Ferdinand Kramer, Adolf Loos, Josef Frank, J. J. P. Oud, Le Corbusier, Mart Stam, Poelzig, Mendelsohn, Theo van Doesburg—and of course Mies, as artistic overseer, and his office colleague Häring. The latter pair revised the list, eliminating Bonatz, Keuerleber, Loos, and Frank and adding Berlage, Henry van de Velde, Bartning, Korn, Hans Luckhardt, and Alfred Gellhorn.[54] Finally the Werkbund produced a kind of compromise list: it included everyone previously suggested except Berlage, Bonatz, and Loos, and introduced Scharoun.[55]

Meanwhile the exhibition had been postponed until 1927. Together with Häring, Mies worked up a preliminary overall plan, which envisioned an unusual development of the sloping property with attached and interlocking forms (plates 90, 91). In the earliest versions the crystallike layers follow the curves of the contour lines, but they gradually take on a more orthogonal arrangement, lying flat against the hillside and fitting together like a kind of Suprematist sculpture dominated by a geometrical, abstract "city crown" of Expressionist memory (plate 93). Many site plans, a view, and a three-dimensional model were produced.

The fact that for this attractive suburban parcel Mies did not revert to either the garden city model (well-known in progressive German circles at least since the building of Hellerau, Dresden, beginning in 1906) or the rationalist model, the *Siedlung* (of which Theodor Fischer had created an early example with his Alte Heide dwellings near Munich, beginning in 1918), reveals his desire to chart a radically new course. More important, it shows his stubborn adherence to the notion of the city, as opposed to the concept of the village or suburb. Although small, the Weissenhof exhibition was to be an urban construct: compact, dense, uniform. Both the drawings and the model conjure up a modern citadel that could have accommodated over 100 tightly nested apartments, accessed by narrow walkways and flights of stairs.

The officials of the Stadterweiterungsamt were nonplussed but also intrigued, especially since the unusual plan appeared to afford an almost sensationally high building density. Stuttgart's respected and rather conservative architectural fraternity was less enthusiastic. On May 5, 1926, articles critical of the plan, one by Bonatz, the other by Paul Schmitthenner, appeared in two important dailies.[56] The tradition-oriented natives called the plan of the nonlocal avant-garde architect "unprofessional, a piece of applied art, and dilettantish,"[57] and warned the city not to permit such nonsense, let alone encourage it. Schmitthenner, who was reminded of "mountain nests in Italy," declared—by no means inappropriately—that the exhibition might well document the new architecture but failed to do what it had set out to do, namely rationalize the housing question. In addition, he noted—again not altogether mistakenly—that the

design set out to "capture in formulas" the international style of the century.[58] Bonatz went even farther: "In a number of horizontal terraces a profusion of flat cubes presses up the slope in uninhabitable density, more reminiscent of some Jerusalem suburb than dwellings for Stuttgart. For the sake of visual appearance the structural elements interlock in various ways, so that each one ends up having to look at the back wall of the one in front, only a short distance away. Construction will cost more than twice as much as a more sensible design would."[59]

These harsh criticisms had their intended effect, especially since they articulated complaints already in circulation. There was immediate ferment in the Werkbund. At a meeting of the Württemberg chapter in June 1926, nearly the entire board of directors was replaced, but this power shift turned out to benefit the modernist faction: although Bonatz stayed on as a board member, Schmitthenner and several other traditionalists were replaced by moderate avant-gardists like Döcker and Schneck. This was only a prelude to a reshuffling of the board of the parent organization that occurred a short time later, in which Bruckmann was named chairman and Mies vice-chairman.

Meanwhile cracks began to form in the modernist front. After some hesitation, Mies had been confirmed as the project's artistic director. Döcker, a representative of the left wing of the Stuttgart school, not altogether unselfishly offered him help in the completion of the construction plans, but simultaneously made a number of critical comments altogether in the spirit of his former mentor Bonatz. Among other things, he complained that the placement of the houses was "often so arbitrarily whimsical that some of the individual spaces can get no light or air."[60] Mies responded sharply, expressing shock at his colleague's "incomprehension" and declaring that he had "produced only a three-dimensional illustration of a general design principle," so that "it is nonsense to speak of a construction plan." In pique, he asked whether the other man could seriously think it possible that he would "build spaces without light or air" and "not give the buildings the proper orientation to the sun." He stuck firmly to his programmatic approach:

I consider it essential that we take a new course there at the Weissenhof, as I am convinced that a new way of living will evolve beyond the traditional four walls. Here it is not a matter of presenting a model development plan in the old sense; instead, as in my own practice, I want to conquer new territory here. To me that is the real reason, the only reason, for our efforts. Everything else we can confidently leave to the likes of Bonatz and Schmitthenner. These gentlemen have stated clearly enough what they consider to be structural problems. I would not waste an hour on that kind of work. Twenty years ago I struggled to build good, decent, and sensible buildings. Since then my ambition has changed. Building is an intellectual activity for me, therefore [I want] to be creative, and not just in details but in the fundamentals.[61]

Politely but firmly, Mies declined the offer of collaboration.

In July 1926, Mies submitted a revised master plan. He had transformed the interlocking sculpture into a lively and actually rather innocuous composition of individual structures, one that was altogether realistic and buildable. Based on this design, a first estimate of the construction costs was made and quickly approved, together with the development plan—meanwhile redrawn once again by the Stuttgart city council. Distribution of the houses to the participating architects began in September. The list had been changed repeatedly by this time, and now contained fourteen names: Oud, Frank, Döcker, Schneck, Hans Herkommer, Heinz Wetzel, Bartning, Gropius, Häring, Hilberseimer, Mies, Rading, Max Taut, and Tessenow.[62] There was still debate about Le Corbusier and Mendelsohn; Loos had disappeared. Although the list was still subject to change, fee negotiations between the architects and the city got under way—and soon led to the break between Mies and Häring and occasioned violent controversy within the Circle. In his capacity as the association's secretary, Häring stubbornly insisted that the dues schedule be followed precisely. Mies felt his demand was unrealistic, and agreed to a compromise—a flat fee—to save the project. He brusquely reminded Häring that the Weissenhof development was not a Circle project but an undertaking of the Werkbund, whereupon Häring and Mendelsohn withdrew under protest from both the Circle and the Stuttgart scheme.

Meanwhile yet another new list of architects had been drawn up: Herkommer, Wetzel, and Bartning had disappeared to make room for Le Corbusier, Mendelsohn, and Stam.[63] Häring and Mendelsohn, as we have seen, withdrew, and Tessenow courteously declined; he was in the process of moving, and under such circumstances the Stuttgart assignment "would require an unreasonable amount of either work or . . . worry."[64] Max Taut requested that his brother Bruno be invited as well, and Behrens asked Mies, a former collaborator and sometime competitor, if he might be permitted to build a terrace house. Scharoun and Poelzig were invited somewhat later, and finally—probably on Van de Velde's recommendation—Victor Bourgeois was added to the list.

While these curiously complex maneuvers were still going on, the staking out of the site began in October 1926. Döcker was engaged as construction supervisor for the entire development. The architects met in Stuttgart for an exchange of ideas, and in December the Werkbund issued a detailed memorandum presenting the exhibition as "a systematic attempt to design the New Dwelling and resolve all the attendant organizational, spatial, structural, technological, and hygienic problems."[65] The architects' plans were submitted, criticized, corrected, and approved. Construction contracts were issued. The groundbreaking ceremony was held on March 1, 1927.

The difficulties were by no means over. There was friction between Mies and Döcker, there were cost overruns (the budget was extremely tight), there was mistrust in the city government with regard to what was in every respect an unusual experiment, and time was growing short. As early as the end of January 1927, Döcker had pointedly declined all responsibility for getting the development finished by the deadline, and as late as the beginning of May it seemed that the Oud and Poelzig houses might have to be scrapped; construction on them had not even begun. Nevertheless, the exhibition opened for viewing on July 23, with the development still unfinished. A brief two months later it was officially declared complete.

The opening involved the customary speeches, and as usual the artistic director kept his brief. After thanking his colleagues, Mies explained "the justification of their work" as follows:

The problems of the New Dwelling are rooted in the changed material, social, and intellectual structure of our time; only in such a context can these problems be understood. The extent of the change in that structure determines the nature and dimension of these problems. They are anything but arbitrary. They are not to be solved with slogans, nor can they be debated away with slogans. The problem of rationalization and uniformity is only a partial problem. Rationalization and uniformity are only means, must never be our goal. The problem of the New Dwelling is in essence an intellectual one, and the battle for the New Dwelling is only a part of the larger struggle for new ways of living.[66]

Speed, the Myth of Traffic, and Big-City Architecture

No sooner had Martin Wagner been named Berlin's building commissioner—in no small part thanks to lobbying by the Circle—than he initiated a major program of housing developments on the city's outskirts. At the same time, this forty-one-year-old architect, who a decade earlier had written his dissertation on green space in cities,[67] took in hand the redesign of the core of the German capital. The main theme of this redesign was the urban traffic flow. This was in keeping both with the actual problems of the city—whose chaos of pedestrians and automobiles had necessitated the installation of Europe's first traffic light, in Potsdamer Platz in 1925, and whose north-south connections were still inadequate—and with the mythology of the time and the architectural thinking that went along with it.

As early as the end of the nineteenth century, Berlage had justified his "impressionistic architecture" in terms of the new kind of perception produced by the speed of modern life, which rendered detailed ornament on urban building facades superfluous.[68] Eugène Hénard, in his studies for the redesign of Paris from 1900 on, carefully considered this same *"mouvement moderne,"* which he saw as the force that would shape the contemporary city.[69] Magne too, writing in 1908, developed his purist aesthetic out of the increasingly rapid flow of traffic.[70] Two years later Behrens summed up such thinking, writing,

It is a question of rhythm when we say that our time moves faster than that of our fathers. A certain haste has taken hold of us that permits no leisure in which to lose ourselves in details. If we race

through the streets of our metropolis in a speeding vehicle, we can no longer appreciate building details, just as cityscapes caught sight of from a speeding express train can affect us only as silhouettes. Individual buildings no longer speak for themselves. The only architecture appropriate to such a way of viewing our surroundings, already a constant habit, is one that produces facades as uniform and unbusy as possible, which in their simplicity present no obstacles. If something particular has to be emphasized, that element must be positioned at the end of the direction of our movement. What is needed is the creation of large surfaces, the design of prominent monuments and broad open spaces that can be perceived at a glance, or the uniform alignment of necessary smaller elements, whereby these, too, take on a certain unity.[71]

Behrens repeated these arguments almost word for word in 1914, in an essay in which he further developed his ideas on the "aesthetics of motion" and derived from them precepts for modern city planning. Given the speed of the traffic that it must facilitate and even encourage, he wrote, the city cannot follow the "medieval principle of irregular, twisting streets and idyllic squares in the resulting angles" but must "proceed according to well-thought-out, comprehensive plans with broad, straight streets extended a considerable distance."[72] He thus conjured up a modern metropolis whose inner commercial core was a "uniform architectural construct," with tall buildings after the American pattern, while its suburbs evolved into a "country house zone" close to nature.

In the first decades of the twentieth century, the swift and dense stream of traffic experienced in the metropolises served as a fascinating symbol of modern life. In his *"Manifeste du Futurisme"* of 1909, Filippo Tommaso Marinetti praised the "beauty of speed."[73] Walter Ruttmann's revolutionary documentary film *Berlin, Symphonie einer Großstadt* (1927) makes the movement of people and automobiles in urban spaces its central focus. In Friedrich Wilhelm Murnau's film *Sunrise* (1927), a kiss to which two people from the country surrender in the middle of the street unleashes a spectacular traffic jam. And in the novel *Der Mann ohne Eigenschaften* (The man without qualities, 1930–42), Robert Musil describes the inhabitants of the capital city of Kakania—that is to say, Vienna in 1913— as swept up in "restless movement," whether of cyclists, tram drivers, or motorists: "cars shot out of narrow, dark

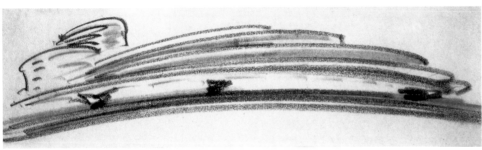

26 (right). Anton Stankowski. *Zeitprotokoll mit Auto* (Time-lapse exposure with car). 1929. Gelatin silver photograph, 9½ x 12" (23.9 x 30.9 cm). Stiftung für die Photographie Kunsthaus Zürich

27 (above). Erich Mendelsohn. Universum Cinema at the WOGA Development, Berlin. 1925–28. Sketch: black, red, and orange pencil on paper, 3½ x 9¾" (9 x 25 cm). Kunstbibliothek Berlin

28 (above right). Erich Mendelsohn. Mosse House Renovation and Addition, Berlin. 1921–23

streets into the lightness of bright squares. The somberness of pedestrians formed wispy tangles."[74]

Architects were by no means immune to the fascination with traffic (figs. 26, 27). On the contrary. Mächler saw traffic as the metabolism of the urban organism (a metaphor by no means lightly chosen), the engine driving the city's economic growth. For Wagner, private cars were seven-league boots that anyone could don in order to reach either the peace of the countryside or the "pulsing" metropolis in only minutes.[75] Mendelsohn went a step farther, deriving from traffic and its dynamism a distinct architectural style that he first demonstrated in his redesign of the Rudolf Mosse House in Berlin (1921–23; fig. 28); he explicitly remarked that his building was "no mere uninvolved spectator of the rushing cars" but finally "an appreciative, collaborating element of movement."[76] With this he had invented a definite—and highly subjective—variant of the specific but international "big-city architecture" whose program Hilberseimer—with different aesthetic implications, to be sure—would articulate in his book *Großstadtarchitektur* of 1927.

Movement, Commerce, and the City: the Alexanderplatz Debate and Redesign (1928–29)

In 1928, a highly publicized competition for the redesign of Alexanderplatz, in the center of Berlin, sparked a discussion of the metropolitan square in general. The newly formed Berliner Verkehrs-Aktiengesellschaft invited six architects to participate in the competition, which was based on a detailed plan that Wagner had worked out himself (fig. 29). Summarizing the principles of the plan in the journal *Das neue Berlin*, of which he was a copublisher, the building commissioner argued that although the designer of a square in a small town could think of "purely architectural issues," this was impossible in a metropolis, where the square was above all a "traffic channel almost constantly filled," a "clearing point for a network of major traffic arteries." Accordingly, "the smooth flow of traffic is the foremost consideration, formal design only of secondary importance."[77] Increases in traffic could not be calculated far in advance—twenty-five years at most—yet a metropolitan square had to be scaled according to expected increases, and its traffic pattern laid out accordingly. After twenty-five years, when the requirements would most likely have changed, it would have to be torn up and rebuilt.

That buildings might be restricted to only brief lives was for Wagner a feature of the modern metropo-

lis. He championed "dynamic urban building,"[78] a city structure that could adapt to changing needs, even if this meant coldly abandoning its existing fabric. As Antonio Sant'Elia had remarked fifteen years before, "each generation" had to create its own city; demolition and construction were two sides of the same coin.[79] Wagner was by no means arguing for a new urban laissez-faire; the reshaping of the city had to be supervised by a central authority (in distinct contrast to the practice of the previous, liberal era), but according to criteria appropriate to a capitalist system. For the commissioner, a social democrat, the city, like any other enterprise, could and should be operated with an eye to profit.

Wagner's concept of the metropolitan square conformed almost precisely to that of the novelist Alfred Döblin, whose serial novel *Berlin Alexanderplatz* would be published in 1929. The writer describes Rosenthaler Platz, a heavily trafficked intersection in east Berlin, as entertaining itself: in his eyes this public urban space is

an independent, complex, but faceless creature sucking in people and automobiles, spinning them around, and releasing them again in every direction. This was not, as his description of the eponymous square in *Berlin Alexanderplatz* shows, without its disturbing fascination:

The police tower over the square. Several specimens of them are standing about. Each specimen casts a connoisseur's glance to both sides, and knows the traffic rules by heart. It has puttees around its legs, a rubber mace hangs from its right side, it swings its arms horizontally from west to east, and thus north and south cannot advance any farther, east flows west, west flows east. Then the specimen switches about automatically: north flows south, south flows north. The copper has a well-defined waistline. As soon as he jerks around, there is a rush across the square in the direction of Königstrasse of about thirty private individuals. Some of them stop on the traffic island, one part reaches the other side and continues walking on the planks. The same number have started east, swimming toward the others, the same thing has befallen them, there is no mishap.

There are men, women, and children, the latter mostly holding women's hands. To enumerate them all and to describe their destinies is hardly possible, and only in a few cases would this succeed. The wind scatters chaff over all of them alike. The faces of the eastward wanderers are in no way different from those of the wanderers to the west, south, and north; moreover they exchange their roles, those who are now crossing the square to Aschinger's may be seen an hour later in front of the empty Hahn department store, just as those who come from Brunnenstrasse on their way to Jannowitz Brücke mingle with those coming from the reverse direction. Yes, and many of them also turn off to the side, from south to east, from south to west, from north to west, from north to east.[80]

The constant flux of the square's public has spread to its architecture: again and again, the street noise that August Endell had celebrated in his 1908 essay "*Die Schönheit der grossen Stadt*"[81] is drowned out by the sound of jackhammers.

Where Jürgens the stationery store was, they have torn down the house and put up a building fence instead. An old man sits there with a medical scale: "Try your weight, five pfennigs." Dear sisters and brethren, you who swarm across the Alex, give yourselves this treat, look through the loophole next to the medical scale at this dumpheap where Jürgens once flourished, and where Hahn's department store still stands, emptied, evacuated, and eviscerated. . . . Thus Rome, Babylon, Nineveh, Hannibal, Caesar, all went to smash, just think of it! In the first place, I must remark that they are digging those cities up again, as the illustrations in last Sunday's edition show, and in the second place, those cities have fulfilled their purpose, and we can now build new cities. Do you cry over your old

29. Martin Wagner, Amt für Stadtplanung, Berlin. General Plan for Redesign of Alexanderplatz. 1928. Competition document. Published in *Das Neue Berlin* 2 (1929): 34

trousers when they are moldy and seedy? No, you simply buy new ones, thus turns the world.[82]

This cynical view, which Döblin presented with ironic melancholy and Wagner with chilly realism, was of profound significance for the Alexanderplatz competition. Like the trousers in Döblin's novel, the life expectancy of the square's architecture was limited from the start, and accordingly the buildings were to have no "lasting economic or architectural values."[83] Nevertheless, the investments required in building them were substantial, and needed to be amortized over a brief quarter century. That meant that the buildings had to be extraordinarily profitable; which in turn meant that they had to be able to attract passersby as potential consumers.

This the buildings could do—to continue Wagner's argument—in two ways. To capture "consumer power," as he sympathetically called it, in shops, department stores, bars, and offices, they not only had to adapt themselves to the "flow lines" of street traffic but also to the "strolling lines" of pedestrian traffic. They also had to be showy, if at the same time cheaply built. In sum: "The most elementary forms, which make a distinct artistic statement during the daytime as well as during the evening hours, are basic requirements of the metropolitan square. Light flooding *in* by day and light flooding *out* by night gives the square an entirely different appearance. *Color, form,* and *light* (advertisements) are the three main structural elements."[84]

The instructions were detailed, and the design that followed them the closest won the prize. Indeed the winning entry, by Hans and Wassili Luckhardt in collaboration with Alfons Anker, was no more than a docile realization of Wagner's ideas (fig. 30). Along the ideal traffic lines, the sides of the square were lined with tall structures, their ground floors reflecting the hypothetical "strolling lines" of pedestrian "consumer power." Two of the streets leading into the square were built over, as suggested in the building commissioner's general plan. Facades were for the most part uniform, in a simplified version of the "Mendelsohn style," and comprised alternating bands of wall, which supported signs, and window. The entire square was a metaphor for the ebb and flow of traffic, a gigantic bauble celebrating modern life—and modern capitalism.

Other competition entries, among them that of Behrens, were also only variations on Wagner's plan. Only Mies's Urban Design Proposal for Alexanderplatz was different, envisioning eleven freestanding structures—sharp-edged prisms of concrete and glass—that almost without exception respected the building lines of the streets on which they stood, but stepped back

from the ideal boundary of the square. Six nine-story buildings, one behind the other, were aligned with a seventeen-story office building. On the opposite side of the traffic circle were four freely positioned structures of the same type, each adapted in width and depth to its site. Between them lay the open square, with its circular flow of traffic and intersecting streetcar lines.

Mies presented his proposal in the form of a sober site plan and two photocollages showing the new Alexanderplatz both from above and from a tram. These images clearly reveal the new structures as offshoots of the Concrete Office Building of 1923. Inset into the first photocollage is a small photograph of the actual Berlin shot from the same bird's-eye perspective used for a charcoal drawing of the square's proposed design; the stifling density shown in the inset makes the design seem all the more spacious. The dematerialization of the metropolis that had begun metaphorically in the design for the Friedrichstrasse Skyscraper here reaches its material culmination: an entire urban district is swept clean. The tabula rasa accorded with contemporary modernist thinking to which Wagner adhered, and which was represented regularly in *Das neue Berlin*, but for Mies it was the basis and provocation for a new urban spatial composition. It was matched by the complex alignment of the uniform prisms to the square and to each other, producing an enigmatic interplay of correspondences and disjunctions.

The result was immediately controversial. After a somewhat prejudiced glance at the five other submissions, Hilberseimer wrote, "Mies van der Rohe's is the only one of the designs submitted that breaks through this rigid system [of matching building lines to traffic flow] and attempts to organize the square independently of the traffic. . . . Mies has designed the square by grouping freestanding building on the basis of architectural considerations alone."[85] The jury

promptly assigned Mies's unaccommodating, idiosyncratic, and in many respects difficult design to last place. In the end it was Behrens—after considerable reworking and reduction of his plan—who would redesign Alexanderplatz (fig. 31). The builder was a consortium financed by American money. The land was not purchased but only leased for fifty years, and the owners retained the right to tear down the buildings and rebuild after a given time.

The Second Competition for a Skyscraper next to the Friedrichstrasse Bahnhof, 1929

In the spring of 1929, the drained and financially pressed Turmhaus-Aktiengesellschaft surrendered its property on Friedrichstrasse, the development of which it had fought for determinedly if not altogether

fairly for nine years, to the same Berliner Verkehrs-Aktiengesellschaft that had sponsored the competition for Alexanderplatz. Before the year was out, the new owners announced a limited competition to which they invited five prominent architects or groups of architects: Alfred Grenander, Heinrich Straumer, Paul Mebes and Paul Emmerich, Mendelsohn, and Mies. What was wanted was a large office building to house the corporation's administration. Bartning and Wagner were among the members of the jury, which decided to award two equal prizes to Mendelsohn (fig. 32) and the office of Mebes and Emmerich. Once again, this time owing to the economic crisis, nothing was built. But once again the competition was not just a waste of time: in particular Mendelsohn, who combined a prismatic shape with a dynamically rounded form, and Mies, who suggested the compact, massive though glazed Friedrichstrasse Office Building Project, produced important and innovative contributions to the theme of the urban skyscraper.

Another Cosmopolitan Square Is Redesigned: The Potsdamer and Leipziger Platz Complex

Potsdamer Platz and Leipziger Platz, like Alexanderplatz, were big-city squares, two separate but functionally interrelated spaces to be redesigned to meet

31. Alexanderplatz, Berlin. Aerial photograph, c. 1935

32. Erich Mendelsohn. Entry in the second Friedrichstrasse skyscraper competition. 1929. Model

Developments that led to the competition for the enlargement of the Reichstag and the redesign of the Platz der Republik (formerly Königsplatz) in 1929 showed that even committed modernists did not altogether abandon the classical principles of architectural composition in favor of metaphors of speed and commerce. In 1927, within the framework of the *Grosse Berliner Kunstausstellung*, the architects of the Circle had presented designs for the Platz der Republik and for breaking through the Ministergärten. The basis for their thinking was the Mächler plan, which

33. Martin Wagner and Felix Unglaube. Project for Potsdamer Platz and Leipziger Platz.1929. Model

34. Marcel Breuer. Project for Potsdamer Platz. 1929. Axonometric drawing. Published in *Das Neue Berlin* 7 (1929): 40

the needs of traffic. Discussion of rebuilding began in 1928, and in various sketches Mendelsohn suggested a uniform arrangement to be produced by groups of high-rises on the important corner lots. This time Wagner chose not to sponsor a competition, but rather worked out a design himself in collaboration with Felix Unglaube: a three-story "carousel" with a subway station at the base, almost wholly a traffic structure (fig. 33). Facades with lighted signs would celebrate capitalist consumption with constantly changing lights and colors.

The same principle lay behind the alternative design by Marcel Breuer, in which traffic was also carried on different levels—albeit without a "carousel"—and the task of bearing advertising fell to the building facades around the square (fig. 34). For Breuer too, the "drama of a metropolis" was traffic: "At the main street intersections the drama reaches its culmination! In the new sense, city squares are only these enhanced sections of the street."[86] He required of the architecture an extreme reserve: "buildings in the simplest forms . . . whose exteriors create only an underlying rhythm for the city's constantly changing, arresting, and highly varied forms of color and light. They are the naked body to be variously clothed in accordance with the changing times."[87]

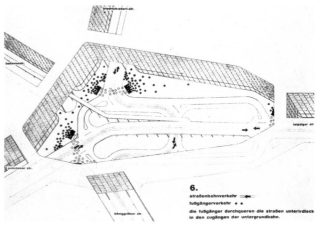

was also exhibited, together with other historical precedents—among them a suggestion by Schinkel from 1840. Häring took over from Mächler the north-south axis, which he renamed Strasse der Republik (fig. 35). He reduced the size of the square by introducing straight rows of monumental ministry buildings, placed a new building for the president of the Reichstag directly opposite the Reichstag itself (beyond an artificially straightened stretch of the Spree), and moved the Victory Column to the Grosser Stern—a step that Speer would actually carry out in 1939. Poelzig proposed a larger square, calmly ringed by ministries (fig. 36). On the whole, these plans were developments and refinements of Mächler's ideas, with Häring making the self-confident claim that new

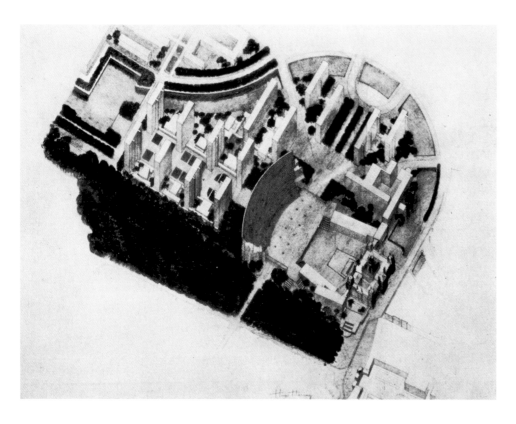

35. Hugo Häring. Project for
Platz der Republik. 1929. Axono-
metric rendering. Published in
Das Neue Berlin 4 (1929): 70

"spiritual values" were being promoted through
architecture and urban design.[88]

In the new republic, Paul Wallot's Reichstag was
proving too small; it needed several hundred more
offices, as well as archival, library, and reading rooms.
A first competition for an addition was announced in
1927. The sole result was the insight that "any building
project associated with the Reichstag can only be
accomplished in the context of a redesign of its surroundings, namely the Platz der Republik."[89] Thus in
the competition of 1929 the square was also included
in the prospectus.

First prize went to Emil Fahrenkamp and Heinrich
de Fries. Included in the final selection were such varied designs as those of Bestelmeyer, Poelzig (who
arranged ten massive prisms into a wreath following
the curving course of the Spree), and Georg Holzbauer
and Franz Stamm. Also noted were the submissions by
Behrens, Häring, Wilhelm Kreis, Schmitthenner—who
proposed an astonishing tower over sixty meters (c. 197
feet) tall—and Eduard Jobst Siedler. The core of the
assignment was the extension of the Reichstag onto

the adjacent, roughly triangular plot next to the Spree,
but ultimately the whole question of urban design was
thrust more and more into the foreground. Paradoxically, from the many suggestions for a redesign of "this
spaceless square, this squareless space,"[90] some of them
quite stunning, a careful observer got the impression
that the only real flaw in the nineteenth-century square
was its sparse landscaping: "If these things are radically
changed, then relatively minor architectural interventions suffice to make out of the Platz der Republik one
of the most magnificent squares in Europe."[91] Werner
Hegemann, who published the results of the competition, did not hesitate to make an alternative proposal of
his own: as a provisional solution, a slender skyscraper
100 meters (c. 328 feet) tall would provide the spaces
required until a definitive rearrangement of the square
was accomplished. After the completion of the final
building complex, this building could be torn down.[92]

Such modesty was not the rule at the time, and
seemed inappropriate to the assignment. In connection
with the debate on the Platz der Republik, the property
owner and investor Heinrich Mendelsohn insisted, in

an unconscious return to the ambitions of the Gross-Berlin competition, that Berlin needed squares that could compete with the place de la Concorde. He scarcely bothered to disguise his nationalistically colored local patriotism: "As showplace of the German Reich and world metropolis, Berlin must break the bonds of the small town."[93] Häring aggressively countered: "A builder for whom the arrangement of things in space had a more profound meaning than merely marking a specific place would have drawn the grand Strasse der Republik from the Alsenbrücke to Kemperplatz, so as first to make a clear and definite stroke through this rulers' axis."[94] In this he was doing little more than supporting his own design from 1926, with its north-south axis borrowed from Mächler.

The End of Something: The Competition for the Expansion of the Reichsbank, 1933

In February 1933, only days before the Reichstag elections that would give 43.9 percent of the votes to Adolf Hitler's National Socialist Party, a competition was announced for the expansion of the Reichsbank in Berlin. Although the assignment involved only one structure, it had large repercussions: for years the Reichsbank had been buying up land between its main headquarters on Hausvogteiplatz and the arm of the Spree at the Kupfergraben. In view of the possible breakthrough of a new east-west street, a question debated since 1927 but still unsettled, the announcement left the relevant urban-design decisions up to the participants.

These were limited to thirty, a restriction occasioning vocal indignation on the part of the German architectural community, almost without exception out of work. The invitees represented a deliberate mix of ideologies: in addition to modernist builders like Döcker, Alfred Fischer, Gropius, Haesler, Mies, Poelzig, Wilhelm Riphahn, and Otto Ernst Schweizer, the list included moderately to outspokenly traditionalist ones like Fritz Becker, Bestelmeyer, Fahrenkamp, Kurt Frick, Fritz Höger, Kreis, Mebes and Emmerich, Ludwig Ruff, and Tessenow. The jury was originally to be made up of Behrens, Bonatz, Fritz Schumacher, and Martin Wagner, but for political reasons, during the eleven weeks between the announcement and the competition's deadline, Wagner was dismissed first from his post as city building commissioner and then from the prize committee. Of the twelve prizes anticipated, only six were awarded—to Becker, Frick, Mebes and Emmerich, Mies, Pfeifer and Grossmann, and Pinno and Grund.

36. Hans Poelzig. Project for Platz der Republik. 1929. Bird's-eye view: charcoal on tracing paper with fixative, 32 3/16 x 18 7/8" (81.7 x 48 cm). Plansammlung der Technische Universität, Berlin

The submissions were presented to Hitler, who had been the nation's chancellor for only a few months but had immediately recognized the implications of the endeavor for both urban design and politics. Hitler dismissed all of the prize-winning designs and selected for execution, with certain changes, the proposal by Heinrich Wolff, the Reichsbank's own building director and author of the prospectus on which the competition had been based.

In the politically disastrous year of 1933, the German architectural profession was in disarray. Arguments between modern, traditionalist, and academic architects, which had only escalated since the Weissenhof affair, took on the shrill tone of ideological harrassment, and a man like Höger was by no means alone in his malicious delight that the "national corruption" and "pestilential ideology" of modern architecture, with its "Moroccan structures," were finally being replaced by a truly German way of building and of life.[95] Given this dismal background, it was surprising that Mies's design for the expansion of the Reichsbank was awarded a prize in the competition and even celebrated by the jury as an "especially splendid solution."[96] Even the conservative *Baugilde* had no qualms about calling the design a "masterpiece of wonderful clarity and logic."[97]

For the irregularly shaped building site between Kurstrasse and the Spree, Mies had suggested a simple, three-part, altogether symmetrical layout that he skillfully adapted to a problematic and heterogeneous situation. Facing Kurstrasse was a ten-story, clearly convex front; to give it a uniform dynamic sweep, the existing bend in the street would have had to be modified. On the side of the building toward the Spree, the structure divided into three separate facades, each also ten stories tall. This more open side of the structure derived its vitality from the precise rhythm of identical volumes. Envisioned in front of the north flank of the complex was a new, elongated square that would have opened onto the extension of Jägerstrasse, and for the sake of which Holzgartenstrasse would have had to be eliminated.

The solution was mainly one of urban design. Mies had devoted considerable effort to refining it, creating countless variations. More and more precisely, he adapted the plan of his large public building to the roughly five-sided site without sacrificing its symmetry or the clarity of its geometry. To retain its monolithic character, he connected it to the old building by a hidden tunnel. In numerous perspective sketches, he investigated the effect of the main facade on the Kurstrasse streetscape; he experimented with the dimensions and sequence of the rear elements facing the water; and again and again he tinkered with the facades, increasingly simplifying them and making them more uniform, until the new building appeared to have been formed at one throw, a huge block created by a single hand, responding with slight variations to the different situations it confronted.

Mies's design sacrificed a great deal to achieve the architect's essential urban vision. The projected height of the building far exceeded that of the Berliner Schloss, in contradiction of the criteria established by the jury. Its main entrance was to be located on the relatively narrow Kurstrasse, and was therefore somewhat unimposing and cramped for space. The view of the building from the Spree side was somewhat forbidding and restless. And the office wings were unfavorably oriented in terms of light.

The architect was undisturbed by such shortcomings. Most of all, his design was a demonstration of urban design. His addition to the Reichsbank—like the Concrete Office Building, the skyscrapers, and the Urban Design Proposal for Alexanderplatz—was imagined as a building block in the ideal modern metropolis he envisioned, one to which he came closer with each new design. The supposed lack of resolution in the structure was in fact a virtually exemplary demonstration of the diversity of that urban ideal, which included both buildings following the street line and areas of urban tension between freestanding structural volumes. Its cohesiveness, or its uniformity, to use Scheffler's term, was assured by the architectural idiom, whose basic elements were simple, smooth concrete parapets and ribbon windows with narrow-mullioned industrial glazing. Mies's ideal city, of course, was never presented as a great coherent utopia, like Le Corbusier's *ville contemporaine* or Hilberseimer's residential or high-rise cities. Rather it is a subtle thread running through designs that are programmatic

37. Albert Speer. Project for North-South Axis, Berlin. 1941. Delineator: K. Friedrich

but at the same time realistic: it is not an urbanistic dogma but an architectural perspective.

Epilogue: The Triumph and Collapse of Megalomania

Against the historical background of urban planning in Berlin between 1910 and 1933, the design for the north-south axis—the Grosse Strasse—that Speer developed between 1936 and 1941, in his capacity as overseer of the redesign of the capital of Hitler's Reich, represented no real break with the past (fig. 37). Its chief precursor had been Mächler's plan, and the models were Paris and Vienna, which Speer intended to surpass. If the Avenue des Champs-Élysées in Paris ran about a mile and a quarter, Berlin was to get a roughly 4½-mile-long boulevard nearly 400 feet wide. At its north end, next to the Spree—here expanded into a lake—was to stand the Grosse Halle, or "Hall of the People." At its southern

end Speer envisioned a triumphal arch in front of the Südbahnhof that would be over 380 feet high—dwarfing Paris's 230-foot-high Arc de Triomphe. On the square, a half mile on each side, between this arch and the train station, which Speer designed in a relatively modernist style, there was to be a trophy allée with captured tanks and cannons. The Grosse Strasse itself, which would have been less a real north-south link than a largely self-contained parade route (from the square in front of the Grosse Halle, for example, there was to be no connection to the workers' quarters in the city's north), would have been flanked along its entire length almost exclusively by monumental governmental and commercial structures. Among others, these would have included the foreign ministry, the opera, the AEG headquarters (designed by Behrens), the headquarters of the army chief command with its soldiers' hall (designed by Kreis), the office of the Reichsmarschall (designed by Speer himself), the complex consisting of the Grosse Halle and the Führer's palace (likewise designed by Speer), the Reichstag building, the police headquarters, the war academy, the headquarters of the navy chief command (designed by Bonatz), the city hall (designed by Bestelmeyer), and finally the Nordbahnhof. All of these buildings were to have been erected without private speculation, within a single, comprehensive plan of the sort carried out by Baron Haussmann in Paris under Napoleon III. A consortium of participating firms was founded in 1941. That same year, however, Speer was forced to abandon any undertakings inessential to the war effort, so that the immense project, understandably kept secret from the public, was stifled at birth.

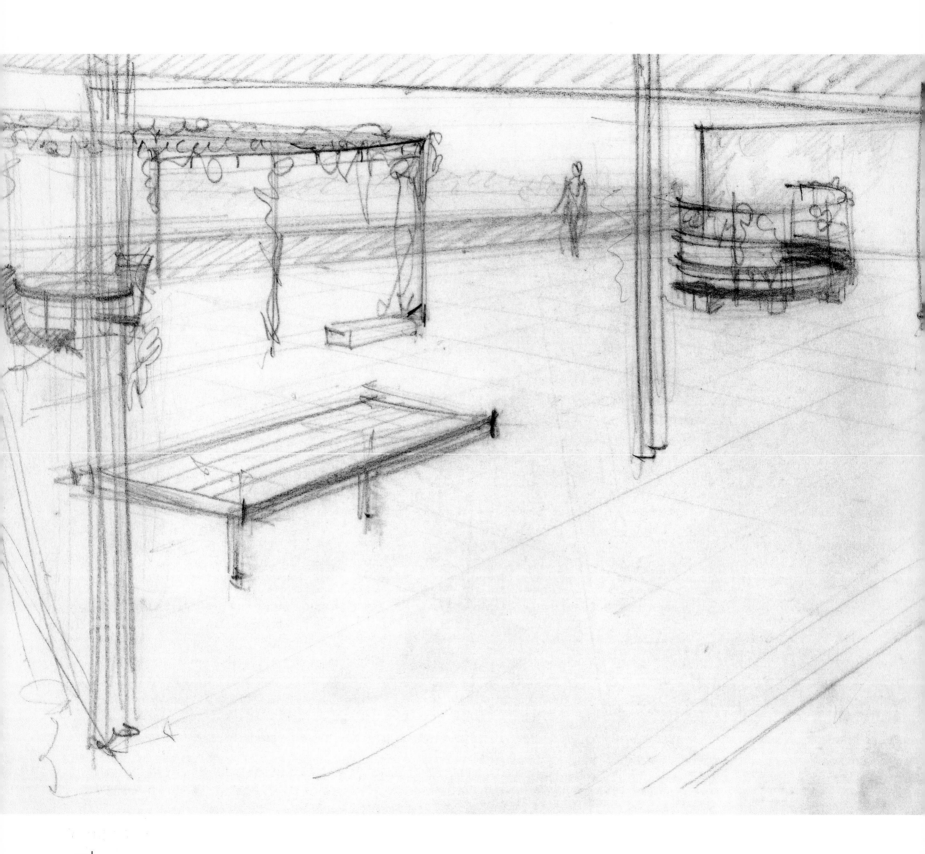

The Nature of Mies's Space

BARRY BERGDOLL

In 1932, in the galleries of The Museum of Modern Art and in the pages of Henry-Russell Hitchcock and Philip Johnson's book *The International Style*, Mies's Tugendhat House, Brno, and German Pavilion, Barcelona, were sheared of their gardens.[1] Only a few lines were erased in the neatly redrawn floor plans, but the omissions were enough to have a radical effect on perceptions of Mies's work. The deletion of the path leading into the grove behind the German Pavilion (figs. 1, 2), and of the outlines of the terrace that creates a podium for the Tugendhat garden facade (figs. 3, 4), severed Mies's buildings from their landscapes and simplified the complex layering of outdoor and indoor space fundamental to his architecture. Mies's inclusion of every piece of furniture on the floor plans for these buildings was respected in the "International Style" exhibition and book (or so it seems at first), but his equally characteristic delineation of plantings was eliminated.[2] Even as Mies was declaring, "We want to investigate the potential residing in the German space and its landscapes," his American champions systematically weeded out plants and vines from his plans.[3] Clearing the trees from the plans of both Barcelona and Brno, they documented an autonomous, universal space, internalized and reproducible anywhere.

These erasures not only altered the nature of Mies's spaces, they blurred most traces of a line of historical development. In place of a meandering path leading back to Mies's interests in the vibrant house and garden reform movements of around 1905–10, Johnson and Hitchcock insinuated a rapid trajectory of avant-garde invention. Meanwhile Mies himself had pruned his oeuvre in the mid-1920s, casting off works that didn't conform to the new avant-garde persona of

"Miës van der Rohe."[4] As with Le Corbusier, a youthful pre-World War I career was all but effaced.

Few who lionized the German Pavilion had actually visited it, and even the Tugendhat House was known primarily through images. Johnson famously declared in his 1947 book on Mies that "no other important contemporary architect cares so much about placing furniture. Mies gives as much thought to placing chairs in a room as other architects do to placing buildings around a square."[5] Yet in 1932 he had no compunction about eliminating the outdoor furniture from the Tugendhat plan, including the built-in semicircular bench and metal trellis on the upper terrace. For Mies, such furnishings were integral to crafting a relationship between the spaces of dwelling and of nature. Exedral benches and vine-covered trellises were also genealogical signs of his engagement with the work of Karl Friedrich Schinkel, for whom these classical elements of garden design were key devices in staging an interplay between architecture and landscape.[6]

The Riehl House: Wohnreform and the Architectonic Garden

To design a house for a philosopher on a steeply sloped site a stone's throw from the Kaiser's Schloss Babelsberg, near Potsdam, was a tall order for a twenty-year-old architectural apprentice only recently arrived in the capital. Historians who have analyzed the Riehl House (1906–7), Mies's first independent commission, have demonstrated how that assured design draws upon readily available models, notably by Mies's employer, the fashionable house and furniture designer Bruno Paul (fig. 5).[7] But Mies's choice of models was anything but capricious. With studied modesty, he declared an engagement with the *Wohnreform* movement, which

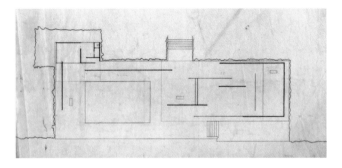

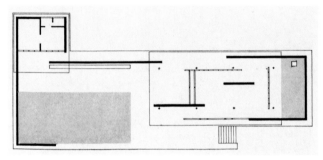

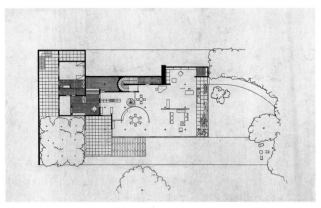

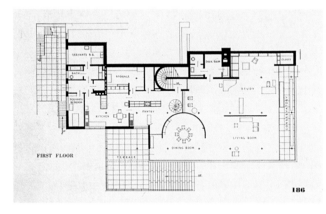

sought a formal and ideological reform of the everyday environment in the faith that new kinds of spaces in the verdant outskirts of the metropolis would bring with them healthful living and an ethical renewal of German culture.

Mies's organization of the interior of the Riehl House around a generously proportioned living hall, or *Halle*, rather than a representational parlor or salon reflects Hermann Muthesius's appeal to models in the English Arts and Crafts movement.[8] The evocation of the local vernacular of the Biedermeier period—the house "wasn't a villa; it was rather like the houses in the local style at Werder, the style of the Mark Brandenburg,"[9] Mies later explained—adroitly fulfills the program most famously associated with Paul Mebes's influential book *Um 1800* (fig. 6). The peaked roof with gable and eyebrow dormers, and the clean stucco walls, painted ocher and all but devoid of decorative embellishments, are fully in the spirit of Mebes's call for a return to "architecture and handicraft in the last century of its natural development."[10] This had been proffered as an escape route from historicist culture and a path to

restoring authenticity to German life and building, even to reforging a unified culture in the face of tremendous social change. It was not long before such buildings, with their frank expression of program, were being labeled *sachlich*, a word that emerged in the turn-of-the-century reform movements as an umbrella term for any matter-of-fact acceptance of the conditions of modern life.

That Alois and Sofie Riehl embraced *Wohnreform* is clear in the distinction between their house and the revivalist villas one passes to reach it, at the end of a cul-de-sac above the picturesque valley of the Griebnitzsee: Italian Renaissance villas, turreted German Renaissance manses, even a towered villa with a frieze of Assyrian lions. The Riehl House, in contrast, turns away from the street toward its walled garden, its narrow gable end and peaked roof visible over a perimeter wall carefully calculated to hide the door from view, and leaving visible a single embellishment: a stuccoed interlace of wreaths in the center of the entrance front, a detail lifted straight from *Um 1800*. The matter-of-factness and English reserve of the house were the

1 (top left). Ludwig Mies van der Rohe. German Pavilion, Barcelona International Exhibition. 1928–29. Preliminary floor plan. Pencil on tracing paper, 19 x 36" (48.3 x 91.4 cm). The Museum of Modern Art, New York. Mies van der Rohe Archive. Gift of the architect

2 (top right). Ludwig Mies van der Rohe. German Pavilion, Barcelona International Exhibition. 1928–29. Floor plan as published in Henry-Russell Hitchcock and Philip Johnson, *The International Style* (1932)

3 (bottom left). Ludwig Mies van der Rohe. Tugendhat House, Brno. 1928–30. Lower-level plan. Ink and pencil on tracing paper, 19 x 32¼" (48.3 x 82 cm). The Museum of Modern Art, New York. Mies van der Rohe Archive. Gift of the architect

4 (bottom right). Ludwig Mies van der Rohe. Tugendhat House, Brno. 1928–30. Lower-level plan as published in Hitchcock and Johnson, *The International Style*

qualities Muthesius advocated for a middle class focused on family and healthful living rather than display. Even the feature that, once discovered, captures and holds our attention—the building's startling transformation from a *bürgerlich* village house on the entrance facade into a temple poised lightly and asymmetrically over a monumental podium on the garden front—can be easily traced to contemporary models (fig. 7; compare with plate 6).[11]

The site stretches to the Kaiserstrasse (today's Karl-Marx-Strasse), a road regularly traveled by the Kaiser, to whom the temple front offered a respectful nod from Professor Riehl, a privy councillor in the imperial government. The house was a pavilion among others in the extensive landscape park of interlocked royal—and now bourgeois—estates that unfold along the banks of the Griebnitzsee, anchored by Schloss Babelsberg to the south and Schloss Glienicke to the north, both masterpieces of the collaboration in the late 1820s and

'30s between Schinkel and the picturesque-landscape designer Peter Joseph Lenné. Mies was belatedly adding another to the famous series of vantage points by which Schinkel and Lenné crafted a network of optical relationships within one of the most extensive of the natural landscapes so appreciated by the German Romantics, one that took in the hills and lakes of Potsdam and its region for many miles.[12]

By 1910, Muthesius was promoting Mies's design as a model, devoting a spread to it in a revised edition of his *Landhaus und Garten* (fig. 5).[13] The book was a programmatic statement of the garden reform movement, launched in the 1890s by such cultural critics as Alfred Lichtwark and Ferdinand Avenarius and taken up after 1900 by architects attempting to extend their vision of a *Gesamtkunstwerk* from the interior to the environment as a whole. Muthesius celebrated recent English garden design, and introduced Germans to its new formality: axial planning, geometric spaces, and

5. Ludwig Mies van der Rohe. Riehl House, Neubabelsberg. 1907. Top left: entrance front from walled garden. Top right: view from street. Bottom left: site plan and floor plans of ground and upper story. Bottom right: view from lower garden. As published in Hermann Muthesius, *Landhaus und Garten*, second edition (1910), pp. 50–51

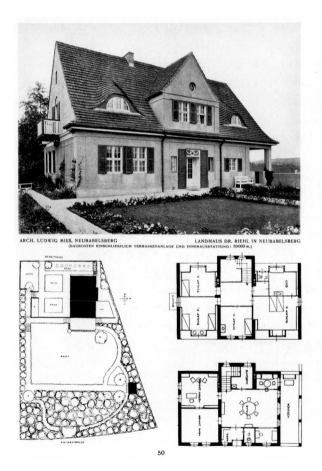

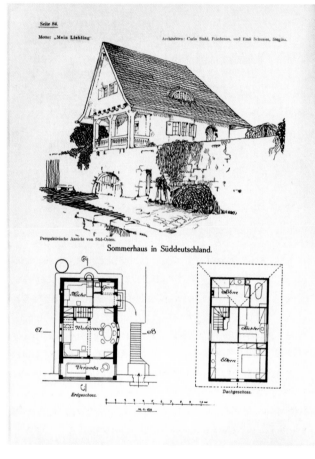

6. Farmhouse near Langfuhr. From Paul Mebes, *Um 1800*, third edition (1908), fig. 17

7. Design for a summer house in southern Germany submitted to a publisher's competition for model houses, 1906. From *Sommer- und Ferienhäuser aus dem Wettbewerb der Woche* (1907), p. 84

borders of native plants, together defining a new aesthetic and ethic of home life outdoors.[14] The revised edition of *Landhaus und Garten* featured recent German examples, missing from the first edition and thus substantiating Muthesius's claim of an impending triumph of the so-called "architectonic" or "architecture" garden. The Riehl House, with its interwoven interior and exterior spatial design, was among his prime examples.

As the architectonic garden had been developed by architects—notably Josef Hoffmann and Joseph Maria Olbrich in Austria, and Paul Schultze-Naumburg and Muthesius in Germany—it was an integral component of *Wohnreform* and constituted a critique of the practice of setting a villa in a picturesque garden, no matter how small the plot. The critique addressed both the false naturalism of drastically reduced versions of the landscaping of aristocratic estates and the tendency of middle-class owners to sacrifice everything in the garden to the representation of status. On only 500 square meters, Victor Zobel wrote, an owner thinks to create a microcosm of nature, taking up the sinuous paths, clumps of trees, and dense plantings of the English picturesque tradition with little regard for the house, or for the way the family uses the garden. In six steps one has taken the tour of the picturesque paths, he noted in parody, and "often there is even a small cement pool, whose form imitates a large mountain lake."[15] Architects should take up the problem of the garden, Muthesius argued, "in order to save the house from the decadence into which it had fallen in the nineteenth century, and to stamp it once again with the mark of artistic unity."[16] He elsewhere announced, "Garden and house are a unity, their characteristics should be infused with the same spirit."[17] Abstraction and geometrization he characterized as closer to a higher, more essential nature than was the banal imitation of nature, thus allying an attack on the naturalistic tradition of landscape design with the critique of historical styles in architecture.

Writing in 1909, Schultze-Naumburg pointed to the Biedermeier garden, and in particular the working gardens of farmers and country vicars, as unpretentious models preferable to exaggerated representations of nature, a fallacy doomed to failure.[18] Olbrich and Henry van de Velde had already associated this functioning garden with the reform of daily life, and Peter Behrens had extended his exploration of the proportional grid as a formative element in architecture into the planning of exterior "rooms" in exhibition gardens at Düsseldorf (1904), Oldenburg (1905), and Mannheim (1907; fig. 8).[19] But it was Muthesius who became the real spokesman for the architectonic garden, defending the role of architects over the young profession of landscape designers. "The house and garden," Muthesius declared, "are so intimately related in their nature, that it is simply impossible that two people unknown to one another,

8. Peter Behrens. Exhibition garden with open-air theater for the *Mannheimer Kunst- und Gartenbauausstellung*, Mannheim, 1907

an architect and a gardener, give form to the house and its surroundings."[20]

Reformers called for a tight relationship between garden spaces and domestic interiors, even designating functions in their garden plans as well as in their floor plans. The age-old logic that placed the kitchen garden adjacent to the kitchen, generally in a sunken service court, was to be extended to a whole series of specialized gardens related to individual facades and often divided from one another by low walls, hedges, or changes in level. The *Wohngarten* (living garden) was the complement to the *Wohnzimmer* (living room); an outdoor dining area might be placed next to a dining room.

The garden was to have a specially designed *Spielgarten* (play garden) for children, and the gendered interiors of the *Herrenzimmer* ("gentlemen's room," or library) and *Damenzimmer* (lady's parlor) would be matched respectively by the conversational garden, sometimes ornamented with sculpture, and the rose garden.

Muthesius spoke of the "continuation of the spaces of the house" in the garden,[21] but the promotion of open-air garden "rooms," or *Freilufträume*, as settings for middle-class life was not merely a concern of architects. By 1905 the popular household handbook of Dr. Anna Fischer-Dückelmann, *Die Frau als Hausärztin* (Woman as home doctor)—over 280,000 copies were printed—declared that if considerations of air and light inside the house were key to a family's health, this priority should be extended to outdoor living. Fischer-Dückelmann proposed open-air bathing facilities (*Luftbäder*) as well as partitions to enable sleeping outdoors. In fine weather the whole sanitary apparatus of the house could find its equivalent in the garden. "The future will certainly bring us a manner of building that in no way disturbs our well-being and that enables the greatest possible ventilation," Fischer-Dückelmann concluded.[22]

In the Riehl House Mies responded impeccably to the reform program. Although the plot of land was ample, he pulled the house as close to the northwest corner of the site as the period's set-back laws allowed, presumably responding to a diagram of Muthesius's demonstrating how such a siting would maximize sunlight in the south-facing *Wohngarten* and *Wohnzimmer*.[23] Rather than setting the house on a podium to be admired from the street—one of Muthesius's chief complaints about historicist villa culture—Mies bound house and garden together to form a podium that is only discovered once one is invited inside. While the kitchen and utility spaces, in the basement, have access to a kitchen court on the north side and to a broad lawn sloping away from the house on the east, the main living floor and the geometrically designed flower garden are pulled into a tight dialogue on the upper terrace. To underscore the fluidity of interior and exterior living, a single low step differentiates the living level from the flower beds, which are laid out to reinforce the underlying order of the house, whose dimensions they echo.

On the facade of the house Mies suggests an underlying tectonic frame through a subtle relief, a frame of pilasters that give rhythm and order to the elevations—an assertion of order that seems to point to the architecture of Schinkel. He mirrors this composition in the geometric ordering of the garden. In the house, for example, there is a subtle asymmetrical tension in the two bays flanking the gabled entrance: the left-hand bay is slightly wider than the right-hand one, which is itself divided between a closed half bay and an open veranda. In the garden this asymmetry is reflected in reverse in the subtly different dimensions of the rectangular rose beds that flank the path to the front door. Barely perceptible in plan, the dynamic tensions of this layout become palpable once one is in the garden itself. The perimeter wall is carefully calculated to create a sense of enclosure and privacy while also offering views of distant trees, landscape, and sky. In spirit as well as letter, the house fulfills Muthesius's call for a dialogue between house and garden:

If the house belongs to architecture, the garden must also. And if one takes the word "architecture" in its most frequent extension, so that it encompasses all manmade images and forms [Gestalten], garden design must also, of necessity, belong to architecture. What is appropriate to human formal invention in every medium is rhythmics, submission to principles. . . . the same fundamental principles that prevail in the house, the same organic relationship of the individual parts one to another, the same unification of the parts into a harmonic whole . . . must also prevail in the garden.[24]

Mies went beyond fulfilling the ideal of the house as a frame for spiritual and physical well-being to create a place, as Fritz Neumeyer suggests, even for the practice of philosophy.[25] The relationship between interior and exterior is explored at several scales. The house/garden podium takes up only the upper third of the site, severed by the sharp line and dramatic change in elevation marked by the great retaining wall shared by house and flower garden. The lower garden is in turn divided into a great lawn bounded by a geometric figure, which yields at one edge to the sinuous line of a garden path and a dense planting of trees penetrated only by a curved path leading to a gate on the Kaiserstrasse below. The geometric dialogue between house and flower garden is thus placed in a larger dialogue with the landscape setting, an expansion of the architectonic garden such as Muthesius admired in the work of Mackay Hugh Baillie Scott, Edwin Lutyens, and Gertrude Jekyll. Muthesius had proposed that the next step in the maturing of the German architectonic garden would be to combine "an orderly layout" with framed views of nature, "i.e. pure nature in the form of woods, meadows, heath, fields, or whatever."[26]

On its sloping site, the Riehl House could hardly avoid vistas over the Griebnitzsee valley, but Mies used garden walls to control this relationship, postponing the full landscape panorama and maintaining a kind of separation that keeps nature at arm's length, an object for self-conscious apprehension rather than a seamless continuum. Instead of arranging a broad terrace to connect the house to nature, Mies—with his great retaining wall—drew a line, which serves optically to compose a panorama that features a dramatic juxtaposition of foreground and distant view. The loss of the middle distance had been a leitmotif of early-nineteenth-century Romantic landscaping, notably in Schinkel's marriage of landscape and architecture. This attitude of discovery and awareness is underscored in the sequence of three photographs presented in *Landhaus und Garten* (fig. 5), which offer glimpses of the essence of a view—such as the open sky seen through the frame of the veranda, and just visible over the garden fence—even while the full drama is repeatedly postponed.

Like the obliquely framed photographs, the garden plan, with its almost perverse refusal of a direct path from the garden gate to the front door (by the 1930s, the owners had replaced the garden parterres with a diagonal path[27]), is embryonic of a strategy in nearly all Mies's German houses: the visitor is generally obliged to turn several times at right angles before the view is fully unveiled. Here, even once the veranda portico is reached, the view is carefully framed, not only by the piers that transform the gable end of the house into a temple portico, but by the parapet wall, which steps up slightly as it passes from *Wohngarten* to veranda to adjust to the floor height within and to maintain the erasure of the middle distance that transforms the landscape into a pictorial experience.

A narrow stair—the only connection between upper terrace and lower garden—is discreetly pushed to the periphery. Approaching the house from below, one discovers the main door framed between high walls (plate 3), a reframing of the everyday that was to become one of Mies's favored landscape strategies. Just as the relationship of mind to world preoccupied Riehl, a neo-Kantian, so Mies staged a discovery of and engagement with the larger environment, one that seems to place his exploration of architecture in dialogue with Riehl's definition of philosophy: "Instead of dealing with nature, which is the object of experimental investigation, philosophy deals with the condition of the knowledge of nature."[28]

Could it have been Riehl who prodded Mies to explore a new dialogue embraced by garden theorists as suggesting a more sophisticated practice of the architectonic garden? In his treatise *Kultur und Natur in der Gartenkunst* (1910), Walter Engelhardt called for a dialogue between a rationalist handling of the garden as a frank expression of human dominance over nature and an appreciation of the larger realm of nature as underscoring the limits of human knowledge—also a theme of Riehl's philosophy. Calling for a new synthesis of geometric "cultural" forms and free "natural" forms, Engelhardt could almost have been describing Riehl's new house when he wrote, "The retaining walls of the terrace of a country house, decorated with orderly flower beds, can also reach out into the picturesque thickets of a natural wood, which, the wilder and more extensive it appears, the more it shows off to its advantage the contrast with the cultural form."[29]

In Babelsberg Mies had discovered not only the Schinkel whom *Wohnreform* advocates celebrated as proto-*sachlich* for his austere handling of classical order and his compositions of pure volumes with clean stucco surfaces, but the Schinkel who developed so much of nearby Potsdam as a landscape of Romantic self-consciousness.[30] In particular Schinkel had made a theme of the high balustrade and viewing platform, introduced to provide ruptures and discontinuities in the landscape that might cause one to reflect on distant, almost pictorialized views, as in the Grosse Neugierde at Schloss Glienicke (fig. 9) or in the spaces of Glienicke's Casino, which at once frames and postpones a panoramic vista, developing a series of spaces bound by open forms parallel to the view (fig. 10). Was it coincidence that Mies treated the space under the Riehl House portico as an extension of the dining space of the *Halle*, just as Schinkel had done in Schloss Charlottenhof, where the portico is at once belvedere, stage, and perch for al fresco dining (fig. 11)? The portico/veranda of the Riehl House is not only a place for private contemplation but a continuation of the interior spaces of entertaining, equipped with a piano and a glazed lateral wall with a curtain that allows space and light to be increased or diminished.

Klösterli, or "little cloister," as the Riehls baptized their new weekend home—both, perhaps, for its walled garden and for its conduciveness to intellectual retreat—became the center of a vibrant intellectual and artistic life in which Mies took part, as attested by the frequent appearance of his name in the house's guest book (p. 314, figs. 5, 6).[31] Many visitors to the house were interested in the relationship of the new practices of garden design to nature at large and to human consciousness. Behrens signed the first page of Klösterli's guest book in 1909, by which time Mies had been working for a year at the older architect's Neubabelsberg studio, where his new employer was laying out a model architectonic garden. Several months later, Walter Gropius, Adolf Meyer, Mies, and Le Corbusier would all be working in Behrens's studio, whose windows gave out on a geometric extension of space, featuring carefully placed benches, latticework pergolas, and statuary as intermediaries between the viewer and the verdant background of the heavily wooded neighborhood.

Perhaps it was also at Klösterli that Mies and Behrens first met Karl Foerster, with whom both would work in the next few years. The Riehls were among the earliest clients of Foerster's young nursery, which was to emerge as a great powerhouse of twentieth-century German gardening, not only for the numerous varieties of perennials it developed but for its implicit philosophy of the garden as a reflection of nature's cycles and larger structures, a philosophy that Foerster traced back to his father's collaboration with the naturalist Alexander von Humboldt.[32] Foerster was also a leading interpreter of the call of garden-reform theorists for a garden of native species that would relate to the local environment, rather than of the specimen trees and exotic plants that had dominated the palette of the late-nineteenth-century natural garden. The pioneering autochromes that Foerster tipped into the copies of his best-selling first book, *Winterharte Blütenstauden und Sträucher der Neuzeit* (1911; p. 315, fig. 7), comprise a homage to the Riehls' early patronage.[33] Here he explained how tall and sturdy perennials could not only enhance the spatial qualities of the architectonic garden but create a role for the garden as an ever-changing

window into the inner workings of nature, whose cycles he made visible in a theory of the seven planting seasons. Attaching trellises to the street elevation of the Riehl elevation, Mies and his clients too sought a close interaction between architecture and nature. Family photographs taken a few years after the house's completion show the retaining wall itself being taken over by vines. Mies's indication of simple rose beds was only partly carried out; period photographs reveal rose borders around grass lawn in the center rectangles of the upper garden, to which Foerster had added a series of perennials and vines that continued the house's blooming season well into the autumn. The Riehl House was the first of a series of designs in which Mies would engineer an abrupt juxtaposition of a planted foreground with a distant view.

Peter Behrens and the Spatial Challenge of Garden Design

Behrens is best remembered for his comprehensive design role at the electrical conglomerate AEG, beginning in 1907, but during Mies's years in his studio the garden too was central to his practice. His article "*Der moderne Garten*," of 1911, seems obliquely to honor the Riehl House. Seeking to expand Muthesius's functional zoning of the garden onto a spiritual plane, Behrens distinguishes here between rooms that should open to a landscape from rooms "whose purpose is not sociability, but rather serve for collecting of one's thoughts, for study, or for withdrawing."[34] Such spaces, he says, should face out on a more enclosed garden court—as Riehl's study does. Behrens also offers practical advice for those planning a garden: a reading of Engelhardt's philosophical tract, and recourse to professional guidance in selecting plants. He does not mention Foerster's newly opened nursery in Potsdam-Bornim, with its demonstration garden,[35] but he directs readers away from the big landscape businesses that would arrive after the fact to landscape the leftover spaces around a house. The garden, he concludes, lies at the heart of the central mission of all of the period's arts:

When the layout of the garden is treated as architecture it is more than a matter of tracing geometric lines, it is an opportunity for forming space [*Raumgestaltung*]. Giving form to space is obviously

12. Karl Friedrich Schinkel. Pavilion, Charlottenburg Palace, Berlin-Charlottenburg. 1824. Ground floor plan with exedral bench in *Gartensaal* (left center). Stiftung Preussische Schlösser und Gärten Berlin-Brandenburg

13. Attributed to Ludwig Mies van der Rohe. Perls House, Berlin-Zehlendorf. 1911–12. Garden plan. Diazotype, 12 x 19½" (29.9 x 48.6 cm). Bauhaus-Archiv Berlin

the highest principle of architecture. To comprehend architecture as a maker of space is the discovery of modern aesthetics as it has been developed since Hans von Marées, Adolf Hildebrand, and others. To create a work of architecture as a spatial form means to exercise true creative artistry.[36]

Marées and Hildebrand, along with August Schmarsow, were figures from the vibrant discussions of space and its relationship to sensation that fell broadly under the name *Einfühlung*, or empathy theory. For Behrens, the garden was a possible site of resolution of one of the most burning debates in architectural theory of the years around 1910: should form be derived from the demands of function, or should function be determined by an outer form. This question

achieved. This interlocking of forms, this aesthetic evaluation of the opposing form, is one of the most important moments in the fine arts in general.[37]

Mies responded to Behrens's challenge in a house he completed in 1912 for the lawyer and art collector Hugo Perls in Zehlendorf, a villa colony on the edge of the Grunewald forest (p. 16, fig. 7).[38] A deepening interest in Schinkel's neoclassical designs, which Behrens led his assistants to visit in these years, is unmistakable in the Perls House. Perls's later claim that he encouraged Mies in that direction is ratified by the design development: what began as a pitched roof neo-Biedermeier villa in the spirit of *Um 1800* quickly evolved toward a stronger geometric volume with a

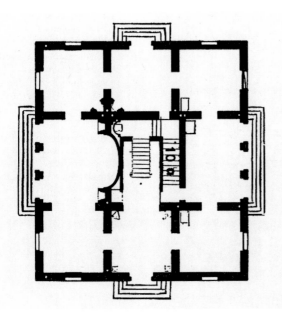

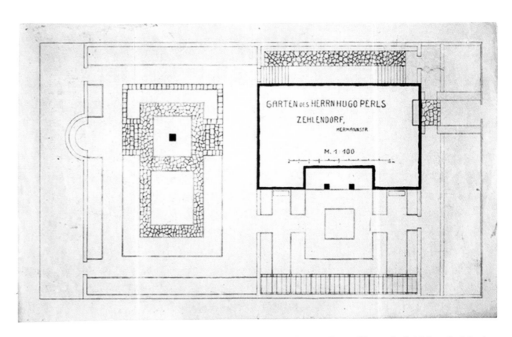

would preoccupy Mies for much of his career. Behrens saw form as the boundary between two inextricably interlocked programs and spatial experiences, those of the house interior and those of its surrounding garden:

The house always forms part of the surrounding site. And it is not inconsequential how the parcel of land that is left over appears as a geometric figure. It is not enough that a few paths in a straight line lead up to a window, instead of being straight or winding. Seen from the outside, the house must appear, no matter how careful its interior planning, as though its walls were only arranged as they are in order to enclose the various areas, beds, ponds, or whatever one has laid out. Only then will there be no leftover little angles, and only then is the task of a harmonic unison of house and garden

taut profile, its low-hipped roof largely hidden behind a prominent attic, as in such Schinkel designs as the pavilion at Charlottenburg (fig. 12, and p. 141, fig. 7).[39] It is by now a truism that Schinkel offered inspiration in Mies's search for an internally consistent and rigorously abstracted tectonic syntax, but a previously unpublished garden plan for the Perls House (fig. 13) makes clear that Mies was equally interested in the spatial lessons of Schinkel's work.[40] Schinkel's self-professed goal was an architecture at once "complete in and of itself" and tied to its environment both formally and experientially, thus "making visible the maximum number of connections" in the interaction between the world of man and the world of nature.[41] The Perls garden plan registers an attempt to take up this dialectic.

As at the Riehl House, the volumes of the house and the spaces of the garden have a taut geometric relationship. The house is pulled as close as possible to the street, and to the northeast corner of the site, to create gardens in maximum sunlight. Its overall perimeter is echoed in the dimensions and layout of the *Wohngarten* to its west, where its volume is rotated ninety degrees and echoed in negative by a sunken garden. There is also a southern garden, facing the loggia, and echoing the building's volume again. Nor is the relationship of interior and exterior space simply one of reflected geometries, for Mies uses the subdivisions of each garden—the western one with stone walls and paths and subtle changes of grade, the southern one with hedges and flower beds—to extend, interweave, and overlap the spaces and functions of the interior rooms. House and garden are autonomous yet interpenetrating.

The garden is almost tartanlike in its overlapping axes and cross-axes. The overall site plan is without a dominant center; tellingly, the only place where both gardens can be enjoyed together is the heart of the house, the dining room. This room was central to both Perls's entertaining and his art collecting; he had murals done here by the Expressionist painter Max Pechstein. From the dining room there is direct access to the loggia, which can be used for outdoor dining and looks out on a garden designed as a veritable open-air room, bordered by low perimeter walls or hedges on its short sides and a vine-covered trellis along the property line (fig. 14). Opening broadly to the living room, the dining room also enjoys a clear axial connection to the *Wohngarten*, so that from it one can enjoy the principal "picture" that Mies composed as an addition to Perls's collection: a view of a sculpture set at the center of the sunken bed, framed by an exedral bench that terminates the cross-axis of the garden and in turn provides a vantage point for admiring the sculpture, the garden, and the house. Characteristically this vista is postponed for visitors, since the entrance to the house from the street is placed off-center, and the vestibule provides only an oblique view into the dining room.

Mies seems to have learned more than an abstract language from Schinkel's pavilion at Charlottenburg; he seems equally to have set himself the challenge of taking up the interplay between the subdivisions of a rectangular figure (Schinkel worked with a square, Mies with a rectangle, a more flexible form in domestic planning) that has axial relationships to a larger environment. In the *Gartensaal* at Charlottenburg, Schinkel placed an exedral bench precisely where the cross-axis of the Baroque garden comes to an end—inside the pavilion, the architectural addition to the landscape. The bench in turn offers a vantage point for a sweeping vista from the interior across the long facade of the palace. Staging the everyday and inviting contemplation, the exedral bench was one of Schinkel's favorite motifs. At the end of a long meadow at Schloss Tegel (fig. 15), he provided an exedral bench from which the villa can be seen as part of a larger landscape. At Schloss Charlottenhof an exedral bench provides a view of the temple front of the house, in juxtaposition with the domed Neues Palais (reflecting a vision of a more authoritarian style of rule) and the plantings of the park (fig. 11). At the Perls House the bench provides a view not only of the garden but of the house, against the green backdrop of the Grunewald. In fact nearly every feature of Mies's garden can be traced to one of Schinkel's gardens, which, however, Mies seems to have understood not as historical sources but as tools for responding to Behrens's challenge for the modern garden:

In my opinion, a garden is as essential a part of a dwelling as a bathroom is, for only in the garden . . . can we find a spiritually purifying union with nature. Only if we have grown together with this fragment of nature, only if we have been influenced by it even as it has been given form by our desires, will we rediscover the relationship to organic being that leads to inner harmony. . . . It doesn't matter how large this piece of ground is; it is equally good if we are awakened in the morning by the twittering of thousands of birds or by a single bird always at the same hour, who appears as a faithful guest to collect his crumb on the breakfast table. Everything is relative.[42]

Behrens's own most complete integration of house and garden was the mansion for the archaeologist Theodor Wiegand, in Dahlem. The garden was actually laid out and planted before construction of the house began, in the autumn of 1910 (fig. 16, and p. 147, fig. 15).

14. Ludwig Mies van der Rohe. Perls House, Berlin-Zehlendorf. 1911–12. View from dining room to garden. Photograph: Kay Fingerle, 2000

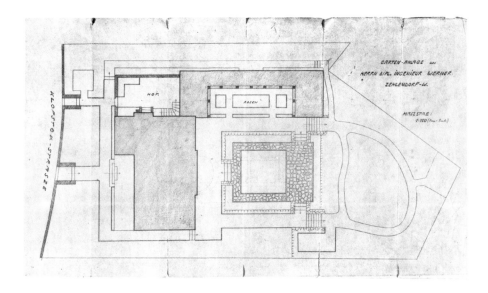

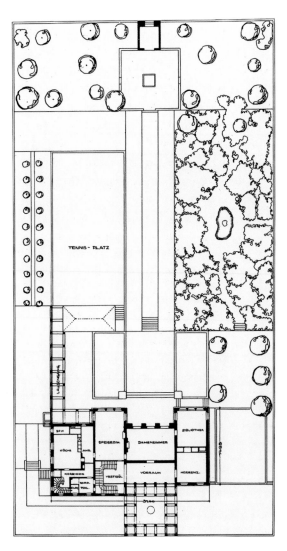

15 (top left). Karl Friedrich Schinkel. Schloss Tegel, Berlin. 1820–24. Memorial column and exedral bench in family graveyard at far end of garden

16 (right). Peter Behrens. Wiegand House, Berlin-Dahlem. 1910. Site plan with garden and ground floor plan (detail). Diazotype, 16 x 12" (40 x 30 cm). Bezirksamt Zehlendorf, Berlin-Zehlendorf

17 (top right). Ludwig Mies van der Rohe. Werner House, Berlin-Zehlendorf. 1912–13. Site plan with garden layout. Pencil and watercolor on diazotype, 14 ¼ x 25 ¼" (35.3 x 63.2 cm). Bauhaus-Archiv Berlin

The project impressed Behrens's employees enormously: the young Le Corbusier took with him from his months in the Neubabelsberg studio his own sketches of the interior layout and a blueprint of the garden,[43] while Mies paraphrased the Wiegand spatial arrangements in the house and garden he designed for Perls's new neighbors the Werners, in 1912–13 (fig. 17).

Architecturally the Werner House evoked the turn of the nineteenth century, and the Prussian manor houses praised by Schulze-Naumburg in *Das Schloss*, the most recent volume of his *Kulturarbeiten* books, which the client collected.[44] But house and garden together mark a development in Mies's thinking about interior and exterior space. The tension between symmetries and asymmetries in the floor plan was adapted from the Wiegand House, as was the hugging of the garden by a shallow U-shaped pergola accessible from the dining room. Even more emphatically than Behrens, Mies juxtaposed an asymmetrical entrance front with a symmetrical garden facade, a reversal of centuries of tradition. Learning from Schinkel's Court Gardener's House (1829–33, figs. 18, 19), from Behrens, and to a lesser extent from Lutyens and Jekyll, Mies established the spatial coherence of the garden by slightly sinking a square parterre, set off-center with regard to the pergola. This court and the garden paths are defined by dry stone walls of the sort recommended by both Schultze-Naumburg and Behrens.

In the tradition of the architectonic garden, dominant axes relate the garden to the house; but the pergola begins to create, as in the Court Gardener's House, a spatial movement around the negative volume of the garden.

The sculpting of the ground plane was extended to the entire site. House and garden are treated as a unity. The kitchen and laundry in the basement communicate with a service court, while the central garden room (*Gartensaal*) and the flanking study (*Herrenzimmer*) and dining room are level with the *Wohngarten*. A low brick wall along the street and a raised terrace before the front door create enough enclosure that even the front garden can be used as a room, as family photographs indicate it was (p. 146, fig. 14).[45] With this design Mies responds directly to Behrens's imprimatur that "in addition to a careful control of the dimensions of breadth and length, one must work also in the third dimension, on height. Only then will an illusion of spatial fullness and palpability be created, only then will the garden become a small world of its own."[46]

These were the years of Mies's contacts with developments in abstract dance and set design in the garden city of Hellerau, outside Dresden. He visited Hellerau often while courting his future wife, Ada Bruhn, who had been one of the first students at Emile Jaques-Dalcroze's famous local institute for eurythmic dance and culture. There is indeed a stagelike quality about the Werner garden, recalling both Schinkel's staging of a portico and trellis in the landscape at the Charlottenhof (fig. 11) and Adolphe Appia's contemporary stage designs for Heinrich

Tessenow's Festsaal at Hellerau (fig. 20).[47] The wooded area behind the house is at a higher elevation, so that the house looks into an irregular grid of tree trunks, presences that might almost be awaiting the draped figures of a modern dance of expression. Pencil notations on the garden plan indicate hesitation over the transition between geometric garden and irregular wood; an early plan indicates that the garden paths were to be laid out only once the trees had been surveyed and perhaps edited. And even once Mies laid out a winding path recalling the transition between culture and nature at the Riehl House, he still hesitated on what the dividing line between the two should be: the abrupt break of a retaining wall with stair access at either side, like a stage, or an exedral form closer to Schinkel's work, and oscillating between eye-catcher and viewing point (fig. 21).

18. Karl Friedrich Schinkel. Court Gardener's House at Schloss Charlottenhof, Sanssouci, Potsdam. 1829–33. Perspective view to west. Engraving from *Sammlung Architektonischer Entwürfe* (1819–40)

19. Karl Friedrich Schinkel. Court Gardener's House at Schloss Charlottenhof. Bird's-eye view with garden and view of Schloss Charlottenhof in distance. Engraving from *Sammlung Architektonischer Entwürfe*

The differences between Behrens's and Mies's proposals of 1911–12 for the Kröller-Müller Villa Project, the most developed integration of garden and house to date in each architect's work, are subtle but telling.[48] Behrens's project (pp. 141–42, figs. 8–10) was Mies's starting point, but when, early in 1912, Mies replaced Behrens in Helene Kröller-Müller's affections, he rethought the design. Behrens had developed his austere, monumental building masses and his garden courtyards and terraces around a single controlling axis anchoring considerable asymmetrical incident. Mies was no stranger to the grand axis; certainly his Schinkelesque project of 1910 for the Bismarck Monument competition involved just such a gesture. But for this nearly flat seaside site, near The Hague, he developed a compositional approach of overlapping major and minor axes, derived in part from his recent discovery of Frank Lloyd Wright's work in the Wasmuth portfolio and in part from Schinkel's Court Gardener's House. These were two great models of the interweaving of interior and exterior spaces, both of them fracturing the hierarchies of academic classical composition.

In Mies's design, each facade generates its own composition of courts, pergolas, and outdoor terraces, echoing the slipping and sliding of the house's almost independent one- and two-story volumes. The scheme comprises overlapping and juxtaposed local symmetries, given formal coherence by the use of a limited set of elements repeated in different configurations. Schinkel's favorite devices abound, notably slightly sunken or raised terraces terminated by an exedral bench that provides a vantage point over both garden and distant landscape. The terrace on the side of the house, for example, faces a striking juxtaposition: a formal garden, centered on a water course, and a view of the dunes beyond. The use of a sunken garden, and of a pergola that provides a platform from which to admire both the landscape and the reflection of the building in water, are inspired by Schinkel's Charlottenhof, but are submitted to greater geometric rigor.

Mies fulfilled in advance the critic Paul Westheim's response to the fashion for Schinkel: that to understand the modernity of the nineteenth-century architect was not to imitate his forms but to capture the spirit of his "remarkable feeling for masses, relationships, rhythms, and form-melody."[49] A signature Mies gesture appears here for the first time—the interlocking of two independent volumes by a slight overlap at the corner. Another signature element appears in Mies's presentation drawings

20. Stage designed for Emile Jaques-Dalcroze in Heinrich Tessenow's Festsaalbau, Hellerau, c. 1912

21. Ludwig Mies van der Rohe. Werner House, Berlin-Zehlendorf. 1912–13. View of garden exedra. Bauhaus-Archiv Berlin

(the earliest surviving for any residential design): his indication of the counterpoint between the house and existing trees, and his rendering of vines and plants growing on and over his geometric compositions. Vines are a key feature of Wright's perspective views, as they are of Schinkel's engravings of the Court Gardener's House. For both Wright and Schinkel this inclusion went beyond picturesque effect—it was an invitation to reflect on the links between architecture's search for a generative formal language and the structures of nature. As Mies would later recall of the impact of Wright's work, "Here, again, at last, genuine organic architecture flowered."[50]

Mies designed two more houses for Potsdam before the war, one the House for the Architect (1914), a sketched project for land he and his wife had purchased at Werder, the other the Urbig House (1915–17), for the banks of the Griebnitzsee. The two buildings seem unconnected, but when one remembers that a lost first design for the Urbig House had a flat roof, like the House for the Architect, they come together as attempts to develop the lessons of the Kröller-Müller project.

For his own house Mies produced two designs, both rendered in bird's-eye views of the type Schinkel had used to illustrate a building's ordering of an entire landscape (fig. 19). Like Schinkel, Mies was interested in exploring two modes of composition, one symmetrical and one asymmetrical. Although he could not have known the precept in Schinkel's words—"Every object with a specific function demands a correspondingly specific order. That order is either symmetry, which everyone understands, or relative order, which is understood only by those who know its principle"—he had grasped it through Schinkel's work.[51] Like Schinkel, Mies would expend much effort on understanding the difficult principle of asymmetrical order; like Schinkel, he would wonder what relationship such an order might have to the order of the natural world. For the simple U-shaped block of the House for the Architect, Mies sketched a garden plan in counterpoint to the building, with a suggestion that it would be sunken and at least partially defined by hedges. In both alternatives the house was to stand in a grove, which would define

an edge behind it, while at the front it would open toward a prospect. The site of the property is unknown, but one can imagine that it faced the Havel River or one of its tributaries. Mies's love of rose gardens emerges in a sketch designating a geometric flowerbed as a "*Rosen-garten*," the only indication of a "function" on the plan.

The Urbig House (figs. 22–25) is an imposing block that largely screens a view of the Griebnitzsee from arriving visitors. Instead this view is commanded from the terraces around the rear and sides of the house, and from the rooftop terraces atop two one-story additions set in counterpoint to the main block.[52] The sliding volumetric composition of the Kröller-Müller design is here largely subordinated to the client's taste for a neo-eighteenth-century manor. But surviving evidence of the garden, on which Mies worked with Foerster, suggests a synthesis of the continual working of the ground plane seen in the Kröller-Müller project with the rupturing of the landscape first explored at the nearby Riehl House.[53] In fact Mrs. Urbig turned to Mies because of her admiration for the Riehl House,[54] but given the difference in spirit between Klösterli and this pilastered house for a banker, one imagines that it was the structuring of the landscape that most captured her fancy.

Street and garden facades are radically different. The formal street elevation is cadenced by tall French windows allowing access to the garden from every room, and by a monumental order of pilasters—severely abstracted, like nearly all the elements of the neoclassical vocabulary that Mies now used. The monumental block sits almost directly on the earth, taking its cue from the eighteenth-century tradition of the *Lustschloss* or country house, of which the renowned local example was, of course, Frederick the Great's Sanssouci. Like that august model, the Urbig House is associated with vines. In an interesting reversal of neoclassicism, Mies sets the French doors atop two travertine steps, a kind of interrupted residual classical stylobate, while the pilasters fall directly into the earth. He interrupts the travertine terrace across the front of the house to carve out negative bases in the form of planters that would eventually allow climbing vines to soften the house's geometry; the vines are echoed in

22 (opposite, left). Ludwig Mies van der Rohe. Urbig House, Potsdam-Neubabelsberg. 1915–17. View of rear (garden) elevation with terrace and loggia, c. 1919. Urbig Family Trust

23 (center). Ludwig Mies van der Rohe. Urbig House, Potsdam-Neubabelsberg. 1915–17. View of bay window with climbing roses and stairs to terrace, c. 1919. Urbig Family Trust

24 (top right). Ludwig Mies van der Rohe. Urbig House, Potsdam-Neubabelsberg. 1915–17. View from terrace toward exedral bench, c. 1919. Urbig Family Trust

25 (bottom right). Ludwig Mies van der Rohe. Urbig House, Potsdam-Neubabelsberg. 1915–17. View of side facade with statue of "Praying Boy," c. 1919. Urbig Family Trust

the reliefs atop the windows, the only contradiction of the proscription on ornament that Mies formulated for the Kröller-Müller design (fig. 23). Within a few years, as family photographs reveal, the framework of the classical language of architecture was being doubled by a natural one.

One of the Urbigs' daughters recalled that client and architect found common ground in their admiration

the main mass is opened up by arcades to connect the dining room to a raised terrace and to the view. On an axis perpendicular to the rear facade, Mies placed an exedral bench that looked back at the terrace above its flight of steps (fig. 24, and p. 148, fig. 16). This was the first of a series of axial moves, both parallel and perpendicular to the axes of the house, that structured garden space and views in relationship to individual

for Schloss Charlottenhof (fig. 11).[55] As in Schinkel's design, the Urbig garden facade does not connect directly with the landscape but is set on a stagelike podium, created by a basement story considerably larger than the house above (figs. 22 and 24). Here was an extension of the theme of the occupiable plinth that Mies might have studied in the work of Friedrich Gilly and Schinkel—enjoying an enormous revival in those years[56]—and that would fascinate him repeatedly right up to the New National Gallery (1962–67). The rear of the house became a complexly leveled manmade landscape of shifting volumes and planes, made all the more dramatic by the late decision to drop the pilaster order, which drawings show were originally to extend to all four elevations.[57] A one-story block set perpendicular to

facades. Indeed an entire sequence of terraced spaces wraps around three sides of the house, as Mies worked the ground planes of the garden to layer outdoor space.

A bronze replica of the famous "Praying Boy"—a Greek figure of a nude youth, thought at the time to embody an ancient prayer to the sun—was set on a pedestal at the critical juncture where the visitor rounding the corner of the house first glimpses the horizon and the opposite bank of the Griebnitzsee (fig. 25).[58] This was the principal view from the study or *Herrenzimmer*, much as the adjacent *Damenzimmer* enjoyed views of the rose garden and the exedral bench (fig. 23). One of the few life-size bronze statues surviving from antiquity, the "Praying Boy" allowed an exploration of the use of freestanding statuary to layer outdoor space optically through a surrogate figure—an approach to sculpture that Mies had discussed with Mrs. Kröller-Müller.[59] The "Praying Boy" moreover had an extraordinary iconographic lineage, beginning with Frederick the Great, who had exhibited it in front of the latticework pavilion at Sanssouci, placed to be visible from his study and to mark the place where the uppermost terrace stepped off toward the horizon. Since 1830 the original had occupied pride of place on an axis with the entrance in Schinkel's Altes Museum in Berlin, but copies of it had been used to structure numerous neoclassical garden ensembles, including Schinkel's at his Casino at Schloss Glienicke (fig. 10). At the Urbig House Mies turned the rear terrace into an artificial precipice, much as he had at the Riehl House, at once dramatizing the picture of nature that unfolds from the house and drawing a line between the structures of mankind and those of the natural world. A sweeping lawn between mature trees framed a view out over the lake.

Avant-Garde Practice and the Garden

Mies remained a popular architect for business and banking clients in Berlin's suburbs through much of the 1920s, even while he achieved artistic fame with theoretical projects in competitions, exhibitions, and avant-garde journals. "The most important projects of our time have not been executed," he noted in 1924,[60] yet his built and his unbuilt works remained linked, just as they had before the war. There are striking continuities between his Concrete Country House Project of 1923 (fig. 26) and the House for the Architect of 1914: the sliding and interlocking of geometric forms, even the play between symmetry and asymmetry, reappear, but in different materials and a different idiom. Seen obliquely from above in a photograph of the model (essentially reproducing the bird's-eye perspective of the drawings for the House for the Architect), the Concrete Country House composition has a spiraling quality that has repeatedly led historians and critics to ally it with Gropius's Dessau Bauhaus of two years later. Yet if we look at the entrance area, where views of the building are actually blocked by a low perimeter wall, it is evident that this composition would never reveal itself as an object in space. Rather, it defines an

itinerary through courts and framed views, continually working the ground plane and controlling the path of movement, which slides along the facades of the building rather than penetrating through it. Both the Concrete Country House and the Brick Country House Project of the following year—Wolf Tegethoff has shown both to be designs for the architect himself[61]—rework the architectonic garden in terms of a new vocabulary of forms, new spatial concepts, and most important the new materials of the technological era.

New materials, particularly glass, were celebrated by the avant-garde as utopian signs of a new, potentially transformative architecture. Mies was aware from the first that they not only overturned traditional laws of composition but enormously expanded the possibilities of relating interior and exterior space. "I cut openings into the walls where I need them for view or illumination," he explained in a laconic text on concrete construction and the Concrete Country House.[62] This was one of a series of texts from 1923 in which he drew a distinction between his own researches and what he saw as the quest for form for form's sake in the work of others, notably Gropius and Hugo Häring. Dismissing both men as formalists, for all the radical differences in their architectures, Mies insisted that form be derivative

26. Ludwig Mies van der Rohe. Concrete Country House Project. 1923. View of model (lost). The Museum of Modern Art, New York. Mies van der Rohe Archive. Gift of the architect

of "the nature of the task with the means of our time," and above all that the "building art is the spatially apprehended will of the epoch."[63] The Concrete Country House and Brick Country House designs were different because of the differing nature of their materials; yet they shared a generative principle. Like different forms in nature, the formal differences among his various designs were not troubling: "A landscape or a wood is not made up of identical formal structures, and a juniper bush goes well with a rose bush; if nature were as formally uninteresting as our architectonic structures, here too a revolution would long since have taken place."[64]

Ten years later Mies concluded a decade-long study of the nature of glass—with its continual shifting from transparent to opaque to reflective—in a prospectus titled "What Would Concrete, What Would Steel Be without Plate Glass?" Here he wrote, "The space-toppling power of both would be undermined, yes, even canceled; would remain empty promise. The glass skin, the glass walls, alone permit the skeleton struc-

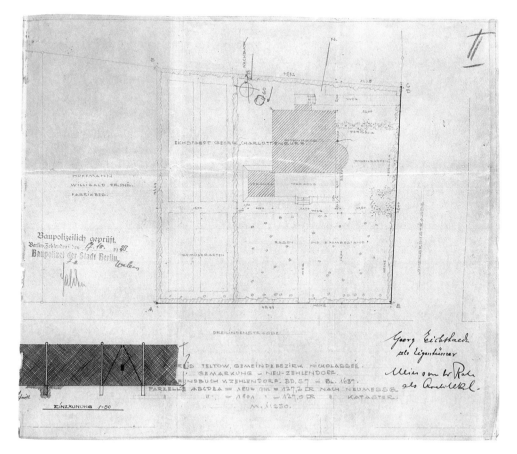

27. Ludwig Mies van der Rohe. Eichstaedt House, Berlin-Nikolassee. 1921–23. Site plan. Diazotype, 12 x 19½" (29.9 x 48.6 cm). Bauhaus-Archiv Berlin

ture its unambiguous constructive appearance and secure its architectonic possibilities." The full consequences would be realized not in factories or other functional buildings, he noted, but in residences, which "permit a measure of freedom in spatial composition that we will not relinquish any longer. Only now can we articulate space freely, open it up and connect it to the landscape."[65] As if to confirm this he had created a series of panoramalike renderings of the Concrete Country House that were wide enough to teeter at the edge of peripheral vision, making palpable something of the effect of the great bands of windows that stretched along the horizontal facades and dissolved the corners of the house's simple concrete building blocks (plates 60, 63).[66]

Mies blamed traditional building materials more than tradition-bound clients for the restraints on the fullest exploration of Behrens's notion that the building envelope was simply the dividing line between interior and exterior spatial design. To juxtapose the Concrete Country House with the Eichstaedt House of 1921–23 is to stage a contrast almost as striking as that between Picasso's *Three Musicians* and *Three Women at the Spring* of the same year. Mies, like Picasso, could simultaneously practice a modern cubism and a modernized neoclassicism, not as creation and compromise respectively but as alternative explorations of overlapping themes. In both projects there is a tight interlocking of exterior and interior spaces, of regularly subdivided and subtly terraced garden elements, in order to create open-air rooms and to frame vistas of nature.

Set in a dense but verdant residential neighborhood where the only views would be unwanted glimpses of the neighbors, the Eichstaedt House features the most hermetic to date of Mies's architectonic gardens. Its original form is best preserved in a 1923 site plan, one of the only ones for this house signed with Mies's new avant-garde persona "van der Rohe" (fig. 27). A perfect cube set asymmetrically on a lot whose perimeter is enclosed by tall hedges, the house is an object in a frame. Naturally it is pulled to the northeast, creating sunny space to the south and west for vegetable and rose gardens and a great lawn dotted with tall existing trees. The only additions to the cube—a square open veranda for outdoor dining at the southwest corner, and a semicircular bay off the *Damenzimmer* (and providing views of the rose garden, as at the Urbig House)—help to separate the functions of the individual gardens designed in relation to each of the house's facades.

The client, Georg Eichstaedt—a bookseller—worried about costs. Use of new materials during the early Weimar Republic's period of rampant inflation was out of the question here. The Concrete Country House, on the other hand, was a hypothetical project. Designed for a site of Mies's choice, where the land sloped gently away toward a natural vista (possibly the Havel, since Mies explored buying several sites here in these years),[67] it too is shifted off-center on its site, and like the Eichstaedt House it blocks the arriving visitor's full view of the lawn and in this case the distant vista. Where the Eichstaedt House is symmetrical, Mies's design for himself takes on the challenge of asymmetry, now influenced by the whole range of avant-garde artistic experiments from De Stijl to Constructivism. The volumes spiral around an open outdoor space, a kind of negative center, as in Schinkel's Court Gardener's House (fig. 19). Regular flower beds and a kitchen garden were important enough to Mies that he recorded them on the model. All evidence of the interior plan of the house is lost, however, if indeed it ever existed.

The Brick Country House is chiefly famous for its abolition of roomlike enclosures in favor of a sense of space "flowing" between rooms and around freestanding walls and L- and T-shaped partitions, a plan exceeding even the daring openness of Wright in his Prairie House–period designs.[68] This vocabulary continues outside the house to create a series of outdoor "rooms" of unprecedented grandeur and openness to the landscape. Any notion that Mies was here exploring a "universal" space of the type associated with De Stijl (although De Stijl certainly stimulated this breakthrough) must be tempered by attention to the role of terracing and low walls in the garden: Mies's linear definition of space here owes as much to the architectonic garden as it does to Theo van Doesburg's *Rhythm of a Russian Dance* (1918), or to other De Stijl compositions of the sort that were juxtaposed with his Concrete Country House design at the Rosenberg Gallery, Paris, in 1923.

As in every aspect of his design work, there is a continual tension between tradition and innovation.[69]

The line of the garden wall in the foreground of the perspective view of the Brick Country House (plate 65) severs any continuity between our space and the representational space of the image, even as it draws a boundary between the garden and the broader landscape.[70] Similarly in the Concrete Country House Mies creates a sharp terracing to cut the same kind of boundary. This hovering cantilever severs viewer from view, pictorializing the vista and promoting a detached contemplation of distant nature. This was a new way of achieving, even on a gently sloping site, something of the dramatic layering of space earlier effected by the retaining wall of the Riehl House.

As in the skyscraper designs of 1921 and 1922, glass in these projects is used as substance as much as absence, an ever thinner membrane between interior and exterior space. As Tegethoff was the first to realize, the large glass planes in the Brick Country House serve opposite but related functions. From the outside they are "impenetrable membranes, either dazzling with reflected light or, as the light wanes in intensity, curtained by the darkness of the room behind."[71] From within, meanwhile, they selectively frame the landscape, not creating a seamless relation to the outdoors but pictorializing key views. Much of this would have been achieved by the insertion of the fenestration in brick walls of unusual thinness, so that almost no shadow lines would be created by overhanging roof sections or window frames. The addition of steel lintels and concrete cantilevers to brick construction would preserve the tactile qualities of brick, and its inherent units of measure and proportion, even while creating walls of a new thinness, so that, as in the Concrete Country House, the view would become virtually part of the wall plane.

Not all experimentation was confined to manifestos. Although evidence of the nine or so house commissions that Mies received between 1919 and 1925 is scant, surviving drawings point to a number of innovations that advanced the searches for both a language of new materials and a new interrelation of interior and exterior space. Both the Petermann (1921) and the Lessing

(1923) houses, planned for Neubabelsberg, extend the concerns of Mies's prewar work. The Petermann House Project (p. 116, fig. 11) proposes cubic brick walls with large windows; presumably Mies intended to introduce steel framing elements of the sort he later worked out for the Esters and Hermann Lange houses in Krefeld (1927–30). The Lessing House Project (p. 116, fig. 12) is the link between Mies's Schinkelesque device of attaching cubic forms to one another at their corners and his later mode of designing a counterpoint between interior rooms and open courtyards. Like the Concrete Country House, the Lessing House centers on a core space composed of an adjacent living hall and a square garden. The garden is flanked on three sides by single-story living quarters of the type Mies increasingly preferred, even as the dialogue of interior and exterior space advocated in the garden reform movement is developed into an integral system of spatial design.

Wright was certainly an inspiration for Mies in these years, as the tectonic language, organizing chimneys, and accents of growing vines make clear in the elevation of the Eliat House Project (1925), planned for a lakeside site at Nedlitz (fig. 28). Here the potential of channeling living space rather than enclosing it is juxtaposed with a sequence of partitioned courts and gardens that echo the recessions and projections of the building volumes. The interlocking of perpendicular blocks at their corners is now integrated with the slipping and sliding of freestanding walls seen in the Brick Country House. Mies's quiet spatial revolution in that most conservative of tasks, the country house, found its most appreciative spokesman in Westheim, whose appreciation of Mies's new sense of space flows naturally from his praise for Mies as the most original of the period's "*Schinkel-schüler*," precisely because "he no longer has anything to do with a so-called Schinkel style":

Mies belongs to those who from the first conceive of the house as a unity. Not a juxtaposition of rooms with a roof over them, but a sort of life blood, a circulation, which leads from space to space. And it is indeed a matter—as in city planning—of ordering the circulation so that the process of domestic life, which the building is to serve, can take place with minimal friction. . . . The individual spaces as such are no longer partitioned. Rather an interlocking of individual spaces is sought. . . . their character derives not from their decoration but rather from their domestic function. The house in the end is nothing but the dressing of this spatial flow. . . . the flat walls, only broken by cuts for doors and windows, are enough for such a house layout, which no longer knows a front and a back, a representative display front, or unsightly side walls.[72]

Westheim captures the extent to which Mies's experiments developed from the demands of prewar

28. Ludwig Mies van der Rohe. Eliat House Project. 1925. Perspective view. Lost; reprinted from *Das Kunstblatt*, February 1927

Wohnreform for a new spatial envelope, even suggesting that Mies created a kind of frame or stage for heightening the awareness of daily living: "Furniture, fittings, colors, forms, made of the room a kind of stage, on which the residents and their guests were the actors."[73] Nor was nature to be any less staged and dramatized. The heart of the Eliat House plan is a switchback spatial sequence that draws the house's living functions into a dynamic pivoting composition even as it stages outdoor views with remarkable dramatic potential. Like the eighteenth-century French *hôtel* plan, which often accommodated an axial shift between entrance court and garden by slippage between two parallel tracks of spaces in the main building block, Mies switches axes on either side of the thickened wall of the entrance vestibule/living hall to turn the visitor's view ninety degrees—a shift, however, that is only accomplished by making three successive turns. Least expected as one approaches the one-story house is the fact that the ground falls away abruptly at the rear, so that both the French doors in the living room and the terrace of the dining room are raised over the landscape, commanding views of the lake. Whereas the *hôtel* plan's change in axis maintained a sense of classical wholeness, Mies assimilates a shift both in axis and in plane to dramatize a cleavage in space and to pictorialize a view—all in the narrow volume of an extended *Landhaus* plan. The Eliat House is at once the germ of Mies's famous houses of the late 1920s—the Wolf, Esters, Lange, and Tugendhat houses—and the flowering of his earlier engagement with the architectonic garden.

It also offers a response to the garden reformers' criticism of the nineteenth-century conservatory, that glass-roofed space that brought light and nature deep into the dense plans of city mansions and country villas. In place of this naturalistic imitation of a landscape within the house, Mies developed the *Wintergarten* as an integral element of the house and of the thin dividing line between interior and exterior. The incorporation of a winter garden into the living room is the only significant change Mies made in the Eliat House plan as he moved from sketches to a fully developed floor plan. As part of this change, he somewhat simplified the complexity of the flowing spaces in the sketches, giving

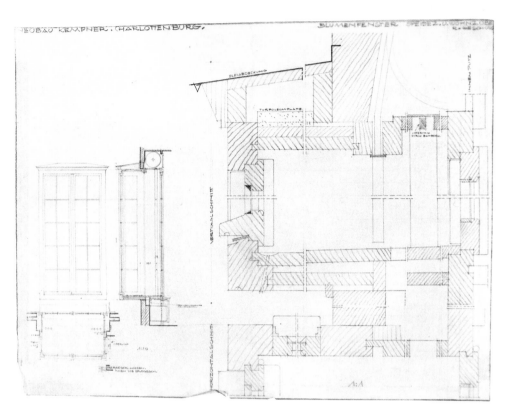

the living room a more roomlike form centered on a fireplace, and replacing the former play of L-shaped partitions with two parallel planes of glass, creating a small greenhouse. While previously the view from the hall to the living room was closed by a solid wall, now it was to be closed by a screen of greenery, as houseplants were pressed into the service of extending the connection between nature and architecture already suggested by vines growing on the elevations.

Just as the wall dissolved into French windows framing a landscape vista, so the winter garden created a picture of nature. In both cases the alternately transparent and reflective quality of glass would offer a continual oscillation between walls dissolved and walls enriched with framed views of nature and of landscape. A building block of Mies's later experiments with the spatial ambiguities of glass in such experimental designs as the Glass Room in Stuttgart in 1927, the winter garden was presaged in some of Mies's most "conservative" work of the early 1920s, notably the Kempner House of 1922, in Charlottenburg, where a projecting *Blumenfenster* (flower window) fully integrates nature even in traditional brick-wall construction (fig. 29).[74]

29. Ludwig Mies van der Rohe. Kempner House, Berlin-Charlottenburg. 1922. Elevation, section, and construction details of *Blumenfenster* (flower window). Graphite on tracing paper, 29 1/4 x 38" (74 x 97 cm). The Museum of Modern Art, New York. Mies van der Rohe Archive. Gift of the architect

30. Ludwig Mies van der Rohe. Wolf House, Gubin. 1925–27. View of garden front of house from below, c. 1927. Gelatin silver print, 2⅜ x 4⅜" (6 x 11 cm). The Museum of Modern Art, New York. Mies van der Rohe Archive. Gift of the architect

31. Tourist brochure showing Gubin skyline. c. 1927. The Wolf House appears at left, above the porticoed facade of the municipal theater

Brick Houses and Gardens: The Wolf, Esters, and Lange Houses

The first building in which Mies was able to bridge the gap between his commissioned work and his ideal projects was designed for an admirer of the Kempner House. In January 1925, Mies was approached by the industrialist and art collector Erich Wolf to design a house for a site dominating the picturesque medieval town of Gubin and the valley of the Neisse River beyond (fig. 30). This long narrow property (formerly a vineyard flanked by two restaurants, one of them called Sanssouci!) had striking similarities to the site of the Riehl House. Over 100 feet wide at its widest point, it stretched between two streets over 700 feet apart and separated by a change in grade of about 65 feet, thus linking a plateau that was one of the highest points in the region with the river bank. The resulting design translates the asymmetrical rhythms of cantilevered solids and shadowy voids seen in Mies's contemporary Monument to the November Revolution (1926) into residential design, while also updating his exploration of the architectonic garden. The house was demolished

in 1945, after extensive wartime damage, but the site, now preserved as a park, still conveys Mies's landscape intentions.

Rugged stone retaining walls spanning the property—left over from the vineyard—became the theme of Mies's building, which seen from below seemed almost to grow out of its site, refining its inherited features into a complex series of overlapping brick planes and volumes. Boundaries between house and garden were as impossible to discern as the radical break between garden and landscape was difficult to breach. This view from below quickly became a local icon, even appearing in the town's publicity brochures (fig. 31). But the Wolf family and their visitors were provided with a carefully staged itinerary constantly inviting them to rediscover the vistas Mies arranged in counterpoint to the planar layering of space. As his site plan of October 1925 reveals (plate 76), Mies designed the house as a vaguely pinwheeling form poised at the edge of the precipice; yet just as in the Concrete Country House, this composition could not be experienced as sculptural form—as "form for its own sake," as Mies would say. Spanning the narrow site and creating party walls with its neighbors, the house barred the vista until the visitor had negotiated a set of spatial switchbacks through both house and garden.

This optical landscaping began on Teichbornstrasse, where the house was announced by a low perimeter wall of finely studied brick masonry. Mies exploited a natural berm to mask the cubic play of his composition from view until the drive had completed its first curve. As the drive approached the house, what first appeared as a play of volumes was now experienced as a set of sliding parallel planes. The entrance was hidden from view, but was announced by the broad cantilevered second-floor terrace, which served as a canopy between the nearly blank wall of the entrance front and the low perimeter wall of a formal garden. In its dimensions, this garden—which was crossed to arrive at the front door, set at right angles to the garden's own entrance— echoed the volume of the house, a scheme going back to the Riehl House. It also updated the earlier architectonic garden through a sophisticated asymmetrical play of rectangular flower beds, paved paths, a bench, and a single tree, which a bird's-eye perspective drawing shows as it would be seen from the terrace that was to serve as a play area outside the children's bedrooms (plate 78).

Mies developed the floor plan of the house from unrealized Eliat House plans of the same year, but the switchback shifts of axis around the walls that structure the space in the plan, sliding past one another more often than forming right angles, have greater complexity. Individual spaces such as the *Herrenzimmer* are isolated by sliding doors. The social standing of the Wolf family is suggested by the sequence of entry, hall, living room, music room, and dining room, but these are arranged not *en filade*, which could have maximized views of the garden, but rather in a nearly slalomlike spatial design that would have withheld the view, presenting it only at key moments. From one's arrival in the living and dining rooms, the house and its garden terraces beyond would continually frame and reframe the panoramic view of the skyline and valley. As in the Eliat plan, French doors allowed free movement between the living room and its terrace. At right angles to that view, the roof slab was cantilevered far beyond its support to create an outdoor dining loggia and to complete the itinerary of arrival begun under the cantilevered balcony of the entry side.

Never before had Mies made the material, compositional, and spatial unity of a house and garden so complete. The brick garden terrace was surrounded by a perimeter wall both defining the space and dramatizing the juxtaposition of manmade foreground and distant view with little perceptible middle ground, a technique reminiscent not only of Schinkel but of the paintings of Caspar David Friedrich. (Wolf had at least one of these in his collection.[75]) The terrace itself was a complex play of levels and slots of space, allowing a descent via a staircase hidden between high walls to land that the family planted as a fruit orchard.

Just as traditional walls were avoided inside, so the garden spaces were created by subtle changes in level, without recourse to hedges, trellises, or dividing walls. This is the most abstract and geometric of all Mies's gardens, its tight compositional control reinforced by the planting of beds of single flowers, for the most part tulips, arranged, the Wolf daughters recall,

in fields of uniform color. Tulips were favored by modernists (they featured prominently, for instance, in Gabriel Guévrékian's garden for the Villa de Noailles, in Hyères[76]) since they grow to a uniform height; seen from above, they compose into planes of color, like fields in an abstract painting. In fact the Wolf garden is the closest Mies came to the transposition of avant-garde painting into garden form—of the type essayed at the Bauhaus by Farkas Molnár, or in several gardens at Germany's first major twentieth-century garden exhibition, in Dresden in 1926[77]—and it is significant that he not only drew these gardens in bird's-eye perspective, he provided rooftop terraces so that they might be seen in their most abstract form, obliquely from above.

Photography of the house was carefully controlled, as it had been at the Riehl House: the same sequence of views, summarizing the key moments of arrival and discovery, was reproduced over and over again. Family photographs taken a decade later reveal that the rigid geometries of the house gradually gave way to lush planting, as vines took over the facades and retaining wall (fig. 32). But the framed view of the town remained, carefully staged to leave most of the industry on the opposite riverbank out of the view, although this was precisely where the hat factory that provided Wolf's fortune was located. Rather, the view was skewed to take in the medieval and neo-Gothic towers of the historic center.

By the late 1920s the concept of *Gestaltung* involved for Mies a comprehensive meshing of interior and exterior space.[78] Furniture and plants were essential building blocks of the organic whole. The office draftsman's notation "Mies reserves the right to design the garden" on an alternative scheme for a terrace at the Esters House[79] is the firmest evidence that even as he juggled commissions in three countries—the Esters and Hermann Lange houses in Germany, the Tugendhat House in Czechoslovakia, and the German Pavilion in Spain were all in design in 1928–29—he remained unwilling to delegate garden design to a professional landscape company. In both the Esters House and the neighboring Lange House, fraternal twins in a then new subdivision, the garden facade develops the theme of the progressive stepping forward of the building mass to provide maximum exposure to the

garden and landscape, while the garden responds, intermeshed with the facade almost like the cogs of a gear (fig. 33).

The designs of the two houses involve serial repetitions rather than mirror symmetry, but Mies conceived of their landscape as a whole. His concern with sunlight here extends back to his earliest designs, and explains why the two houses step back to open themselves up to the southwest. Each house has a terrace anchored at its eastern end by a one-story loggia, a place for outdoor dining that also communicates directly with the indoor dining room. In the latter, too, the wall is pierced in both houses by a window, allowing morning light to filter through and enhancing the sense of the brick walls as a thin skin. By this time Mies had read Siegfried Ebeling's *Der Raum als Membran* (Space as membrane), a book that gave a new urgency to Behrens's earlier call for house and garden to relate to one other like form and mold.[80]

Early designs for the Esters House foresaw an extensively glazed facade, but as this was abandoned for brick walls generously punctured by windows, Mies developed interior and exterior spaces in tandem around a series of framed views that telescope out. Not only do individual windows of these houses frame landscape views so large as to be essentially brought indoors, and displayed in juxtaposition with art (of which Hermann Lange especially was an avid collector), but perspectives are constructed through the wide

but staggered openings of one room into the next, so that long vistas of overlapping planes extend from interior to exterior. Besides developing complex systems of steel framing to allow for these large picture windows, Mies here employed two new window types, the famous *Senkfenster*, which can be lowered completely into a trough, and hinged banks of windows in which each frame can be folded back, reducing the frame to a thin band. From the terrace, under the right conditions of light, the windows allow layered views back through each house and even, at some points, right through the building to the front garden.

Like the Wolf House, the Krefeld houses are developed almost as horizontally extruded planes that traverse their plots even as they nestle into the site. Both have full basements that are revealed only on the short elevation, where the service spaces within them face into sunken courts defined by brick walls, as the building sections carefully work the ground levels of the flat meadow landscape. The development company for the subdivision required a broad front garden and proscribed enclosing it in the iron gates and fences of nineteenth-century villa suburbs. Yet Mies designed this garden as a distinct space, separating it from the sidewalk with a low brick wall doubled by a low hedge of the type common in the fields of the nearby North Rhine landscape. Perhaps in response to the work of Le Corbusier, which Mies had come to know intimately while working on the

Weissenhof Housing Colony Master Plan for Stuttgart (1925–27), the broad front gardens of the Esters and Lange houses are the first to have their paths defined by the movement of the car rather than the perceptual speed of a pedestrian. Mies's vigorous drawings of automobile trajectories dividing the garden parterres constitute an experiment, exceptional for him, with the technological culture that fascinated many of his contemporaries in the 1920s (fig. 34). But the speed slows considerably once the planar facades of the houses are traversed. In fact the rear terraces are carefully studied to frame views from built-in furniture, the heights of the walls that define them being determined from the point of view of a seated visitor, whether in the interior or exterior living rooms.

The rear facade of each house provides a series of oblique views that create an experience of the building as a composition in a sweeping perspective such as that set up by the staggered room sequences within. In a lesson that ultimately derives from Schinkel, Mies refuses axial access to the garden terrace, instead positioning stairs parallel to the rear facade and set between walls, channeling diagonal views (fig. 33). (At the Riehl House two decades earlier, he had created axial symmetrical views with similar means.) The result underscores the sharp division between the garden, governed by geometries, and the view of nature beyond. Archival research done in conjunction with the recent restoration of the two gardens reveals that at least in the case of the Esters garden, Mies was reworking an earlier scheme.[81] The Esters family had enjoyed their site for several years before turning to Mies, and had laid out paths among their majestic chestnut trees. Mies eliminated these paths to create a sweeping lawn. At the bottom of the garden he cut selective views in the trees to allow glimpses of the meadow landscapes beyond, which were then intact. (These views have since been allowed to grow in as the residential neighborhood has become denser over the years.) He also framed the lawn on either side with paths echoing the widths of the side sections of the terraces, and continuing their perspective lines toward the horizon (fig. 35).

Mies was fascinated with playing off the hard-edged geometry of his asymmetrical compositions against nature. In studies for the Esters garden, he ultimately opts for climbing roses rather than tall-stemmed standing roses, a first hint that he intended the house walls to be partly overgrown eventually with flowering vines. Early photographs, including those with oblique viewpoints of the type Mies seems to have stage-directed over and over again for presentation photography, show vines spilling out of planters along the second-story terraces. In another frequently published view, geraniums, hollyhocks, and tall shrubs play against the planar composition of garden walls and stairs.[82] As in Schinkel's Court Gardener's House, the effect was not confined to charm but went to the heart of the search for an architectural language with an organic wholeness comparable to but distinct from the natural realm. Much as Schinkel's Court Gardener's House offered a panorama of nearly all the ways in which trabeated and arcuated architecture could be conjugated with flowering nature, so at the Esters and Lange houses Mies developed a tectonic language for modern brick construction with a thoroughness that even led him to calculate his walls in brick lengths, or at least to give the appearance of having done so.

Nature and the Critique of Technology: The German Pavilion, Barcelona, and the Tugendhat House

The words "consciousness" and "awareness" pepper Mies's lectures and notes of the years 1927–30, as his

34. Ludwig Mies van der Rohe. Esters House, Krefeld. 1927–30. Sketch site plan showing driveway. Graphite and colored pencil on tracing paper, 11¾ x 19¼" (27.6 x 49 cm). The Museum of Modern Art, New York. Mies van der Rohe Archive. Gift of the architect

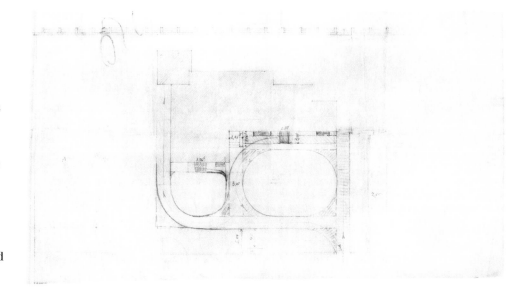

35. Aerial view of Krefeld showing Esters and Lange houses at upper right. 1930

position of architects such as Häring. By late 1927 he was reading the neo-Catholic texts of Rudolf Schwarz, another former Behrens pupil, and had met the Catholic philosopher Romano Guardini, with whom he might already have crossed paths at Klösterli or through the Kempners. "There are people who would like to make a Ford Factory out of nature," Mies writes in a notebook of 1927–28, almost a spiritual catechism for reestablishing authentic experience and consciousness in the new conditions of scientific and technological culture.[84] In the important lecture "The Preconditions of Architectural Work" (1928) he concluded, "We have to become master of the unleashed forces and build them into a new order, an order that permits free play for the unfolding of life. Yes, but an order also that is related to mankind. . . . We do not need less science, but a science that is more spiritual. . . . All that will only become possible when man asserts himself in objective nature and relates it to himself."[85]

Mies was preoccupied with these issues in the months before receiving the commissions for the German Pavilion at the 1929 International Exposition in Barcelona and the Tugendhat House in Brno. "We want to give things their meaning again," he copied from Guardini's *Letters from Lake Como* (1926),[86] and "There is a totally untouched nature, and the longing for it, is itself a cultural phenomenon. . . . Nature is truly affecting only when it begins to be dwelled in, when culture begins in it. Piece by piece nature is formed. Man creates in it his own world, not only of a natural need, but with a deliberate purpose, serving spiritual ideas."[87] The German Pavilion, as Neumeyer has brilliantly argued, was Mies's attempt to make his own contribution to these philosophical ruminations through the media of structure and space.[88]

Mies seized the opportunity of a commission virtually free of programmatic demands to craft a new paradigm for design as a structuring of the world that humanity can create. And as in Behrens's earlier exhibition pavilions and gardens, the German Pavilion is at once a building and a landscape, a house and a temple, a measuring of space and an expansion of consciousness. Destroyed in 1930, it was re-created on the same site in 1981–86, and insofar as its experiential complexities

personal reading program in philosophical literature and his exploration of new building materials came together with a number of important commissions. Even as he assumed a leadership role in the Deutscher Werkbund, with its debates on the relationship of artistic creation to industrial production and consumer culture, and even as he began to experiment with the products of advanced German industries, from plate glass and steel to linoleum, chrome, and industrialized textiles, he began to question the place of technology as a driving force in modern culture. "We agree with the direction [Henry] Ford has taken, but we reject the plane on which he moves. Mechanization can never be a goal, it must remain a means. A means toward a spiritual purpose," he had warned as early as 1924.[83]

Mies collected Raoul Francé's popular books on the underlying structures and productive capacities of plants, but he never fell into the visual metaphors linking architecture and nature that underscored the have since then sponsored diverse interpretations, it has fulfilled just what Mies intended: a place in which the capacities of the new architecture opened new horizons of thought.[89] Nor was this lost on visitors at the time, even if the interpretation of the building as a demonstration of the rational architecture made possible by new technological capacities was rapidly made dominant by powerful critics like Hitchcock and Johnson—neither of whom had seen the pavilion. One reviewer admired Mies's invitation of the visitor "to some shorter or longer period of rest and contemplation"[90] in the only space in the fairgrounds where emptiness and quiet replaced a cornucopia of displays and new techniques of recorded sound and images. And the English architect Raymond McGrath celebrated the pavilion as a seminal moment in structuring perception, and Mies as "to-day's Brunelleschi," an architect making us aware that "the limiting and seeming expansion of space in building are facts to be taken into account not only physically but in theory." McGrath noted,

This Garden House was clean and open—unlike the other buildings of the Exposition. Its rooms and walled square had nobody living in them. To see it was like coming face to face with someone strange and beautiful. This building, with its glass and water, its bright columns and its quiet girl in stone, was a place for the mind's play more than for the business of living.[91]

In the German Pavilion Mies defined two building blocks for an architecture understood as constructing a reality parallel to but separate from nature: the free-standing wall and the freestanding column. In effect, he set free two elements that the Renaissance architect Leon Battista Alberti had considered intimately related. He married this innovation with a renewal of the experiment in forming space out of panels of transparent and colored glass that he had first essayed in the Glass Room two years earlier, where he had given physical form to Ebeling's call for "space as membrane." Both the Glass Room and the pavilion were ambiguously structure and space, for like the reflective surfaces of the walls, they could oscillate perceptually between those roles. While the freestanding walls channeled and directed space, the cruciform columns provided a palpable reading, a gauge or measure of space.

The evolution of the design demonstrates that the grid was not a generative force, as it had been earlier for Behrens; indeed Sergius Ruegenberg recalled that the design was studied principally in a Plasticine base in which the walls could be moved at will.[92] Instead the grid was a late addition, a fine-tuning of visual experience: recorded insistently on the travertine surface of the podium shared by house and garden, it is an aesthetic and optical device to anchor the eye as it scans space. The walls do much of the work of carrying the roof,[93] but they too serve as measures and anchors of space, both guiding the body in motion, through their famous sliding compositional relations, and anchoring the body in stasis by channeling views through various glass filters to the garden, the exposition, and even the city beyond, whose traffic often reflects on the glass walls with the movement of the sun. As Ruegenberg recalled in both sketches (fig. 36) and an unpublished memoir, Mies insisted that the greatest difference between his own and Le Corbusier's staging of a prospect through expanses of glass was the use of a spatial grounding that could be felt bodily, even when it was outside the eye's peripheral field. "I must have a wall behind me," Mies is said to have explained, in one

36. Sergius Ruegenberg. Caricature portrait of Mies: "I must have a wall behind me." c. 1925. Graphite and colored pencil on paper, 5¾ x 8½" (14.2 x 21 cm). Berlinische Galerie

of his most telling extensions of the German tradition of empathetic analysis of the psychology of space.[94]

The spatial paradigm of the pavilion is indeed new, but many of Mies's clients of the 1920s would recognize elements of their homes in what McGrath called, quite unself-consciously, a "garden house." In the earliest plan, a space for this experiment in shifting planes and viewpoints is carved out of the site by a hedge, a wavy line on the plan (fig. 1). Although Mies replaced the hedge, instead relying on the architectural (and instant rather than slow-growing) means of freestanding walls of glass, marble, and travertine, the link with nature—and with the origins of these walls in the garden devices of his earlier career—was reinforced by incorporating planters for vines into the very structure of the travertine walls partially enclosing the larger pool, which was itself planted with water lilies.[95]

Set at one end of the short axis of the exhibition's cross-shaped plan, the pavilion is approached axially, its composition of volumes, voids, and sliding planes appearing through a freestanding row of Ionic columns (since demolished) that was a given of the site, along with the dense greenery behind (fig. 37). But access to the podium is oblique, up a broad flight of stairs set at right angles to the edge of the podium. This is the first of a series of switchbacks the visitor must make to move through staggered planes and openings, the eye coming to land on spatial anchors in the form of Mies's famous Barcelona chairs or of sculptures set on pedestals (three were called for in the early stages of the design; one was installed).

The path describes an itinerary but the endpoints are multiple: the pool with Georg Kolbe's figure *Dawn*, set in a pool bathed in early light; the path leading axially to the grove behind the pavilion, which turns out to be centered on the podium and thus on the exhibition's cross-axis, previously so emphatically denied; or the terrace, with its long travertine bench overlooking a shallow pool that reflects both the setting sun and the pavilion itself. The hinge space between them all, at precisely the center of the rectangular podium—a space neither wholly indoors nor wholly outdoors, under the protective canopy of the cantilevered roof, and free of membranes to the outside world—is clearly the

37. International Exposition, Barcelona, 1929. Aerial view of fairgrounds with Mies's German Pavilion at center right

descendant of the outdoor dining areas in most of Mies's earlier garden houses. As in Krefeld, a translucent wall provides a soft, glowing illumination both here and inside the pavilion, where it is seen in counterpoint to the great object of display, a stunning warm-rose onyx wall.

The pavilion has a formal front facade and a more reserved back garden (fig. 38), but Mies—having arranged his sliding planes directly across a secondary entrance to the fair, and on the short route to the popular Pueblo Español, the Spanish village display—realized from the first that his building would be encountered from both sides. In fact he blocked the simple path through with a deep green wall of marble, so that moving in either direction would require a detour into the spaces of contemplation, whether roofed or open air. Mies's construction staged a heightened "world in itself"—the very demand Behrens had made of the architectonic garden. Set among the fair's abundant icons of historicist culture, the pavilion, a modernist propylaeum, was a place of transition between worlds.

"Our task is to progress further to a new, albeit critically tested unity," Mies underlined in his copy of Guardini's *Letters from Lake Como*; and "consciousness is part of culture, is perhaps its prime prerequisite; the basis from which it rises. Culture presupposes a distance from immediate reality."[96] Guardini recommends "increased awareness of the body by rhythmical culture," an argument resonant with Mies's earlier interests in the theories of rhythm and abstraction taught by Jaques-Dalcroze. Regretting the "loss of the symbolic meaning of space," Guardini calls for a new awareness of "the most self-understood things, the everyday actions, which contain that which is most profound."[97] No wonder, then, that the encounters between Mies and Grete and Fritz Tugendhat were so passionate and engaged. At one meeting at Am Karlsbad 24, Mies's Berlin office and home, on December 31, 1928, they missed a New Year's Eve dinner because Mies kept them talking until 1 A.M.[98]

Grete Tugendhat had lived for four years in Berlin, where she frequented the circles of the Marxist cultural historian Eduard Fuchs, who had purchased the Perls House and in 1928 had Mies design an extension to it. She was intensely involved with the thinking of Martin Heidegger and his evolving critique of technology; two close friends were pupils of the philosopher, and she attended the lectures leading up to the publication of *Being and Time* in 1927.[99] Just married, the Tugendhats were planning to return to their native Brno to build a house in the Černá Pole villa quarter, on a commanding site carved from the garden of Grete's parents. The house commission would involve not only the pragmatic and aesthetic decisions of an architect/client negotiation but an attempt to address a concept in the philosophies of Heidegger and Guardini: the belief that an active engagement with the environment was a way of constituting the self.

In 1969, Tugendhat gave a compelling account of working with Mies:

I had always wanted a spacious modern house of clear and simple forms, and my husband had been most horrified by the interiors of his youth, stuffed with trinkets and lace. After we had decided to have a house built, we made an appointment with Mies van der

38. Ludwig Mies van der Rohe. German Pavilion, International Exposition, Barcelona. 1928–29. View of rear or garden facade and corner of the reconstruction of 1986. Photograph: Kay Fingerle, 2000

Rohe. And from the very first moment we met him, it was clear to us that he should be the one to build our house, so impressed were we by his personality. . . . the way he talked about his architecture gave us the feeling that we were dealing with a true artist. He said, for instance, that the ideal measurements of a room could never be calculated; rather, one had to feel the room while standing in and moving through it. He added that a house should not be built starting from the facade, but from the inside, and that windows in a modern building should no longer be holes in a wall but fill the space between floor and ceiling, thereby becoming elements of the structure.[100]

Together Mies and the Tugendhats visited Krefeld and Gubin. "We particularly liked the most recent one . . . belonging to a Mr. Wolf. At first our house was meant to be built of brick as well, but it turned out that there was no beautiful brick to be had in Brno, and no bricklayers who were able to work flawlessly." As Tugendhat makes clear, her house was planned from the first as a kind of staging of the existing site: "Of course Mies was delighted with this site, which offered a view over Brno and the Špilberk" (a picturesque castle overlooking not only the cityscape but the convergence of the Moravian heights and the plains toward Vienna), and "this view was preserved by the gap between the house and the garage and determined the composition of the building masses."[101] The decision was made to adopt steel-frame construction, a technique that Mies had used just once before, in the Weissenhof Apartment House, but that expanded the possibilities for relating interior and exterior spaces. At first he thought to cantilever out the masses of the extensively glass-enveloped building, opening the view while severing a direct relationship with the sweeping lawn and existing trees, but he soon rejected this idea in favor of a technique closer to his earlier practice: a high podium on which volumes shift and interpenetrate, creating rooms that cluster around outdoor areas, marrying the architectonic garden with the new possibilities for spatial freedom.

Mies manipulated the building's masses not only compositionally but experientially, in terms of different individual and communal activities. Many modern-movement houses obscure older patterns of separating the spaces of reception and of family living, but the Tugendhat House is traditional in this respect, to such an extent that it stages different experiences of space for visitors and for family members.[102] The family quarters are primarily on the upper level, where the bedrooms give directly onto a terrace. This terrace wraps around to the street side of the house, under the portico, yet for all its openness it is hidden from visitors, who are discouraged from approaching the tempting view by a thin metal bar. Mies considered planting a square of lawn across the opening under the portico, much as he extended a carpet between spatial dividers at Barcelona. This would have divided front and back terraces, but more important would have juxtaposed a foreground greensward (had the lawn thrived in shadow) with the framed picture-postcard view of the Špilberk, a collage effect almost surreal in its exploration of the Romantic landscape's loss of middle ground. Mies also suggested a line of widely spaced boxed shrubs before the front facade—a natural equivalent of the Ionic columns before the German Pavilion—and an interpretation of the perimeter hedge that would have left the grid laid out in the paving clear to view (fig. 39).

39. Ludwig Mies van der Rohe. Tugendhat House, Brno. 1928–30. Sketch perspective of entry approach with unrealized proposal for plantings. Pencil on diazotype, 19½ x 29¼" (49.5 x 74.2 cm). The Museum of Modern Art, New York. Mies van der Rohe Archive. Gift of the architect

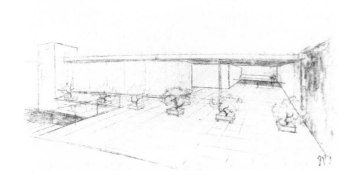

The dramatic view presented to visitors as a snapshot disappears as they are received in a formal entry hall. This frosted-glass vestibule is furnished with the three fundamental building blocks of the house: a single chrome cruciform column, specially designed tubular steel furniture, and a potted plant, all bathed in the "shadowless light" that Mies first created in the Glass Room. To arrive on the main floor, visitors and family descend a relatively dark curved stair, only to emerge in the active light of a great space freed of traditional walls. Despite the room's later fame (based largely on photographs) as an exercise in "universal" space, the actual experience here is one of channeled views, rhythms of light, and compression and release. Our eyes do not roam about unguided; the space is zoned, functionally and optically. Far from opening to a boundless panorama, the main floor commands a view skewed toward the southeast, and thus away from the villa of Grete's parents, which once was largely hidden behind a grand weeping willow (fig. 40). The vista is broader than on the floor above, but is carefully framed between curved banks of trees laid out in consultation with the local landscape architect Grete Müller-Roder, whom the Tugendhats had hired to help them relandscape this remnant of Grete's parents' garden (fig. 41).[103] The willow features prominently in Mies's earliest bird's-eye sketches of the building; along with the view of the Špilberk, it determined the house's planning every bit as much as the sequence of domestic functions. Its loss, first on paper in Johnson and Hitchcock's floor plan and then in actuality to old age, has fundamentally altered understanding of the Tugendhat House.[104]

As at Barcelona, Mies transposed the dialogue between indoors and outdoors into the architecture itself, making this dialogue more powerfully the kind of pairing of opposites with which he liked to design and think. The glass membrane that surrounds the living floor on two sides often collapses the view into reflections on the surface of the building, momentarily pictorializing it. And although the space is always said to be zoned by freestanding elements (the famous onyx wall and ebony alcove), spatial divisions are also achieved by furniture and other, more ephemeral means. The fundamental difference between Mies's exploration of

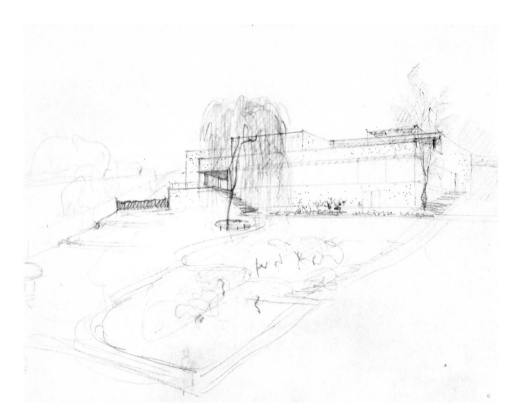

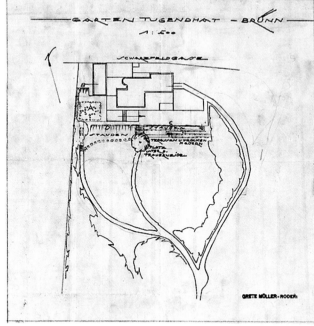

the free plan and Le Corbusier's lies in Mies's insistence on positioning the furniture, and thus fixing bodies in conversation or contemplation. Fabric, nature, and reflections also provide changing boundaries in a space that is alive to the rhythms of the body and of nature. Curtains, some opaque, some translucent, can be drawn to set off individual spaces; Grete Tugendhat, her daughter recalls, claimed that the family used them often, and described them as "creating and delimiting their own private space at will." She noted, "My mother told me that this experience of space was an essential quality of life in the house: while providing seclusion and privacy there was feeling of belonging to a larger totality at the same time."[105] The great glass wall facing the garden and the vista—in Mies's fullest development of the idea of enclosing space with but a breathing membrane—is not an undifferentiated plane; the Tugendhats enthusiastically endorsed Mies's suggestion of employing two expansive and expensive sinkable windows of the sort first essayed in the Lange House, but now combined with the idea of the floor-to-ceiling glass membrane introduced at Barcelona. If the

membrane was for Ebeling an organic metaphor, here it is really living, responding to the time of day and season.

This domestic use of the curtain wall is dramatic, for not only can silver-gray silk drapes be drawn or withdrawn, but the glass can partially be made to disappear, rather theatrically transforming the living room and the dining room into open belvederes. These removable panels are perfectly aligned with the living and dining spaces, pendants as it were to the onyx wall and ebony alcove and thus completing, paradoxically by absence, a delineation of spaces with entirely new means. Freely open to view, the dining room was aligned with the willow, so that the great arc of the tree over the lawn once more or less completed the half-circle of the exedral alcove. The dining table is fixed in place by a diminutive cruciform column. Mies also designed lightweight movable tables, one of which a family photograph shows being used for a picnic in what the architect, on his plan, named a *Platz unter der Trauerweide*, a roundel of space under the willow tree, where several garden paths come together (fig. 42).

Nature is everywhere brought inside, beginning with the layering of greenery between the double

40. Ludwig Mies van der Rohe. Tugendhat House, Brno. 1928–30. Sketch perspective of house and garden with weeping willow tree. Drawing: Sergius Ruegenberg. Pencil on paper, 11 x 14" (28 x 35 cm). Berlinische Galerie, Hanna-Hoech-Archiv

41. Grete Müller-Roder. Garden plan for Tugendhat House, Brno. 1928–30. Pencil and colored pencil on tracing paper, 11 x 10¾" (28 x 27.3 cm). The Museum of Modern Art, New York. Mies van der Rohe Archive. Gift of the architect

thickness of glass that forms the winter garden, in the last half bay of the main floor. This arrangement frames the study between pressed plants on one side and the onyx wall on the other. The planned and fortuitous reflections created by the parallel planes of glass continually intermingle elements of interior and exterior, as household plants and garden plants visually exchange places, layering real space and the space of

42. Ludwig Mies van der Rohe. Tugendhat House, Brno. 1928–30. The Tugendhat family dining under the weeping willow, c. 1933. Photograph: Fritz Tugendhat. Collection Daniela Hammer-Tugendhat

the imagination. These shifting refractions were recorded in photographs by Fritz Tugendhat, who captured the reflections not only in the glass and chrome of the architectural space but in the planes and surfaces of the furniture, from Mies's glass coffee table to desk lamps used throughout the house—clear glass spheres filled with water to multiply reflections.[106] The entire space is a kaleidoscope of changing reflections and light effects. The onyx wall is highly polished, and Mies carefully supervised the patterns in the stone and was delighted when the lowering sun caused the rear side of the panel to glow with a reddish hue, rendering ephemeral and beautiful interior pictorializations of nature.

Everywhere the house plays between the freedom of the open plan and the use of nature to direct the view. The broad landing at the top of the monumental flight of steps leading down to the garden, and parallel to the rear facade, could serve as a dining area, as in Mies's earlier hillside houses. In an echo of the architectonic garden, it is paired with a square garden of nearly identical dimensions (fig. 43). Mies studied a variety of compositions for this garden, using pergolas, gridded groves of trees, and parallel beds of perennials (figs. 44, 45). Eventually, perhaps, this formal garden was to fill with a grid of tall trees, creating a green wall that would add screening to the house's translucent glass (fig. 3).

Ruegenberg pointed to Le Corbusier's Villa Stein, at Garches (1927), as the inspiration for the grand garden stair, although in many respects it resembles the podium stair at the German Pavilion. Massive and grounded to provide a contrast with the open volume above, it also ties the layering of the spaces in the house to the layering of the spaces in the garden, a technique that goes back to the Riehl and Perls houses. The stair comes to rest on the uppermost of a series of stepped terraces that span the upper garden nearly from side to side, connecting the spatial layers of interior and exterior. Any easy axial connection is severed, however, for the stairs have no direct access to the lawn. The uppermost terrace recalls the exedral bench at the Urbig House in that Mies terminated the cross-axis created by the stair with a roughly apsidal indentation in a leafy planting of trees. Here he strategically placed a suite of garden furniture, which, like the groupings of furniture inside the house, invites both conversation and contemplation of a calculated view. The base on which the house sits, a world of servant spaces as in the Riehl House, was designed—as Tugendhat's photographs record (fig. 46)—to disappear from view as vines planted along it grew, freeing the belvedere of the house from this solid base, just as the space was meant to free the mind for thought.

In providing a rooftop garden on the upper terrace, Mies was no doubt rivaling Le Corbusier, but he was also readdressing his own long-standing engagement with the dialogue of interior and exterior. The house might almost represent a strategy for achieving what he

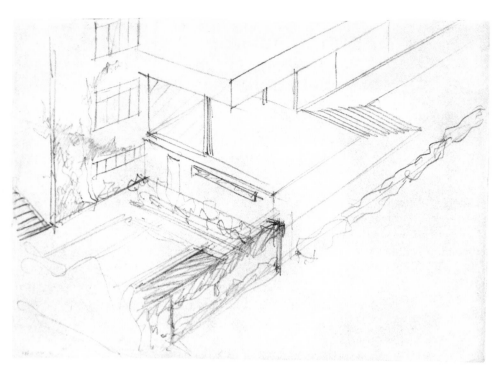

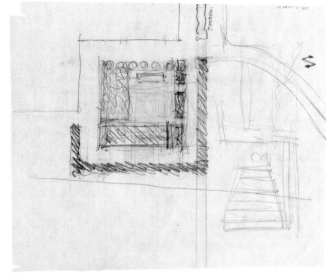

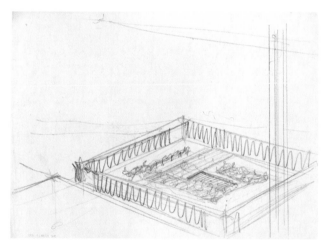

had called for in his 1928 lecture "The Preconditions of Architectural Work": "It must be possible to solve the task of controlling nature and yet create simultaneously a new freedom."[107] On the roof, Mies returned to precisely the symbols of his earlier engagement with Schinkel, the exedral bench and the vine-covered trellis (frontispiece). Rendered frankly in the materials of the steel-framed house, these elements also signify a retrieval of the humanistic connection with nature, a concern for Mies in the wake of his anxieties over the limits of technology. It is striking to note that while the configuration of space, and even furniture, in the interior was decided early on, Mies tinkered long with the interrelation of the bench, the trellis, a possible built-in table, and either a water basin or a sandbox in this rooftop garden. In continuity with the *Spielgärten* of the *Wohnreform* movement, bench and trellis created an area for children to play, while also linking the two interrelated elements of Mies's architectural thought: architecture as a frame for consciousness and the tectonic frame. Could Mies have known the lithograph in which Schinkel related precisely these two themes, juxtaposing a vine-covered trellis with two exedral benches, in a project at the heart of his reconstruction of Pliny's villa (fig. 47)?

The debate over the question "Can one live in the Tugendhat House?," published in *Die Form* between a group of architecture critics, the architect Ludwig Hilberseimer, and the clients has become infamous. In many respects it turned around the question of consciousness or awareness as a valid program for modern architecture.[108] Disturbed to see the elements of a state exhibition building in Barcelona transferred into a private dwelling, the critic Justus Bier complained that there was no privacy in a space without walls; and since there was no place to hang pictures, the personal

43 (above left). Ludwig Mies van der Rohe. Tugendhat House, Brno. 1928–30. Sketch perspective of southwest corner with garden. Pencil on paper, 8¼ x 11¾" (20.9 x 29.6 cm). The Museum of Modern Art, New York. Mies van der Rohe Archive. Gift of the architect

44 (above right). Ludwig Mies van der Rohe. Tugendhat House, Brno. 1928–30. Sketch plan of southwest corner garden. Pencil on paper, 10 x 12" (25.4 x 30.5 cm). The Museum of Modern Art, New York. Mies van der Rohe Archive. Gift of the architect

45 (left). Ludwig Mies van der Rohe. Tugendhat House, Brno. 1928–30. Sketch perspective of southwest corner garden. Pencil on paper, 8¼ x 11½" (21 x 29.2 cm). The Museum of Modern Art, New York. Mies van der Rohe Archive. Gift of the architect

tastes of the residents could not counteract the strong patterns of stone and wood grain, in which Bier saw the aggressive presence of the architect. Could the residents abide the space's exaggerated pathos without ultimately rebelling? Would not this new kind of "*Ausstellungswohnen*" (exhibition living) result in a suppression of personal life? The Marxist architectural critic Roger Ginsburger criticized the "immoral luxury" and even the effect of sacredness in the great room:

This awe and bemusement is exactly what takes hold of us when we enter a church or a palace. . . . The aim is the same: to give the impression of affluence, of particularity, of something never experienced before. . . . I willingly do admit that the onyx and the precious wood of the walls are amazingly beautiful materials to look at, as beautiful (and for the same reason so) as a face of rock in the Alps in whose layers and cracks we recognize the effects of powerful natural forces. . . . But you do not have to have such things placed in your room to delight in them again and again, simply because the pleasure is soon dulled, but above all because there is more to life than just looking at onyx walls and veneers of precious woods.[109]

dwarfing but in a liberating sense. . . . For just as one sees in this room every flower in a different light and as every work of art gives a stronger impression (e.g. a sculpture in front of the onyx wall), individuals too and others stand out more clearly against such a background."[110] She continued by confirming an earlier comment of Hilberseimer's—that "one can obtain no impression of this house from photographs. One has to move in the space, its rhythm is like music"[111]—and to describe this rhythm as so strong that small changes of furniture make no difference to it. Finally she refuted the notion that the house creates a total merging of inside and out. "The connection between interior and exterior space is indeed important," she explained, "but the large interior space is completely closed and reposing in itself, with the glazed wall working as a perfect limitation. Otherwise, too, one would find that one would have a feeling of unrest and insecurity. But the way it is, the large room—precisely because of its

46. Ludwig Mies van der Rohe. Tugendhat House, Brno. 1928–30. View of garden facade, c. 1935. Photograph: Fritz Tugendhat. Collection Daniela Hammer-Tugendhat

47. Karl Friedrich Schinkel. Stibadium in the Tuscan Villa of Pliny, drawn by Schinkel, lithography by V. H. Mützel, lithograph 1841. First published in *Architektonisches Album* (Berlin 1841)

By the end of the year Grete Tugendhat felt compelled to respond: "What has the architect given us?," she asked rhetorically, and responded, "An important feeling of existence [*Daseinsgefühl*]," clearly evoking Heidegger, whose call on us to ask the all-important question "What is it, to be?" seemed to her readily contemplated in this space. "I have never," she went on, "experienced the rooms as possessing pathos. I find them large and austerely simple—however, not in a

rhythm—has a very particular tranquillity, which a closed room could never have."[112] The full complexity of Mies's space, with its oscillations between enclosure and a self-conscious, pictorialized, but always distanced contact with the natural realm, could hardly have found a more sympathetic client; for Grete Tugendhat found her house a vehicle for contemplating self in the natural realm.

A New Perspective on Nature: Houses of the 1930s

By the time Mies emigrated to the United States, in 1938, he had built but two single-story houses, one the ephemeral Exhibition House at the German Building Exhibition in Berlin (1931), the other the modest Lemke House (1932–33). Yet the single-story house had emerged as an ideal, the foundation of his pedagogy at the Bauhaus, and a recurrent theme both of houses he sketched for himself and of designs for clients. He had made some of the most significant contributions to modernism's exploration of the free plan, yet unlike Le Corbusier or Adolf Loos, he remained all but indifferent to the freedom in sectional composition made possible by the very technologies of construction he celebrated in his "manifesto" houses of 1923–24. The implied juxtaposition of single- and double-height spaces in the Brick Country House elevations remained stillborn. Even the stair nearly always remained an enclosed volume, usually set near the periphery to allow a free plan its fullest expanse. Nothing like the open ramp seen in Le Corbusier's internalized "promenades" of the 1920s ever interested Mies.

Mies's drawings are overwhelmingly concerned with the viewpoint of an ambulant observer. He never embraced the fashion for the axonometric view. In the 1930s the pursuit of the single-story house and the cultivation of a tradition of panoramic perspective drawing going back to Gilly and Schinkel went hand-in-hand, as Mies began to sketch perspectival views *from* his houses, views that until then had apparently been left for discovery in the finished building.[113] He would move from bird's-eye sketches as he appraised a landscape to perspective views that follow an invisible eye through the spaces in almost cinematographic frames. These broad perspectives, with their high horizon lines, became not merely graphic representations but veritable building blocks of his work, for the views from Mies's houses were no less essential characteristics of his architecture than the elements of structure and of furnishings. With his earliest extant perspectival views toward the horizon (p. 328, fig. 10), for the Krefeld Golf Club Project (1930), came also the frequent use of outdoor figurative sculpture to create a

human presence in the landscape, a technique anticipated at Barcelona but so important to Mies in the 1930s that he even drew sculpture *in elevation* on his floor plans to indicate whether a recumbent or standing figure would serve as our surrogate in a given space. Order and a human presence in nature were necessarily paired.

The experience of the horizon, and new possibilities of bringing the pictorialized landscape into domestic space through walls of glass (indeed it was now nearly impossible for Mies to draw a perspective of a house interior without taking in exterior space), allowed the architect to explore a syntax of architecture in which landscape was integral. The full liberation of interior space—seen as a void between two horizontal planes whose resolution can be imagined only in the distance, outside the architecture—was fully established in the Tugendhat House but first depicted in the drawings for the Golf Club. At Brno, Mies specified enormous sheets of white linoleum, making the floor virtually a reflection of the ceiling. In the German Pavilion he had continued the grid over the entire podium, but at the Tugendhat House he reserved the grid for one term in a spatial duality, demarcating architecturally structured space outdoors, outside any enclosure. Like the water in the German Pavilion, the grid at the Tugendhat House is in dialogue with the sky, setting a scale against which to measure immensity (as it has since the Renaissance) and structuring views toward the horizon. This graphic code for space-making became a standard element of Mies's plans for the next decade.[114]

In two houses designed for lakeside sites in Berlin in 1932–33, Mies took up the architectonic garden anew as he developed this new spatial paradigm. The site of the Gericke House Project was on the Wannsee, the largest of the lakes in the Romantic landscape between Berlin and Potsdam. The client, Herbert Gericke, was the director of the Deutscher Akademie (German academy) in Rome. (Mies would later be particularly despondent over Gericke's final decision not to pursue the design, for there was a significance in the fact that the director of a center for the study of classical culture desired a house expressive of contemporary culture.) The Gericke site is steeply sloped, and Mies designed for it a house on two levels. But the floors are treated remarkably independently of each other, suggesting that for Mies any freedom in section was to be developed more as a landscape proposition than as an internalized architectural promenade (fig. 48). Both levels create outdoor space through linear extensions—hedges, solid walls, glass-enclosed volumes, gridded pathways. These grammatical parts, conjugated, create a rich sequence of open-air rooms—entrance court, service court, *Wohngarten*—closely linked to interior spaces. At the same time, they channel views so as to convert unprecedented floor-to-ceiling expanses of glass into a landscape panorama.

As at Brno, Mies designed a house that is entered on the upper story, which is largely devoted to enclosed bedroom and service spaces and given a plastic accent by a sweeping curve of opaque glass announcing an enclosed stair. Entry requires turning away from a view of the lake, which cannot be approached, since the axis of entry, a path aimed like a runway at a manmade drop, is cut short by a glass-enclosed vestibule, even while the eye is allowed to continue its journey to the horizon. Arrival on the lower level again involves an eruption of open space, although the view has been shifted obliquely and the resulting panoramic sweep takes in not only the lake but a series of interior and

exterior spaces defined by opaque and transparent walls, some inside, some out.

The program for Gericke's unusual private competition required a house "in the simplest form of our period and pleasantly connected with the landscape and with the garden."[115] Was it this that led Mies to return to a dualism of interior and exterior space? Planned to occupy the site of a late-nineteenth-century villa demolished to make way for a house "of our period," the space of the sitting room and dining room is a merger of the great room of the Tugendhat House with the subtle interplay between staggered interior spaces and exterior terraces and gardens of earlier designs. The focal point is the living room, which lacks opaque exterior walls, its relationship to the outdoors being defined by walls of glass and by the upper and lower framers of the panorama defined by the terrace floor and the roof plane. The design in fact suggests how essential the flat roof was for Mies; once it came under attack in the next few years, his entire philosophy of architecture and landscape was at stake.

The layering of indoor and outdoor space had interested Mies since his earliest work in this region; he rendered it in the Gericke project with an unprecedented transparency, and recorded its complexity from every angle in a series of perspective panoramas that offer a virtual home movie of this new kind of space. The living room remained central to the staging of landscape, and in four of the five frames that Mies drew—labeling them "*Blick*" (View), a term reminiscent of Schinkel—this interior caught between planes of glass is seen in a changing dialogue with exterior space. Tellingly, the only vista Mies did not render was the view from the living room directly toward the lake; the interaction of garden, dwelling space, and vista had become as much the building blocks of the architecture as the physical elements of chrome columns, curtain walls, and freestanding wall planes.

The Gericke drawings place natural materials and architectonic means in a dialogue so complete that they sometimes trade places, even as they would do, with kaleidoscopic richness, in the house's future daily life of transparency and reflection. In an early sketch (fig. 49) Mies imagined inserting a freestanding fireplace wall

48. Ludwig Mies van der Rohe. Gericke House Project, Berlin-Wannsee. 1932. Sketch perspective bird's-eye view. Pencil on paper, 8 1/4 x 11 3/4" (21 x 30 cm). The Museum of Modern Art, New York. Mies van der Rohe Archive. Gift of the architect

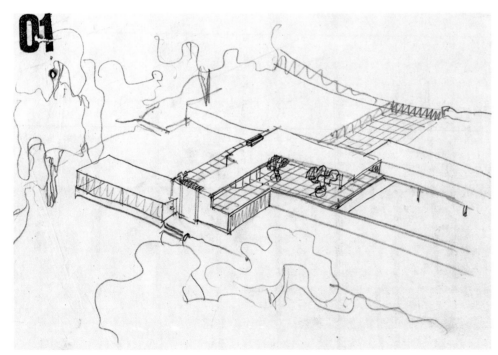

inside the glass box of the living room, both to anchor the furniture composition and to close lateral views. In the final version, however, Mies replaced this wall with a narrow winter garden, which closes the short end of the glass box and merges visually with a hedge in the adjacent garden (plate 235). The fireplace in turn was shifted to the opaque wall of the sitting room/dining room area, a wall that characteristically obscures any axial discovery of the vista from the viewer arriving at the foot of the stair.

The vista through as well as from the glass room is now carefully framed between a hearth and conservatory, between a wall of fire and stone and a wall of greenery and glass. The return of the hearth, missing from the Tugendhat House, might be related to the pinwheel compositions of Wright's that Mies admired, and echoes of Gottfried Semper also come to mind, but all of this is given a new, spiritual dimension by Mies's reading of Guardini, who had written of the open hearth, "We have here something that is bound up with the deepest roots of human existence: seizing open fire and putting the flame to use to warm us. Mind and spirit are at work here; nature is put to human use. . . . With some exaggeration we might say that being human means lighting a fire at a protected spot." Electricity had rendered the relationship with nature abstract: with electrical heat, "nothing burns at all, but a current comes into the house and gives warmth in some way. The manifestation of culture has gone, the link with nature has been cut, a totally artificial situation has been created. Everything that was achieved by human existence before an open fire is a thing of the past."[116] Ruegenberg suggests that Mies required a "warm wall" to organize space in his buildings—a fireplace wall, or a wall of rich materials.[117] This would make the architect's freestanding walls at once signs of a break with tradition and attempts to find a reconciliation with nature in the language of modernity.

Of Mies's frames of the Gericke House, *Blick vom Wohngarten ins Haus* (View from the living garden into the house, plate 239) renders the interchangeability of interior and exterior spaces most dramatically. Here for the first time we are made aware of the house's two stories, which become another dualism established with

great poetic resonance. For by moving the fireplace to serve as the opaque center of the house's "facade" toward the lake, Mies aligns it with the open vine-covered trellis on the upper terrace. Just as the living room is made possible by a grid of thin columnar supports, creating an open frame, the trellis too is a space-making tectonic frame, as well as a frame for self-conscious reflection on nature beyond.

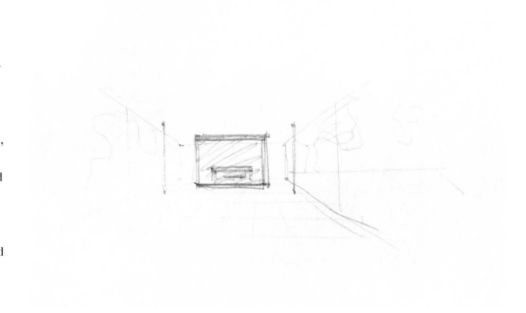

In the spring of 1932, Mies proposed another two-story design—the architect's last—for Karl Lemke, who had purchased a pair of adjacent sites on the gently sloping banks of a small artificial lake created in the late nineteenth century during the laying out of the villa quarter of Hohenschönhausen. Lemke, who owned a Berlin printing works and was active in the arts and in communist politics, rejected this two-story scheme— a compact box with outdoor spaces excavated in its open steel frame—in favor of a smaller, cheaper, single-story layout. This project too was revised; "I have the notion that on fair-weather days the living space, in reality restricted, should extend into the garden," Lemke explained in a letter rejecting it.[118] In place of a series of loosely connected blocks with generously proportioned

49. Ludwig Mies van der Rohe. Gericke House Project, Berlin-Wannsee. 1932. Sketch perspective interior view of living room with fireplace (detail). Pencil on paper, 8 ¼ x 11 ¾" (21 x 30 cm). The Museum of Modern Art, New York. Mies van der Rohe Archive. Gift of the architect

rooms defining a pattern of interior and exterior spaces on all sides, the client asked for a minimal-existence dwelling pushed as close to the street as building regulations would allow to preserve the terrain for a garden leading down to the lake, where Mies was to design a boat dock set among weeping willows. The final scheme compressed the interlocking blocks into a tight, subtly jagged profile that focuses the main spaces of the

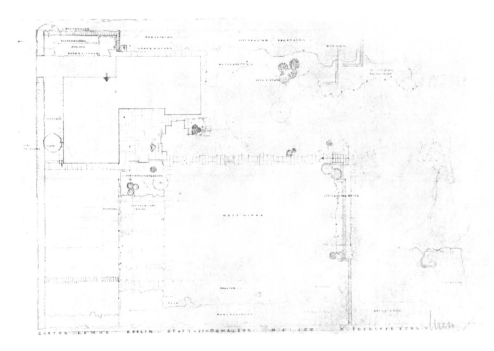

50. Karl Foerster Associates. Garden plan for Mies's Lemke House, Berlin-Hohenschönhausen. 1932–33. Diazotype, 18½ x 28¾" (47.3 x 73.1 cm). The Museum of Modern Art, New York. Mies van der Rohe Archive. Gift of the architect

house around an exterior terrace whose dimensions echo those of the adjacent built volumes.

This incunabulum of the court houses of the 1930s was in large measure the result of an architect-client negotiation. Lemke, an enthusiastic but strong-willed client, had served as printer to the Werkbund, from which he seems to have acquired many of his progressive notions about architecture, and he was eager to administer his limited budget to ensure that money saved on building would allow him a space equipped with Mies's new tubular-steel furniture, which must have impressed him at the German Building Exhibition in Berlin in 1931. The two principal living spaces are nearly fully glazed facing the terrace but are anchored at the corner by a brick wall section, which is echoed outside by a single tree, providing both shade and a spatial anchor in the larger composition. An early photograph shows Mies's

Tugendhat chairs and a tubular-steel table arranged to take advantage of this open-air room (plate 247).

It was Lemke who decided that Mies should work again with Karl Foerster, with whom he had not collaborated since his youthful works in Neubabelsberg. Although Georg Gardner, who had consulted on the garden and landscape design for the Building Exhibition, solicited the job, Lemke turned instead to Foerster's Bornim nursery, which by the early 1930s had expanded to include a design department under the landscape architects Herta Hammerbacher and her husband Hermann Mattern. The extent to which Mies and Foerster had diverged in fifteen years is dramatically apparent in both the disjointed site plan—house and garden come from different formal universes—and the detached and sequential process of design (fig. 50). It was only in January 1933, when construction on the house was well advanced, that Lemke sent Mies's assistant Ernst Walther the Foerster proposal, designed by Hammerbacher. The garden incorporated the softening of borders, the predominance of planting over geometric design, and the attentiveness to the existing contours of a site that became the hallmark of the so-called *Bornimer Kreis* (Bornim circle) around Foerster in the 1930s, a school increasingly sympathetic to the organicism of Hans Scharoun, with whom Hammerbacher and Mattern often worked. Although adamantly nonideological, this new organicism soon found resonance with the revival of the "German" garden under the National Socialists, especially as it was developed by Foerster's onetime associate Willy Lange.[119] Given that the *Bornimer Kreis* made a principle of the belief that the house should take its cue from the site, and therefore that the garden design should precede the architectural project, the Lemke commission was as much a compromise for Hammerbacher as it was for Mies.

Many have seen Mies's development of the so-called court house—a term it seems he never employed himself in his German years—as a retreat from the world while the black cloud of National Socialism spread. Yet Mies's work was no more a direct response to political events than was the distant contemplation of nature he proposed as a palliative to the larger modern condition. The problematic of the court house is already implicit in the Exhibition House of 1931, and the concept was established as a pedagogical tool at the Bauhaus even before Hitler's rise to power. In the most developed of Mies's designs in which interior and exterior spaces are bound in dialogue by a perimeter wall, that perimeter serves the same purpose that garden walls, whether mineral or botanical, had always played in Mies's designs. They are devices for controlling the vista, and for making contemplation of the horizon, of what lies just outside daily existence but is readily accessible to heightened awareness, integral to architecture.

Like the Gericke House, the Hubbe House Project, on which Mies worked for much of 1935, began as an attenuated composition of parts held together by a thin canopy that provided a datum line of the vista to the horizon, in this case a view of the Elbe River. The house, on an island in the Elbe at Magdeburg, was to be financed by real estate development on the back half of the property, and Mies worked simultaneously on the main house and on the Hubbe Court-House Studies, a proposal for serial dwellings. For these he studied numerous variants of a party-wall house in which an enclosed court would offer a fragment of nature and a framed view of the sky, providing the natural equivalent of that spirit of "heightened emptiness" or "*betonte Leere*" that had been part of his aesthetic since Barcelona and Brno.[120] For Mies, even minimal existence was to be linked to expanded spiritual horizons. This solution quickly suggested a way of dealing with landscape issues for the main house as well, as Mies explained in a text accompanying a beautiful series of perspective drawings in *Die Schildgenossen*, the Catholic journal that Guardini and Schwarz had stamped with the program of questioning the relationship between technology and nature, modernism and humanism. Mies's text is terse, but its every word was resonant with meaning for readers of the journal, who could understand them as signs for a whole realm of thought developed at greater length by the journal's philosophical writers. Mies begins by describing the site,

under old beautiful trees with a far-reaching view. . . . It was an unusually beautiful place for building. Only the exposure presented problems. The beautiful view was to the east, to the south the view was dull, almost disturbing. . . . For that reason I have enlarged the living quarters by a garden court surrounded by a wall and so locked out this view while allowing full sunshine. Toward the river the house is entirely open and melts into the landscape. . . . a beautiful alternation of quiet seclusion and open spaces . . . also corresponds to the dwelling needs of the client, who, although living alone in the house, wanted to cultivate a relaxed social life and hospitality. This is also reflected by the interior arrangement. Here also the required privacy combines with the freedom of open room forms.[121]

What sounds like simple notes takes on greater resonance when we hear the same insistence on nature and freedom, landscape and seclusion, in one of Schwarz's key texts on the challenge of technology, from a few years earlier:

There is something called spirit. . . . There is not only brute force, and there is not only "soul," there is also "spirit" . . . something quite ultimate . . . and it is this that is in tune with nature, and in it inanimate nature discovers its worthy adversary. . . . This necessitates that we become free; that we stand at each moment both within time and above it. This demands an awareness that can say even today: I am the master. This demands that we commit ourselves to absolute freedom.[122]

The exterior courts of the Hubbe House, and of the Ulrich Lange House Project planned in the same year (neither was built), are Mies's ultimate refinement

51. Ludwig Mies van der Rohe. Ulrich Lange House, Krefeld. 1935. Sketch perspective. Pencil and colored pencil on paper, 8¼ x 11½" (21 x 29.3 cm). The Museum of Modern Art, New York. Mies van der Rohe Archive. Gift of the architect

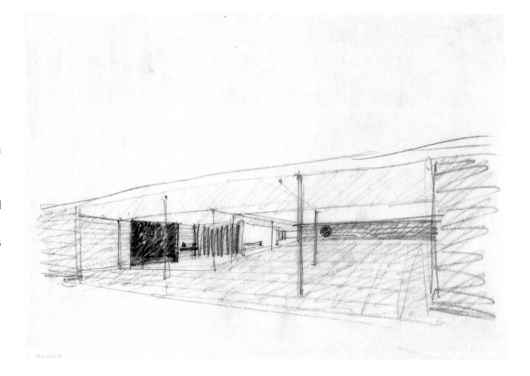

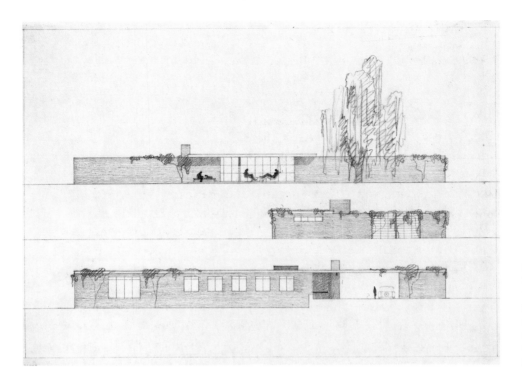

52. Ludwig Mies van der Rohe.
Ulrich Lange House, Krefeld.
1935. Elevations. Pencil on
tracing paper, 16¼ x 23¾"
(41.3 x 60.4 cm). The Museum
of Modern Art, New York. Mies
van der Rohe Archive. Gift of the
architect

during his German years of the dialogue between interior and exterior (figs. 51 and 52). The interior enjoys framed views to both a garden court and a landscape panorama, both open to the sky, both with horizon lines carefully calibrated against an interior construction of space. No less essentialist is the equipment of the garden: a single statue, a shrub, a tree, and some vines playing in counterpoint to the geometries of the architecture. With a minimum number of elements Mies constructs a dialogue between symmetry and asymmetry, nature and architecture, dwelling and consciousness, every bit as rich as Schinkel's in his country villas in Potsdam.[123] At the same time, one feels almost as though Behrens's 1911 program for the modern garden might be read as a description of Mies's forms of nearly twenty-five years later:

The house must appear, no matter how carefully considered its interior planning, as though its walls were only composed as they are in order to enclose the various places, flowerbeds, water basins . . . one has laid out. . . . only then is the task of a harmonic unison of house and garden achieved. . . . a garden is as essential a part of a dwelling as a bathroom. . . . Only if we have grown up together with this fragment of nature, only if we have been influenced by it even as it has been given form by our desires, will we rediscover that relationship to organic being which leads to inner harmony. . . . it is equally good if we are awakened in the morning by the twittering of thousands of birds or by a single bird always at the same hour.[124]

Behrens had elsewhere noted, "The realm of art begins at the point where an object that has been simplified into a sovereign form becomes the universal symbol for all similar objects."[125] So juxtaposed, a tree and a cruciform column alone could begin to anchor space both for dwelling and for spirit.

Architectures of Becoming:
Mies van der Rohe and the Avant-Garde

DETLEF MERTINS

Already recognized as a promising young talent before the Great War, Mies submitted his ambitious yet unrealized Kröller-Müller Villa Project of 1912–13 to Berlin's first architectural exhibition after the war—and was rejected. Sponsored by the Arbeitsrat für Kunst (Workers' council for art) and organized by Walter Gropius, the *Ausstellung für unbekannte Architekten* (Exhibition of unknown architects) was held in late March and April of 1919.[1] Intended to question prevailing conceptions of architecture and to foreground new visions, the show featured visual artists along with architects. While before the war the protagonists of Jugendstil and its neoclassical successor had held that a new style, suitable for all scales of cultural production, would emerge first in the decorative arts, the Arbeitsrat looked to visual artists to break with academic architectural conventions. In his brief exhibition statement, Gropius went so far as to declare, "There are no architects today, we are all of us merely preparing the way for he who will once again deserve the name of architect, for that means: lord of art, who will build gardens out of deserts and pile up wonders to the sky."[2] Given this focus, it is not surprising that he rejected Mies's neoclassical Kröller-Müller project, saying, "We can't exhibit it; we are looking for something entirely different."[3]

No formal list remains of the artists and works in the exhibition, but the critic Kurt Gerstenberg wrote an overview of the show's structure and highlights.[4] The first of the four rooms presented "the architects of former battles" and metropolitan architecture, understood in relation to the United States and featuring skyscraper designs adapted to the German context. The other rooms held colorful fairy tales constructed on paper. Hermann Obrist was presented as the spiritual forefather

here, with photographs of tombstones and stalactite agglomerations that inaugurated a dissolution of form.

Among the rest, Gerstenberg identified four groups. The first were master-builders in glass and steel, spurred on by the vision of glass architecture proffered by the Berlin humorist and fantasist poet Paul Scheerbart before the war. An exhibition building by Wenzil Hablik rose into the sky—a tower in which each segment of the construction stepped in from the one below and rotated on its axis to form a spiral crystal. Oswald Herzog presented a spherical temple of crystal forms; Arnold Topp showed a temple of death in glass and steel with a vermilion exterior, an inner wall of blue glass, and violet lighting within. He also showed a tower resembling a glass mountain. A more painterly orientation was represented by César Klein's colorful stage-set, while an approach derived from Cubist painting appeared in Johannes Molzahn's prismatic pyramid (fig. 1).

The most significant and sensational part of the show was the final group, whose images resembled no previous architecture. Here were houses by Hermann Finsterlin, doughy masses suggesting mushrooms, mollusks, and sea creatures in countless variations (fig. 2). These works presented a new way of shaping architecture and a labyrinthine feeling for space, without the traditional sense of proportion, stability, or symmetry. In Gerstenberg's eyes they substituted the playful invention of the unconscious for the regulation of the conscious. Here too were Jefim Golyscheff's formless drawings and collages, which the critic Adolf Behne, the secretary of the Arbeitsrat, described as having nothing in them of the Expressionist hankering for mystic soulfulness, but as "bringing—as small as they are! Greetings from the greater world!," the larger world beyond the human, the cosmos of mysterious and fundamentally unknowable life (fig. 3).[5]

Opening of First International Dada Fair, gallery of Dr. Otto Burchard, Berlin, June 30, 1920. Mies stands with back to camera; Johannes Baader points to image of Flatiron Building, New York. Berlinische Galerie, Hannah-Höch-Archiv

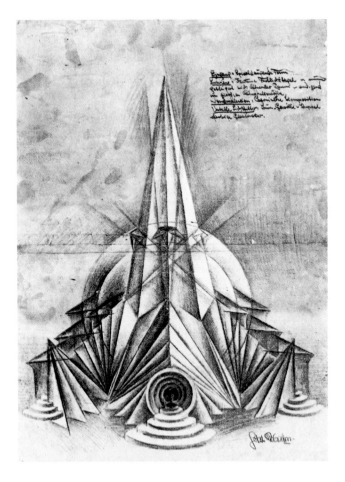

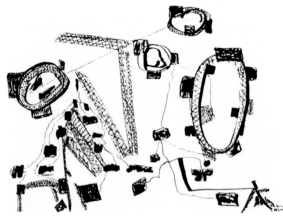

1. Johannes Molzahn. Untitled. 1918. Charcoal and graphite on tracing paper, 24¾ x 18½" (62.7 x 47 cm). Molzahn Bequest, Munich

2. Hermann Finsterlin. *Das Haus der Atlantiden*. 1919. Black and white ink on paper, 5¾ x 7¾" (14.5 x 19.5 cm). Sammlung Siegfried Cremer/Hamburger Kunsthalle

3. Jefim Golyscheff. Untitled. c. 1919. Ink on paper. Location unknown; published in *Der Cicerone* 9 (1919)

In writings since 1914, Behne had become critical of Expressionism, promoting instead the creation of an artistic paradigm that would realize the potential for an entirely new environment in the epochal revolution inaugurated by Cubism. More precisely, Behne sought to fuse the pure architectonics of Cubist painting with Scheerbart's technological cosmology. In *Die Wiederkehr der Kunst* (The return of art, 1919), he forecast the renewal of true art—overcoming materiality, engaging the unknowable world beyond the human one, and producing a new kind of individual through a "spiritual revolution." He called the activity of building a cosmic Ur-force and life-force, a world art and an elemental art. Indeed "the becoming of the world," Behne declared, "is a building."[6]

Behne identified Bruno Taut, Gropius, and Henry van de Velde as the key architects of the prewar period; from the war years themselves he considered Lyonel Feininger the most important artist.[7] After the exhibition he focused on Golyscheff as exemplary of the aesthetic regeneration signaled by Cubism, a "return of art" now understood as a continuous cultural revolution—"never a fixed state" but a ceaseless process of inauguration, destroying and rebuilding again and again in the unending pleasure, even intoxication, of creation. Even when Behne turned away from the paper fantasies of 1919—toward first the revolutionary art of Russia and then the sober abstraction and rationalism of de Stijl—he retained his conviction that a utopia of new beginnings and becomings could be achieved through pure artistic means.

The artists and works in the *Ausstellung für unbekannte Architekten* overlap with those of Bruno Taut's Crystal Chain group but are hardly identical with them. Gerstenberg makes no mention of Hans Scharoun's colorful eruptions, Max Taut's prismatic interiors, Wassili Luckhardt's glowing crystals, or Taut's own Alpine architecture. In fact many of the most familiar images from Taut's circle, including some by Finsterlin, Hablik, and Taut himself, were produced only after the exhibition and may even have been prompted by it.[8] The show prompted others as well to speculate on a future world capable of redeeming modern times in a vitalist utopia. Certainly this dream was an impetus for Gropius in the first years of the Bauhaus at Weimar; while hiring artists like Feininger, Paul Klee, Georg Muche, and Johannes Itten, Gropius nevertheless made the creation of a new architecture—a new total environment—the aim of the school.

László Moholy-Nagy too invoked the idea of glass architecture to describe his work of 1921–22 (fig. 4), based on pure color and overlapping geometric forms and inspired by the Suprematist works of Kasimir Malevich, on the one hand, and Behne's *Wiederkehr der Kunst* and the Dadaists, on the other. Unlike the Dadaists, however, Moholy pursued liberation through the creative rather than the destructive capacity of the artist. He believed in the need for a new order based on rationality, technology, and the discovery of natural laws of construction and vision. The idea of glass architecture as a disembodied utopia, unrealized and

AKTIVISTA FOLYÓIRAT

4. László Moholy-Nagy. *Glass Architecture III*. 1921–22. Cover of *MA*, May 1, 1922

at the time unrealizable, continued to inform his work throughout the 1920s as he explored qualities of transparency and interpenetration, not only in paintings, lithographs, and woodcuts but in mechanically reproduced media—photographs, photomontages, photograms, and films—and in designs for stage sets and exhibitions that approached the status of architecture. Like Malevich, El Lissitzky, and László Péri, Moholy-Nagy understood the project of modern art to have the scope of world reconstruction, beginning with a new architectonic in painting but heading toward a new spatial environment.[9]

As the program of glass architecture became absorbed within a broader field of projects that straddled architecture and art, Scheerbart's catalytic role continued to be acknowledged. In an article of 1926 on the properties, potentials, and technical development of glass construction, Gropius linked the newly completed Dessau Bauhaus to Scheerbart when he wrote that "glass architecture, which was just a poetic utopia not long ago, now becomes reality without constraint."[10] The previous year, Theo van Doesburg had written of the significance of glass in bringing the new architectural image into harmony with the needs and tempo of modern life. He had mentioned Gropius, and also Adolf Loos and Friedrich Kiesler in Austria and Mies in Germany, as leading the way to a new architecture that would be light, open, and clear.[11] The house van Doesburg designed for Léonce Rosenberg in 1923 negotiated a Scheerbart-like path between the Purism of Le Corbusier and the fantasy of Bruno Taut's Alpine architecture. In a letter to Rosenberg he explained, "Your atelier must be like a glass cover or like an empty crystal. It must have an absolute purity, a constant light, a clear atmosphere. It must also be white. The palette must be of glass. . . . Your atelier must have the cold atmosphere of mountains 3,000 meters high."[12]

Arthur Korn's 1929 book *Glas im Bau und als Gebrauchsgegenstand* (Glass in building and as object of utility) summarizes the development of glass architecture to that point. His introduction again alludes to Scheerbart: "A new glass age has begun, which is equal in beauty to the old Gothic windows . . . [that] afforded glimpses of paradise in luminous colors." It is the special characteristic of glass, he continues, that it is "noticeable yet not quite visible. It is the great membrane, full of mystery, delicate yet tough. It can enclose and open up spaces in more than one direction. Its peculiar advantage is in the diversity of the impressions it creates." To illustrate his contention that "the visible depth behind the thin skin of glass is the exciting factor," Korn cites Mies's glass architecture as well as Gropius and Adolf Meyer's Bauhaus at Dessau. Although Mies himself never referred to Scheerbart, Korn begins his book with Mies's Friedrichstrasse Skyscraper and Glass Skyscraper projects of 1921 and 1922 and with the Concrete Office Building Project of 1923, treating these as the architectonic origin and Scheerbart's writings, at least implicitly, as the literary origin for the entire subsequent production of international constructivist architecture.[13]

The New Mies

Mies's rejection by Gropius in 1919 marked his subsequent relationship to both the artistic and the architectural avant-gardes in several ways.[14] He began to interact more with artists in relation to his work, and this at a time when Berlin was becoming a European center for radical art.[15] He changed his approach to design, making industrial materials and constructive techniques his departure point and the affects of post-Cubist art his goal. He also wrote manifestos against predetermined forms, advocating instead an openness to life, to the unformed, the emergent, the process of becoming. Employing the means characteristic of the age, Mies suggested, was the precondition for genuine form-creation or *Gestaltung*. These means, in their pure state, constituted an architectonics of becoming. In a word, Mies set out on his own quest for the crystalline, post-Cubist, and technological architecture that Behne had said should be the mission of art. Without becoming an artist himself, as Le Corbusier had, Mies developed a second line of practice, experimental and theoretical, through which he participated in the discourse of the artistic avant-garde. He published widely in art journals, both mainstream publications and small magazines. As he attracted more adventurous clients—clients who were often patrons of modern art— he drew on his experiments to inform actual building commissions. He negotiated a place for his work in two

distinct circles: avant-garde artists, especially those who aspired to a new architecture and a new urbanism, and the reform architects of *das neue Bauen* (the new building), especially those inspired by the revolution in modern art.

Mies became an active member of both the Novembergruppe and the Deutscher Werkbund, as well as of smaller, more radical groups of artists and architects, such as the circle around *G* magazine and the group of architects called the *Zehnerring* (Circle of ten).[16] He joined the Werkbund in 1925 and was its vice-president from 1926 to 1932. For him, the purpose of the organization was "to illuminate the spiritual and concrete situation in which we find ourselves, make it visible, order its currents, and thereby direct it."[17] It was through his affiliation with the Werkbund that he became the artistic director of its 1927 exhibition *Die Wohnung* (The dwelling), in Stuttgart, which included the Weissenhofsiedlung, the permanent colony of modern housing that would prove the most significant part of the show. *Die Wohnung* extended Mies's reputation from emerging Berlin architect to leading figure on the international stage, someone capable of drawing together the architectural avant-garde. It was the success of the housing exhibition that led to Mies's commission for the German Pavilion at the International Exposition in Barcelona (1929), his most celebrated and influential project.

The Novembergruppe was an organization of radically minded artists in the fields of painting, sculpture, architecture, theater, music, literature, and film. Founded in 1919 and active until 1933, it was less radical in its politics than the Arbeitsrat, but shared much of the same reform agenda and became influential through its exhibition program. Mies joined in 1922 and was president from 1923 to 1925. In the group's 1923 exhibition he showed drawings and models of the Concrete Office Building and Concrete Country House projects, as well as drawings of an interior and of a brick house; his contribution to the group's 1924 exhibition was his design for the Brick Country House Project.[18] Correspondence shows that he was active in organizing the architectural components of the Novembergruppe exhibitions during these years.[19]

Even before Mies joined the Novembergruppe he had begun to associate with one of its early members, the artist and filmmaker Hans Richter. From 1923 to 1926 he contributed actively (financially as well as intellectually) to Richter's journal *G: Material zur elementaren Gestaltung*, and his studio became a second center, next to Richter's own, for the group of pan-European avant-garde artists participating in the journal. *G* sought to collect evidence of an emergent culture characterized by the multifaceted notion of elementary *Gestaltung*. That culture bridged a diverse array of post-Expressionist artistic research, cut across disciplines, and broke the barrier between art and engineering. Founded by Richter and the filmmaker Viking Eggeling, the original *G* circle consisted of Hans Arp, Ludwig Hilberseimer, Tristan Tzara, and van Doesburg, but soon expanded to include Walter Benjamin, Naum Gabo, Werner Gräff, Georg Grosz, Raoul Hausmann, Frederick Kiesler, Lissitzky, Man Ray, Mies, and Antoine Pevsner. The magazine featured new car engines and bodies, men's clothing designed by Hausmann, poems by Kurt Schwitters, painting by Piet Mondrian, sculpture by Constantin Brancusi, films by Fernand Léger and René Clair, and the art of the insane as presented by Hans Prinzhorn. It embraced Dadaists and Neo-Plasticists, Constructivists and Surrealists. The third issue (June 1924) included Benjamin's translation of a short essay by Tzara on the photograms of Man Ray as well as Mies's call for a more effective embrace of industrialization in building. Through improved synthetic materials and the reorganization of the trades to combine factory production with on-site assembly, Mies hoped to realize the potential of rational "montage" fabrication. His participation in the Novembergruppe and the *G* circle consolidated his reputation as a leading architect who understood the implications for architecture of the revolution in art.

Coinciding with his new artistic turn, Mies changed his name around 1921 from Ludwig Mies to Ludwig Miës van der Rohe, adding the Dutch and seemingly aristocratic "van der"; his mother's maiden name, "Rohe"; and the umlaut in "Miës."[20] While the umlaut tempered the disagreeable associations of the German word *mies*, which means "wretched," "miserable," and "rotten," "*roh*" has the double connotation of "raw" and "pure." The new name may be understood, then, as a play of words, without specific meaning but with a host of associations. The invention of new personas was not uncommon; van Doesburg was using two pseudonyms around this time, Dadaists and members of the Crystal Chain had all assumed additional names, and Charles-Édouard Jeanneret had taken the name "Le Corbusier" for his architecture while keeping "Jeanneret" for his art. In the same period in which Mies changed his name, he also changed his life, leaving his wife and children to become a bachelor. In the wake of his rejection from the *Ausstellung für unbekannte Architekten*, Ludwig Mies transformed himself into Miës van der Rohe, the architect history has come to know as a master of modernism who, like Le Corbusier and Gropius, reinvented architecture through a fusion of modern technology and modern art that it was hoped would forge a new human subject, a new society, and a new nature.

New Language

A photograph from the opening of the First International Dada Fair (*Messe*), on June 30, 1920, shows Mies among the assembled Dadaists and their supporters—among, that is, the most outspoken antagonists of Expressionism and the most politicized critics of bourgeois art, politics, and society (frontispiece). Where the Expressionists had responded with soulful anguish to their sense of a loss of organic wholeness under the conditions of modernity, Dada took "the mechanization, the sterility, the rigidity, and the tempo of these times into its broad lap."[21] Where the Expressionists had put their hope for the future in art, understood as a refuge from reality—speculative, occult, medievalist—Dada opposed the isolation of art from society and sought direct engagement with the present. Where the Expressionists had looked to the deep inner nature of the "New Man" to provide the strength for a messianic overcoming of the fragmented and uncertain modern world, Dada rejected this sense of transcendental and intoxicating subjectivity and reworked the New Man into an inorganic, historically and materially contingent figure who "carries pandemonium within himself . . . for or against which no one can do anything."[22]

The Dadaists enacted the New Man by adopting fictional personae with which to parody social structures and conventions, often shocking their audiences in the streets and in the press as well as in the art gallery. Internalizing contradiction, chaos, flux, and chance, Dada saw itself as "one with the times, it is a child of the present epoch which one may curse, but cannot deny."[23] In photocollages, montages, and assemblages—techniques derived from modern technology and developed in opposition to the media of painting and sculpture—they transformed the work of art into a piece of reality, albeit one embodying a heightened awareness and a transformative potential. For them, art was to be a diagram of the inherent structure of reality and a map of cosmic consciousness. Using the techniques of mass media (advertising, headlines, slogans, photomontage), they created works in which bits of photographs, texts, and found objects were cut from their contexts, disassembled, abstracted, and recombined into new configurations that provoked an expanded understanding of the original. Both meaning and matter were taken to be in flux, and man was conceived no longer as the center of a humanist universe but simply as "a thing among things."

The fair of 1920 was itself a montage, or more precisely a montage environment (fig. 5). A microcosm of the metropolis engulfed the visitor with works that took the form of posters, political slogans, and advertising—a swirling chaos of photographs, headlines, broken typography, bits of images covering the walls, and a mannequin with a pig's head hanging from the ceiling. Offering a dizzying array of stimulations and provocations, the images and assemblages were jarring, aggressive, and disjunctive. There was no rest for the eye, no peace for the soul. Nothing could seem farther from Bruno Taut's paradisal Glass House (1914). Yet both provided an immersive experience that was both disorienting and reorienting, and aimed to forge a new human subject capable of grappling with the modern world. Where Taut's pavilion was radically interiorized, however, dissociating visitors from the world outside by immersing them in a regenerative atmosphere of filtered light and kaleidoscopic abstraction, the fair brought reality in, abolishing any operative distinction between

inside and outside. It placed the observer in a complex relational field within which to seek orientation and identity. Perception here was not passive, it was an active negotiation between subject and object, organism and environment. Dada montage served to recalibrate the viewer's perceptual apparatus to operate more effectively within the mediating conditions of the new optics of photography and publicity. The cognitive value of vision was directed not toward an idealist cosmology but toward living through the traumas, conflicts, and hidden politics of everyday life in the industrial metropolis.

5. First International Dada Fair, Berlin, 1920. Raoul Hausmann and Hannah Höch are on the left. Bildarchiv Preussischer Kulturbesitz

Here then stands the thirty-four-year-old Mies, within a pandemonium staged to declare the end of art and to thrust artistic activity directly into the maelstrom of modernity. He seems at ease in his tweed suit, clearly engaged by the scene and in animated conversation with Johannes Baader, the Oberdada or President of the Globe, architect, provocateur, and messiah. What did Mies, the seeker of order, make of this immersion in chaos? Was he already then, as later, fearful of being overwhelmed by the disorder that Baader personified and exacerbated? Would he, like Oskar Schlemmer, have interpreted the Dada enterprise as simply a playful upsetting of the established order?[24] Or did he recognize the serious agenda of critique and transformation that underpinned the fair? How did he understand Baader's montage architecture, *Das Grosse Plasto-Dio-Dada-Drama: Deutschlands Grösse und Untergang* (The great plasto-dio-Dada-drama: Greatness and downfall of Germany, 1920; fig. 6)? Identifying himself as a modern Christ, Baader defined his role as building a new society from a present in which perception and consciousness were shaped by the mass media. Firmly grounded in the present, his montage architecture was to direct the spirit into the future—an aspiration that would later be echoed by Mies, echoing the modernist theologian Romano Guardini. What did Mies make of Baader's pile of poster poems, declarations, machine parts, and building blocks, surmounted by a stovepipe? And what relationship might this construction have had to their conversation? For at the moment of the shutter's release, Baader was directing Mies's attention to the cover of the June 1917 issue of the proto-Dada journal *Neue Jugend*—an issue featuring a sharply profiled photograph of the Flatiron Building in New York. Unlike the photographs by Edward Steichen in which the building is shrouded in the mysterious mist of a dark

metropolis, here it stands out strongly—objective, elemental, an almost pure extrusion of its triangular site.

Where the Expressionists had theorized pure artistic means—pure color, line, and plane—as preconditions for art, the Dadaists accepted found objects as their raw materials and spoke of a new materiality in the concrete manifestations of metropolitan experience. Hausmann understood the individual psyche as fragmented and absurd, at one with the cosmos only through contact with its surrounding environment, even if that environment appeared hostile.[25] Only by regaining vision, or more accurately by cultivating vision to be adequate to the conditions of the times, could humanity grasp its perceptions of the world and its relations to that world as a totality.[26] For Hausmann, the New Man required a language different from the language of representation: a cosmic language for a secular society. This was to be a new language drawn from the experience of the metropolis, a concrete, primitive language that reduced found materials to their elemental state, then recombined them into new configurations.

Following Ernst Mach's belief that reality exists only in experience and is composed purely of sensations and combinations of sensations, Hausmann created an onomatopoeic word-art (*Wortkunst*) and explored its visual counterpart first in optophonetic poetry and then in constructions of pure articulation, formation, sensation, and matter (fig. 7). He outlined the theoretical underpinnings of this approach in his book *Materiel der Malerei, Plastik und Architektur* (1918). Informed by Ernst Haeckel's notion of a universal substance in which matter and spirit coincide, Hausmann understood the language he sought as cutting across the boundaries of the arts (painting, sculpture, and architecture), providing an energetic medium for free form-creation (*Gestaltung*) and genuine experience (*Erlebnis*).

Hausmann made ambiguous structures, using a vocabulary of autonomous forms that could be read as landscapes, architecture, or human features (fig. 8). He was guided by Carl Einstein's suggestion that the elements of form in a "primitive" composition constituted a more valid reality than did naturalistic representation. "Every part," Einstein had written, "must become

6. First International Dada Fair, Berlin, 1920. Johannes Baader standing beside his assemblage *Das Grosse Plasto-Dio-Dada-Drama: Deutschlands Grösse und Untergang* (The great plasto-dio-Dada-drama: Greatness and downfall of Germany, 1920)

plastically autonomous and deformed" in order for the totality to be absorbed into the form.[27] This "plastic vision" entailed a combination of reduction and reintegration, of formal clarification and reconnection. Transposed into the world of modern industry and media, these procedures and principles served to underpin the art of montage as developed by Georg Grosz, Hausmann, John Heartfield, Hannah Höch, and others. Rather than relating meaning to a fundamental idealism, Dada recognized that the material and social world confers meaning as a function of relationships—relationships that they sought to change. The reduction of language, art, and culture to their pure material existence was taken to be the precondition for works that provided access to true experience. Hausmann's poster poems, for instance, were composed of disconnected vowels and consonants pictorially arranged without ever forming recognizable words.

Given the Dadaists' animosity toward Expressionism, their admiration for Scheerbart may at first seem surprising. Yet they had initially been part of the circle around Herwath Walden's gallery and magazine *Der Sturm*, which had presented Scheerbart's writings to the Berlin artistic community. The Dadaists considered themselves the "diapered children" of a new age, and Scheerbart their spiritual father.[28] Höch had an extensive Scheerbart library. In March 1919, Hausmann and Baader renamed Club Dada the Club zur blauen Milchstrasse (Club to the blue Milky Way)—a homage to Scheerbart. The philosophers most associated with Dada, Anselm Ruest and Salomo Friedländer, helped fuel Scheerbart's reception after the war. Where the Expressionists mobilized Scheerbart in support of a new techno-organicity in the mountains, the Dadaists were inspired by his biting satires, nonsense poetry, and engineering fantasies, as well as by his metropolitanism and bohemianism.

As early as September 1919, Hilberseimer, a Dada supporter who would be a lifelong friend and colleague of Mies's, had cautioned against misappropriations of Scheerbart by architects.[29] Without mentioning the *Ausstellung für unbekannte Architekten* or any specific figures directly, Hilberseimer's critique was clearly directed at Taut, Gropius, and Behne, who had claimed Scheerbart's legacy as they assumed the leadership

of the Arbeitsrat für Kunst. While Hilberseimer too admired the scope of Scheerbart's fantasy—"The entire cosmos is material for his form-creation"—he saw the new explorations in architecture as translating the writer's ideas too directly from literature into buildings. Like Behne, he warned against the "naturalistic misunderstanding of cubistic pictures" in "crooked houses" and "crashing streets." These visions, he explained, failed to consider the material world in which we live, and the media of construction. They would, he contended, never make it beyond the paper on which they were drawn. Even reinforced concrete, celebrated as a plastic material that could realize any fantasy, required discipline if architects were not to succumb to picturesque effects. Implying a need for greater *Sachlichkeit* (objectivity), Hilberseimer dismissed Scheerbart's followers as imitators and false interpreters. Quoting Scheerbart, he emphasized that the work of art should be like an opal whose every side offers new leaves of

7. Raoul Hausmann. *Grün* (Green). 1918. Graphite on paper, 11 x 8¹¹/₁₆" (28 x 22 cm). Musée National d'Art Moderne, Centre Georges Pompidou, Paris

8. Raoul Hausmann. Untitled. c. 1917. Woodcut for *Materiel der Malerei, Plastik und Architektur* (Berlin: Barthe, 1918), 12³/₁₆ x 7½" (31 x 19 cm). Collection Marthe Prévot, Limoges

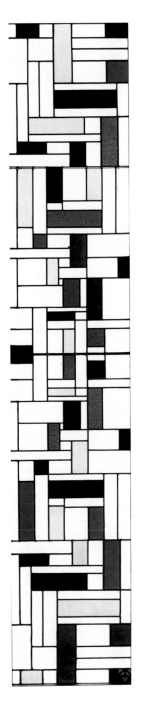

color, yet whose simple mass contains all these fleeting, colorful stories.[30] Even into the late 1920s he continued to honor Scheerbart for having recognized in glass the potential for an entirely new architecture. At the same time, he continued to reiterate his critique of Expressionist architects for ignoring the "constructive premises" of building in glass and steel in their "unarchitectonic, decorative fantasies."[31]

Hilberseimer's appreciation of Scheerbart's rationalism—of the attention to the discipline and nature of construction as the basis of a technical, even scientific kind of fantasy so evident in his 1914 book *Glasarchitektur* (Glass architecture)—coincided with a shift within Dada from negation to affirmation, from destructive impulse to constructive play. In 1919, Hausmann depicted a light, whimsical structure of scaffolding and cranes in bright colors. By 1920 his conception of the New Man had shifted to engineers and inventors. He began to portray the new technics of building and technical drawings, taking practicality and conventionality as means to achieving a "synthesis of spirit and matter" that he called "*Présentismus*."[32] Later, in his "In Praise of the Conventional" of 1922, he opposed the fantasy of "*artistes*" with "the fantasy of the technician, the constructor of machines . . . the scientific experimenter . . . the watchmaker, welder, or locomotive engineer."[33] Le Corbusier had already promoted the engineer's aesthetic in 1920, in the pages of *L'Esprit Nouveau*. Van Doesburg too had begun to write about the machine that same year. More than any other avant-garde artist of the time, in fact, van Doesburg had staged the dualism of destruction and construction when he assumed a Dadaist persona (I. K. Bonset) without relinquishing his leading role in the constructively oriented de Stijl movement; in 1922, he sought to bring the two groups together in congresses at Düsseldorf and Weimar. Hausmann too became a key figure in this shift, helping to write the first Elementarist Manifesto in October 1921 with Arp, Ivan Puni, and Moholy-Nagy—bringing Berlin and Zurich Dada together with Russian and Hungarian Futurism and Suprematism.[34]

The fair of 1920, then, turned out to be the ultimate Dada event after which the group dissolved, with several of its key figures turning increasingly toward forms of constructivism. It was precisely at this moment that Mies entered the scene, beginning to circulate among artists who sought to create a new, all-embracing architecture, an elemental artistic paradigm distilled from the conditions of the emerging age. According to Richter, it was van Doesburg who first introduced him to Mies. Richter's story suggests that this meeting took place sometime in 1921, probably soon after van Doesburg himself had met Mies and before the announcement of the competition for the Friedrichstrasse Skyscraper, on November 1, 1921.[35] Van Doesburg had spent the fall of 1920 largely in Berlin, where he had met Richter, Eggeling, and other experimental artists and architects through Behne, whom he had met earlier that year when Behne had visited Holland.[36] In early 1921 he moved to Weimar, hoping to secure a teaching appointment at the Bauhaus. When it became clear that Gropius would not hire him, he began to offer private instruction nearby, to Bauhaus students among others. From a vantage outside the Bauhaus, he launched a campaign against its Expressionism, the indulgent subjectivism and mysticism promoted, he argued, by Itten and Gropius. Van Doesburg's critique helped shift the school toward a more objectivist and collectivist orientation, one that Mies would soon share (fig. 9).

Richter had been reluctant to take up van Doesburg's suggestion that he meet Mies, having little interest in architecture, his father's profession. But van Doesburg insisted, explaining that the plans of a house that Mies was then designing for Neubabelsberg resembled drawings by Mondrian as well as Richter's own graphic experiments toward abstract film, his "Präludium" (1919–20; fig. 10). Since little remains of Mies's work from this period it is difficult to know what project so excited van Doesburg, but the Petermann House of 1921 would appear a close fit, although only one image of it survives (fig. 11).[37] The design proposed an elemental main block with several similarly abstract, unornamented, smaller blocks attached, not unlike the Frank Lloyd Wright–type designs that J. J. P. Oud, Jan Wils, and Robert van't Hoff had been making, or that van Doesburg's Weimar students would produce in 1922.[38] The plan was probably composed of interlocked or abutting rectangles. Mies's later Kempner House

(1922), Eichstaedt House (1921–23), and especially the Lessing House (1923; fig. 12) share precisely such compositions. Even earlier projects by Mies—the Kröller-Müller Villa Project (1912–13) and the House for the Architect (1914)—used similar devices. The decade before World War I was in this respect an important prelude to elementarism, for the architectonic neoclassicism of Peter Behrens and Heinrich Tessenow in those years was already characterized by unadorned elemental volumes regulated by underlying geometric structures. It seems apt that the sole images to survive of the Petermann and Lessing projects were those published by Paul Westheim in an article of 1927 for

the first time linking Mies with Karl Friedrich Schinkel. Westheim called Mies one of Schinkel's most talented and original students, taking from the nineteenth-century master not a style or set of forms but his "remarkable feeling for masses, relationships, rhythms and form-melody."[39]

Upon visiting Mies in his apartment, Richter concurred with van Doesburg's assessment and declared that Mies's plans resembled music—"visual music, which we were discussing at that time, toward which we were working, and which we were realizing in film" (fig. 13). For Richter, Mies's project represented more than a floor plan, "it was a new language, precisely one that appeared to draw our generation together."[40] The metaphor of music was of course familiar from Romantic and Expressionist aesthetics, while the idea of a new nonrepresentational language had a history from the rationalist aesthetics of Gotthold Ephraim Lessing in the late eighteenth century to Hausmann's optophonetic poetry. What is interesting here is that Richter both linked the metaphors of language and music and privileged film, a medium of time, movement, and sequence. He also saw architecture as playing a unifying role akin to that of language. The metaphor of language served as a guarantor of unity among the arts. Where the idea of the *Gesamtkunstwerk*, or total artwork, relied on collaboration and the metaphor of

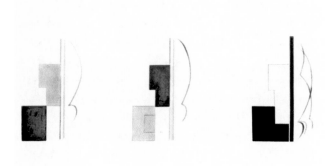

10. Hans Richter. *Präludium* (detail). 1919. Ink on paper. Staatliche Museen zu Berlin. Kupferstichkabinett

11. Ludwig Mies van der Rohe. Petermann House, Potsdam-Neubabelsberg. 1921. Perspective. Published in *Das Kunstblatt*, February 1927

12. Ludwig Mies van der Rohe. Lessing House, Potsdam-Neubabelsberg. 1923. Plan. Published in *Das Kunstblatt*, February 1927

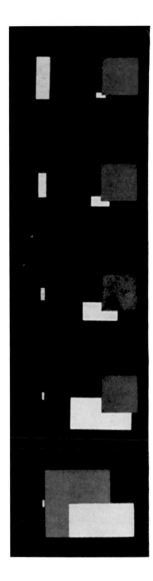

13. Hans Richter. Still from *Rhythmus 21*. 1921. From Richter, *Filmgegner von Heute, Filmfreunde von Morgen* (Berlin: Hermann Reckendorf, 1929)

fusion,[41] the notion of language posited unity through a common structure of mediation. More neo-Kantian than Romantic, this assumed that the conditions of the possibility of knowledge would be manifest in homologous ways in different spheres, each of which would remain autonomous, i.e., self-regulating with respect to the defining and limiting conditions of its own medium. The aesthetician Conrad Fiedler had already adapted the metaphor of language to visual cognition in the 1870s. In neo-Kantian aesthetics and art history, the metaphor of language took on a structural and structuring role, which was historicized by Alois Riegl and Heinrich Wölfflin. Expanding beyond vision, it came to encompass spatiality, feeling, and also technology.

In a short reminiscence on *G* published in 1967, Richter focused almost exclusively on Mies, suggesting the extent to which the architect was immediately absorbed into discussions of a new universal language and contributed to them from an architectural perspective. More than any of the others with whom Richter started the journal—more than van Doesburg, Lissitzky, and Gräff—it was Mies he would remember as crucial for the first issues: "The truth is that his personality, his work, and his active participation in *G* became more indispensable and important than those of all the others."[42] Perhaps the reverse was also true—that the discourse of *G* became indispensable to Mies, not only in the 1920s but later in America as well. Certainly his Weimar-period career was forged within the collective discussion of elementarism, which was most intense between 1921 and 1924. Although he only invoked the metaphor of language later in life, he spoke on many occasions in the 1920s and '30s of the necessity of employing the means of the age, turning them into the means of elementary *Gestaltung*. At the same time, he dedicated his experimental work to the development of new types, much like Arp's development of a typological visual language. When Mies finally did refer explicitly to architecture as language, he echoed Richter's focus on the new structural paradigm and its potential for a new poetics.

Glass Prisms

After 1919, Mies resumed his practice as an architect of private houses in the suburbs of Berlin. Yet when a competition for a skyscraper on the Friedrichstrasse was announced in late 1921, he decided to enter, and produced the remarkable shimmering monolith known as the Friedrichstrasse Skyscraper Project of 1921—the very first proposal for a high-rise building clad entirely in glass.

Although Mies's house projects had already demonstrated a high degree of formal abstraction, it was with the skyscraper that he first ventured a pure elemental prism. While the design was surely informed by the crystalline cubism of the Arbeitsrat für Kunst and the Taut circle, Mies appears to have heeded the warnings of both Behne and Hilberseimer not to imitate Cubist painting literally. His skyscraper is neither a "paper pagoda" nor a "fantasy" but a fully architectural proposition, potentially realizable through new building technologies. It was his first engagement with both a metropolitan building type (the high-rise office building) and a metropolitan building site (adjoining a major train station), as well as with modern materials and technical forms (concrete frame, plate glass skin, and elevators). Conceived in the very moment when Mies was being absorbed into the post-Expressionist quest for a new elemental language, the Friedrichstrasse Skyscraper was a pure crystalline mass of unprecedented scale and monumentality—primitive and raw, yet constructed with the most advanced building technologies and capable of producing visual effects of dissolution and dematerialization traditionally associated with cathedrals.

In the manifesto Mies wrote to accompany the first publication of the project—in Bruno Taut's journal *Frühlicht*, in 1922—he set it in relation on the one hand to American skyscrapers and on the other to the task of finding modern equivalents to inherited conceptions of architectural beauty. The "bold constructive thoughts" of the "high-reaching steel skeletons," Mies explained, are the "necessary basis for artistic form-giving" for the skyscraper. Echoing a general sentiment among progressive architects in Germany, he went on to note that in America this skeleton was "annihilated and frequently smothered by a meaningless and trivial jumble of [traditional] forms."[43] Although still relatively unfamiliar with skeleton-and-glass construction, Mies

proposed a direct, elemental extrusion of the site, like the Flatiron Building. But where that New York example was still encumbered with stone decoration, Mies offered a clarified form, a pure expression. Abandoning the weight and mass of stone in favor of a continuous glass surface hung like a curtain over the frame, he replaced the aesthetics of stone molding—classical architecture's play of light and shadow—with a new aesthetic specific to glass.

To "avoid the danger of lifelessness that often occurs if one employs large glass panels," Mies broke the tower into three triangular segments joined at the center by an elevator core. The sides of each of these segments were broken in turn into two continuous twenty-story planes of plate glass, set at slight angles to one another to produce a "rich interplay of light reflections." Without undermining the integrity of the geometric form, the reflections in the glass were to enliven the surface and thereby animate the object along a trajectory of growth and transcendence. Anxious to avoid accusations of arbitrariness, Mies went on to explain how the irregularly curved contours of the second version of his skyscraper design, the Glass Skyscraper Project of 1922, were "the result of many experiments on the glass model." The curves, he continued, "were determined by the need to illuminate the interior, the effect of the building mass in the urban context, and finally the play of the desired light reflection." Echoing the call of *das neue Bauen* to "give form to the new task out of the nature of this task,"[44] Mies nevertheless went beyond reductive functionalism to explore the possibility of a new kind of beauty, one commensurate with the "constructive thoughts" of "skin-and-bones architecture," as van Doesburg would call it. This new beauty was to be comparable to the old beauty of stone but specific to the properties of the new materials—their architectonic logics, scale, and spatiality.[45]

In *Frühlicht* Taut presented two photographs of the model of Mies's second, curvilinear proposal, one showing a highly transparent tower emerging from the historical urban fabric, the other a view from below, with the context dropped away (fig. 14). In this second view the tower appears as an opaque prism with only a

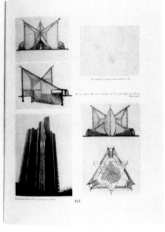

14. Spread and following page from *Frühlicht* 1, no. 4 (1922), showing Mies's Glass Skyscraper and Friedrichstrasse Skyscraper projects with works by Bruno Taut and others

hint of transparency at one edge and a tiny play of reflection near the top. On the same page Taut included drawings of his own project for a glass cinema, similarly triangular in plan but with wings rising up into a three-dimensional star. On the next page, accompanying Mies's text, was the charcoal perspective of the first, faceted tower, a luminous phoenix rising from the dark metropolis. Once again Taut combined it with designs by others: an advertising pavilion for the Swedish ballet on the Potsdamer Platz and a shop in Schöneberg. The first is sculpturally prismatic and cubistic while the second is more painterly, and would have produced a disorienting, kaleidoscopic effect, a whirl of circles and shards (presumably in brilliant colors) dissolving the plane of the storefront into an abstract landscape. Clearly Taut was trying to absorb Mies's designs into his own understanding of the quest for a new architecture, but Mies's differ significantly from the others in maintaining their volumetric integrity. Rather than composing with shards or fragments, Mies demateralizes the perfectly regular form of the tower, through the surface play of the glass, without undermining its corporeal integrity.

The crystalline character of the Friedrichstrasse Skyscraper, its date, and its publication in *Frühlicht* have led historians to interpret it as "Expressionist"—as Mies's one foray into subjectivism and mysticism. Yet Mies never described the project in such terms, and continued to work on it well after the competition—in other words,

15. Sergius Ruegenberg. Caricature of Mies with model of Glass Skyscraper. c. 1925. Graphite and colored pencil on paper, 6⅞ x 8¼" (17.5 x 21 cm). Berlinische Galerie

after the general turn toward a *neue Sachlichkeit* (new objectivity) and after beginning his more obviously elementarist projects. A caricature from 1924–25 by Mies's assistant Sergius Ruegenberg shows the architect still preoccupied three or four years later with the perceptual effects of his glass model, stooping down to examine it as it would be perceived from the street, just as he would later study the models of his American skyscrapers (fig. 15).[46] In fact Mies consistently allowed the Friedrichstrasse Skyscraper to be presented as the beginning of the glass architecture that became the hallmark of his career and achievement—of his attempt to transmute the raw technical forms of modern building into symbols of transfiguration and transcendence.[47] One might well ask, after all, how critics might have interpreted the project had the site been square or rectangular.

It should also be remembered that the movement toward a new architecture was not yet divided into the competing isms that would later be codified by historians. As the first avant-garde architecture journal after the war, *Frühlicht* published a broad range of approaches. Even "Expressionism" was originally an umbrella term for all post-Impressionist modern art. Moreover, Mies's glass skyscrapers lent themselves to a complex set of affiliations, for they looked both forward and back. Related on the one hand to the cult of nature and the utopian delirium of 1919, they also promoted the more sober technological rationalism that would become dominant by the mid-1920s. Unlike Finsterlin's plastic expressions or Scharoun's explosions of color, Mies's skyscrapers relied on inorganic metaphors rather than organic ones. His geometry was simpler than that of Hablik's glass towers; his glass was clear as reason rather than colored with feeling; and his crystalline form had affinities with the cold clarity of Behrens or Tessenow, whose school at Hellerau, for Emile Jaques-Dalcroze's eurythmic dance and culture (p. 17, fig. 10), Mies had known quite well before the war.[48]

Mies's skyscrapers were more transcendental than ecstatic, more monumental than kaleidoscopic, more frames for the rhythmic union of body and soul with the *Weltall* (universe) than representations of it. Rising like modern-day cathedrals or "city crowns" for the industrial metropolis, luminous and dissolving into the heavens, they offered to reconcile the antinomy between technology and nature. Mechanical, industrial, and raw, they also prefigured a new, second nature, synthetic in origin, forged from human intellect through a spiritualized technology. The large drawings and photocollages that Mies made after the competition stage a powerful, almost theological or alchemic drama of darkness becoming light, solid melting into air, matter transmuting into spirit, detritus into gold. Although the skyscrapers might well be considered together with Erich Heckel's *Glassy Day* (1913), Feininger's prismatic woodcuts of crystalline cathedrals, or even Scheerbart's *Lésabendio* (1913), a story of a cosmic tower, they would also have to be placed beside not only Moholy's glass architecture paintings but Hausmann's engineers, constructions, and angels. Within this field they are distinguished as neither the projections of a utopian fantasy nor recourses to the myth of pure nature, but as transformations of given conditions. Working with and beyond the givens of modernization and civilization, Mies refashioned the high-rise office building into images of its immanent and natural self-fulfillment, figured as a pure physiognomy, simultaneously rising from the ground and dissolving into the ether. Like Baader and Schwitters, Mies accepted his historical circumstances and sought to transform them. But unlike Schwitters, he made his model of transformation not a fusion of opposites from which a new third term was to emerge, but a purification, elementarization, and dematerialization of what was already given—finding what was natural in it and raising it into spirit. For Mies, transcendence was immanent within reality.

The glass skyscrapers' history of publication and exhibition reveals that they were quickly accepted as important early experiments within international constructivism. In 1923, for instance, the curvilinear skyscraper was featured, together with the Concrete Office Building, in the *Internationale Architektur* show curated by Gropius as part of the Bauhaus exhibition that summer in Weimar (fig. 16). This was the show that signaled the school's shift from the Expressionism of Itten to the constructivism of Moholy-Nagy. Here Gropius placed Mies's models near his own rationalist design for the Chicago Tribune Competition, and when he published his follow-up book, *Internationale Architektur*, in 1925, he again included the second version of the skyscraper, the only building with a curvilinear plan.[49]

Mies's Glass Skyscraper was shown again in 1923, in the fall, this time in the de Stijl exhibition at Rosenberg's Galerie L'Effort Moderne in Paris (fig. 17). The show was dedicated to "The Architects of the de Stijl Group, Holland," but the program lists one project from Germany, by an architect who had recently adapted his name to the Dutch-sounding Miës van der Rohe. Mies's project is identified as a "skyscraper,"[50] and correspondence makes clear that it was this project, and its favorable reception among van Doesburg's friends in Paris, that led to Mies's invitation to participate in the show.[51] Mies also sought to include the Concrete Office Building, "in order to show the effect of the two buildings in relation to one another,"[52] as had been done in the *Internationale*

16. Installation view of *Internationale Architektur* exhibition, the Bauhaus, Weimar. 1923. The models for Mies's Glass Skyscraper and Concrete Office Building projects are on the left. Hochschule für Architektur und Bauwesen, Weimar

17. Installation view of de Stijl exhibition, Galerie L'Effort Moderne, Paris. 1923. Institut Collectie Nederland, Rijswijk

Architektur exhibition that summer. Last-minute shipping problems precluded sending the models, and Mies's contribution ended up consisting of a perspective and two photographs of the model for the Glass Skyscraper, along with a perspective, an elevation, and sections of the Concrete Office Building and a perspective of the Concrete Country House.[53]

The model photographs and perspective could well have been the same as those published the year before in *Frühlicht*. Yet in the context of de Stijl—of van Doesburg's collaborations with Cornelis van Eesteren, and of buildings by Oud, Wils, and van't Hoff—they demand a different reading. What does it mean for our understanding of Mies's skyscrapers that they could be so readily absorbed into the "collective construction" of de Stijl, as van Doesburg and van Eesteren subsequently called their effort to extend the momentum of the exhibition?[54] For van Doesburg the Glass Skyscraper belonged to elementarism, meaning not only Mies's own elementarist projects but an entire movement seeking to reconstruct the world according to reason, objectivity, and spirit. In fact the large perspectives of the Glass Skyscraper and the Concrete Office Building, like the models that Mies had coupled for the Bauhaus show, may be read as a pair: both are large monumental charcoal drawings employing an oblique perspective that invites the viewer to step into a dark metropolitan scene in which the proposed building stands out like a beacon of redemption. Both buildings appear to rise out of the ground like a natural growth; both exceed their context in scale and formal clarity; and both employ new structural systems and new modes of cladding.

The following year saw further publication of the two skyscrapers in journals that were explicitly elementarist and constructivist in orientation. The second skyscraper was featured on the cover of the third issue of *G* (June 1924), appearing in elevation as an abstract vertical rectangle overlapping the geometrized silhouette of a typical Berlin building (fig. 18). As a composition, this cover image has a certain affinity with Moholy's "Glass Architecture" cover of *MA* (fig. 4). In staging a confrontation between the new and the old,

18. Cover of *G* no. 3 (June 1924), showing the elevation study for Mies's Glass Skyscraper Project (1922). The Museum of Modern Art, New York. Mies van der Rohe Archive. Gift of the architect

it also bears comparison with an image by Nathan Altmann inside the journal showing Suprematist planes invading St. Petersburg's Uritizki Square, an image marking the first anniversary of the October Revolution. (Malevich himself would produce an image of this kind with his *Architecton against Manhattan as Background*, 1926.[55]) Richter's introduction in this issue was also illustrated with one of Mies's photo-based perspectives of the first skyscraper, to document the new, elemental material culture that Richter was suggesting could be discerned within industrial civilization. Not only did it stand for this new way of life, it also rendered it operational, providing an architectonic frame for the unfolding of new forms of existence, life processes, and subjectivities—unsentimental and at the same time unwilling merely to affirm the chaos of the present.

In articles in the same issue of *G*, Mies and Hilberseimer offered further discussion of the open and luminous spatiality they envisioned for glass architecture, imagined as industrial structures with thin glass membranes supported on light steel frames. Gräff's essay on new technics pointed to the design of car bodies and engines as exemplars of design with which the skyscraper could be compared. Hausmann's designs of loose-fitting shirts, coats, and hats applied a similar logic to the design of men's clothing, which he called "exterior expressions of the body." Just as Prinzhorn, in a letter to Mies, had explained that the mentally ill, like children, tribal peoples, artists—and presumably elementarist architects—were weak in the naturalistic depiction of reality but rich in free expression, Richter now explained that while the poetry and art of Arp, a friend of Prinzhorn's, had been called schizophrenic, it touched something elementary, which he associated with the irrational and outrageous creativity of the unconscious.[56] Arp's poetry communicated not through narrative prose but through unexpected sequences of mental images, word sounds, and rhythms, and his reliefs and graphic works developed what he called an "object language" of abstract organic shapes that connoted aspects of the human figure in ambiguous yet humorous and suggestively poetic ways (fig. 19). The poetry of Schwitters was also included, to demonstrate the proposition that the letter, rather than the word,

19. Hans Arp. *7 Arpaden-Mappe*. 1923. Left to right: "Mustache Hat," "The Sea," "A Navel," "The Navel Bottle," "Mustache Watch," "Eggbeater," "Arabic 8." Lithographs published in *G* no. 3 (June 1924). The Museum of Modern Art, New York. Mies van der Rohe Archive. Gift of the architect

was the original material of poetry. In this company Mies's skyscraper may be understood as a pure expression of a dreaming unconscious, a machine designed from the inside out, and a reduction of architecture to its originary mute materiality.

G also presented evidence of a new, technologically mediated visuality that may be seen as another context for understanding Mies's skyscraper. Aerial photographs suggest something of the panoramic, near-abstract visuality that the skyscraper would have afforded its occupants daily. More purely abstract landscapes were also opened up by the new optics of paintings by Mondrian and van Doesburg, which achieved unity, harmony, and equilibrium through an elementarization of color and form. Meanwhile photograms by Man Ray used light to produce phantasmatic images, and films by Richter and Eggeling sought a unified gestalt over time through the rhythmic orchestration of elemental lines, forms, and colors in motion. Mies himself described the rich play of reflections and transparencies that he expected the skyscraper to create from the outside. From the inside too it must be imagined as an optical instrument producing panoramic vistas of the city. In the following issue of *G* (March 1926), Hilberseimer republished the charcoal perspective of the triangular Friedrichstrasse Skyscraper, concluding his review of an exhibition of American architecture with a call for a new "light architecture" of glass and steel.

The curvilinear version of Mies's skyscraper was also published in 1924, in Schwitters's journal *Merz*, in an issue edited jointly with Lissitzky and titled *Nasci* (fig. 20). *Nasci* is Latin for the English "becoming" and the German "*Gestaltung*." Here Mies's project was juxtaposed with a human femur and a cubic pavilion by Oud. Mies's maxim from *G* no. 2 (September 1923)—

"We know no forms, only building problems. Form is not the goal but rather the result of our work"[57]—was presented as a line on the page, graphically linking the skyscraper to the bone, as if to imply that while each addressed a different problem of construction, their approach to form was the same.

In this respect it is interesting to note how much Mies's manifesto was indebted to Lissitzky's text "Proun," written in 1920 and published in *De Stijl* in June 1922.[58] It was also Lissitzky who drew the bone in *Nasci*, copying it from a book by the popular science

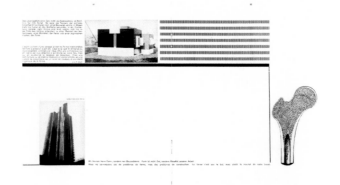

20. Spread from *Merz* no. 8–9 (April–June 1924), edited by Kurt Schwitters and El Lissitzky, and titled *Nasci*. The model for Mies's Glass Skyscraper Project (1922) appears with a pavilion by J. J. P. Oud and a human femur

writer Raoul H. Francé. Inspired perhaps by an excerpt of Francé's book *Die Pflanze als Erfinder* (Plants as inventors) in the January 1923 issue of *Das Kunstblatt*,[59] Lissitzky had taken Francé's theory of construction in nature as the underlying basis for the works assembled in *Nasci*, and had even wanted to dedicate the issue to him.[60] One of the first pages in the journal presents a graphic summary of his proposition that seven Ur-forms underpin all creation, human as well as natural: crystal, sphere, plane, rod, ribbon, screw, and cylinder (fig. 21). More than geometric abstractions, these are understood as the fundamental "technical forms" that are employed "in various combinations by all world-processes, including architecture, machine elements, crystallography, chemistry, geography, astronomy, and art—every technique in the entire world."

The plates that follow, beginning with one of Lissitzky's own Prouns, evidence this biotechnical system at work in modern art—in paintings by Malevich, Mondrian, and Léger; collages by Schwitters, Arp, and Georges Braque; sculpture by Alexander Archipenko; photograms by Man Ray; and architecture by Vladimir Tatlin, Oud, Mies, and nature. The sequence concludes with an unidentified microscopic image punctuated by a question mark, suggesting something of the formlessness from which all form emerges, or perhaps of the biotechnic future to which the assembled works were understood to be leading. In this context both of Mies's skyscrapers become demonstrative of nature's means of construction, understood as fundamentally the same for both organic and inorganic life, and as employing

21. Spread from *Nasci* juxtaposing a list of Raoul H. Francé's "seven Ur-forms of creation" (crystal, sphere, plane, rod, ribbon, screw, and cylinder) with one of Lissitzky's Proun compositions

both curvilinear forms and orthogonal or prismatic ones. While the metaphor of architecture as organism had long been a staple of architectural theory, the idea that architecture should emulate nature's construction methods was here updated to a systemic theory that Francé described as biotechnics and that the constructivist avant-garde assimilated to its theory of elementary *Gestaltung*.

Mies himself collected Francé's books, a fact that places his thinking in an extensive yet disparate biocentric discourse that included, as Oliver Botar has shown, artists (Hausmann, Moholy-Nagy, Lissitzky,

Ernó Kállai, Schlemmer, Schwitters), scientists (Haeckel, Hans Driesch, Jakob von Uexküll, Francé), philosophers (Friedrich Nietzsche, Henri Bergson, Georg Simmel, Ludwig Klages, Oswald Spengler), and architects (Mies, Hannes Meyer, Siegfried Ebeling, Hilberseimer).[61] Mies's interest in the structure of nature began early: while still a young man in Aachen, he came across a pamphlet on the mathematician and physicist Pierre-Simon LaPlace and the journal *Die Zukunft*.[62] We do not know what triggered Mies's interest in LaPlace, but LaPlacian physics was distinguished by an attempt to account for all phenomena, whether on the terrestrial, molecular, or celestial scale, in terms of forces between particles that could either attract or repel. The biocentric discourse, monistic and holistic in orientation, reiterated this quest for homologies across all scales of creation.

The idea of structures repeating at different scales, or of a nested hierarchy of harmoniously integrated systems, was seen as being graphically revealed in scientific photography (microscopic and telescopic), and was appropriated by artists like Moholy-Nagy as a key to a new vision potentially able to reconcile humanity with technological modernization. Francé held up nature's processes and inventions as both origin and model for engineering, architecture, and art, which was of special consequence for those seeking to overcome the antinomy between organism and mechanism that had structured architectural thinking since 1800. He took nature's laws of economy, individuality, unity, harmony, proportion, and number to be exemplary for cultural works of all kinds, and even for ways of living. He also posited that all creation was the product of a unifying vital life force or "plasma," similar to Bergson's "*élan vital*," Klages's "*kosmogoner Eros*," Haeckel's "*Seele*," and Max Scheler's "*kosmovitale Einfühlung*," all of which reiterate in one way or another Aristotle's "*Entelechie*."[63] Francé extended Haeckel's ecological studies of the relationships between organisms and their environments, not only in the realms of plants and animals but also in human society and culture. He considered cultural history to be tied to natural history. If *Heimat* was understood to be the habitat or environment of humanity, civilization was the rebuilding of this habitat into an optimally functional and artistic *Biozönose*, and culture was the harmony between artistic *Biozönose* and the totality of experience. It was in experience, the realm of sensations, that reality was ultimately to be found. The theory of staged evolution helped to account for the struggles of the present as a period of transition (new against old, idealism against materialism) along a historical trajectory that operated through transformation and mutation.

By the mid-1920s, then, Mies's first glass prisms had been widely presented as elementarist and constructivist experiments understood in terms of both van Doesburg's antinaturalist emphasis on art as the manifestation of spirit and Lissitzky's promotion of a holistic and biological world view in which nature and humanity were undivided.[64] The projects were taken to demonstrate nature's laws and methods of construction, reconciling technology and nature less in their image or form than as the result of a process of elemental *Gestaltung* that relied solely on technical means and was mediated by the new structural order of montage. Their skin-and-bones construction had become emblematic of an architecture of life and for life, which Mies continued to develop in one project after another—from the Concrete Office Building to the S. Adam Department Store Project (1928–29), the Bank and Office Building Project (1928), the Urban Design Proposal for Alexanderplatz (1929), and finally the built office buildings of the 1950s and '60s. Mies's embrace of life and life processes was never at odds, however, with his conception of architecture as the expression of spirit. Moreover, he understood architecture as making possible the apprehension of spirit with a new beauty.[65]

Rhythmic Constructions

In his catalogue for the exhibition *Cubism and Abstract Art*, at The Museum of Modern Art in 1936, Alfred H. Barr, Jr., placed Mies's plan for the Brick Country House alongside a painting by van Doesburg entitled *Rhythm of a Russian Dance* (1918; fig. 22).[66] Barr's juxtaposition fixed the link between Mies and de Stijl into architectural culture so firmly that it has rarely until recently been questioned or probed.[67] Equally important, it established the pedigree for some of Mies's best-known

designs: the German Pavilion, Barcelona, of 1928–29, and its domestic counterpart, the Tugendhat House in Brno, Czechoslovakia, of 1928–30. Although Mies denied that his projects were derived from Neo-Plastic painting, the idea stuck, and even gave rise to an erroneous period division between his earlier "de Stijl" work in Germany and his later "classicist" work in America.

A second, less well-known interpretation of Mies's relationship to de Stijl was made by Philip Johnson in presenting his own Glass House (1949) in *Architectural Review* (fig. 23), where Johnson placed his building in a family of modern architecture that included Mies and Le Corbusier, Malevich and van Doesburg, Schinkel and Claude-Nicolas Ledoux.[68] This genealogy focused on groupings of prismatic masses rather than planes, and broadened out the category of elementarism to include its neoclassical precursors as well as Suprematism and Purism. More specifically, Johnson compared the site plan for his own glass box to a composition of four rectangles by van Doesburg and an exercise for a design in a Chicago park that Mies had set students at the Armour Institute of Technology shortly after becoming its director of architecture, in 1938.

Johnson's juxtaposition was in fact consistent with the presentation of Mies's work in the pages of *G* (fig. 24). Van Doesburg's four rectangles had appeared on the

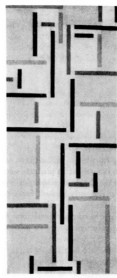

162 (52) Doesburg: Russian dance, 1918 (*not in exhibition*); *cf.* Picasso, fig. 27

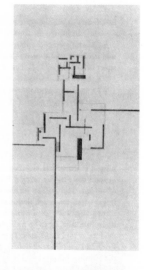

163 (305) Mies van der Rohe: Project for a brick country house, plan, 1922

22. Spread (detail) from the exhibition catalogue *Cubism and Abstract Art*, by Alfred H. Barr, Jr. (New York: The Museum of Modern Art, 1936), showing Theo van Doesburg's *Rhythm of a Russian Dance* (1918) next to the plan for Mies's Brick Country House Project (1924), p. 157

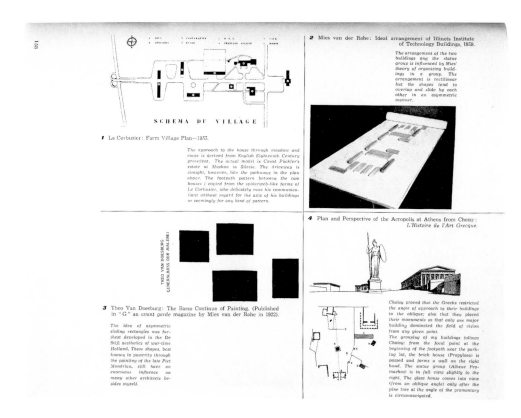

2 Mies van der Rohe: Ideal arrangement of Illinois Institute of Technology Buildings, 1939.

The arrangement of the two buildings and the statue group is influenced by Mies' theory of organizing buildings in a group. The arrangement is rectilinear but the shapes tend to overlap and slide by each other in an asymmetric manner.

SCHEMA DU VILLAGE

1 Le Corbusier: Farm Village Plan—1933.

The approach to the house through meadow and copse is derived from English Eighteenth Century precedent. The actual model is Count Pückler's estate at Muskau in Silesia. The driveway is straight, however, like the pathways in the plan above. The footpath pattern between the two houses I copied from the spiderweb-like forms of Le Corbusier, who delicately runs his communications without regard to the axis of his buildings or seemingly for any kind of pattern.

THEO VAN DOESBURG
GENERALBASS DER MALEREI

4 Plan and Perspective of the Acropolis at Athens from Choisy: L'Histoire de l'Art Grecque.

3 Theo Van Doesburg: The Basso Continuo of Painting. (Published in "G" an *avant garde* magazine by Mies van der Rohe in 1922).

The idea of asymmetric sliding rectangles was furthest developed in the De Stijl aesthetics of war-time Holland. These shapes, best known to posterity through the painting of the late Piet Mondrian, still have an enormous influence on many other architects besides myself.

Choisy proved that the Greeks restricted the angle of approach to their buildings to the oblique; also that they placed their monuments so that only one major building dominated the field of vision from any given point. The grouping of my buildings follows Choisy: from the focal point at the beginning of the footpath near the parking lot, the brick house (Propylaea) is passed and forms a wall on the right hand. The statue group (Athene Promachos) is in full view slightly to the right, The glass house comes into view (from an oblique angle) only after the pine tree at the angle of the promontory is circumnavigated.

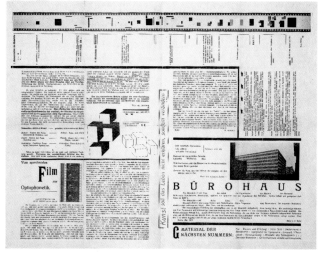

---

23 (above left). Page from Philip Johnson's article "House at New Canaan, Connecticut," *Architectural Review*, September 1950, showing a village plan by Le Corbusier, a teaching exercise by Mies, a composition by Theo van Doesburg, and the Acropolis, Athens

24 (above right). Spread from *G* no. 1 (July 1923), showing the perspective for Mies's Concrete Office Building Project (1923), Theo van Doesburg's diagrams "Basic Elements of Sculpture" and "Basic Elements of Architecture," and a film strip from Hans Richter's *Rhythmus 21* (1921). Collection Elaine Lustig-Cohen, New York

first page of the first issue of the magazine (July 1923), accompanying his manifesto "*Zur Elementaren Gestaltung.*" Identified as the "general basis for painting," van Doesburg's composition led, on an inside spread, to two axonometric projections taken to represent the equivalents for sculpture (with shadows) and architecture (without)—variations on the theme of pure elementary means for pure expressions in three different mediums.[69] The facing page featured Mies's Concrete Office Building Project, its rectangular mass appearing to materialize van Doesburg's "general basis for architecture" in concrete and glass, as a new framework for modern office life.[70]

Using an eye-level perspective rather than an axonometric projection, Mies showed the building as a unitary block inserted into the urban fabric of Berlin. By expanding the space in front, he created an open urban plaza (his first), inviting the observer to move between and around the buildings. His sketch for the perspective makes even clearer the importance he assigned to vision in motion, and signals a silent debt to the picturesque urbanism of the Austrian Camillo Sitte

and his German followers.[71] Then again, one of Sitte's own suggestions for modifying the modern rectilinear system of streets to create variety and picturesque effects curiously resembles later de Stijl compositions.[72]

A film strip from Richter's abstract animation *Rhythmus 21* (1921) stretches along the top of the same spread in *G* that features Mies's Concrete Office Building and van Doesburg's rectangles. Considered together, this constellation of works suggests that Mies's project was party to another concept of motion and another kind of visuality, one that effectively updated the arts of building and city planning to the paradigm of elementarist cinema.

Soon after first meeting Richter, in Berlin in December 1920, van Doesburg published an article on the studies for abstract films that Richter was making with Eggeling. In fact *Rhythmus 21* is in many ways the cinematic counterpart of van Doesburg's compositions of planes and lines, playing with black-white contrasts, figure-ground inversions, and the recessional effects of color fields. And just as van Doesburg treats four rectangles as the "general basis" of painting, the film treats black and white rectangles as the "general basis" of film, albeit these are in motion—advancing and receding, sliding across the frame, and overlapping to generate effects of depth and space. Underscoring the affinity between van Doesburg's two-dimensional compositions and Richter's projection into four dimensions, each artist contributed further essays on film to *De Stijl* over the next two years, focusing increasingly on the medium's unique characteristics in terms of movement, light, and time. More studies by Eggeling and Richter were published with these and other essays, as were filmic scrolls by Gräff, the young protégé of van Doesburg and Richter who collaborated on *G* and later with Mies.[73]

Van Doesburg's and Richter's texts on film of 1923 firmly installed the notions of movement, time, and light into the concept of modern space, which they thereby linked to the still expanding discourse on the fourth dimension.[74] In Richter's words,

The distinctive sphere of film is that of "moving" space, the "moving" surface, the "moving" line. Moving: that means space, surface, line many times over and one after another.

This space is neither architectonic nor sculptural, but rather time-based, i.e. light forms through alternation of qualities (light, dark, color). Light-spaces which are not volumetric but are only spatial through sequence.[75]

Richter's compositions and texts of 1923 were produced while van Doesburg was collaborating with van Eesteren in Paris on the house and studio projects for Rosenberg's de Stijl exhibition. With the help of the young Bauhaus graduate, van Doesburg finally made the breakthrough to the formless, post-Cubist, coloristic architecture that he had sought through many years of work with other architects—principally Oud and briefly C. R. de Boer.[76] By applying pure colors to van Eesteren's axonometric of interlocking cubes, van Doesburg transformed the walls into abstract colored planes, making planarity a common denominator between architecture and painting (fig. 25).

As Yve-Alain Bois has observed, however, the goal of de Stijl was a combination of elementarization *and* integration. This was first achieved in painting by Mondrian, in canvases of 1920 in which figure and ground became indissoluble, in a single unified pictorial structure producing an oscillating perception of depth.[77] Distinguished from concepts of unity that relied on boundary, hierarchy, and centrality, this new unity was a spatio-optical effect of the interplay of figure and ground, planes and grids. A similar kind of unity was attained in van Doesburg's House for an Artist (1923), whose unity was conceived in terms of simultaneity. As Nancy Troy puts it, van Doesburg's "notion of coloristic

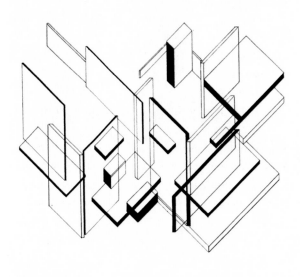

25. Theo van Doesburg. *Counter Construction*. 1923. Pencil and ink on transparency, 21 x 15" (53 x 38 cm). Published in *De Stijl* 6, nos. 6–7 (1924): 93. Nederlands Architectuurinstituut, Rotterdam

movement . . . was understood not simply as movement in space or movement through time, but as the fusion of these concepts in a far more abstract realm where color functions to reveal time as the fourth dimension of space."[78] For the historian and critic Sigfried Giedion, writing later in the 1930s, van Doesburg's Counter Constructions of 1923 inaugurated the paradigm of the "open construction" in which the building as a whole held together through the same connective logic or inner force that was evident in Analytical Cubism and photomontage. Unlike van Doesburg, however, Giedion suggested that in architecture, cognition of the whole was contingent on the movement of the observer around and through the ensemble of elements, amalgamating these perceptions into a single mental image. The unity of such a construct remained necessarily relative, indeterminate, and open to changing experiences.

For Richter, similarly, the aim of film was to organize the parts (rhythm and counterrhythm) synthetically so that the whole was indivisible, to construct a whole that was not a simple sum of spatial parts but produced a "new quality." This "time-unity" was understood to relate to space "as space-unity does to surface."[79] Here then was a new paradigm of a unity that was no longer formal, static, and bounded but contingent on time, motion, and perception. It demanded an interchange between subject and object—mediated by technology— in which the observer experienced and felt space as an expansion of perception and heightened awareness, charged with implications of transcendence and transfiguration. Gilles Deleuze considers Richter's "movement-image" exemplary of the German school of montage as distinguished from the American, French, and Soviet schools, and especially from the dialectical montage of Sergei Eisenstein, who sought "the qualitative leap which made the whole evolve." For the

attachments to the material, the organic, and the human, to detach itself from all the states of the past, and thus to discover the spiritual abstract Form of the future (Hans Richter's *Rhythms*)."[80]

The essays van Doesburg and Richter published in *De Stijl* in May 1923 were accompanied by two of Richter's compositions consisting of floating horizontal and vertical planes, similar to van Doesburg's Counter Constructions but shown in perspective rather than axonometric views (fig. 26). Titled *Filmmoment*, they bear strong affinities with the architectural experiments of Gerrit Rietveld and Vilmos Huszar, as well as with Lissitzky's Prouns, Péri's Space Constructions, and Moholy-Nagy's Glass Architecture, all of which had been published in previous issues of the journal (fig. 27).[81] These images by Richter point to the cinematic dimension of elementarist architecture, in de Stijl, in international constructivism, and by implication in the work of Mies. Like his films, Richter's architectural compositions suggest an immersive, fluid, and abstract spatiality in which the observer is suspended without gravity in an endless and timeless play of expansion and contraction, light contrasts and rhythmic movements. For Richter, the montage principle of film was regulated by rhythm, flow, and sequence, properties previously associated with music and dance.

With his theoretical projects for the Concrete Country House and the Brick Country House, Mies articulated his own version of the new spatial order in which interior and exterior were to be interwoven fluidly and dynamically, drawing aspects of Schinkel and Wright together with the experiments of the elementarist avant-garde. In relation to the constructs proposed by artists such as Lissitzky, Mies's experimental houses appear more architectural, while still manifesting an open, dynamic, rhythmic spatial unity. Although the Concrete Country House spins and floats like a Proun, it does so to a lesser degree, remaining bound to gravity and close to the ground. The Brick Country House does not float at all, but rather reconfigures the ground as the primary plane on which a new life is to unfold. Designed in keeping with the logic of their materials and methods of construction, these projects achieve their abstract quality through the geometrization of

26. Cover of *De Stijl* 6, no. 5 (May 1923), showing Hans Richter's *Filmmoment* (1923). Canadian Centre for Architecture, Montreal

27. Cover of *De Stijl* 5, no. 6 (1922), showing one of El Lissitzky's Prouns. Canadian Centre for Architecture, Montreal

HANS RICHTER   FILMMOMENT
87

EL LISSITSKY (MOSKAU)   PROUN'
81

Germans, on the other hand, Deleuze suggests that "the whole is on high, and is identical to the summit of a pyramid which, in rising up, constantly pushes down its base. The whole has become the truly infinite intensification which is extracted from all sensible their materials. Freestanding walls and interlocking volumes are treated as precise geometric figures suppressing the moldings, edgings, and frames of traditional construction. The color renderings of the Concrete Country House suggest that even these one-material projects would have been developed as abstract coloristic environments.[82]

At the same time, the dimensions and arrangements of the spaces, and the locations of fireplaces, entrances, and terraces, are all suggestive of how the buildings were to be lived in. As Mies once explained, he wanted to "open a new land," full of light and air, for a new way of living that would entail a greater exchange between inside and outside, organism and environment.[83] In an article on Mies in 1925, Richter explained that the floor plan of the Brick Country House was not a mathematical abstraction but a sensuously legible complex that brought the process of living into visibility.[84] A new world, society, humanity, intellect, and beauty were all to flow from this new sensuousness (*Sinnlichkeit*). Where other architects of the period were repeating old conventions but with new modernist facades, Mies, Richter held, represented a new type of master builder able to forge a new way of building commensurate with a new way of living.

Although Mies did not mention film in his writings or lectures, from his first meeting with Richter in 1921 he was exposed to a discourse in which film was treated as paradigmatic of the consciousness of the emerging age. In *G* nos. 5–6 (April 1926), for instance—the journal's last issue, dedicated to the "new landscape" of film[85]—Richter suggested that the younger generation was working toward a new optical and space-time consciousness that would constitute a strengthening of consciousness as such. From its first issue to its last, *G* promoted a rethinking of architecture in relation to new media, just as it promoted the analysis of media in terms of their inherent architecture. In 1925 Mies was involved in organizing a film matinee for the Novembergruppe and in securing funds for the first Berlin screening of Léger's film *Ballet mécanique* (1924).[86] He was still vice-president of the Werkbund when it mounted the *Film und Foto* exhibition in 1929. And he, like Richter, belonged to the Deutsche Liga für unabhängige Film

(German league for independent film), a group that lobbied for experimental cinema against the increasing popularity of Hollywood movies. In Mies's years in Chicago, he still owned a copy of the German edition of Bergson's *Evolution créatrice* (Creative evolution, 1911), which treats the cinematograph as paradigmatic of scientific attempts to model the fluid process of becoming through the exigency of capturing movement in a sequence of fixed images, or, more precisely, of denoting a fixed aspect of reality in an arrested form.[87] In *Nasci* Lissitzky likewise drew an analogy with photography to explain his theory of becoming, derived in large part from Francé: "Every form is the frozen instantaneous picture of a process. Thus a work is a stopping place on the road to becoming, not the fixed goal."[88]

The Glass Room that Mies designed with Lilly Reich for *Die Wohnung*, the Werkbund exhibition in Stuttgart in 1927, should properly be considered in sequence with the renowned experimental projects from 1921–24.[89] Like them, it explored the potential of a new material to realize a new building type with a new formal and structural paradigm. Among the display of building products and domestic fittings that occupied most of the main exhibition, the Glass Room demonstrated the potential not only of plate glass but of glass architecture as such. Arranged as a series of vaguely domestic tableaux experienced along a twisting path, it had walls made exclusively of freestanding glass sheets: clear, etched, mouse gray, and olive green. A ceiling of stretched fabric provided an even and shadowless light. And a floor in white, gray, and red linoleum articulated the otherwise flowing space into a pattern of rectangles recalling the colored versions of Richter's compositions.[90] Unlike de Stijl environments, however, the Glass Room used colors and other optical effects that were integral to the material rather than applied as surface treatments. At the same time, these materials were themselves of such minimal depth and material substance as to be almost pure surfaces, abstractions.

Of all Mies's projects, the Glass Room is the most readily interpreted in terms of a new optics bridging painting, photography, film, and architecture. The arrangement of glass screens is clearly indebted to

28. Jan Kamman. *Architecture.*
From László Moholy-Nagy, *Von
Material zu Architektur* (Passau:
Passavia Druckerei, 1929), p. 236

Richter's *Filmmoment* (1923), and to that film's
precursors in van Doesburg's transparent Counter
Constructions and Lissitzky's Prouns. The colors and
tones of the glass have affinities as well with the abstract
photograms of Man Ray, the light constructions of
Ludwig Hirschfeld-Mack, and the photograms and
transparent paintings of Moholy-Nagy. Although Richter
had prepared a color study for a film to be titled *Orchestration der Farben* (1923), his films *Rhythmus 21* and
Rhythmus 23 relied strictly on black and white, and
did not include planes perpendicular to one another.
Nevertheless, they suggest something of the receding,
advancing, and overlapping spatiality of the Glass Room.
Comparison with Moholy-Nagy's film *Light Play*
(1930) is also revealing, even though it dates from several years later: its swirling screen of hypnotic light
effects and reflections is the clearest expression of
Moholy's quest for a dynamic architecture of transparency, interpenetration, and space-creation
(*Raumgestaltung*), which he had pursued in various
media since 1922. As evident in his book *Von Material
zu Architektur* (1929), he thought of this work as the
nonsubstantial or virtual generation of spatial and volumetric configurations. The final image of that book is a
barely legible negative double exposure simply titled
Architecture (fig. 28).[91] The caption reads, "From two

superimposed photographs (negatives) emerges the
illusion of a spatial interpenetration, which only the
next generation will be able to experience as reality—
as glass architecture."[92] Clearly Moholy's project still
referred to Scheerbart, and implicitly extended the
immersive and transformative milieu of Taut's Glass
House of 1914 into the medium of film, which was
frequently being described as "light architecture" in
those years.[93]

Situated somewhere between Taut's Glass House
and Moholy's *Light Play*, the Glass Room differed from
these more idealist milieus by remaining a space of
dwelling. It was a site in the world of everyday life,
reformed into a new synthetic nature and raised to
the realm of art, culture, and spirit. This ethereal elementarist rendition of a domestic interior—at once
materialist *and* idealist—offered a piece of the future
into which the audience was invited to wander. Like
Surrealist photography and film—Léger's *Ballet
mécanique*, René Clair's *Entr'acte* (1924), Man Ray's
Emak Bakia (1926; fig. 29), Richter's *Rennsymphonie*
(1928; fig. 30)—its transparent walls of translucent
and tinted glass combined abstraction and realism,
estrangement and play. Its filtered and layered transparencies engendered a montagelike visuality in which
visitors became both actors and audience in a mobile
mise-en-scène—a continually shifting configuration of
people engaged in an ambiguous interplay with the
glass walls and sparse furnishings, and with the sculpture, an enigmatic torso, sealed in its vitreous courtyard.

By 1926, the techniques of photography and film—
superimposition, distortion, dissolution, cropping, and
rapid cutting—were being used to generate poetic
and Surrealistic effects. While critical of Surrealism's
tendency toward the mysterious, Benjamin later called
these effects profane illuminations, revelations of a
higher reality (a sur-reality) within the welter of everyday experience—in the industrial harbors, construction
sites, factories, and avenues of the metropolis.[94] As Tzara
pointed out in an essay that Benjamin translated for *G*
no. 3,[95] on Man Ray's folio of photograms *Champs déli-
cieux*, photography had made it possible to create
images entirely removed from naturalistic representation, belonging to a phantasmatic world of light and

shadow, in this case generated by placing objects on photographic paper and exposing them to light in the darkroom. But much of the new photography of the late 1920s produced similar abstractions by means of crops, close-ups, and angles of view, revealing abstraction within the surfaces of appearances. For Lissitzky, Moholy-Nagy, and others immersed in biocentric thought, abstraction came to figure the underlying order of creation, allowing an experience of the vital life force itself. Richter described the fluid movement between abstract and representational imagery in his *Filmstudie* of 1926 as dissolving the border between artistic and natural life, giving new content to things through association. "With the elements of association," he explained, "we have a language of images—the means of film poesy."[96]

In his book *Filmgegner von Heute, Filmfreunde von Morgen* (1929), Richter described how the medium of film could be used to produce a "film poesy" going beyond naturalistic representation to the creation of "hitherto unknown events." Film poesy, he explained, first turns to fantasy, for instance to the fantasy of a head detaching itself from its body, spinning around, and flying through the air. Multiplying eyeballs and profiles of heads could also create unfamiliar forms. In films without plots or realistic settings, a strong sense of rhythm was needed to create unity, to orchestrate the montage of scenes so as to orient the consciousness of the viewer. "In film poesy it is rhythm that provides the clear, memorable structure that becomes the content of the film."[97]

A key topic within the discourse of cultural renewal, "rhythm" must have become familiar to Mies before the war, perhaps during his courtship of his future wife, Ada Bruhn, in 1912–13, when she was enrolled in the Dalcroze school of eurythmics in Hellerau. Originally conceived to enhance the teaching of music, Jaques-Dalcroze's curriculum of rhythmic gymnastics was expanded at Hellerau into a program of educational reform for the "rhythmization" of human life in response to the cultural disruptions of modernization.[98] Later, in 1919, van Doesburg had explained how, for an artist, the experience of a body in motion (a cow or a Russian dancer) could be absorbed in a

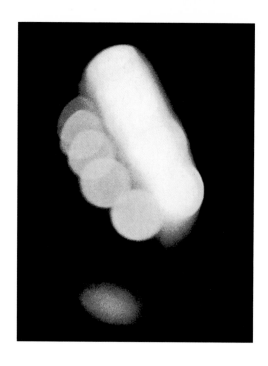

work of art only by raising movement from the physical to the abstract, transforming it into "rhythm."[99] For Richter, as we have seen, it was rhythm that provided structural unity in film. In *G* in 1926, the filmmaker Clair suggested that a rhythmic value could be discerned in every film, although the inner movement of most films remained impoverished and disjointed. Clair defined rhythm as "a sequence of events in time that call up an impression of certain relations in the mind of the viewer," and identified three factors that contributed to a film's specific rhythm: the duration of the image; changes of scene, or of motive for action; and the movement of objectively photographed things. He concluded by questioning the application of logic and regularity to the domain of images, associating cinematic rhythm, as others had, with the "wonderful barbarism" of the "endless Ur-world" or "nature," an "untouched land" beyond rule.[100] Discussing the question of a new subjectivity, Ebeling, a student of Moholy-Nagy's at the Bauhaus, began his book *Der Raum als Membran* (1926) by declaring, "The rhythmic human being breaks free of the chains of the past."[101]

While Mies later laughed at the fear of glass expressed by the sponsors of his German Pavilion in Barcelona,[102] he also cautioned against using glass

alone, being careful, he said in an interview of 1955, to combine it with other materials.[103] Having played with its reflective properties in the skyscrapers, explored its translucencies and colors in the Glass Room, promoted its "fairy tale effects"[104] for the Adam Department Store, and developed it into an urban tableau in the Alexanderplatz proposal, he now turned to a mixed and richer palette of materials. He even went so far as to use the oldest and most venerated substance in Western architecture, marble—in combination with synthetic materials, like glass and steel, and lush fabrics (a red velvet curtain, a black woolen carpet, white leather upholstery). Like the Glass Room, the German Pavilion should be included among his experiments with materials, although in this context it might more appropriately be called the Marble Pavilion, or even the Mixed-Media Pavilion.

In the Glass Room, walls, ceilings, and floors had become abstract surfaces. Stretched white fabric sheets, colored linoleum, and plate glass had been made into transparent, translucent, and tinted rectangles of color, as thin as a sheet or a strip of film. The German Pavilion by contrast reclaims flesh, staging a transformation of matter into spirit. As in the skyscraper projects, abstraction here is as much verb as noun. Everywhere the signs of fabrication are suppressed, so that matter itself can assume the appearance of its underlying form—sharp, precise, mathematical. Where the planes of the Glass Room lacked depth, in Barcelona the eye sinks into the walls and floors. The observer dwells in the hollow interior of matter. The travertine plinth provides a geometrized ground whose thickness is apparent not only from outside but from within, in two pools of water. The surfaces of these basins may be as taut and slick as a mirror, but they are the outer membranes of deep dark pools, whose uncertain depth and viscosity draw the viewer in. The travertine is naturally pockmarked and flecked with holes, allowing us to see, even feel, its substance. The pull is even stronger with the onyx wall, a honey-colored ocean enticing the eye to swim, get lost, dissolve.

Against their dark and variegated green ground, the white veins of the Tinos marble are mesmerizing, enveloping like the living walls of a garden frozen in a photograph—an image that threatens to come alive at any moment. Against the leaves of the trees that rustle above the wall, the stillness of the marble, the water, and the bronze figure create mystery. The pattern of the marble might also suggest a photographic enlargement of the skin of an animal, the weave of a fabric, or even the texture of cellular tissue. Its materiality is paradoxically immediate yet distanced; its tactility is mediated by vision, more precisely by the new optics of photography, film, microscopes, and telescopes. The haptic is subsumed into the optic, nature into culture.

In the German Pavilion, matter is both fixed and in motion, both calm and restless, caught in a tense state of vibration, a frozen moment of becoming. The substance of the building alternatively asserts itself and dissolves, liquefying to the touch of the eye. The cruciform chrome columns are palpable yet self-effacing. Like phantoms they materialize and evaporate in the play of reflections, making the observer do the same. Fragments of our mirror image flash by momentarily as we pass them—cropped slivers of ourselves, barely recognizable, distorted and multiplied by the curves, glimpses of ourselves that surprise and provoke.

In the Glass Room the eye could pass through every wall except the enclosing walls of the exhibition room itself. In effect, the observer could grasp the whole at once, simultaneously, even though to experience each space in turn enhanced understanding of the parts and their relationship in a unified organism. In Barcelona, however, the eye passes through only a few of the pavilion's internal walls, while others block vision and entice movement. But the eye also extends above the walls, beyond the interior, and also, where the enclosing walls are discontinuous or replaced by glass, beyond the building's podium. Mies creates a rich interplay of closed and open, interior and exterior, transparent and opaque. Without absolute boundaries, the experience of the pavilion has no clear beginning or end.

Stepping up onto the podium, one is removed from the surrounding city. Thrown back into it on leaving, one has been immersed in an extraordinary new beauty—a pocket of transcendent aesthetic experience, at once magical and existential. This is a space of solitude and self-reflection but also of connectivity. It offers no resistance yet slows the pace, to promote self-discovery not from within as much as in relation to the milieu. One's effortless glide through its interwoven complex of rooms, terraces, passages, and alcoves—rich and larger than life—sharpens the senses and expands the horizon of experience. Awareness is heightened to the point of expectancy. A space without hierarchy, center, or narrative, it is a labyrinth in which to search and discover, to wander and wonder and be struck with wonder. Both sacred and profane, this is a house of the gods that mortals can enter and experience— rich yet poor, full yet empty, austere yet magical, a space of transformation.

As in Richter's films, the elements and spaces assume coherence and unity through the rhythm with which they move the observer through and around them (fig. 31). Yet at the same time, something of van Doesburg's simultaneity also remains in effect— combining synchronic and diachronic conceptions of rhythm and unity. Reflections on the marble, glass, and water intensify the ambiguity between inside and out, up and down, reinforcing the cohesion of the whole by folding the parts onto themselves—establishing identity while precluding any stable image (fig. 32). If one looks along the dark glass wall that separates the sculpture court from the reception space inside, the court

appears doubled onto the interior, the dark pool outside mapping almost perfectly onto the black carpet inside. Georg Kolbe's *Dawn* can be seen reflected not only in the pool but in the walls behind it and in the glass panels in front of it. Again and again from different vantage points, the statue is multiplied and dislocated, a symbol and symptom of the ongoing fracturing and recombination of identity feared in Expressionism and then celebrated in Dada and Surrealism.

The pavilion engenders a kind of timeless perpetual motion, both physically and psychically. It places the observer in a state of suspended animation and reverie that is nonetheless marked by movement, and by a combination of self-estrangement and self-integration. For Bergson and later philosophers of life, it was precisely this combination that underpinned life's endless process of becoming. As Richter had suggested, the architects of Mies's generation found themselves in a transitional period of history and their work understood as the necessary architectural expression of transition—"a stopping place on the road to becoming,"[105] at once old and new, familiar and strange, a mutation and a catalyst.

In reading Bergson's *Evolution créatrice*, Mies paused at a discussion of the difference and discord in rhythm between the relentless mobility of life and the tendency of particular manifestations to lag behind. As Bergson expresses it,

Evolution in general would fain go on in a straight line; each special evolution is a kind of circle. Like eddies of dust raised by the wind as it passes, the living turn upon themselves, borne up by the great blast of life. They are therefore relatively stable, and counterfeit

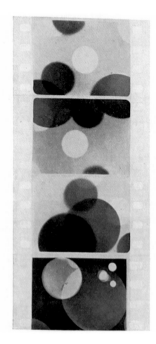

immobility so well that we treat each of them as a *thing* rather than as a *progress*, forgetting that the very permanence of their form is only the outline of a movement. At times, however, in a fleeting vision, the invisible breath that bears them is materialized before our eyes. We have this sudden illumination before certain forms of maternal love, so striking, and in most animals so touching, observable even in the solicitude of the plant for its seed.[106]

Mies's only mark in the book begins at this point in the text:

This love, in which some have seen the great mystery of life, may possibly deliver us life's secret. It shows us each generation leaning over the generation that shall follow. It allows us a glimpse of the fact that the living being is above all a thoroughfare, and that the essence of life is in the movement by which life is transmitted.

Mies's annotation and Bergson's thoughts on this dynamic continue with an image that is striking in relation to the German Pavilion considered as a living form—a rhythmic construction for the transition to a new world. Bergson explains,

Absorbed in the form it is about to take, [the species] falls into a partial sleep, in which it ignores almost all the rest of life; it fashions itself so as to take the greatest possible advantage of its immediate environment with the least possible trouble. Accordingly, the act by which life goes forward to the creation of a new form, and the act by which this form is shaped, are two different and often antagonistic movements. The first is continuous with the second, but cannot continue in it without being drawn aside from its direction, as would happen to a man leaping, if, in order to clear the obstacle, he had to turn his eyes from it and look at himself all the while.[107]

Mies's pavilion provided a setting for the active yet listless drama of becoming, offering its visitors not a blueprint for the future but a piece of it, proleptically achieved as a threshold and transformer. It reformulated the mission of glass architecture: to transform humanity by participating in its natural evolution, overcoming anthropomorphism and the problems of modernization in a new stage of development, a biocentric age of harmony and tranquillity. By the late 1920s, as Mies absorbed the theories of historical change proffered by Guardini and his architect colleague Rudolf Schwarz, these aims became conflated with the task of creating the conditions for spirit within a secular, materialist, and industrial society, a society of the masses, of mass production and mass media. While Richter made films like *Vormittagspuk* (Ghosts before breakfast) of 1928, in which cinematic techniques were exploited to make miracles and epiphanies a part of everyday life, Mies's pavilion staged a similar cinematic poesie in which visitors participated in a performance of self-estrangement and rediscovery on a higher plane of existence. They found themselves wandering effortlessly and aimlessly in a rich and dazzling milieu of *almost* pure abstraction—an immersive, labyrinthine environment in which matter had been formed into polished rectangles of varied colors, textures, and transparencies, and assembled into an open construct that was both finite and infinite. Suspended in a state between reality and delirium, liquefaction and crystallization, visitors experienced themselves and their world in a way that was both detached and connected, their identity now contingent on their multiple and fluid relationships to the context. While abstraction and alienation were understood to be problematic effects of instrumental rationality and industrial capitalism, here they were harnessed precisely to overcome these problems and usher in a new stage of modernity. In fusing the technological and the artistic means of the age, Mies produced a space for going beyond it, a space of expectancy and emergence.

Catching the Spirit: Mies's Early Work and the Impact of the "Prussian Style"

WOLF TEGETHOFF

German society in the 1890s and early 1900s, when Mies was growing up in Aachen, was far from homogeneous. All the higher ranks and professional positions in politics, public service, and the military were still the domain of the old aristocracy. Industry and capital may have ruled the market, but to rise to the nobility was generally aspired to as the highest step on the ladder of social prestige. Next came the prosperous middle classes, composed of successful entrepreneurs, executives, and academics, followed by the petit bourgeoisie or so-called *Kleinbürgertum*—independent craftsmen, shopkeepers, clerks, and lower civil servants. Mies's family—his father was a master stonemason, running his own small business—belonged to this latter group, which sought to distinguish itself strictly from the working classes at the bottom of the social scale, who were considered a permanent threat to the fragile stability of all late-nineteenth-century industrial societies. Social mobility based on either economic success or academic education had been increasing throughout the nineteenth century, but remained largely restricted to the middle classes.

Patriotism, a euphemistic word for what would today be called outright chauvinism, was considered a civic virtue in all European countries. In Germany, as a consequence of the Franco-Prussian War (which had ushered in national unification, in 1871), it was additionally seasoned by an irrational craze for the military. National self-definition took place in part as a counterreaction to Europe's rapidly growing economic integration, which seemed to jeopardize preestablished national identities. Even so, there was, at least in the upper social strata, a great deal of intellectual and cultural interchange among the different countries, making the modern movement of the turn of the century a truly European phenomenon.

Information on Mies's youth is sparse, and is based for the most part on what he himself chose to reveal in his later recollections. Aachen was the seat of a respected *Technische Hochschule* (technical institute) where architecture was taught, but a university career was out of reach for Mies, who never enjoyed a higher education. His family background gave him an early introduction to the building trade, where he received some basic training in draftsmanship and building as such, although he apparently never went through any final examinations.[1]

From 1901 to 1905 Mies was apprenticed to two architects in Aachen, while simultaneously attending evening classes at the municipal vocational school. Of his first employer only the family name Goebbels is known; the second one was Albert Schneider, who seems to have run a busy office around the turn of the century, and who, in around 1905, functioned as an associate of the Berlin architects Bossler and Knorr in the planning and construction of the Aachen branch of the Tietz department store.[2] While working on the project, and obviously inspired by the professionalism of his new colleagues from Berlin, Mies decided to leave Aachen for the bustling German capital. Acting on advice from an acquaintance at Bossler and Knorr, he found a job as a draftsman with a certain John Martens, head of the municipal building department in Rixdorf, then a booming and still independent city in the greater Berlin area. Rixdorf had just set about building a new town hall, designed by Reinhold Kiehl. The construction drawings and site supervision were to be handled by the municipal offices, which were therefore in need of additional staff.[3] When Mies boarded the train for Berlin, sometime in 1905, it was probably the first time he had left Aachen.

Karl Friedrich Schinkel. Orianda Palace Project, Crimea. 1838. General view: color lithograph, 23 x 32 11/16" (58 x 83 cm). Getty Research Institute

Mobility was an obvious symptom of the industrial age. In the nineteenth century, particularly in its closing decades, all of the major German cities experienced enormous population increases, principally caused by migration from rural areas and small towns. The young, the venturesome, and the ambitious were of course the first to take the risk; so there was nothing unusual about a talented nineteen-year-old turning his back on his hometown and moving to Berlin. Once Mies had exhausted the limited opportunities that Aachen had to offer him, the booming and intellectually challenging German capital must have seemed the place to go. By the turn of the century, too, Berlin had overtaken Munich as Germany's artistic center, and artists were moving there from other parts of the country. Among these—having changed their profession to architecture—were Bruno Paul and Peter Behrens, who had started their careers in Munich, as visual artists, before settling in Berlin. Both men were instrumental in shaping Mies's architectural talents, which had not yet found an outlet.

As an illustrator, Paul had been a partisan of Jugendstil, the German equivalent of Art Nouveau. As a designer of furniture and interior decorations he soon became a key figure in the diverse reform movements that animated the cultural debates of turn-of-the-century Germany.[4] His design for the German section at the St. Louis World's Fair of 1904 was enthusiastically received and won him an international reputation. In 1907 he became a founding member of the Deutscher Werkbund, a group that united the most progressive representatives of the arts and crafts and of architecture. That same year he was appointed director of the educational department of the Berlin Kunstgewerbemuseum (Museum of industrial and applied arts). Mies's work in Rixdorf was short-lived; soon after arriving in Berlin, he found employment in Paul's architectural office, work that brought with it the chance to attend occasional classes at the museum's art school. This was the first time he had come in personal contact with a leading figure of the modern movement. His employment can hardly have lasted much over a year, and affected him stylistically very little; almost no traces of Paul's influence can be detected in his later oeuvre. But he may well

have learned from Paul's mastery in the use and handling of materials, particularly wood.

It was while Mies worked for Paul that he received his first private commission, for a small family house in Neubabelsberg, on the outskirts of Potsdam, that Paul quite generously let his young trainee handle (fig. 1). The house was to be for Alois Riehl, a professor of philosophy at Berlin's Friedrich-Wilhelm university and a neo-Kantian thinker who was also an early and fervent partisan of Friedrich Nietzsche.[5] Though obviously impressed by the seriousness and ardor of his young architect, Riehl was somewhat reluctant at first to hand the project over to a newcomer in the field. It was therefore decided to send Mies on a tour of Italy at the client's expense, in order to broaden his scope.

In its overall appearance and restrained furnishing and decoration, the Riehl House is well in line with the so-called neo-Biedermeier style then fashionable in Germany and particularly in Berlin. Its most spectacular feature is a prominent retaining wall that terraces the upper part of the steeply sloping site and runs flush with the pillars of the loggia and the eastern gable of the building proper, for which it functions as a kind of podium. The plan, by contrast, is fairly conventional, the central hall adjoining a staircase being a rather common feature by then, although its simultaneous function as a dining room seems somewhat unusual. The general arrangement of the interior, with the main living rooms on the ground floor and the sleeping quarters upstairs, is also traditional. Kitchen and service rooms occupy the basement floor, but thanks to the eastern terrace wall, which they abut, they are well lit and enjoy an ample view of the lower garden. The house was published in two leading German periodicals and in the English-language *Studio Year-Book* of 1911, an extensive coverage that seems rather surprising for the first work of a young and unknown architect.[6] And yet, the qualities of the Riehl House notwithstanding, it is the hindsight of the historian that gives it a prominence in Mies's oeuvre—a prominence that he himself was later unwilling to concede.

In 1907, Mies had his first commission in his pocket and was thus firmly settled on the career of an architect. He must soon have discovered, though, that working

1. Mies in the garden of the Riehl House. c. 1915. The Museum of Modern Art, New York. Mies van der Rohe Archive. Gift of the architect

with an interior designer like Paul would hardly make up for his lack of professional training. Accordingly, sometime in 1908, he joined the office of Behrens, who had recently established himself firmly in Berlin as the chief designer for the electrical conglomerate Allgemeine Elektricitäts-Gesellschaft (AEG). This move must be considered the real turning point in Mies's early career. Whoever else supported his decision, Paul Thiersch, Paul's chief project manager, is said to have had a hand in it.[7] Clearly Mies was no longer a provincial lad trying to find a place for himself in the metropolis; he had already developed a keen notion of where architectural trends were heading.

Behrens had trained as a painter and illustrator, and had been among the select group of artists, architects, and artisans invited to join the Darmstadt artists' colony in 1899.[8] It was there that he made his debut in architecture, the house he built for himself in the colony being in fact the only one there not designed by Joseph Maria Olbrich, chief architect of the town's 1901 Mathildenhöhe exhibition grounds. After a brief interlude in Nuremberg, Behrens became director of the Kunstgewerbeschule (Arts and crafts school), Düsseldorf, in 1903, and artistic adviser of the AEG, Berlin, in 1907. At the AEG, which was then rapidly expanding toward market dominance, Behrens's position was that of an

industrial designer *avant la lettre*. The person responsible for what today would be called the company's corporate identity, he was also in charge of all its major building programs. During the widespread turn toward neoclassicism around 1910, Behrens advanced to a key position within the German architectural profession. His style was indebted to Karl Friedrich Schinkel and the early-nineteenth-century Prussian tradition (fig. 2), but it had genuinely progressive aspects nevertheless, adapting itself well to the new and increasingly sophisticated demands of an industrialized society.

It was at Behrens's office in Neubabelsberg that Mies first met Walter Gropius and perhaps also Charles-Édouard Jeanneret, later known as Le Corbusier. But this trio of future heroes of the modern movement apparently never came very close during these years. In an office swamped with new commissions, Mies and Gropius were assigned to different projects; Le Corbusier worked as a trainee with Behrens from November 1910 to April 1911, but both Gropius and Mies had left in the spring of 1910 (Gropius in March, Mies a month or two later). Mies returned to Behrens's employ in 1911,[9] but was immediately sent to Russia to supervise the construction of Behrens's German Embassy in St. Petersburg (fig. 3); so he and Le Corbusier at this point may barely have known each other.

No reliable documentary evidence survives to suggest what projects Mies worked on in Behrens's office, apart from the St. Petersburg embassy and the Kröller-Müller Villa Project. He supposedly designed the courtyard facade of the famous AEG Turbine Factory, Berlin, of 1908–9,[10] and according to local hearsay he also had a hand in the design of interiors and furniture for the Cuno and Schröder houses in Hagen (1908–10). He was certainly not involved in the Mannesmann Administration Building in Düsseldorf, nor in the Wiegand House in Berlin-Dahlem, both dating from 1911–12, when he was fully occupied in St. Petersburg. Upon his return from Russia Behrens set him to work on the Kröller-Müller Villa Project in Wassenaar, The Netherlands, which ultimately led to a serious quarrel between the two men and caused his final dismissal from the office.

For the period between early 1910 and early 1911, Mies briefly returned to Aachen, where he sought to establish himself as an independent architect.[11] Two projects came forth during that interlude, only one of which, the Perls House in Berlin-Zehlendorf (1911–12), was built, eventually bringing him back to the capital. The other project, more prestigious and daring in its overall conception, failed to materialize but nevertheless won Mies a succès d'estime, strengthening his self-confidence. In 1909, a nationwide competition for a monument to Otto von Bismarck, the "father" of German unification, had been announced. The site chosen was the Elisenhöhe, a hill above the town of Bingen, where the river Nahe meets the Rhine from the south. The deadline for the competition was set first as July 1, 1910, then extended to November 30 of the same year. The inauguration was to be on April 1, 1915, the 100th anniversary of Bismarck's birth, but the project turned to nothing long before that. The project that Mies turned in with his brother Ewald made it through four successive rounds of a selection process that reduced the 379 original submissions to twenty-six, but was finally cast out on the assumption that it would cost considerably more than the 1,800,000-mark limit.[12]

Participants in the competition were given a free hand as to how to position the monument on the Elisenhöhe. A good many commentators had objected

to the location on the grounds that a monument here would offer an ungainly sight from immediately below; Mies solved the problem with the help of an enormous substructure that pushed the main mass of the building beyond the edge of the lower cliff, giving it a prominence from the river bank that few other entries could match. The nature of this substructure is not altogether clear. A large colored presentation drawing giving the side elevation from the northwest suggests thin layers of rough-cut stone topped by a crisp frieze and cornice, and with a regularly spaced row of trimmed trees on the terrace above (plate 9). A photocollage, by contrast—a worm's-eye perspective of the (lost) plaster model from the east, ingeniously

3. Peter Behrens. German Embassy, St. Petersburg. 1912. Main entrance facade

combined with detail shots of the actual site—gives the impression of a monolithic bloc hewn from the natural rock of the cliff, which in turn is overgrown by wild vegetation (plate 12).

Crowning this substructure, the monument itself appears simple at first sight: a semicircular exedra flanked by massive pylons, which in turn are attached to a pair of long, lower parallel wings. Exedra and wings have square-cut openings at regular intervals, and these openings and the wall spaces between them are the same width, so as to resemble a continuous row of pillars with a kind of abstract entablature on top. In consequence, the basic composition of cylinder, cube, and horizontal block tends to transform into a tectonic post-and-lintel structure, the resulting unresolved ambivalence being no doubt intentional. The same ambivalence holds true for the general plan, which is symmetrical but would hardly have appeared so in the two principal views of the building that would have been obtained from up- and downriver. From each of these sides, one of the pylons would have functioned as a pivotal core, with the long low colonnade balancing the cylindrical mass of the exedra on the pylon's opposite side. Judging by the photocollage, the model seems to have been telling in this respect, with the colonnade virtually cutting into the pylon so as to underline its independent volumetric mass.

The main approach is from the southwest, and leads along the shoulder of the ridge, a central axis terminating in a gigantic statue of Bismarck in the exedra. This statue was probably to be the contribution of Mies's older brother Ewald. The sunken courtyard between the wings functions as a kind of agora, while the wings themselves are reminiscent of an antique stoa. The classical qualities of the project, and its spectacular position on a height overlooking the river valley beneath, strongly point to the inspiration of Schinkel. His grand concept for a royal palace on the Acropolis in Athens (1834), and, even more so, his ideal project for an imperial Russian summer residence at Orianda in the Crimea (1838), almost immediately come to mind (frontispiece).[13] In its basic volumetric disposition and the almost archaic handling of the wall openings, however, Mies's Bismarck Monument is essentially pre-Schinkelesque and therefore closer to the thinking of Friedrich Gilly, which Moeller van den Bruck—a German author very popular at the time—characterized as follows: "Gilly never was up for refinement, but searched for the spiritual. [The German word for 'spiritual,' *Vergeistigung*, strongly recalls key phrases in Mies's own later writings.] He no longer built upon columns and pilasters, but treated them as a rare accessory: out of intersecting planes he assembled a cubic universe, a four-dimensional universe, to be sure" (fig. 4).[14] Be that as it may,

4. Friedrich Gilly. Project for a Monument to Frederick the Great. 1797. Perspective view: ink and gouache on paper, 23 7/16 x 53 1/4" (59.6 x 135.2 cm). Staatliche Museen zu Berlin. Kupferstichkabinett. Sammlung der Zeichnungen und Druckgraphik (Schinkel-Archiv)

by around 1910, and no doubt through the mediation of his teacher Behrens, Mies had been strongly infected by the Prussian neoclassical tradition.

Mies's second project of this period was the Perls House in Berlin-Zehlendorf.[15] The client, Hugo Perls—an acquaintance of Riehl's—was a junior lawyer in the German foreign office but was soon to leave public service in order to become an art dealer in Berlin. The application for the building permit is dated September 1911, suggesting that the project did not take form until well after Mies's return to Berlin from Aachen (fig. 5).[16] Even then it was subject to major alterations, as an elevation drawing of October 6, 1911, clearly reveals (fig. 6).[17] Even more surprising, this drawing is signed "F. Goebbels, Arch[itect]." The name calls to mind the obscure Aachen architect for whom Mies had worked a decade or so earlier; the man in question, however, was most certainly Ferdinand Goebbels, another architect in Behrens's office. In any case there can be no question that the main author of the Perls House was Mies. While the planning of the project may already have been underway in the second half of 1910, the actual construction dates must run from the end of 1911 until well into 1912, when both Mies and Goebbels, the latter probably functioning as Mies's associate, were working for Behrens.

Whereas the drawing included in the building-permit application bears a certain resemblance to the Mosler House of 1924–26, it is the revision of October 6, 1911, that introduces some of the design's most striking features: the replacement of a steep hip roof with a relatively shallow one, and the insertion of a low parapet wall above the main cornice. Minor alterations affect the proportioning and general arrangement of the windows, particularly on the street front, where those on the upper floor are enlarged and given shutters. Another new feature is the austere string course above the ground-floor entry and windows, which organizes the otherwise plain stucco facade somewhat more symmetrically. A similar element tops the pillars of the loggia, giving it a tectonic quality reflecting its interior structure.

The interior plan is again unspectacular. It follows the conventional scheme of a single-family house of the

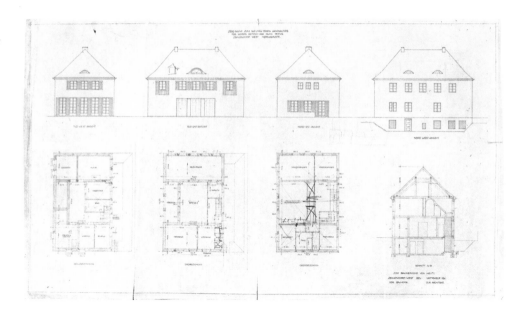

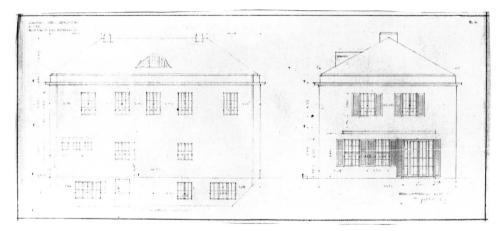

time, with its tripartite sequence of reception rooms on the ground floor, kitchen and service spaces in the basement, and bedrooms upstairs. The facades are basically symmetrical, although slight asymmetries are deliberately introduced wherever required by the interior layout. As with the Bismarck Monument, the building's essential quality lies in its volumetric massing. This massing is counterbalanced by the loggia, with its pillars and its interior post-and-lintel applications indicating a structural framework hidden beneath what pretends to be but a tightly stretched skin. The impact of Schinkel, as Fritz Neumeyer has shown, goes far beyond the iron railings of the French windows on the upper floor, almost a direct quote from the staircase of the Altes Museum in Berlin (1822–29). In addition, the

5. Ludwig Mies van der Rohe. Perls House, Berlin-Zehlendorf. 1911–12. Elevations, plans, and section: diazotype, 18½ x 32¼" (47 x 81.8 cm). The Museum of Modern Art, New York. Mies van der Rohe Archive. Gift of the architect

6. Ludwig Mies van der Rohe. Perls House, Berlin-Zehlendorf. 1911–12. Northwest and north-east elevations: diazotype, 12½ x 29" (31.9 x 73.4 cm). The Museum of Modern Art, New York. Mies van der Rohe Archive. Gift of the architect

concept of the inset loggia refers directly to Schinkel's Pavilion at Charlottenburg (1824; fig. 7), built as a private residence for the Prussian king; so do the elongated proportions of the windows with shutters, and the parapet wall above the projecting cornice.[18]

By the end of 1911, when construction of the house must already have been underway, Mies, whose engagement with the St. Petersburg Embassy had come to a close, was simultaneously working on another major Behrens project in Wassenaar, near The Hague. The clients were Helene Kröller-Müller, a wealthy German heiress, and her Dutch husband, A. G. Kröller, who ran a successful trading company in Rotterdam.[19] The Kröllers wished to build for themselves a sumptuous villa that would also contain an extensive gallery for their art collection. According to Helene Kröller-Müller's former secretary, Salomon van Deventer, the decision to go back to work for Behrens must have ripened in Mies while he was working on his Bismarck Monument proposal: in that very year of 1910 "he became aware of the greatness in Behrens, felt that he was the only one from whom he could learn as an architect."[20]

Behrens's project for the Kröller-Müller Villa, which is known from the illustrations in Fritz Hoeber's early monograph,[21] proposes an extensive, irregular, two-story ashlar structure in the neoclassical style (fig. 8). The main block, with its open portico between projecting wings, centers on a large pond with flanking garden parterres. The axis continues on the back of the house across an open courtyard into the adjoining wood (fig. 9). The entrance to the house, through a portal or porte cochere at the side of the left wing, leads to a flight of reception rooms. A semidetached one-story structure at the rear contains the dining room and pantry, which, unusually, are served from a kitchen on the upper floor of the adjoining wing. The central part of the house, which is slightly higher than the rest of the building, is reserved for the family's private living rooms. A separate lady's apartment occupies the adjoining right wing, and faces an intimate *giardino secreto* closed off toward the front by a greenhouse and surrounded on the other sides by the large sky-lit picture gallery and the family's sleeping quarters (fig. 10).

7. Karl Friedrich Schinkel. Pavilion in the park at Charlottenburg. 1824–25

8. Peter Behrens. Kröller-Müller Villa Project, Wassenaar. 1911. Perspective view. From Fritz Hoeber, *Peter Behrens* (Munich: Georg Müller und Eugen Rentsch, 1913), p. 202

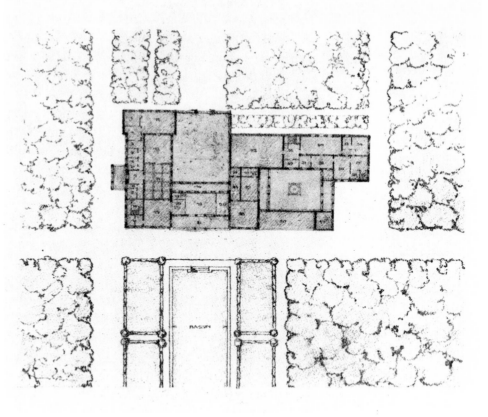

The plan no doubt has shortcomings, the complicated interior layout being in part the result of a heterogeneous program requiring that public, semipublic, and private spaces, in various stages of transgression of these roles, be housed in a single building. According to Hoeber, the clients had expressed a desire for the coziness of Dutch family life—a wish almost impossible to fulfill in an elaborate country house, large parts of which were to be used for entertaining guests at all kinds of formal occasions. Helene Kröller-Müller, enthusiastic but irresolute and susceptible to the opinions of others, could not make up her mind. So, on her husband's insistence, a one-to-one model of Behrens's project was built on the site sometime in the winter of 1911—probably the point where Mies came in, having been sent to The Hague by Behrens to supervise the construction. Once the wooden framework was up and covered with canvas walls, however, the client felt even more unsure, and Mies obviously shared her reservations: when the Kröllers suggested that he come

up with a proposal of his own, he accepted. By then at the latest the split with Behrens, which finally took place in January 1912, would have been inevitable.

For the next eight months Mies worked in The Hague, where an office was allotted to him at the Lange Voorhout, and where Helene Kröller-Müller visited him almost daily to discuss their plans. Despite his client's emphatic support, however, Mies had not yet secured the commission. On the recommendation of the art critic H. P. Bremmer—Helene Kröller-Müller's mentor since 1907, and, as her constant adviser, a substantial contributor to the formation of her famous van Gogh collection—the Dutch architect Hendrik Petrus Berlage was also invited to submit a proposal. Berlage, whose Amsterdam Bourse of 1897–1903 had won him an international reputation equal to that of Behrens (figs. 11, 12), was a major player in early-twentieth-century modern architecture and thus a mighty challenge for the twenty-six-year-old Mies, who, later on, always spoke of his work with great admiration. The date for turning in their respective projects was set for early September 1912. Although Mies must have been aware of the danger of losing, he could hardly have expected the devastating criticism his entry would face.

With the exception of a hand-colored blueprint—a perspective now in the Kröller-Müller Museum, Otterlo—only photographs of the drawings and model for Mies's project have survived. The design shows an elongated two-story core structure with symmetrically arranged French doors and windows that cut into the walls without any framing device. The central block interlocks with lower wings of different size and height, projecting at a right angle from either side. The larger one, to the right, is windowless on the outside,[22] so presumably houses the main art gallery, whereas the wing opposite, on the left, contains reception spaces and the large dining room toward the front.[23] The wings are connected by an L-shaped colonnade, demarcating an extensive courtyard or rose garden into which two canopied doorways open symmetrically from the main block of the house. A portico in the form of an open cube loosely attached to the farther edge of the left wing serves as the main entrance. The principal approach is thus from the rear, the other sides being blocked by a formal flower garden on the left, a huge rectangular pond—almost the size of the building—in front of the colonnade, and what appears to be a kind of kitchen garden between the gallery and a low annex that houses a winter garden or hothouse. The surface is ashlar, regular-sized blocks of cut stone. A slender cornice demarcates the roof line of the main block, and a friezelike course of much larger blocks or slabs crowns the lateral wings.

Mies's design is certainly indebted to Behrens's proposal, but emanates more tranquillity and repose. The compact cubic mass of Behrens's design is deeply recessed, even squeezed, into the surrounding woods, and so is the center block in relation to its lateral wings, leaving it barely room to breathe. Mies, on the other hand, chose a site immediately in front of the woods, and gave the main body of the building a dominant horizontal orientation parallel to the dense line of trees behind it, which thus were to serve as a backdrop for the architecture. The idea as such, however, must be credited to Helene Kröller-Müller herself, who had voiced her preference for such a placement as early as the summer of

11. Hendrik Petrus Berlage. Bourse, Amsterdam. 1897–1903. Exterior perspective from southwest: watercolor and india ink wash on paper, 47½ x 70¹⁵⁄₁₆" (120.7 x 180.2 cm). Delineator: H. J. M. Walenkamp, 1901. City of Amsterdam, Collection Beurs van Berlage

12. Hendrik Petrus Berlage. Bourse, Amsterdam. 1897–1903. Interior perspective: watercolor and india ink wash on paper, 35½ x 47⅜" (90.2 x 120.9 cm). Delineator: H. J. M. Walenkamp, 1901. City of Amsterdam, Collection Beurs van Berlage

1910.[24] She later said that she always liked to feel some sheltering prop behind her and an expanse of open space, preferably a simple meadow, in front of her: "Were it a painting, or were I able to paint, I would always put [the house] against some kind of a background."[25] Another deviation from the original Behrens scheme is the subordination of the lower, lateral wings to the main body of the house. Their shape and layout balance the strict symmetry of the house but nonetheless create some correspondence, which is underlined by the connecting colonnade and the formal setting of the large pond stretching in front of them. Furthermore, their staggered arrangement contravenes a frontal vista and invites a diagonal point of view instead, as is indeed implied by almost all of the perspective drawings and photographs.

Virtually all of the formal elements of Mies's proposal are derived from Behrens's stripped neoclassical repertoire, but the refined, seemingly effortless disposition of the cubic masses is more akin to Schinkel's stylistic handwriting. By 1912, Mies had learned the lessons of the earlier architect well, although without ever lapsing into the particular kind of verbatim adaptation that, in the previous century, had proven a dead end to architectural creativity. The use of a subtle play of irregular components to counterbalance a basically symmetrical architectural body must in any case be credited to Behrens. It is certainly found in the work of other contemporary architects as well, and particularly in that of Berlage, which Mies later held in so much higher esteem than he did Behrens's; yet he clearly didn't need the experience of the Amsterdam Bourse to get the message.

Great expectations came to nothing in virtually a moment. In September 1912, upon the presentation of Berlage's and Mies's proposals, Bremmer coined his vote for Berlage as a simple crushing sentence: "This is art—and this is not!"[26] Helene Kröller-Müller, more diffident and variable of opinion than ever, fell into a long depression. Mies—deeply irritated, and probably more to reassure himself than to advance his case—sought to procure the expert opinion of the German art critic Julius Meier-Graefe, who wrote him a long letter of support.[27] A. G. Kröller, always ready to cater to his wife's whims, decided in favor of another full-scale mockup,

which, like Behrens's earlier one, was put on rails so as to test alternative positions on the site.[28]

The leafless trees in the photograph (plate 26) suggest a time in winter, and therefore late in 1912 or early in 1913. By March of 1913 at the latest, Mies's project was definitively rejected. His ensuing letters to Helene Kröller-Müller speak openly of the disappointment and even shock that her decision, though not completely unexpected, had inflicted on him, but also show his respect and admiration for a client who had been generously prepared to grant him every possible chance.[29]

As an irony of history, Berlage's winning proposal was not to materialize either. Berlage did build a sumptuous hunting lodge for the Kröllers at their estate at Hoenderloo (1914–19), but the commission for the villa was finally passed to Henry van der Velde. His present Kröller-Müller Museum in Otterlo (1925–1938, without the later extension) began as a project for a temporary museum to house the Kröller-Müller's art collections, which were donated to the Dutch state in 1928, when the family company underwent some serious trouble.

————————

Back in Berlin by the end of 1912, his earlier hopes shattered, Mies took time to digest his disappointment. At least for a while, he seems to have set his mind on a typical middle-class life-style, accepting commissions that, in his later days, he rather preferred not to mention. He also soon got married, on April 10, 1913, to Ada Bruhn, whom he had met in the social circle of the Riehl family. The young couple took residence in the Berlin suburb of Lichterfelde, where three daughters were born to them, in 1914, 1915, and 1917; sometime during World War I they moved to a new, apparently more spacious flat at Am Karlsbad 24, in the center of Berlin. But although they never officially divorced, the marriage was not to last: around 1921, Ada Mies moved out, taking the children with her. From then until his emigration from Germany, in 1938, Mies led the life of a bachelor at Am Karlsbad 24, now largely turned into drafting rooms for his increasingly radical architectural practice (fig. 13).[30]

Before World War I, though, Mies's career focused on projects like the Werner House, a medium-sized

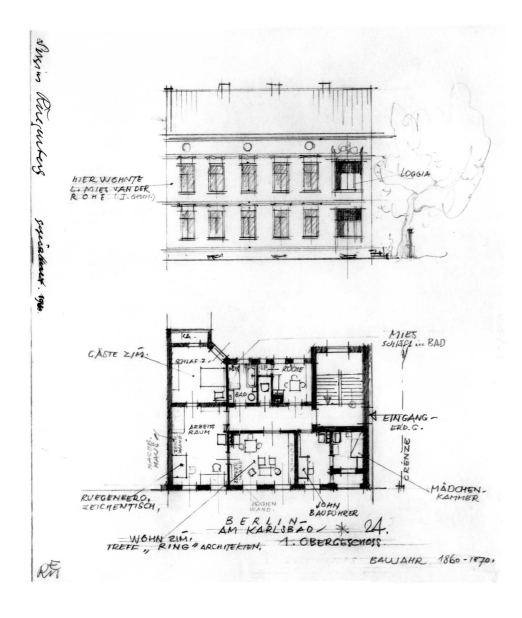

HIER WOHNTE
L. MIES VAN DER
ROHE (I.GESCH.)

LOGGIA

MIES
schläft im BAD

KÄ.
GÄSTE ZIM.
SCHLAF 2.
SP. ROHE
BAD
EINGANG
ERD.G.
ARBEITS
RAUM
NACHB.
HAUS
GRENZE
RUEGENBERG,
ZEICHENTISCH
ZEICHEN
WAND
JOHN
BAUFÜHRER
MÄDCHEN-
KAMMER
WOHN ZIM.
TREFF "RING" ARCHITEKTEN
BERLIN
AM KARLSBAD ✳ 24.
1. OBERGESCHOSS
BAUJAHR 1860-1870

13. Mies's home and office at Am Karlsbad 24, Berlin. Plan and elevation: graphite on tracing paper, 9 5/16 x 8 1/8" (23.7 x 20.6 cm). Delineator: Sergius Ruegenberg, c. 1960. VG Bild-Kunst, Bonn

temporarily abandoned his more ambitious ideas and was ready to comply with whatever a prospective client was looking for is hard to tell; it could have been Goebbels who was basically responsible for the overall design of the Werner House—a possibility that might explain why Mies never made any claims to its authorship.[32] In any case, the colored perspective drawing now in the Bauhaus-Archiv in Berlin shows no sign of his typical handwriting.

Following a familiar principle of the English country house but also a Prussian tradition going back to the eighteenth century, the upper floor, with its gabled dormer windows, is covered by a steep gambrel roof that gives the appearance of a one-story structure (fig. 14). The street front is unspectacular, and the projecting kitchen wing makes it slightly L-shaped. The garden facade is in contrast strictly symmetrical, and its central, two-story, projecting front section, with its rows of three French windows on each floor, bestows upon it a rather noble and decidedly neoclassical character. Attached to it at the right, and to be entered from the adjoining dining room, is a square-shaped porch or loggia, from which a pillared colonnade continues along one side of the property, then turns at a right angle to end in an open pavilion facing the main building. Between the pavilion and the house is a sunken rose garden, an arrangement much favored by Behrens and reappearing over and again in Mies's oeuvre until late in the 1920s. As a matter of fact, the whole layout of the Werner House is basically a blunt copy of Behrens's Wiegand House of 1911–12 (fig. 15). Mies had more or less left Behrens's office by then, but Goebbels was still an employee; these simple facts as such will hardly settle the question of authorship, but the closeness of the respective plans seems to provide a strong argument in favor of Goebbels. Mies must have been familiar with the Wiegand House, but was certainly not the man to borrow a preconceived scheme unchanged, as the Kröller-Müller affair shows. And by 1912–13 his attitude toward Behrens had become critical enough to guide him along his own lines of thought. In any case, whatever his share in the Werner House design may have been, it was one of

country villa that he and his former associate from the Perls House commission, Ferdinand Goebbels, had been asked to design for the engineer Ernst Werner.[31] The surviving application drawings are dated February 8, 1913, and the building was probably finished by the end of that year. The site in Berlin-Zehlendorf immediately adjoins the Perls property, which may help explain the client's choice of architects. Yet the Perls and Werner houses bear almost no resemblance to each other, the Werner House in fact being stylistically much closer to the earlier Riehl House. Whether, with the definitive failure of the Kröller-Müller project, Mies only two commissions he received before the outbreak of World War I, and thus a major source of income to provide for his family.[33]

On the eve of the war, after two decades of rapid growth, private building activity in Germany showed unmistakable signs of stagnation; under the wartime economy it virtually came to a halt. Between June 1915 and November 1917, however, the Berlin banker Franz Urbig constructed a sumptuous villa in Neubabelsberg, proving that there is always an exemption for big money, whatever the rules may be. The project also indicates that Mies was by and large spared the terrible atrocities of the Great War, which left millions of his generation dead and millions more permanently traumatized. He was drafted in October 1915, but served most of the following eighteen months in an office position at his regimental headquarters in Berlin, an assignment that, even interrupted by periods of illness and convalescence, apparently left him enough time to handle the Urbig commission. In the spring of 1917 he joined an engineering unit in Romania, but by then the military campaign in this part of the continent had already come to a standstill.[34]

The Urbig House design was finished in the rough by November 16, 1915, but construction was not completed until almost exactly two years later.[35] Once again the commission had come through the Riehl circle. Urbig was a director of the Deutsche Bank in Berlin, and he and his wife had become fond of the Riehl House and of the suburban district of Neubabelsberg, with its lake, the Griebnitzsee, which bordered the site of their future home. Mies's associate or more likely assistant on this prestigious project was a certain Werner von Walthausen, who according to his obituary worked for Heinrich Tessenow, Mies, German Bestelmeyer, and Behrens before establishing his own office in Berlin in the early 1920s.[36] A building permit was applied for on June 15, 1915. There is also some mention of a preliminary project, supposedly a one-story building with neoclassical features, of which, however, no visual documentation has survived.[37]

The Urbig House, which recently underwent some careful restoration,[38] presents itself as a rectangular two-story block with a hipped roof and dormers. Lower

annexes containing the service area and dining room wing project from the side and rear, but are barely visible from the front, which is strictly symmetrical and centered on an arched main entrance topped by a small balcony. The house seems to sit on a flat travertine base or plinth, but at its narrow ends the slope of the site reveals a basement floor that then extends into a kind of podium for a paved terrace overlooking the lake. The front facade is divided into seven shallow bays framed by a grand order of abstract pilasters without an entablature, so that they run straight up to the projecting cornice, making it clear that they have no structural meaning but serve purely as a decorative and rhythmic device. The order of pilasters does not continue on the other sides of the building, which have plain stucco walls with a suspicious notch at the corners, as if thin slabs were attached to some solid body beneath.[39] The travertine window frames thus gain additional prominence against the deep pink plasterwork, the present color of which supposedly conforms to the original rendering. The square-cut jambs and lintels of these frames are flush with the walls, but are set off from them by a deep groove or reveal and, above the ground-floor French windows, by inset panels with relief carvings of swags, seeming to confirm an independent tectonic character for the window elements.

Like the main facade, the interior layout of the house is quite formal. An ample vestibule opens through two freestanding columns into a transverse hallway that serves as the main circulation area for the reception rooms on the ground floor. Straight ahead is the salon or reception room, and to the left is the main staircase to the upper floor. At the far right end of the transverse hall, a door leads into the library or *Herren-zimmer*. The salon in turn connects by double doors to a lady's parlor or boudoir on the right and to the dining

15. Peter Behrens. Wiegand House, Berlin-Dahlem. 1911–12. View from garden, with entry court visible from the side. Published in *Innendekoration* 24 (1913)

room wing on the left, which ends in an arched loggia projecting to the front edge of the terrace. The dining room may also be entered directly from the staircase through a kind of anteroom, which is again separated from the main space by a set of flanking columns. Beyond the dining room is a pantry connected by a service elevator and a separate staircase to the kitchen and scullery in the basement. On the first floor, from

the upper landing of the main staircase another transverse hallway extends to a private living room, with the Schinkelesque motif of flanking columns here repeated a third time. The hallway gives access to the family bedrooms, except for the two guest bedrooms and the nurse's chamber, which are entered directly from the staircase landing. Each of the guest bedrooms opens onto a roof terrace, on top of the pantry and dining room annexes respectively.

Today most of the rooms retain their original woodwork, marble or parquet flooring, and stucco decoration, as well as some pieces of built-in furniture, now meticulously restored. In the main drawing room, Fritz Rumpf's decorative landscape paintings and overdoors are still in situ, and even the basement kitchen, with its inset landscape panels on tiles, is largely intact.[40] The neo-Empire character of the furnishing creates a noble ambience, but is rather traditional for its time, and more conservative than the exterior would lead one to expect.

The Urbig House is an eclectic mix of early Prussian neoclassicism spiced noticeably by the work of Schinkel, but it also includes modern elements that seem to anticipate Mies's mature work. Many features can be traced back to local precedents; recessed relief panels and a screenlike interpretation of the wall surface, for example, can be seen in the Marmorpalais in Potsdam (Karl von Gontard and Carl Gotthard Langhans, 1787–97), while the row of French windows giving access to the front lawn and garden terrace point to the possible prototype of Schloss Sanssouci, Potsdam (Georg Wenzeslaus von Knobelsdorff, 1745–47). Pilasters of a grand order without a proper entablature also occur in the local eighteenth-century vernacular, and the motif of flanking columns is of course directly derived from Schinkel. As for the features evoking Mies's projects of the later 1920s, one that recalls the Wolf House in particular is the formal terrace stretching in front of the main reception rooms (fig. 16). Flanked on one side by the projecting dining room wing, it encourages one to take a meandering approach to the garden by walking all the way through the dining room, then continuing on the terrace along the whole length of the building before finally reaching the broad flight of stairs that leads down to the garden proper.

and window framings is interesting in its way, but leads nowhere when considered from the point of structural clarity and honesty. Whatever the merits of its general arrangement and, in particular, of its approach to the key question of how to relate interior and exterior,[42] the Urbig House does little to suggest the major role that Mies was later to play in the history of modern architecture.

The collapse of the German empire and the proclamation of the Weimar Republic on November 9, 1918, initiated a phase of radical transformation in German society and its political institutions without, however,

Apart from its local references, the design also seems to make a subliminal one to the early work of Frank Lloyd Wright, which Mies knew quite well from the Wasmuth portfolio published in Berlin in 1910.[41] The flat plinth of the facade facing the street, for instance, strongly recalls the Winslow House of 1893, in River Forest, Illinois, where Wright too played on the contrast between a strictly symmetrical facade and a more freely arranged one (fig. 17). Similarities in the interiors of the Winslow and Urbig houses are less apparent, but a transverse hall or passage is a common element, and so is a bay window. (The Urbig House has one in the lady's parlor.) More interesting than these similarities as such, however, is the fact that it was one of Wright's earliest and most formal designs that caught Mies's attention, while the revolutionary character of his Prairie Style houses at this point passed unnoticed.

While the Urbig House clearly reveals the range of interest and curiosity that in one way or another influenced Mies's early work, it falls decidedly short of constituting a masterpiece of early-twentieth-century architecture—even when considered generously, given the prevailing circumstances of the war years. Though certainly a very convenient and comfortable house to live in, and no doubt of the highest architectural standard in detailing and execution, it remains an ingenious kind of pastiche, and lacks both the charming simplicity of the Perls House and the aesthetic consistency of the Kröller-Müller project. The formal treatment of the walls

bringing about a comparable change in the nation's overall mentality—which tended to remain conservative, antidemocratic, and submissive to public authority. The social hierarchies were still in place, but, like the old aristocracy, had been deprived of their former political function. At the same time, a vast majority of the lower middle classes, whose security had largely been based on personal savings and public bonds, fell victim to the hyperinflation that reached its peak in the fall of 1923 before being brought to a final halt by a reform of the currency. Outspoken supporters of the Weimar Republic consequently formed a rather fragile minority, and belief in social and cultural progress became the almost exclusive domain of a small intellectual elite. As a consequence of the devastating economic situation and the financial collapse of the middle classes (the main pillar of all real estate investment), the suspension of nearly all building activities during the Great War continued well into the early 1920s. Commissions for architects, especially young and unknown architects, were rare, while at the same time the demand for cheap rental housing was constantly increasing, and was becoming an important political issue.

Taking all this into account, the aims and objectives of the self-declared architectural avant-garde between 1919 and early 1922 may come as a surprise. Just by their choice of names, artists' associations such as the Berlin Arbeitsrat für Kunst (Workers' council for art) and the Novembergruppe (named for the revolutionary events of November 1918) suggested a political—i.e., left-wing—orientation, but the individual projects they proposed, and the topics they discussed, seem to tell a different story: the brief "Expressionist" phase in postwar German architecture indulged in romantic visions of cosmic harmonies, and in philanthropic concepts of a highly utopian nature. The pressing needs of a society and country in turmoil and even despair were ignored.[45]

So where was Mies? Where did he place himself in that context, with whom did he affiliate himself, and what were his personal ambitions and concerns? Documentary evidence for the early 1920s in the Mies van der Rohe Archive is rather marginal, and so is information on his early postwar oeuvre. For all we know, he was never a member of the Arbeitsrat, and he only joined the Novembergruppe in early 1922, long after it had lost its radical impetus and become a mere lobbying group promoting the local avant-garde. Before that year he seems to have made no public appearance at all, neither publishing anything nor participating in the debates that helped to shape the Berlin architectural scene. Nor did he exhibit any of his works, not, at least, after his attempt to show his Kröller-Müller project in the *Ausstellung für unbekannte Architekten* (Exhibition of unknown architects) in February 1919 was flatly denied by Walter Gropius.

By 1922, though, Mies had come a long way. The protégé and young friend of a distinguished professor of philosophy, the disciple of Germany's foremost prewar architect, the should-be-happy head of a family and husband of a woman from a respectable family, had climbed the ladder to success and social prestige. Riehl had introduced him to the intellectual world of literature and, still more important, to the higher strata of Berlin society and thus to many a future client; Behrens had made him see and understand Schinkel, and had taught him the secrets of a personal style suiting his Hanseatic *haut bourgeois* frame of mind; and his wife, Ada Bruhn, who came from a well-to-do middle-class background, had granted him a certain degree of financial security.

As an architect, too, and even though he lacked an official diploma, Mies was doing much better than the majority of the profession, who were fighting hard for the few jobs available at the time. His first postwar commission seems to have been the Eichstaedt House in Berlin-Nikolassee, a rather plain, cubical stucco building of two stories, stylistically in line with the Perls House but more modest in scale and interior layout. The completion of the Urbig House in 1917 brought further commissions from Urbig's acquaintances and banker colleagues: the Kempner House in Berlin-Charlottenburg (1921–22; destroyed in 1952), the Feldmann House in Berlin-Grunewald (1921–22; severely damaged during World War II, and later demolished), and the Mosler House in Potsdam-Neubabelsberg (fig. 18). All three of these follow the basic layout of the Urbig House, with a two-story rectangular central element crowned by a steep hip roof with dormer windows and flanked by lower annexes at the sides. In all of these houses except the Kempner House, the arrangement of the windows on the main facades is strictly symmetrical and centered on the entrance doors, but neoclassical detailing and ornamentation is significantly absent. The plain but carefully calculated brickwork of the Kempner and Mosler houses adds a new quality to the architectural surfaces (fig. 19); it may also suggest a distant link to Mies's projects of the second half of the 1920s, when brick or more precisely clinker became his favorite cladding material. Even so, the Wolf House of 1925–27 and the

Hermann Lange and Esters houses of 1927–30 are worlds apart from the slightly earlier Mosler House.

Mies's rise to spearhead the modern architectural movement took a longer time than Philip Johnson was willing to admit in his monograph of 1947, the first the architect authorized.[44] The mental turning point, however, can be dated quite precisely, and there are many signs to tell us that it reflected a deliberate effort on Mies's part to break with the past. In around 1921–22, he separated from his wife and family to devote himself fully to his professional work; at about the same time, he changed his name from Ludwig Mies to Ludwig Miës van der Rohe. He also became actively involved in professional organizations like the Novembergruppe, the prestigious Bund Deutscher Architekten (Association of German architects), and the Deutscher Werkbund, all of which provided an effective platform for his future career. Most important, he came forth with a couple of imaginary projects, too radical and utopian ever to be built; made sure they were shown and published in the right places; and even forced himself to declare his thoughts in a sequence of keynote statements, terse, salient, seemingly radical, yet vague enough to pass along as manifestos of a new spirit in architecture. The ensuing break almost completely obliterated Mies's early work, which he himself later held in rather low esteem when looking back on his own revolutionary achievement.

The question still to be asked is how far the grappling with Schinkel, and with the Prussian neoclassical tradition, set the course for Mies's mature work. Paul Westheim, writing in 1927 and consequently in full awareness of the architect's recent shift into modernism, considered him Schinkel's most talented and pristine disciple.[45] According to Westheim, Mies had left the neoclassical repertoire behind and proceeded beyond formal imitation to the very essence of Schinkel's work: the mastery of volume, proportion, rhythm, and formal harmony, and most important of all, the granting of priority to an interior arrangement imposed by the building's intended function. Abstract qualities like these, however, may of course be legitimately claimed for any great piece of architecture throughout history. Mies's early work clearly shows that Schinkel was far from his only point of reference and source of inspiration; he had also developed an interest in the local late Baroque, and in neoclassical traditions predating Schinkel, while at the same time remaining almost completely indifferent to the most advanced solutions in contemporary house planning.

Like everyone of his generation, Mies was deeply aware that the conditions of family life had undergone a radical change in the course of the preceding century, and that the increasing demand for privacy imposed new requirements on the general plan of a house. So when, with his Concrete Country House and Brick Country House projects of 1923 and 1924 respectively, Mies finally decided to abolish the traditional enfilade of rooms in favor of a continuous sequence of interior spaces, which he opened up to the garden and landscape outside, it was the more contemporary model of Wright's Prairie houses that came to the fore. His break with Schinkel and with his own neoclassical oeuvre could not have been more radical. Yet it is precisely here that the "spirit" of Schinkel makes itself felt more strongly than ever before: the various framing and screening elements for openings ingeniously devised to serve as visual demarcation lines between interior and exterior, the terraced buffer zones, and the indirect, meandering approach to the garden from inside the building are all, in one way or another, indebted to the great Prussian architect. For Mies really to understand Schinkel, and so to proceed beyond the level of mere formal imitation, however, he apparently needed the lesson of Wright, which took him over a decade to digest.

Plates

All architectural drawings and related images were the gift of the architect to the Mies van der Rohe Archive, The Museum of Modern Art, New York, unless otherwise identified or recently commissioned. Much research remains to be done on the drawings in the Archive; sketches and studies are usually in Mies's hand, but the delineators of other drawings are not always known. They are identified in the captions where they are known with certainty.

Photographs of built projects were also the gift of the architect to the Archive, unless otherwise identified or taken after the architect's death, in 1969. Medium and dimensions are provided for vintage photographs but not for later copies. Photographers are identified where they are known.

In the dimensions, height precedes width precedes depth.

Riehl House, Potsdam-Neubabelsberg, 1906–7

"The work is so faultless that no one would guess it is a young architect's first independent work," a critic remarked of the house that Mies, then aged twenty, had designed for Alois and Sofie Riehl in the smart Potsdam suburb of Neubabelsberg. Sometime in 1906, according to Mies's own later recollections, Sofie Riehl had visited the office of Bruno Paul and been referred to the young apprentice from Aachen. Within a matter of days, Mies was hired to design a small house on a prominent but difficult sloped site, with commanding views over the Griebnitz lake.

Mies planned a radical relandscaping and a house and garden very much in the neo-Biedermeier style. The property was divided into two unequal parts: a flat upper terrace shared by the rectilinear house and flower garden, and a lower sloped lawn cut out of a grove of trees. The house itself, in essence a retaining wall, formed the radical break between the two. What appears from the street as a modest one-and-a-half-story stucco building—with a hint of grandeur only in its illusionistic representation of a simple trabeated frame, cadenced by pilasters and entablatures cut into the stucco walls—reveals itself from the lower garden as a monumental porticoed temple set asymmetrically atop an expansive podium base. The base in fact nearly spans the site, underscoring the tight interweaving of house and garden.

The interior displays an allegiance to the German interest in the contemporary English Arts and Crafts–style country house and its organization of social spaces around a great living "*Halle*" or hall. But the abstraction of the gridded wall paneling in the hall, and the alcoves for dining and for Sofie Riehl's writing desk (separated only by a curtain from the main space), seem prophetic of Mies's later designs and open plans. The Riehls intended this weekend and summer house to serve as both a quiet retreat and a center for the entertaining of a large circle of intellectual and artistic friends. Both house and circle, of which Mies became very much a member, would come to be known as the Klösterli, or little cloister.

No drawings or correspondence survive from the house's original design, and the house was sold in the 1930s. Sometime shortly thereafter the loggia was glazed, and remained so during an otherwise thorough restoration of the house between 1998 and 2000. —*Barry Bergdoll*

1. Ground-floor and upper-garden plan. Delineator: Amanda Reeser, 2001. 1: parlor. 2: study. 3: living hall. 4: loggia.

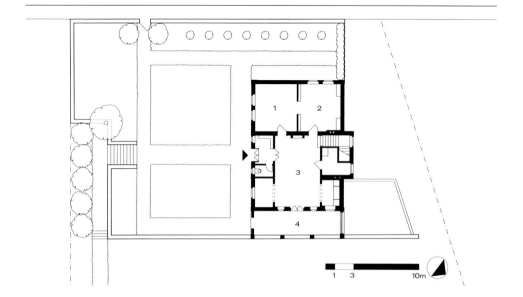

2. View of entrance facade. c. 1907

3. View of entrance facade from beyond garden stairs. Gelatin silver photograph, 11 13/16 x 17 11/16" (30 x 45 cm). Photograph: Kay Fingerle, 1999

4. View of living hall. c. 1907.

5. View of fireplace, living hall.
Chromogenic color photograph,
17 11/16 x 11 13/16" (45 x 30 cm).
Photograph: Kay Fingerle, 2000

6. View from lower garden.
c. 1907

7. View from lower garden.
Gelatin silver photograph,
15¼ x 19 11/16" (40 x 50 cm).
Photograph: Kay Fingerle, 1999

8. View of service area, rear
facade. Gelatin silver photograph,
11 13/16 x 17 11/16" (30 x 45 cm).
Photograph: Kay Fingerle, 1999

Bismarck Monument Project, Bingen, 1910

Plans for a monument to Otto von Bismarck, Germany's first chancellor, began to take shape in early 1907. The monument was to be unveiled on April 1, 1915, the centennial of Bismarck's birth, and the site finally chosen for the location was the Elisenhöhe, an impressive height rising over 400 feet above the banks of the Rhine at Bingen. The site resembled that of Leo von Klenze's imposing Walhalla (1830–42), a Bavarian Parthenon above the Danube near Regensburg. Bingen was also a symbolically significant location in its proximity to the long-disputed border with France.

A competition for the monument was announced in September 1909. Any German-speaking architect, artist, or sculptor could participate. Due to the extraordinary nature of the site, each entrant received a plan and five photographs of the Elisenhöhe, views that many would use either directly (in photocollages) or indirectly (as the bases for drawings) in developing the perspectives required. Entrants could also submit a model of the site, at 1:500 scale. The competition drew an enormous response: by the deadline of November 30, 1910, 379 entries had come in.

These models, paintings, drawings, and photocollages were assembled in sixty-four rooms of the Düsseldorf Kunstpalast, where the competition jury viewed them on January 23, 1911. First prize was awarded to German Bestelmeyer (architect) and Hermann Hahn (sculptor), but a debate between jurors ensued, and in December 1911 a second vote was taken, this time awarding the commission to Wilhelm Kreis. The outbreak of World War I postponed realization of the project.

The participants in the blind competition included not only many of the most prominent architects of the Wilhelmine period but also some of the most significant of the next generation, including Walter Gropius, the young Mies (then aged twenty-four), and Hans Poelzig. Mies's entry, a collaboration with his brother Ewald, was code-named "*Deutschlands Dank*" (Germany's gratitude), and was one of twenty-six designs singled out by the jurors for special merit. According to the competition catalogue, they found the Mies brothers' solution "both very simple and very impressive," but considered it financially untenable: "The indispensable terraced area alone would necessitate a significant excess over the cost allowances."

Mies's proposed structure, which was to be placed on a massive podium, comprised an unroofed court defined by two long parallel colonnades joined at the end overlooking the river by a semicircular section within which Ewald's statue of Bismarck was to be placed. The proposal fulfilled the Wilhelmine taste for heavy masonry and monumental design, at the same time that its simplicity of form and restrained ornamentation anticipated modern developments. A perspective view of the court shows a romanticized use of color and a bold axial symmetry that attest to Mies's early debt to the Prussian neoclassicist Karl Friedrich Schinkel, and the relationship between Mies's monumental structure and the dramatic setting exhibits similar affinities to Schinkel's unrealized Schloss Orianda project for the Crimea, a project with repeated echoes in Mies's later designs. Schinkel's influence on Mies at this time was undoubtedly filtered through the sober neoclassicism of Peter Behrens, Mies's intermittent employer since 1908.

Construction on a Bismarck monument on the Elisenhöhe did not begin until two decades after the competition was announced, in the politically altered climate of 1933.

—*Adrian Sudhalter*

9. Longitudinal elevation.
Pencil and colored pastel on
tracing paper, 39¾" x 7' 1½"
(99.5 x 214 cm)

10. View from below.
Collage of site and plaster
model. Location unknown

11. View of plaster model. Gelatin silver photograph, 1 ½ x 2 ½" (4 x 6.5 cm)

12. View from below. Collage: gelatin silver photograph, direct carbon photograph, and ink on illustration board, 30 x 40" (76.5 x 102 cm)

13 (opposite). Perspective view of courtyard. Gouache on linen, 55 ½" x 7' 10 ½" (140 x 240 cm). The Museum of Modern Art, New York. Mies van der Rohe Archive. Robert Beyer Purchase Fund, Edward Larrabee Barnes Purchase Fund, Marcel Breuer Purchase Fund, and Philip Johnson Purchase Fund

DEUTSCHLANDS DANK

Perls House, Berlin-Zehlendorf, 1911–12

Mies's second independent commission—a small villa for the lawyer and art collector Hugo Perls—moved away from the Prussian vernacular of the 1906–7 Riehl House and was the first of Mies's executed buildings to pay overt homage to Karl Friedrich Schinkel. This was true of both the overall form and such details as the distinctive wrought-iron window rails, which unmistakably paraphrase those used by Schinkel at the Altes Museum in Berlin.

A set of drawings for a building-permit application is dated September 14, 1911, and is signed "F. Goebbels"—most likely Ferdinand Goebbels, a colleague of Mies's in the office of Peter Behrens, and presumably his associate in the project. The drawings describe a house with a tall pitched roof and a pediment over the long garden facade to announce the inset loggia below. But the house built in 1911–12 is a two-story cubic volume of stuccoed brick (in an ocher color recalling Schinkel's Potsdam work) with a shallow hip roof and a quiet uninterrupted roofline. With the exception of an offset entry on the street elevation, the four facades are treated symmetrically. The entry leads into a small vestibule and then to the dining room, which opens level with the garden via an inset three-bay loggia, reminiscent of Schinkel's pavilion at Schloss Charlottenburg. A study, library, and music room complete the formal ground floor, with bedrooms on the first floor.

Although the vocabulary of the exterior is indebted to neoclassical precedent, Mies handles an austere classical language with a notable spirit of reduction and abstraction. The cornice is dropped below the roof edge, forming a suspended line that hovers just below the top of the wall. In a similarly abstract gesture, a molding of simple profile above the windows on the east, entrance facade pulls the windows and doors into a composition but stops short of the edges of the building. The walls of the dining loggia are scored to suggest the trabeated order of classical pilasters, with the hint of a fragmentary pilaster emerging from the inner corners of the recess, a detail that recalls the famous corner pilasters of Bramante's cloisters.

The Perls House was conceived at an interesting moment in Mies's early career. He had been working for Behrens, who was then designing a house for the archaeologist Theodor Wiegand. Though much grander than Perls's house, the Wiegand House was similarly a reinterpretation of Schinkel's Berlin residences and an exercise in an intimate geometric linking of house and garden design.

In 1928, Mies designed an addition to the house for a new client [see p. 228]. —*Amanda Reeser*

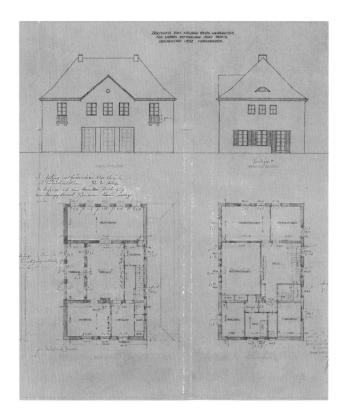

14. Elevations and floor plans (detail). Architectural print, 18½ x 30¾" (46 x 77 cm). Bezirksamt Zehlendorf von Berlin

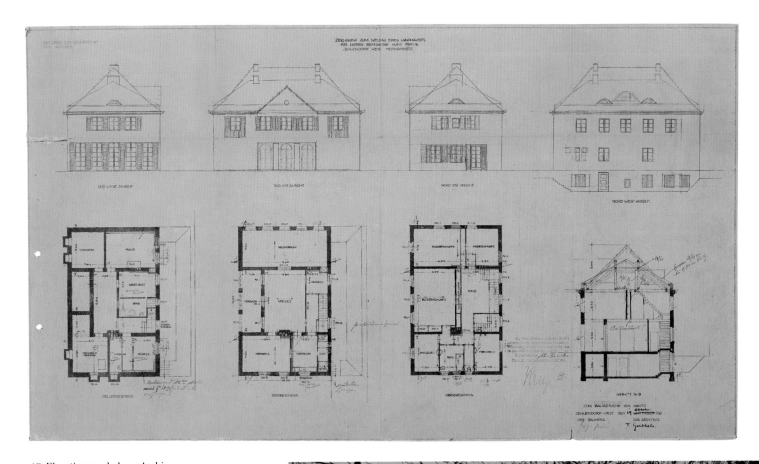

15. Elevations and plans. Architectural print with modifications, 18⅛ x 30⁵⁄₁₆" (77 x 46 cm). Bezirksamt Zehlendorf von Berlin

16. View of southeast facade. Chromogenic color photograph, 15¾ x 19¹¹⁄₁₆" (40 x 50 cm). Photograph: Kay Fingerle, 2000

17. Detail of ironwork. Gelatin
silver photograph, 17$\frac{11}{16}$ x 11$\frac{13}{16}$"
(45 x 30 cm). Photograph:
Kay Fingerle, 1999

18. View from dining room into
loggia. Gelatin silver photograph,
11$\frac{13}{16}$ x 17$\frac{11}{16}$" (30 x 45 cm).
Photograph: Kay Fingerle, 1999

19. View of loggia from east.
c. 1930

20 (below). View from south.
Gelatin silver photograph,
11 13⁄16 x 17 11⁄16" (30 x 45 cm).
Photograph: Kay Fingerle, 1999

21 (above). View from southwest, with, in the foreground,
the exedra at the Werner House.
Gelatin silver photograph,
19 11⁄16 x 15 3⁄4" (50 x 40 cm).
Photograph: Kay Fingerle, 2000

Kröller-Müller Villa Project, Wassenaar, 1912–13

The Kröller-Müller Villa is named after A. G. Kröller and his wife, Helene Kröller-Müller, who in 1912 commissioned Mies to design a house and art gallery on their estate, called Ellenwoude, in Wassenaar, The Netherlands. The house was never built, but is documented by a series of prints made after perspective drawings, by photographs of a plaster model and of a canvas mock-up, and by a sketch of the layout that Mies made some twenty years later.

Kröller was the director of a shipping and trading company; Kröller-Müller devoted her energy to establishing an impressive art collection. The house was to serve not only as a residence but as an appropriate place for Kröller to entertain his business connections and for Kröller-Müller to house her art. The couple intended to make their house a museum and to leave it to the Dutch nation.

Mies's version of the Kröller-Müller project was the third of four. The first design was done by the local architect L. J. Falkenburg, the second by the Berlin architect Peter Behrens, for whom Mies worked at the time. To get an impression of the house and of its relationship to its environment, the Kröllers had Behrens's design executed as a full-scale canvas mock-up at the intended site. They subsequently rejected it, passing the commission to the young Mies and simultaneously to H. P. Berlage, in effect making the two men competitors. Like Behrens's, Mies's design was executed as a full-scale canvas mock-up. Despite Helene Kröller-Müller's affection for it, and for Mies himself, it was Berlage's design that was accepted— but never built.

The arguments over the four designs are poorly documented. Presumably part of the problem was that the Kröller couple were in new territory: they were in the process of developing an awareness of the architectural qualities available to them, and wanted a clear departure from the bourgeois environment with which they were familiar. Remarks by relative outsiders, the art critics Julius Meier-Graefe and Fritz Stahl, hint at the arguments that may have puzzled them: Meier-Graefe admired the way Mies had managed to combine the living spaces with the art spaces, making the gallery not an isolated element but an essential part of the layout; he also praised the asymmetrical qualities of the plan. Stahl, on the

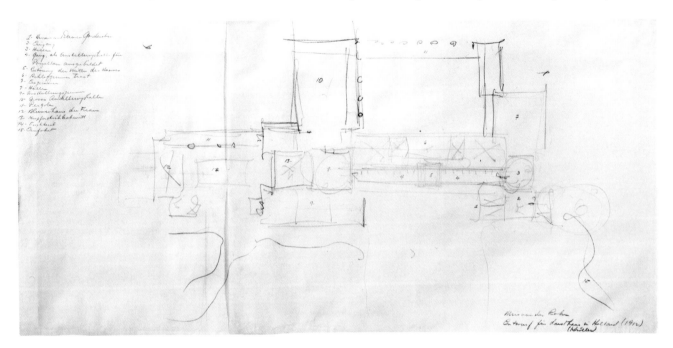

22. Sketch plan of ground floor. c. 1931. Pencil on tracing paper, 8⅜ x 17⅜" (21.3 x 44.7 cm). The Museum of Modern Art, New York. Mies van der Rohe Archive. Gift of the Estate of Howard B. Dearstyne

23. Perspective view from
garden, with pergola and large
gallery in foreground.
Pastel and watercolor on print,
17⅞ x 55¼" (45.4 x 141.5 cm).
Kröller-Müller Museum, Otterlo,
The Netherlands

other hand, disliked Mies's play with different architectural volumes, and proposed combining all functions under one roof.

Both Mies and Behrens produced designs for the surrounding park. Mies's model suggests that he considered the house and its surroundings as one unit; their dimensions clearly relate to each other. Both Mies and Behrens also placed an entrance on one of the short sides of the house instead of in the middle of the front facade. This is one of a number of elements that demonstrates the dependency of Mies's design on Behrens's preceding one, but it simultaneously shows his

departure from Behrens in that he made the entrance a portico, giving it a spatial volume of its own. He also introduced walls without windows, emphasizing the sculptural aspects of his design.

Although Mies's project was never built, he remained proud of the design, submitting the drawings to Walter Gropius's *Ausstellung für unbekannte Architekten* (Exhibition of unknown architects), in Berlin in 1919, and later donating them to the Kröller-Müller Museum, which was finally built in Otterlo by Henry van de Velde in the 1930s. —*Johannes van der Wolk*

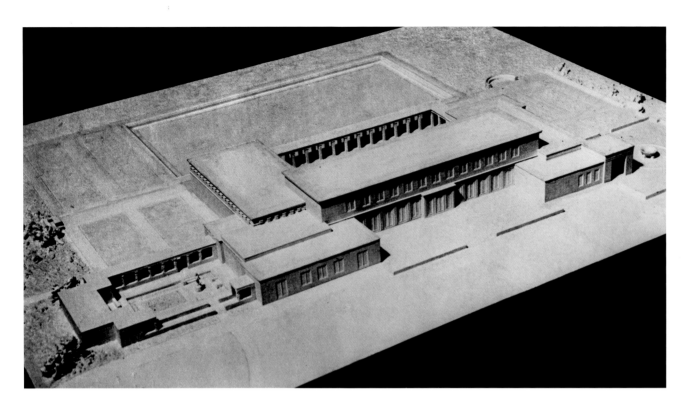

24. View of model, entrance
facade. c. 1913

25. View of model, garden
facades. c. 1913.

26. View of full-scale cloth-and-
board mockup, with pergola
and large gallery in foreground.
1912. Gelatin silver photograph,
8⅜ x 10⅜" (21.3 x 26.9 cm)

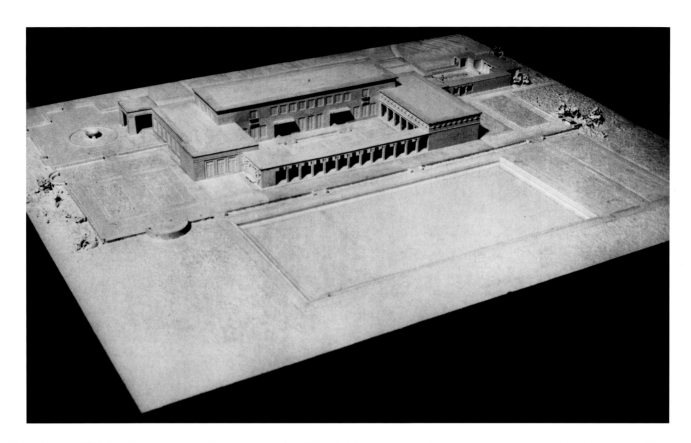

Werner House, Berlin-Zehlendorf, 1912–13

Ernst Werner was an engineer who acquired a narrow wooded plot in Zehlendorf in September of 1912, intending to build a country house there—a structure he imagined as following the restrained pattern of the late-eighteenth-century Prussian farmhouse. He invited two architects to submit preliminary designs, Friedrich Blume and Mies, and it was Mies (working with Ferdinand Goebbels, as he had on the Perls House) whose plan was adopted. The final design was ready by February of 1913; construction began in mid-March, and the family moved in on September 16, 1913.

In plan the house is a rectangle divided into two parallel rows of three rooms each, plus a kitchen wing protruding toward the street. A two-story projection with a triangular pediment dominates the elevation facing the garden. Outside this formal facade, a gambrel roof dominates the building, its tiles completely covering the second floor; only the ground floor is stuccoed. The detailing recalls local precedent. Mies also designed the interior woodwork and helped with furniture and decor.

The house is oriented toward the garden. Here the main feature is a square sunken flower bed, screened off by a roofed pergola with a garden house at the opposite end from the house. Mies designed this area to make house and garden together a single unit. (Later changes were made by the owners and the garden architect Hans Solbrig.) House and garden were restored in the early 1990s, and are now part of a school.

Traditional in many ways, the Werner House does not fit current interpretations of Mies's work. But it is the first project in which the architect conclusively shows himself able to combine a great variety of sources, especially those of local character, into a convincing whole. If the house looks historicist now, it was progressive in 1913, without, however, being "protomodern." —*Christian Wolsdorff*

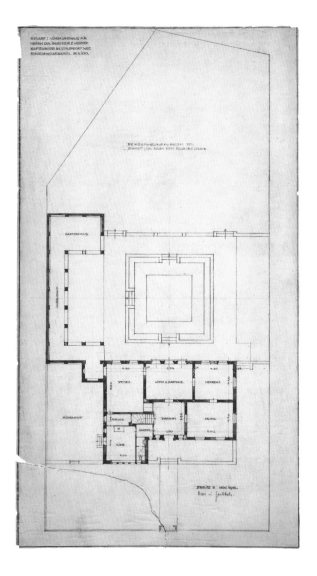

27. Ground-floor and garden plan. Pencil and watercolor on tracing paper, 25¼ x 14¼" (63.2 x 35.3 cm). Bauhaus-Archiv Berlin

28. Perspective view from street. Pencil and watercolor on tracing paper, 10¾ x 21¼" (27 x 54.2 cm). Bauhaus-Archiv Berlin

29. View of entrance facade. c. 1915. Gelatin silver photograph, 3½ x 5¾" (8.9 x 14 cm). Photograph: Thedor Born. Bauhaus-Archiv Berlin

30. View of living room. 1914. Gelatin silver photograph, 8¾ x 6¾" (21.9 x 17 cm). Photograph: Carl Rogge. Bauhaus-Archiv Berlin

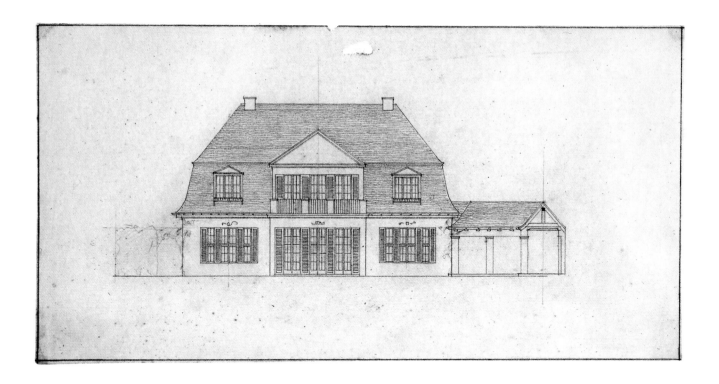

31. Garden elevation, preliminary design. Pencil and colored crayon on tracing paper, 12¼ x 28½" (20.1 x 39.1 cm). Bauhaus-Archiv Berlin

32. View of garden facade and pergola. Chromogenic color photograph, 11¹⁵⁄₁₆ x 17¹¹⁄₁₆" (30 x 45 cm). Photograph: Kay Fingerle, 2000

33. View of house and garden
from southwest. 1920–22. Gelatin
silver photograph, 3½ x 5¼" (9 x
14.1 cm). Bauhaus-Archiv Berlin

34. View of garden and pergola,
with Perls House beyond.
Chromogenic color photograph,
11¹³/₁₆ x 17¹¹/₁₆" (30 x 45 cm).
Photograph: Kay Fingerle, 2000

House for the Architect Project, Werder, 1914

Shortly after his marriage, in 1913, Mies bought a tract of land near Werder, a picturesque "island" town south of Potsdam on the Havel River. Two variant designs of 1914 for a house on this site are known only in bird's-eye perspective sketches published by Paul Westheim in *Das Kunstblatt* in 1927, in the first overall study of Mies's career. One variant calls for a two-story rectangular main block with an asymmetrically placed single-story wing set at right angles to form an entrance court, the other side of which is formed by dense planting. The other design features a symmetrical U-shaped scheme uniformly of two stories and thus creating a more formal entry court.

Mies's inclusion of sunken gardens and an orchardlike copse of trees in relationship to the house in both designs points to his early coupling of landscape and architectural design. The flat roofs of both designs are important formal links between Mies's early interest in Karl Friedrich Schinkel's Potsdam lake-land-villa ideal and Mies's later modernist practice. Schinkel's influence can also be felt in the dynamic asymmetrical relationship of the built masses to the garden's negative spaces. —*Katherine Howe*

35. Aerial perspective view (lost). Originally published in *Das Kunstblatt*, February 1927

36. Aerial perspective view
(lost). Originally published in
Das Kunstblatt, February 1927

Urbig House, Potsdam-Neubabelsberg, 1915–17

In 1915 Mies designed a house for the wealthy Berlin banker Franz Urbig and his wife, who were admirers of the nearby Riehl House. The last and by far the grandest of Mies's designs from before and during World War I, the Urbig House was not completed until 1917, by which time daily supervision of construction had been taken over by another architect, Werner von Walthausen, while Mies was in military service.

The two-story neoclassical villa stands at the crest of a sloping site leading down to the Griebnitzsee, the lake where Mies also designed a boathouse and advised on the layout of a garden. (The boathouse was demolished in 1961, when the Berlin Wall was built along one edge of the site). Mies conceived a house entered directly at ground level on the side of the formal entrance, while the rear facade, where the main reception rooms are, overlooks a raised terrace and then the garden and lake. The dining room is housed principally in a one-story wing set at a right angle to the main block of the house; it communicates directly with a covered arcaded loggia. All of the reception rooms enjoy access to the terrace.

The street facade is treated with greater formality, cadenced by large two-storied pilasters. The original contract drawing of June 15, 1915, called for fluted pilasters on all four facades with a paired order setting off the principal entrance, but the building as executed features plain pilasters equally spaced on the street facade alone. The pilaster order, in addition to abandoning classical fluting, is severely abstracted by the much reduced suggestion of an entablature and capital. At the ground, instead of resting on a solid base, each pilaster falls directly into a rectangular planting bed intended for vines, which were to be trained up the pilasters. Gradually, then, house and planting scheme would merge, much as the

interior layout was complemented by an elaborate series of raised and sunken terrace spaces on the exterior.

Another distinctive feature is a reveal inscribed in the rose-colored stucco finish around each of the windows, making them appear almost as sculptural solids set in a frame. The technique recalls Mies's interest in Karl Friedrich Schinkel, who suggested the volumes of pilasters by cutting recesses around them in the Altes Museum, Berlin. Carving away the pilaster not only accentuates the window frame but reveals the deceit of the apparently solid wall, thus indicating the origins of one of the most famous of Mies's later constructive details in one of his seemingly most conservative early commissions.

—*Amanda Reeser*

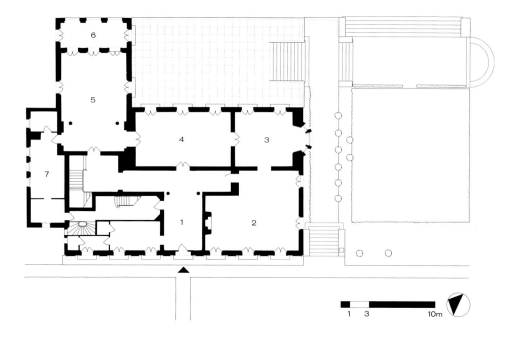

37. Ground-floor and garden plan. Delineator: Amanda Reeser, 2000. 1: entrance hall. 2: study (*Herrenzimmer*). 3: parlor (*Damenzimmer*). 4: reception room. 5: dining room. 6: loggia. 7: butler's pantry

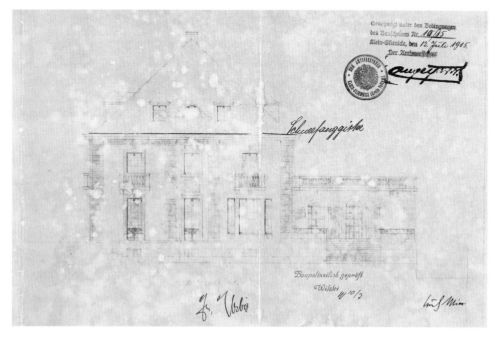

38 (above). View of entrance.
c. 1918. Collection Franz Urbig
Trust

39. View of entrance facade.
c. 1918. Collection Franz Urbig
Trust

40. South elevation. Architectural
print with notations, 10½ x 14"
(26.7 x 35.7 cm). Stadtverwaltung,
Potsdam

41 (above). View from Griebnitzsee. c. 1918. Collection Franz Urbig Trust

42 (left). View of terrace. c. 1918. Collection Franz Urbig Trust

43 (right). View of bathroom.
c. 1918. Collection Franz Urbig
Trust

44 (left). View from entrance hall
toward main stair. Gelatin silver
photograph, 15¾ x 19¹¹⁄₁₆"
(40 x 50 cm). Photograph:
Kay Fingerle, 1999

Friedrichstrasse Skyscraper Project, Berlin-Mitte, 1921

Mies's contribution to one of Germany's first skyscraper competitions, in 1921, secured him a central position among the architectural avant-garde. Nothing in his previous work had prepared for this breathtaking image of a shining cliff emerging triumphantly from the architecture of the past. Although a glass curtain wall had appeared as the facade of Bernhard Sehring's Tietz department store in Berlin (1900), and large expanses of glass were under construction at the Friedrichstrasse railway station, Mies's idea of sheathing an entire building in a glass skin was novel in Europe and would not become technically feasible for several decades. The triangular site lay on Berlin's central north-south axis, in the heart of the commercial and entertainment district and facing the Friedrichstrasse station, the main gateway for visitors to the German capital.

The aesthetic power of Mies's design stands in polemical contrast to his matter-of-fact explanation: "The building site was triangular; I tried to make full use of it. The depth of the site compelled me to split the fronts, so that the inner core received light." In fact the approach Mies chose—a star-shaped plan with three arms stretching into the site's corners—appeared frequently in other entries to the competition. By widening these arms or wings almost to cover the plot, however, Mies tried to secure maximum square footage, while high ceilings, transparent exterior walls, and courtyards would maximize natural light. By stacking twenty floors up to the suggested height of eighty meters (c. 262 feet), he provided 70,000 square meters (over 753,000 square feet) of floor space—almost twice the area provided by any other entrant's design. The competition brief had called for commercial and circulatory spaces on the first floor; Mies's design offered nine large stores and a system of passages between them, accessible by three major and six minor entrances.

Although Mies professed to be "overwhelmed" by the skeletal frames of contemporary skyscrapers under construction, and marveled at the way glass revealed them, his drawings suggest an anticipation that the structure of the Friedrichstrasse Skyscraper would be concealed by the reflectiveness of its glass walls. In any case, he neither showed nor specified the construction method he intended. His code word for his entry, "*Wabe*" (honeycomb), was perhaps a reference to Louis Sullivan's use of the term in the essay "The Tall Office Building Artistically Considered," of 1896.

A smaller, more conservative design won the competition, and nothing was ever built. But Mies continued working on the scheme, exhibiting a perspective drawing at the *Grosse Berliner Kunstausstellung* (Great Berlin art exhibition) in 1922. His project was soon recognized as an important contribution to an expanding architectural debate. After the disaster of World War I, Germany was gripped by a veritable skyscraper fever; thousands of unbuilt projects were put forth, some influenced by visions of glass cathedrals in recent Expressionist art, others intended as monumental symbols of a conservative national rebirth. While Mies's design certainly displays the influence of expressionistic ideas and its own brand of monumentalism, it transgresses these references by defining the building through transparency and reflection—ultimately negating traditional architectural form as such, and foreshadowing the most radical developments of the future.

—Dietrich Neumann

45. Perspective view from north.
Photomontage, 55⅛ x 39⅜"
(140 x 100 cm). Bauhaus-Archiv
Berlin

46. Perspective view from north. Charcoal and pencil on tracing paper mounted on board, 68¼ x 48" (173.5 x 122 cm)

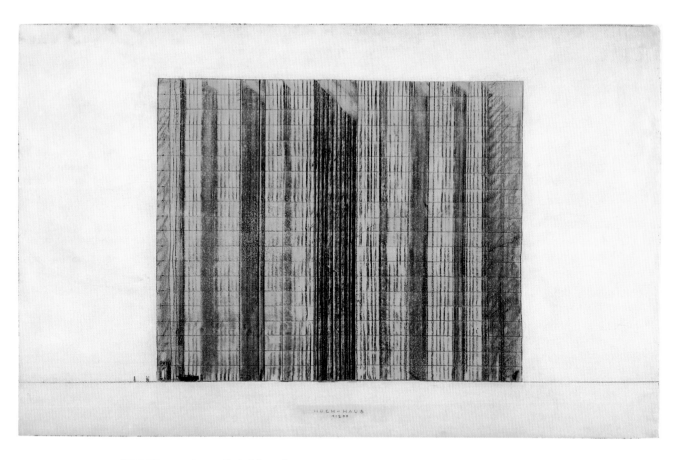

47 (right). Elevation study.
Charcoal and graphite on tracing
paper mounted on board, 21¾ x
34½" (55.3 x 87.5 cm). The
Museum of Modern Art. Mies
van der Rohe Archive. Gift of
Mary Callery

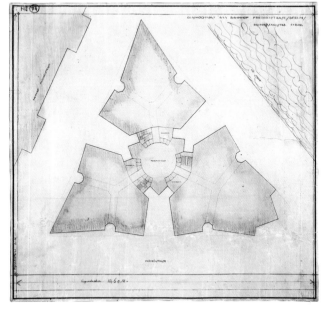

48 (left). Typical floor plan.
Vandyke print with pencil, 23½ x
25¼" (60 x 64 cm)

Eichstaedt House, Berlin-Nikolassee, 1921–23

Mies's Schinkelesque design for a house for the Berlin bookseller Georg Eichstaedt and his family was completed in 1923. The house was one of the architect's first commissions after World War I, and its construction reflected Germany's growing economic stability after the chaos of the immediate postwar years.

The two-story structure sits on a relatively small corner plot among other houses of similar scale and social ambition just off the main road from Berlin to Potsdam in the suburb of Nikolassee, where Hermann Muthesius had built a number of houses. The house is sited toward the edge of the plot, but perimeter hedges and a fence screen it and its gardens from the picturesquely named streets to the south and east—Tristan- and Isoldestrasse respectively. It is placed to create a series of outdoor spaces, defined by a pergola, the hedges, and the facades of the house itself. This *Architectonischegarten* once included a vegetable garden, a flower garden, a yard, and an entrance allée.

Indoors, the spaces of Mies's proposed design flow from the entrance through a foyer and an entry hall to a south-facing main living and dining room, designed to take full advantage of the attendant outdoor spaces. Running the width of the house, this main room is connected by three French doors to a terrace along its length. At its eastern end it terminates in an apselike space, with a grand piano, that projects into the flower garden; a single-story garden pavilion to the west, open on all four sides, balances this eastern projection, being joined to the main block of the house by intersecting corners. Like Mies's House for the Architect Project of 1914, this unusual example of architectural massing derives from the work of Karl Friedrich Schinkel.

If the overall plan of the house reflects Mies's ongoing interest in the English garden house, the low profile, stuccoed cubic mass, and detailing recall the Perls House of 1911–12, which also owes a debt to Schinkel. Subsequent alterations to the entrance, the garden pavilion, and the interior layout have greatly changed its appearance. —*Terence Riley*

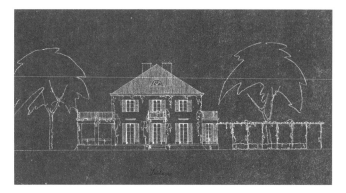

49. Garden elevation. Blueprint, 9¼ x 17" (23 x 42.5 cm). Bauhaus-Archiv Berlin

50. Ground-floor plan (detail). Blueprint, 7¼ x 14½" (26.2 x 36.4 cm). Bauhaus-Archiv Berlin

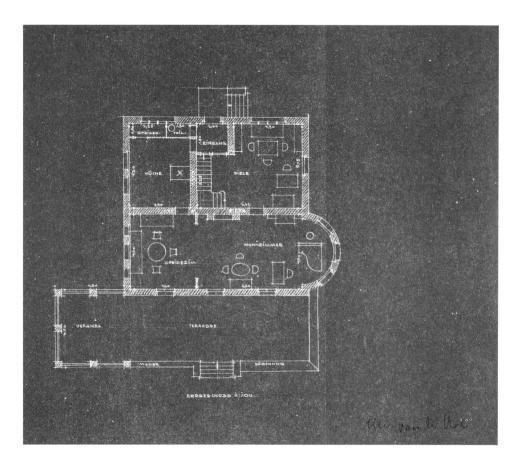

54 (below). View from dining
room toward living room. c. 1925.
Gelatin silver photograph, 7¼ x
5¼" (18 x 12.8 cm). Bauhaus-
Archiv Berlin

51 (top). View from east, with
Georg Eichstaedt and daughter.
c. 1925. Gelatin silver photograph, 5¼ x 7¼" (12.8 x 18 cm).
Bauhaus-Archiv Berlin

52 and 53 (center and bottom).
Views of garden facade. c. 1925.
Gelatin silver photographs, 5¼ x
7¼" (12.8 x 18 cm). Bauhaus-
Archiv Berlin

Glass Skyscraper Project, no intended site known, 1922

The Glass Skyscraper Project carried Mies's Friedrichstrasse Skyscraper competition entry of 1921 into new aesthetic and structural territory. Photographs of a model show a slender tower whose glass curtain walls describe soft meandering curves. In various collage photographs the skyscraper appears alternatively quite transparent and strikingly reflective. The plan shows open offices, a central hall, two circular staircases, and nine elevators, as well as restroom facilities and a doorman's office. Mies described how he had continued to work here with the key elements of the earlier design: "I placed the glass walls at slight angles to each other to avoid the monotony of overlarge glass surfaces. I discovered by working with actual glass models that the important thing is the play of reflections, not the effect of light and shadow as in ordinary buildings. . . . At first glance the curved outline of the plan seems arbitrary. These curves, however, were determined by three factors: sufficient illumination of the interior, the massing of the building viewed from the street, and lastly the play of reflections."

To ensure interior light, Mies minimized the size of the floors. To compensate for this lost space, he increased the height of the building to thirty stories (a twenty-one-story version also exists). While he did not specify the construction method, friends and contemporaries (Mart Stam, Bruno Taut, Ludwig Hilberseimer, and Heinz and Bodo Rasch) identified the design as an experiment with so-called "concrete mushroom columns." This new construction method had recently been presented in a German architecture magazine as providing "better distribution of light and air" and allowing easier application and reuse of the wooden forms typically used in reinforced-concrete construction. Instead of setting ceiling beams across individual supports, here the architect uses central posts with a capital to carry all loads beneath a continuously flat ceiling. A circular plate being the ideal shape for such a support, Mies's design implies a cluster of mushroom structures of different perimeters (which, in reality, would have been enormously difficult to execute). The columns in the model are placed roughly in the centers of the circular sections that might have informed the plan.

Mies's emphasis on lighting conditions and viewpoints suggests that he had a location in mind, but both the site plan and the surrounding buildings in the model are inconclusive. One photomontage of uncertain origin places the project on the site of the Friedrichstrasse Skyscraper.

An alternative floor plan shows an attempt at a different internal layout and structural solution, possibly in both steel and reinforced concrete. Here ceiling beams connect a grid of fifty-two columns, whose shadows Mies carefully traced in a separate sketch. This floor plan avoids the first version's rather arbitrarily shaped lobby, unconvincing placement of elevators, and circular staircases, which the German building code in fact prohibited at the time. Instead, a round lobby with eleven elevators, two straight emergency staircases, and a third street entry adopts central ideas of the Friedrichstrasse Skyscraper design.

American critics who saw the design in 1923 were amazed: "The plan . . . is so fantastic and impractical and so impossible to divide into any kind of usable or desirable offices or apartments that it is not likely that it would ever be executed," wrote one, while another described it as "a picture of a nude building falling down stairs," referring to Marcel Duchamp's famous painting of 1912. —*Dietrich Neumann*

55. View of model. Airbrushed
gouache on gelatin silver photograph, 7⅜ x 5⅛" (18.8 x 13.7 cm).
Private collection, New York

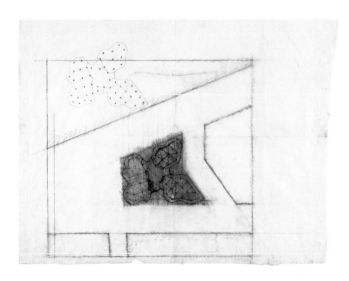

56. Site plan with structural studies. Pencil and chàrcoal on tracing paper, 30½ x 37¾" (77.4 x 95.8 cm)

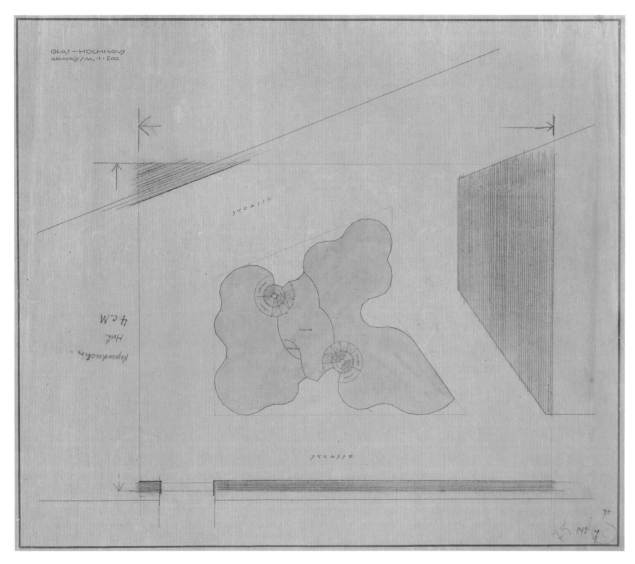

57. Typical floor plan. Vandyke print with watercolor, pencil, and wax pencil, 21 x 24½" (53.1 x 62.2 cm).

58. Reflection study. c. 1922.
Gelatin silver photograph, 4 x 3⅛"
(10.3 x 8 cm)

59. Elevation study. Charcoal,
Conté crayon, and pencil on
paper mounted on board,
54½ x 32¾" (138.5 x 83.2 cm).
The Museum of Modern Art.
Mies van der Rohe Archive.
Gift of George Danforth

Concrete Country House Project, no intended site known, 1923

Mies first exhibited this project at the *Grosse Berliner Kunstausstellung* in 1923, along with the Concrete Office Building Project. He had probably designed the house shortly before, perhaps for himself, for a site he had acquired in Potsdam. Two photographs survive of a model, along with two large-scale black-and-white and two pastel perspectives. They show a one- and two-story building with wings extending in four directions, partly surrounding a raised courtyard. The house's most striking features are its essentially flat roof, untreated concrete surfaces, and long ribbon windows. A projecting canopy protects a grand entrance, a second the southern terrace of the enormous living room. All of these elements made the design distinctly different from any other German residence of the time.

In September 1923, Mies explained in a short text accompanying a photograph of the model in the magazine *G* that he had hoped to save material by concentrating the load-bearing elements on a few points in the structure: "The main living area is supported by a four-post truss system. This structural system is enclosed in a thin skin of reinforced concrete, comprising both walls and roof. The roof slopes downward slightly from the exterior walls toward the center. . . . I have cut openings in the walls wherever I required them for outside vistas and illumination of spaces." As the model photograph shows, Mies carefully combined and calibrated the slight roof inclinations in order to connect drains and load-bearing posts. By

moving the support system inside, he hoped to gain maximum flexibility in both the internal layout and the design of the facades. Mies lacked experience with concrete, and his understanding of its qualities was still rudimentary; his intended structural unity of wall and roof would have been problematic. Nevertheless, the ribbon windows he proposed here—earlier than anyone else—became a trademark of the emerging architectural style. Similarly, the pinwheel motif of building components protruding in different directions—perhaps inspired by some of Frank Lloyd Wright's residential designs—was soon a frequently adopted compositional principle of the modern movement. —*Dietrich Neumann*

60. Perspective view of garden facade. Colored pastel and pencil on paper, 33¾" x 7'6" (85.8 x 228.5 cm)

61. View of model (lost), garden facade. c. 1923

62. View of model (lost), entrance facade

63. Perspective view of garden facade. Colored pastel and pencil on paper, 28½" x 7'2½" (72.3 x 219.3 cm)

Concrete Office Building Project, no intended site known, 1923

Only Mies's perspective drawing, a small sketch in a letter, and a photograph of a model (p. 120, fig. 17) have survived of this project, which was shown for the first time in the *Grosse Berliner Kunstausstellung* of 1923. Its radical horizontality and the openness of its wide interior spaces were unprecedented.

When Mies published the design in the magazine *G* in July 1923, he laconically presented it as the mere result of rational calculation, remarking that in each five-meter-wide bay a sixteen-meter-long (c. 52 1/2 feet) ceiling beam extends four meters (c. 13 feet) on each side beyond two supporting pillars eight meters apart. "This system carries the floor slab, which turns upward at its edges to become the outer skin and the wall behind the shelves, which are removed from the interior of the room and placed at the outer walls for the sake of openness. Above these two-meter-high shelves is an uninterrupted ribbon window up to the ceiling." From these numbers and Mies's perspective drawing one can confidently deduce the building's layout and section.

Toward each corner, the rhythm of the visible ceiling beams changes, demonstrating the ninety-degree turn of the structural system. The sixteen-meter-deep wings and the visible forty-nine-meter-wide (c. 160 feet) facade suggest a building with a seventeen-meter-wide courtyard. The changing size of the corner windows reveals that each floor protrudes about eight inches farther than the one below. Apart from providing a more dynamic appearance, this upward growth of the building probably resulted from a detailed structural analysis: the load on vertical stanchions decreases with each ascending story, but the wooden forms for the cast concrete would customarily be reused—resulting in uniform columns increasingly oversized for the weight they would have to bear. Mies probably sought to put this effect to use by adding weight in the form of additional floor space.

Berlin's six-story height limit is exploited to its fullest: the first floor is lifted above the ground in order to allow light into the basement. The building's topmost ribbon window is narrow, suggesting a dark attic (which would have been legally permitted), but this floor might have been intended to receive additional light from above and thus be fully functional. Flanked by open spaces on either side, the office building stands as a solitaire in stark contrast with its historicist neighbors. Its size of forty-nine meters by at least sixty-seven meters (c. 220 feet; the photograph of the model even suggests a length of over 525 feet) and height of almost thirty meters (c. 98 feet) predict a new urban scale, characterized by uniform and monofunctional city blocks. One of the units in Mies's Urban Design Proposal for Alexanderplatz, of 1929, seems a direct derivative of this design. —*Dietrich Neumann*

64. Perspective view. Charcoal
and crayon on paper, 54 $\frac{1}{2}$" x
9' 5 $\frac{1}{4}$" (138.8 x 289 cm).

Brick Country House Project, Potsdam-Neubabelsberg, 1924

This residential design, perhaps intended for Mies himself, was the last of a group of experiments with new materials and building types that later critics saw as constituting something of a manifesto (along with the Friedrichstrasse Skyscraper, the Glass Skyscraper, the Concrete Office Building, and the Concrete Country House projects). All of the original drawings are lost; only prints of a perspective and a plan survive. They show a low one- and two-story building with a flat roof, set on a gently sloping site defined and divided by long garden walls. The perspective does not fully correspond to the plan, and is atypical of Mies's drawing style; another draftsman may have executed it. The version of the design exhibited in 1925 at Mannheim, of which a photograph survives in the collection of the Kunsthalle there, bears an inscription indicating that the house was planned for Neubabelsberg, where Mies had built several houses, and was then at work on a conservative design for the Mosler family.

Many critics have pointed out a resemblance between the plan and Theo van Doesburg's abstract painting *Rhythm of a Russian Dance*, of 1918. More striking still, however, is a fundamental rethinking of residential design: traditional doors and windows are redefined as sheer openings between uniform wall slabs, and the roof is a horizontal plate, protruding and receding as needed. The main part of the house (labeled on the plan simply as "*Wohnräume*," or living spaces) could accommodate the spatial sequence of the typical social evening's pre- and after-dinner ritual. Instead of the traditional axial lineup of hall, living room, library, and dining room, however, this sequential route would proceed via the corners of openly connected spaces, requiring a series of

180-degree moves around protruding walls. (This open spatial arrangement foreshadowed later Mies buildings in Barcelona, Brno, and Berlin.) The utilitarian wing ("*Wirtschaftsräume*") would provide spaces for a kitchen, a maid, storage, and a back entrance. The second floor would have housed two bedrooms, reached by a staircase from the living room.

Uninterrupted walls of uniform thickness abandoned the usual differentiations between inside and outside, load-bearing and partitioning walls. While the attention to structural qualities seen in some of Mies's earlier projects was probably not a priority here, the uniform wall thickness might have stemmed from the modular application of the newly standardized metric brick sizes, as suggested by two (albeit much later) versions of the floor plan, executed in around 1964 or 1965 in Mies's Chicago office. —*Dietrich Neumann*

65. Perspective view and floor plan (lost). Gelatin silver photograph, 6 11/16 x 7 1/2" (17 x 19.1 cm). Städtische Kunsthalle, Mannheim

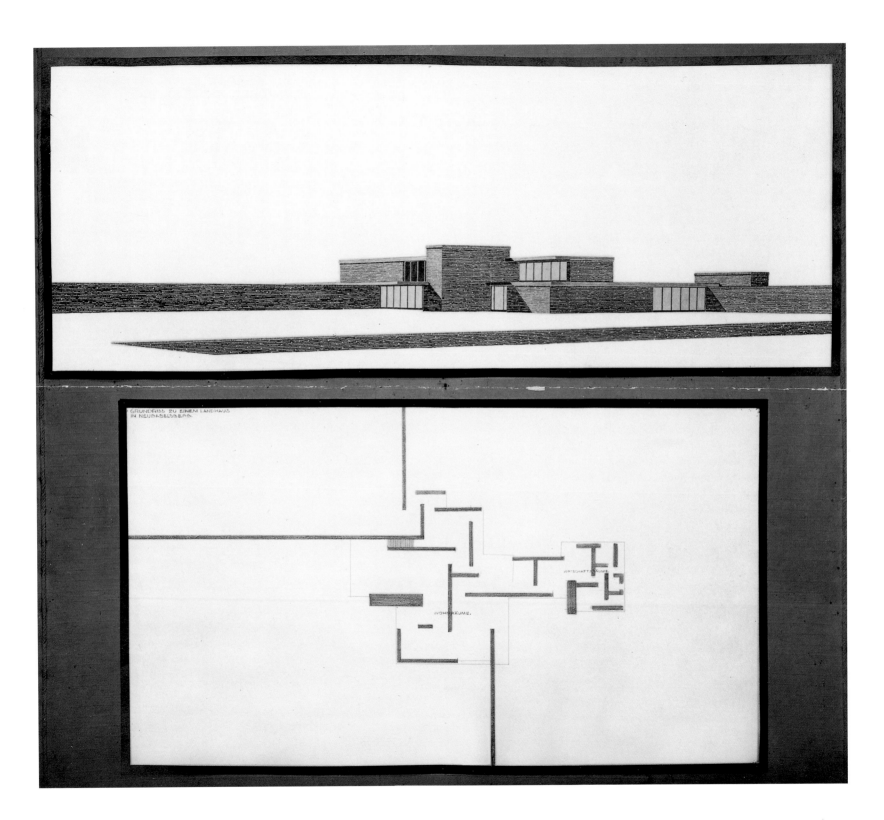

GRUNDRISS ZU EINEM LANDHAUS
IN NEUBABELSBERG.

WOHNRXUME.

WIRTSCHAFTSRXUME.

Gymnasium Addition to Frau Butte's Private School, Potsdam, 1924

In 1924, Mies accepted the commission to add a one-story gymnasium wing to the heavily ornamented, neo–German Renaissance–style school building of one of Potsdam's private academies. Among the least-known of his more "traditional" works, the project developed in the studio alongside the famed "manifesto" designs of the early 1920s. Hidden in a courtyard off the Alexandrinenstrasse (now Helene-Lange-Strasse), the design reflects Mies's continued interest in Karl Friedrich Schinkel's classical vocabulary even while Mies was beginning to explore new spatial concepts and new material images. It recalls Schinkel's neoclassical designs in its tall vertical windows, pronounced moldings, deep reveals, and flat roof, all developed in striking contrast to the ornamental classicism of the original building. These not only provided this minor structure with a monumental scale but flooded the exercise hall, and its built-in gymnastic equipment, with natural light.

The addition of two more floors for classrooms above Mies's building in 1930 led to a restructuring of the complex's facade, and Mies's vocabulary, as well as its striking contrast to the original building, was lost under a uniform stucco finish, a process accentuated in postwar renovations of the building. Mies's design is preserved only in two recently discovered drawings in the archives of the Denkmalamt in Potsdam.

—*Katherine Howe*

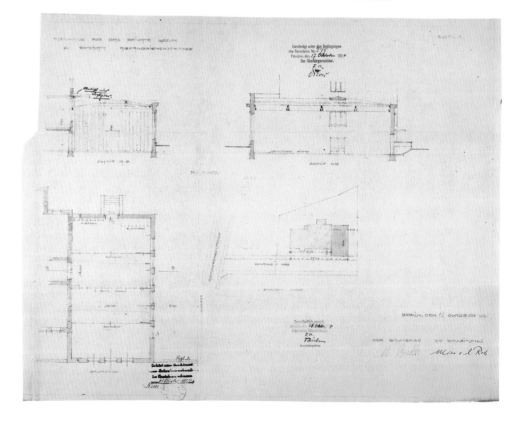

66. Plan and sections.
Architectural print, 18½ x 23¹³⁄₁₆"
(47 x 60.5 cm). Stadtverwaltung,
Potsdam

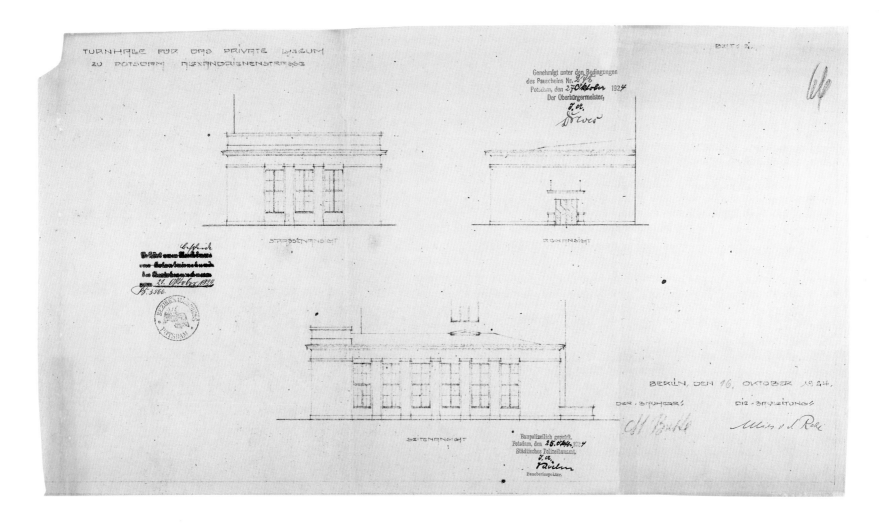

67. Elevations. Architectural
print, 13 x 24" (33.5 x 59.8 cm).
Stadtverwaltung, Potsdam

Dexel House Project, Jena, 1925

The unrealized Dexel House commission of 1925 resulted from Mies's inclusion in a 1924 architecture exhibition mounted by the Jena arts society and curated by the well-known painter Walter Dexel. Dexel and his backer canceled the project after less than three months, complaining of Mies's inability to meet their stringent deadlines; they subsequently hired another architect. The Dexel House drawings are among the most compelling of Mies's quick studies, although four sheets of plan sketches and five of small perspective views (with thumbnail plan diagrams) are all that remains of the project.

Two variants of the plan both show ground and upper floors in similarly conventional layouts. In both versions of the second-floor plan, five bedrooms are arranged off a central hallway. The ground floor in both schemes contains a large rectangular living and eating hall with a series of openings to the outdoors. (These openings were probably to be filled with French doors.) Perpendicular to this space is a studio wing of roughly equal size. The studio is in turn subdivided into workroom and office, with a large veranda adjacent to the garden doors of the main house block. The two building volumes are arranged in relation to a small grade change bisecting the building plot; the studio wing steps down with the grade, while the living block rises to two-story height on slightly higher ground.

This layout reappears in the accompanying perspective drawings, but only as the base element of a more complex design. The five sheets of loose charcoal sketches show the low-slung studio in the foreground (to the north side of the site) flanked by the living block and a tall rectangular stack, perhaps a large chimney. Four of the sheets show a third volume to the west, a counterpoint to the long low profile of the studio wing. The massing of these sketches suggests a considerably larger and more complex building than the plan layouts provide. A progression in the drawings is also evident; three of the five sheets show thumbnail plans of the two perpendicular volumes, together with more complex elaborations of the same ideas in plan and in three dimensions. The remaining two sheets show considerably more developed sketches of the multivolumed massing already described. Interestingly, the scheme developed by the architect Dexel hired to replace Mies, Adolf Meyer, occupies a footprint remarkably similar to one of these two sheets of sketches; it would appear that Mies's work on the house did not go entirely to waste, although Meyer's project too remained unbuilt. —*Claire Zimmerman*

68. Lower-level sketch plan. Graphite on paper, 8⅛ x 13" (20.6 x 33 cm). Canadian Centre for Architecture, Montreal

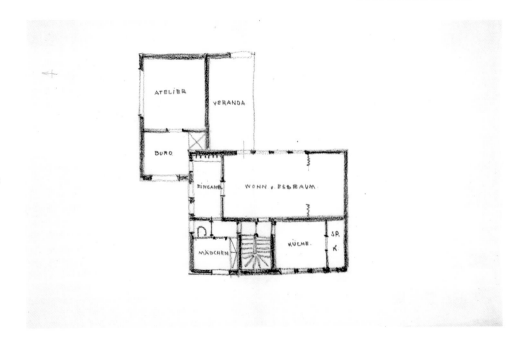

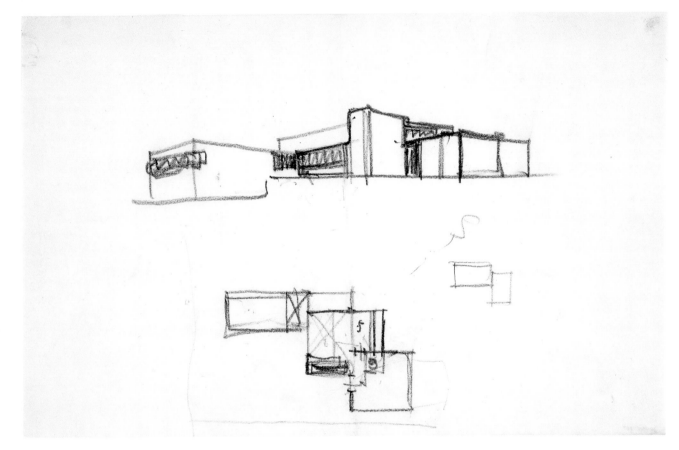

69. Sketch plan and perspective. Graphite on tracing paper, 8¼ x 13" (20.9 x 33 cm). Canadian Centre for Architecture, Montreal

70. Sketch plans and perspectives. Graphite on tracing paper, 8¼ x 13" (20.9 x 33 cm). Canadian Centre for Architecture, Montreal

71. Upper-level sketch plan. Graphite on paper, 8¹³⁄₁₆ x 13" (20.8 x 33 cm). Canadian Centre for Architecture, Montreal

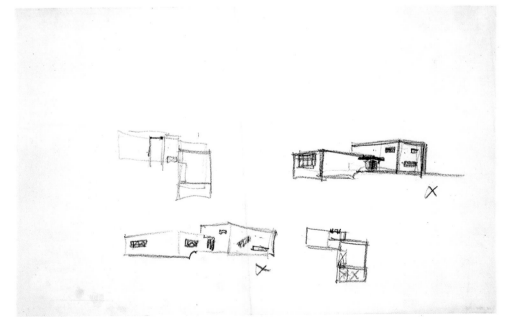

Eliat House Project, Potsdam-Nedlitz, 1925

The scant remaining evidence for the house of the Berlin banker Ernst Eliat depicts a generous compound on a site adjoining the Fahrlander lake, near Potsdam. While the overall site design is unfinished, the design of the house itself appears relatively complete, with minor discrepancies between plan and elevation in the three sheets of extant drawings known. The generosity and extent of this site design are unusual in Mies's work, and illustrate his interest in the interpenetration of architecture with natural topography and landscaping. In this case the extended automobile court, flanked by landscape elements that complete its rectangular geometry, enhances an otherwise modest country villa, giving a grander scale than the house alone would supply. This near inversion of the traditional hierarchy of architecture and landscape (where landscaping subordinately complements architecture) appeared in many Mies projects, with bold siting turning modest designs into dramatic tours de force. The Eliat House might in this respect be compared to the Riehl House of 1906–7 and the contemporary Wolf House in Gubin.

The plan of the residence is centrifugal, with spaces radiating out from a central core, as in many of Mies's plans. Each of three discrete building volumes commands views of the landscape; each is appended to the central square block containing vestibule, butler's pantry (with dumbwaiter), and stairs. A lower level housing storage, kitchen, and servants' accommodations is half embedded in the slightly sloping site. The building is thus interwoven with landscape elements in three senses: in plan, with an architectural massing that extends fingers of building out into the site; visually, in the discrete construction of views; and sectionally, in the burial and emergence of the building, two-storied on the lake side and single-storied on the automobile court. This interweaving almost certainly reflects the influence of Frank Lloyd Wright, an influence also evident in features such as the continuity between indoor and outdoor space in the front hall and dining room, and the massive yet decorative fireplace blocks.

—*Claire Zimmerman*

72. Sketch site plan. Pencil on tracing paper, 21 ¾ x 39 ½" (55.2 x 100.4 cm)

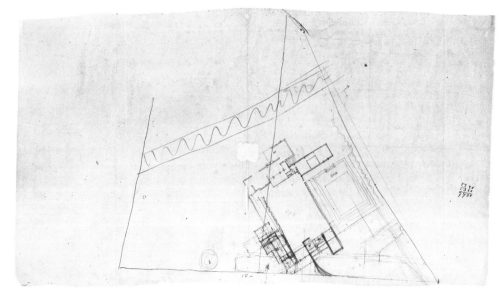

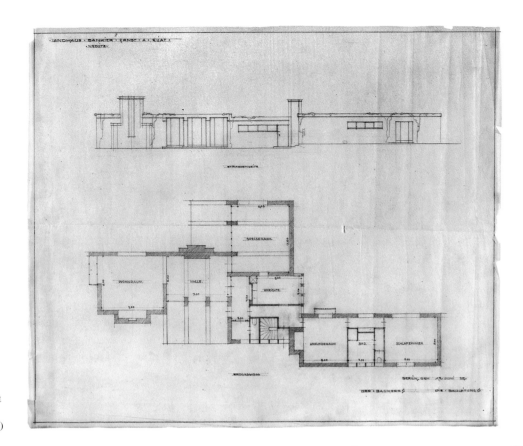

73. Ground-floor plan and street elevation. Pencil on tracing paper, 17¼ x 21" (44.1 x 53.5 cm)

74. Upper-level plan and water-front elevation. Pencil on tracing paper, 17¼ x 20¾" (44.1 x 53.1 cm)

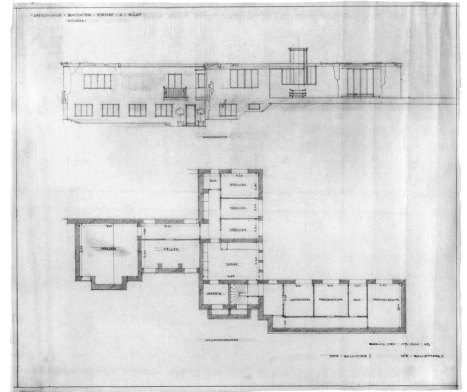

Wolf House, Gubin, 1925–27

The Gubin textile merchant and hat manufacturer Erich Wolf met Mies through the Kempner family, for whom the architect had designed a house in Berlin in 1922, and promptly commissioned him to build a three-story house in Gubin. Situated not far from the Old Town, at the top of a narrow sloping lot, the squarish brick structure perched above the Neisse River, overlooking an industrial suburb and a panoramic view. The literature has repeatedly noted that the structure drew on theoretical work Mies had done in 1923 and 1924—that in the Wolf House, even more than in the later Esters and Hermann Lange houses, Mies managed to incorporate notions of space that he had developed experimentally in his Concrete Country House and Brick Country House projects. For Mies the commission provided an opportunity to experiment with new forms, and the result differed substantially from his villas of a few years earlier.

The Wolf House was an asymmetrical arrangement of different-sized rectangular spaces. An open, fluid floor plan and a linking of indoors and outdoors, later increasingly important for Mies, are already evident in this design, which wherever possible broke down the notion of separate enclosed rooms. In fact, if one studies the plans in chronological order, it becomes apparent that the architect moved from a still more fluid ground plan to a more traditional one, presumably to accommodate his client. The outside walls, however, were opened up with large windows, and a series of preexisting stone terraces created a clear connection between the house and the natural surroundings.

Approaching the house from the east along a narrow, slightly curving driveway, the visitor would only have been aware of its considerable height. The structure also took up the entire width of the lot, completely hiding the dramatic views to the west. It thus divided the lot into an exposed front yard to the east and a private terraced garden in the back. The only exterior connection between the two was a short corridor along the house's south side.

The main entrance was on the east side, barely noticeable beneath the cantilevered second-floor terrace. The visitor arrived in a large entrance hall from which a staircase led to the two upper floors, with their bedrooms, children's rooms, and maids' quarters—all traditional enclosed spaces. The early drawings of the ground floor show a more open concept—with the living and dining rooms combined—than was ultimately built.

From the living and dining area one could step out onto the terrace. The orthogonal, unornamented design of the brick facade was continued here: the parapet, the paving, and the stairs echoed the forms and materials of the house itself. Despite the predominance of the brickwork, the layout synthesized architectural and natural forms, mainly through plantings and especially through the sunken flower bed. This motif had appeared in earlier projects such as the Perls, Werner, and Eliat houses, but in the Wolf House it was more dominant. The flower bed, and its visual relationship to the surrounding greenery of the slope, underscored the interpenetration of architectural and natural spaces.

As in other projects, Mies designed not only the house and its surrounding spaces but also the furniture. Family photographs show that several rooms contained tables, sideboards, and chairs of Mies's design; the dining room suite resembles the one he built when he refurnished his Berlin apartment in the mid-1920s. For the Wolf House as for later interiors, he collaborated with the designer Lilly Reich.

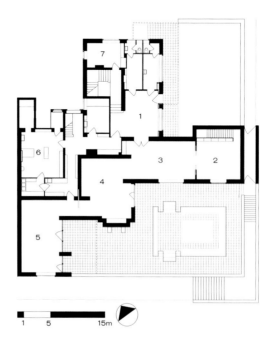

75. First floor and garden plan. Delineator: Amanda Reeser, 2001. 1: entrance and stair hall. 2: study/library. 3: music room. 4: living room. 5: dining room. 6: kitchen. 7: parlor

89. View of balconies along
lateral facade. Gelatin silver
photograph, 15¾ x 19¹¹⁄₁₆"
(40 x 50 cm). Photograph:
Kay Fingerle, 2000

Weissenhof Housing Colony Master Plan, "Die Wohnung" Exhibition, Stuttgart, 1925–27

Mies's plan for the Weissenhof Housing Colony in Stuttgart, an exhibition of built projects, placed buildings by several architects in an awkward plot of land stretched along a north-south axis. From narrow frontage on Friedrich-Eberts-Strasse the site ballooned outward, narrowed, then bulged out again; it also rose steeply from the southwest to the northeast. Within this difficult terrain Mies arranged a collection of detached and double houses, row houses, and apartment buildings, accommodating both the housing needs of the city and the program specified for the exhibition.

Mies emphasized the work of Le Corbusier by locating his double house at the southwest corner of the site, like a billboard facing the city below. On one side of this building, the sharp angles and planes of cuboid detached houses by Ludwig Hilberseimer, Hans Poelzig, Richard Döcker, and Max Taut were locked into straight strips of retaining wall, forming a single ensemble stepping up along the slow ascending curve of Rathenaustrasse. To the other side, a steep stair led into the

site, lined with houses by Le Corbusier and Adolf Schneck— a propylon of talent opening onto an acropolis of modern architecture. The stairs entered Bruckmannweg, which jogged through the site. On one side of this street were houses by Walter Gropius, Max and Bruno Taut, Döcker, and Adolf Rading; on the other, row houses by J. J. P. Oud, and Mies's own Weissenhof Apartment House. The street was punctuated by a small square on which a group of low-cost experimental designs faced each other, including Oud's row houses, a prefabricated house by Gropius, and a worker's house by Bruno Taut. From here, the long volume of Mies's apartment building was set back from the higher side of the street. Along the lower side, the cuboid volumes of houses by the Taut brothers and Döcker adjoined the street, contrasting the multiple- with the single-family dwelling. Rading's house concluded the sequence.

In the bulge of the site to the north, the northwest and northeast corners were established respectively by Peter Behrens's large apartment building and Hans Scharoun's small

90. Preliminary site plan. October 14, 1925. Diazotype with colored pencil and charcoal, 13 x 32¼" (33 x 82 cm)

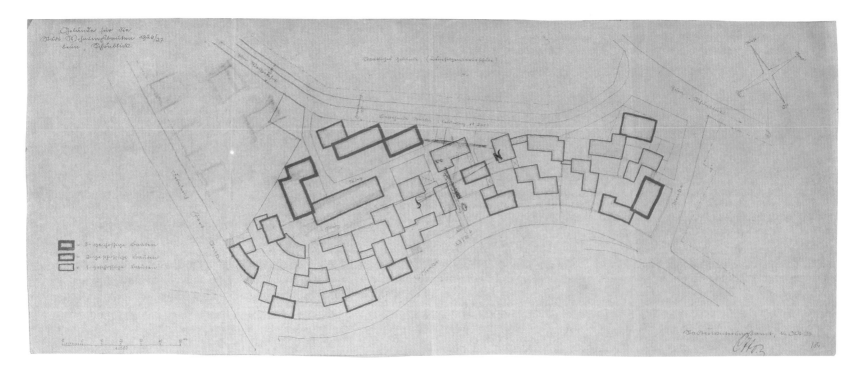

91. View of clay model (lost), preliminary scheme

but lively house. During the exhibition, Scharoun's corner was staked out with banners on tall masts, acknowledging its importance. Down the hill, the curve of Rathenaustrasse set off Josef Frank's house, while on the other side of the site, Mart Stam's row houses slid away from the street at the angle of Am Weissenhof to extend the open courtyard of Behrens's block.

With this design, Mies capitalized on the site's awkwardness to bring unity to an otherwise various group of projects. He provided the colony with an overall shape by arranging buildings of different configurations and heights on the angled streets along the raised western flank, while setting the cuboid houses and two double houses along the lower, eastern part and Rathenaustrasse. He used the neighborhood's angled and curved streets and hillside terrain to compose local groupings of buildings, and he implied a sequence through these arrangements that set off the individuality of the designs and suggested certain attitudes to them. A vigorously conceived order underlay what appeared open and casual.

The project involved compromise. With the initial assistance of Hugo Häring, Mies produced a first site plan in September 1925, working without knowledge of the terrain. This plan has not survived. A clay model and related drawings from October 1925 depict a citadel of taller buildings above a tightly nested array of low houses, raised on terraces, opening on walled gardens, and reached by narrow footpaths and stairs. Most of the buildings join others at their corners, hook around their gardens in L-shaped arrangements, and face south for sunlight. Since access favors pedestrians more than vehicles, the colony is "something like a medieval town," as Mies later said. He created this interconnected layout not only because it was "artistically valuable" but because it would subordinate individual architects' projects to the whole.

The design had few connections with the two dominant approaches in early-twentieth-century German planning. The intermingled ideals of Camillo Sitte and the English garden city—widely employed in German housing projects before

World War I, and still in use in the 1920s—advocated curvilinear arrangements adapted to the topography. But these designs were more open and less compactly urban than Mies's. Equally foreign to the project was a plan introduced in the early 1920s, the so-called *Zeilenbau* system, in which straight parallel streets were laid out on a north-south axis without regard to topography, to provide maximum sunlight, air, quiet, and a leveling equality.

Instead, Mies drew on the tradition established around 1900 by the Artists' Colony in Darmstadt, and specifically on Joseph Maria Olbrich's long studio building there, laid across the top of the hill, and Behrens's conflation of Mediterranean vernacular with abstract and stereometric form in a series of house designs from before World War I. Related to these approaches were Bruno Taut's plans for Hohenhagen, a colony of villas for artists and industrialists; Theodor Fischer's ideas for impressive buildings crowning the Stuttgart hills; and the variations on Fischer's scheme by Adolf Muesmann and Döcker. Mies's project can be seen as an assimilation and critique of these site plans.

A revision of July 1926 responded to the city's requirements for automobile access, less terracing, and the possible sale of individual houses. Mies reduced the group of buildings at the top of the colony to a single long block of two- and three-story houses; straightened and isolated the buildings by eliminating the L-shaped extensions; and introduced a wider road. Aspects of the clay model remained, but now architecture dominated the landscape instead of melding with it.

More than any consideration of building type and site design, the limited repertory of formal principles accepted by the modernists became the means of unifying the site's architecture. In his model of October 1925, Mies had already depicted most of the site's buildings as an interlocking set of cubes; his presentation may have been a less schematic and more specific formal strategy than has generally been assumed. —*Christian F. Otto*

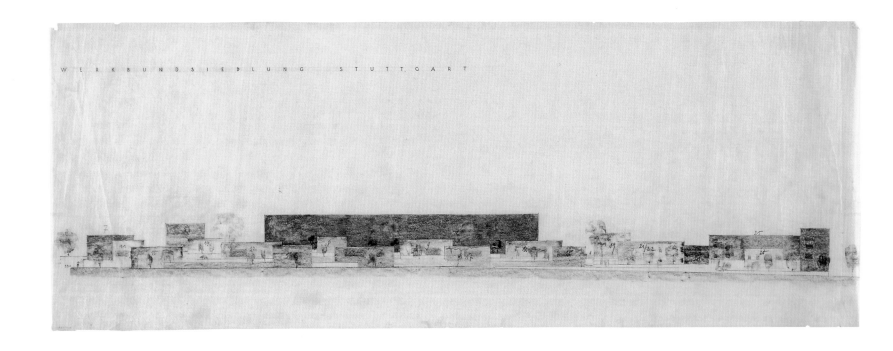

92. Site elevation study from
east. 1926. Pencil on tracing
paper, 16½ x 45¼" (42.3 x 114.6
cm)

93. Site plan study with housing
types. July 1926. Pencil and
colored pencil on paper, 41½ x
59" (105.3 x 150 cm)

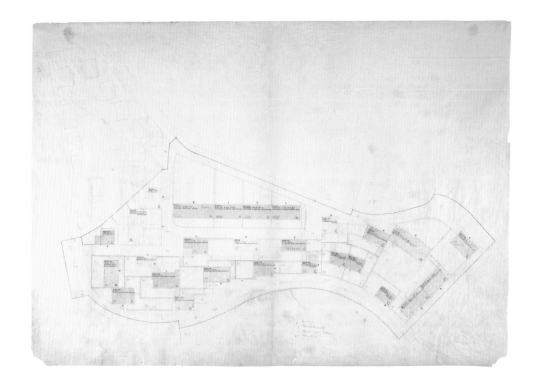

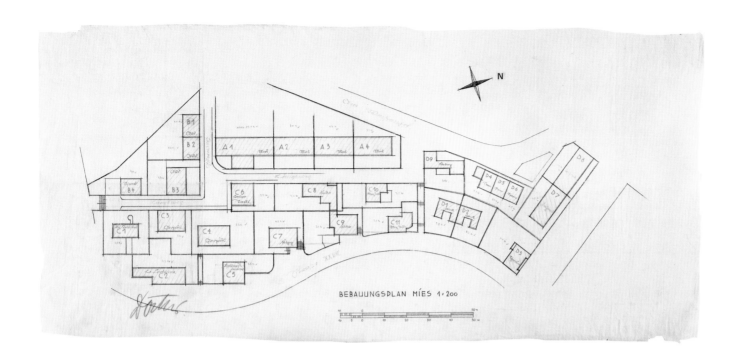

94. Site plan with architects'
assignments. Pencil and colored
crayon on paper, 27½ x 58¾"
(69.6 x 148.9 cm)

95. Aerial view. c. 1927

Weissenhof Housing Colony Master Plan | 209

Weissenhof Apartment House, "Die Wohnung" Exhibition, Stuttgart, 1926–27

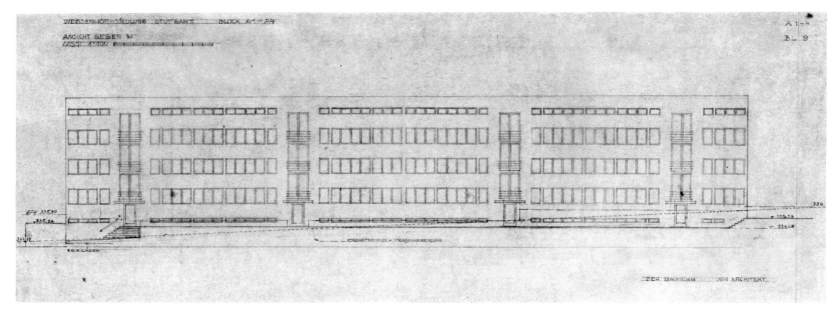

Sheer size made Mies's Apartment House the dominant building at Weissenhof; a white wall extending along the top ridge of the colony, it was by far the largest project in the exhibition. Although committed to industrial practices in building, Mies felt that architecture was to illuminate not merely material but spiritual life. "More important than the demand for material quality is that for spiritual quality," he asserted during the exhibition. The purpose of his project was to demonstrate how freedom could be achieved within a standardized, rational building.

The long narrow structure contained twenty-four apartments aligned north-south, permitting east and west exposures. Four stairways were arranged to serve two apartments on each floor. On the top level, laundries and storage were interspersed with roof gardens. The building stood on flat ground won by carving out and filling in a site that slanted uphill to the north, adjusting the land to the structure, just as a Greek temple was placed on a leveling stylobate. The placement of windows, doors, and balconies was determined by the symmetrical composition of the facades; in some of the groups of triple windows, two serve one apartment, the third its neighbor. The autonomous regularity of the exterior, though derived from H. P. Berlage, Otto Wagner, and the writings of Karl Scheffler, supported Mies's conviction about the impersonal nature of modernity: "Here the fundamental anonymous character of our time is apparent."

The Apartment House was a significant step in Mies's exploration of how to combine a regularized structure with an open and flowing space, a scheme he would next pursue in the Tugendhat House in Brno (1928–30) and in the German Pavilion in Barcelona (1928–29). The catalyst for his plan and facade was the steel frame, which he employed at Weissenhof for the first time in a built project. He acknowledged but did not literally reveal the frame on the exterior by employing the grid in relation to his organization of the facades. Since 1921, he had seen the frame as the "basis of all artistic design," yet visible structure was absent in his idealized projects from these years. At Weissenhof, he employed the frame to join "standardized and rationalized construction" with the "steadily increasing variety of our living needs" and to realize flexible spaces within the apartments.

While the Weissenhof Apartment House reflected the *Zeilenbau* of the period—monumental apartment blocks placed in rows that were oriented to the sun rather than the street pattern—it nonetheless retained elements of a standard nineteenth-century plan, notably in the disposition of stairs, kitchens, and bathrooms. Also, whereas the egalitarian attitude of *Zeilenbau* planning entitled all occupants to the same sun, street, facade, and grounds, treated as continuous green swards, Mies included individual gardens for some apartments, conflating housing types. —*Christian F. Otto*

96. West elevation. Pencil on tracing paper, 29½ x 35½" (74.7 x 90 cm)

97. View of west facade.
Chromogenic color photograph,
15¾ x 19¹¹⁄₁₆" (40 x 50 cm).
Photograph: Kay Fingerle, 2000

98. View of east facade.
Chromogenic color photograph,
17¹¹⁄₁₆ x 11¹³⁄₁₆" (45 x 30 cm).
Photograph: Kay Fingerle, 2000

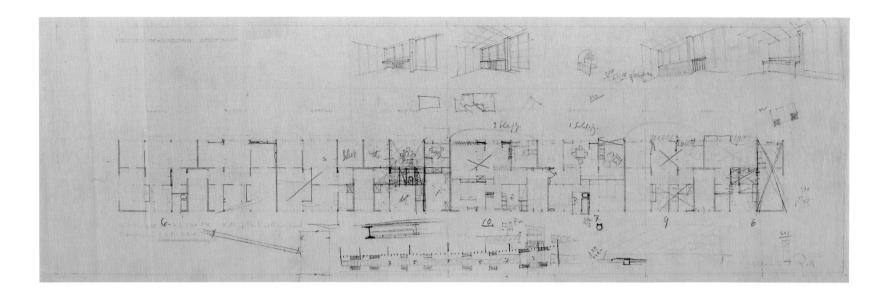

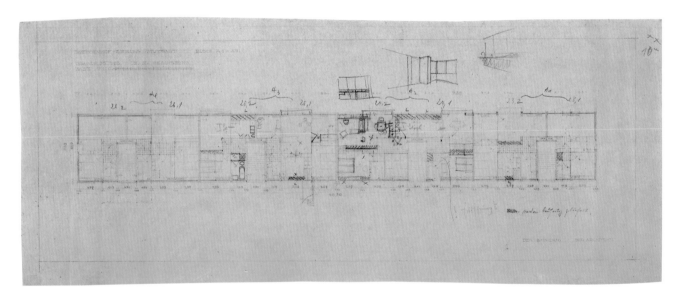

99. Ground-floor plan with apartment layout studies and interior perspective sketch views. Diazotype with pencil and colored pencil, 12 ½ x 39 ¼" (32.1 x 99.8 cm)

100. Second- and third-floor plans with apartment layout studies. Diazotype with pencil and colored pencil, 13 ½ x 33 ½" (34.5 x 84.9 cm)

101. Ground-floor plan with fenestration studies. Diazotype with pencil, 13 x 39" (33 x 99.3 cm)

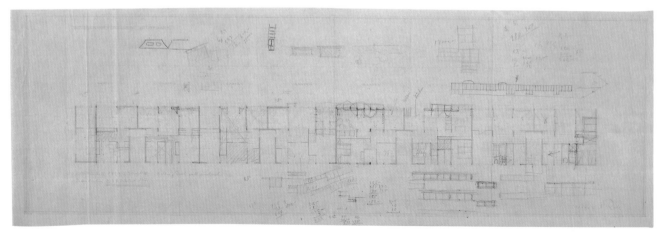

102. View of living room. c. 1927.
Gelatin silver photograph,
6⅝ x 9⅛" (16.7 x 23 cm)

103. Handrail (detail), stair hall.
Gelatin silver photograph,
17¹³⁄₁₆ x 11¹³⁄₁₆" (45 x 30 cm).
Photograph: Kay Fingerle, 2000

104. View of bedroom. c. 1927.
Gelatin silver photograph,
6⁹⁄₁₆ x 9³⁄₁₆" (16.7 x 23.4 cm)

Monument to the November Revolution, Berlin-Lichtenberg, 1926

The Monument to the November Revolution, in Berlin's Friedrichsfelde cemetery, came to Mies through Eduard Fuchs, an art historian, collector, and Communist Party member, and memorialized Karl Liebknecht and Rosa Luxemburg, the martyrs of the 1918–19 Spartacist Revolt. Since some of the revolutionaries had been lined up against walls for execution, Mies imagined the monument as a monolithic brick wall. The monument's German title, "Denkmal der Revolutionsopfer," means "Monument to the victims of the revolution." These "victims" were both concrete and abstract, for the monument attested to the heroism not only of Liebknecht and Luxemburg but of the many revolutionaries buried in the cemetery.

Dedicated on Luxemburg's birthday—June 13, 1926—the monument was Mies's only purely sculptural work. A rectangular block stood roughly twenty feet high, forty feet long, and thirteen feet wide (six by twelve by four meters). Its architectonic monumentality derived from a shifting surface of rectilinear masses of brick, simultaneously lending the structure a sense of motion and stability. Mies chose rough brick salvaged from destroyed buildings to imbue the monument with the harshness of the executioner's wall.

The monument originally bore an inscription: "*Ich bin, Ich war, Ich werde sein*" ("I am, I was, I will be"). Some of Mies's drawings also included the motto "*Den toten Helden der Revolution*" ("To the fallen heroes of the revolution"). There was a flagpole and a steel star with a hammer and sickle, which Mies had to construct independently as the Krupp steelworks refused to fabricate a leftist symbol. For reasons unclear, the inscription disappeared around 1931.

The Monument to the November Revolution raises a question about the relation of Mies's architecture to politics. Here he designed a structure that became a rallying point for Germany's left. Only eight years later he participated in a competition sponsored by the Nazi government, for the German Pavilion at the International Exposition in Brussels. For Mies, clearly, architecture was an end unto itself, superseding political ideology.

In response to the monument's significance for German leftists, the Nazi government destroyed it shortly after coming to power in 1933. —*Katherine Howe*

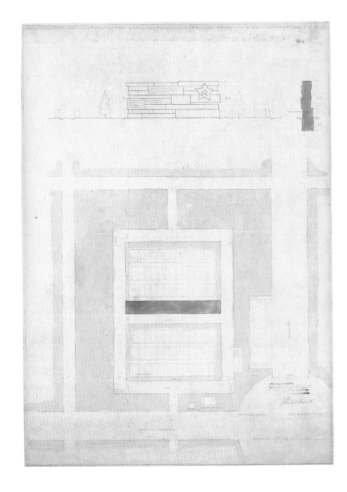

105. Site plan, section, and elevation. Diazotype with watercolor and pencil, 26¼ x 19¼" (67.9 x 48.8 cm)

106. Frontal view. c. 1926

107. Oblique view. c. 1926.
Gelatin silver photograph,
8⅞ x 6⁹⁄₁₆" (22.5 x 16.7 cm).
Photograph: Arthur Köster

108. Lettering study. Pencil on
tracing paper, 19¾ x 39½"
(50.2 x 100.4 cm)

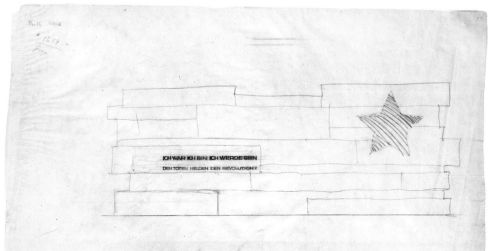

Hermann Lange House and Esters House, Krefeld, 1927–30

The Lange and Esters houses in the Rhineland city of Krefeld mark a change in direction in Mies's development, joining traditional elements to a new spatial openness. In late 1927 the architect was commissioned to design two imposing residences, on neighboring lots, for the textile manufacturers Hermann Lange and Josef Esters. The selection of the architect was made by Lange, a distinguished collector of modern art. The two houses were designed simultaneously and balanced against each other in their general layout and in many of their details. Construction of both was begun in the fall of 1928 and completed in early 1930.

The houses are built of complex steel skeletons skillfully faced with subtly varied dark-red brick, the qualities of which are highlighted in a masterly if somewhat rhetorical way. The architecture combines elements of the classical villa, such as a podium on the garden side, with a franker functional expression, visible in the facades of both houses' eastern service courts. The houses were clearly conceived as an ensemble; a common garden wall runs in front of both, creating a single low barrier between the street and the two gardens, and the main facades of the houses are similarly blank, with few openings for windows and doors.

On the southern, garden side, the volume of each house diminishes in steps, the dense block of the service wing to the east dropping to a shallow, single-room depth on the west. The facades, which are bracketed by terraces opening onto the adjacent gardens, show a modulated interplay of nearly room-high windows on the ground floors and repeating window and door motifs on the upper floors. These large openings, and the variety of the terraces (some of them covered and semi-enclosed), make the garden facades more porous than the street facades and spatially integrate interiors and exteriors.

The interiors of the Lange House are characterized by an interplay of walls painted an almost pure white, with darker tones appearing in the travertine window seats and in the walnut and oak of the door and window frames, radiator covers, and parquet floors. A more dramatic macassar wood appears only on the two entrance doors and in the women's sitting room. Contrasting with the imposing breadth of the ground floor, the upper story features a simple row of relatively small bedrooms and adjacent bathrooms, and in tune with this more sober character the doors and woodwork are painted a light gray. Yet large windows and access to various terraces create a

109. Site and ground-floor plans, Esters House and Hermann Lange House. Delineator: Amanda Reeser, 2001. 1: living hall. 2: dining room. 3: nursery. 4: parlor (*Damenzimmer*). 5. living room. 6: study (*Herrenzimmer*). 7: staff room

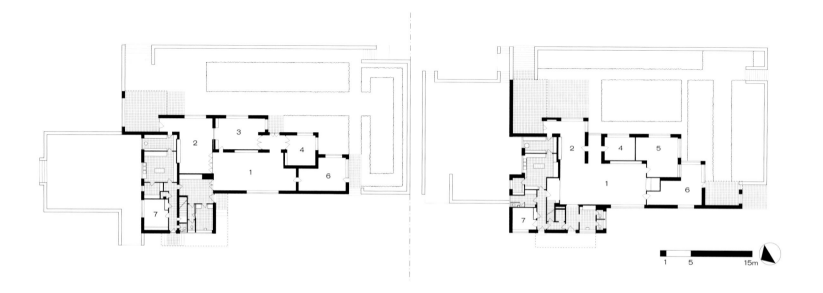

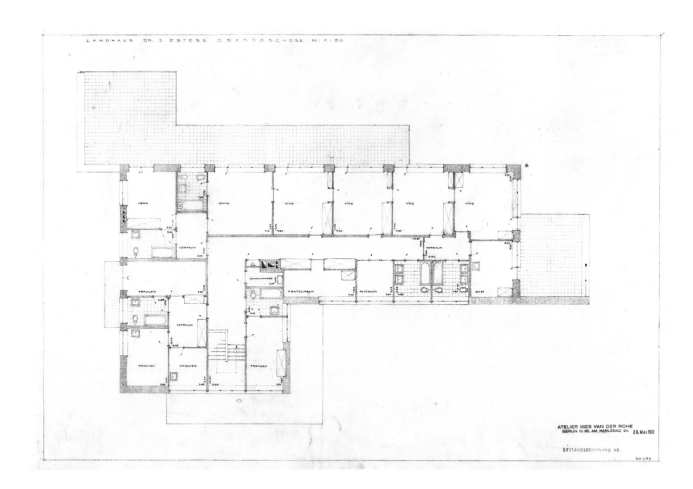

LANDHAUS DR. J. ESTERS. OBERGESCHOSS. M 1:50

ATELIER MIES VAN DER ROHE
BERLIN W. 35, AM KARLSBAD 24.   2 8. Mai 1931

BESTANDSZEICHNUNG NR.

110. Upper-level plan, Esters
House. Pencil on tracing paper,
27½ x 37¾" (70.3 x 96.1 cm)

strong tie to the outdoors, as they do downstairs. In the service wing, with its kitchen, workrooms, and servants' quarters, the disposition of spaces is wholly functional.

The interior organization and finishing materials of the Esters House are on both floors essentially like those of the Lange House, but the traffic pattern is rather more varied, with numerous changes of direction, changing light relationships, and retarding threshold elements structuring the gradual interpenetration of interior and exterior space. All the rooms except for Esters's study are connected by room-high openings. The hall is less dominant in relation to the smaller rooms, creating a greater harmony in the spaces, as the diagonal axis builds toward a climax on the garden side. In the Brick Country House Project of 1924, Mies had tried to develop "a series of spatial effects rather than a row of individual rooms"; that goal is only partly realized in Krefeld, and more so in the Esters House than in the Lange House. One does not experience a carefully modulated, unified flow of space of the kind apparent

in the German Pavilion in Barcelona and the Tugendhat House in Brno, which were designed around the same time, but rather a staggering of clearly separate rooms.

The Lange House was occupied by the Lange family until roughly 1948. It has been used since 1955 for changing exhibitions of contemporary art. With some interruption in the period after World War II, the Esters house was occupied by the family until the 1970s, and, like the Lange house, has been used for exhibitions since 1981. While neither house has been changed structurally, the transformation into exhibition space occasioned the removal of many elements originally built in, such as room dividers and cupboards. Both houses and their gardens were extensively restored in 1998–2000.

—Julian Heynen

111. Perspective study of street facade, Esters House. Pencil and pastel on paper, 16¼ x 22¾" (41.2 x 60.2 cm)

112. View of street facade, Esters House. c. 1930. Gelatin silver photograph, 6 1/16 x 8½" (15.4 x 21.6 cm)

113. View from south (detail), Esters House. c. 1930. Gelatin silver photograph, 6⅜ x 9" (16.2 x 22.9 cm)

114. View of terrace and garden facade, Esters House. Chromogenic color photograph, 15¾ x 19¹¹⁄₁₆" (40 x 50 cm). Photograph: Volker Döhne, 2000

115. View of living hall, Esters House. After 1930. Gelatin silver photograph, 3³⁄₁₆ x 5³⁄₁₆" (8.2 x 13.2 cm). Collection Joachim C. Heitmann

116. View of garden facade, Esters House. Chromogenic color photograph, 11¹³⁄₁₆ x 17¹¹⁄₁₆" (30 x 45 cm). Photograph: Kay Fingerle, 2000

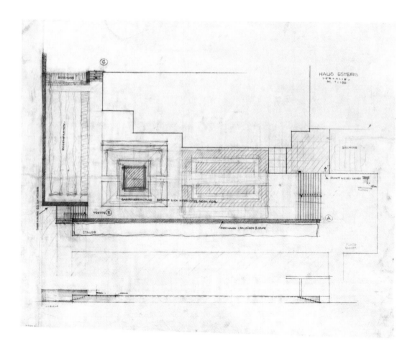

117. Garden plan and podium elevation, Esters House. Pencil on tracing paper, 19½ x 24" (49.3 x 61 cm)

118. View of Hermann Lange House from Esters House. Chromogenic color photograph, 11¹³⁄₁₆ x 17¹¹⁄₁₆" (30 x 45 cm). Photograph: Volker Döhne, 2000

119. East and west elevations, Hermann Lange House. Pencil on tracing paper, 14½ x 23" (36.3 x 58.6 cm)

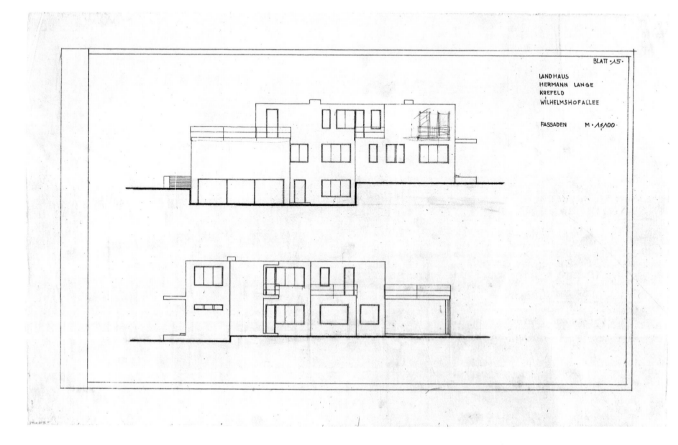

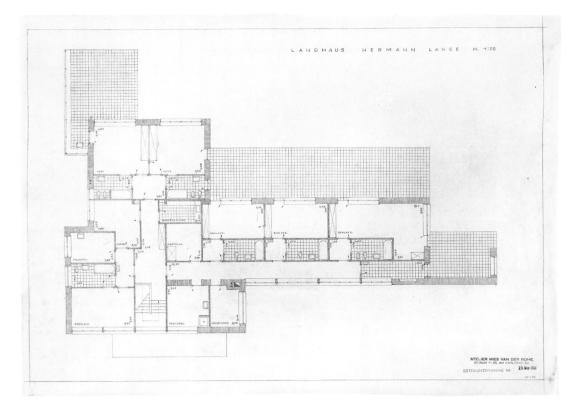

120. Upper-level plan, Hermann
Lange House. Pencil on tracing
paper, 25½ x 36¼" (64.7 x
93.3 cm)

121. View of street facade,
Hermann Lange House.
Chromogenic color photograph,
11¹³⁄₁₆ x 17¹¹⁄₁₆" (30 x 45 cm).
Photograph: Volker Döhne, 2000

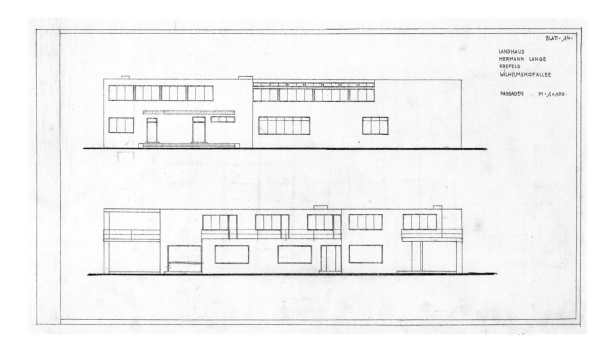

122. North and south elevations,
Hermann Lange House. Pencil
on tracing paper, 14¼ x 25"
(36.5 x 63.4 cm)

123. View of living hall,
Hermann Lange House. After
1930. Published in *Museum der
Gegenwart* 1, no. 4 (1930–31)

124. View of covered terraces,
Hermann Lange House. Gelatin
silver photograph, 17¹¹⁄₁₆ x
11¹³⁄₁₆" (45 x 30 cm). Photograph:
Volker Döhne, 2000

125. View of garden facade,
Hermann Lange House.
Chromogenic color photograph,
15¾ x 19¹¹⁄₁₆" (40 x 50 cm).
Photograph: Kay Fingerle, 2000

126. View from west through
covered terrace, Hermann Lange
House. Gelatin silver photograph,
17¹¹⁄₁₆ x 11¹⁵⁄₁₆" (45 x 30 cm).
Photograph: Kay Fingerle, 2000

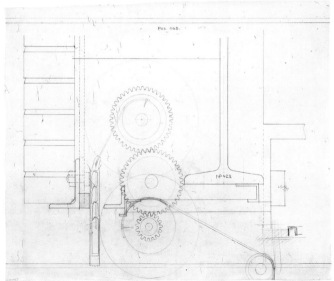

127. Section detail of shutter
mechanism, Hermann Lange
House. Pencil on tracing paper,
22 x 26½" (55.6 x 67.5 cm)

Fuchs Addition to Perls House, Berlin-Zehlendorf, 1928

Not long after Mies completed his house of 1911–12 for Hugo Perls, it was sold to Eduard Fuchs, the art historian and collector, in exchange for five paintings by Max Liebermann. In 1928, when Fuchs needed additional space for the display and storage of his art, he too hired Mies, to whom he had earlier steered the commission for the Monument to the November Revolution (1926). Now Mies was faced with the difficult task of marrying his ideas in 1928 with his design of seventeen years earlier. Drawings indicate that he explored different facade treatments, but held fast to the principle of a mostly detached wing connected to the main building by a cantilevered roof slab.

The addition is a flat-roofed volume that connects to the earlier house at its northwest corner. Five French doors open onto the garden, in a gesture toward the earlier house's loggia, but the language is otherwise considerably reduced from the first neoclassical form. The plan is consistent with Mies's work at the time, with shifted and layered enclosures and an asymmetrical, nonaxial layout. A roof terrace covering most of the addition is reached via a stair at the back of the gallery.

—Amanda Reeser

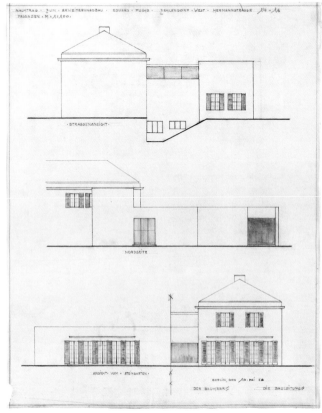

128. Elevation studies. Pencil on tracing paper, 19¼ x 15¼" (49.2 x 38.9 cm)

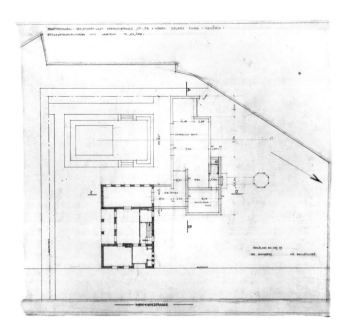

129. Ground-floor and garden plan. Pencil on tracing paper, 22 x 23¾" (56.1 x 60.3 cm)

130 (below). View from north.
Chromogenic color photograph,
17¹¹⁄₁₆ x 11¹³⁄₁₆" (45 x 30 cm).
Photograph: Kay Fingerle, 2000

131. View from garden.
Chromogenic color photograph,
15¾ x 19¹¹⁄₁₆" (40 x 50 cm).
Photograph: Kay Fingerle, 2000

132. Detail of connecting
structure between addition and
house of 1911–12. Gelatin silver
photograph, 17¹¹⁄₁₆ x 11¹³⁄₁₆"
(45 x 30 cm). Photograph:
Kay Fingerle, 1999

Bank and Office Building Project, Stuttgart, 1928

From August through December 1928, Mies participated in a competition to design a building that was to include both a banking hall for the competition's sponsor, the Württembergische Landesbank, and rentable retail and office space. The site was bounded by Lautenschlagerstrasse and Schillerstrasse, and lay at the prominent intersection where these streets flowed into the Hindenburgplatz, the square facing the monumental railroad station that had recently been completed to the historicist designs of Paul Bonatz and Friedrich Eugen Scholer. A jury of bank and city officials and local professors of architecture awarded two first-place prizes, along with other distinctions; Mies received an honorable mention. Neither winning design was built—the commission ultimately went to Bonatz and Scholer, who had won third prize in the competition, and constructed on the site the building today called the Zepellinbau.

Like his S. Adam Department Store Project, completed earlier in the same year for Berlin, Mies's design was based on an open plan; the drawings for the concrete structure show uninterrupted floor plates for maximum flexibility. But the program for the Stuttgart project called for what would today be called a mixed-use building, and Mies worked on the premise that the "banking house should be clearly separated from the business building." His submission therefore comprised two, parallel structures: an eight-story block fronting on Lautenschlagerstrasse, with retail space on the street level and office space above; and a three-story structure behind, facing an interior court, for the banking hall. Threading the gap between the two horizontal buildings were four slender towers housing stairways and bathrooms.

The twenty-eight-meter-high (c. ninety feet) facade was to be an uninterrupted glass-and-stainless-steel curtain wall, an idea the jury deemed "interesting but problematic." Mies specified transparent glass for display windows on the street level, which was to include the retail space as well as the entrance to the banking hall beyond, while the upper levels were to be clad in matte glass, so as to appear like a glowing prism. While this suggestive image closely recalls the Adam Department Store design, in Stuttgart Mies emphasized its role in addressing the competition requirement that the facade accommodate advertising signs. A model of the project suggests that the names of the buildings' tenants were to be affixed to the building's metal frame, where they would have been backlit by the matte glass, melding architecture and media in a prescient expression of a growing consumer culture.

—*Terence Riley*

135. Street-level plan (detail). Pencil and colored pencil on tracing paper, 17⅜ x 35⅛" (44 x 90.5 cm). Collection Albrecht Werwigk, Tuttlingen

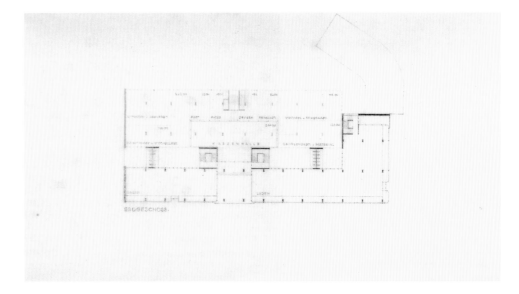

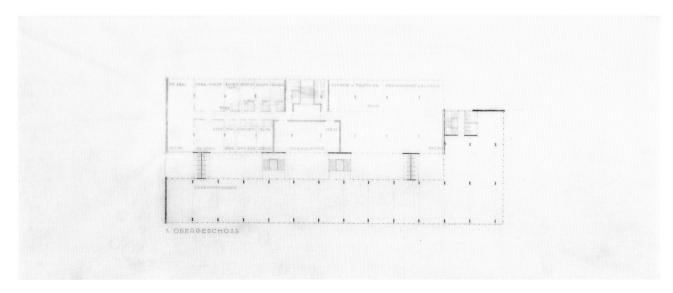

1. OBERGESCHOSS

136. Second-floor plan. Pencil and colored pencil on tracing paper, 17⅜ x 35⅝" (44 x 90.5 cm). Collection Albrecht Werwigk, Tuttlingen

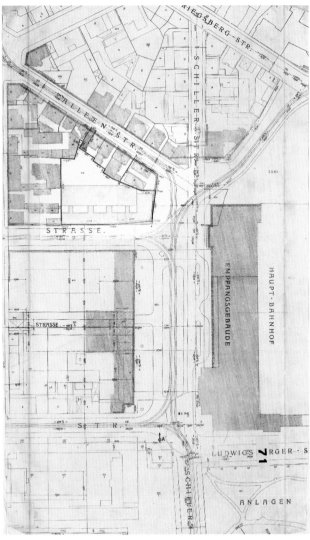

137. Site plan. Pencil and colored pencil on print, 35⅝ x 20⅞" (90.5 x 53 cm). Collection Albrecht Werwigk, Tuttlingen

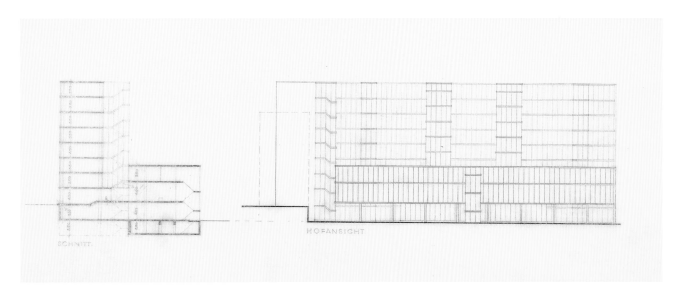

SCHNITT.

HOFANSICHT

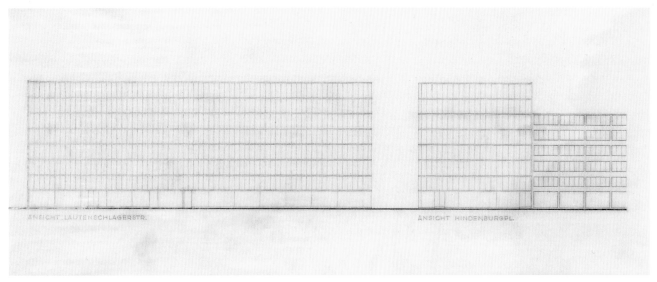

ANSICHT LAUTENSCHLAGERSTR.

ANSICHT HINDENBURGPL.

138. Transverse section and elevation facing interior court. Pencil and colored pencil on tracing paper, 17⅜ x 35⅝" (44 x 90.5 cm). Collection Albrecht Werwigk, Tuttlingen

139. Street elevations. Pencil and colored pencil on tracing paper, 17⅜ x 35⅝" (44 x 90.5 cm). Collection Albrecht Werwigk, Tuttlingen

140. Perspective view from
Hindenburgplatz. Photomontage,
37 13/16 x 59 1/8" (96 x 150 cm).
Collection Albrecht Werwigk,
Tuttlingen

German Pavilion, International Exposition, Barcelona, 1928–29

Mies's famous "Barcelona Pavilion" has had a dual life. Words and images alone constructed perceptions of the building for many years, thanks to its demolition in 1930. The building was reconstructed in 1986, and its experiential propositions can once again be tested against its now historic two-dimensional representations, initiating a third phase of its history.

The architectural elements of the German Pavilion are well-known. Finished in four varieties of stone (two green marbles, travertine, and onyx doré), tinted glass (green, gray, white, and clear), and chromed metal, the building constituted an early effort to disengage structure from enclosing wall surfaces, using a newly discovered design technique to radicalize spatial experience. Marble-clad and glass walls choreographed an uninterrupted spatial sequence punctuated by the slim lines of cruciform chrome columns set against walls of intense reflectivity. The absence of the pavilion's steel and glass doors (left out of nearly all the original photography) was critical to the reading of spatial continuity, further defamiliarizing the experience of the building. Within the display of slick yet ornamental surfaces, an oversized statue of a woman (Georg Kolbe's *Dawn*) provided a figural reference somewhere between cult image and modern icon. Its arms raised gracefully from the midst of a dark pool in the building's rear court, the statue transposed its classical prototype from hieratic deity into evocative nude. A larger pool greeted the visitor in the building's outer court, open to the street from the raised podium on which the whole structure stood; in this case lily pads growing in the water and creepers trailing down the wall behind provided other recognizable figures counterposed against the abstractly rendered fields of water and textured stone.

Mies himself selected the site for the pavilion (rejecting one offered by the Spanish authorities), a critical decision for this contextual, site-dependent building. The German Pavilion established a gateway between the grandiose, eclectic architecture of the Exposition proper and the picturesque "Spanish village," the Pueblo Español, on the hill behind the German site. Located at the terminus of an important cross-axis partway up the exposition's ceremonial spine, the building was shielded quietly behind a screen of Ionic columns at the end of a long plaza. Critical reference to its pendant at the other end of the plaza—the neo-Renaissance pavilion of the City of Barcelona—echoed gently in its two enclosing end walls, traces of an eviscerated neoclassicism.

Germany's Weimar government had symbolic intentions for its Barcelona exhibits and pavilion, articulated by General Commissioner Georg von Schnitzler as reflecting "our desire to be absolutely truthful, giving voice to the spirit of a new era." In addition, Germany's economic intentions were openly instrumental, as it sought new markets in Spain and the Americas. For the pavilion this was a representational matter, as its primary function was the successful advertisement of a newly democratic Germany. The aesthetic and spatial achievements of the pavilion existed within a sociopolitical framework, where the building symbolized Germany's progressive stance in cultural and material terms.

The commission for the German Pavilion was in Mies's office in the late summer of 1928, and the building was constructed between March and May of 1929. This hurried schedule was complicated by a brief work stoppage and a subsequent budget shortfall that led to several cost-cutting measures. The pavilion was planned as a project employing new building technologies, but much of its construction had to be adapted to the resources of 1929 Barcelona, based largely in nineteenth-

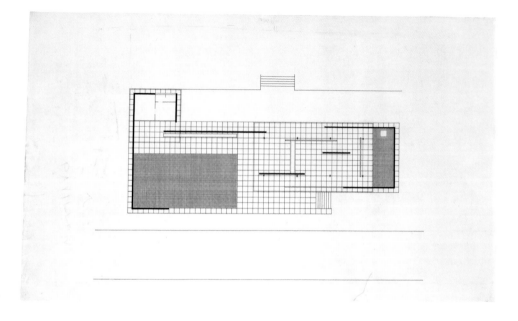

141. Floor plan. Ink and pencil on paper, 22 ½ x 38 ½" (57.6 x 98.1 cm)

142. Sketch perspective view of principal facade (detail). Pencil and colored pencil on tracing paper, 8⅛ x 10⅜" (20.6 x 27 cm). Drawing: Sergius Ruegenberg. Preussischer Kulturbesitz/ Kunstbibliothek, Berlin

143. Sketch perspective view from west (detail). Graphite on tracing paper, 8¹/₁₆ x 10½" (20.5 x 26.7 cm). Drawing: Sergius Ruegenberg. Preussischer Kulturbesitz/ Kunstbibliothek, Berlin

century methods. Subsequently considered a manifesto for the new architecture, the project was part of Mies's ongoing effort to develop a paradigm for the steel-framed building, in this case challenged by a difficult schedule, an insufficient budget, and a number of technological compromises. Conceptually clear, Mies's first essay into a new structure/enclosure paradigm was still, of necessity, a constructional hybrid.

Images of the pavilion and the pavilion itself have proved remarkably absorbent of multiple interpretations. It was championed by modernist critics as the quintessential example of spatial abstraction in architecture, a masterwork independent of context. More recent interpretations, however, have focused less on the object value of the building, emphasizing transactions between building and site, or building and user. The building has been understood, for example, as reinterpreting a Greek temple, as picturesque landscape, and as a machine for simultaneously producing and destroying symmetry. In any case, the reconstructed German Pavilion now sits astride a body of historiographic material that virtually ensures its continued yet shifting status as a "canonical" building.

—*Claire Zimmerman*

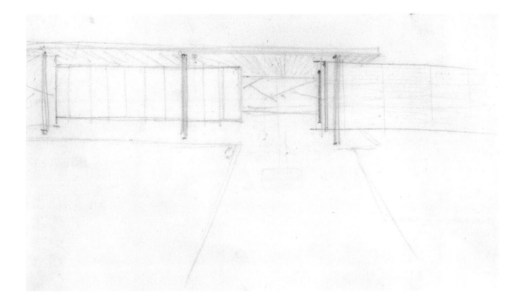

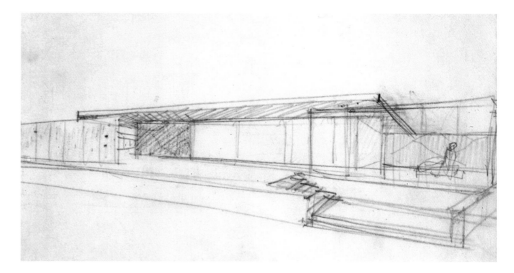

144 (right). Sketch perspective view of principal facade (detail). Pencil and colored pencil on tracing paper, 8⅛ x 10⅝" (20.6 x 27 cm). Drawing: Sergius Ruegenberg. Preussischer Kulturbesitz/Kunstbibliothek, Berlin

145. View of principal facade, with German flag. 1929. Gelatin silver photograph, 6½ x 8¹³⁄₁₆" (16.3 x 22.4 cm)

146. View toward pavilion (the reconstruction of 1986) over main reflecting pool. Chromogenic color photograph, 19⅝ x 15¼" (50 x 40 cm). Photograph: Kay Fingerle, 2000

148. View of secondary entrance from west. 1929. Gelatin silver photograph, 6⁵⁄₁₆ x 8⅞" (16 x 22.6 cm)

149. View of secondary entrance looking toward attendants' lodge. 1929. Gelatin silver photograph, 6¼ x 8¹³⁄₁₆" (16 x 22.3 cm)

147. View of main entrance with doors removed. 1929

150. Sketch perspective view of interior with table and stools. Graphite on tracing paper, 8¼ x 10¾" (20.4 x 27.4 cm). Drawing: Sergius Ruegenberg. Preussischer Kulturbesitz/ Kunstbibliothek, Berlin

151. View of interior (the reconstruction of 1986) looking toward light wall. Chromogenic color photograph, 19⅝ x 15¾" (50 x 40 cm). Photograph: Kay Fingerle, 2000

152. Interior perspective view (unfinished). Crayon and pencil on illustration board, 39 x 51¼" (99.1 x 130.2 cm).

153 (near right). View of onyx
wall (the reconstruction of 1986).
Chromogenic color photograph,
19⅜ x 15¾" (50 x 40 cm).
Photograph: Kay Fingerle, 2000

154 (far right). View of interior
light wall (the reconstruction of
1986). Chromogenic color photograph, 19⅜ x 15¾" (50 x 40 cm).
Photograph: Kay Fingerle, 2000

155 (far left). View of courtyard
reflecting pool and interior
(the reconstruction of 1986).
Chromogenic color photograph,
19⅜ x 15¾" (50 x 40 cm).
Photograph: Kay Fingerle, 2000

156 (near left). Reflection study
(the reconstruction of 1986).
Chromogenic color photograph,
19⅜ x 15¾" (50 x 40 cm).
Photograph: Kay Fingerle, 2000

Tugendhat House, Brno, 1928–30

Grete and Fritz Tugendhat commissioned Mies to design a house in Brno in mid-1928, following Grete Tugendhat's frequent visits to the Perls House in Berlin. In a 1969 lecture, Mrs. Tugendhat cited the Weissenhof Housing Colony in Stuttgart as a precedent for the selection; the clients also visited the recently completed Wolf House in Gubin. Heirs of wealthy, German-speaking Jewish industrialists in the former Austro-Hungary, the Tugendhats occupied the building until 1938.

The house presents a modest single story to the street, its front door shielded by a curved milk-glass volume. By contrast, a distant view of Brno's picturesque Špilberk fortress, framed by a cutout in the building mass, lies directly ahead of those arriving. The house thus immediately presents itself as a frame for viewing. Inside, the semipublic zone of the building takes one down spiral stairs to the main living level, where one emerges into a large open space subdivided by a single onyx wall and a nearly semicircular wall of ebony, punctuated by cruciform columns and wall-size silk and velvet curtains in several colors. The choreography of the bourgeois house nevertheless remains—dining room, living room, study/library, music room, conservatory—and is reinforced by the placement of furniture and textiles designed by Mies and Lilly Reich, in some cases explicitly for this commission. The abolition of space-enclosing walls provides grandeur without excess; each individual spatial cell is modestly proportioned, acquiring generosity from the continuity of the surrounding space. In addition, the transparency between spaces extends to the outside: enormous sheets of plate glass bound the living area from the garden, and two of these windows sink completely into the floor. The living area is thus simultaneously interior and exterior. It can be transformed again by its large curtains, partitions providing further spatial mutability. This mutability should be juxtaposed to the spatial fluidity of the contemporaneous German Pavilion in Barcelona, another revolutionary aspect of Mies's achievement.

In comparison to the main level, with its transparency and openness, the family bedrooms are carefully screened from viewers. Although positioned at street level, with a terrace overlooking the site below, they paradoxically occupy the building's most private zone. They are also conventionally discrete, a series of closed rooms for sleeping and bathing.

Similarly, the service spaces on the main level below are concealed and separated behind another stretch of milk-glass wall. The house thus carefully screened the private life of its owners. According to the testimony of the Tugendhats, the grandeur of the living space accommodated itself well to the private needs of the family.

The Tugendhat House, like the German Pavilion, indicates a development in Mies's design practice that can be traced back to the 1927 Glass Room in Stuttgart: the assemblage of freestanding walls and other architectural elements according to compositional and spatial values, virtually without regard to structural necessity. A grid of slender steel columns distinguishes structure from enclosure. Commonly related to Le Corbusier's 1926–27 articulation of the free plan, Mies's own discovery of this separation also dates to Stuttgart and 1927, where it is present, if only nominally expressed, in his Weissenhof Apartment House. The Tugendhat House unites two elements still separated at Stuttgart: it is a steel-framed building in which columnar supports are clearly distinguished from space-defining walls.

157. Entrance-level plan. Ink and pencil on tracing paper, 19 x 32¼" (48.3 x 82 cm)

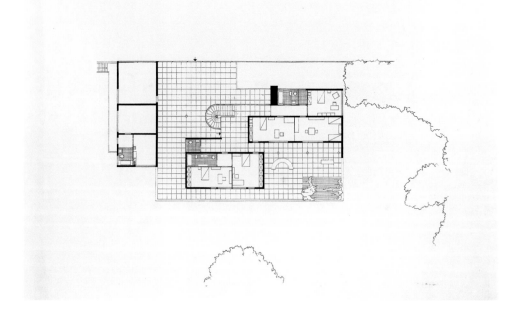

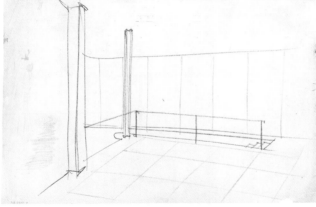

158 (above). View of street facade. c. 1930. Gelatin silver photograph, 6 x 8¾" (15.3 x 22.1 cm)

159 (top right). Framed landscape view from entrance court. Chromogenic color photograph, 11¹³⁄₁₆ x 17¹¹⁄₁₆" (30 x 45 cm). Photograph: Kay Fingerle, 2000

160. Sketch perspective view of entrance hall with stair to main level. Pencil on paper, 8⁵⁄₁₆ x 13" (21.1 x 33 cm)

161. View up stairwell. Chromogenic color photograph, 17¹¹⁄₁₆ x 11¹³⁄₁₆" (45 x 30 cm). Photograph: Kay Fingerle, 2000

The relationship between landscape and architecture at the Tugendhat House continued a theme in Mies's work that would be further developed in the Gericke House Project of 1932. The sinkable (*versenkbar*) glass window-walls on the garden facade transform the living area into a giant terrace, while the winter garden along the east side of the same space captures a natural tableau within architectural confines. Carefully shielded from contact with the street above, the garden side of the house enacts the "Virgilian dream" articulated by Le Corbusier in his description of his Villa Savoye (1929–31). Classical model notwithstanding, this dialogic relationship between architecture and landscape was for Mies linked to German precedents, and to a strain of German idealism dating back to the last century. In contemporaneous debates on architectural modernism, the Tugendhat House was invoked to signal the move away from radical functionalism toward a new vision of architecture, one raised to the "realm of the spirit," in the words of the critic Walter Riezler. It thus also marks the point at which Mies's common cause with other German modernists, from Walter Gropius to Bruno Taut, began to weaken. He committed himself instead to a search for new spatial paradigms and new construction practices, with a corresponding ideological neutrality that would mark the rest of his work, both German and American.

—*Claire Zimmerman*

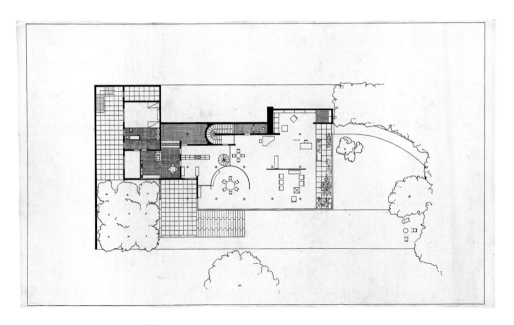

162. Main-level plan. Ink and pencil on tracing paper, 19 x 32 ¼" (48.3 x 82 cm)

163 (top right). View between onyx wall and dining area partition. Chromogenic color photograph, 11 ¹³⁄₁₆ x 17 ¹¹⁄₁₆" (30 x 45 cm). Photograph: Kay Fingerle, 2000

164 (below). View of dining area. c. 1930. Gelatin silver photograph, 6 ½ x 8 ¹³⁄₁₆" (17.5 x 23.4 cm)

165. View along south glass facade. Chromogenic color photograph, 17 ¹¹⁄₁₆ x 11 ¹³⁄₁₆" (45 x 30 cm). Photograph: Kay Fingerle, 2000

166 (below). Perspective view of
living room. Pencil on tracing
paper, 17 x 24" (43.4 x 61 cm)

167 (right). View of study toward
dining room. Chromogenic color
photograph, 19 11/16 x 15 3/4"
(50 x 40 cm). Photograph:
Kay Fingerle, 2000

168 (below left). View of living
area with library beyond. c. 1930.
Gelatin silver photograph, 6 7/16 x
8 15/16" (16.2 x 22.6 cm)

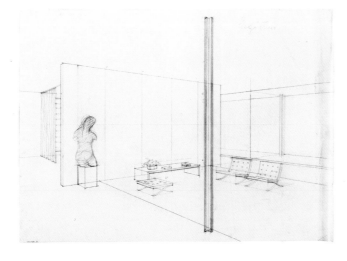

169 (below right). View of library.
c. 1930. Gelatin silver photograph,
6 5/8 x 8 15/16" (16.8 x 22.7 cm)

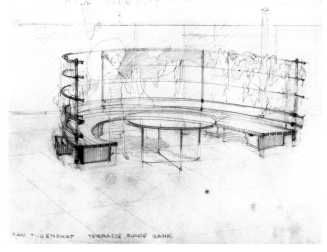

170 (above). View of terrace with exedral bench and pergola above. Gelatin silver photograph, 11 $^{13}/_{16}$ x 17 $^{11}/_{16}$" (30 x 45 cm). Photograph: Kay Fingerle, 2000

171 (above right). Sketch perspective view of exedral bench on terrace. Pencil on paper, 11 x 14" (27.9 x 35.6 cm). Drawing: Sergius Ruegenberg. Preussischer Kulturbesitz/ Kunstbibliothek, Berlin

172 (below left). View of winter garden. Chromogenic color photograph, 11 $^{13}/_{16}$ x 17 $^{11}/_{16}$" (30 x 45 cm). Photograph: Kay Fingerle, 2000

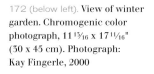

173 (below right). Perspective view of winter garden from living room. Pencil on paper, 11 x 14" (27.9 x 35.6 cm). Preussischer Kulturbesitz/ Kunstbibliothek, Berlin

174. Night view of garden facade. Gelatin silver photograph, 15¾ x 19¹¹⁄₁₆" (40 x 50 cm). Photograph: Kay Fingerle, 2000

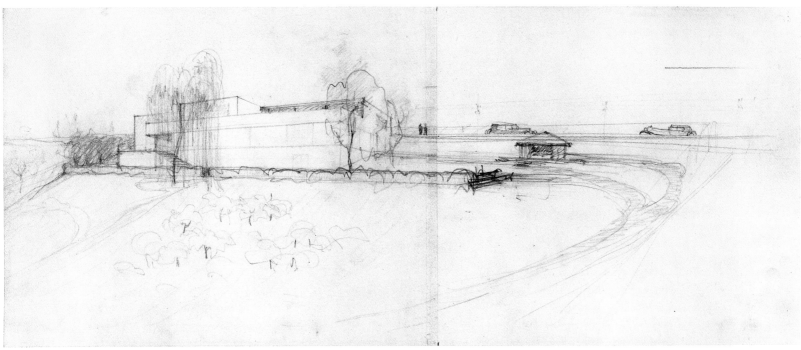

175 (left). Aerial perspective view from southwest. Charcoal on tracing paper, 15¾ x 29¼" (40 x 74.5 cm)

176 (above). Perspective view from garden. Graphite on tracing paper, 8 x 20³⁄₁₆" (20.3 x 51.2 cm). Preussischer Kulturbesitz/ Kunstbibliothek, Berlin

Urban Design Proposal for Alexanderplatz, Berlin-Mitte, 1929

In November 1928, Martin Wagner, the head of Berlin's planning department, presented the Berlin City Council with a preliminary proposal for a remodeling of Alexanderplatz, one of the city's busiest intersections. The redesign of the streets and buildings above ground was to correspond with construction on the U-Bahn subway system below; Wagner's primary aim was to facilitate the flow of traffic, with architectural redevelopment the means. The council approved a competition, and by January 1929, six architectural offices had been invited to participate: Peter Behrens, Hans and Wassili Luckhardt with Alfons Anker, Paul Mebes and Paul Emmerich, Mies, Heinrich Müller-Erkelenz, and Johann Emil Schaudt.

The jury, which met on February 5, 1929, awarded the first prize to Luckhardt and Anker, whose designs most completely fulfilled the competition requirements. Mies's entry placed last. Unlike the other five participants, who essentially presented variations on Wagner's model (a symmetrical arrangement of buildings of uniform height, including a semicircular enclosure built over two roads), Mies flagrantly ignored the competition requirements, instead designing entirely freestanding buildings asymmetrically arranged around the traffic roundabout. Of Mies's eleven proposed buildings, the seven pictured in his perspective photocollage, which looks south along Alexanderstrasse, were even rectangular blocks, the tallest of them rising to seventeen stories (with a double-height ground floor), the others to nine stories. The four buildings on the other side of Alexanderplatz reflected the irregular shapes of the city blocks, but maintained relatively regular rectangular forms and a consistent height of eight stories. All of the buildings were to have glass facades, like those Mies was proposing for his Bank and Office Building project in Stuttgart and S. Adam Department Store in Berlin at around the same time; the street levels, where colonnades would offer protection from the elements, would be lined with transparent glass, the upper levels with opaque glass.

Despite the proposal's ranking in the competition, Wagner hardly dismissed Mies's solution, publishing Ludwig Hilberseimer's defense of it in the February 1929 issue of his journal, *Das Neue Berlin*. Hilberseimer argued that "Mies van der Rohe's project is the only one of the designs submitted that breaks through this rigid system [of frontages conforming to traffic flow] and attempts to organize the square independently of the traffic. The traffic lanes maintain their function, yet Mies has designed the square by grouping freestanding buildings according to architectural principles alone. By opening the streets wide, he achieves a new spaciousness which all the other projects lack."

In May 1929, much of the Alexanderplatz property that had been owned by the city was transferred to private ownership. The new investor, Bürohaus am Alexanderplatz GmbH, rejected Luckhardt and Anker's plans as too expensive. Behrens was asked to submit an alternate proposal, which resulted in the construction of his Alexanderhaus and Berolinahaus office buildings of 1930–32. —*Adrian Sudhalter*

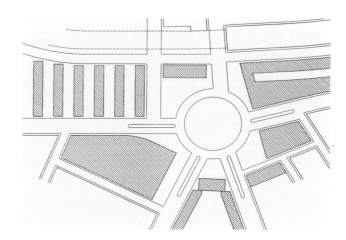

177. Site plan. Drawn after 1938. Ink on illustration board, 22 x 30" (56 x 76.3 cm)

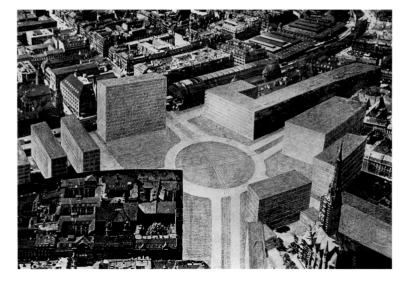

178. View of model (lost). Originally published in *Das Neue Berlin*, February 1929

179. Aerial perspective view. Photomontage (lost). Originally published in *Das Neue Berlin*, February 1929

180. Axonometric drawing. 1928. Pencil on tracing paper, 9⅞ x 11¼" (25 x 28.5 cm). Art Institute of Chicago

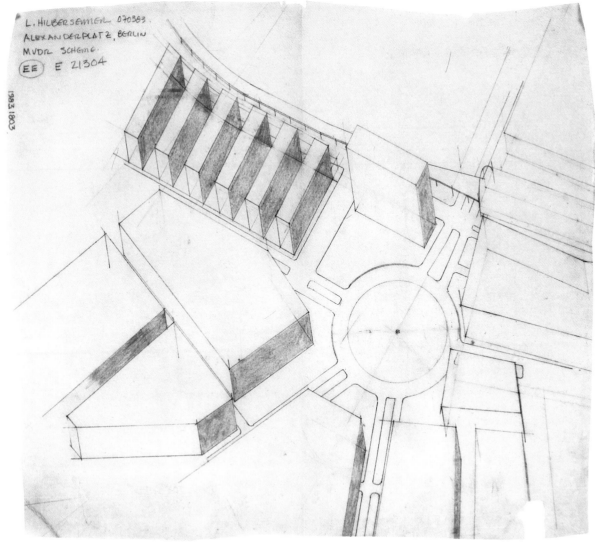

Nolde House Project, Berlin-Dahlem, 1929

In 1929, the Expressionist painter Emil Nolde commissioned Mies to design a house on a small sloping lot opposite a small park in Dahlem. Nolde was an important social connection of Mies's and had brought him into contact with clients such as Margarete Hubbe and Ernst Henke. Holdings in the Mies Archive indicate that Nolde's house was ready for construction when Mies canceled the building permit, apparently because its cost was too high.

The house, to be steel framed with walls of masonry infill, testifies to Mies's continuing interest in steel-frame construction. In its use of cruciform columns and glass walls, it relates directly to contemporaneous projects such as the Tugendhat House and the German Pavilion in Barcelona. The plan falls into three zones, of which the southern is the largest and includes living spaces for Nolde and his wife. The service spaces are distributed on either side of a central corridor, with kitchen and guest room in the middle and staff accommodations at the back. Entry is also from the back, into a glass-walled vestibule with Nolde's gallery immediately to the left, possibly through a double glass or milk-glass wall. Directly ahead, but entered around the ends of two staggered east-west walls, is the living space. Both of these large ceremonial spaces, each about 15 by 7.5 meters (50 by 25 feet), includes cruciform columns and almost no other spatial divider, but the gallery, separated from the living space by Nolde's studio, has few windows, and was presumably to be lit either by a skylight not shown in the drawings or by artificial lighting. The living room, by contrast, is sheathed in a double layer of glass along its southern face, in a room-length winter garden, a development of motifs that Mies had used in the Tugendhat House design. Where the Tugendhat winter garden runs along a side wall, however, here the narrow conservatory would have screened the living room's southern front from visual access, presenting a mural-sized natural scene as the focus of view, set against the greenery of the park across the street.

—*Claire Zimmerman*

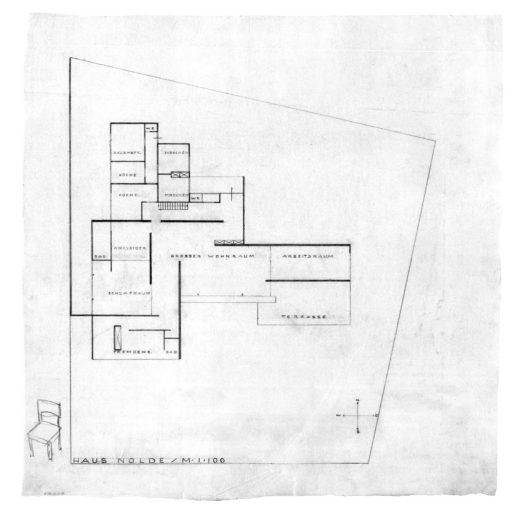

181. Site plan with floor plan. Pencil on tracing paper, 21¼ x 21¼" (54 x 54 cm)

182. East and west elevations.
Pencil on tracing paper, 22¼ x
28½" (56.5 x 72.4 cm)

183. South and north elevations.
Pencil on tracing paper, 22¼ x
28½" (56.5 x 72.4 cm)

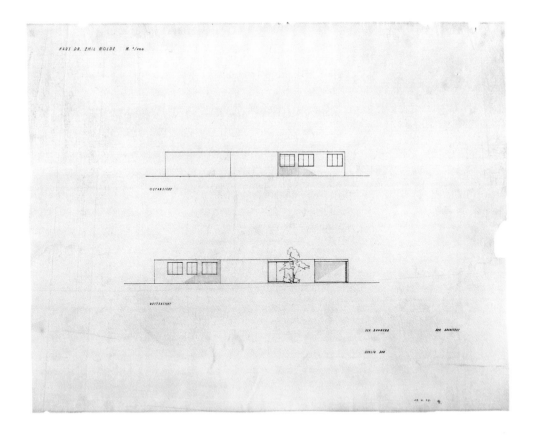

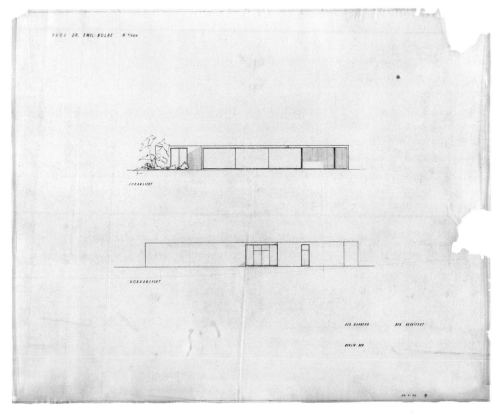

Friedrichstrasse Office Building Project, Berlin-Mitte, 1929

In 1929, the Berlin Traffic Authority announced a competition for the development of a site it oversaw on Friedrichstrasse, one of a series of projects the organization initiated in the late 1920s to reorganize pivotal traffic and commercial centers in the city. The project called for an office building to house a variety of functions and services connected to the Friedrichstrasse railway station and the surrounding urban infrastructure. The site—between the station and the Spree River, close to the city's cultural and political center—was the same one for which Mies had developed the Friedrichstrasse Skyscraper Project of 1921, allowing him the opportunity to reconsider the program of his earlier proposal. Of the five entries submitted, prizes were awarded to the team of Paul Mebes and Paul Emmerich and to Erich Mendelsohn.

Repeating the general program of the 1921 proposal, Mies organized three repeated units around a central core, but the new design's horizontal emphasis, incorporation of traditional materials, change in plan, restricted height, and subtle hierarchical differentiation were clear departures from the earlier project. The articulation of the ground level with floor-to-ceiling glass panes provides a sense of scale. It also suggests both that the interior was intended for retail space and that Mies was concerned to relate the building to the streetscape. The upper levels of the facade are rendered as alternating transparent and opaque bands, and were primarily designated for office space. Mies's code name for the project, *Rote Kreis* (Red circle; the competition was anonymous), and his later use of brick in the Reichsbank Project of 1933, suggest that the opaque strips were intended to be red brick. The blocklike banded structure invites comparison with Mies's Concrete Office Building Project of 1923 and Urban Design Proposal for Alexanderplatz of 1929 (also sponsored by the Berlin Traffic Authority).

The height of the nine-story building would have assured it a prominent place in the largely nineteenth- and turn-of-the-century urban landscape, and would have allowed sweeping views of the city from the upper levels and the roof gardens or terraces. A collage emphasizes the relationship between the building and the surrounding landscape, and it is notable that the structure with which Mies's proposal holds the greatest sympathy is the sleek glass-and-steel shed of the Friedrichstrasse station. The convex curve of the facades, the fluid lines of a sketch for the project, and the pull of the lateral slabs away from the central core allude to the building's role as a fulcrum in the traffic-filled city. Further, the attention to and articulation of movement recall contemporary work by Mendelsohn.

The triangular core, obscured in elevation but visible in plan, was to be linked to the slabs by corridors off which were located the main circulation routes. Drawings indicate that in addition to office and retail space the building was to provide a hotel and underground access to the subway. Mies's sketches for storefronts (one includes a storefront for Chrysler automobiles), his detailed organization of the hotel, and the attention given to the upper terraces suggest that his intention was not merely to provide a multiple-use shell but to resolve a series of spatial and functional relationships within a single unified composition attuned to the dynamism of the modern city.
—*Lucy M. Maulsby*

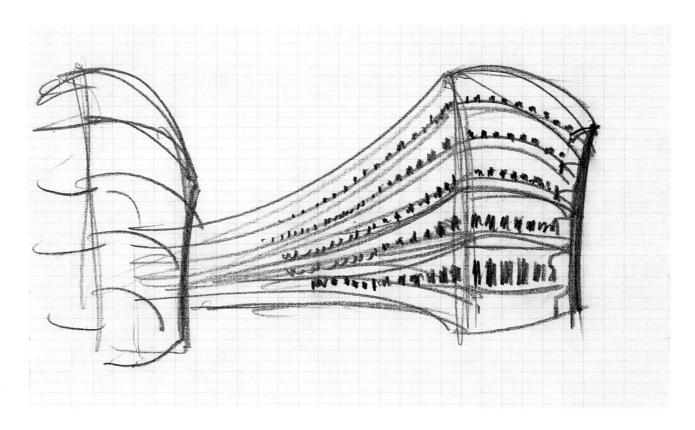

184. Sketch perspective view (detail). Pencil on graph paper, 8¾ x 11¼" (22.2 x 28.3 cm)

185. Massing and plan sketches. Pencil on paper, 8¼ x 11⅝" (20.9 x 29.6 cm). Canadian Centre for Architecture, Montreal

186. Massing and plan sketches. Pencil on paper, 8⅝ x 11⅛" (21.9 x 28.2 cm). Canadian Centre for Architecture, Montreal

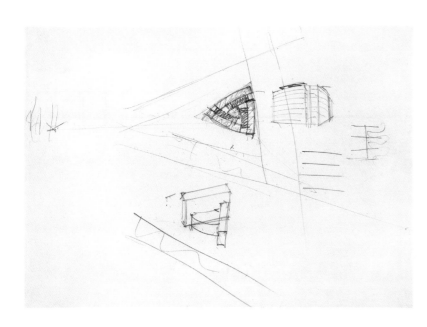

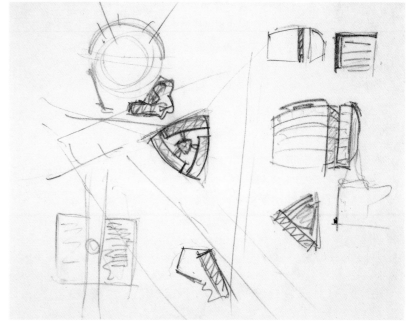

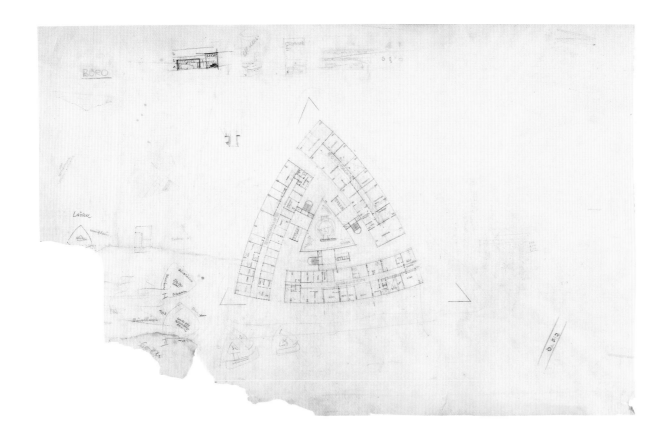

187. Plan of typical floor with office layouts. Pencil and colored pencil on paper, 28¼ x 39½" (71.8 x 100.6 cm)

188. Plan of lower level and connecting passageway to U-Bahn. Pencil and colored pencil on paper, 21½ x 39½" (54.8 x 100.5 cm)

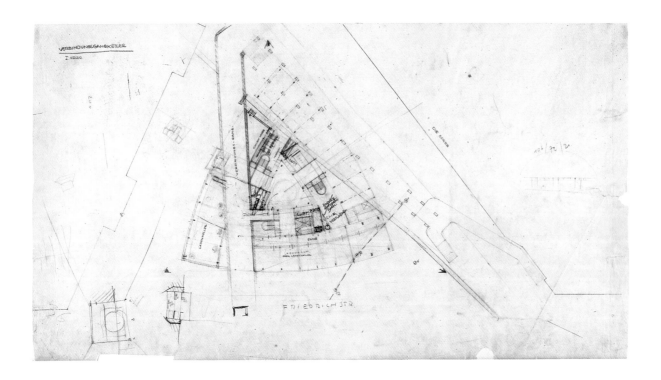

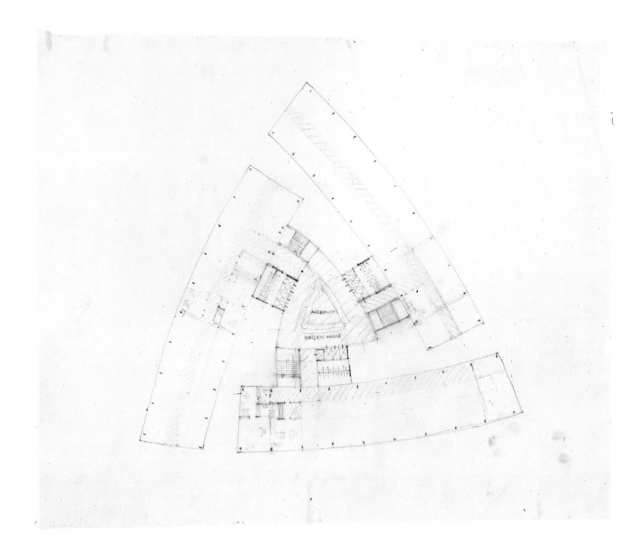

189. Plan of typical floor, circulation study. Pencil on tracing paper, 18 x 21½" (45.7 x 54.4 cm).

190. View from west. Photomontage (lost). Originally published in *Wasmuths Monatshefte für Baukunst und Städtebau*, April 1930

191. View from north (detail). Photomontage (lost). Originally published in *Wasmuths Monatshefte für Baukunst und Städtebau*, April 1930

Neue Wache War Memorial Project, Berlin-Mitte, 1930

In April 1930, Mies was invited to take part in a state competition to create a war memorial inside Karl Friedrich Schinkel's Neue Wache (1816–18), the then unused royal guardhouse on Unter den Linden. Accounts of Mies's architecture during this period have been so preoccupied with the famous projects at Barcelona and Brno that, with a few notable exceptions, they have paid relatively little attention to the design that Mies submitted to the committee in July of that year. Yet Mies's striking reinterpretation of the classical monument did not suffer from critical neglect in its own day. In addition to the proposals of each of the competitors (Peter Behrens, Erich Blunck, Hans Grube, Mies, Hans Poelzig, and the eventual winner, Heinrich Tessenow), we have as a record of the competition the written opinions of the jurors—a distinguished group that included both government officials and prominent members of the Berlin architectural community—as well as the observations made in the contemporary press by *Frankfurter Zeitung* feuilletonist Siegfried Kracauer, *Das Kunstblatt* editor Paul Westheim, and architectural critic Adolf Behne, among others.

The competition program made two specific demands: for a sign of contemplation ("*Denkzeichen*"), and for a central atrium open to the sky—according to the program, the layout least in conflict with the building's symmetrical plan. The site was a space that had once included the guardhouse's interior courtyard but had since been roofed over, so that the program now called for the creation of a new aperture in the ceiling. At some point during a brief but intense period of preliminary sketching, however, Mies realized that an atrium open to street noise and the elements would ultimately detract from his main objective, which was to lead the viewer through and eventually beyond this interior space by means of an enhanced awareness of the room's perspectival recession.

The preparatory drawings reveal the major strategies with which Mies experimented: a monolith (or sometimes a freestanding wall) set near and parallel to the room's far wall, suggesting the continuation of space behind it; the dedication "To the Dead" ("*DEN TOTEN*"), inscribed on the monolith so as to accentuate the composition's vanishing point; linear elements to the side, such as glass walls and benches, leading the viewer toward the back of the room; a horizontal slab on the floor that in foreshortened perspective renderings draws one's attention away from the ceiling and toward the rear door; richly textured surfaces of various patterns and materials (green Tinian marble, black granite, travertine); and finally a low ceiling, possibly made of glass or fabric, permitting a diffuse and somber light.

By eliminating the adornments typical of war commemoration—wreaths, torches, figurative statuary—and by heightening the visitor's perception of spatial extension (going so far as to create a rear exit linking the interior of the memorial to the rest of the site, a landscape consisting of a grid of trees), Mies's monument proposed that death can never be grasped in the form of familiar icons, but only indirectly, as the beholder became conscious of the distance between the dead and the living, the past and the present. It was this psychic distance—to which the architect alluded by using the abstract, conceptual code name "Space" ("*Raum*") for his anonymous submission—that the Neue Wache project attempted to make visually palpable. —*Paul Galvez*

192. Sketch interior perspective view. Pencil on paper, 8¼ x 13" (20.8 x 33.3 cm)

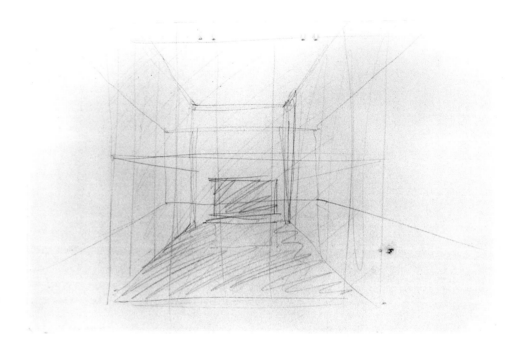

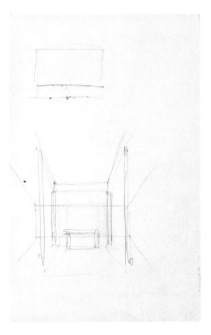
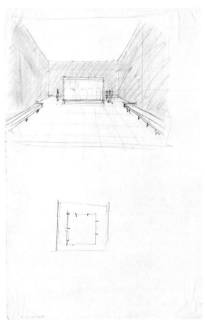
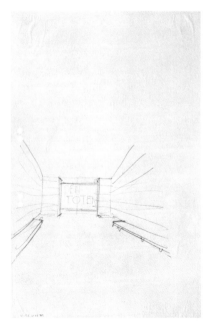
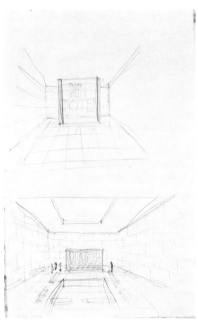

193. Sketch plan and interior
perspective view. Pencil on
paper, 13 x 8¼" (33.3 x 20.8 cm)

194. Sketch interior perspective
view and plan. Pencil on paper,
13 x 8¼" (33.3 x 20.8 cm)

195. Sketch interior perspective
view. Pencil on paper, 13 x 8¼"
(33.3 x 20.8 cm)

196. Two sketch interior perspective views. Pencil on paper,
13 x 8¼" (33 x 21 cm)

197. Floor plan and sections
study (detail). Pencil on
tracing paper, 41¼ x 41¾"
(104.5 x 106 cm)

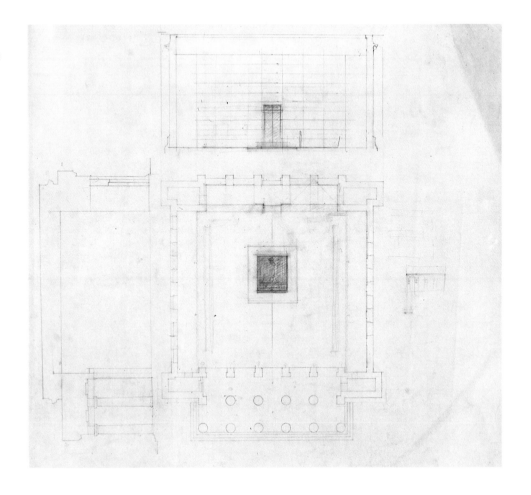

198. Section study through hall.
Pencil on tracing paper,
17 x 22¾" (43 x 57.7 cm)

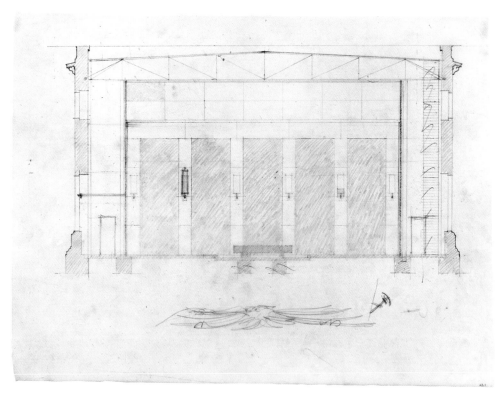

199–202. Sketch interior
perspective views. All pencil on
paper, 8¼ x 13" (20.8 x 33.3 cm)

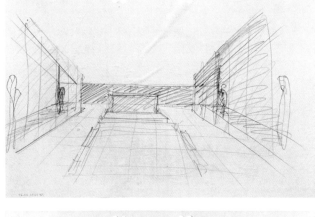

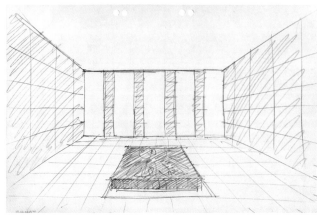

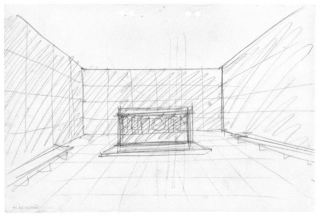

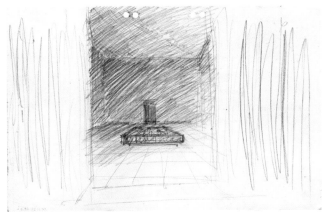

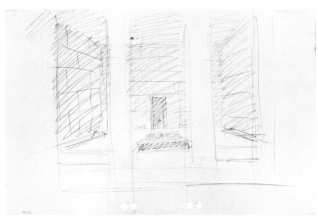

203–6. Sketch interior perspective views. All pencil on paper, 8¼ x 13" (20.8 x 33.3 cm)

207. Interior perspective view. Drawing: Sergius Ruegenberg, 1930. Location unknown, originally published in *Das Kunstblatt*, September 1930

Golf Club Project, Krefeld, 1930

In the summer of 1930, as a result of his connections with the Verseidag silk company, Mies was invited to participate in a limited competition for the new Krefeld Golf Club. Two preoccupations emerge from the statement accompanying his submission: the separation of different activities in the building's plan, and a sensitivity to the local weather. These two themes—careful zoning in the plan, and the relationship of building to natural setting—were recurrent themes in Mies's work. The Golf Club Project provided a focused opportunity to explore both, since the design would have to accommodate a number of disparate activities (changing rooms, social rooms, administrative and service spaces, living accommodations) and also to serve as a staging area for ritualized forays into nature—the sculpted parkland of the golf course.

The building design consists of a series of separate volumes centrifugally organized under a sheltering roof plane that covers exterior as well as interior spaces. The glass-walled *Saal* or reception hall, adjacent to the bridge rooms and bar, is perpendicular to and turned away from the block of changing rooms, just as both the administrative offices and groundskeeper's residence turn their primary faces away from the center of the complex. The freestanding glass pavilion emerged more fully here than in the German Pavilion in

Barcelona the year before; it would recur in the Gericke House Project (1932) and was finally built as the Farnsworth House in Plano, Illinois (1949–50).

Mies prepared at least two versions of the Krefeld project, and automobile access figures prominently in both; in the final version it is accommodated through an extended porte cochere under a long roof plane continuous with the roof of the building. This prominent device underscores the idea of the building as a base of operations to be repeatedly left and returned to. The distended organization of the plan seems to do the same: the building is represented as a series of pieces pulled away from each other by the attractions of landscape and sport, and held together by the anchoring plane of the roof.

—*Claire Zimmerman*

208. Floor plan study (preliminary version; formerly catalogued as Tugendhat House). Charcoal on tracing paper, 17¾ x 26¼" (45 x 66.6 cm)

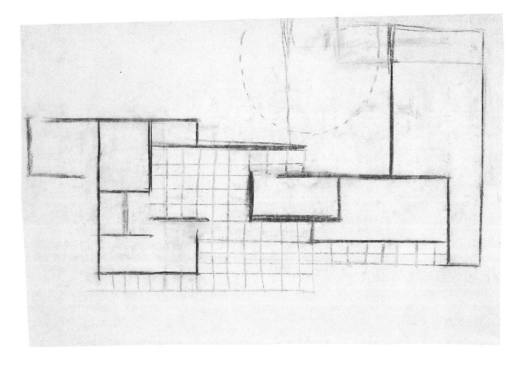

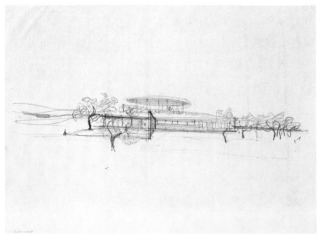

209–11. Sketch perspective
views (preliminary version).
All pencil on paper, 8¼ x 11½"
(20.8 x 29.5 cm)

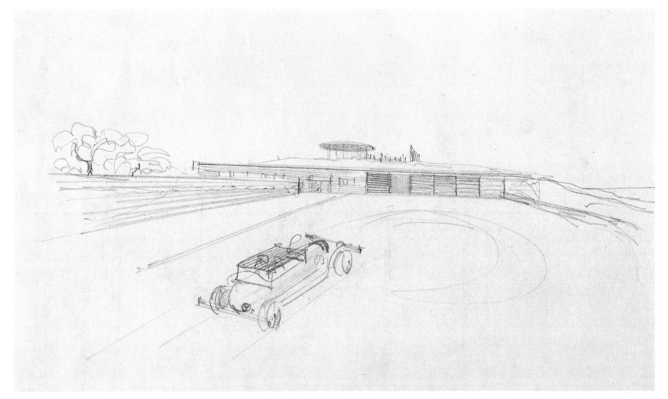

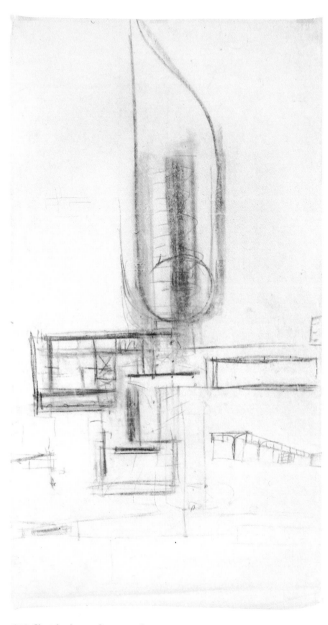

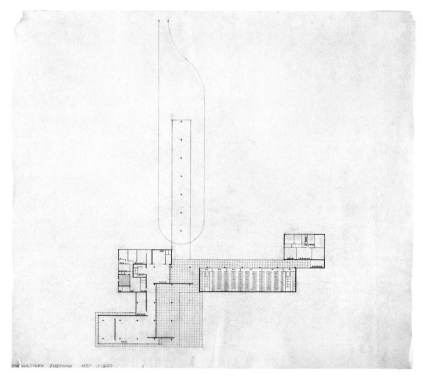

213. Floor plan (final version).
Pencil on tracing paper, 27 x 31"
(68.4 x 79.3 cm)

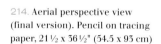

214. Aerial perspective view
(final version). Pencil on tracing
paper, 21½ x 36½" (54.5 x 93 cm)

212. Sketch plan and perspective
views (final version). Charcoal
on tracing paper, 39½ x 21½"
(100.4 x 54.5 cm)

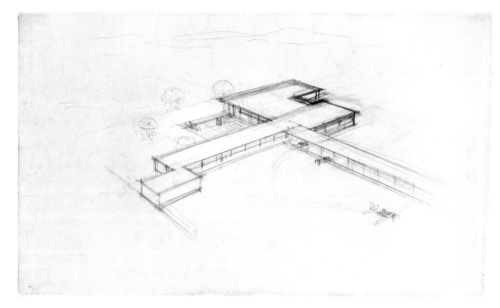

215. Perspective view from
beneath canopy (final version).
Pastel and pencil on tracing
paper, 21½ x 42¼"
(54.6 x 107.5 cm)

216. Perspective view of terrace
and clubhouse beyond (final
version). Pencil on tracing paper,
28½ x 39½" (72.6 x 100.6 cm)

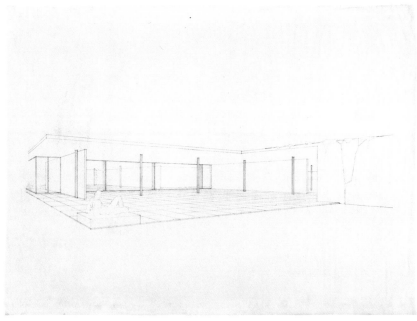

Exhibition House and Apartment for a Bachelor, German Building
Exhibition, Berlin, 1931

The Exhibition House expanded upon the radical spatial experimentation that Mies had begun with the Brick Country House Project of 1924 and realized in 1928–30 in the German Pavilion in Barcelona and the Tugendhat House in Brno. Conceived as a residence for a childless couple, the house was exhibited in *Die Wohnung unserer Zeit* (The dwelling of our time), a section of the German Building Exhibition directed by Mies and offering different architects' solutions to contemporary housing needs. The structure was a low rectilinear pavilion, its roof slab supported by a steel-frame skeleton of fifteen columns arranged in a strict grid. Intersecting the grid were nonstructural, partition-like walls interrupted by expanses of glass. Extending beyond the roof, these walls connected the interior with the surrounding courtyard areas and reflecting pool, creating what Mies called "attached garden rooms." The design effectively collapsed the division of inside and out, revealing Mies's interest in blurring the boundaries between architecture and nature. The open-plan interior was organized by the arrangement of the furnishings, most of them designed by Mies. Interior doors were for the most part eschewed in favor of hanging fabric partitions.

Also installed in *Die Wohnung unserer Zeit* was Mies's Apartment for a Bachelor. The design clearly responded to Germany's ongoing discussion of the *Existenzminimum*, the minimum needs for human existence (and here, specifically, the minimum spatial requirements), but Mies's characteristic choice of rich materials like rosewood, leather, and silk for the furnishings proved that "smaller" need not mean "lower quality." The apartment was a free-flowing space, with the placement of furniture defining different areas: dining and work spaces; living and sleeping areas, divided by a bookcase/storage unit; and a bathroom, kitchen, and utility room, all in a space less than seven by nine meters square (c. 23 by 29½ feet).
—*Marianne Eggler-Gerozissis*

217 Ground-floor plan with furniture layout, Exhibition House. Pencil on tracing paper, 15¼ x 32¾" (38.8 x 83.3 cm)

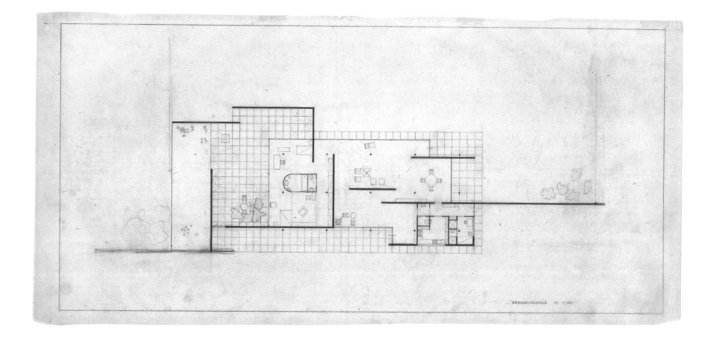

218. Perspective view study, Exhibition House. Charcoal and pencil on tracing paper, 21½ x 33¾" (54.8 x 85.9 cm)

219. Exhibition House as shown on cover of *Die Form*, June 15, 1931

220. Sketch aerial perspective view, Exhibition House. Pencil on paper, 8¼ x 11¾" (20.9 x 29.6 cm)

DIE FORM

ZEITSCHRIFT FÜR GESTALTENDE ARBEIT

6. JAHR

HEFT 6

15. JUNI 1931

VERLAG HERMANN RECKENDORF G.M.B.H. BERLIN SW 68

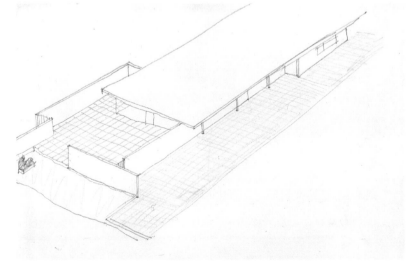

221. View of entrance hall, Exhibition House. 1931. Gelatin silver photograph, 6⅜ x 8⅞" (16 x 22.5 cm)

222. View of living area, Exhibition House. 1931. Gelatin silver photograph, 6⅝ x 9" (16.8 x 22.9 cm)

223. View from court, Exhibition House. 1931. Gelatin silver photograph, 8³⁄₁₆ x 11³⁄₁₆" (20.9 x 28.4 cm). Photograph: Emil Leitner

224. View of court with
reflecting pool, Exhibition House.
1931. Gelatin silver photograph,
6⅜ x 8⅞" (16 x 22.5 cm)

225. Interior view, Apartment
for a Bachelor. 1931. Gelatin
silver photograph, 6⁹⁄₁₆ x 9"
(16.7 x 22.8 cm). Photograph:
Curt Rehbein

226. Elevations and sections
of wardrobe, Apartment for a
Bachelor. Pencil on tracing
paper, 21¼ x 29¼" (54 x 74.3 cm)

227. Floor plan with furniture
layout and elevations of doors
and cabinets, Apartment for a
Bachelor. Pencil on tracing
paper, 21½ x 28¾" (54.5 x 73 cm)

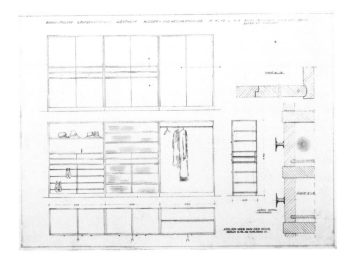

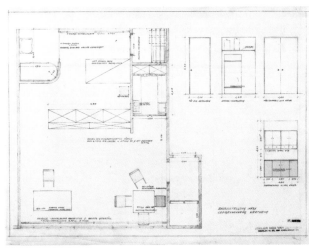

Gericke House Project, Berlin-Wannsee, 1932

The Gericke House Project was produced for an unusual private competition administered by the architect Werner March for Herbert Gericke, director of the German Academy in Rome. The house site was on Grosse Seestrasse, near the Potsdamer Chaussee, looking across the Wannsee to the shores of Berlin's affluent southwestern suburbs. The new building was to occupy the site of an earlier Italianate villa, where demolition had left three terraces stepping down toward the water. In the three weeks available, Mies produced a series of elegant, sparely drawn renderings. None of the four entrants (Mies, Bruno Paul, and two who are not known) built the dwelling, which Gericke described in later correspondence as a "small bungalow-style house" with room for five live-in staff.

The Gericke House Project comprises three elements: the landscape, with its beautiful stands of old trees; an existing building site, the remnant of an earlier architectural culture; and Mies's new proposal. That design consists of a series of discreet pavilions, sitting long and low in the site, and surrounded by green. The pavilions are tenuously connected to one another at their corners or linked by a common roof, as at the Krefeld Golf Club of 1930; but here the centrifugal plan is distributed over two levels and a basement. The building also recalls the Brick Country House Project of 1924, except that here, walls extending beyond the limits of the interior are retaining walls built against the cavity of the old mansion. Thus Mies links extension into the landscape to a sectional change, literally embedding the architecture in the site.

The Gericke commission should also be considered in the context of the Tugendhat House design of 1928–30, as it proposed a similar plan distribution within a very different building form. The Tugendhat site had dictated a street-level entry with bedrooms above and living floors below. Here Mies went farther, both with familiar elements like the sinkable window and the winter garden, and with a more integrated approach to architecture and landscape. At Wannsee, the stipulation that the outdoors be directly accessible from the interior, with no steps to intervene, led Mies to minimize the division between architecture and garden, in a building where spatial flow would extend fully to the outside. The court-house designs, whether theoretical or sited, would provide an arena for exploring this theme further. But what makes the Gericke project a compelling house design is its centrifugal, distended layout, with tentacles of building extending into the landscape and waves of green extending into and over the architecture.

—*Claire Zimmerman*

228. Entrance-floor plan. Pencil on illustration board, 19½ x 25½" (49.5 x 64.8 cm)

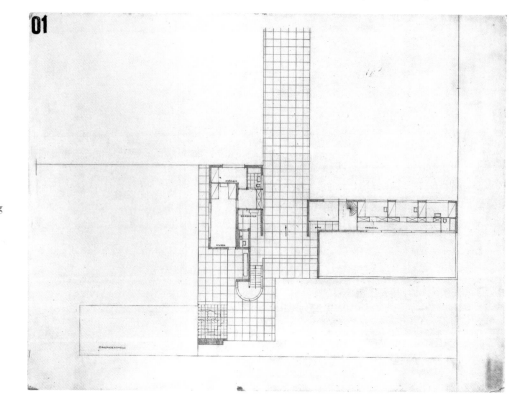

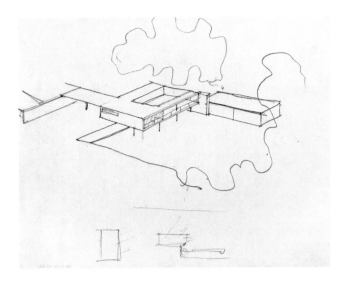

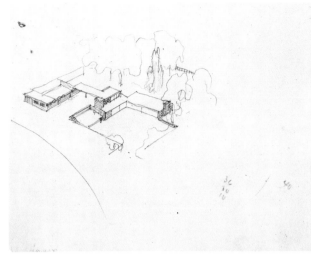

229–30. Sketch perspective
views. Pencil on paper, 8¼ x
11¾" (20.8 x 29.7 cm)

231. Two sketch perspective
views. Pencil on paper, 8¼ x
11¾" (20.8 x 29.7 cm)

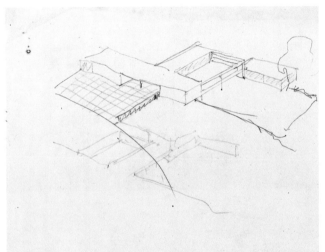

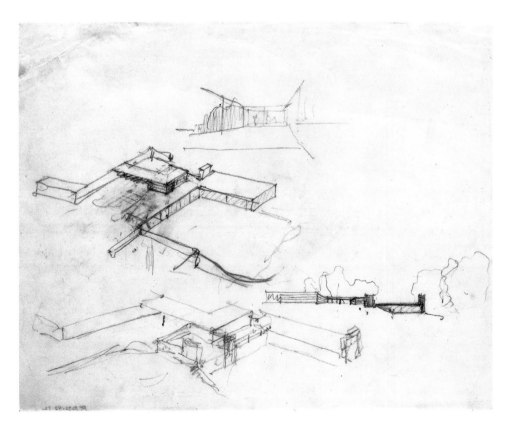

232. Sketch perspective views.
Pencil on paper, 8¼ x 11¾"
(20.8 x 29.7 cm)

269

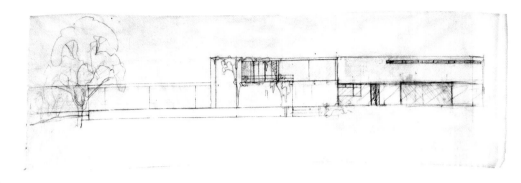

233 (left). Sketch perspective
view. Pencil on paper, 8¼ x
11¾" (20.8 x 29.7 cm)

234 (above). Elevation study
facing Wannsee. Pencil on tracing
paper, 7⅞ x 23¾" (20 x 60.4 cm).
Private collection, Chicago

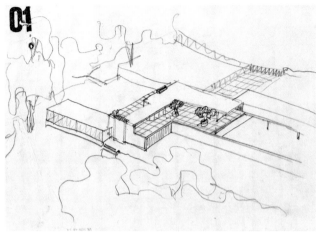

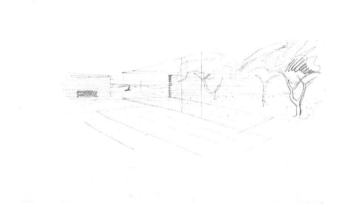

235 (above). Interior perspective
view from foot of stair. Pencil on
paper, 8¼ x 11¾" (20.8 x 29.7 cm)

236 (right). Main-floor plan.
Pencil on illustration board,
19½ x 25½" (49.5 x 64.8 cm)

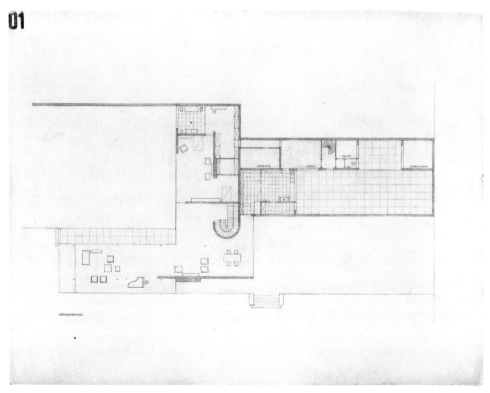

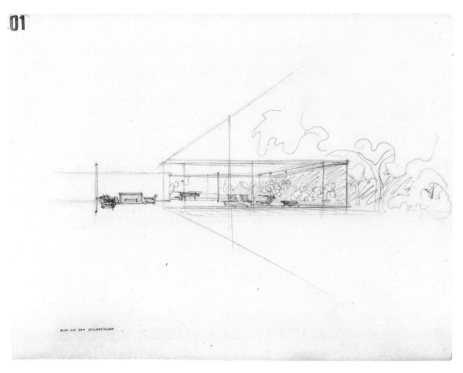

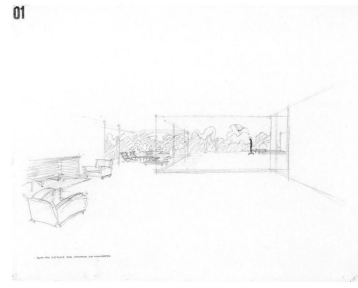

237. Perspective view of sitting area and living room from master bedroom. Pencil on illustration board, 19 ½ x 25 ½" (49.5 x 64.8 cm)

238. Perspective view of sitting area, living room, and court from dining area. Pencil on illustration board, 19 ½ x 25 ½" (49.5 x 64.8 cm)

239. Perspective view of dining area (at left), sitting area, and living room (at right) from court. Pencil on illustration board, 19 ½ x 25 ½" (49.5 x 64.8 cm)

Lemke House, Berlin-Hohenschönhausen, 1932–33

In its modest scale and program, the Lemke House, Mies's last completed house before his emigration to the United States, offers a glimpse of his architectural thinking during a significant shift in his career. In February 1932, Karl Lemke, the proprietor of a printing business, solicited from Mies a design for a new house to be built on two adjacent lakeside lots in the eastern Berlin district of Hohenschönhausen. Lemke, with limited ability or willingness to spend, imposed on Mies the minimum program for a bourgeois house of the time: a bedroom, a living room, an *Arbeitszimmer des Herren* or gentleman's study, a *Zimmer der Dame* or ladies' parlor, a guest room, and the service spaces (*Wirtschaftsräume*). Lemke also made clear his need, for fiscal reasons, to have the structure completed by October of the same year; interior work and landscaping continued into 1933.

Over the next few months, despite all the programmatic, budgetary, and scheduling constraints, Mies produced several sketches that mark a transition in his residential architecture from the centrifugal houses of the 1920s to the more geometrically bound court-house designs of the 1930s. One notable scheme is a design for a two-story block with a living space defined by a large glass wall and variations on the Tugendhat House stair. Another is for a one-story house with fully or partially enclosed courtyards. Particularly in perspective sketches for the latter, Mies manipulates walls and roofs to frame the landscape. Telescopically extending the boundaries between interior and exterior space, he makes interior and exterior values relative, a point emphasized in their interchangeability over a series of sketches.

Volumetrically the entire building can be described as an L-shaped configuration of two blocks, each in turn containing an L-shaped arrangement of cells around a larger courtyard-like room. The brick is ordinary (and affordable) in quality, lacking the impeccably uniform color and texture of Mies's earlier houses, but it reinforces the sense of massing. Its modesty, too, would have been appropriate for the client, who was a member of the Communist Party.

A *Halle* or living hall forms the dominant space in the entire composition of the Lemke House through Mies's deft treatment of the walls and windows, resulting in a complex but clearly articulated juncture of material and mass. This space is defined on the one side by the block containing the living room and on the other by the volume of the bedroom. A full expanse of glass connects the two masses and divides the *Halle* from the courtyard. The slight recess of the window plane from that of the bedroom reinforces the *Halle*'s sense of spatial extension into the courtyard. Where the glass expanse of the *Halle* joins the living room block, it separates the plaster on the inside from the brick on the outside. The plaster wall itself is coplanar with the glass doors of the foyer, revealing the corner of the living room.

Mies and Lilly Reich designed the furniture, which is mostly of wood with leather upholstery. Sharp lines and right angles characterize the tables and bookcases, while the armchairs and desk chairs taper slightly. Steel and its more slender proportions are absent, while glass is limited to the sliding doors on the bookcases. —*Josef Asteinza*

240. Sketch floor plan (preliminary version). Pencil and colored pencil on tracing paper, 14¾ x 25½" (37.7 x 64.7 cm)

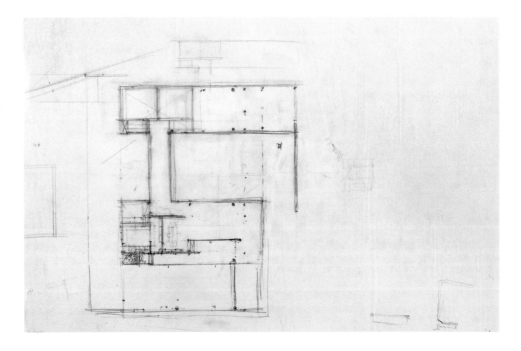

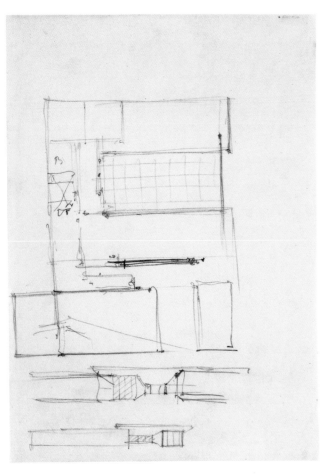

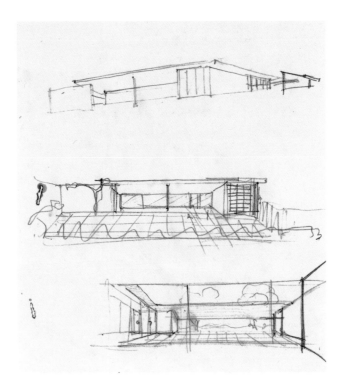

243 (below). Sketch elevation
and plan (two-story version).
Pencil on paper, 8¼ x 11½"
(20.9 x 29.5 cm)

241 (above). Sketch plan and
perspective views (preliminary
version). Pencil on paper, 11½ x
8¼" (29.5 x 20.9 cm)

242 (above right). Three sketch
exterior perspective views
(preliminary version; detail).
Pencil on paper, 11½ x 8¼"
(29.5 x 20.9 cm)

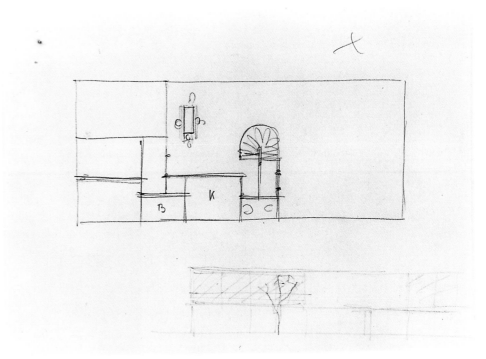

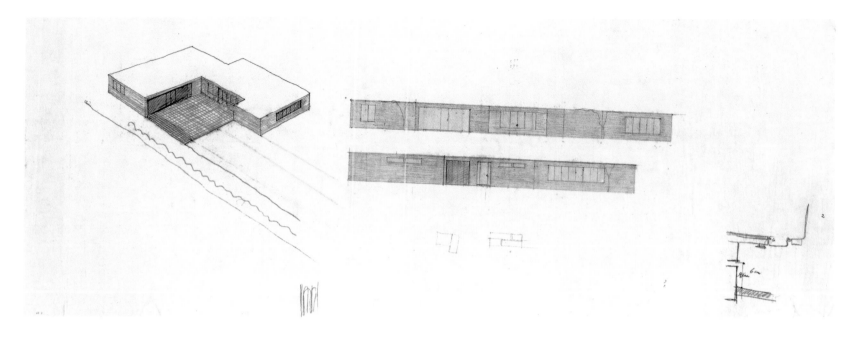

244. Aerial perspective view,
elevations, and sketch studies.
Pencil on tracing paper,
16 x 42¾" (40.6 x 108.6 cm)

245. View from garden.
After 1933

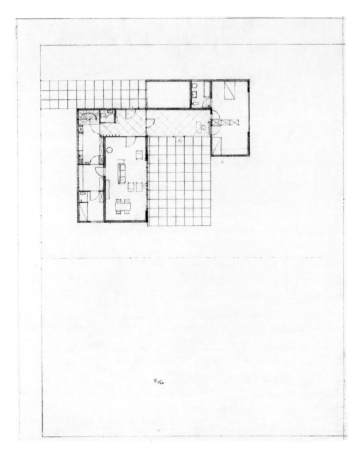

246. Plan (final version). Pencil on tracing paper, 23¾ x 9¼" (61.5 x 23.1 cm)

247. View of terrace. After 1933

248. View from garden. After 1933

Reichsbank Project, Berlin-Mitte, 1933

In February of 1933, Mies was one of thirty architects invited to participate in a national competition to design an extension of the Reichsbank building from Kurstrasse to the Spree Canal. The extension, which required the demolition of existing buildings and street patterns, was to provide for the bank's expanding needs and enhance its presence in the capital. The scale and location of the new building suggest that it was also to extend the monumental center of Berlin and provide an architectural testimonial to the anticipated economic growth of the nation. The competition entries were submitted to a jury in May of 1933, and Mies's project was one of six awarded a prize. The projects were exhibited and published, but none of them was executed.

In plan, Mies's proposed building reads as an isolated urban block. (It was to be connected to the existing building through an underground passage.) The curved main facade is set slightly back from the street; to the rear, three connected rectangular units project toward the canal. The main facade is dominated by axial symmetry and is broken into three primary units. The base is articulated by a three-story brick face, broken at ground level by two narrow strips of glass windows (one to each side) and at the second story by a double-height projecting glass wall centered over the primary entrance. The upper levels of the ten-story facade are composed of bands of glass and brick; the uppermost level includes a roof garden or terrace.

In both style and scale, this facade presents a sharp contrast to the existing urban landscape, but the use of brick, the continuation of established floor heights, and the treatment of the site as a unified block are sympathetic to Berlin tradition. The rear facade, again composed of glass and brick bands, appears from the far side of the canal as three independent structures, but maintains the monumental tenor exhibited in the main facade. Its three blocks deny a single vantage point, inviting the viewer to move through the city; the composition demonstrates an affinity with the panoramic interventions of Karl Friedrich Schinkel, most notably in his design for the Packhof (1829–32), demolished by Mies's time but originally located along the same branch of the Spree River.

The internal organization of the Reichsbank demonstrates Mies's concern to reconcile the bank's diverse functional and representational needs within the overall design program. The brick entrance hall, reached by ascending a split staircase that rises from the main entrance, extends the entire length of the front facade, offering a panoramic view of the existing Reichsbank building through the double-height glass window, as well as access to three equally monumental adjacent banking halls and to the offices on the upper floors. The banking halls are separated from the entrance hall by floor-to-ceiling glass walls with doors at their bases. Used for official functions as well as employee relaxation, the various roof terraces frame views of Potsdamer Platz and Liepziger Platz, the commercial center of modern Berlin, and also look toward medieval Berlin, centered around the Mollen Markt and Rathaus. Again sensitive to context, Mies orients the building to exploit these views, locating the Reichsbank within the commercial history of the city.

The monumentality of the Reichsbank project has encouraged scholars to understand it as a rupture in both ideological and formal terms from Mies's domestic and urban projects of the 1920s, and as a response to the changing political climate: Hitler had been appointed chancellor less than a month before the project was announced. But the project can also be understood in terms of Mies's continued interest in the urban landscape and the role of the office building in the modern city. The success of Mies's solution lies in its ability to address the complex functional needs of the bank and to offer a mode of engagement with the city that transcends the building's status as a monument. —*Lucy M. Maulsby*

249. Sketch site plan with massing studies. Diazotype with pencil and colored pencil, 23½ x 26¾" (59.7 x 68 cm)

250. Sketch diagram (detail). Pencil and colored pencil on tracing paper, 10 x 10½" (25.3 x 26.6 cm)

251. Sketch diagram (detail). Pencil and colored pencil on tracing paper, 13½ x 7¾" (34.3 x 19.8 cm)

252. Sketch site plan. Colored pencil on paper, 10¾ x 8½" (27.6 x 21.9 cm)

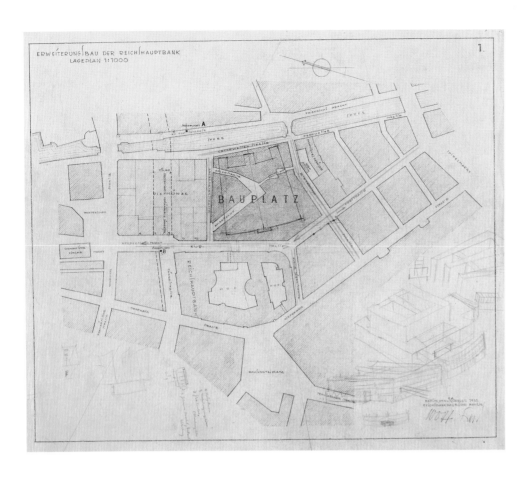

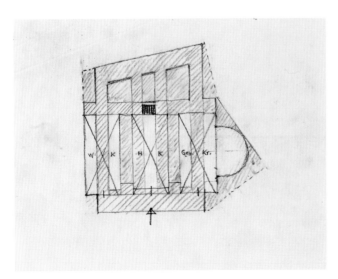

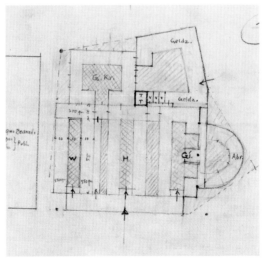

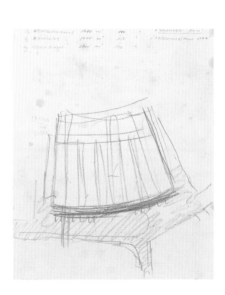

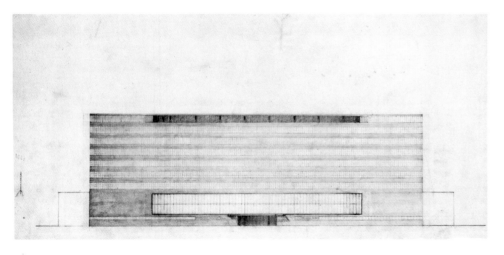

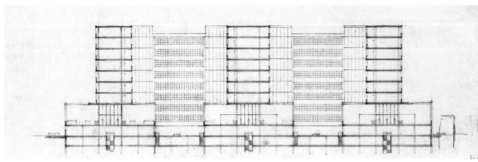

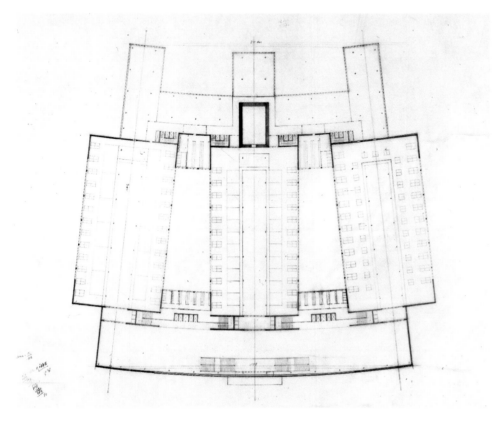

253. Principal facade. Pencil on tracing paper, 14½ x 33½" (37.1 x 85 cm)

254. Transverse section. Pencil on tracing paper, 9¾ x 31½" (24.8 x 80 cm)

255. Second-floor plan. Pencil and colored ink on tracing paper, 35 x 41½" (89.2 x 105.5 cm)

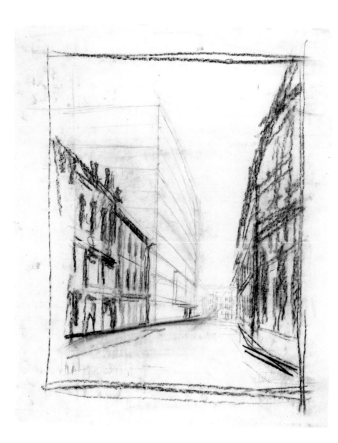

256 (left). Perspective view study of principal facade. Charcoal on tracing paper, 38¼ x 30¾" (97.2 x 78.1 cm)

257 (below left). Sketch perspective view of principal facade (detail). Pencil on tracing paper, 6 x 5¾" (15.1 x 14.5 cm)

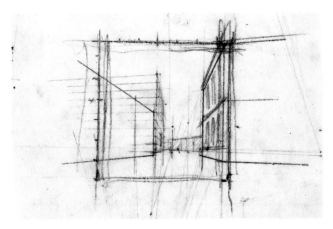

258 (right). Perspective view study of rear facade. Charcoal on tracing paper, 28¼ x 35¾" (71.4 x 90.8 cm)

Mountain House Studies, no intended site known
(possibly Merano, South Tyrol), c. 1934

After the closing of the Bauhaus in Dessau in 1932, Mies reopened the famed institution in Berlin, as a private school of architecture. The Gestapo closed it again in the spring of 1933, and in August of the same year Mies preempted their final decision on the matter by permanently shutting the school down.

Immediately thereafter Mies decamped for a few months with his collaborator and companion Lilly Reich and a few students to Lugano, Switzerland, where he ran an informal atelier away from the tumult of the German capital. For some time after this trip, he periodically returned to drawings for a house for himself, thought to be intended for an Alpine site near Merano, in northern Italy, where he and his family had earlier spent summer vacations. The drawings are notable for the extent to which they translate his personal circumstances into an architectural vision. Of the several schemes that Mies generated as part of this exercise, the most elaborated version features an L-shaped structure wrapping two sides of an open court. The approach to the house is on the opposite side from the court; the outside corner of the structure would have faced the visitor. While the facade facing the court is rendered in sheets of glass, the facade facing the approach is rendered in rough stonework, battered like an archaic fortification. A massive oak tree is part of the composition, standing like an immovable sentry before the entrance to the fragile glass house within.

Although catalogued separately by historians, the Glass House on a Hillside—a single sketch that directly influenced the work of Charles Eames, Philip Johnson, and many other "Miesian" architects—and the House on a Terrace appear to be all part of the same exercise. Whatever their circumstances, both of these represent variations on the theme of a theoretical house project designed for a sloping site. In his 1947 retrospective exhibition at The Museum of Modern Art, Mies gave pride of place in his installation design to this relatively unheralded, unbuilt, and very personal design.
—*Terence Riley*

259. Sketch perspective view.
Pencil on paper, 8¼ x 11¾"
(20.8 x 29.7 cm)

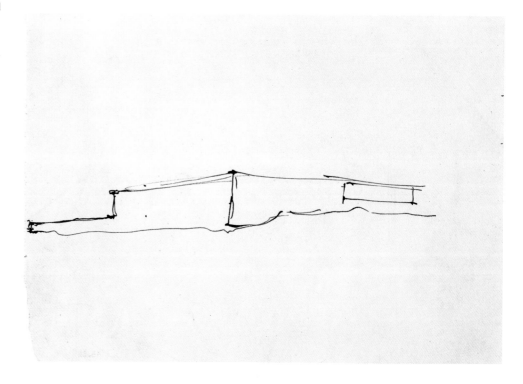

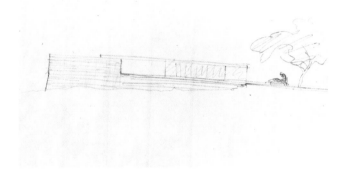

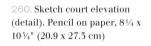

260. Sketch court elevation
(detail). Pencil on paper, 8¼ x
10¾" (20.9 x 27.3 cm)

261. Entrance elevation sketch.
Pencil on paper, 8¼ x 10¾"
(21.1 x 27.4 cm)

262. Aerial perspective view.
Pencil on paper, 8¼ x 11¾"
(20.8 x 29.7 cm)

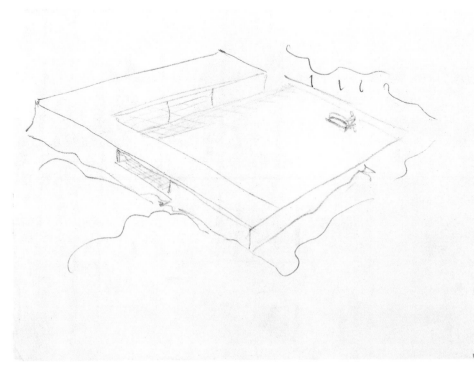

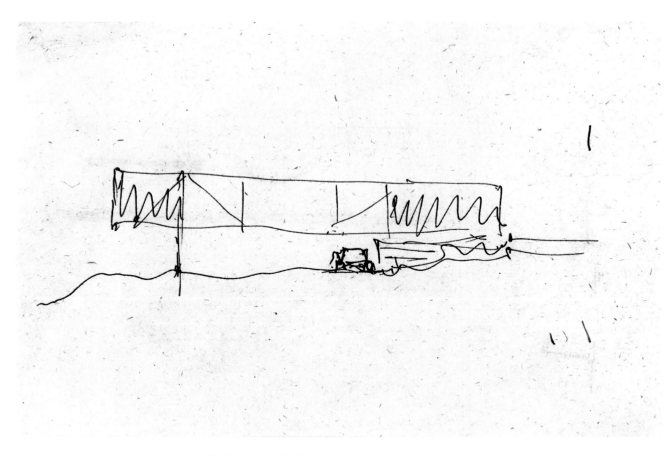

263. Sketch elevation for "Glass House on a Hillside." Ink on paper, 4 ½ x 8" (10.7 x 20.3 cm)

264. Sketch section and perspective view for "House on a Terrace." Pencil on paper, 8 ¼ x 10 ¼" (21 x 27.5 cm)

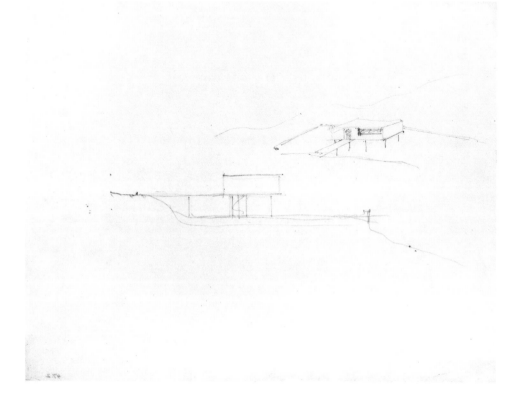

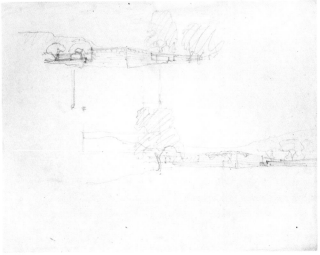

266. Entrance elevation sketch (detail). After 1938. Pencil on paper, 9 x 11½" (22.8 x 29.2 cm)

265. Aerial perspective view. After 1938. Pencil on paper, 8¾ x 11¼" (22 x 28.1 cm). Canadian Centre for Architecture, Montreal

267 Perspective view. After 1938? Charcoal and pencil on tracing paper, 21 x 40" (53.3 x 101.5 cm)

German Pavilion, International Exposition, Brussels, 1934

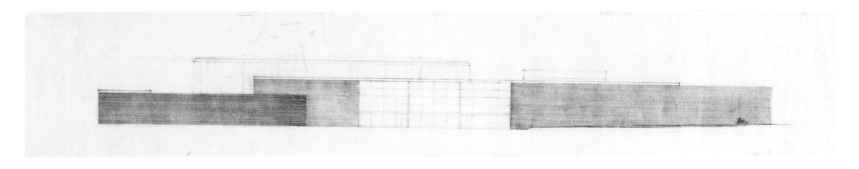

In 1934, the National Socialist government invited Mies and five others to compete for a pavilion for the 1935 Brussels International Exposition. Mies's design was not selected; Ludwig Ruff, architect of the vast, unbuilt Kongresshalle at Nuremburg (1934), won the commission. Construction had begun when Germany withdrew from the exhibition, in late 1934.

Mies's competition submission became government property. While design drawings and project correspondence remain, presentation drawings and model photographs are presumed lost. These lacunae leave certain details of the design unclear. Although the claim (by Mies's employee Sergius Ruegenberg) that Mies's drawings were relegated to the floor of Hitler's office during the review cannot be confirmed, his entry certainly did not win the competition, and he was never invited to design another government building for the National Socialists.

The competition brief included generic program needs as well as specific representational requirements, most prominently the inclusion of the new regime's symbols, including the swastika. Like the German Pavilion at the Barcelona Exposition in 1929, this building would represent the German government internationally, in political and economic terms. Otherwise the project differed from Barcelona in important respects. First, representational and industrial exhibits were to occupy the same space, requiring a much larger building; and second, the symbolic and representational character of the building was not left to the architect's judgment but was clearly dictated in the brief. Formal elements like the "Court of Honor" (*Ehrenhof*) and its flanking "Hall of Honor" (*Ehrenhalle*) were to contrast with such exhibits as "Cross-Section of German Creative Activity in the Context of the Third Reich." In response, Mies produced a design clearly related to Barcelona and other projects, but on a monumental scale. He treated the formal requirements much like other discrete, free-plan elements. Thus the Court of Honor, bearing clear similarities to his own and Heinrich Tessenow's schemes for Berlin's Neue Wache (1930), sits as a spatial object within a matrix of cruciform steel columns.

The site design includes familiar motifs. Both of the two main entrances are flanked by a forecourt, each with a small pool similar to Barcelona's. The brick walls of the building spread into the site in full-height bounding walls and low retaining walls accommodating the grade change, rising from west to east, and increasing the monumental presence of a large but understated building. A restaurant on the lower level is directly accessible from the west. Other program elements—a building for the machine and electrical industries and a small cinema and café—lie east of the main building, along with a grove of trees and a court promoting the upcoming 1936 Berlin Olympics.

The project left Mies on the horns of a stylistic dilemma, torn between the emerging aesthetic conservatism of the National Socialists and his own growing reputation as a leading avant-garde designer. Although the government's cultural policies were not thoroughly defined by the summer of 1934, the outcome of the recent Reichsbank competition showed a clear preference for the static and monumental in important public buildings, with a taste for overtly classical models. On the other hand, Mies was famed for his aesthetic experiments as a modernist and could expect that the international audience of the Brussels Exposition would look to him for an innovative design. The struggle to accommodate both conditions manifests itself in the site design and the internal layout. Specifically, the Court of Honor, approached head-on from the south, provides the building with a static central focus. Yet west of this focus, asymmetrical, freestanding walls loosely define another center. Around this implied center (with its own entry sequence to the north) Mies arranges the exhibits of industry; around the Court of Honor he places the propaganda exhibits, including "People and Empire," "World View," and "Peasant and Soil" (used instead of the National Socialist slogan "Blood and Soil"). The split between these two centers is not emphasized; instead the second exists as an alternative to, or an echo of, the first. Nevertheless, the difference between two spatial conceptions—one static and grandiose, the other dynamically elliptical—makes for an uneasy composition, even within the forgiving matrix of the free-plan grid.

—*Claire Zimmerman*

268. Lateral elevation. Pencil on tracing paper, 7½ x 42¾" (18.9 x 108.5 cm)

269. Sketch interior perspective view. Pencil and colored pencil on paper, 8¾ x 11½" (22.7 x 29 cm)

270. Two plans, three elevations, and one perspective sketch. Pencil on paper, 11¼ x 8¾" (29 x 22.7 cm)

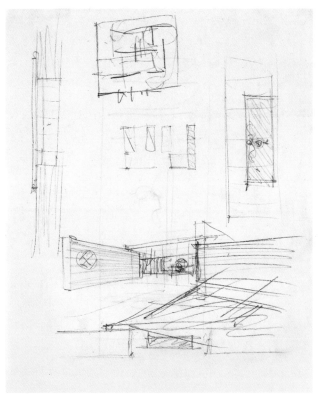

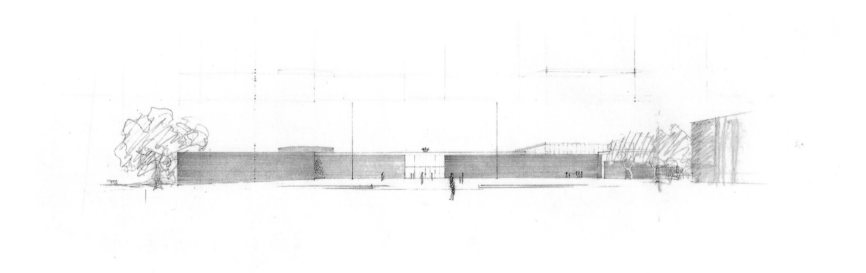

271 (above). Perspective view of
principal facade with female
figure in foreground. Pencil and
colored pencil on tracing paper,
11¼ x 41¹¹⁄₁₆" (28.6 x 103.3 cm).
Private collection, courtesy Max
Protetch Gallery, New York

272 (right). Sketch perspective
view of principal facade, detail
with flags. Crayon on paper,
8½ x 11⁷⁄₁₆" (21.6 x 29.1 cm).
Private collection, courtesy
Max Protetch Gallery, New York

273 (below left). Floor plan and
elevation study. Pencil and
colored pencil on tracing paper,
30¾ x 27½" (78.6 x 70 cm).

274 (below right). Sketch partial
floor plan and perspective view
of principal facade. Colored
pencil on paper, 8¼ x 11¾"
(21 x 29.7 cm)

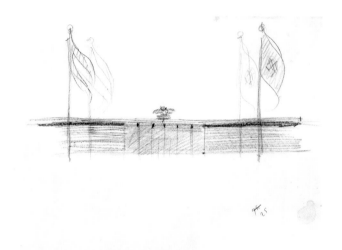

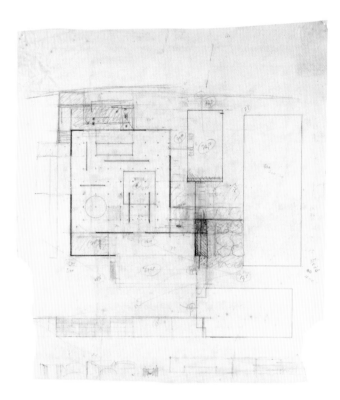

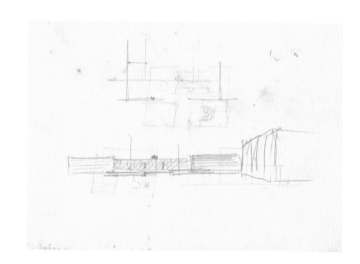

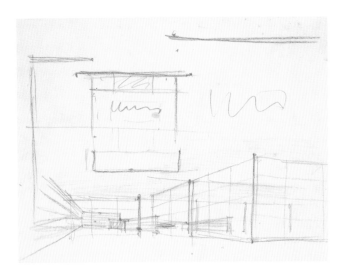

275. Sketch floor plan and interior perspective view. Colored pencil on paper, 8¾ x 11½" (22.7 x 29 cm)

276. Interior perspective view study. Pencil on tracing paper, 10½ x 17¼" (26.4 x 43.9 cm)

277. Interior perspective view study. Pencil on paper, 11¹⁵⁄₁₆ x 17⁷⁄₁₆" (29.9 x 19 cm). Private collection, courtesy Max Protetch Gallery, New York

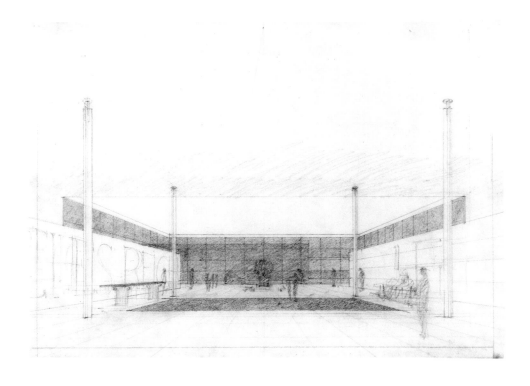

Hubbe House Project, Magdeburg, 1934–35

Like most of Mies's projects of the 1930s, the house he designed for Margarete Hubbe was never built. Little is known of Hubbe other than her membership in the Deutscher Werkbund and her friendship with the artist Emil Nolde, for whom Mies had also designed a house, also unexecuted, in 1929.

Hubbe's property bordered the eastern side of a low-lying river island, the Elb-Insel, in the city of Magdeburg. The site had not been chosen as the ideal spot for a house; the property had been inherited, and had a number of demerits, including existing structures that Mies proposed to demolish and an upstream view that Mies considered "dull." Nonetheless, Mies also favorably noted the distant view across the river, and the "beautiful trees," when he published the project—already abandoned—in *Die Schildgenossen* in August of 1935.

In what appears to be an early site plan, the house is composed of several freestanding and semiattached elements arranged in a pinwheeling fashion. The main entrance pavilion is joined to what appears to be a bedroom wing by a wall that creates an enclosed space between them. As in the Tugendhat House and the Gericke House Project, a semicircular enclosure stands out in the otherwise orthogonal plan.

Mies generated the final plan from a number of different basic schemes, many of them extending along an axis parallel to the river and all of them single-story structures, presumably to be made of brick. Views outward to the landscape are frequently balanced with views into enclosed and semienclosed courts and yards. While the final plan appears to have been pared back from previous versions, the house was to have been commodious, with open, flowing spaces punctuated by cruciform steel columns. In most of the plans, visitors would pass through a central entry on the inland side of the house, between a bedroom wing and a wing for services and staff. Moving around a screening wall, they would come to a glazed living and dining area projecting toward the river. Most of the plans also show a wall extending from the house and enclosing a court to the east of the living area, effectively screening the offensive view, with numerous variations to the west.

In the later schemes the plans become less extended and more condensed, and the principal spaces focus on enclosed courts, except where there is a view across and down the river. In this regard it is important to note an apparent plan to subdivide the property west and north of the house. Thus the increasingly introspective character of the design may be attributed as much to the client's increased need for privacy as to Mies's developing interest in finding a balance between what he called quiet seclusion and open expanse.
—*Terence Riley*

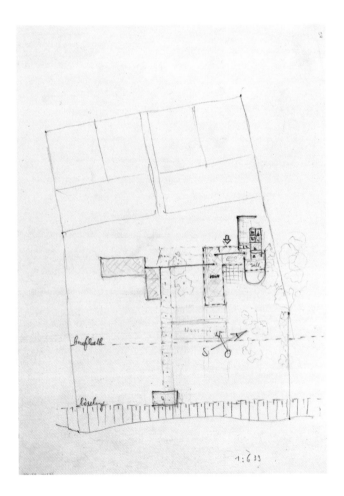

278. Site plan with surrounding land parcels (preliminary version). Pencil on paper, 11 ½ x 8 ¼" (29.6 x 21 cm)

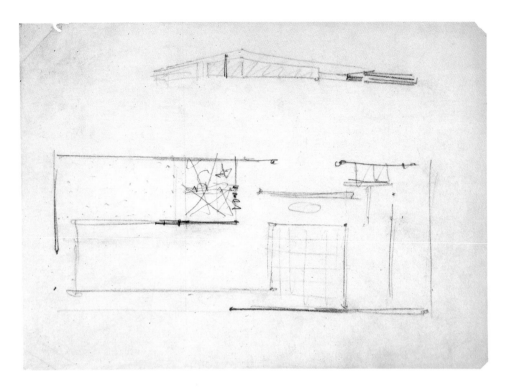

279. Sketch floor plan and exterior perspective view. Pencil on tracing paper, 8½ x 11¾" (21.5 x 29.8 cm). Getty Research Institute, Los Angeles

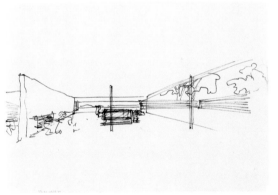

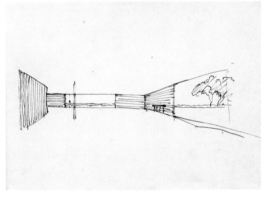

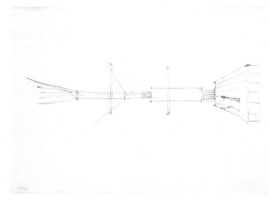

280 (above). Sketch interior perspective view. Ink on paper, 8¼ x 11¾" (20.8 x 29.7 cm)

282 (above right). Sketch interior perspective view. Ink on tracing paper, 8⅜ x 11¾" (21.3 x 29.7 cm)

281 (above center). Sketch interior perspective view. Pencil on tracing paper, 8½ x 11¾" (21.5 x 29.8 cm). Getty Research Institute, Los Angeles

283 (right). Sketch floor plan. Pencil on tracing paper, 11¾ x 21½" (30 x 54.5 cm)

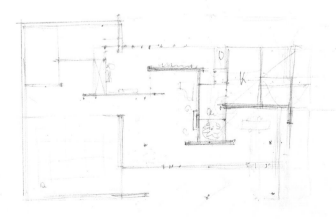

284. Sketch perspective view
of winter garden (detail). Pencil
on tracing paper, 8½ x 11¹¹⁄₁₆"
(21.5 x 29.7 cm). Deutsche
Architektur Museum, Berlin

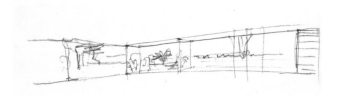

285. Perspective view of foyer
from entrance portico. Pencil on
illustration board, 19 x 26½"
(48.2 x 67.4 cm)

286. Floor plan with furniture
placement (final version). Pencil
on illustration board, 19 x 26½"
(48 x 67.3 cm)

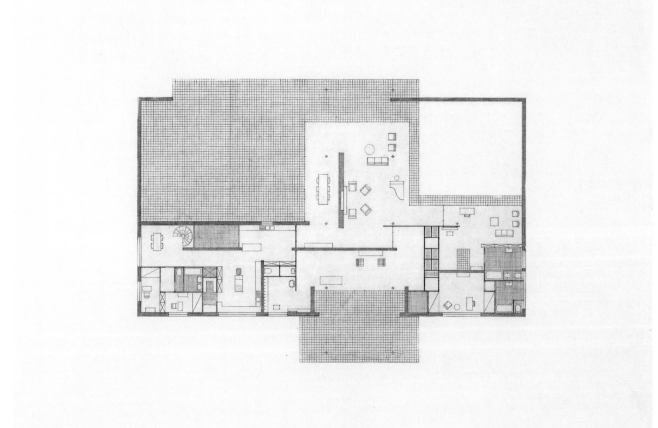

287. Perspective view of living room and court. Pencil on illustration board, 19 x 26½" (48.2 x 67.4 cm)

288. Perspective view of living room and terrace. Pencil on illustration board, 19¼ x 26½" (49.2 x 67.4 cm)

289. Perspective view of court from living room terrace. Pencil on illustration board, 19 x 26½" (48.2 x 67.4 cm)

Court-House Studies, 1934–35

Mies's court-house concept arose out of his teaching at the Bauhaus, where he regularly gave younger students the problem of designing a "settlement" of economical houses with individual gardens and courts on small plots defined by perimeter walls. Under his tutelage, the court-house became an increasingly refined housing strategy that Mies brought with him to America when he began teaching at the Illinois Institute of Technology in Chicago.

In rare instances Mies pursued the concept in his own architectural work, as in the 1934 Court-House with Garage, which shows him extending the original court-house idea into a freestanding house. This project is also highly uncharacteristic in its undulating geometries, which incorporate the turning radius of the automobile, winding its way into a garage at the heart of the house. Besides various plan studies, the best-known of which postdates the project, no other views exist of Mies's singular design, which he may have intended for himself. The designs for houses for Margarete Hubbe and Ulrich Lange similarly adapt the court-house scheme for larger, more luxurious freestanding houses, although both of them reflect other influences as well.

In addition to these adaptations, Mies also worked on a single project for a "settlement" of court-houses. In 1934, he produced a number of drawings showing various ways of subdividing a property owned by Hubbe in Magdeburg, as well as adjacent parcels to the north. Early sketches illustrate his basic strategy: a larger parcel facing the river was reserved for Hubbe's own house, while smaller parcels lay to the north and west.

The most finished plans show that Mies intended the settlement to consist of up to sixteen court-houses. The lots are deeper than they are wide, with brick walls defining their perimeters. As uniformly rectangular as the site permits, they vary in size, with the total area of each one noted on Mies's plans. In the more definitive plans, the size of the lots increases with their proximity to the river.

Mies generated dozens of sketch plans of individual houses corresponding in scale and proportion to his subdivision plan. The houses vary in size, number of bedrooms, and other spatial amenities, with the total area again noted on each plan. But all are related in terms of their basic scheme.

Each house is relatively small, and enclosed in glass. It spans the width of the lot, which is defined by brick walls abutting the house, as in many plans produced by Mies's Bauhaus students. A large open area, planted with grass and vines, provides a relatively expansive view from the main living areas, and distances the house from the street. Smaller, paved courts at the back of the lot are more introspective and bring light and air into the more private areas of the house. The number and size of the paved courts reflect the complexity and scale of the individual house types. —*Terence Riley*

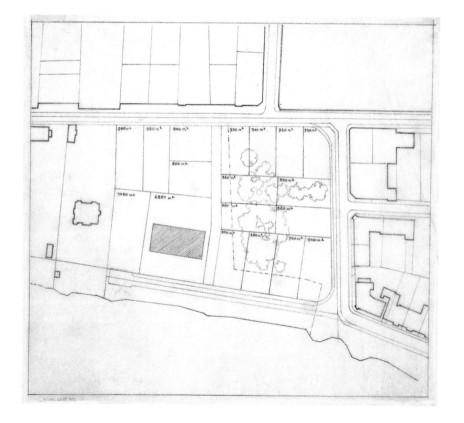

290. Site plan with subdivision plan, Hubbe Court-House Studies. Pencil on tracing paper, 11 x 12" (28 x 30.5 cm)

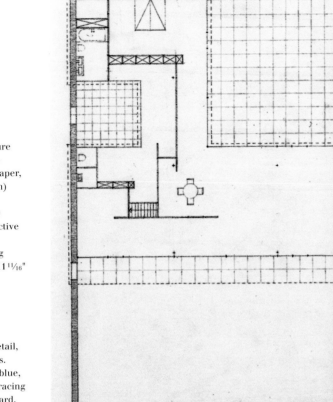

291. Floor plan with furniture layout, Hubbe Court-House Studies. Pencil on tracing paper, 16½ x 11¾" (41.9 x 29.8 cm)

292. Sketch floor plan (259 square meters) and perspective views, Hubbe Court-House Studies. Graphite on tracing paper on cardboard, 8⁷⁄₁₆ x 11¹¹⁄₁₆" (21.4 x 29.8 cm). Canadian Centre for Architecture, Montreal

293. Sketch floor plan (255 square meters) and detail, Hubbe Court-House Studies. Graphite with additions in blue, red, and yellow pencil on tracing paper laid down on cardboard, 8⁷⁄₁₆ x 11¹¹⁄₁₆" (21.5 x 29.8 cm). Canadian Centre for Architecture, Montreal

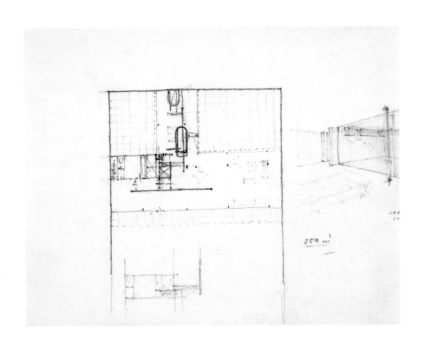

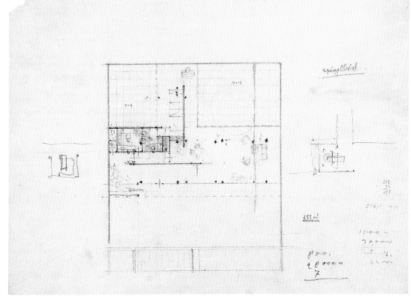

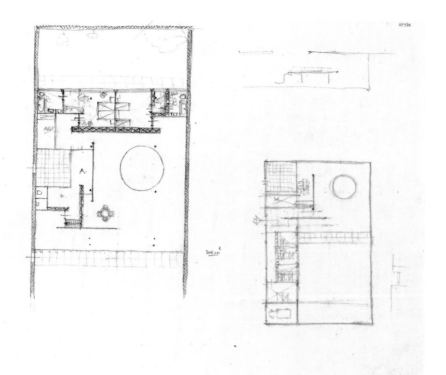

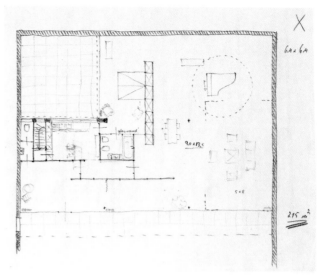

294. Sketch floor plans, Hubbe Court-House Studies. Pencil on tracing paper, 15¾ x 21½" (40 x 54.4 cm)

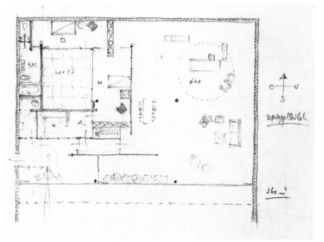

295–97. Sketch floor plans (215, 260, and 230 square meters), Hubbe Court-House Studies. All pencil on paper, 8¼ x 11¾" (20.9 x 29.7 cm)

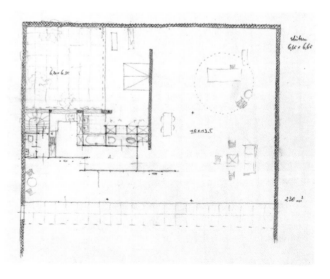

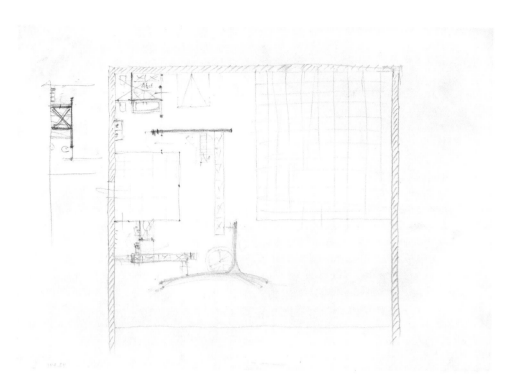

298. Sketch floor plan, Hubbe Court-House Studies. Pencil on tracing paper, 8¼ x 11¼" (20.9 x 29.7 cm)

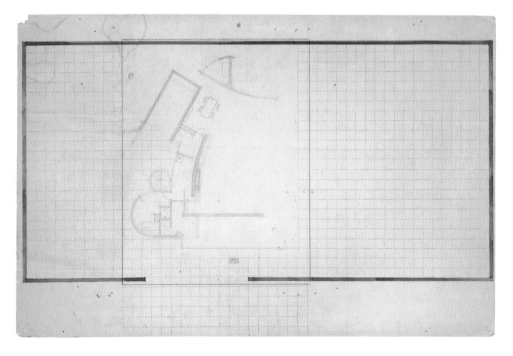

299. Floor plan, Court-House with Garage Project. Graphite, ink, and colored pencil on cardboard, 12⅞ x 19¹¹⁄₁₆" (32.7 x 50 cm). Canadian Centre for Architecture, Montreal

Ulrich Lange House Project, Krefeld, 1935

Mies received the commission, prepared two finished schemes, and made presentations to the Krefeld building department for a house for Ulrich Lange all in a year's time. The project was abandoned by early 1936, when Mies was sorely in need of work. While documentation is scarce, the Krefeld building authorities apparently objected to the design's unadorned modern facades and flat roofline. Permission was given to build only if an earthen berm was erected to shield the house from the neighbors, causing Mies to withdraw from the project.

The first of Mies's two schemes is for a single-story brick house comprising two wings—connected by a glass-enclosed foyer—and a freestanding garage. The first wing contains the main living and dining areas and the kitchen; the second contains the bedrooms, a sitting room, and a gallery. Brick walls and hedges extending from the structures create a service court between the kitchen and the garage and enclose a garden between the two wings of the house.

The second scheme maintains certain aspects of the first, but makes a number of notable changes. Now the extensions of the brick walls nearly enclose the house within a single rectangle, which is clearly bisected to create a service wing, including the garage, and a living area. The latter is comprised of a semienclosed paved court with two flanking volumes: a wing with brick-enclosed bedrooms, and a large, open living and dining area glazed on two sides. A freestanding wall, shaped like an S in plan, separates this living and dining area from the kitchen. The geometry of the curving partition is uncharacteristic of Mies's work of the 1930s, and his series of studies showing abstract polychromatic designs for its surface is even more so.

Many years later, Mies would refer to his 1935 design as a "court-house," that is, a house wholly enclosed by perimeter walls. While the design, like that of the near contemporaneous Hubbe House Project, would have balanced inward views to the enclosed courts with views out to the rural landscape, the Ulrich Lange House remains the most introverted of Mies's designs for freestanding houses. The curving geometries, the place devoted to the automobile, and the overall organization suggest some relationship to the Court-House with Garage, a project of which virtually nothing is known other than the drawings themselves, dated to 1934. —*Terence Riley*

300. Transverse section/ elevations (first version). Pencil on tracing paper, 10 x 20½" (25.6 x 52.3 cm)

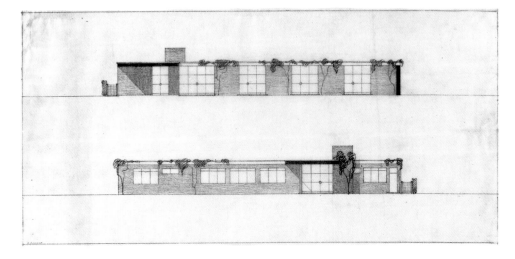

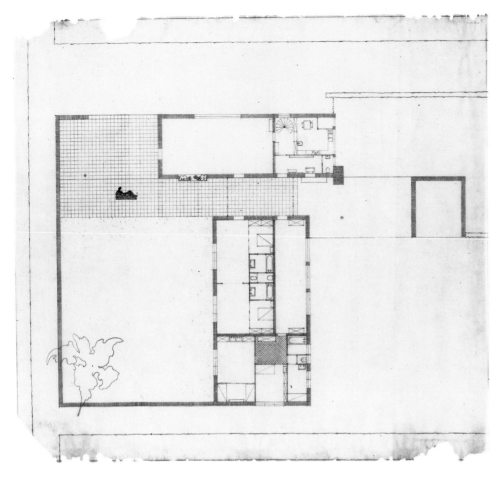

301. Plan (first version). Pencil
on tracing paper, 18½ x 20½"
(47.1 x 52.3 cm)

302. Sketch floor plans. Pencil
on tracing paper, 10¾ x 21¼"
(27.6 x 53.8 cm)

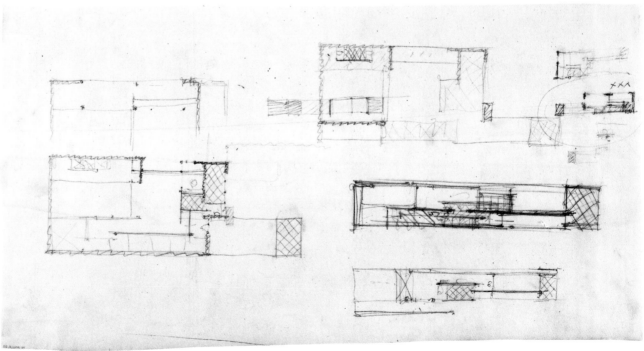

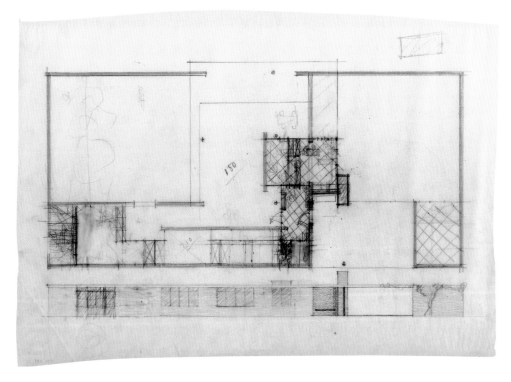

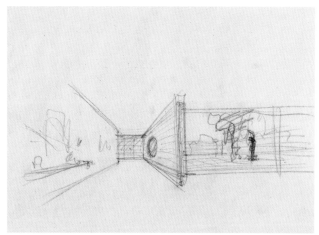

304. Sketch perspective view
(second version). Pencil on
paper, 8¼ x 11½" (20.9 x 29.3 cm)

303. Plan and elevation study
(second version). Pencil and
colored pencil on tracing paper,
15 x 21¼" (38 x 54 cm)

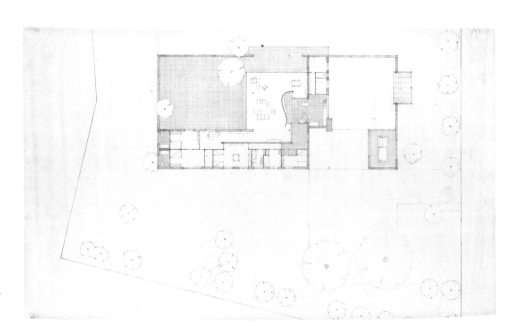

305. Floor and site plan with
furniture layout (second version).
Pencil on tracing paper, 21¾ x
37¾" (55.7 x 96.2 cm)

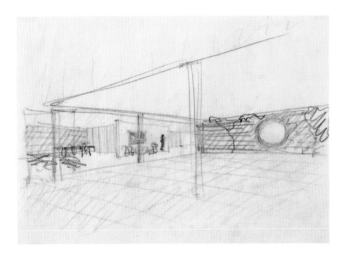

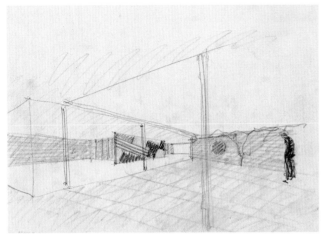

306–08. Studies for freestanding
partition (second version). All
pencil and colored pencil on
paper, 8¼ x 11½" (20.9 x 29.3 cm)

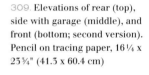

309. Elevations of rear (top),
side with garage (middle), and
front (bottom; second version).
Pencil on tracing paper, 16¼ x
23¾" (41.3 x 60.4 cm)

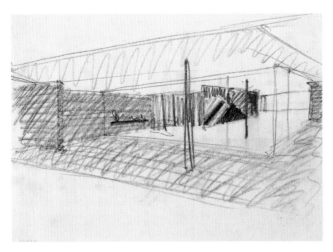

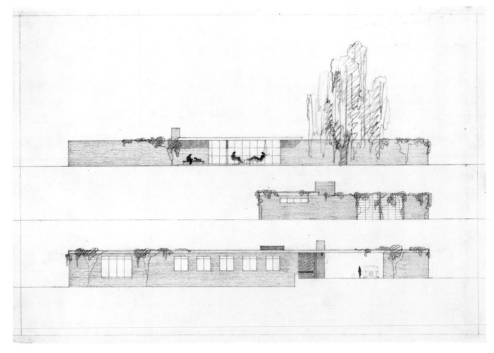

Verseidag Administration Building Project, Krefeld, 1937–38

The last project Mies undertook before emigrating to the United States was for the Administration Building of the Verseidag corporation, a Krefeld textile company. Mies had designed Verseidag's factory building in 1930–31, and the Administration Building, which was never executed, should be understood as part of his ongoing involvement with the development of the corporation's industrial and administrative infrastructure.

In its general massing and footprint, the building bears similarities to Mies's Reichsbank competition project of 1933. The clear repetition and reworking of the earlier project suggest both Mies's commitment to particular architectural motifs—the use of industrial materials, for example, and of courtyard spaces—and his willingness to adapt these themes to a given context. For the primary office space, two straight four-story blocks are joined by a curved four-story block along the rear elevation. The front elevation repeats the rear curved unit, but a single-story glass-enclosed passage provides limited office space and is raised on pilotis. The two curved units are connected by a block that divides the internal space into two landscaped courtyards and establishes the main entrance to the upper-level offices. In contrast to Mies's earlier office projects, this main entrance is set back from the street by a large terrace. Mies also begins to disengage various elements (outbuildings, stairwells) from the building mass, dispersing them to compose an architectural landscape—an interest that will reappear in his project for the Illinois Institute of Technology, Chicago, of 1940–41.

A series of perspective drawings, made by Mies's assistant Eric Holthoff and shaded by Mies, provides the most detailed record of Mies's intentions. Building and compound are secluded from their environment. Narrow windows, towerlike stairwells, and a low wall along the rear perimeter reinforce this sense of isolation. Yet the visual transparency imparted by the use of pilotis and glass on the main facade, and the continuity of the landscaping in the courtyards and terrace with the landscaping in adjacent lots, suggest a concern to incorporate the Administration Building within the existing industrial topography. —*Lucy M. Maulsby*

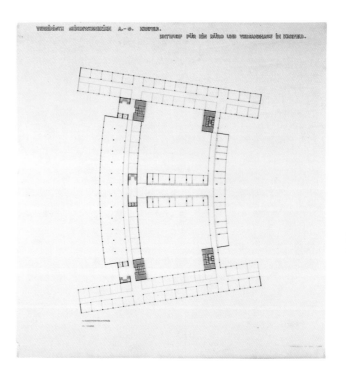

310. Second-floor plan. Ink and pencil on tracing paper, 38¼ x 36¾" (97 x 93.4 cm)

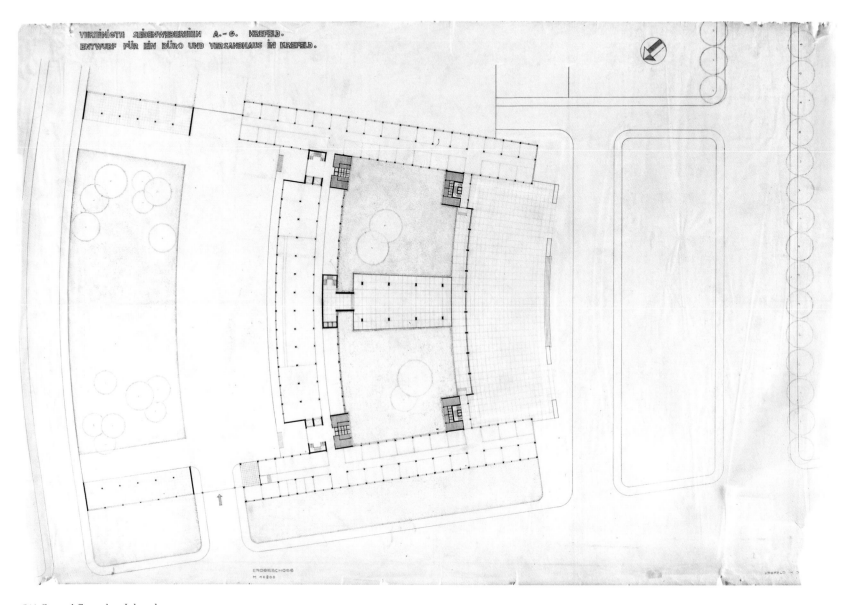

VEREINIGTE SEIDENWEBEREIEN A.-G. KREFELD.
ENTWURF FÜR EIN BÜRO UND VERSANDHAUS IN KREFELD.

ERDGESCHOSS
M. 1:200

311. Ground-floor plan. Ink and
pencil on tracing paper, 39 ¼ x
59" (99.6 x 150.2 cm)

VEREINIGTE SEIDENWEBEREIEN A.-G. KREFELD. ENTWURF FÜR EIN BÜRO UND VERSANDHAUS.

SCHAUBILD VON DER GIRMESGATH

KREFELD IM JULI 1938.

312. Perspective view from south. Pencil on illustration board, 28⅜ x 40⅛" (72.7 x 109.9 cm). Delineator: Eric Holthoff. The Museum of Modern Art, New York. Mies van der Rohe Archive. Departmental Purchase Funds

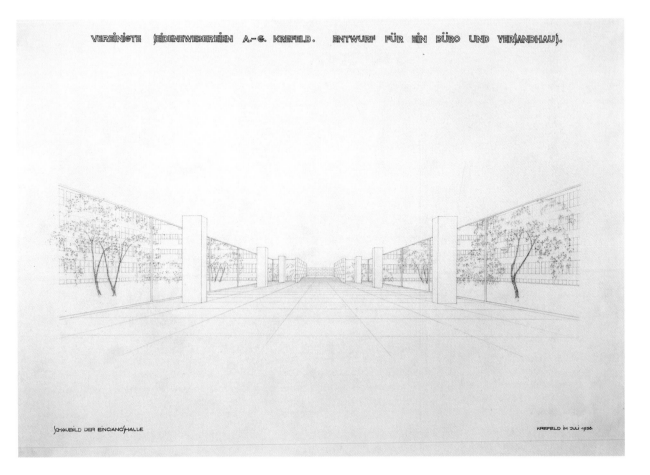

313. Perspective view of principal facade. Pencil on illustration board, 28⅜ x 40⅛" (72.7 x 109.9 cm). Delineator: Eric Holthoff. The Museum of Modern Art, New York. Mies van der Rohe Archive. Departmental Purchase Funds

314. Perspective view of entrance portico. Pencil on illustration board, 28⅜ x 40⅛" (72.7 x 109.9 cm). Delineator: Eric Holthoff. The Museum of Modern Art, New York. Mies van der Rohe Archive. Departmental Purchase Funds

VEREINIGTE SEIDENWEBEREIEN A.-G. KREFELD. ENTWURF FÜR EIN BÜRO UND VERSANDHAUS.

ANSICHT VOM HINDENBURGPLATZ

KREFELD IM JULI 1938.

VEREINIGTE SEIDENEWEBEREIEN A.-G. KREFELD. ENTWURF FÜR EIN BÜRO UND VERSANDHAUS.

SCHAUBILD DER EINGANGSHALLE

KREFELD IM JULI 1938.

Resor House Project, Jackson Hole, Wyoming, 1937–38

At the time of the "International Style" exhibition at The Museum of Modern Art in 1932, Mies failed to respond to numerous invitations by Philip Johnson to come to the United States, despite the financial crisis in Germany. By 1937, however, his personal and professional situation under the Nazi regime was such that he overcame his ambivalence. On the suggestion of the Museum's director, Alfred H. Barr, Jr., Mr. and Mrs. Stanley Resor had invited him to the United States for the purpose of designing a vacation home for them in Wilson, Wyoming, near Jackson Hole. Mies arrived in New York in August of 1937, and shortly thereafter departed for Chicago and the West.

The site presented both opportunities and limitations. The house was to span a stream, Mill Creek, that branched off the Snake River. To the north and east, the Teton Range loomed in the distance, with scattered camp structures in the foreground—as near to a European's vision, no doubt, of the vast spaces and rustic wildness of the American West as can be imagined. Working with another architect, the clients had already decided that the house would span the stream, and a service wing, sheathed in cypress, had already been constructed on the water's western edge when disagreements between architect and client halted the project. Reluctantly accepting the work already in place, Mies prepared designs for a two-story house that would balance the somewhat awkward service wing with an entry and bedroom wing to the east. The upper level was to be clad in cypress, the lower in rugged fieldstone. An open-plan living and dining room with expanses of glass on the north and south sides was to span the stream. Reminiscent of the Mountain House that Mies designed for himself around 1934, the Resor House design contrasted rugged materials with more ephemeral ones.

Before beginning the final drawings, Mies generated dozens of schemes, eventually focusing on a single approach with several variants. The final construction drawings were completed in March 1938 in New York, in association with two American former Bauhaus students who also acted as Mies's interpreters. In the most developed scheme, the ground-level entrance appears as a glazed volume beneath the projecting upper level, the stone garage being tucked behind. A stair leads from the entry to a second-story hall that opens onto a covered terrace and separates the bedrooms from the main living areas.

Mies's freehand sketches document a complex sequence of arrival, reminiscent of the Gericke and Hubbe Houses: a turn to the stair upon entering, another turn at the top of the stair, a momentary framed view out to the landscape, and yet a final turn around a massive stone chimney-stack before reaching the main living areas and the expansive views to the mountains.

After the construction drawings were complete, and emboldened, perhaps, by a worsening situation at home and his success in working in a foreign country, Mies accepted an offer to head the architecture department at the Illinois Institute of Technology, Chicago, and sailed for Europe with the intention of wrapping up his affairs in Berlin. A telegram from the Resors, received aboard ship, informing him of the project's cancellation did not sway his resolve.

After returning to the United States in the fall of 1938, Mies revised his designs for the Resor House, although it is unclear how much the Resors supported these efforts. In terms of materials and proportions, his models and collages for a single-story variant are more polished than the version previously settled on; exhibited and published widely, they are also now better-known than the rustic project, Mies's last before emigrating, designed during his eight-month odyssey in the New World. —*Terence Riley*

315. Ground-floor plan. Pencil on paper, 15 x 24" (38.1 x 61 cm). Delineators: John Barney Rodgers and William Priestley

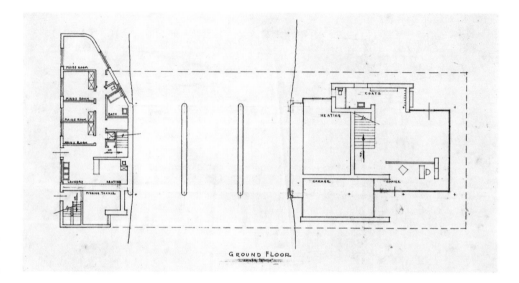

GROUND FLOOR

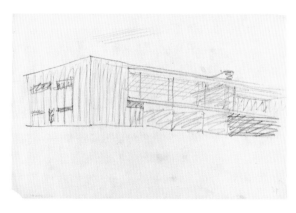

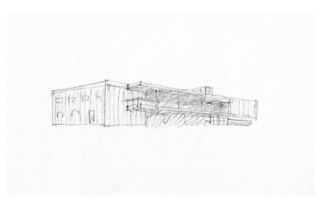

316. Facade study. Pencil and
colored pencil on paper, 8½ x 13"
(21.5 x 33 cm)

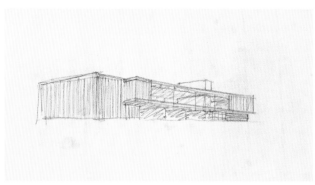

317–18. Facade studies (details).
Both pencil and colored pencil on
paper, 8½ x 13" (21.5 x 33 cm)

319. Upper-level plan. Pencil on
paper, 15 x 24" (38.1 x 61 cm).
Delineators: John Barney
Rodgers and William Priestley

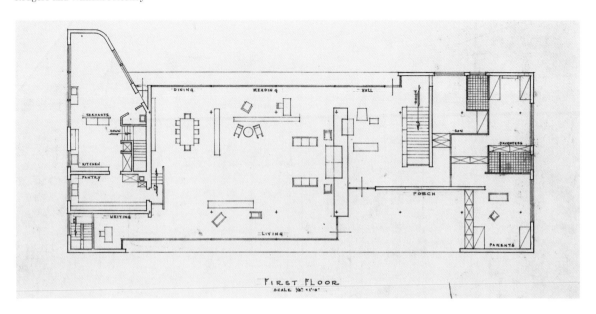

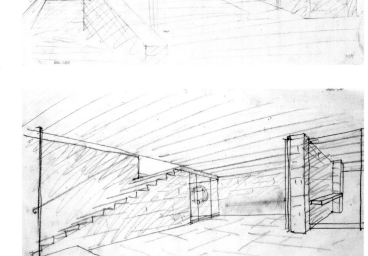

320 (right). Sketch interior perspective view of upper-level stair hall with fireplace. Pencil on paper, 8½ x 13" (21.5 x 33 cm)

321 (below). Sketch perspective view of entrance. Pencil on paper, 8½ x 13" (21.5 x 33 cm)

322 (below right). Sketch interior perspective view of entrance hall and staircase. Pencil on paper, 8½ x 13" (21.5 x 33 cm)

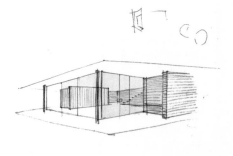

323 (below). Elevation study (detail). Pencil and colored pencil on tracing paper, 22 x 48¼" (55.9 x 123.8 cm)

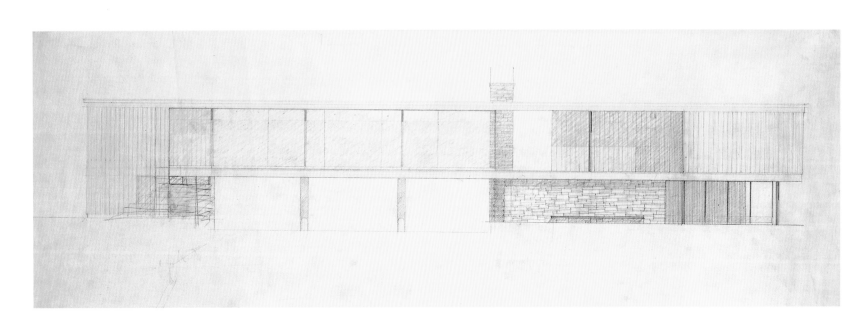

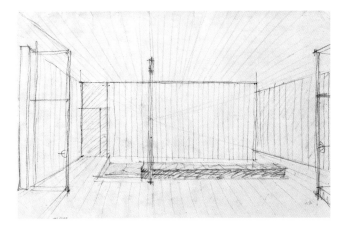

324. Sketch interior perspective view of upper-level stair hall. Pencil on paper, 8½ x 13" (21.5 x 33 cm)

325. Perspective view of living area. Pencil on paper, 17¼ x 23¾" (43.8 x 60.3 cm). Delineators: John Barney Rodgers and William Priestley

326. View looking out from interior (detail). Gelatin silver photograph and pencil on illustration board, 20 x 30" (50.7 x 76.2 cm)

Research
Essays

Mies's First Project: Revisiting the Atmosphere at Klösterli

FRITZ NEUMEYER

The Riehl House—Mies's first commission—was built in Neubabelsberg in 1907, when Mies was twenty-one. Like all of Mies's early architecture, it has long been overshadowed by the glorious structures that made him famous. Mies himself was largely responsible for this; looking back on his life and work, he would speak of his early houses dismissively, and they were accordingly thought to be of little interest. The late Mies who strove to elevate modern steel-and-glass construction into a universal architectural grammar apparently considered his early villas a mere biographical footnote. Only recently have scholars begun to develop an appreciation for the early Mies, and to consider these buildings, too, as paradigmatic objects, giving rise to interesting speculations about their historical roots and even about the historical character of modernism in general.

The Riehl House (fig. 1), although occasionally mentioned and even illustrated in the major monographs on Mies that have appeared since Philip Johnson's book of 1947, has remained relatively undiscovered. My own study of 1986, *The Artless Word*, was the first to discuss its architecture in detail, and I also suggested there something of the relationship between Mies and his first client, Alois Riehl, which continued into the 1920s and certainly influenced his thought. New research now makes it possible to provide more specific observations on that relationship.

Riehl died on November 21, 1924, at home in the house Mies built. An entry in the architect's notebook shows that he designed the gravestone.[1] The stone has not survived, but from correspondence between Mies's office and the contractor we learn that it was a simple one with incised letters and a flat base, the whole probably executed in travertine.[2] Two postcards from Riehl's widow, Sofie, that ended up in Mies's business correspondence indicate the close personal ties between the two. The first concerns the stone; on a card dated June 5, 1925, under the salutation "Dear Ludwig," Sofie begs Mies to "pursue the matter energetically and attend to all the details." She signs herself "Your faithful Sofie Riehl."[3] Another, later card

1. Ludwig Mies van der Rohe. Riehl House, Potsdam-Neubabelsberg. 1906–7. View from lower garden, c. 1907

gives us a glimpse of social customs in the Riehl House: Mies is requested to "come by on Tuesday at the accustomed hour for tea if it suits you."[4]

It is unclear just what motives led the Riehls (whose own children had died, in infancy and in adulthood) to ask the very young Mies to design their home, entrusting themselves to an "architect" who, although trained as a craftsman and at work in the atelier of Bruno Paul, had basically nothing to offer but his personality. They certainly did not choose him for his artistic signature, for at that point he was still a tabula rasa. Yet perhaps that was an advantage for Alois Riehl,

whose academic career was coming to an end and who may well have felt he could realize his own, quite definite concept for the house more readily with a young architect than with an established one. The idea of being used as a guinea pig in the interest of some fashionable architect's principles may also have been less than appealing. Riehl placed his trust in Mies. His experience as an educator was long, and he apparently felt he had found a gifted, sensible, and intelligent pupil who would develop into something in the right hands and surroundings. This deduction is surely supported by the fact that, as Mies himself said, Riehl sent his protégé on a six-week study trip to Italy at his own expense.

When planning their house, on a picturesque sloping lot on the Griebnitzsee, the clients envisioned less a proper villa than an unassuming summer house, a philosopher's hermitage or *studiolo*, a retreat from the bustle of the metropolis, and most of all a home for their old age. That they wished to live in idyllic isolation is apparent from the name they gave their house from the start: "Klösterli," or "Little Cloister." In its secluded setting, the house was to give them a spot for reflection, allowing them to live quietly but not standoffishly. They seem to have maintained a city apartment in Berlin even after the Neubabelsberg house was completed.[5]

Born in Bolzano in 1844, Alois Riehl (fig. 2) assumed his first professorship in Graz in 1878, then transferred to Freiburg in 1882, to Kiel in 1895, and to Halle in 1898. He was appointed professor of philosophy at the University of Berlin only in 1905, near the close of his academic career. Riehl had made a scholarly name for himself as an exponent of a brand of philosophy based on Immanuel Kant. Termed "critical

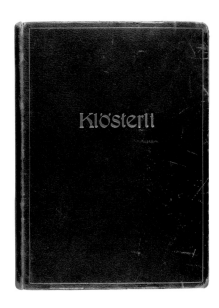

realism," his approach challenged both speculative idealism and ordinary realism; receptive to positivism, it was concerned with reconciling idealism and materialism, the arts and the sciences. To Riehl this seemed to be what was called for by the times, given the development of thought over the course of the nineteenth century. (One seems to hear echoes of Riehl's basic thinking in Mies's inaugural lecture at the Armour Institute of Technology, Chicago, in 1938, when he presents the "path from material through purpose to creative work," and calls for an "organic principle of order," a synthesis between the idealistic and the mechanistic, "to create order out of the hopeless confusion of our days."[6]) Before Riehl's appointment, philosophy in Berlin had been steeped in Hegelian idealism, and there were those who felt he was an unsuitable successor to the famous Wilhelm Dilthey. Carl Stumpf, an equally controversial appointment, joined the philosophy faculty at about the same time, leading Berlin wags to complain—punning on the expression "*Stumpf und Stiel*" (root and branch)—that Berlin philosophy had been destroyed, "*Stumpf und Riehl*."[7]

Mies's encounter with Riehl was undoubtedly an educational experience of the first rank, and he must have taken away from it any number of ideas that influenced his later thinking. His assertion that his endeavor as an architect was basically to reconcile old and new values, for example, sounds virtually identical to Riehl's philosophical stance; the professor's distinction, in the eyes of his professional colleagues, was "that he points backward and forward at the same time, connecting two eras that understand each other with such difficulty in so many ways."[8] Unpublished sources now allow more precise speculations on the influence of this first client, and on what crucial intellectual experiences Mies had in his house. The document that opens the door a crack farther into the great architect's inner world is the Klösterli guest book, which only surfaced three years ago,[9] and which runs from August 19, 1909, to September 1924 (fig. 3). The entries in the book make it possible to reconstruct a network of Mies's social connections, at least in outline; for after the house was completed, he was included in the Riehls' intimate circle, and thus became acquainted with an important group of intellectuals—colleagues and students of the professor's who often visited him. One can imagine what it must have meant for the young Mies to be here

(fig. 4), if only as a listener, or to find himself sitting next to such figures at table. This was a better entrée to the world of the intellect than any university seminar.

To suggest Riehl's importance for Mies, it is worth recalling a parallel from architectural history: the case of Palladio, who found a crucial patron and champion in his first client, Count Trissino, a scholar with a name as a philosopher. In fact it was thanks to this first client that the stonecutter Palladio was able to develop a career in architecture. Mies met his Trissino in the philosopher Alois Riehl, who decisively influenced the youthful architect (also trained as a stonecutter) not only in his thinking, by drawing him into a new intellectual world, but in his professional practice, by introducing him to social circles in which other clients would subsequently appear. Finally, and this must not be overlooked, Mies forged personal bonds in the Riehl House. It was there that he came to know Ada Bruhn, a friend of Riehl's grandchildren who was studying dance at the Jaques-Dalcroze school in Hellerau. At the time she was still theoretically the fiancée of the art historian Heinrich Wölfflin, but Mies—perhaps with a little urging from the lady of the house[10]—married her in 1913. They separated in the 1920s.

The reconstruction of the social network centered on Klösterli would be an exercise in intellectual and cultural history in its own right. Wölfflin's importance for Mies would itself justify a study, one in which the Riehl House would play a role. This essay will provide at least a glimpse of this complex web.

Wölfflin had studied under Dilthey in 1885–86. In 1901 he became a professor at the University of Berlin, where he taught until 1911. Aside from the delicate problem of stealing Wölfflin's fiancée, Mies could only have viewed the great art historian with interest and respect. Peter Behrens, Mies's employer after 1908, highly admired Wölfflin, and was admired by him in turn.[11] Wölfflin had treated architecture in a highly original way as early as his dissertation of 1886, *Prolegomena to a Psychology of Architecture*. Inspired by Friedrich Nietzsche's idea of the "grand style," he developed a theory of the "grand form" that brought him extraordinary respect among architects, including Behrens. Asked in the 1960s what he had learned from Behrens, Mies replied, "In a single sentence I would perhaps say that it was there I learned the grand form"[12]—a sign of exactly the context of art-historical thinking established by Wölfflin during his years in Berlin.[13]

There is no document of any personal contact between Riehl and Wölfflin, or of visits by Wölfflin to Riehl's home. Yet the two men must surely have met. Even before the Riehl House was built, Wölfflin was often on a neighboring property, the home of his longtime friends the archaeologist Friedrich Sarre and his wife, a daughter of the archaeologist Carl Humann. He

would thus have been aware of the building of the Riehl House, and contact with the Riehls would have been established through his engagement to their friend Ada Bruhn. (Mies's library contained a first edition of Wölfflin's famous *Klassische Kunst* [1908], with the handwritten dedication "November 1909 from H. W."—presumably intended for Bruhn, not Mies.[14]) And although Wölfflin's name does not appear in the Klösterli guest book, such a book only reliably documents special occasions; ordinary teatime calls and other passing visits would not be recorded here.

Then, too, Riehl could hardly have been without interest for Wölfflin, for he was the first academic philosopher to embrace Nietzsche, and published one of the first monographs on this philosopher of art and artists, in 1897.[15] Translated into various languages and repeatedly reprinted, the book contributed greatly to the appreciation of Nietzsche around the turn of the century. Riehl had shown an early interest in aesthetics and the philosophy of culture, inspired in part by the Munich cultural historian Wilhelm Riehl, whose home he had often visited as a student.[16] Wölfflin too had known the older Riehl. It was Alois Riehl's interest in aesthetics that had led him to Nietzsche, to whose work he had been introduced by one of his students, Heinrich Rickert.[17] In the 1890s, Rickert, twenty years his junior, succeeded him as professor of philosophy in Freiburg. Rickert signed the Klösterli guest book on three occasions, the first on November 26, 1911, presumably his first visit. The second was a week later, on December 3, 1911; directly below his signature is that of Mies. The two names appear again on March 5, 1912, an evening of dancing that brought together the

Riehls' younger circle of friends, we read, from five in the afternoon until eleven-thirty at night.

Riehl was strongly attracted to Nietzsche, the conqueror of Schopenhauerian pessimism. Born in the same year, 1844, both had been swept up in a passionate enthusiasm for Wagner in their early years, only to turn away from him later. As thinkers, both opposed idealism and nourished scientific, predominantly physiological interests. Like Nietzsche, Riehl considered mountainous country his ideal landscape; he also favored

Nietzsche's philosophical pace, working out his thoughts not at the writing desk but while walking or hiking.[18] His interest in Nietzsche was not simply academic, it was motivated by his struggle with the problem of perception, which occupied him from the 1870s on. This was why he became interested in the 1890s in the aesthetic theory then being developed by Conrad Fiedler and Adolf Hildebrand, an involvement documented in the essay "*Bemerkungen zum Problem der Form in der Dichtkunst*" (Remarks on the problem of form in poetry), published in 1897, the same year as his Nietzsche study.[19] All of this would have been more than enough to create a bond between Riehl and Wölfflin.

More important than connections like these for the study of Mies, however, is Riehl's role as client and mentor, particularly in his writings on philosophy and aesthetics. Riehl apparently entertained no architectural ambition to affect the form and style of his future house, yet he must have had a clear idea of the kind of dwelling he wanted and at least an abstract notion of its structure. He did not engage an important modern architect; he seems to have had all the contact he wanted with the "young generation of the '90s" and its cry for "life, more exultant life."[20] A leading architect of this generation, and a promoter of Jugendstil, was Henry van de Velde, an ardent Nietzschean and founder of the Weimar Kunstgewerbeschule (School of applied arts), later to form part of the Bauhaus. Van de Velde had overseen the redesign of the Nietzsche-Archiv in Weimar; Riehl had spoken at the dedication of the facility, on October 15, 1903.[21] Perhaps he had looked at van de Velde's "exalted" approach to design, and had taken it as a warning; for he considered the

reform movement in the applied arts altogether repugnant. Like Adolf Loos, he argued that art, like all great things, was not there simply "for our amusement." Turn-of-the-century artists who championed the marriage of art and everyday life, with the goal of an increase in daily sensual pleasure, were suspect to him, for he was convinced of the need to banish hedonism not only from ethics, following Kant, but also from aesthetics.[22]

It is easy to imagine, then, that Riehl may have felt more confident of obtaining the house he envisioned—a calm, contemplative house, not overrefined—from an untried architect of the youngest generation rather than the more aesthetically extravagant generation before. This cultural perspective may also explain his attachment to the younger generation, for as a responsible thinker he considered it his personal obligation "to carry philosophy to safety beyond the 'ebb tide' of the most recent past."[23] Convinced that that unfortunate period was drawing to a close, he placed his trust in young people and gathered about him a number of promising talents of Mies's generation—proof of his instincts as a teacher—who would go on to have impressive careers. Two of the more notable examples were the philosopher Eduard Spranger, who would distinguish himself as Riehl's successor at the University of Berlin from 1920 to 1946, and the classical philologist Werner Jaeger, who would make a name for himself even beyond academic circles in the 1920s as the champion of a "third humanism."

Mies knew both of these men, and the guest book shows that he enjoyed their company repeatedly. Beginning in 1910, Spranger especially was a frequent guest at Klösterli, where

he received, as Erich Jaensch writes, a "warm, paternal friendship." "Taken up into that household deprived of children as a virtual son," he "let no week go by without presenting himself at the quiet 'Klösterli' out in Neubabelsberg."[24] Indeed, of all the names in the guest book, Spranger's appears most often—a total of eleven times. Mies follows with nine. Their names appear together for the first time on April 27, 1914, Alois Riehl's seventieth birthday. That the two were part of the couple's most intimate circle is shown by the entry of August 5, 1922, on the eve of a family wedding. Spranger was then at the height of his academic career. In 1911 he had been appointed a professor at the University of Leipzig, where he taught alongside the distinguished colleagues Wilhelm Wundt and Johannes Volkelt, but in the spring of 1920 he had returned to Berlin as a "replacement professor for my fatherly friend Riehl."[25] His chief work, *Lebensformen: Geisteswissenschaftliche Psychologie und Ethik der Persönlichkeit* (Life forms: Psychology as a liberal art and the ethics of personality, 1914), had appeared in an expanded edition in 1921; Mies owned an edition of it from 1922, and his markings indicate that he read it.[26]

Carl Siegel writes that the Riehl household for several decades included "sons of the house,"[27] and one can assume that in around 1910, Mies and Spranger were the two in whom Riehl placed particular trust. With them, he may have felt, he had put his house in order—with Mies, the young architect, into whose thinking he had injected intellectual depth and scope, and with Spranger, the philosopher, who would carry on his sense of the human as a structure of thought, and would even succeed him in his professorship. The supposition that Riehl hoped to show the way, and even smooth it if possible, for a new generation is reinforced in Mies's case from another side, namely architectural criticism. In 1910, presumably with Riehl's support, Anton Jaumann published an article in the magazine *Innen-Dekoration*, meaningfully titled "Of New Artistic Blood" and stamped by its author's astonishment at the unexpected atmosphere of restrained composure that had confronted him on a visit to the Riehl House. Doubtless exhausted with the prolific frenzies of the waning Jugendstil, or perhaps expecting a pompous bourgeois villa, Jaumann was virtually nonplussed by the simplicity that the Riehl House presented as the message of a new artistic generation. The extent to which Mies may have been expressing Riehl's preferences in this instance is neither here nor there. Jaumann responded to the odd absence of contemporaneity in Mies's first house with the perceptive comment that it looked as though the young, in order to purify architecture, were jumping backward over the generation of their fathers. "Astonishingly," he writes, "it is the young who are now preaching moderation, correcting their teachers, outdoing them in flawlessness, in perfection.... What do these young people want? They are striving for maturity, calm, balance, they abhor all radicalism, they are searching for the 'golden mean' between old and new. Their works thus serve as a silent accusation against what came before, a kind of censure."[28]

The calm architectural realism of the Riehl House does indeed represent a kind of censure, if only implicitly, for it is not some bold unique form but a perfectly conventional dwelling clad in simple, almost Biedermeier garments. The abstract clarity of its spatial structure is not immediately apparent, and the architectural message is not of formal audacity but of logically integrated spaces. If one chooses to find an architectural statement here, it is that specific forms and details matter less than their relation to an overall context, a whole. The house owes its considerable impact to just such thinking, and its artistic excellence lies in its subtle yet opulent way of nestling in the landscape.

Mies's signature as a master of space, capable of creating spatial sequences unlike anyone else's with the most unassuming elements, appears here for the first time, but is already flawless. The modest Riehl House is the first instance of Mies's adaptation of the classical solution of podium and pavilion. The motif is realized at a higher level in the German Pavilion, Barcelona, in 1929, in the medium of steel and glass, manifesting a new, modern sense of space and demonstrating the capabilities of modern architecture. It would continue to be a Miesian motif up through his last project, the New National Gallery in Berlin (1962–68).

In that the Riehl House sits on a podium, it is oriented in space toward the horizon, invoking a large spatial continuum to which the rooms relate and into which they are absorbed. The notion of peaceful participation in a greater whole has a philosophical validity as well as an architectural one, and one must ask to what extent Riehl's thinking contributed to Mies's rebirth of an art of space—an art leading back, on the architectural side, to Karl Friedrich Schinkel and his rediscoverer Behrens, on the theoretical side to thinkers like Hildebrand and August Schmarsow. As close a student of Riehl's philosophy as Spranger identified space as "Riehl's real problem."[29] Riehl had dealt with the perception of space from a physiological and epistemological point of view as early as 1877, in his essay "*Der Raum als Gesichtsvorstellung*" (Space as an idea of the visual sense). A critic of Kant's a priori concept of space, he was concerned with the relationship between the perception of space and the idea of space, and with three-dimensionality as form. Understandably, he enthusiastically welcomed Hildebrand's 1893 book *Das Problem der Form in der bildenden Kunst* (The problem of form in the visual arts), which fit in with his own epistemological premises in its distinction between "actual form" and "perceived form."

Riehl thought Hildebrand correct in suggesting that we always imagine the structure of a whole in terms of space. We can only imagine a whole as a spatial or more precisely "architectural" construct, one made up, in our minds, of different perceptual forms—the close-up and the more distant view—and modeled accordingly. Hildebrand understands the term "architecture" in this general, psycho-physiological sense. Kant, with his famous phrase "*Das Ganze ist gegliedert und nicht gehäuft*" (The whole is structured, not simply piled up), had insisted that the a priori "existence form" of the intellect was a kind of reason that worked architecturally. Hildebrand formulates a corollary to Kant's "architecture of pure reason," one related to perception and image, in that he refers to an architecture in our imagination that is based on physiology and functions virtually unconsciously. He speaks of this "architectural feeling" as a general artistic urge at work in us, "the instinctive need to form a whole that can be visualized out of fragments of experience." Needless to say, Hildebrand is using the term "architecture" here in an abstract sense, "as the structure of a formal whole, independent of the formal idiom."[30]

At the heart of Hildebrand's thinking is the notion that all image-making can be derived from the psycho-physiological conditions of spatial seeing and imagining, and that the artistic creation of a self-contained formal whole is therefore always governed by ideas of space. To Riehl this idea seemed of such fundamental importance that it might be applied to nonvisual art forms as well, for example poetry. In *"Bemerkungen zum Problem der Form in der Dichtkunst"* he explores the theories of Fiedler and Hildebrand and declares his profound agreement with them. He discusses their insight into the necessary relationship between appearance and imagined form, between visual impressions and their spatial significance, and explains what it means in terms of epistemology. From Hildebrand's theory Riehl derived a central insight: "The theme of space is the artistic 'idea' of the work, which gives rise to its formal content and to which the substance of the work is subordinate."[31] One might also posit this principle as the central feature of the Riehl House (or even, to some extent, of all of Mies's buildings), and of the brilliance with which its spaces, however modest, are attuned to those of the landscape, so that close-up and distant views are equally pleasing.

It can be assumed with some certainty that Riehl passed on to his young architect the insight that space is the decisive notion behind all art: both Fiedler and Hildebrand were represented in Mies's library.[32]

In Mies's first entry in the Riehls' guest book one senses the gratitude of an apprentice: with almost self-effacing modesty he signed himself "Klösterli's collaborator. October 25, '09. Mies" (fig. 5). In his second entry, from the summer of 1910—by which time he had already worked for Behrens, and within the next year would go to St. Petersburg to oversee the construction of the architect's German Embassy there—he is similarly reticent, and so grateful that he seems reluctant to take credit for the house: "I hate leaving Klösterli but do so confidently, and sincere thanks once again for the possibility of its creation. June 8, 1910. Mies."

Just as Riehl took Mies in hand, so did his wife, Sofie. This is apparent from *Historie vom Klösterli—1911*," a seven-verse poem presumably composed for the guest book on the occasion of a party celebrating Mies's engagement to Bruhn, on January 6, 1912. Here Klösterli is again described as a collaborative effort:

> A young architect
> And a kind fairy
> Together built a cloister
> On the Babelsberg above the lake.
>
> With art and taste
> They embellished house and garden,
> Delighting the many noble guests
> Who have come to see them.[33]

The fairy, the poem later seems to suggest, is not Alois but Sofie.

Mies had clearly become a member of the Klösterli family, a circle, as Riehl's biographer puts it, in which "warm good fellowship flour-

ished."[34] Alois, called "Lusso" within the group, had been fated to survive his own children, which may in part explain his paternal fondness for the younger generation. Mies reveals himself as a "son of the house" when he signs the guest book no longer as "Ludwig Mies" but as "Ludwig Klösterli," adopting the name shared by all those in the inner circle: "October 15, 1911, the Klösterli family celebrated. Lusso and Sofie Klösterli Lou Klösterli Heidi Klösterli Ada Klösterli Ludwig Klösterli" (fig. 6).

As the Riehls hosted philosophical evenings, evenings of music with the "Klösterli Trio," and tea and evening dances, the guest book soon became filled with famous and not-yet-famous names.[35] The famous include such prominent figures as the politician Hans Delbrück, the industrialist Walther Rathenau (head of the AEG electrical conglomerate), and the economist Gustav Schmoller.[36] The African explorer Leo Frobenius makes a brief appearance; his book *Das unbekannte Afrika* (The unknown Africa, 1923) would later be seen on the drawing table in Mies's office at all times, along with Schinkel's designs for Orianda.[37] Naturally Behrens and his wife, who lived nearby, also visited.[38] Among the names that would only attain prominence later are Jaeger and the psychologist Kurt Lewin, both of whom, like Mies, would emigrate to the United States in the 1930s.

Riehl had long been interested in creating a "lecturers' seminar" that would help to fund young scholars in their researches. He proposed such a project in 1910, and in 1914, on his seventieth birthday, a foundation was created for the purpose, with the German government offering to donate a site. The plans were halted by the outbreak of World War I.[39] We learn from the guest book, however, that Riehl hosted informal "philosophical evenings" at Klösterli from the beginning,[40] and that he still held seminars there in the 1920s.[41] As a "son of the house," Mies would have met leaders of the younger academic generation, perhaps explaining the presence of specific authors in his library.[42]

Mies was soon receiving recognition in print. The house first appears in the professional literature, along with the name of its architect, in the summer of 1910, when *Innen-Dekoration* published its illustrated essay by Jaumann. Shortly afterward the journal *Moderne Bauformen* published generous visual coverage of the house, which that same year was also included in Hermann Muthesius's *Landhaus und Garten* (p. 69, fig. 5).[43] In 1911 the house, or rather its garden, appeared in a color photograph—still a rarity at the time—on the cover of a book by the well-known nurseryman and writer Karl Foerster (fig. 7). The photograph shows a corner in the upper part of the garden, teeming with yellow flowers in the second autumn after its planting; across a white bench, perhaps designed by Mies, lies a long black robe, cascading in picturesque folds to the ground, as if the owner of the house had just removed his philosopher's gown and stepped away for a moment. A splendid garden was clearly more important to the Riehls than a splendid villa, and they not only consulted Foerster but commissioned him to work on their garden. It is not surprising, then, that this apparently model "garden of Prof. Riehl, Neubabelsberg" is represented in his book with several illustrations, some with partial views of the house.[44]

7. Karl Foerster. *Winterharte Blütenstauden und Sträucher der Neuzeit* (Hardy blooming shrubs and bushes of today; Leipzig, 1911). On cover: the Riehl House garden, in an autochrome by Foerster

Clearly the Riehls' house and garden quickly became a minor sensation, and visitors were moved to write graceful compliments in the guest book. In an allusion to Diogenes and his tub, Schmoller praised "the impressive tub dwelling…so well suited to its splendid occupants."[45] The atmosphere of soothing seclusion at Klösterli inspired some to poetry: "Modern cloister / Klösterli! / Wayfarer, as you enter here, / Shake off the dust of all discord / And tune your strings / In harmony."[46] The philosopher Adolf Lasson, a colleague of Riehl's whose translation of Aristotle's *De Anima* was also among Mies's books,[47] composed the following charming lines on May 4, 1914: "This house—built by Alois Riehl— / Was conceived in high style. / It is tamed nature, / Shaped with spirit as a cultured refuge. / May the years pass happily here, / In spiritual creation, spiritual enjoyment."[48]

The philosopher Max Dessoir signed in on July 6, 1913, with the formulation "To builders of houses, stones are bread! In admiration of house and garden." He appears a second time at a social event in mid-May of 1914, when Delbrück,

Rathenau, and Lewin left their signatures as well. A lecturer in the philosophy department of the University of Berlin, Dessoir was as committed to the occult as to aesthetics. His first book, from 1888, was on hypnotism, and in his essay "*Das Doppel-Ich*" (The double I) a short time later he coined the term "parapsychology." From his interest in the borderline between psychology and physiology, he then turned to aesthetics, and in 1905 founded the journal *Zeitschrift für Ästhetik und Kunstwissenschaft*, which he edited from 1906 to 1943. He also created a research society that sponsored, on October 7–9, 1913, the first "Congress for Aesthetics and General Art History," at which Behrens spoke in place of Schmarsow, who was unable to attend. Riehl, like Behrens, was a member of the committee that organized the congress,[49] but by the time it convened he had left for Princeton, where he delivered a lecture on October 23.

Dessoir, a friend of Behrens and of the architect Hermann Muthesius, was by no means unknown to Mies: from 1910 on, along with Muthesius, Rathenau, and the sculptor August Gaul, he served on the jury for the Bismarck Monument competition, to which Mies submitted a design.[50] In his autobiography, *Buch der Erinnerung* (Book of memory, 1946), Dessoir repeatedly mentions Riehl, who apparently opposed his appointment at the university—unsurprisingly, for Riehl would have had little in common with the author of such books as *Vom Jenseits der Seele* (From the other side of the soul, 1917).[51] Mies likewise seems to have had no interest in Dessoir's writings, although he had a mystical bent of his own, as is suggested by the nearly complete collection of the writings of Raoul H. Francé in his library. Francé believed that man was not the only creature capable of artistry, and Mies's passing interest in the early 1920s in biology, and in a way of building based on organic structures—he was after all a representative of "skin and bones" construction—owed something to his reading of these works.

The architect Erich Mendelsohn indirectly complimented Mies on the Riehl House, which he visited on June 15, 1919. At that point he did not know Mies's name, yet he wrote in a letter the following day, "In the evening . . . in the Riehl House, which is very charming and illustrates the striking thesis of my garden requirement."[52]

Some of those whom the Riehl House guest book shows Mies meeting at the beginning of his career remained intellectually important to him two decades later. One such was Jaeger, two years younger than Mies and a brilliant representative of the Berlin intellectual life of his time. In 1912, at the age of twenty-two, Jaeger graduated from the University of Berlin summa cum laude, a distinction that had not been awarded for a dissertation for the previous forty years. In June 1914 he qualified as a university lecturer. Following in Nietzsche's footsteps, the young philologist first accepted a position at the University of Basel, then transferred in 1915 to Kiel. In 1921 he assumed what was probably the most highly respected chair in classical philology in the world, succeeding the famous Ulrich von Wilamowitz-Moellendorff at the University of Berlin.

On May 27, 1911, while Jaeger was still a student, he visited Klösterli for a philosophy evening. Perhaps it was his attempt at a neo-Kantian interpretation of Plato that brought him to Riehl's attention; in any case, his inscription in the guest book praises the house in high-flown terms as a place where "harmonious spaces" and the spirits of their inhabitants melded into a kind of divine miracle: "The spirit of this house—that of an *ousia* / The inhabitants of its harmonious spaces—two rare *hypostases* / This ideal two-in-oneness is a *theieon mysterion* / that made the most profound impression on the Neoplatonist Dr. Werner Jaeger on his first—hopefully not last—entrance into this house." Jaeger, who would visit the Riehl House often before his move to Basel,[53] naturally met the architect who had created this cosmos. Mies and Jaeger appear together in the guest book for the first time on August 6, 1922, as guests at a wedding celebration. Spranger was also present. All three were again in attendance on Alois Riehl's seventy-ninth and eightieth birthdays, in 1923 and 1924.

In the 1920s, Jaeger became the leading representative of what Spranger termed the "third humanism," the first having flourished in the Renaissance, the second in the era of Goethe. The "third humanism" was a Weimar Republic social current advocating a renewed interest in Hellenism as a way of overcoming the cultural crisis that followed World War I. Spranger named the movement in a speech in 1921, explaining that it differed from its predecessors "in the breadth of the questioning and understanding that we moderns are capable of mustering."[54] Mies in turn, in statements beginning in the late 1920s, pledged himself to the task of uniting the new, modern breadth of consciousness with classical humanistic values.

For Jaeger, antiquity represented the ideal example of a living intellectual history with a normative claim to validity even in the present. To renovate the underpinnings of Western culture, he argued, it was necessary to turn with new awareness to Plato, the teacher of humanistic values. Jaeger's Hellenism involved a concept of an essentially moral human nature developed only through life in the community—that is, in relation to state and society. As such it was not without problems; for all its idealism, Jaeger's humanism was capable of a political reading. In 1933, in fact, he attempted to tie his movement to National Socialism—without success, however. And although it would be unjust to conclude that the "third humanism" developed as a social movement in parallel to Nazism, Jaeger was one of the few intellectuals officially permitted to accept an invitation to teach abroad—this although in 1931 he had married a Jew, the daughter of Georg Heinitz, director of the Mosse Foundation. Jaeger emigrated to Chicago in 1936, two years before Mies. In 1939 he moved to Harvard, where he taught until 1960. His chief work was his famous *Paideia: The Ideals of Greek Culture*, the first volume of which was published in 1934, the second and third volumes in the United States in 1943–44. The book was translated into various languages, and was adopted at Harvard as part of the General Education Program.[55] Needless to say, Mies owned a copy.[56] Whether or not the two came into contact while they were both in Chicago is uncertain.

In *The Artless Word* I discussed the increasing importance of Platonic thought for Mies's notion of order, beginning in 1926. This was in large part a result of his acquaintance with and readings of Romano Guardini, a philosopher of religion at the University of Berlin. Guardini's name is absent from the Klösterli guest book, and whether it was Riehl who brought him to Mies's attention is unknown. A lecture Mies gave at Berlin's Kunstbibliothek at the end of February

1928, "The Preconditions of Architectural Work," shows that Guardini provided the architect with a number of catchwords. The lecture is important evidence that an engagement with antiquity had come to interest Mies as a step toward the renewal of culture and even of architecture. It is therefore legitimate to link Mies's argument for a new intellectual consciousness and reordering of values directly to the Neoplatonic revival of humanism represented in the 1920s by Guardini, Spranger, and Jaeger.

In around 1928, the synthesis of classical form and modern technology in the creation of a new sense of space became Mies's guiding principle, one that would remain valid up to his last building, the New National Gallery in Berlin. Embodied in this paradigm is a kind of architectural humanism, later paraphrased by Mies in the statement that each of his buildings demonstrated the notion "that it must be possible to harmonize old and new strengths in our civilization."[57] The work of Alois Riehl exhibits a similar endeavor.

Perhaps the most impressive demonstration of this Miesian tenet is the German Pavilion in Barcelona, which celebrates the Dionysian freedom of a dynamic modern spatial arrangement, opulently realized, while resting on the foundation of a classical podium, Platonic and Apollonian. And in this blending of the classic and the modern, the Barcelona Chair serves as the ideal furnishing. With its dynamic, chrome-plated version of the ancient St. Andrew's cross, it could be a chair for a twentieth-century Plato.

A document from 1928 shows that in the period when Mies was working on the Barcelona Pavilion, he was definitely receptive to the "third humanism" championed by Jaeger and Spranger, another "son of the house" at Klösterli. In light of the Klösterli guest book, the importance of that document becomes even greater. It is a note from the Herdersche bookstore, dated July 23, 1928, that fell into my hands as I leafed through a copy of the journal *Die Antike* in Mies's library in Chicago. It contains the message: "The above issue includes Jaeger, Plato's Position." In other words, Mies had ordered the journal in order to read Jaeger's essay *"Platos Stellung im Aufbau der griechischen Bildung"* (The place of Plato in the development of Greek culture), probably providing the title of the essay he wanted but not the specific issue number. This is why the bookshop made a point of indicating the contents of the issue it delivered to him.[58]

Looking again at buildings of Mies's like the Barcelona Pavilion or the National Gallery, both of them twentieth-century temples in their way, one definitely senses in them an echo of the "spiritual presence of antiquity" advocated by Jaeger. Antiquity was to be thought of not as mere tradition, a frozen, classicist ideal, but rather as a living cultural idea. One needed to encourage the vital penetration of this cultural idea from within, to regenerate it constantly out of the root from which it grew, and thereby to re-create oneself.

In Mies's case, as I have tried to show, this process began in the home of Alois Riehl. Spranger, another "son of the house," looking back on his "access to the house of the noblest man I ever met," wrote words that might just as well have come from Mies: "In the atmosphere at Klösterli on the Griebnitzsee, my appreciation for humanity became more profound."[59]

Building for Art: Mies van der Rohe as the Architect for Art Collectors

JAN MARUHN

Art historians in recent years have become increasingly interested in the study of art collections—the fates of individual collections, the collaboration between dealers and buyers, the development of taste, the social background of art-collecting. They have managed to reconstruct the activities of some important German collectors, including Ludwig and Rosi Fischer (Frankfurt),[1] Ida Bienert (Munich), Alfred Hess (Erfurt), Bernhard Koehler (Berlin),[2] and Hermann Lange (Krefeld),[3] but have particularly focused on those in Berlin, the destruction of whose culture under National Socialism is painfully clear. Even before World War I, many in the well-to-do Berlin bourgeoisie, most of them Jews, collected the modernist art of France and the Expressionism of Dresden and Munich, in direct defiance of the taste of Kaiser Wilhelm. In the 1920s they looked toward both France and their own city, amassing collections of high quality. Many of these collections barely survived a decade; some succumbed to the world financial crisis of 1929, and most of the rest were broken up after 1933, as politically and racially persecuted owners jettisoned their works to raise money for exit taxes and exile. Art prices fell drastically, particularly for contemporary art but even for old masters, and many collections were literally given away.[4] Marta Huth's unique photographs of upper-class Berlin interiors illustrate what was lost, including Curt Glaser's outstanding ensemble of works by Edvard Munch, Victor Hahn's late Gothic sculptures, and Paul von Mendelssohn-Bartholdy's Pablo Picasso group.[5]

The last vestiges of this culture were erased during World War II and the ensuing Russian confiscations. Only a few collections survived from Berlin's great years of private connoisseurship, and what disappeared was not just the artworks but the collectors, a whole segment of society—and also the buildings in which they lived with their possessions. Even less has survived of the settings of these collections than of the collections themselves. Villas built to house art, homes arranged both for living and entertaining and for displaying art, are part of the history of private collecting. If every work of art reflects its time, even more so do structures built for art express the social framework of their builders.

Mies and Le Corbusier were the only modern architects to build significant numbers of residences for art collectors. Mies's European work consists in large part of villas. He designed thirty-two private homes, half of which were built. His designs, generally for a wealthy clientele, differed little in size from the houses of such competitors as Alfred Breslauer and Otto Rudolf Salvisberg. With their smoking rooms, salons, and boudoirs, they also adhered to the traditional divisions of the bourgeois German household both before and after World War I, deploying the classical separations of male from female realms,[6] of living spaces from sleeping spaces, and of household help from their employers. Even in his revolutionary open plans, Mies never abandoned the conventions of bourgeois domesticity. The display of art in the home was assumed, whether in private rooms, reception rooms, separate galleries, or throughout the house—and all of these options were used by Mies, for whom the relationship between architecture and art was clearly much influenced by the wishes of his client.

Before Mies emigrated to the United States, in 1938, he owned only two paintings, by Max Beckmann and Wassily Kandinsky. In America he acquired more—paintings by Paul Klee, Kurt Schwitters, Picasso, and Georges Braque, and prints by Munch—but he was never a passionate collector.[7] As a young man newly arrived in Berlin, however, he was quickly received into well-to-do, art-loving circles. This cultivated, academic, and philosophically minded milieu sharpened his eye for fine art, and it was also here that he found his first patrons.

During his years in Germany, Mies designed eight homes to accommodate art collections, beginning with his second commission, from the collector, attorney, and art dealer Hugo Perls. When Perls met the twenty-four-year-old architect, in the summer of 1910, his impressive collection included works by Picasso, Henri Matisse, and Munch.[8] With its asymmetrical entrance, the outwardly unimposing structure that Mies produced for Perls's site in Berlin-Zehlendorf recalls the floor plans of Hermann Muthesius,[9] but it is otherwise reminiscent of Prussian classicism. Apparently Perls's sensibility, by his own later admission "all too conservative," limited Mies's freedom.[10]

Perls wanted to display his collection in three ground-floor reception rooms whose severely neoclassical decor and light, muted wall tones would set off the paintings' bold colors and forms. Mies worked out the house from the exterior facade to the interior design in minute detail—to the ultimate detriment of the collection, for the paintings and drawings came to seem mere decoration. For the dining room, however, a "lovely, Schinkel-like room" in Mies's conception,[11] Perls, without consulting his architect, hired the well-known Expressionist painter Max Pechstein to produce a cycle of canvases completely filling the walls and ceiling (fig. 1).[12] Female nudes in luxuriant landscapes dominated the room, overwhelming the somewhat delicate environment Mies had created. Essentially the Perls House was not truly a collector's house: paintings were displayed in its reception rooms, but a deeper relationship between art and domesticity was not achieved, and doubtless was not intended. Mies's architecture and his client's collecting had little to do with each other.

In February 1911, while Mies was occupied with the Perls House and especially with work on the German Embassy in St. Petersburg, designed by his then employer, Peter Behrens, the German/Dutch couple Anton Kröller and Helene Kröller-Müller commissioned Behrens to design a villa in Wassenaar, near The Hague. Mies went to Holland as Behrens's assistant, but suddenly found himself in competition with his boss when Kröller-Müller asked him to plan the house himself. Neither architect's design was finally approved. Kröller-Müller's ideas were reflected in both: the house, which was to contain the couple's art collection, was to be quite long, largely unornamented, and to stand on a meadow against the background of nearby woods. Instead of a separate gallery, Kröller-Müller preferred a skylit exhibition hall in the middle of the living area.[13]

In its size and complexity, the Kröller-Müller Villa Project occupies a prominent place among Mies's private commissions, challenging him to design a livable museum for a collection even then well-known, especially for its rich holdings of van Gogh. His "museum-house,"[14] combining the functions of entertaining, living, and exhibition, shows many similarities to Behrens's design, in the distribution of structural masses, the facade arrangement, and various details. Like his mentor, Mies drew on the country houses of Karl Friedrich Schinkel and

his followers. The asymmetrical floor plan with one shorter wing recalls Schinkel's Schloss Glienicke (1824–27), near Berlin, where an entrance set well off the building's axial system led into a collection of antiquities—sculptures, reliefs, and architectural fragments.[15] In Wassenaar too, Mies placed the approach to the Kröller-Müller treasures in an off-center corner, calling attention to it with a square portico.

1. Ludwig Mies van der Rohe. Perls House, Berlin-Zehlendorf. 1911–12. Dining room, with murals by Max Pechstein. Courtesy Ute Frank

Following the entry hall and dining room in the north wing were reception rooms and smaller and larger galleries for paintings, small sculpture, and porcelain, culminating in a central picture salon.[16] The art historian Julius Meier-Graefe congratulated Mies on avoiding the "questionable isolation" implicit in separating galleries from living space: "The gallery seems an essential part of the architectural whole, chiefly because of its handsome asymmetrical arrangement."[17] It was Mies's Kröller-Müller design that established his reputation among art collectors as an architect with a gift for theatrical

settings. But Mies would not again win a commission for a museum/home like this one, with its skylit salon borrowing from the classic nineteenth-century gallery. The only thing that would come close to it was the Hermann Lange House in Krefeld.

Late in 1927, Lange and Josef Esters, the directors of Krefeld's Verseidag Silk Weaving Mills, asked Mies to build an ensemble of neighboring houses for them, symbolizing their friendship.[18] Before World War II, Lange was one of Germany's most important patrons of art and architecture.[19] As early as the turn of the century, he and his father had commissioned reformist architects and textile designers, among them Behrens and Henry van de Velde, to design fabrics for their silk factory.[20] Some ten years later he began to collect modern art, focusing on the Cubists, Wilhelm Lehmbruck, and the *Brücke* and *Blaue Reiter* painters, but giving French and Germans equal importance.[21] He was involved in various ways in the German art world—as a member of the Deutscher Werkbund, for example, and as a patron of Berlin's National Gallery, to which, after 1929, he was an important lender of modern art.[22]

Lange had begun looking for an architect as early as 1924, and had in fact commissioned Theo van Doesburg and Cornelis van Eesteren to design for him an "ideal house, fully furnished."[23] In 1921–23, van Doesburg, van Eesteren, and Gerrit Rietveld had planned a residence with a separate art display space in the garden for the Paris gallerist Léonce Rosenberg (fig. 2).[24] The project was never realized, but it apparently sparked Lange's interest in modern architecture: he was a client of Rosenberg's gallery, L'Effort Moderne,[25] and here, in 1923, he saw the

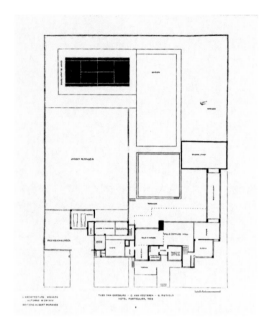

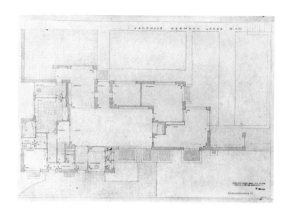

exhibition *Les Architectes du groupe de Stijl*, which included the model for the Rosenberg project—alongside Mies's design for the Concrete Country House Project (1923).[26] Through the Werkbund patron Count Kilmannsegg, who was trying to interest industrialists in modern architecture,[27] Lange met van Doesburg and van Eesteren and corresponded with them about building a house for him in Krefeld. Van Doesburg visited the site in 1925, and arranged for another meeting with Lange in Paris "to discuss everything in detail and look at the plans."[28] But for reasons now unknown, neither sketches nor plans were ever submitted.

The Esters and Lange ensemble is among the finest in the history of modernist architecture—yet the two villas were neither reviewed nor illustrated in contemporary architecture journals. Mies took charge of his own publicity, and always reserved the rights to photographs of his buildings.[29] Many of his exhibition designs were published in newspapers and books, and photographs of the Wolf House, built only a little earlier, appeared in various journals, but apparently he saw to it that buildings he felt he had already surpassed were not presented in the way that his path-breaking structures (*Stützenbauten*) in Brno and Barcelona were. Perhaps he felt that the Krefeld houses were more conservative than

those programmatic showpieces, although they were all created at about the same time.[30] The Lange House (but not the Esters House) became widely known first in America, in 1932, when Philip Johnson and Henry-Russell Hitchcock both included it in their show *Modern Architecture: International Exhibition*, at The Museum of Modern Art (an exhibition of which Lange was a patron), and illustrated it in their influential book *The International Style*.[31] The only German publication of the Lange House was in the art journal *Museum der Gegenwart*, where the essay, interestingly enough, was devoted less to the architecture than to its contents: Lange's collection.[32]

With its reception rooms, bedrooms, and service wing, the Lange House has all the attributes of the classic family villa. Yet the building's real function was to house Lange's collection of over 300 sculptures and paintings.[33] Behind the close-laid-brick exterior lie living rooms that double as galleries (fig. 3). Lange shunned theatricality,[34] and there is no single dominant space. The original plan led the visitor through a modest entryway into a central hall, which gave access to the first-floor salons and the stairs (fig. 4). With its large expanses of wall, this rectangular space formed a counterbalance to the other reception rooms, where picture windows, which slide down to disappear into the floor, open on the garden.[35] The arrangement of space, then, was nothing like the open, fluid floor plans of the German Pavilion in Barcelona (1928–29) and the Tugendhat House (1928–30). Mies was doubtless constrained by Lange's need for walls on which to hang his pictures.

Forgoing open spaces allowed Lange to group parts of his collection as independent units. In the central hall, for example, were large-scale paintings including Marc Chagall's *Hommage à Apollinaire, Walden, Cenudo, Cendras* (1911–12), Ernst-Ludwig Kirchner's *Potsdamer Platz* (1914), and Franz Marc's *Shepherds* (1912), as well as Lehmbruck's sculpture *Woman Looking Backward* (before 1914) and several medieval Madonnas.[36] In the study, smaller Cubist paintings by Picasso, Braque, and Juan Gris formed an intimate grouping with sculptures by Rudolf Belling and Ernst Barlach. The music room was dominated by Kirchner's *Women Bathing* (1911), over six feet wide, to the side of which hung a small painting by Christian Rohlfs.[37] Mies's design let the collector show his favorite works; picture rails let him rearrange the paintings easily throughout the house. The gallerylike nature of the rooms was emphasized by their spare furnishings. Mies had originally envisioned groups of Barcelona chairs on islands of carpet, but Lange preferred old family

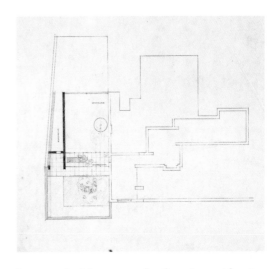

5. Ludwig Mies van der Rohe. Wolf House, Gubin. 1925–27. Dining room

6. Ludwig Mies van der Rohe. Wolf House, Gubin. 1925–27. Plan (c. 1927) with gallery addition proposed after construction: pencil and colored pencil on tracing paper, 22 x 21¼" (56 x 54 cm). The Museum of Modern Art, New York. Mies van der Rohe Archive. Gift of the architect

furniture, which Mies supplemented in the ladies' sitting room and the dining room with a few wooden pieces of his own design.[38] The hall was virtually empty, its only furnishings a row of low built-in cupboards and a seating area on an oriental carpet.

The Lange House gave Mies the unique opportunity to realize a private house as a museum, and for one of the most important collections of the prewar era. Lange was so pleased with the result that he became Mies's most important client, asking the architect to produce designs (not all of them realized) for an apartment for his daughter, Mildred, in Berlin-Südende (1930–31); the Krefeld Golf Club, of which Lange was the director (1930);[39] a Verseidag factory producing linings for men's hats (1930–31);[40] a house for Lange's son, Ulrich, in Krefeld-Traar (1935); and finally Verseidag's Administration Building in Krefeld (1937–38), which, with its symmetrical structure, anticipated the architect's American period.[41]

Another faithful client of Mies's was the Gubin hat manufacturer Erich Wolf, considered "one of the finest connoisseurs of European porcelain"[42] and a collector of antique rugs and mostly nineteenth-century paintings.[43] The Wolf House, on a site high above the Neisse River, was finished in 1927. Shortly after the completion of the interiors, the architect and his client agreed on an addition for the art collection.[44] Since no rooms were set apart for the collection in the main house, pictures, vases, and sculptures were everywhere (fig. 5), and the bulk of the art remained in Wolf's late-nineteenth-century villa in Gubin.[45] To resolve the problem Mies designed a separate space, abutting the main building but dramatically different from it.[46] The main house featured diagonally interlocking spaces; the gallery addition was to consist of a single open space with a winter garden like that in the Tugendhat House (fig. 6). With its simple right angles, paved terrace, flower bed, and another terrace capitalizing on the view, it was to be closed off from the house and garden by solid exterior walls and a retaining wall. In short, the architect here anticipated characteristics of his court-house projects of the 1930s such as the Hubbe House in Magdeburg (1934–35). Since the Wolf House was destroyed during World War II, it is impossible to evaluate it fully, especially its interior.[47]

In 1913, the Perls House was acquired by the historian and collector Eduard Fuchs,[48] who had become famous for his *Illustrierte Sittengeschichte vom Mittelalter bis zur Gegenwart* and was an expert on Honoré Daumier.[49] His collection included many paintings and some 20,000 drawings and prints, including over 6,000 Daumier lithographs,[50] fifteen paintings and a portfolio of drawings by Max Liebermann,[51] works by Giovanni Bologna, Luca della Robbia, and Rodin, and a library of over 7,000 volumes. Yet his collection had about it something of the quality of "the sort of curio cabinet popular in the Baroque period, but nothing museumlike,"[52] filling the house to the roof and leaving no room for appropriate display.

In 1928, then, Fuchs asked Mies to add a gallery wing to his own earlier structure. The two men had known each other since at least 1926, when, as secretary of the Communist Party, the collector had steered to the architect the commission for the Monument to the November Revolution.[53] The annex abuts the residence and is set well back from the road. A simple structure, it is dominated by a large gallery, above which is a smaller gallery space and an extensive roof terrace. One enters the large gallery through a music room and library. Except for the flat roof, the exterior resembles the earlier building down to small details, and the interior too is a logical extension of the house. With the annex, Mies skillfully extended the house's ground plan into an L shape. One reaches the gallery without fanfare, but the sequence of spaces builds toward a culmination here, providing an ideal "residence for an art lover and scholar surrounded by the art treasures that provide his inspiration."[54]

Between January and May 1929, Mies designed a house and studio for the painter Emil Nolde.[55] The project went unrealized, probably for financial reasons.[56] Strictly speaking, this was to be the house not of a collector but of a working painter. For a site in Berlin-Dahlem Mies designed a single-story building with a large living room, small bedrooms, and an apartment for a housekeeper. Adjoining the living room, which faced south and was opened up by glass, he planned a hall (*Saal*) of equal size, facing the street but largely closed off from it.[57] On entering the house, however, one was to get a view

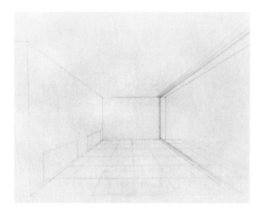

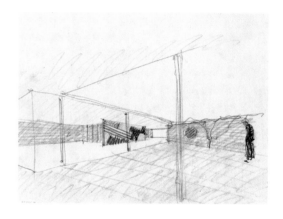

7. Ludwig Mies van der Rohe. Henke House Addition, Essen. 1930. Interior perspective of gallery with retractable window on right: pencil on tracing paper, 17¼ x 20⅞" (43.8 x 53 cm). The Museum of Modern Art, New York. Mies van der Rohe Archive. Gift of the architect

8. Ludwig Mies van der Rohe. Ulrich Lange House Project, Krefeld. 1935. Perspective sketch: pencil and colored pencil on paper, 8¼ x 11½" (20.9 x 29.3 cm). The Museum of Modern Art, New York. Mies van der Rohe Archive. Gift of the architect

into the exhibition studio through a glass wall. In the Hermann Lange House, the central hall had been the house's focus, and anyone wanting to see the art had had to enter it; in the exhibition *Die Wohnung* (The dwelling) in Stuttgart in 1927, Mies had placed a Lehmbruck sculpture out of reach in the Glass Room he designed with Lilly Reich (p. 354, fig. 8). In the Nolde House he brought these ideas into harmony. Although positioned off-axis, the artist's studio was to be the house's center. The glass through which visitors were to see into it was in effect a display window, but they would have had to follow a different route to enter it. Had the Nolde House been built, this play of proximity and inaccessibility, exterior and interior space, would have opened up new possibilities in modernist architecture.

In 1930 Mies was commissioned to add a gallery onto the house of the industrialist Ernst Henke, in Essen-Bredeney. A cofounder of Essen's Museum Folkwang, Henke owned a large collection notable for German post-Expressionism, with such paintings as Oskar Schlemmer's *Festive Twelve*,[58] Otto Dix's *Self-Portrait with Ursus and Jan*,[59] and Nolde's *The Magi*.[60] Henke's relatively modern 1920s house had become too small for the collection, and Mies placed a two-story, L-shaped addition against its garden facade.[61] The addition was destroyed during the war, and no photographs of it remain, but over 400 surviving letters between client and architect attest to minute discussion of the relatively modest assignment:[62] unlike the letters relating to the far more ambitious Lange House, these deal with such details as the choice of carpet (brown and

yellow wool from the Dessau Bauhaus), drapes (lattice-design tulle), built-in furnishings, and small iron armchairs. Henke also visited the Lange House with Mies and Nolde.[63] On the ground floor, the gallery opened onto a projecting terrace. Travertine floor tiles tied the interior to this outdoor space, from which it was separated only by a large glass pane that could be lowered into the floor (fig. 7). As in the central hall of the Lange House, bookcases were built into the walls in the large room, and also as in the Lange House, the gallery with its two seating areas doubled as a room for entertaining. The elevated main floor above the garden, its continuous windows, and the second set-back story borrowed from the Tugendhat House. The absence of more detailed plans prevents fuller analysis of this project.

In 1935, having married, Lange's son Ulrich decided to build a house in the Krefeld suburb of Traar. In the first design stage, Mies developed a blocklike structure divided into a living wing and a wing with bedrooms and servants' quarters. The final design featured a fluid open space of striking clarity—a combination of closed and open rooms, glass and stone walls, within a framing rectangle (fig. 8). Ulrich Lange's house was also to house a collection.[64] The floor plan of the preliminary design shows a gallery attached to the bedroom wing, but in the final design a larger space combines the functions of living area, dining area, and exhibition room. While applying an entirely different concept of architectural form, Mies here returned to the idea of the private residence as museum that he had earlier realized for Hermann Lange.

Views of a later design-stage show the main wall of the living room with a wall painting,[65] and freestanding sculptures appear throughout the plans and views. The terraces and inner courtyards set off recumbent figures in the manner of Aristide Maillol; other figures stand or stride forward. Mies also sketched in works by his favorite sculptors, Georg Kolbe and Lehmbruck, enhancing the notion of the house as a small museum. Unfortunately the design was never realized. After the war, Ulrich Lange tried to revive Mies's interest in the project, but was unsuccessful; the commission eventually went to another architect.[66]

A collector's house often limits the freedom of architects, preventing them from realizing their ideal interplay of art and architectural structure. There are exceptions: when Le Corbusier built a house for Raoul La Roche in Paris in 1923, he was already helping his client to acquire Cubist and post-Cubist art (steering some of his own paintings into La Roche's collection, as well as works by Amédée Ozenfant and Gris), and the painter-architect had a strong say in how they were hung.[67] When Mies was relatively free of a client's preconceptions, however, he developed a very different interplay between art and architecture: by placing a single sculpture in an otherwise ascetically empty space, he would create a templelike atmosphere. In the debate over the primacy of painting or sculpture, an argument since the Renaissance, Mies came down on the side of sculpture early on. He admired Kolbe, but was particularly devoted to Lehmbruck, a close friend of his.[68]

Mies first made this kind of use of sculpture in the Glass Room in *Die Wohnung*, the exhibition of 1927. The architecture consisted of walls of different-colored glass, with Lehmbruck's *Torso of a Girl* in a transparent central *cella*.[69] The contrast with the inviting but inaccessible physicality of Lehmbruck's sculpture heightened the glass's coolness, while Mies simultaneously managed to glorify the human form by setting it apart, like an image of a deity in a shrine. In the German Pavilion, similarly, the architecture, dramatic and fluid, reveals itself step by step, and only after changing direction several times does the viewer glimpse Kolbe's elegiac female figure, her matte bronze finish set off by a dark wall of green marble. This symbolist figure, *Dawn*, rises up from a pool, untouchable. Architecture, sculpture, and the sculpture's very name suggest the new modern Germany that the pavilion was intended to promote.

In Grete and Fritz Tugendhat Mies was blessed with clients who gave him the freedom to realize his ideal synthesis of architecture and art.[70] The Tugendhat House has all the attributes of bourgeois domesticity, with one exception: despite the size of the living room—around 3,000 square feet[71]—not even a modest art collection can be accommodated here, for there are no walls. More important, though, the combination of decor and architecture amounts to a kind of *Gesamtkunstwerk* that allows of no additions. Lehmbruck's *Woman Looking Backward* was the only artwork Mies permitted in his carefully crafted space,[72] its melancholy stylization offering a counterpoint to the severity of the architecture, and its light stone contrasting with the yellow-gold onyx wall behind it. Whether the sculpture was placed in response to the archi-

tecture or the architecture was created as a setting for the sculpture is hard to tell. As in the Lange House, the visitor arrives in the center of the structure. An unimposing staircase winds down to the main floor. By contrast Mies staged the route from the house of Grete Tugendhat's parents, at the bottom of the steep garden, to lead directly to the living room. The glass house crowns the slope like a temple, and the Lehmbruck torso is its spiritual center.

———

The domestic museum was an unusual assignment for modern architects, and played no ideological or theoretical role at all. Even Mies, who designed eight houses for art collections and built five of them, developed no distinctive concept for this type of structure. He largely neglected to document his collectors' houses photographically, and showed little interest in having them published, perhaps feeling that his clients' furnishings and picture arrangements were not in keeping with his architectural ideals. The collectors may also have forbidden the publication of their treasures. In any case, the only interiors he published were of the Hermann Lange House.[73]

Technological and pragmatic considerations played a greater role in Mies's houses for collectors than in his other villas. The exhibition of art required walls, which had to be painted in light colors. Picture rails are still in place in the Lange House and are documented in the Henke House.[74] Lange also asked for a covered slot in the floor through which pictures could be lowered into a downstairs storeroom;[75] the Nolde House was to have a similar fixture. Climate control was not an issue in those days. Little is known about the lighting in these houses, but Mies generally

installed regularly placed lamps in the ceiling, bathing the space in a uniform light; he had no interest in highlighting specific works.[76] There would also have been side illumination through the large windows. Only for the Kröller-Müllers—and possibly for Nolde—did Mies design skylit exhibition spaces.[77]

In terms of type, Mies's collectors' houses have little in common. The architecture gives no hint of the nature of the collection, whether old master or modern, sculpture or painting. In Krefeld Mies reflected the variety of Hermann Lange's large collection through a complex arrangement of rooms, which, however, could only be accessed from the central hall. The Kröller-Müller Villa was also to have an exhibition hall, but around it living and gallery spaces were to alternate. By contrast, the additions to the Wolf, Fuchs, and Henke houses have the look of museum pavilions—single empty spaces with a maximum amount of wall surface. Only the preliminary design for the Fuchs Addition to the Perls House shows a more fluid floor plan with freestanding walls.[78] Of all these houses, the final design for Ulrich Lange came closest to the more open design of the German Pavilion in Barcelona and the Tugendhat House. One has to wonder how many paintings it could have accommodated. Only with his New National Gallery (1962–68) in Berlin, at the end of his life, did Mies realize a structure that accommodates art in an uncompromisingly open spatial continuum. The sunken exhibition floor is crowned by a steel-and-glass temple that no longer glorifies a single work, like those in Stuttgart, Barcelona, or Brno, but celebrates the very idea of the museum—and even more, the architect's own life's work.

Mies and Photomontage, 1910–38

ANDRES LEPIK

Mies's prominence in our perception of the architecture of modernism is largely due to his ability to capture programmatic ideas in pictorial form. Like Le Corbusier, by the beginning of the 1920s Mies knew how to create a public image of himself as a leading modern architect. To do so he devised impressive presentations of his work, both in exhibitions and in print, and carefully supervised the creation and reproduction of pictures and texts on his projects. He early on assumed responsibility for the image the public would form of him.

Mies's surviving drawings record virtually nothing of his first designs, from the period 1905–10. There are no drawings clearly identified as his relating to the Riehl House (1906–7) or any other project of the period, whether he worked on it independently or as an employee in the offices of Bruno Paul or Peter Behrens. Yet his training in an Aachen trade school had certainly given him experience as a draftsman well before he even considered a career as an architect.[1] It was his confidence in his drawing skills that led to his first paying job, which itself gave him practice in drawing: every workday for two years, he stood at a drafting board preparing working drawings for stucco architectural ornaments.[2]

Over 3,000 drawings from 1910–38 are preserved in The Museum of Modern Art's Mies van der Rohe Archive.[3] Of these, the vast majority date from after 1921. Whether at the Museum or elsewhere, only a few finished renderings survive from earlier years, and these generally exhibit nothing of Mies's characteristic signature. (He weeded out a lot of his papers in the 1920s.[4]) In view of these numbers, it is striking that for Mies's first competition entry, for the Bismarck Monument proposed

for Bingen in 1910, there survive not only two large-format, color presentation drawings of exterior and courtyard views (plates 9, 13) but also his first photomontage.[5]

In incorporating his drawings in photomontages, Mies took up a form of architectural presentation initially used mainly in competition situations. Around 1900, Friedrich von Thiersch and other architects preparing competition submissions began the practice of mounting a drawing on a photograph of a building's possible setting, making for greater realism and a more convincing simulation than the standard perspective drawings these images supplemented.[6]

1. Ludwig Mies van der Rohe. Bismarck Monument Project, Bingen. 1910. Perspective, downstream view: gelatin silver photograph, direct carbon photograph, and ink on illustration board, 30 x 40" (76.5 x 102 cm). The Museum of Modern Art, New York. Mies van der Rohe Archive. Gift of the architect

Subsequently, as the use of photography to present architecture both in professional journals and for more general audiences became increasingly widespread, the addition of drawings to photographs became more common. Wherever Mies first encountered the technique,[7] he adopted it as

ideally suited for the presentation of architectural concepts in the growing number of publications available to him.

The Bismarck Monument

For the proposed Bismarck Monument, we have, in addition to Mies's large presentation drawings and a photomontage (fig. 1), a preliminary drawing (fig. 2) that seems to have been made as a guide for the person who made the montage. In the upper section of this horizontal sheet is a view of the monument, its base beginning halfway up the high hill that at this point defines the riverbank. The drawing is summary in its details, but the form of the structure seems to have been finalized. It is shown at an angle from below, as if the viewer were approaching it on foot. Below the image of the monument is a diagonal dotted line indicating where drawing and photograph were to join. In the lower third of the sheet, the footpath is roughly sketched in, just as it would appear in the photograph. On the left is another section set off by a dotted line, marking an area where the photograph was to be extended with an additional drawing: the photograph chosen for the montage,[8] of a path between vineyards, was apparently too small to cover the full width of the proposed image, so additional vines needed to be sketched in to stretch it.

Mies's inclusion on the drawing of the numerals 1, 2, and 3, as well as of the dimensions he envisioned—"mat size 1.00 x 0.50 size of actual picture 0.91 x 0.72"—suggests that the montage was to be executed by someone else. His detailed directions show how carefully he wanted his draftsmanship to be juxtaposed with the photograph.[9] His talent for presenting his ideas is obvious if one compares his submission with that of Gropius, for example, which adopts a quite similar point of view and is formally quite close to his, but fails to attain the same realism, appearing more two-dimensional.[10] Mies deliberately used photomontage in addition to or perhaps even instead of his own large-format colored drawings (whether these drawings were actually submitted to the competition is unclear) to simulate the effect of the structure in an actual setting. He manipulated photographic "reality" to create an impression.

After the Bismarck Monument, it was a while before Mies created another photomontage. In his commissions for private homes like the Perls House (1911–12), the Werner House (1912–13), and the Urbig House (1915–17), traditional views, cross-sections, and floor plans were adequate for the communication between architect and client. Photomontage was more public in function, and it only reappears in Mies's drawings to illustrate the visionary building ideas that he began to develop in the early 1920s. The actual construction of these buildings was improbable at the time, but the publication and distribution of the designs for them were important to him. These designs would only become well-known through such theatrical presentation.

Mies's interest in publishing may have been inspired by the architectural books and journals of his day, particularly the important series of portfolios of works by contemporary architects begun by Wasmuth, Berlin, in 1900. The Wasmuth collection *Ausgeführte Bauten und Entwürfe von Frank Lloyd Wright* (Executed buildings and designs by Frank Lloyd Wright), along with a Berlin exhibition of its illustrations, was largely responsible for making Wright influential in Germany.[11] Beginning in 1922, with his shrewd publications of designs and accompanying statements in the journals *Frühlicht* and *G*, Mies became actively engaged in the theoretical discussions of his time. Allergic to writing as he was, his statements tended to be concise,[12] so that the reproductions that accompanied them took on added importance, not just as illustrations to the texts but as independent statements.

The Friedrichstrasse Skyscraper

Mies's photomontages of the skyscraper he envisioned for a site next to Berlin's Friedrichstrasse

2. Ludwig Mies van der Rohe. Bismarck Monument Project, Bingen. 1910. Preliminary drawing for perspective, downstream view: pencil on tracing paper, 26 x 35¼" (65.8 x 90.7 cm). The Museum of Modern Art, New York. Mies van der Rohe Archive. Gift of the architect

train station are among the crucial incunabula of architectural presentation in the twentieth century. To the best of our knowledge, they were not included in the material Mies submitted to the 1921 competition for the site; made in unusually large formats—and therefore surely unacceptable as competition submissions— they only make sense as later creations for the purposes of exhibition and publication.[13] These montages, frequently reproduced both in their final form and in earlier stages, reveal an evolution from a basically photorealist style to one of Expressionist exaggeration.

The basis for the series was a single enlarged photograph of Friedrichstrasse, a dramatic perspective looking south along the street. Into this image Mies inserted a drawing of his sharp-edged glass skyscraper, a transparent, almost ethereal vision.[14] The contrast between the late-nineteenth-century facades on both sides of the street, recognizable as real by the shop signs if nothing else, and the delicately rendered glass structure could not be greater, and in the earliest known version of the montage (fig. 3) it breaks the photographed reality and the visionary drawing virtually into different picture planes. In capital letters along the bottom edge is a caption, which is incomplete—"BLIK VON DER OBEREN FRIEDRICHSTR . . ." (View of Upper Friedrichstr . . .)—suggesting that this early montage, now lost, was an abandoned first stage. When it was published in *G*, in June 1924, the lower edge was cropped,[15] as it was in subsequent publications.[16] The fold across the middle, visible even in the reproduction, suggests that this montage, like the later ones, was routinely folded for transport to exhibitions.

In a subsequent version, still working with the same enlargement, Mies managed to bring the planes of photograph and drawing closer together, melding them into a unified whole (fig. 4). He did so by darkening the forms in the photograph with thick crayon, which made them more abstract, while at the same time adding details to the skyscraper, including an

indication of individual floors. In this version the darkening of the photograph does not fully cover it; a lighter border is left at the bottom and along the right side. Apparently Mies was already considering cropping the image—as he did in the final stage, at all four edges, so that the skyscraper dominates the picture (fig. 5). Comparing this version (first reproduced in *Frühlicht* in 1922[17] and now in the collection of The Museum of Modern Art) with reproductions of it in early publications, one notes that at some point its focus was further narrowed by a second cropping of the edges. There is another, important difference between this final image and the earlier stages: this image is entirely a drawing. Not only has the photograph's record of reality been reduced to a schematic frame, it has been transferred into an image drawn in charcoal. From the earlier versions of the montage, in which the dominant impression is the simulation of an actual street scene, Mies ultimately arrived at an autonomous image.[18]

In reworking his montage in this way, Mies was developing a presentation medium for his designs that was all his own. His goal, clearly, was not a photorealist simulation of the

project but the strongest possible image. In fact everything suggests that this entire series of large montages and drawings was produced for either publication or exhibition, each one moving farther from the original context of the architectural competition. This helps to explain why questions of technical feasibility appear to have concerned Mies barely at all in these buildings.[19] During this period, he was employing the same presentation technique of framing an architectural vision with darkened older structures for his Concrete Office Building Project (1923), also published in *G* and shown at exhibition, and produced independently of any competition.

Around 1922, Mies had a model made of his Glass Skyscraper Project, perhaps a second design for the Friedrichstrasse site. He photographed this model in settings both simulated and real, then published the photographs (fig. 6; p. 353, figs. 5, 6).[20] These images, with their caricaturish depiction of older structures supposedly surrounding the skyscraper, immediately remind one of Expressionist architecture in the German film of the period, for example Hans Poelzig's crooked clay huts in *The Golem* (1920). Here Mies made no attempt to reproduce Friedrichstrasse as it actually was; the illustration was programmatic. The photographs took the process of simulation one step farther. Meanwhile, in a charcoal drawing from the same year (fig. 7), Mies reverted to a more familiar medium, which, however, he used to create an expressive, visionary presentation in the form of a monumental rendering.

Although these diverse representations show Mies exploring an Expressionist exaggeration of the view from the pedestrian perspective, in the charcoal drawings embedded in them he completely abandons the notion of simulating realistic views. These images present his

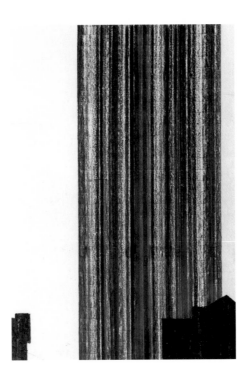

6. Ludwig Mies van der Rohe. Glass Skyscraper Project. 1922. View of model: airbrushed gouache on gelatin silver photograph, 7⅜ x 5⅛" (17.7 x 12.7 cm). Private collection

7. Ludwig Mies van der Rohe. Glass Skyscraper Project. 1922. Elevation study: charcoal, Conté crayon, and pencil on paper mounted on board, 54½ x 32¼" (138.5 x 83.2 cm). The Museum of Modern Art, New York. Mies van der Rohe Archive. Gift of George Danforth

designs as virtually abstract structures, looming up out of architectural surroundings that are either merely suggested or omitted altogether. Mies rarely signed his drawings, but he signed the second of these ones, suggesting that he ascribed particular value to it. This was the drawing he used as the cover of the third issue of *G*, in June 1924 [21]—the issue he financed himself, at the request of the journal's editor, Hans Richter (p. 121, fig. 18).

Dada

Montage and collage were favored mediums of expression for Berlin Dadaists such as Hannah Höch, Raoul Hausmann, and John Heartfield, all of whom used the two techniques from 1919 or so onward. Mies's attendance at the opening of Berlin's First International Dada Fair—on June 30, 1920, in the salon of Dr. Otto Burchard (p. 106, frontispiece)—suggests his personal relationship with the Dada community in Berlin; with Höch especially he was on friendly terms for many years, beginning around 1919.[22] But despite these connections, his montages bear little relation to Dadaist thinking.[23] Those artists used montage and collage mainly to

dissect existing pictorial realities and then to rearrange them into new, ambiguous unities. For them, drawing was an unimportant conventional skill.[24] Mies's montages, on the other hand, derived their strength from drawing, and preserve an inner axial and spatial unity.

In a larger sense, however, there is a quality of Mies's montages that links them to Dada: their self-promotional aspect. The Dadaists were famous for their exploitation of newspapers and journals, for example *Neue Jugend* (beginning in 1917), *Die Pleite* (beginning in 1919), and *Der Gegner* (beginning in 1920), all published by Malik Verlag. In the immediate postwar period, when actual building commissions were hard to come by, many architects resorted to print to express their ideas. Bruno Taut's *Stadtkrone* (City crown) and *Alpine Architektur* books both appeared in 1919. In 1920, Le Corbusier began publishing his journal *L'Esprit nouveau*; Taut's journal *Frühlicht*, which represents the culmination of visionary Expressionist architectural theory, began publication in 1921. It was in *Frühlicht*, in 1922, that Mies published his first skyscraper design for the Friedrichstrasse site, allowing himself

to be associated with the exalted, almost mythic vision of glass architecture that had been developing since 1914.[25] This was by no means the context in which he wished to be understood; yet none of the many Dadaist publications, all propagandistically antibourgeois, provided the right platform for his ideas either. Mies had no desire to shock his clients, to whom he had owed profitable commissions even during the war. So it was that in 1923 he declared his commitment to Richter's *G*, a far less political forum in which he published some of his core ideas and designs of the period. With its experimental typographic design, the journal, to which Mies also provided financial support, resembled the short-lived publications of the Dadaists, and occasionally made room for their contributions. It was also inspired in part by the Dutch journal *De Stijl* and by the Russian Constructivists.

Mies often used montage in his presentations even after 1922, for example in his Urban Design Proposal for Alexanderplatz (1929; plate 179) and in his S. Adam Department Store Project in Berlin (1928–29; fig. 8). He also submitted a montage to the competition for a Bank and Office Building in

8. Ludwig Mies van der Rohe. S. Adam Department Store Project, Berlin. 1928–29. Photomontage: airbrushed gouache on gelatin silver photograph, 8⅛ x 6¼" (20.3 x 15.2 cm). Private collection

Stuttgart (1928; plate 140), as also did Paul Bonatz, Alfred Fischer, and various other architects; in fact, since all of these submissions were based on the same photograph, it seems likely that such a presentation was required.[26] In presenting his designs for the Friedrichstrasse Office Building Project in 1929, Mies again superimposed drawings on photographs of the existing urban fabric (plates 190, 191). Dramatic as these images are, they all use the same technique that Mies had worked out in 1910, in his montages of the Bismarck Monument.

From Inside Out

Until 1928–29, Mies used montage exclusively in exterior views of his major projects. After 1930, however, he developed another type of montage to show interiors, giving otherwise straightforward perspective drawings, albeit of fluid spatial arrangements structured by walls, columns, and glass, a wholly different aura by inserting into them photographs of real works of art. This practice is most evident after 1938, but foreshadowings of it can be seen in Mies's drawings—in an interior view for the German Pavilion, Barcelona, of 1928–29, and in another for the Tugendhat House of 1928–30 (fig. 9), for example, in both of which Mies draws a sculpture by Wilhelm Lehmbruck. From the time of his design for the Krefeld Golf Club Project (1930) onward,[27] Mies's drawings increasingly represent architecture from the inside out, and in a drawing for the Golf Club, a delicate perspective of a pavilionlike interior and an outdoor courtyard barely separated from each other by a glass wall, we again see a recumbent sculpture in the manner of Lehmbruck (fig. 10), much as the Georg Kolbe figure *Dawn* had appeared in a courtyard at the German Pavilion. The sculpture serves as a point of reference or orientation in the representation of interior versus exterior. The perspective indicated by a square grid marked in the floor creates an effect of large space, and the vanishing point for these lines is not in the center of the drawing but decidedly to one side.[28]

In a number of his court-house designs of the 1930s, Mies returned to montage as a way of creating "pictures" to represent his ideas in exhibitions. Some of these presentations include real wood veneer, and reproductions of sculptures (for example fig. 11, which shows a standing figure by Lehmbruck from 1919) or paintings. All of these montages were created after 1938, some of them perhaps a decade or so later, in preparation for the exhibition of Mies's work at The Museum of Modern Art in 1947.[29] From the late 1930s on, Mies included reproductions of art in his drawings so regularly that it must have been a favorite presentation technique. One thinks of the familiar montages for the Resor

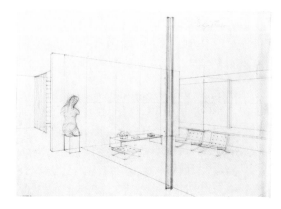

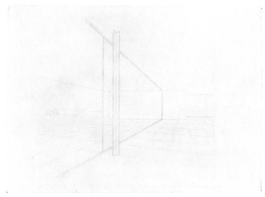

9. Ludwig Mies van der Rohe. Tugendhat House, Brno. 1928–30. Perspective of living room: pencil on tracing paper, 17¹¹⁄₁₆ x 24" (43.4 x 61 cm). The Museum of Modern Art, New York. Mies van der Rohe Archive. Gift of the architect

10. Ludwig Mies van der Rohe. Golf Club Project, Krefeld. 1930. Interior perspective looking toward main hall, with reclining statue outside: pencil on illustration board, 28½ x 40" (72.6 x 101.6 cm). The Museum of Modern Art, New York. Mies van der Rohe Archive. Gift of the architect

11. Ludwig Mies van der Rohe. Court-House Project. After 1938. Interior perspective: pencil and cut-out reproductions (of Wilhelm Lehmbruck's *Standing Figure* and an unidentified painting) on illustration board, 30 x 40" (76.2 x 101.6 cm). The Museum of Modern Art, New York. Mies van der Rohe Archive. Gift of the architect

12. Archigram Architects. Pool Enclosure for Rod Stewart. 1972. Photomontage. Archigram Archives

House Project (1937–38), the Museum for a Small City Project (1942), the Concert Hall Project (1942), and the Convention Hall Project (1953–54).[30] In fact Mies used the technique as late as his last major commission, the New National Gallery in Berlin (1962–68).

Montage, clearly, was one of Mies's favorite methods of presentation,[31] and his pictures were so effective that some of his pupils adopted the technique as well.[32] A generation later, in their effort to deconstruct his legacy, postmodern critics of modernism have used montage themselves[33]—or, as in the case of the polemical architectural group Archigram, have brazenly reinterpreted his montages for their own ends (fig. 12).[34] The architect Renzo Piano, in a corner view showing his recent design for a high-rise on Potsdamer Platz in Berlin, clearly alludes to Mies's first montages of the Friedrichstrasse Skyscraper of 1921.[35]

While Mies's writings tend to be laconic and abstract, his montages are highly expressive, a quality owed largely to their elegant draftsmanship. Anything but products of "chance,"[36] they are a logical complement to his theoretical statements and his more traditional drawings. Although Mies destroyed any number of drawings from his early years, he shrewdly preserved his montages, selecting them carefully for the various publications he oversaw, or into which he had input—even including the book accompanying his exhibition at The Museum of Modern Art in 1947. Even our view of the structures he actually built is influenced by these images, to the extent that we occasionally find a straightforward photograph of one so dramatic that we suspect it of being a montage.

From Bauhaus to Court-House

TERENCE RILEY

One of the architectural models in Mies's 1947 exhibition at The Museum of Modern Art represented his Group of Court-Houses Project, which a wall label described as "the furthest development of Mies's 'court-house' scheme of 1931."[1] In the book accompanying the exhibition, the curator Philip Johnson provided a historical framework and a definition for the court-house concept: "From 1931 to 1938 Mies developed a series of projects for 'court-houses' . . . in which the flow of space is confined within a single rectangle formed by the outside walls of court and house conjoined."[2] A sequence of ten drawings serves to illustrate Johnson's chronological framework, beginning with a freehand "Sketch for a court-house. c. 1931" and concluding with the floor plan of the same Group of Court-Houses Project, which dates from 1938 (fig. 1).[3] Since Johnson's exhibition and the publication of his book, the court-house has been canonized as a fundamental element of Mies's architecture of the 1930s and later. Yet all of the projects and most of the illustrations that Johnson selected to illustrate the court-house idea raise basic questions regarding some aspect of their provenance.

Although Johnson's essay is authoritative in tone, the definition and chronology he offered did not represent established views of Mies's work but were being put forward for the first time. In fact his essay also introduced the term "court-house" itself, a term today near universal in the lexicon of modern architecture. Anglophone readers in 1947 might have presumed that this hyphenated locution[4]— which Johnson set off in quotation marks—was German in origin, but the German word that serves today as its equivalent, *Hofhaus*, does not appear in any of Mies's published writings from his time in Berlin, nor even in any standard dictionary. Indeed the limited use of *Hofhaus* in the contemporary German vocabulary (or rather in the vocabulary of German-speaking architects) actually derives from the German translation of Johnson's text, in 1956, which again sets it in quotation marks.[5] Yet if

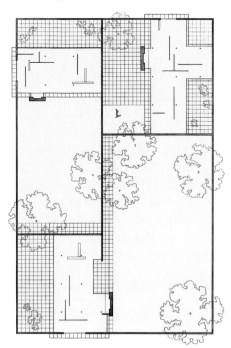

1. Ludwig Mies van der Rohe and Ludwig Hilbersheimer, with IIT students. Group of Court-Houses Project. 1938. Plan: ink and dot pattern on illustration board, 40 x 30" (101.6 x 76.2 cm). The Museum of Modern Art, New York. Mies van der Rohe Archive. Gift of the architect

Hofhaus is simply a direct translation of "court-house" into German, the term "court-house" does appear to have a more subtle linguistic antecedent, related to Mies's teaching, in the German language. Howard Dearstyne, an American student of Mies's when the architect was the director of the Bauhaus, much later described a 1930 project by a fellow student, Eduard Ludwig, as a court-house.[6] Yet Ludwig no more used the word *Hofhaus* than Mies did—it appears in none of his drawings, nor for that matter in any other document in the Bauhaus archives.[7] He did, however, give the projects he designed under Mies's tutelage the title "*Flachbau mit Wohnhof*," or "Low structure with living court." Directly translated, Ludwig's title is somewhat inelegant but quite appropriately describes the structures called "court-houses" in the exhibition. It is not known who suggested the court-house neologism, and George Danforth, one of Mies's first students in America, recalls that Mies did not use the term before the 1947 exhibition and only rarely afterward, even as his students adopted it from Johnson's widely circulated catalogue. It should be noted, however, that the linguistic leap from the workmanlike "*Flachbau mit Wohnhof*" to the more mellifluous "court-house" was well within the abilities of Johnson, who was fluent in German, though not necessarily of the Mies of 1947.[8]

In his pages on the court-house concept, Johnson illustrates three freehand drawings described as "sketches for court-houses. c. 1931," in addition to a plan, an elevation, and a collage perspective (fig. 2) of a project for "row houses,"[9] also dated 1931 in the caption. The presence of these images seems to suggest that Mies was generating not just exploratory drawings but a completed project for a court-house in that year. A close look at the freehand drawings, however, shows that they are actually

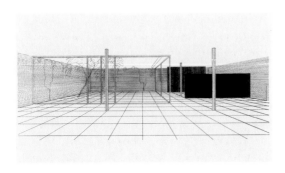

cal court-house collages, published in numerous books on Mies since 1947, were made in America by his students at IIT. Even so, Danforth's perspective quite closely resembles another, not included in Johnson's essay, and drawn again not by Mies but by Ludwig, in 1931, as part of his *Flachbau mit Wohnhof* project (fig. 3). The two images describe extremely similar plans, which they view from similar vantage points.

caption.[13] The name of this project, like the term "court-house," was invented at the time of the exhibition. Rather than being an independent project, the House with Three Courts has roots in a scheme that Mies developed in 1934 for a subdivision on and adjacent to property owned by Margarete Hubbe in Magdeburg. While Johnson and many later chroniclers of Mies's work have examined the architect's unrealized Hubbe

studies for the Gericke and Hubbe house projects, of 1932 and 1934–35 respectively. The plan and elevation of the row houses also deserve scrutiny: the caption's 1931 date notwithstanding, both drawings were made by Danforth while he was a student at the Illinois Institute of Technology (IIT), shortly after Mies began teaching there in 1938.[10] Nor do these seem to be "clean" drawings of a previous project, for there is no document in the Mies van der Rohe Archive to suggest that the architect had a client for a row house in 1931. Meanwhile, at least two other row house plans by Mies's American students, virtually identical in proportion, structure, circulation, and program to the plan in Johnson's book, exist respectively in the Mies van der Rohe Archive at The Museum of Modern Art and in the archive of the work of Mies's students at IIT.[11]

The collage perspective of the row house interior, one of the many such drawings that came to be seen as iconic representations of Mies's work of the 1930s, also raises questions. Despite its purported date, it is drawn on an American product, Strathmore illustration board.[12] Conversations with Danforth reveal what appears to have been a well-known fact among Mies's colleagues: all of the now canoni-

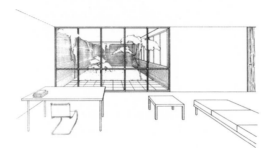

2. Ludwig Mies van der Rohe with George Danforth, after a 1931 project by Eduard Ludwig. Court-House Project, c. 1940. Collage interior perspective: pencil and wood veneer on illustration board, 30 x 40" (76.2 x 101.6 cm). Delineators: Danforth and Mies. The Museum of Modern Art, New York. Mies van der Rohe Archive. Gift of the architect

3. Eduard Ludwig. House C—*Flachbau mit Wohnhof* (Low structure with living court; Bauhaus student project, studio master Mies van der Rohe). 1931. Interior perspective: ink on paper, 16 7/16 x 23 3/8" (41.7 x 59.3 cm). Bauhaus-Archiv Berlin

4. Ludwig Mies van der Rohe. House with Three Courts Project. c. 1940 (based on Hubbe Court-House Studies, 1934–35). Plan: pencil on illustration board, 40 x 30" (101.6 x 76.2 cm). Delineator: George Danforth. The Museum of Modern Art, New York. Mies van der Rohe Archive. Gift of the architect

Johnson's court-house illustrations continue with another plan (fig. 4) and an interior collage (also drawn by Danforth) for a project titled "house with three courts" and dated 1934 in the

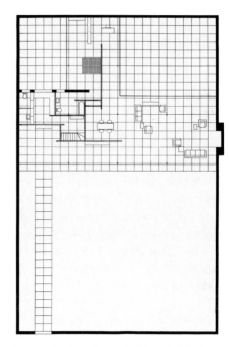

House design, intended for Hubbe herself, virtually nothing has been said of the extended Hubbe Court-House Studies project, which in its most definitive form would have included up to sixteen houses.

The penultimate project in the sequence— the "court-house with garage" (fig. 5)—is dated 1934 but was drawn, like the "house with three courts," by Danforth from an existing drawing

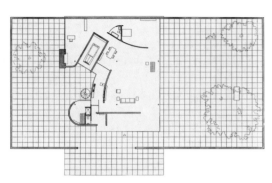

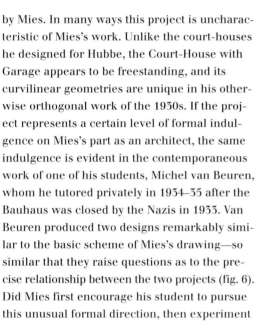

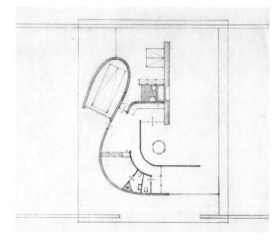

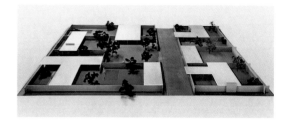

5. Ludwig Mies van der Rohe. Court-House with Garage Project. 1934. Plan: ink on illustration board, 30 x 40" (76.2 x 101.6 cm). Delineator: George Danforth, c. 1940. The Museum of Modern Art, New York. Mies van der Rohe Archive. Gift of the architect

6. Michel van Beuren. Student project, tutor Mies van der Rohe. 1934–35. Plan: pencil and colored pencil on tracing paper, 12¾ x 10" (32.4 x 25.4 cm). Bauhaus-Archiv Berlin

7. Ludwig Mies van der Rohe and Ludwig Hilberseimer, with IIT students. Group of Court-Houses Project. Photograph of lost model. The Museum of Modern Art, New York. Mies van der Rohe Archive. Gift of the architect

by Mies. In many ways this project is uncharacteristic of Mies's work. Unlike the court-houses he designed for Hubbe, the Court-House with Garage appears to be freestanding, and its curvilinear geometries are unique in his otherwise orthogonal work of the 1930s. If the project represents a certain level of formal indulgence on Mies's part as an architect, the same indulgence is evident in the contemporaneous work of one of his students, Michel van Beuren, whom he tutored privately in 1934–35 after the Bauhaus was closed by the Nazis in 1933. Van Beuren produced two designs remarkably similar to the basic scheme of Mies's drawing—so similar that they raise questions as to the precise relationship between the two projects (fig. 6). Did Mies first encourage his student to pursue this unusual formal direction, then experiment with it himself? Or vice-versa?

While it may never be clear what relationships exist between van Beuren's projects and Mies's, it is clear that they represent an interlude shared by teacher and student. By and large, Mies declined to pursue the experiment in his practice, with a few minor exceptions. A faint echo of Mies's and van Beuren's projects can be seen in the single curving partition in Mies's contemporaneous project for a house for Ulrich Lange (plate 305). The equally uncharacteristic

Y-shaped partition in the Court-House with Garage also appears in the sketches for both the Ulrich Lange House and the Hubbe Court-House Studies, although they do not appear in the final designs.

The reader of Johnson's book would probably have assumed that the origin of the Group of Court-Houses lay in Mies's architectural practice, whether it was a commission or a self-initiated project. A previously unpublished photograph in the Mies van der Rohe Archive, however, shows another model that is virtually identical in materials and construction to the one in the exhibition, although it is larger, and consists of two clusters of houses astride a roadway, where the model that was used shows only one (fig. 7). The similarities between the two models raise various questions as to the nature of the project. Although the drawings related to the latter are catalogued among his works in the archive, Danforth confirms that both were IIT student projects, directed by Mies and his colleague Ludwig Hilberseimer.

At this point it seems obvious that some of the questions surrounding Johnson's selection of illustrations might be answered by heeding Mies's words of 1962: "I made these projects at the Bauhaus."[14] There is no reason to believe that Mies was referring to projects that he, as an

architect, designed in the Bauhaus atelier; rather, surviving documentation of his students' work clearly suggests he was speaking of their studio projects. While those familiar with pedagogical practices in schools of architecture today might look askance at Mies's proprietary attitude toward his students' work, his words accurately reflect a philosophy of teaching and a relationship with his students that in his day was more the norm than the exception.

Mies ran his Bauhaus studio as a master class. Working with the advanced students on a one-on-one basis, he would sit with them at the drafting board and sketch over their drawings in progress. While he emphasized individual effort, his students' projects show that he did not emphasize independent work. Of the projects of which he kept photographs,[15] those by the more advanced students increasingly converge on a single architectural language reflecting his own preoccupations at the time. In terms of overall image, Ludwig's *Diplomarbeit*, or final project, for a Dessau department store (fig. 8) directly quotes Mies's 1928 design for a Bank and Office Building Project in Stuttgart. Pius Pahl's interior perspective equally reveals Mies's influence on the level of details—cruciform columns, the placement of sculpture, a grand piano (seemingly ubiquitous in Mies's

8. Eduard Ludwig. Borchardt Department Store Project, Dessau, Kavalierstrasse facade (Bauhaus *Diplomarbeit*, or final project). 1932

9. Howard Dearstyne. House A (Bauhaus student project, studio master Mies van der Rohe). 1930. Plan

10. Eduard Ludwig. House A (Bauhaus student project, studio master Mies van der Rohe). 1930. Plan, site plan, elevations, perspective view of street facade

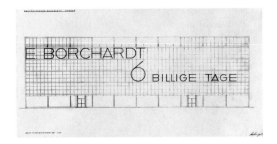

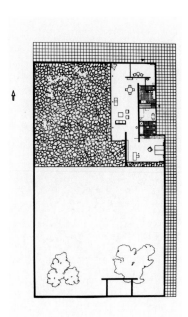

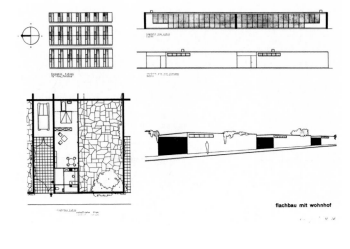

flachbau mit wohnhof

projects of the 1930s), and an arrangement of Mies's furniture.

Except for the students' final projects, virtually all of the studio's output was devoted to the problem of the house.[16] Under this umbrella, however, an extended inventory of types emerged, involving increasingly complex functional problems: weekend house, garden house, single-family house, house for a music lover, house with a doctor's office, etc. Variations in structural and technical complexity can be seen in the assignments of one- and two-story, attached and detached, single and serial buildings. Spatial complexity and scale ranged from the bachelor's studio to the multibedroom family house. The students' consecutive assignments—referred to as House A, B, and C—varied in their requirements, emphasizing the role of the program in determining the form and scale of each house.

A direct connection between Mies's Bauhaus work and his putative "'court-house' scheme of 1931" appears in the recollections of Howard Dearstyne, who joined Mies's first Bauhaus architecture class in 1930, along with Ludwig and four others.[17] In Dearstyne's account, "Mies started us off with a simple problem, the design of a single bedroom 'court house,' a house, that is, facing a walled garden" that was to be conceived of as a unit of a larger grouping of

houses—a "settlement," to use Dearstyne's word.[18] By the time of this essay, published in 1993, the term "court house" was enshrined in the architectural lexicon, accounting for Dearstyne's use of it here; as mentioned earlier, it does not appear in the Bauhaus archives. Still, a court-house-like concept was clearly part of Mies's teaching from the start—although comparison of Dearstyne's and Ludwig's projects suggests that in 1930 the concept was still loosely defined (figs. 9, 10): while Ludwig's first project prefigures the interdependence of interior and exterior spaces that would come to characterize the court-house, Dearstyne's is less resolved, the house appearing as a marginal figure on an open ground. Ludwig's first three projects are more systematic and more closely related to one another than are those of his classmate; in addition to the typical floor plan and elevations, each of them features a hypothetical site plan showing the houses connected in groups, and calculating the efficiency of the plan in terms of population per hectare. Each site plan also shows the orientation of the units with respect to the sun, and the third of them includes a diagram calculating the sunlight in the court at various times of day. Ludwig also gives all three projects the same typological label, "*Flachbau mit Wohnhof*."[19]

Ludwig's expression of traditional domestic values—privacy, sun, air—recurs in the student work of the following years. Where Ludwig's projects seem more overtly functional, more *sachlich*, than one would have expected of Mies's students, later efforts appear to retain the basic values of the exercise even as they refine it and express it more recognizably in Mies's architectural language. Indeed, projects such as the House A designs of Günter Conrad (fig. 11) and Egon Hüttmann clearly reflect Mies's description of the court-house thirty years later: "The use of freestanding walls and large glass areas within a peripheral enclosing wall gave these plans a great richness, even when the house was quite small."[20] A look at these two students' respective plans shows that the systematic rigor of the serial *Flachbau mit Wohnhof* had become part of a shared language in Mies's studio. The similarity between their plans also indicates that their focus had narrowed to more qualitative issues rather than the quantitative ones that Ludwig had addressed.

In both designs the house has a long narrow footprint. The entrance from the street is on its shorter side, and it stands between a yard or garden in front and a small paved court in the rear. The narrow site is less spatially efficient than are Ludwig's designs, but permits a greater

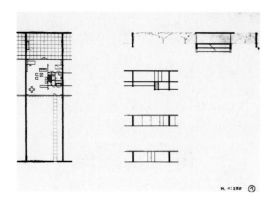

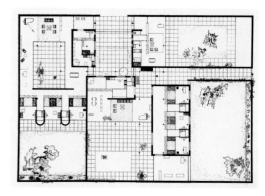

distance between the interior of the house and the street. The differences in scale and in the treatment of the open spaces further suggest a more developed subjective language: the longer yard offers more of a garden, a surrogate landscape view, while the court, compressed between the house and the far wall, is more introspective in character (fig. 12).

While all of the court-house illustrations in Johnson's book have some unspoken relationship to Mies's teaching, the House with Three Courts, presented as a theoretical exercise by the architect, also has a previously unexplained relationship to his practice. In 1934, the year after the closing of the Bauhaus, Mies produced drawings showing various ways of subdividing the Hubbe property in Magdeburg and an adjacent parcel to the north.[21] The most definitive plans illustrate his basic strategy: to reserve a parcel facing the river for the Hubbe House, and to establish smaller parcels to the north and west. The purpose of the exercise is unclear, although developing the property may have been a way to finance the cost of the main house. Dozens of sketch plans of individual houses, until now catalogued in the Mies van der Rohe Archive as court-house studies without reference to the Magdeburg project, correspond in scale, orientation, and proportion to Mies's subdivision plans.

The most finished plans show the site subdivided into various lots, all of which—like the Conrad and Hüttmann plans—are deeper than wide, with the entry facade on the narrow end. Furthermore, all of the sketches for individual houses show Conrad's and Hüttmann's basic House A arrangement of a garden in front of the

11. Günter Conrad. House A (Bauhaus student project, studio master Mies van der Rohe). 1932. Plan, section, elevations

12. Günter Conrad. House A (Bauhaus student project, studio master Mies van der Rohe). 1932. Interior perspective

13. Frank Trudel. Cluster of Three Houses with Shared Service Court Project (student project, tutor Mies van der Rohe). 1934–35. Plan

house and a more compressed paved court at the rear. In the Magdeburg sketches, however, Mies expands on the repertory of configurations of the rear court.[22] Various sketches show him systematically exploring a single court spanning the width of the plot, a single court in one of the corners, and two separate courts—the latter eventually developing into the House with Three Courts in the 1947 exhibition.

Where the projects of Mies's students consisted of repetitions of a single house type,[23] his Magdeburg plans included a range of programs and sizes, reflecting the irregular shape of the property but also a more mature vision of how court-houses might be clustered to form larger patterns of housing. The plans also go beyond the simple back-to-back row house arrangement typical of his student's projects and of earlier Bauhaus plans: in the more finished versions, Mies ran some of the projects side by side but rotated others, forming a cluster of up to twelve houses north of the Hubbe site and a smaller cluster of four houses opposite the main house.

While the Hubbe project was ending, one of Mies's private students, Frank Trudel, designed a project for a *Gruppenwohnblock*, a cluster of court-houses (fig. 13). The design is not very accomplished, but reflects Mies's strategy for

the Hubbe property rather than the back-to-back row house configuration. Even so, Mies seems to have pushed Trudel to consider new possibilities inherent in the clustering of the houses. He himself, while accommodating various scales and sizes in his Magdeburg studies, had used a uniform proportion and basic schema. Trudel's project, in contrast, comprised a range not only of sizes but of proportions and house types. The overall plan of the cluster remained rectangular, as did the individual units, but the composition of the lots was more dynamic than in either the Magdeburg project or the systematically structured earlier projects of Mies's students.

The Group of Court-Houses provides an interesting link between Mies's students in Germany and in America. The two IIT models show clusters of three houses of varying size (fig. 7), nestled, as in Trudel's project, within the larger rectangular perimeter of the *Gruppenwohnblock*. Another correlation might be noted: in addition to the three houses and their respective private courts, Trudel included a fourth space, a common kitchen court that services all three houses. In the second, previously unpublished model, both clusters, on either side of the road, also have a shared open space.

The Group of Court-Houses proposes a number of types of house, each with some variation of a grassy lawn and a paved court. In the project presented in the exhibition, one house clearly replicates the proportions and the garden/house/court scheme of Conrad's and Hüttmann's designs (fig. 1). The long thread of this basic schema continues through Mies's tenure at IIT, appearing again, for example, in a project by

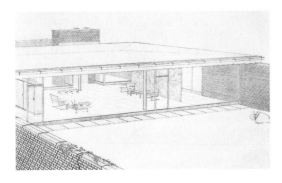

14. Carter H. Manny, Jr. Court-House (IIT student project). 1947. Aerial perspective: pencil on illustration board, 30 x 40" (76.2 x 101.6 cm). Art Institute of Chicago

15. Philip Johnson. Johnson House, Cambridge, Mass. 1942. View from living area into court

Carter H. Manny, Jr., produced for a 1947 course in construction (fig. 14).

———

To recapitulate, of the ten drawings Johnson selected to illustrate the development of the court-house, three are misidentified sketches for other projects; three are drawings made by IIT students, and related, most likely, to the work of Mies's students at the Bauhaus; three are drawings made by IIT students and based on earlier projects, unidentified or of unclear origin, by Mies; and one is a project developed by a number of Mies's students at IIT. This long recitation of unexpected provenance is designed to question not Mies's intellectual authorship of the court-house idea, however, but current perceptions of the role of the court-house in his architectural production of the 1930s, as well as its role, previously unexplored, in his teaching. The repositioning of the court-house relative to Mies's practice and teaching also requires that we reconsider commonly held historical interpretations of the court-house.

The most important revision would be the recognition that the court-house was not the dominant motif in Mies's architectural practice of the 1930s but an abstract problem within his teaching. Indeed, his studies for the Hubbe property are among the very few instances in which he proposed to build court-houses for an actual client, and the Court-House with Garage—which he may have designed for himself—is the only self-initiated court-house project. But Johnson's selection of illustrations to document the court-house tended to suggest

otherwise, as did his text, wherein he claimed, "During the same years [1931–38] Mies designed five adaptations of the court-house idea for clients."[24] He identifies two of these, the Lemke House (1932–33) and the Mountain House Studies (c. 1934), and the other three, by inference, would most likely be the two designs for the Ulrich Lange House and the Hubbe House project. Yet the Lemke House and the Mountain House seem to have little if any relationship to the court-house concept, and while the designs for the Ulrich Lange House (the second much more than the first) and for the Hubbe House do resemble the court-house idea, its influence stops well short of being singular. The constant and fluctuating dialogue in those projects between point-load columns and free-standing partitions, enclosure and free-flowing space, transparency and opacity, views inward and views out to the landscape, is keenly evident in both the Exhibition House of 1931 and the German Pavilion for Barcelona of 1928–29.

If it seems contrary to common perception that Mies's only German clients for court-houses were Hubbe and Ulrich Lange, it may be equally surprising to recognize that Mies neither proposed nor built a court-house for either a client or himself during his three-decade-long career in America. While the court-house remained a part of his teaching at IIT, it is clear—in retrospect—that by 1947 the concept was a historical one as far as he was concerned. Perhaps the Group of Court-Houses Project of 1938 represented a kind of personal as well as intellectual closure on the problem: just as Mies began to collect the avant-garde art

of the 1920s after he emigrated to America, his regeneration of the court-house theme at IIT has the air of both historical summation and retrieval of a lost moment. Meanwhile, however, in his teaching throughout the 1940s he turned increasingly to the problem of the tall building and the long-span structure, both of which would influence his architecture more fundamentally than the court-house ever did.

Johnson's text clearly set the stage for the belief that Mies's architecture of the 1930s was dominated by the court-house, but subsequent misidentifications of Mies's drawings also played a part. Mies had with him in the United States a cache of drawings from his 1930s projects that included a good many of the sketch plans from the Hubbe Court-House Studies. His plans for the subdivision of the site (plate 290), however, were not among them. Hence the key drawings demonstrating that the dozens of sketch plans were all made in the space of a few months, for a single project, were not available until after Mies's death, in 1969. In the meantime The Museum of Modern Art and other institutions misidentified these sketches as independent projects, contributing to the idea that Mies designed a multitude of freestanding court-houses. Furthermore, the court-house took on a life of its own in America after 1941 as many of Mies's followers, with Johnson first among them (fig. 15), did in fact build "Miesian" court-houses.[25]

If a new perception of the court-house must recognize how closely its development is interwoven with Mies's years as a teacher, we cannot fully understand it without considering its benefit to his students. Mies never spoke of it in these terms, but the court-house problem was an ideal student exercise, for it focused on a limited number of issues commensurate with the fledgling skills of young architects. The sites imagined for these projects were generally flat and featureless, limiting the student's need to consider more complex contextual issues; the inward orientation of the court-house emphasized spatial flow more than outward appearance; and the low-rise construction signified by the term "*Flachbau*" required only low-tech solutions. The structural and mechanical implications of the court-house could be grasped intuitively and the single-story layout was decidedly less complex than a multistory project. And even while the court-house was not an overwhelming challenge to the student's technical skills, it reflected universal themes: the individual, the family, the basic building block of society. Indeed the ingenuity of the court-house as a teaching device should be considered as great an accomplishment on Mies's part as any of his students' evident contributions to the development of the theme.

To see the court-house as principally a product of Mies's teaching practice rather than his architectural office requires a more complex perception of its development. Perhaps this complexity even accounts for the lack of reference to Mies's teaching in Johnson's book, which aspired, after all, to introduce forty years of prolific practice to a wide audience in relatively few pages. Indeed the apparent fluidity with which details, plans, and even entire projects migrated between Mies's teaching and his architectural practice suggests a rich though obviously unequal relationship between Mies

and his students—some of whom became his employees—that cannot be described with any degree of certitude. Both at the Bauhaus and at IIT, his dominating presence and his professional accomplishments inevitably and obviously influenced his students' designs. At IIT, his contemporaneous designs for the school's campus were primary sources for his students, who, however, also had access not only to his cache of drawings from his German career but to selected photographic reproductions of the work of his Bauhaus students, all apparently sent from Berlin by Lilly Reich.[26] A distinction emerges between the work of Mies's Bauhaus students and that of his students at IIT: in the projects of the Bauhaus students, the essential characteristics of the court-house can be seen unfolding under his guidance; while individual projects are uneven, the trajectory from conception to first flowering to accomplished rendition is evident in the photographic record. The urban implications of the scheme (which reflect the influence of Hilberseimer as much as of Mies), and the systematic refinements in the project for a Group of Court-Houses, are principally developed by Mies's IIT students.

A reappraisal of the role of the court-house in Mies's work and thought involves more than a parsing out of historical fact. The perception that the court-house was the central paradigm in Mies's work of the 1930s may have originated in the presentation of his work in the 1947 exhibition and book, but it was certainly expanded by subsequent students of Mies's work. Repeated in virtually every chronicle thereafter, Johnson's history has fueled a whole bibliography of interpretations that see the court-house as Mies's response to the political

crises of Nazi Germany. A publication of a dozen years ago is typical: "Where, ten years earlier, he had explored the possibilities of outward flowing space (in his country house projects of 1923 and 1924), he now understood, like so many of his fellow countrymen, that respite—in architecture, as in life—came only from turning within."[27] While such an interpretation might fairly describe Mies's dilemma in an increasingly compromised political climate, it does not accurately characterize the bulk of his work of the 1930s.

If the standard historical interpretations of the court-house now seem overreaching, it might be asked if there is any other interpretation, other than the pedagogical, that might give some insight into Mies's architectural philosophy in the 1930s. If, as we have seen, a definitive original *project* does not exist, was there an original *idea* that might be considered "Mies's 'court-house' scheme of 1931"? The circumstances of Mies's arrival at the Bauhaus, and the work his students produced in that first year, provide a speculative answer.

Mies's appointment to head the Bauhaus, in the fall of 1930, was suggested by Walter Gropius to depoliticize the school after the two years in which it was directed by Hannes Meyer, whose left-wing politics had inflamed conservative opposition to the publicly financed institution. The students and faculty who had supported Meyer greeted Mies's appointment with dismay, claiming that he had "built mansions for the wealthy when he should provide dwellings for the poor."[28] The criticism of Mies as a politically conservative designer of luxurious private homes in the midst of dire economic circumstances no doubt stung, but was not easily shrugged off. In

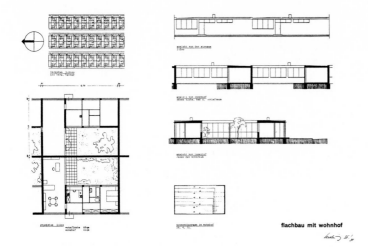

flachbau mit wohnhof

addition to having recently completed the richly realized Tugendhat House, Mies, unlike many of his colleagues, did not pursue social housing commissions except for two apartment blocks in Stuttgart and Berlin, the Stuttgart commission a prestigious exhibition project.

While many of the projects of Mies's students might be retroactively and incorrectly associated with sophisticated and often luxurious latter-day Miesian court-houses such as Johnson's, Ludwig's first projects demonstrate that the *Flachbau mit Wohnhof* reflects the values of reform housing as established by earlier figures such as the English Arts and Crafts architect Mackay Hugh Baillie Scott.[29] Like Scott's Terrace House B, the plan of which recalls Johnson's definition of a court-house, each of Ludwig's three houses— two one-bedroom plans and one two-bedroom plan (fig. 16)—can be seen as offering a reduced version of the amenities of the typical freestanding petit-bourgeois house, itself reducing

grander visions: identity, privacy, fresh air, sunlight, exterior space. The logic of Ludwig's designs might even be seen in Scott's words: "Where only a limited sum of money is available for the making of a home, it will be the best wisdom to spend as much as we can afford in securing a thoughtfully designed and well-built house, and as little as may be required for essential furnishings, and nothing at all in decoration."[30]

The larger plans demonstrated how densely these sorts of minimized houses could aggregate, maximizing land use and thereby containing costs.[31] The *Flachbau* or single-story principle was intended not only to ensure that each court received sunlight, as in Ludwig's diagrams, but to simplify construction and keep costs low. Thus the term *Flachbau mit Wohnhof* was not simply a formal description but represented a comprehensive planning strategy intermingling formal, spatial, tectonic, economic, and social issues. Needless to say, such a strategy was far

beyond the skills of a fledgling architectural student. Of this strategy Mies is surely the author.

In the months leading up to his appointment as director of the Bauhaus, Mies delivered a talk at the Deutscher Werkbund meeting in Vienna. He ended his remarks by emphasizing what he called "spiritual" values as essential to architecture: "The meaning and justification of each epoch, even the new one, lie only in providing conditions under which the spirit can exist."[32] Mies's words defined the essential gap between himself and Meyer, an empiricist and materialist who believed that "building is nothing but organization: social, technical, economic, psychological organization."[33] "Mies's 'court-house' scheme of 1931," then, may well have been his architectural response to his critics at the Bauhaus; rather than a demonstration of *Existenzminimum*, he proposed a strategy to create a house that could create a city— *Existenzmaximum* with minimal resources.

Mies and Exhibitions

WALLIS MILLER

Anyone even modestly familiar with Mies's architecture will associate his time in Germany with exhibitions. A list of his important works of the period might begin with a building such as the Tugendhat House (1928–30), but exhibition projects, such as the German Pavilion in Barcelona (1928–29) and the Weissenhof Housing Colony Master Plan in Stuttgart (1925–27), would soon follow. A moment's more thought would likely conjure up the five projects of the early 1920s—the Friedrichstrasse and the Glass skyscrapers, the Brick and the Concrete country houses, and the Concrete Office Building; not all of these projects were designed for exhibitions, but their existence depended on their being exhibited, in the pages of books and journals as well as in galleries. Mies's collaborations with Lilly Reich add more projects to this list: they worked together on the Glass Room and the Velvet and Silk Café, for exhibitions in Stuttgart and Berlin in 1927; on *Die Wohnung unserer Zeit* (The dwelling of our time), at the 1931 German Building Exhibition in Berlin; on various displays at the *Deutsches Volk, deutsche Arbeit* (German people, German work) exhibition in Berlin in 1934; and on other exhibits of German industry. Mies's unrealized design of 1934 for the German Pavilion at the upcoming International Exposition in Brussels, and his position, early in his career, as director of the Novembergruppe—which primarily existed to produce exhibitions—might complete a list of important German projects were it not for another event that cannot be omitted: Walter Gropius's refusal to include Mies's Kröller-Müller Villa Project of 1912–13 in the *Ausstellung für unbekannte Architekten* (Exhibition of unknown architects, 1919), on the grounds that it was too conservative. As Richard Pommer has pointed out, the moment was prophetic: while it might have been the last time Mies's work would be rejected from a modern show, it was the first of many times that he distanced himself from other members of the modern movement—especially Gropius—with work that was different, even if it would not always be labeled "conservative."[1]

Although many scholars move easily between the exhibition projects and the others, comparing, for example, the German Pavilion in Barcelona to the Tugendhat House, the exhibition projects may constitute a separate genre of work. Did the nature of an exhibition project—its focus on certain issues and its freedom from addressing others—allow Mies to produce designs that he would have been unable to create otherwise? Or were exhibition projects only distinguished from the others by their venue?

In some cases—the Velvet and Silk Café, the expositions in Barcelona and in Brussels—Mies was asked to design exhibition contexts for a variety of objects and ideas: textiles, beer, glass, national identity. In others—the Novembergruppe exhibitions, the Weissenhof Housing Colony, the German Building Exhibition, and Mies's design for his own retrospective at The Museum of Modern Art, New York, in 1947—he put architecture itself on display. But one might say that architecture was on display at all of these events, for Mies's approach to exhibition design blurred the distinction between the content of the display and the context he created for it. One of the first to recognize the architectural value of these designs was Philip Johnson, in his review of *Die Wohnung unserer Zeit*, which Mies designed and directed: "The art of exhibiting is a branch of architecture and should be practiced as such. Mies has designed the entire hall, containing houses and apartments by the various architects, as itself one piece of architecture. The result is a clear arrangement inviting inspection, instead of the usual long central hall, with exhibits placed side by side."[2]

The German Building Exhibition was a huge show dedicated to all sectors of the German building industry, with *Die Wohnung unserer Zeit*, sponsored by the Deutscher Werkbund, representing architecture (figs. 1–3). The design that enabled Johnson to understand "the art of exhibiting" as "a branch of architecture"—rather than as a series of display armatures, or as a representation of an architectural context that existed elsewhere—enveloped twenty-three full-scale displays of housing in a context that overwhelmed any reference to their existence on other sites and in other conditions. All of these units were on the main floor of the exhibition hall; six freestanding units stood at the center of the space, while the rest were on the perimeter, tucked under a balcony. The exhibit brought together one-room flats, duplexes, single-family homes, and a Boarding House or apartment hotel, designed mostly by architects and artists allied with the Werkbund's modern faction (among them Hans and Wassili Luckhardt, Hugo Häring, Gropius, Reich, Josef Albers, Marcel Breuer, and Erwin Gutkind). The Prussian government's building administration was also represented, with a display of "alternative dwellings" that included dorm rooms and prison cells.

The exhibition's official guidebook suggested that the housing would be quite diverse. Some units were defined by their physical attributes—

"an apartment for two people in a multistory apartment house in an east-west orientation," "a single-story row house with a southern exposure," "a two-story apartment in a tower," "a four-room apartment," "a minimal apartment"; others were identified by the social situations of their occupants: houses for couples with and without children, "bachelor's apartments," "an apartment for

two working women," "a house for an athlete," and "an apartment for an intellectual."[3] Despite the promise of variety, however, what visitors saw was a unified sea of white surfaces and expanses of glass. Rather than letting the exteriors of the exhibits betray their different designers, Mies rendered them identically, with a limited palette of materials and proportions. Although the flats and houses under the balcony were not designed to be contiguous, Mies orchestrated their facades as a rhythmic composition, eliminating any simple separation between them. This continuous perimeter seems to have expressed a concern for the coherence of the exhibition context rather than for the authenticity of a display of housing.

Mies also obscured the varied origins and purposes of the units at the center of the hall. Otto Haesler and Karl Völker's duplex apartment, for example, was presented as a freestanding unit; its only concession to its intended location in an apartment tower was that steel columns lifted it one story off the ground. These columns could have been mistaken for part of the unit

1. Ludwig Mies van der Rohe. *Die Wohnung unserer Zeit* (The dwelling of our time), German Building Exhibition, Berlin, 1931. In the right foreground, Mies's Exhibition House; beyond it, Lilly Reich's Ground-Floor House; in the background, Otto Haesler and Karl Völker's duplex; to the left, the Boarding House

2. Ludwig Mies van der Rohe. *Die Wohnung unserer Zeit.* In the foreground, Hugo Häring's house; to the left, Haesler and Völker's duplex; in the right background, the Boarding House

3. Ludwig Mies van der Rohe. *Die Wohnung unserer Zeit.* Plan: pencil on tracing paper, 21½ x 29¾" (54.6 x 75.6 cm). Mies's Exhibition House is #48; Reich's Ground-Floor House is #31. The Museum of Modern Art, New York. Mies van der Rohe Archive. Gift of the architect

rather than part of the armature of display; a stair to the apartment did not appear to be a part of either. In fact the columns, reminiscent of pilotis, and the stair together made this display of a tower apartment look like a single-family

house, as one contemporary reporter wrote: "The section of the apartment tower . . . won't be misunderstood only by laypeople: people think it is a single-family house that the architect in some crazy mood placed on stilts."[4]

Subordinating the different origins and purposes of the housing units to the exhibition's formal unity, Mies wove the structures into the

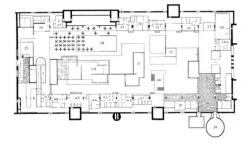

new context created by the exhibition design. Underscoring this appropriation of content by context, he created continuities between the exhibits and elements of the exhibition hall: the facades of the units around the hall's perimeter rose up to become the parapet of the balcony and a ramp connecting the two levels; the balcony became part of the environment around the housing units, an "exterior landscape"; and this landscape itself evolved into a space of display (in an exhibit sponsored by the Wertheim department store). Having all but lost its connection to the "real world"—to the site or any other part of the network of constraints and interests that ultimately determine the forms of all built work—the content of the exhibition ceased to be representative, derivative, or even displaced; it was itself a part of a new work of architecture, and its spaces, being at full scale, could be immediately and thoroughly experienced.

4. Ludwig Mies van der Rohe and Lilly Reich. Glass Room. *Die Wohnung* (The dwelling) exhibition, Stuttgart, 1927

5. Ludwig Mies van der Rohe and Lilly Reich. Deutsche Linoleum Werke exhibit. *Die Wohnung* exhibition, Stuttgart, 1927

While Johnson's characterization of exhibition design as architecture was apt for *Die Wohnung unserer Zeit*, it did not apply to another exhibit at the Building Exhibition, designed by Gropius for the unions representing the building trades.[5] Working with László Moholy-Nagy and Herbert Bayer, Gropius filled his space with interactive exhibits that transformed countless statistics into exciting visual experiences. One could say much about these exhibits, but little about Gropius's spatial arrangement of them, except to describe his section as a set of "exhibits placed side by side." Moreover, the footprints and arrows that accompanied visitors through the exhibit indicated a directional intention that the spatial design did not fulfill.

Objects

"The clear arrangement inviting inspection" was the hallmark of all of Mies's exhibition work. The relationship among the various display

elements was as important as their individual design; visitors could enter his exhibition environments as they would his built architecture and have a complex but coherent spatial experience. Several of these designs were collaborations with Reich, who, as Matilda McQuaid writes, "altered the prevailing custom of presenting raw materials and techniques as a mere adjunct to the finished product by choosing material and process as the essence of her installation."[6]

The Werkbund exhibition *Die Wohnung* (The dwelling, 1927), whose most celebrated component was the Weissenhof Housing Colony, also included exhibits in a series of halls in central Stuttgart. Mies and Reich worked together on two installations here, the Glass Room (fig. 4) and the adjoining display for the Deutsche Linoleum Werke (German linoleum works, fig. 5; in fact Reich was in charge of eight of the nine areas in this part of the exhibition). In both of these exhibits Mies and Reich showed that space need not be defined by architectural elements alone: the lines they traced in plan and section could be undermined as easily as reinforced by the materials out of which the elements were built. If anything could challenge the boundary established by the abstract notions of wall, floor, and ceiling, it was glass, and in the Glass Room Mies and Reich exploited the effect of subtle variations in the medium's tint to connect, divide, and loosely associate various residential spaces. These effects were enhanced by the upholstery and veneers on the furniture. In the linoleum exhibit they used a material that could cover large surfaces without interruption to shape space visually through changes in color. Sliding around the walls and floor of its exhibition area and back into the Glass Room, the

6. Ludwig Mies van der Rohe and Lilly Reich. Velvet and Silk Café. *Die Mode der Dame* (Women's fashion) exhibition, Berlin, 1927

linoleum often ignored the physical boundaries constructed by the architecture.[7]

A shifting relationship between the material on display and the architectural elements that defined the space was not just a peculiarity of the Stuttgart shows. That same year, Mies and Reich also collaborated on the Velvet and Silk Café, at *Die Mode der Dame* (Women's fashion), an exhibition in Berlin (fig. 6). Here they used velvet, in black, orange, and red, and silk, in black and lemon yellow, to define the relatively intimate spaces of the café, which was located in an exhibition hall wrapped in 10,000 meters of blue tulle and 8,000 square meters of gold paper.[8] As in the glass and linoleum exhibits in Stuttgart, the café's intense juxtapositions of color and texture affected the perception of its spaces. In addition, the flexibility of velvet and silk affected the design. First, it freed the spaces from rectilinear form, defining them through a series of graceful curves that did not quite intersect.[9] While each curve gathered up a few tables, it never completely obscured the patrons' view

7. Ludwig Mies van der Rohe and Lilly Reich. Hackerbräu beer exhibit. International Exposition, Barcelona, 1929

8. Ludwig Mies van der Rohe and Lilly Reich. Textile exhibit. International Exposition, Barcelona, 1929

of the rest of the crowd. Second, the materials' soft malleability suggested that the walls could be easily displaced.[10] As in Mies's Weissenhof Apartment House, the shifting boundaries and flowing space could at least theoretically be created by anyone.

In 1929 in Barcelona, Mies and Reich collaborated again. The Germans were represented here by twenty-five industrial exhibits, as well as by Mies's German Pavilion; because they could not afford to build an independent exhibition hall, all but one of their industrial exhibits were integrated into thematically oriented halls shared by different countries. The exception was the exhibit of the German electric utilities, which had its own pavilion designed under Mies's direction.

Reich was the overall director of the industrial exhibits, which were praised for their unified presentation despite their varying contents.[11] She and Mies designed some of the exhibits together, but it is unclear which: according to McQuaid, they probably collaborated on the

exhibit for Hackerbräu beer (fig. 7); according to Sonja Günther, they also produced textile and chemistry exhibits (fig. 8).[12] In these displays, devices of repetition, stacking, and draping transformed objects and materials into walls, partitions, and columns of various heights and thicknesses. These in turn were placed to define the flow of space, perhaps most strikingly in the beer exhibit, where two long shelves of bottles mounted several feet off the ground opened up and affected the scale of the exhibition space, which was physically enclosed by three white walls. The objects and materials on display in these exhibits would not have been recognized as typical materials of architecture, and so made more subtle statements about materials and the difference between drawing or planning and actual building than had their predecessors in the Glass Room, the linoleum exhibit, and the Velvet and Silk Café.

Mies's and Reich's next significant collaborations were at *Die Wohnung unserer Zeit*, in 1931. Visitors following the prescribed sequence would enter this exhibition on the balcony level, where a *Materialienschau* (Materials show) designed by Reich was the preface to the main floor below (figs. 9, 10).[13] Here Reich displayed twenty-four different finishing materials, fittings, and furnishings, such as glass, wood, paint, carpet, upholstery, clocks, and chairs. Like previous exhibition displays Mies and Reich had designed, the *Materialienschau* exhibited not so much the applications of materials as their inherent visual characteristics and their malleability into a variety of forms. The exhibits were organized in a progression from two to three dimensions: the first half of them were of surface materials—marble (in a display

9. Lilly Reich. Wood exhibit. *Materialienschau* (Materials show), *Die Wohnung unserer Zeit* (The dwelling of our time), German Building Exhibition, Berlin, 1931

10. Lilly Reich. Textile exhibit (on balcony). *Materialienschau*, *Die Wohnung unserer Zeit*. View from the Boarding House

designed by Mies), wood and veneers, flooring, carpeting, wallpaper, paint, and lacquer—until a textile display served as the transition to three-dimensional objects such as clocks, hardware, and furniture. The sequence ended with an exhibit of plate glass, whose complex reflections emphasized its three-dimensional presence.

Although the displays in the *Materialienschau* encouraged visitors to move around them, it was only downstairs that visitors passed through a well-defined set of spaces. Most prominent here were the houses by Mies and Reich respectively. Unlike many of the apartments on display, whose modernity was signified by the furniture more than the space, these two houses were clear examples of open-plan design. But there was a difference: while the spaces of Reich's house were certainly open to each other, those in Mies's were almost entirely continuous and

11. Ludwig Mies van der Rohe. Exhibition House. *Die Wohnung unserer Zeit* (The dwelling of our time), German Building Exhibition, Berlin, 1931

interwoven (fig. 11). In his Exhibition House, the shifting boundaries of the space redefined fundamental distinctions between public and private, inside and out. The difference was clearest from the exterior: where Reich's house was completely enclosed, Mies's appeared as a series of overlapping planes and spaces.[14]

If the resemblances between the spaces of Mies's Exhibition House and of his and Reich's exhibition collaborations suggest that he was probably primarily responsible for the spatial design of the exhibits, the *Materialienschau* suggests that Reich was primarily responsible for the individual displays. Here—as in the shop

windows she designed in her early career, and in her exhibition work in Frankfurt, Stuttgart, Barcelona, Berlin, and Paris—she reduced an object to its formal properties, which she then exposed to public view, often in new ways. She saw materials and objects as visual opportunities that she could exploit with her armatures, display cases, pedestals, and arrangements of stacks, rows, and groups. Her designs coaxed materials and objects into forms that viewers could only appreciate from multiple vantage points. Like Mies's architecture, her work demanded movement.

By making Reich's *Materialienschau* the preface to *Die Wohnung unserer Zeit*, Mies suggested that the materials and fixtures in a building were not merely embellishments but necessary to the generation of architectural space.[15] The reviews of the full-scale units on the main floor were filled with descriptions and photographs of the new furniture, cabinetry, and surface treatments, whose rich textures and colors immediately captured the public's attention.[16] Of all the units here, Mies's Exhibition House worked with the most restrained material palette, yet he used paint, wood, fabric, stone, glass, and chrome in such a way that the spatial configuration of the project could not be understood without them (fig. 12). The fabric that hung as curtains over every glass wall and across some of the spaces changed the experience of the space implied by the plan. Two dark heavy curtains spanning interior sections of the house could be moved to affect the entry sequence; others, either by displacement or by their transparency, redefined the boundary between inside and out in the living and dining spaces as well as in the bedrooms.[17] In addition, the use of wood

veneer on the wall of the living space, combinations of chairs with both dark and light upholstery, a glass-and-chrome Tugendhat Table, and a dark carpet challenged the ability of the plan of the Exhibition House to represent the project fully, evocative though it is. With Reich's *Materialienschau* looming on the balcony above, visitors could have seen these finishes as a complex combination of colors, textures, and

12. Ludwig Mies van der Rohe. Exhibition House. *Die Wohnung unserer Zeit*, German Building Exhibition, Berlin, 1931. Interior view

shapes determining their perception of the space around them. Rather than simply emphasizing what was delineated in the drawing, the glass, veneer, curtains, and carpets would have allowed the spaces to join and separate, expand and contract, seem deeper and shallower.

The sequence of *Die Wohnung unserer Zeit*, beginning with the *Materialienschau*, challenged the architectural method of defining space representationally, for example through drawings and plans, by introducing the public to space-making elements at full scale. When they finally reached Mies's house, which was at the end of the sequence, visitors might have shared Johnson's impression: "This three-dimensional type of composition defied photography or even appreciation from but one point of view. Only by walking through the building can an idea of its beauty be obtained."[18] Architectural space emerged here from the direct perception of the materials that defined it, rather than from the conventions and standards of good drawing. This made it difficult, however, to interpret the units' smooth white exterior surfaces. While the presence of Reich's *Materialienschau* might have seemed to suggest that these facades were covered in white paint, their detailing did not seem robust enough to sustain any weathering. Rather, *Die Wohnung unserer Zeit* seemed to be composed of a series of interwoven planes whose appearance originated in a model made in the architects' studio. It was unclear whether the exhibit showed buildings or models of buildings. This ambiguity appeared in all of Mies's exhibition projects, and characterized his attitude toward relationships definitive for architecture: between architectural design and technology and between representation and building.

Three years after *Die Wohnung unserer Zeit*, Mies and Reich collaborated again, in the same exhibition hall, on *Deutsches Volk, deutsche Arbeit*. Now, during the Nazi period, their exhibits revealed the tension between two spatial strategies: the asymmetry and balance associated with modernism and internationalism, and the symmetry and axial organization generally associated with nationalism and the representational projects of Hitler's Germany. Mies's and Reich's design for the mining exhibit in this show consisted of mural-sized photographs and

13. Ludwig Mies van der Rohe and Lilly Reich. Mining exhibit. *Deutsches Volk, deutsche Arbeit* (German people, German work) exhibition, Berlin, 1934

walls of coal and salt (fig. 13).[19] The surrounding exhibition hall was organized around a strong central axis, which was anchored by a staircase at one end and an abstracted German eagle at the other; two large walls in the mining exhibit seemed to reinforce this axis. In front of these walls, however, Mies and Reich slid lower walls of different thicknesses and materials (a strategy recalling the Stuttgart linoleum exhibit of 1927), and with these and the partitions they set in the exhibition spaces to each side, they seem to have put their uncertainty with their new context on display: the lower walls suggest that they were using their modern preference for balanced composition to challenge the central axis and symmetry associated with Nazism.

It was in that same year of 1934 that Mies designed his competition project for the German Pavilion at the International Exposition to be held in Brussels the following year. (Mies lost the competition to Ludwig Ruff, whose project, however, was never built.) The program for the pavilion had two components: one section was to exhibit industrial progress, the other, national

ideology. As Claire Zimmerman has observed, Mies accommodated the program by conceiving of the two components as alternatives and giving the square building two centers.[20] One, defined symmetrically, was to contain a "Court of Honor" displaying exhibits called "People and Empire," "World View," and "Peasant and Soil"; the other, for the industrial exhibits, involved a series of asymmetrically disposed walls.

The few existing drawings of the project indicate that Mies's conceptual strategy echoed the Nazi party's acceptance of a modernist, asymmetrical style for industrial projects but desire for a more conservative, symmetrical design for representation. Rather than letting the two parts confront each other, however, Mies separated them, so that they could have coexisted harmoniously under the same roof. In fact the symmetrical Court of Honor was to float asymmetrically in the pavilion, and the overall design confirmed Mies's commitment to asymmetry, balance, and modernism. Symmetry again shared space with asymmetry in Mies's and Reich's last collaborative exhibition design, for the 1937 *Reichsausstellung der deutschen Textil- und Bekleidungswirtschaft* (Imperial exposition of the German textile and garment industry) in Berlin. Here one-third of the exhibits were disposed about a central axis (fig. 14), in a symmetry that was undisturbed by the asymmetry of the rest of the exhibit because it governed only one end of the room, which was mainly concealed behind partitions.[21]

Pavilions

In *Die Wohnung unserer Zeit*, as we have seen, the exterior surfaces were uniform; in the German Pavilion in Barcelona two years earlier,

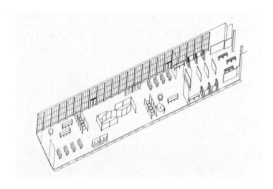

14. Ludwig Mies van der Rohe and Lilly Reich. *Reichs-ausstellung der deutschen Textil- und Bekleidungswirtschaft* (Imperial exposition of the German textile and garment industry), Berlin, 1937. Axonometric drawing: ink on Mylar. Delineator: Craig Konyk, 1996

almost every surface was clad in a material rich in color and pattern. (Only the roof, when viewed from the ground below, resembled one of the white planes of the later exhibition.) These were among the characteristics that would earn the building a place in the canon of modern architecture. "With unsurpassed precision," wrote Sigfried Giedion, "[Mies] used pure surfaces of precious materials as elements of the new space conception."[22] The lesson of the German Pavilion, however, was all too easily forgotten. Contemporary critics noticed that in the pavilion an "absolute material emptiness is filled by a harmony of color and form," and marveled at "the sensual joy of the secret magic of real material," but they discussed Mies's Exhibition House of 1931 only in terms of its practicality.[23] By that time the urgent need for housing had probably gotten in the way of any appreciation of the project's experiential value.

The reaction to the German Pavilion suggests that the plan, despite its graphic power,

could not have adequately represented a building whose materials so transformed the experience of its spaces. The reflections and shadows in polished marble and colored glass, the ripples on the surface of water, the curtains blowing in the wind, created continuities and discontinuities that redefined the spaces made by the building's solid boundaries, challenging the absolute power of ceilings, floors, and walls to enclose space. With the aid of a black carpet, or a basin of water lined with black glass, white floors opened up to suggest infinite depth.[24] While Mies's Exhibition House, and his overall design for *Die Wohnung unserer Zeit*, would register some uncertainty about the ultimate influences on the definition of architectural space, the German Pavilion showed his appreciation of the effect of materials in a direct encounter with the building, an effect that could not be fully anticipated in the architect's studio.[25]

Besides designing the German Pavilion in Barcelona, and collaborating with Reich on various industrial exhibits there, Mies also designed a pavilion for the German electrical utilities, a three-quarter white cube tucked between two of the older exhibition halls (figs. 15, 16).[26] The design of the exterior emphasized its role as an enclosure with the placement of four I-beam-shaped steel verticals mounted on both of the building's side walls like pilasters. These beams anticipated those in the Seagram Building, New York, a few decades later (1954–58), although here they were carried to the ground, and could not have been mistaken for window mullions because they were attached to smooth white walls. Like the exterior walls of the units in *Die Wohnung unserer Zeit*, the outside walls of the Electric Utilities Pavilion showed no evidence

of gutters, flashing, or any other functional change in materials. Only a row of small square openings between the I-beams at the top of the building might have admitted air or light to the inside. As the Farnsworth House (1949–50) and the Seagram Building would do, the pavilion pushed its structural elements—or rather their expression—to its edge, calling attention to the boundary between itself and the rest of the world.

The design of the interior, executed by Fritz Schüler under Mies's supervision, underscored this emphasis on enclosure. Only a wide low opening cut into the facade provided entry, to what Fritz Neumeyer has described as a support-free space that gave the illusion of being open on all sides. The interior of the windowless cube, Neumeyer writes, was completely covered with large-scale photographs depicting various aspects of the German power industry. Together these images gave the illusion of a three-dimensional panorama, seeming to open the space toward an imaginary horizon.[27] It was as if the walls that might have divided the interior space had been pushed to its edges, where they were clad in photographs rather than by a typical facing material such as plaster. Some of the photographs even wrapped around the building's corners, dissolving the perception of a limited, interior space. The colored and textured walls of the German Pavilion were here exchanged for large-scale images emulating a real view, and thus shaping the space of the pavilion—as large photographs would in the *Deutsches Volk, deutsche Arbeit* exhibition five years later, as paintings would in Mies's Museum for a Small City Project of 1942, and as floor-to-ceiling views so often would in his modern work. The transformation of boundaries so crucial to his architecture was now clearly shown to affect the definition of the wall itself, which at once contained and flattened space. For Mies, the exhibition pavilion, at least in Barcelona, became a way to reconsider the nature of enclosure. While he used the German Pavilion to investigate the location as well as the physical character of a building's enclosure, in the Electric Utilities Pavilion he concentrated on the relationship of enclosure to periphery, simultaneously emphasizing and dissolving it in a way that foreshadowed his American work.

Drawings

In all of these exhibition designs, Mies privileged actual space, rejecting the use of small scale to suggest a full-scale design. By contrast, his first five modern designs took the form of drawings and scale models. The Friedrichstrasse Skyscraper, the Glass Skyscraper, the Concrete Office Building, the Concrete Country House, and the Brick Country House projects were all exhibited as part of the Novembergruppe section of the Grosse Berliner Kunstausstellung exhibitions of 1922, 1923, and 1924, and were displayed in rooms containing drawing, graphics, painting, and sculpture. Unlike Mies's other exhibition work, these projects were impossible to enter, but the size of his drawings suggests that, like the murals he later used in Barcelona and Berlin, they may have transformed the exhibition space at its edges.

Working at full scale was part of Mies's early career. As a fifteen-year-old draftsman in an Aachen stucco factory, he drew ornaments of all styles, he said in a later interview, on "huge drawing boards that went from floor to ceiling and stood vertically against the wall." Like most

15. Ludwig Mies van der Rohe. Electric Utilities Pavilion, International Exposition, Barcelona, 1929

16. Ludwig Mies van der Rohe with Fritz Schüler. Electric Utilities Pavilion. Interior with photomurals

shop drawings, his were big, as close to life-size as possible: "We made drawings the size of an entire quarter of a room ceiling." The process of making these drawings seems to have had as much in common with Mies's later work as did their size: "You couldn't lean on or against them; you had to stand squarely in front of them and draw not just by turning your hand but by swinging your whole arm," he explained.

Making the drawings required more than visual acuity; it engaged his body. At least for the draftsmen, the ornament was palpable even before it was built.[28]

Mies's unusually large renderings of some of his architectural projects may be indebted to his experience in the stucco factory. He made his biggest drawings for competition entries and ideal projects that were to be exhibited in some way but not necessarily ever built. His renderings of the Bismarck Monument Project (1910), the Concrete Country House, and the Concrete Office Building were extraordinarily large, the first two being over 7 feet long and the third reaching a size of almost 9 1/2 feet long and over 4 1/2 feet high. The photomontages of the Friedrichstrasse Skyscraper and of the Bank and Office Building Project in Stuttgart (1928), and the elevation of the Glass Skyscraper, were somewhat smaller, although all had one dimension of at least 4 1/2 feet. These large renderings, which include four of the five projects that marked the beginning of Mies's modern career, suggest an attempt to give the projects palpable existence, for himself as well as for his audience.[29] While the renderings could not literally be entered, their size made them transform the space in which they were displayed.

Before Mies exhibited his work with the Novembergruppe, one critic voiced his frustrations about architecture exhibitions: "It really is preposterous to present architecture in exhibition halls. Architecture can only be experienced in nature, its complete effect can only unfold if it is built as it should be and placed in the natural environment for which the building is intended and in which it belongs."[30] Mies directly challenged this attitude, and continued to do so even after he left Germany: in his show at The Museum of Modern Art in 1947, he used floor-to-ceiling photographs to pull the exhibition space into his projects. A photograph of him standing with Johnson in front of a mural-scale photograph of the Tugendhat House living room reveals a continuity between the space of the exhibition and the space of the house, a continuity due both to the composition and cropping of the photograph and to its human scale.[31] Standing before it, Mies is enveloped by the space of the house even as he remains in the space of the gallery (fig. 17).

Mies's project of 1934 for the German Pavilion in Brussels is unusual in that it was not realized at full scale in any medium. Perhaps this is because Mies only had a month to prepare it; perhaps he expected to win the competition and build his design, so that he felt it unnecessary to produce large-scale drawings. The drawings he submitted are lost, but they must have been smaller than any of the perspectives he exhibited in the Novembergruppe shows ten years earlier.[32]

17. Ludwig Mies van der Rohe and Philip Johnson at *Mies van der Rohe*, The Museum of Modern Art, New York, 1947. To the right, the photomural of the Tugendhat House

In the end, the German Pavilion for Brussels, along with the Reichsbank competition design that Mies had produced the year before, was among the few of his German exhibition projects that offered no promise of a full-scale experience.

Buildings

Like the Artists' Colony in Darmstadt (its predecessor of 1901), the Weissenhof Housing Colony of 1927 was referred to as a "built exhibition" or an "experimental housing development." The expectations raised by the project, as well as the responses to it, reflected the contradictions inherent in these names.[33] As soon as the Stuttgart city council and the directors of the Werkbund approved the project, in 1925, they made it clear that they had two goals that could not easily be reconciled: on the one hand the project was to bring fame, both to Stuttgart (for the city officials) and to the "New Building" (for the Werkbund); on the other it was to provide housing for low- and middle-income families.[34]

The hope of fame favored experiments catering neither to the needs of housing nor to the standards of economic construction. From the beginning, city officials and Werkbund members were as attracted to the "lavish design" of Mies's site plan and its promise of a departure from tradition as they were to the task of providing livable housing.[35] The authors of a program for the exhibition, written late in 1926, may have seen Weissenhof as "an experimental colony to determine the principles of mass production," but they were clearly more interested in the differences likely to emerge within an experimental group of buildings designed by fifteen different architects than in a repetitive strategy suited to mass production. Identifying the "main principle of the project" as

"the determination of new ways of living as a consequence of using new materials," they said that "the colony cannot present rational methods of mass production itself but can only be a model."[36] In addition, "experiments cost money," as the architect Max Taut put it, while social housing depended on low budgets.[37]

Mies sought to extract himself from the contradiction inherent in the phrase "built exhibition" by differentiating his contribution from that of the builders: his responsibility was "as a voluntary artistic director, as the author of a building plan, and as an architect responsible for the design of an apartment block," as he put it two months before the exhibition opened. During the construction phase of the project, he responded to problems by claiming that "most of the architects have seriously concentrated on technical questions for months and it is not their fault if there is so little at hand that is technically reliable."[38] Mies elaborated on this point after the exhibition, assigning any responsibility for inadequate construction to the contractors, and claiming that "we were free only in dealing with the spatial problem, that is to say, the real architectural [*baukünstlerischen*] issue."[39]

Blaming the local contractors did not alleviate Mies's frustration with existing construction practices; a few years later, *Die Wohnung unserer Zeit* implicitly charged the entire building industry with technological stagnation. The German Building Exhibition occupied eight halls, with the first hall containing an "International Planning and Housing Exhibition." Mies's architecture exhibit followed; then came several halls of exhibits on materials, fabrication, and construction, and finally an outdoor courtyard filled with completed buildings. The sequence took on a narrative function, then, suggesting that the various building trades had a responsibility to realize the designs of the architects, which came first. Nothing could have accommodated Mies's position better. The irony was that many of the objects shown in the exhibition's demonstrations of construction techniques, and most of its completed buildings outside *Die Wohnung unserer Zeit*, looked nothing like what he and his Werkbund colleagues had proposed in their own section of the exhibition. None of the reviews directly addressed the disjointed nature of the presentation, but Mies's characterization of *Die Wohnung unserer Zeit* echoed his complaints about Weissenhof: in the press, he introduced his section with the claim that "one will not see [here] the dwelling of yesterday, but that of tomorrow," and exposed the builders to the same charge he had levied against them at Weissenhof—that they were still "behind the times."[40]

Many critics have remarked that all of Mies's modern work from this period exposed the division between his architecture and contemporary building practices. Beatriz Colomina, for example, describes the "enormous gap between the flowing architecture of Mies's published projects and his struggle to find the appropriate techniques with which to produce these effects in built form."[41] Wolf Tegethoff similarly distinguishes Mies's built work from his unbuilt projects; referring to the Wolf, Esters, and Hermann Lange houses, he argues that "obviously the technical and structural means at [Mies's] disposal proved disconcertingly inappropriate to what he intended to say in architecture."[42] Robin Evans sees the German Pavilion in Barcelona as showing how Mies resolved the difference between architecture

and construction that characterized other modern German projects; for Mies, Evans writes, truth was based not in the consistency of structure and form, as it was for other modernists, but in appearance: "This is what happens when things are made to be looked at."[43]

Exhibition projects freed Mies from the awkwardness of dealing with existing building practices and let him concentrate on "the real architectural issue." A similar focus is suggested in his foreword to the book accompanying the Weissenhof exhibition, where he describes the new housing as "a problem of the building art [*Baukunst*], in spite of its technical and economic aspects."[44] This turn away from construction and embrace of *Baukunst* coincided with a more general shift in his position. As early as 1926, according to Neumeyer, Mies had relinquished his earlier faith in new materials and their power to transform technology and architecture[45] and described architecture as "a spiritual problem." "'Building art as spiritual decision' presupposes an order," explains Neumeyer, "and indeed an order that does not anchor the spiritual in the immanence of things, in circumstances, but first of all in the consciousness of man, in will and in idea."[46]

If Mies's exhibition work allowed him to practice the "building art" more freely than his commissioned work did, it was because it allowed him to exploit the access to the future granted by works of art. "We stand in the middle of a transformation, a transformation that will change the world," Mies wrote in 1928. "To point to this transformation and further it, that will be the task of the upcoming exhibitions."[47] This was exactly what he did in his exhibition designs, using them to offer an immediate

experience of what technology could only promise for the future. Exhibition contexts also allowed him to reveal the "spiritual decisions" that determined his designs, especially after 1927, without him having to worry about offending the building conventions and functional standards typically associated with commissioned work.

In *Die Wohnung unserer Zeit*, for example, Mies explicitly laid claim to the future by identifying "our time" with tomorrow. But the atectonic exteriors of the units on display made the point that architecture was not a product of technological invention. Reich's *Materialienschau* reinforced this point by using materials to affect spatial perception rather than represent new building technologies. This emphasis on perception, along with Mies's general preoccupation with the "spirit of the time," wrested attention away from function. As Neumeyer points out, Mies had claimed a few years earlier that "the apartment is a use item. May one ask for what? May one ask to what it relates? Obviously only to bodily existence. So that all may proceed smoothly. And yet, man also has a spiritual need to transcend his walls, which can never be satisfied by responding to physical demands."[48] A contemporary reviewer, Wilhelm Lotz, could immediately understand that the function shaping the space of Mies's Exhibition House was spiritual: "The human has become the measure of space in a spiritual sense. Here, the artistic aspect of spatial formation, so to speak, has been expressed in a new way."[49]

Mies's Exhibition House proposed that functional activity could change one's point of view in both a physical and a spiritual sense. Physical functions here can be understood as opportunities to position and reposition the body, as in Reich's displays above, whose complex design required viewers to hold certain postures and move in certain directions. In the visually rich spaces of Mies's house, however, functional activity helped one to establish a perspective figuratively as well as literally. Inspired by the Catholic intellectual Romano Guardini, Mies had argued in a speech of 1930 that the development of a perspective on the modern world was a vital spiritual issue: "We do not want to overestimate mechanization, typification, and standardization. Even the changed economic and social conditions we will accept as facts. All these things go their fateful, value-blind way. What is decisive is only how we assert ourselves toward these givens. It is here that the spiritual problems begin."[50]

The year before, in the German Pavilion in Barcelona, Mies had overtly challenged fact with perception. As visitors moved through the building, its facts—best documented in plan and section—gave way to the effects of light, color, and natural phenomena like wind and rain, which transformed its surfaces and altered the perception of the spaces they defined. The pavilion made a ready association between tangible experience and the intangible connotation generated by its representative function. Here and in the Exhibition House, perception, or the development of a perspective on one's surroundings, was at once a physical and a metaphysical activity—one of the many dualities essential to Mies's architecture.

Exhibitions

If Mies's exhibition designs implicated display objects in a new context, they also gave them new meanings. In many of the nonarchitectural exhibits he designed with Reich, the new context affected the formal and spatial characteristics of the objects, but in projects in which architecture was on display, the new context had social implications, whether these were intended or not.

In his first site plan for Weissenhof, Mies proposed that the lots should overlap, making the properties indistinguishable from each other. This design made it impossible for the colony's various architects to conceive of their projects independently, and thus focused attention on the entire complex, over which Mies had control. Although Mies sought sympathetic "left-wing architects" for the project, he wanted to control the image of the event.[51] Upon submitting the scheme, he emphasized its formal unity, which he later assured by stipulating that the basic color of the building exteriors had to be a "broken white."[52] This site plan had the effect, however, of eroding privacy. Mies's impulse in seeking a unified scheme appears to have been purely visual, but the design carried other implications for the Stuttgart politicians, who insisted that Mies provide discrete lots "to avoid 'legal problems'" and "make it easier to sell the villas."[53] Reading the plan as a threat to privacy, city council members were clearly unprepared for the radical change in the relationship between the public and private realms that Mies's design implied.

Mies created a unified context more completely at *Die Wohnung unserer Zeit*, probably because this indoor, temporary exhibition involved no prospect of occupancy. The continuity of the exhibition design was underscored by the articulation of Mies's Exhibition House, whose planes and spaces seemed potentially to extend infinitely across the landscape. Also, a wall ran from this house to Reich's, a vestige of an early scheme in which all of the units had been linked by similar walls. The exhibition established a context, then, in which works of architecture were not independent but reflected a continuous transformation of one project into another.

If the physical and consequently social continuity of *Die Wohnung unserer Zeit* was lost on an audience preoccupied with shelter (few of the critics seemed to notice the site plan or the general loss of privacy), another freestanding building, the Boarding House, presented visitors directly with the new social configurations reflected in Mies's first Weissenhof scheme. Because its units were not designed for traditional families, this building type could only have emerged in a new metropolitan environment. Within a single structure, Reich, Albers, the interior designer Hermann Gerson, and the Munich architectural teams of Vorhoelzer and Wiederanders and Schmidt and Hacker designed apartments for a childless married couple, a single man, a professional woman, two women, and someone who worked at home, perhaps an intellectual.[54]

Despite the unorthodox nature of this community, Mies's design for the building was almost perfectly regular.[55] Neither the facades nor the shape of the building revealed the variety they contained. But even if Mies's intention was purely formal, someone—possibly Mies himself—realized that the design posed some sort of a threat and issued a warning in the guidebook, disassociating the exhibited project from any real proposal: "Neither in its entirety nor through its technical details should the Boarding House be seen as a complete example of a realistic project. There is only an attempt to identify and solve a few tasks that arise during the construction of a boarding house."[56] Out of all of the projects in *Die Wohnung unserer Zeit*, the Boarding House was the only one that seemed to require explanation. The program did not mention its social implications, but another reason for the disclaimer is hard to imagine. Not only did the warning expose the conservative nature of the exhibition's sponsors, it confirmed the power of Mies's exhibition design to bring another world to life.

As works of architecture, Mies's exhibition designs escaped the contradiction of most such projects: the commitment on the one hand to the origin of the object on display and on the other to the truth of the exhibition, which depends on excising objects from their original contexts. Mies's exhibition work could be characterized neither as an in situ display, which would have maintained a visual continuity between objects and their original environments, nor as an "in context" design reflecting the fact that the objects in an exhibition have been removed from their source.[57] Mies's exhibitions did not contain fragments of worlds left behind, but implicated every object they contained in his vision of a world to come—or one that should have already arrived.

Colomina argues that exhibitions, for Mies, were definitive of his modern work. "The Friedrichstrasse skyscraper was modern," she writes, "precisely *because* it was produced for . . . [an exhibition] context."[58] This suggests not only that Mies's modern designs emerged out of his efforts to publicize his vision of architecture, but also that exhibitions gave him a new working context separate from building. The full-scale character of his exhibition work suggests that he was using it to realize his ideas without waiting to build them, a particularly significant choice given that he generally made large-scale renderings of perceptible views of projects that might not otherwise become permanent buildings.[59] One might suggest that Mies transformed the concept of realization in architecture from one dependent on technology, and on the fulfillment of contemporary social needs, to one contingent simply on the possibility of experience. Many of his exhibition designs in fact presupposed technologies and ways of life that did not yet exist. At Weissenhof and the other exhibitions, Mies extended human experience into the future in a tangible way, as he did with the full-scale mock-up, in canvas and board, that was made of the Kröller-Müller Villa Project in 1912. One of the first projects of his career, the Kröller-Müller Villa was also the catalyst for his first exhibition experience—Gropius's rejection of the design from the *Ausstellung für unbekannte Architekten*. That rejection may in turn have catalyzed Mies's entry into modernist architecture. The project and its full-scale incarnation were indeed prophetic.

Mies's exhibition work not only shows his interest in transforming space without necessarily building but also evidences his confrontation with modern architectural practice (broadly defined) and its reliance on scaled representations, especially the drawing. It was the scaled representation, its conventions, and the standards that emerged from them that distinguished the work of architects from that of builders. This was crucial for the professionalization and thus the modernization of architectural practice as early as the Renaissance. But Mies's work in full scale, which grew out of his experience making shop drawings for builders, revealed to him aspects of his designs that he could not have anticipated in a smaller-scale drawing. Against the abstraction and order of scaled plans stood the rich and unsystematic perceptual effects of his exhibition spaces. If Mies's modernism emerged in an exhibition context, it was because exhibitions allowed him to explore the uneasy relationship to the modern reliance on technology, to social and spiritual change, and, in a broader sense, to representation that characterized his entire career.

Mies and Dark Transparency

ROSEMARIE HAAG BLETTER

Mies's architecture is synonymous with modernism and modernism is synonymous with glass. Glass is also commonly associated with the presumed rationalism of modern architecture. Yet the mythic trajectory of glass follows a more oblique route than the simple modernist storyline that connects, for instance, Joseph Paxton's Crystal Palace to Mies's glass pavilions and skyscrapers. Mies's first public discussion of his projects occurred in *Frühlicht*, a short-lived Expressionist periodical edited by the architect Bruno Taut. Although Mies was not generally associated with the Expressionists, his brief encounter with them was significant for his subsequent use of glass, which addresses more than its pragmatic property—the admission of light—and hides strange conceptual spaces and irrational passages.[1]

Expressionism, like most labels, is not altogether self-evident as a designation. Although, as commonly assumed, it did stress the emotive over the objective, it dealt no more with self-expression than, say, Cubism or de Stijl. Architectural Expressionism was strongest during the two years immediately after World War I, a period of political upheaval. It tended, then, to have more social content than prewar Expressionist painting had had—but architecture is by its nature embedded in social questions. At the same time, because Germany's economic condition forestalled almost any chance to build, architectural energy was poured into utopian projects on paper, allowing a degree of experimentation and vision that a stronger economy and the normal architect-client relationship would have displaced. With the rise of the *Neue Sachlichkeit* (New Objectivity) around 1923, artists, architects, and critics—including many

former Expressionists—began to reject Expressionism.[2] Although *Neue Sachlichkeit* and *Sachlichkeit* alone became popular terms, and were used in opposition to the "subjective" intent of Expressionism, the division between the two movements loses clarity when we examine the often self-serving polemics of artists intent on being part of a quickly advancing avant-garde.[3]

The novellas and short stories of the prewar Expressionist writer Paul Scheerbart (fig. 1) explore glass architecture in a whimsical, mystical manner indebted to the Romantic tradition, while also satirizing the rational modernism of the day. Scheerbart's writing strongly affected

1. Oskar Kokoschka. *Paul Scheerbart*. Published in *Der Sturm*, 1910

the Expressionist circle around Taut.[4] His nonsense poem "Kikakoku" also inspired Dada sound poems,[5] and the cultural critic Walter Benjamin responded to him by radically reinterpreting his ideas.[6] Scheerbart was associated with the group of Berlin anarchists who published in the periodical *Die Aktion*.[7] The drollery of his writing appealed to later Dadaists, but his satirical vein and cosmic settings tend to obscure his work's serious political aspect.

Glasarchitektur (Glass architecture, 1914) is today Scheerbart's best-known book, although its quasi-scientific polemic is atypical of him.[8] Reflective and seemingly mobile, glass is used in the book to support the notion of an unstable architecture, and architectural flexibility itself appears as a metaphor for cultural change. Glass architecture signifies the transformation of a staid Europe into an international culture of evolved human beings. Inspired by the power of colored glass in medieval cathedral windows, and by the technical achievement of the large nineteenth-century greenhouses, Scheerbart is concerned not with total transparency but with the darker, translucent effects of polychrome glass. New technology is only a means to an end, the overcoming of a prosaic, rationalized reality through synaesthetic pleasure. This nervous optical intensification borders on states of emotion. Scheerbart parodies many gender conventions, and in the context of his time, his preoccupation with sensory and emotive effects suggests the irrational, a quality then commonly associated with the feminine, and used to counter the perceived masculine world of progressive rationalism. The synaesthetic effects in Scheerbart's stories are not so much escapist as attempts to retrieve the life of the senses to which the modern world of science gives short shrift.

The transformational features of Scheerbartian glass architecture are proto-Expressionist in addressing the fragmentary in modern culture. He also shared with the Expressionists a fascination with the preindustrial Middle Ages, but he had been more deeply affected by the Arabic tradition of the paradisal garden. Although we cannot be certain that he was familiar with the ancient mystical traditions concerning glass and crystal in Arabic and Jewish folklore, which later influenced the Holy Grail legends and the Gothic cathedral, those traditions in fact form an almost continuous story line with his early-twentieth-century glass fables, and with the role of glass in early modernist architecture. This tradition is primarily a literary one, embracing magical properties in glass that cannot be available within the pragmatic restrictions of construction. As an iconographic tradition, it includes a whole constellation of materials of similar optical impact—glass, crystal, water, reflective materials such as gold or silver, and jewels—that it uses interchangeably as a single metaphor.[9]

Literary Sources for Glass Symbolism

The source for the earliest known versions of the glass metaphor lies in the Old Testament, and specifically in the person of that great mainstay of power coupled with arcane wisdom, King Solomon. The biblical description of Solomon's Temple was to become the germ of an allegorical apocrypha of fanciful legends concerning his architectural feats. In a number of Jewish legends and subsequent Arabic stories inspired by them, Solomon is said to have built a palace of glass to reveal to him whether the visiting Queen of Sheba was a real woman or, as was suspected, a genie. Indeed the Queen of Sheba, unfamiliar with the illusory effects of glass, believed that the king was sitting in a pool and lifted her skirts to step across it, exposing her legs—which were unnaturally hairy, a genie trait.[10] In this legend glass reveals what would otherwise remain hidden: Sheba's true, supernatural nature. The tale was then codified in the Koran.[11]

In Arabic legends of the early Middle Ages, Solomon becomes the patron of a truly fantastic glass architecture: he is said to have commanded genies to construct for him an underwater dome of glass shielding a city of crystal "a hundred thousand fathoms in extent and a thousand stories high."[12] No longer just the wise and powerful ruler of the Bible, Solomon is imbued with supernatural powers—in fact he has taken on the very powers of sorcery attributed to the Queen of Sheba, as if, in unmasking her, he had acquired her magic for himself. There are, of course, erotic implications in Solomon's apparent immersion in water and in Sheba's lifting her dress to get to him.[13] Her hairy legs, proof of her magic powers, can be read as a "male" attribute that she surrenders by succumbing to him.

Echoes of these stories appear in Islamic architecture, in the Revelation of St. John in the New Testament, in Grail and other legends, and in the Gothic cathedral. As one might expect, the most fantastic examples are again to be found not in built architecture but in literature. A twelfth-century addition to the *Letter of Prester John*, for example, describes a *capella vitrea*, a magical glass chapel that expands to accommodate as many worshipers as enter it.[14] Wolfram von Eschenbach's *Parzifal* (1205–14) depicts the Holy Grail as a precious stone, dislodged from the crown of God by Lucifer's lance when he was cast out of Paradise, then hidden by Adam in a cave. The allusion to a stone containing the spark of divine light, hidden in the bowels of a dark cave, bears Gnostic and alchemic overtones.[15] The Grail story here comprises a dualistic image of light and dark—a contrast also signified by the names of the protagonists, Lucifer (bearer of light) and Adam (earth). This mystical dualism will recur in later Romantic lore. Evidently the glass/crystal metaphor was associated not only

with the clarity of light but with the darker aspects of the psyche.

The Gothic stained-glass program absorbed the biblical and Koranic traditions in which translucent and reflective materials symbolize transmutation, spirituality, and divine wisdom. In the secular literature of the later Middle Ages, however, the imagery reveals increasingly personal concerns. Gottfried von Strassburg's *Tristan* of the early thirteenth century describes a bed of crystal, housed in a grotto, that is said to stand for pure and transparent love.[16] The combination of crystal bed and grotto is still quite comparable to the light/earth metaphors in *Parzifal*, but these ideas would eventually separate: in Chaucer's *House of Fame* (c. 1381), the temple of Venus, goddess of love, is a temple of glass alone; meanwhile folk legends from around 1300 onward, usually attributed to the *Minnesinger* Tannhäuser, depict the abode of Venus as the dark interior of a mountain. The syncretism of Grail and secular love legends corresponds to the quasi-religious but individualized quest of the medieval alchemist,[17] for whom the philosophers' stone, a personalized grail, was to bring the discovery of transubstantiation, a transformation of materials promising self-knowledge and individual metamorphosis. The imagery has now lost the architectural dimension of both the Solomonic myths and the Gothic cathedral; reduced to the size of a stone, it represents only the transmuted self. It will be resurrected by the Romantics in the nineteenth century, as a symbol of introspection.[18]

The mystical tradition of the transformation of the self can still be discerned in philosophical and literary works of the later nineteenth century. Nietzsche, for example, in *Thus Spake*

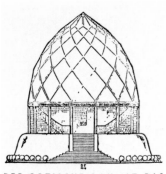

DER GOTISCHE DOM IST DAS
PRALUDIUM DER GLASARCHITEKTUR

Zarathustra, uses the Gnostic light/dark dualism to describe the road to self-knowledge. The Stone of Wisdom represents the self and the mind.[19] In the French Symbolist writer Alfred Jarry's *Exploits and Opinions of Doctor Faustroll* (1895), the philosopher's stone is literally located in Vincent van Gogh's brain. Jarry would be published by the Futurist Filippo Tommaso Marinetti and admired by the Surrealists.[20]

Glass Symbolism in Modern Architecture

The architect Peter Behrens recovered the glass/crystal imagery in the opening festivities he produced for the Darmstadt artists' colony in 1901, where a *Zeichen* (sign) in the form of a crystal was borne by a priestlike figure. The last section of Nietzsche's *Zarathustra* is entitled "The Sign," but Behrens referred more directly back to the alchemic nature of the crystal: just as mere carbon can under intense conditions become a diamond, so the power of art was to transform everyday life into "resplendent life filled with meaning."[21] When Mies worked for Behrens in prewar Berlin, Behrens had apparently moved away from his belief in the transformation of the everyday through aesthetics toward the presumed rationalism of the Deutscher Werkbund and his commissions for the AEG; but similar attitudes were subsumed within this corporate imagery.[22]

It is not until the early manifestations of Expressionism, however, that the glass/crystal iconography is again associated with architecture. Scheerbart's *Glasarchitektur* was dedicated to Taut, whom Scheerbart knew, and in the same

2. Bruno Taut. Glass House, Deutscher Werkbund exhibition, Cologne. 1914. Elevation. From *Glashaus—Werkbund-Ausstelling Cöln 1914* (Berlin, 1914), n.p.

3. Bruno Taut. *Alpine Architektur*. 1919. Illustrated book. Plate showing Alpine peaks decorated with crystalline formations and, in foreground, glacier with lanceolate blades of glass

4. Bruno Taut. *Die Auflösung der Städte* (The dissolution of the cities). 1920. Illustrated book. Page titled "Different ways of living produce different habitats"

year it was published, 1914, Taut dedicated to Scheerbart his Glass House, a pavilion at the first Deutscher Werkbund exhibition, in Cologne. Here, for the first time since the Gothic cathedral, the literary iconography of glass was reified as built form. The gemlike Glass House, with its polychrome glass dome, Luxfer prisms, reflective tiles, stained glass, and illuminated fountain and cascade, all reiterate Scheerbart's glass fables (fig. 2).[23] The cupola room at the top was bathed in colored light; at the bottom was a dark tunnel, faced in blue velvet, and a cavelike "kaleidoscope" room in which abstract light patterns were projected onto a screen. The Glass House thus mirrored the alchemic dualism of dark and light. The critic Adolf Behne, a friend of Taut's, compared it to a "sparkling skull."[24]

The Werkbund exhibition was closed prematurely because of the beginning of World War I, and Scheerbart died in 1915. His ideas were transmitted to the postwar generation of architects by Taut, who would become the catalyst for several Expressionist groups, including the Arbeitsrat für Kunst (Workers' council for art) and the *Gläserne Kette* (Crystal chain).[25] The

utopian books Taut published between 1919 and 1920, primarily pictorial treatises, address glass architecture as the sign of a changed, international, pacifist society. Here, transmitting ideas through rough sketches accompanied by captions, Taut could incorporate transformational effects even more directly than in the Glass House (a building in which functional requirements had been minimal). In *Alpine Architektur* (1919), for example, whole mountain ranges are reordered, and peaks are decorated with colored glass (fig. 3); in *Der Weltbaumeister* (The world architect, 1920), structures continually dissolve and regroup, as if in a giant kaleidoscope.

The images in these books cannot be read as real proposals. Little building was possible when they were produced, and Taut himself described them as "naturally only a utopia and a little joke."[26] His restructuring of mountain ranges can be read as a giant earthwork, a reshaping of a reality that is found wanting.[27] In *Die Auflösung der Städte* (The dissolution of the cities, 1920), glass imagery is less prominent, and the book is more clearly anarchist in its rejection of governments, schools, marriage, and cities (fig. 4). Short quotations mostly from socialists and anarchists, ranging from Rousseau to Lenin, Engels, and Kropotkin, augment the images without providing a coherent political agenda; in general, however, Taut had moved from the self-referential Glass House to an interest in social transformation. From 1920 on, and especially after 1923, when Germany's economic condition stabilized somewhat, the use of glass and crystal as mythic metaphors

disappeared with the resumption of building. In Taut's case the myth was reified in the many, unusually polychrome housing estates he built largely in the vicinity of Berlin. As building became actuality, translucent glass was replaced by opaque colored stucco, used not just for aesthetic effect but to attain urbanistic continuity. Taut also used color perceptually and psychologically, to enhance the reading of the structures.[28]

Within the glass/crystal tradition, then, ideas of metamorphosis had themselves transformed. In the early Jewish and Arabic legends and again in the Gothic cathedral, they were expressed through architectonic concepts, which, in alchemy, Romanticism, and turn-of-the-century Symbolism, they later shed, adopting crystalline form as the notion of change became identified with the personal and the self. In Expressionism, particularly after the war, the metaphor returned to a proto-architectural and social subtext. Not all Expressionist designs used this imagery, of course; architects also turned to biomorphic forms, which were linked with the organicism of Art Nouveau. This is especially evident in the fantasies of Hermann Finsterlin, in the projects and buildings of Eric Mendelsohn, and in Hugo Häring's and Hans Scharoun's organic functionalism. One could argue that these biomorphic designs echo the metaphor of crystalline transformation by suggesting metamorphosis through their fluid forms.

Mies's designs for his Friedrichstrasse Skyscraper Project (1921) and Glass Skyscraper Project (1922) appeared with a brief text in Taut's *Frühlicht* in 1922 (p. 118, fig. 14).[29] *Frühlicht*,

published from 1920 to 1922, reflects the transition between the Expressionism of the immediate postwar years and *Neue Sachlichkeit*. After Taut became chief city planner of Magdeburg, in 1921, the magazine showed an increasing interest in executed schemes, city planning, housing, and international trends such as Dutch de Stijl and Russian Constructivism. Competition designs for the Friedrichstrasse site by Behrens, Mendelsohn, Taut, and Scharoun, among others, were published in the issue of Spring 1922. It is possible that Mies, seeing this, submitted his designs for publication in the following issue.

Scheerbart's ideas were promoted after the war not only by the Arbeitsrat but in the pages of *Frühlicht*. Mies could in any case have encountered them either directly or indirectly through the Expressionists. He was not an overt participant in the postwar Expressionist groups— he joined the Novembergruppe only in 1922, after it had lost its revolutionary zeal[30]—but he experimented with Expressionist elements in his use of both crystalline and biomorphic forms. In his brief text in *Frühlicht* he states that the disposition of these forms should be conditioned less by the effects of light and shade than by the play of reflected light, a remark closer to Expressionism than to the modernist concern with complete transparency. The skin of the Glass Skyscraper is expressed as continuous, uninterrupted by a structural frame or mullions. In some renderings this glass skin is represented as if it were a freestanding curtain. Thus glass assumes a primary visual definition, through which the supporting structure is revealed only

intermittently, depending on the reflective play of light. Mies did also stress the pragmatic conditions that led to this unusual design: "At first glance the contour of the ground plan appears arbitrary, but in reality it is the result of many experiments on the glass model. The curves were determined by the need to illuminate the interior" (figs. 5, 6).[31] His empiricism here sounds defensive, however, especially considering the schematic nature of the plans.

Soon after producing these designs, Mies turned to the orthogonal aesthetic of de Stijl. By 1923, like most other members of the avant-garde, he had embraced *Sachlichkeit* and rationality, an attitude that was intensified through his direct involvement with the periodical *G*, which rejected aesthetic formalism and emphasized building as a scientific process. As a result, the Expressionism of his glass skyscraper projects came to seem like a momentary interlude. But the antirational features of Expressionism lingered on in his whole redefinition of glass in architecture, as well as in darker recesses of his work. To start with, any claim to reject aesthetics and only to express the immediate tasks of building is highly suspect. Architecture can never be a purely scientific enterprise. Further, although de Stijl relied on the right angle, it was developed as an expression of Platonic and theosophical ideas (of which, however, Mies may not have been aware).

The 1922 Glass Skyscraper not only uses the glass skin in a way that suggests Expressionism, but contains in its plan an odd, narrow, elliptical shape that is hard to explain as a functional

interior (plate 57). Similar narrow spaces recur in Mies's later work of the 1920s, buildings that have become iconic images of modernism. The German Pavilion in Barcelona (1928–29), for instance, contains a rectangular enclosure too narrow and small for circulation. It is glazed with milk glass and lit from within, lending it a strange volumetric presence, like a mysterious light-box.[32] In the Tugendhat House (1928–30), a narrow glazed corridorlike space along the eastern garden facade contains a "winter garden" with plants and a water basin, but cannot be sat in; it is barely wide enough to service the plants. Instead it is meant to be seen, "nature" imprisoned in glass, a filtering screen with the garden visible beyond. The Glass Room at the 1927 *Die Wohnung* exhibition in Stuttgart, which Mies designed with Lilly Reich, also had an enclosed winter garden corridor, as well as a sealed-off glass chamber containing a female torso by Wilhelm Lehmbruck (figs. 7, 8). The critic Siegfried Kracauer found the Glass Room somewhat unsettling: "Every fixture and every movement in . . . [neighboring rooms] conjures up shadow-plays on the wall—immaterial silhouettes that hover through the air and become mixed with the mirror images from the glass room itself. The raising of this impalpable glassy ghost, which transforms itself like a kaleidoscope or light reflex, signifies that the new dwelling is not the last solution."[33] This interpretation hardly suggests a rational space.

Mies's floor-to-ceiling plate glass windows that retract into the floor are on the one hand sophisticated technological devices (for the period) in keeping with an orthodox view of modernism. On the other, they can be read as a complete abstraction of the tactile, material basis of architecture, recalling the kind of transformational, flexible space that Taut had proposed in *Die Auflösung der Städte* for a house with walls and enclosures that could be altered according to one's mood. They are also reminiscent of Scheerbart, whose technological proposals were designed to achieve results outside the realm of science. In Mies's case the implication is of a malleable interior-exterior relationship, and a definition of the interior that is far more ambiguous than the idea of a universal space with which he is often associated. Most prominent in the Tugendhat House, retractable glass windows also appear in the Hermann Lange House (1927–30), the Henke House Addition (1930), the Exhibition House at the German Building Exhibition, Berlin (1931), and probably the Gericke House Project (1932).[34]

Other features evoking Scheerbart and glass/crystal iconography are Mies's frequent inclusion of pools of water—the reflecting pool in the German Pavilion's internal courtyard was lined with black glass[35]—and other reflective surfaces. His use of onyx and polished marble suggests the association of such materials with the Grail and troubadour legends. Mies has it both ways: his unornamented definition of materials creates the appearance of a rational, objective treatment, without symbolism, yet the exoticism and reflectivity of these luxurious stones point to the sensory effects of Expressionism. By 1926, in any case, Mies had begun to shift away from the antiaesthetic of the mid-1920s and toward Dionysian, Nietzschean ideas that dealt with space not as structure but biologically and spiritually, as a breathing membrane between the organic dwelling and the cosmos.[36] This concept of the flexible glass skin recalls the magical *capella vitrea* of medieval legend, as well as Scheerbart's and Taut's notions of metamorphosis.

Critical Assessments

Rationalist approaches, and a belief in glass as completely transparent, had been present earlier in the century alongside the antirationalist tradition of Taut and Scheerbart. The Werkbund's prewar concern with window display, the department store, and advertising, for example, is a telling instance of its commercial interests, and of the relationship of glass to the display of commodities. An essay in the Werkbund yearbook of 1913 acknowledges the abstraction introduced by the modern plate glass window, which erases tactile immediacy, making the store window just an advertisement competing with other advertising. The spectator, then, must be seduced with still greater intensity.[37] Mies's project for the S. Adam Department Store (1928–29) in Berlin, with its set-back, continuously glazed store windows, can be understood in this context.

For Benjamin, writing on the store window of the 1920s, the "collective, dreamlike unconscious of the modern industrial age was to be found in precisely this apparently rationalized realm of glass transparency."[38] Yet for Hannes Meyer—the director of the Bauhaus in 1928–30, and well-known for his Communist beliefs, his insistence on scientific planning principles, and his rejection of aesthetics and symbolic meaning—the extensive use of glass in his and Hans Wittwer's design for the League of Nations competition (1927) would have the effect of providing "no back corridors for backstairs diplomacy but open glazed rooms for the public negotiations of honest men." His and Wittwer's competition program further states that "the building does not symbolize anything but is the truthful expression of its program intended for work and collaboration."[59] Meyer's stance has been accepted by the contemporary neo-Marxist critic Michael Hays as a "posthumanist" precursor of postmodern culture.[40] Winfried Nerdinger, however, has argued that Meyer's political and social beliefs during the 1920s were less carefully considered than those of Taut and Behne, and that symbolic values never quite disappeared from his thinking—in 1932, for instance, he defended Soviet architecture's search for national expression.[41] Nevertheless, much contemporary criticism validates his supposed "posthumanism" through his Communism. At the same time, Expressionists and Taut in particular are depicted as more conservative than they were. Taut's trips to the Soviet Union during the 1920s; the visits of the Soviet commissar Anatoly Lunacharsky to see his housing in Berlin; his work in Moscow in 1931–33; his blacklisting by the Nazis as early as 1933—all these have been brushed aside, no doubt because he never adopted Meyer's hard-core materialist slogans or joined the Communist Party.

Detlef Mertins has shown the continued influence of Scheerbart in the 1920s, especially in Benjamin's reworking of Scheerbart's anarchist ideas into a Marxist ideology.[42] (Discussing Scheerbart in 1933, Benjamin wrote of glass in a way not altogether different from Meyer's approach in 1927: "It is not for nothing that glass is such a hard and smooth material upon which nothing attaches itself. Also a cold and concise material. Things made of glass have no aura."[43]) Yet Mertins also sees Expressionism becoming submerged in a bourgeois belief in organic wholeness and harmonious utopias. To be sure, the Expressionists' expectations of change after the fall of the Wilhelmine empire were ecstatic, utopian, romantic, and even naive. Faced with the actual political and economic chaos of the postwar period, however, their attitudes were full of contradictions, and Taut's utopias are hardly harmonious—any suggestion of order is constantly reconfigured. Rather than constituting statements on an ideal life, these books comment on the tense Berlin of the time, when work could not be found, food was hard to come by, and the streets were filled with both left- and right-wing demonstrators. At best, Taut's utopias are temporary palliatives—he himself called them "only" utopias—for a chaotic contemporary context. They also resemble the utopian fragments proposed in 1918 by the Marxist philosopher Ernst Bloch,[44] who suggested broadening the concept of utopia beyond the critique of present conditions to include inspirational fragments from dreams and fairy tales.

In fact a number of recent studies have criticized Expressionism from a neo-Marxist vantage as essentially bourgeois.[45] Regine Prange concludes that the symbolic function of the glass/crystal metaphor is a self-reflection that produces only abstraction.[46] Her interpretation relies mostly on the Romantic and turn-of-the-century meaning of crystal symbolism, and she does not deal with the problem of whether a concept of abstraction can really be applied to the field of architecture—her argument seems to derive from painting. Further, she makes no distinction between Taut's utopian drawings and his later housing estates. Nor does she see his housing estates as practical applications of social ideas, describing his Hufeisen (Horseshoe) Estate (1925–31) not as an urbanistically conceived space but as an abstract pattern. At any rate, her discussion leads her to associate Expressionism with commodity culture, as if Paxton's Crystal Palace, Taut's glass utopias, and commercial skyscrapers formed links in an unbroken chain. In this reductive approach, pleasure and enjoyment cannot be part of an architectural experience without suggesting bourgeois attitudes, and all that is translucent or reflective is from the outset condemned as the phantasmagoric illusions of capitalist culture. Why are abstraction, the illusory, and the immaterial tied to capitalism? Prange's argument implies that only an architecture that is not "abstract"—whatever that may mean—is resistant to commercial culture. This assumption may be the ultimate illusion, the fata morgana, of this unreflective, harsh neo-Marxism.

Today's political critiques of Expressionism retread many of the arguments of Georg Lukács from the 1920s and '30s, although his particular, politically complicated role is rarely addressed. Lukács, the Communist (and by the '30s Stalinist) literary critic, saw Neoclassicism as the proper mode of art. In 1934 he denounced Expressionism as counterrevolutionary, a product of imperialist capitalism and therefore sharing responsibility for the onset of fascism. His attack on Expressionism's forms, however, was intimately connected with his political convictions. Lukács coupled his critique of Expressionism with an attack on a political party, the Independent Social Democrats (USPD), whose attitude toward revolution, like that of the Expressionists, he considered half-hearted. The USPD and the Communists (KPD) had shared an uneasy alliance that by the late 1920s had become an extreme doctrinal split.[47]

Both the USPD and KPD were working-class parties. The KPD, however, had more unskilled and unemployed workers, and the two parties' programs reflected their different makeups: the USPD sought to develop Marxism into a popular socialism within the capitalist system; the KPD, by contrast, demanded radical change, and regarded any reform as illusory. Much of the energy of the labor movement was dissipated in the enmity between these parties. After 1928, the Soviet Communist Party and the Comintern imposed complete separatism on the KPD, which became openly confrontational with the USPD.

Although Taut was a socialist and his friend and colleague Behne was a member of the USPD, not all the Expressionists shared their politics. For Lukács to blame the Expressionists and the USPD for fascism is in any case absurd and self-serving.[48] If responsibility for the rise of fascism is to be meted out, a share of it must go, for example, to conservatives who never embraced the Weimar Republic—and also, surely, to the Communists, for their refusal to form an alliance with the Socialists. Lukács's argument was countered in the late 1930s by his former friend Bloch, who argued that Expressionism did in fact question the society's basic values, and asserted the constructive value of utopianism. Fredric Jameson, in his important exposition of

the Lukács/Bloch debate, regards them as adversaries of equal stature but pointedly asks whether Lukács's Realism is resistant to commodity culture.[49] (It must be said, however, that Bloch defended Expressionism long after most Expressionist artists had moved on from it.) Bertolt Brecht later joined the debate, considering Lukács's essays valuable but viewing him as remote from reality and formalistic.[50] Given the attention these texts have received, it is surprising that so many contemporary critics and historians present only the Lukácsian argument. Prange's critique of Expressionism, for example, mimics that of Lukács.[51] It is perhaps significant that Lukács's one-sided ideology has become a litmus test for politically correct art and architecture. Lukács's dogmatic theory of realism exhibits a fear of the irrational, and dismisses "the *entire* avant-garde as prone to fascistization."[52]

Georg Simmel, the teacher of both Bloch and Lukács, had anticipated the subjective responses of Expressionism in his essay "The Future of Our Culture" (1909). Discussing the widening chasm between the "culture of things and the culture of men," a chasm that robs the observer of an inner, unified relation to culture, he adds that "no systematic politics can sweep away the tragic discrepancy between a limitlessly expanding objective culture and an only very slowly developing subjective culture. It can, however, [prepare] the individual more expeditiously to transform the contents of present-day objective culture into a subjective culture."[53] He establishes a forceful dialectic between the objective and the subjective life, in which the subjective can no longer be satisfied because of the overwhelming tension produced by the hypertrophy of objective culture.[54] While his ideas are not a

recipe for artistic action, they give substance to the Expressionists' attempt to vanquish this monster of modern culture.

Mies himself shared neither Scheerbart's and Taut's political and social ideas—he was a political opportunist[55]—nor their progressive thinking about gender. On the contrary, his use of female torsos in the Glass Room, the German Pavilion, the Tugendhat House, and the German Building Exhibition reveals a conflict between the solid but immobile female sculptures and the open, fluid glass membrane of the "masculine" structure.[56] This conception of the dwelling may be seen as echoing Solomon's entrapment of Sheba, with Mies, like Solomon, appropriating Sheba's magic power. Similarly, he incorporates the antirationalist features of Expressionism while suppressing them under the guise of the rational. In fact his glass structures of the 1920s become modernism's most complete architectonic expression of the glass myth.

Another, more social aspect to the discussion of glass architecture is relevant to Mies's work. Benjamin believed that the transparency of glass constantly exteriorizes the interior,[57] and Jacques Derrida—reacting to Scheerbart and Benjamin—has written, "What terms do we use to speak about glass? . . . The terms of transparency and immediacy, of love or of police, of the border that is perhaps erased between the public and the private, etc.?"[58] The Expressionist glass projects of Scheerbart and Taut would not have been subject to this problem of transparency, because of their use of colored glass. The question is present, however, in Mies's glass structures—not so much in the glass skyscraper schemes as in the glass pavilions and residences such as the Tugendhat House and

9. Siah Armajani. *Glass Room*. 2000. Stainless steel, wood, bronze, aluminum, glass, and Plexiglas, 9'6" x 8'10" x 10'7" (289.6 x 269.3 x 522.6 cm). Walker Art Center, Minneapolis

the Exhibition House. The delimitation between public and private is not always apparent here. In the Tugendhat House the problem is dealt with through the use of translucent milk glass to enclose the stairwell facing the street, and through the opaque barrier formed by the service quarter along the house's west side. Along the truly transparent sides, the south and east, the large garden and the narrow winter garden maintain privacy. In the Exhibition House both the glazed entry area and the translucent space of the living room are screened with a curtain, while the bedroom faces a walled courtyard. Mies's court-house projects of the 1930s also make the transparent walls of the houses face inward-looking spaces defined by high walls.

Colin Rowe and Robert Slutzky, in "Transparency: Literal and Phenomenal" (1963), question the complete transparency associated with the modernism of the later 1920s and the International Style, comparing the "literal" transparency of a building like Walter Gropius's Bauhaus with the more complex, Cubist-inspired shallow depth that Le Corbusier developed through spatial means.[59] In retrospect, their argument for a translucent spatial screen seems a prelude to the redefinition of modernism shown in the exhibition *Light Construction* at The Museum of Modern Art in 1995, curated by Terence Riley.[60] In most of the contemporary projects included in that exhibition, exterior walls are defined by perforated metal screens or patterned glass panes. Technology is present but not emphasized, and while the designs allude to early-twentieth-century modernism, the asceticism of the International Style is ban-

ished by means of translucent (rather than fully transparent) screens that hide the interior more than they reveal it. Scheerbart's glass/crystal fables here merge with the harder, metallic modernism of Sigfried Giedion and Benjamin, perhaps a signal that the several early-twentieth-century modernisms that then seemed incompatible can now be addressed together.

There is a more indirect relationship to Scheerbart's and Taut's utopias in the work of American environmental sculptors. The Earth art of Robert Smithson's *Map of Glass* (1969), or James Turrell's Roden Crater project (begun in 1972), involves the sort of reworking of the landscape and the use of mysterious light effects that Scheerbart described and Taut proposed in *Alpine Architektur*.[61] The ambiguous spaces and reflections of Dan Graham's proto-architectural sculptures similarly appear rationalist but delve deeply into the irrational. Siah Armajani too has turned to works of glass—a glass room (fig. 9), a glass bridge, a glass garden.[62] The glass garden in particular seems to recall the troubadour legends and Scheerbart.

Such present-day allusions to the glass/crystal tradition pose a difficult question. Is Earth art meant as a critique of contemporary culture? Is the use of glass as a material an ironic response to the illusions created by modern commercial communication? Smithson, for instance, saw the crystalline as evidence of fragmentation and disintegration.[63] Using Benjamin's concept of the aura as a point of departure,[64] contemporary critics have also spoken of the "re-auratization" of glass, and one has written that "the re-auratizing *Glanz* (reflection) of glass tends to interfere with

(even as it is harnessed to serve) mass suggestion; as a gateway between interior(ity) and exterior(ity), it possesses the ability to reflect an unreality beyond its material existence."[65] This argument assumes that Benjamin was correct when he wrote that glass has no aura, a point that might be contested. And this trust in materiality as resistant to capitalist phantasmagoria seems both elitist and ideological.

Mies finally emigrated to the U.S. in August 1938. Just three months later, a very different kind of glass imagery broke into international consciousness with Kristallnacht, the government-sanctioned pogrom that convinced the world as never before of the horror of the Nazi regime. (*Kristallglas* was a name used for commercial plate glass windows.[66]) In the political culture of today, the idea of "transparency"—a general metaphor for clarity over centuries[67]—appears with increasing frequency. It was used by German politicians in a literal sense during the debate about new government buildings for Berlin, in the somewhat misguided belief that glass and its transparency would guard against the symbolism of Nazi masonry buildings. Such statements as "the government's refusal to hold transparent elections" are a better example of the generalization of this metaphor within political discourse. But when transparency is proclaimed as a sign of openness, its use may suggest something more opaque. The "transparency" of the glass architecture of the Expressionists and of Mies included from the outset its obverse—dark translucency and the antirational.

New National Gallery, Berlin, 1962–68

Mies returned to Berlin to begin his last major project at the age of seventy-six. There he was able to execute a design that culminated more than ten years of work on several projects at a variety of scales. Seen first in sketches for the Fifty by Fifty House Project (1950–51), this building type consisted of a deep flat roof supported by no more than two columns per side (and by one in the smaller projects). The footprint was square, and a flat slab supported the structure, covering a basement filled with the building program absent above. This open pavilion on a podium was finally realized in the New National Gallery.

Sited on the wide expanse of open land adjoining the Tiergarten, a formerly busy section of Berlin scorched by World War II bombing, the New National Gallery was part of West Berlin's "*Kulturforum*" (Culture forum), a development of new cultural institutions for the divided postwar city, replacing older institutions that had fallen east of the Berlin Wall. Mies thus took part in the effort to rebuild the maimed city in which he had built his reputation and practice. The New National Gallery is within close reach of Mies's old street, Am Karlsbad.

The wide expanse of the *Kulturforum* is reflected in the plinth of Mies's building, raised only a few steps above adjacent Potsdamerstrasse but deepening along the sides of its sloping site to include, at the back of the building, a full story above ground and an enclosed sculpture court. Inside, on the upper level, four nonstructural spatial dividers containing ductwork and service areas are the sole occupants of a vast hall with fully transparent walls, 54 meters (c. 177 feet) per side. Stairs descend to a rectangular room adjoining a square exhibition space, itself leading to a large gallery next to the garden court. The placement of staff offices and storage, mechanical, and service spaces creates a species of poché in which the public spaces on the lower level seem to have been carved from a solid subterranean mass. The deliberate choreography of these spaces contrasts with the undetermined movement privileged in the open gallery above.

The raising of the National Gallery roof in a single day was a media event, attended by Mies in a car pulled under the edge of the monolithic welded roof plate as it was slowly raised by hydraulic jacks from a height of four to twenty-nine feet, dragging its eight pin-jointed cruciform columns behind. Composed of box girders welded into a lattice, the roof uses

different qualities of steel to meet required differences in sectional strength caused by the double cantilever. The plate can thus remain totally flat. Scholars have related the gridlike underside of the lattice to classical coffering, a nod to nineteenth-century neoclassicism. The project might be compared to Friedrich Gilly's project for a Monument to Frederick the Great (p. 139, fig. 4; planned in 1797 for nearby Leipziger Platz, but never built), processed through the industrial language of an architect/engineer like Albert Kahn, whose work for American industry had proved inspirational to Mies in his thirty-year sojourn in the United States. —*Claire Zimmerman*

1. Site plan. Pencil on paper mounted on illustration board, 36 x 46" (91.4 x 116.8 cm)

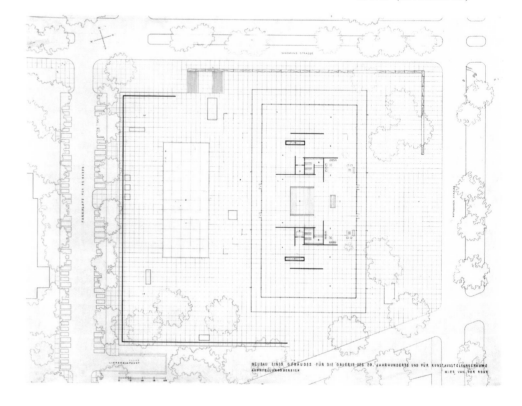

2. Exterior view. Gelatin silver photograph, 3⁷⁄₁₆ x 9⁹⁄₁₆" (9 x 24.3 cm). Photograph: David Hirsch

3. Exterior view. Gelatin silver photograph, 6¹¹⁄₁₆ x 9⁹⁄₁₆" (17 x 24.3 cm). Photograph: David Hirsch

4. Exterior view. Gelatin silver photograph, 5³⁄₈ x 9¼" (14.3 x 23.5 cm). Photograph: Balthazar Korab

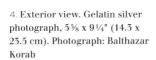

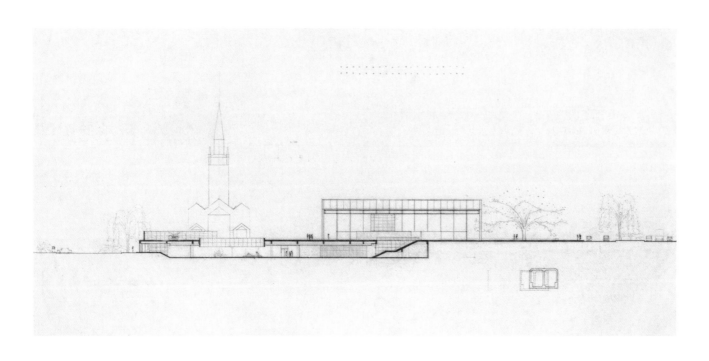

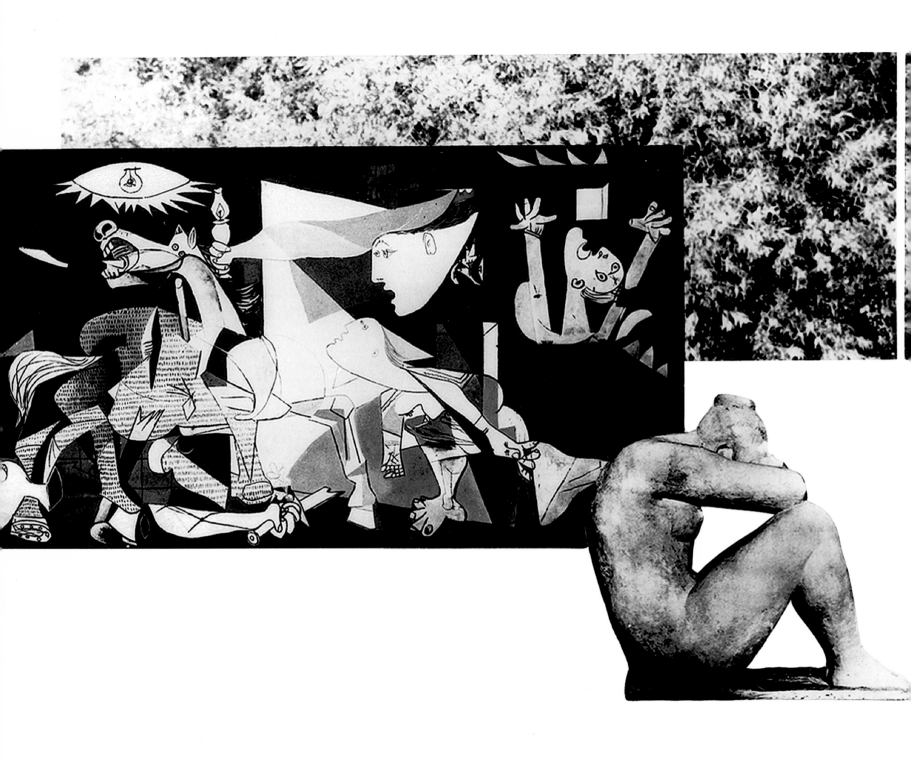

German Desires of America: Mies's Urban Visions

JEAN-LOUIS COHEN

A skyscraper inscribes its geometric outline into the night sky of the metropolis. Its facade is punctuated by the rectangular openings of its tiers of windows, while its base plunges down into a checkerboard of streets lit by the beams of automobile headlights. This striking image of the modern metropolitan condition might seem to evoke the Seagram Building, on New York's Park Avenue, yet it has nothing to do with Mies's tower of steel and glass from 1954–58; in fact the drawing, by Kurt Szafranski, illustrates a brochure published in 1912 by the *Berliner Morgenpost*, discussing the possibility of a "third dimension" for the German capital, namely, a city center of skyscrapers (fig. 1).[1]

The texts and image of this brochure of 1912 mark the opening episode—German, but looking toward the American model—of investigations of Mies's that would ultimately make the New World their theater. Exploring how a building type that had emerged since the 1890s in Chicago and New York might make its appearance in Berlin, the *Morgenpost* invited remarks from three important figures in the city's modern culture: Walther Rathenau, Bruno Möhring, and Peter Behrens. For Rathenau, then the director of the Allgemeine Elektricitäts-Gesellschaft (AEG), "Nothing as imposing as the city of New York has been created since the Middle Ages. . . . For the first time, the creation of these facades that rise to assault the sky manifests the birth of a new constructive idea in architecture." He contrasts this radically new idea with the "compromises" of contemporary building in Berlin.[2] The architect Möhring had visited the United States, and saw nothing innately exotic in the American example; "the constitution of the Berlin soil," he argues here, "is in no way an obstacle for buildings of any height. Chicago rests in part on the alluvial deposits of Lake Michigan, and we have never

seen skyscrapers collapse there."[3] Berlin could therefore rely on the "American experience," which Möhring would later put to use by initiating the 1921 competition, in which Mies would participate, for a skyscraper on Friedrichstrasse. Nearer still to Mies was Behrens, in whose Neubabelsberg studio the young architect had recently worked. In the *Morgenpost*, Behrens relies on his own reactions to America, remarking that he cannot remember "a stronger impression than the one experienced on entering the port of New York, when the city appeared on the horizon like a light fog, creating a sort of enveloping mirage." He sees the skyscraper as proclaiming a different architecture (fig. 2):

What made the greatest impression on me in America, in terms of aesthetics and in general, was precisely the towering business buildings. The country otherwise displays little independent artistic development; official buildings are all frozen in a sugary classicism, and even country houses are with few exceptions patterned after either the English cottage style or the American Colonial style. But these business buildings, thanks to their bold construction, have in them the germ of a new architecture.[4]

For Behrens the skyscraper went beyond architectural aesthetics, for, better than the isolated square or building, it posed the problem of the "horizontal territory" of the metropolis, which "calls for matter, a body, that can only be found in the establishment of vertical and compact masses."[5] In each of these three analyses, in fact, the question of the skyscraper is linked to that of the modernization of the city in its entirety. Indeed, in the transatlantic dialogue on architecture and the metropolis that had begun with the Columbian Exposition in Chicago in 1893, the representation of cities is itself inscribed in a specular relationship: the parallel proposed by Möhring between the soil of Chicago and that of Berlin is only one example of the almost constant comparison between the Porkopolis on Lake Michigan and the Elektropolis on the river Spree, both continental cities subjected to intense immigration in the last three decades of the nineteenth century, and in the years leading up to World War I.[6]

The reverberations of German *Amerikanismus*, often discussed mainly in terms of the local reception of the architecture of H. H. Richardson and Frank Lloyd Wright, are actually far more complex.[7] From Walter

BERLINS DRITTE DIMENSION

Gropius to Erich Mendelsohn, many architects whom Americans saw as the European messengers of the modern were in their own country conscious agents of Americanism (fig. 3). It is harder to place Mies in this context, despite the fragmentary signs provided by the surviving volumes of his personal library.[8] A fundamental register of Americanism, however, as Reyner Banham showed, was an interest in American industrial buildings,[9] and it is clear that the designers in Behrens's

1 (far left). Kurt Szafranski. Cover, *Berlins dritte Dimension*. Brochure published by the *Berliner Morgenpost*, 1912. Staatsbibliothek Berlin

2 (near left). Peter Behrens. Vertical city landscape, cover for *Das Plakat* 6 (June 1920). Canadian Centre for Architecture, Montreal

studio, even after they left it, were receptive to the architecture of the "Motherland of Industry," which Gropius celebrated in the annals of the Deutscher Werkbund in 1913 (fig. 4).[10] The effect of this architecture was not instantaneous, but developed for close to twenty years, under changing modalities. It was a syndrome that Mies did not escape.

When Mies conceived his Concrete Office Building Project, in 1923, he was primarily interested in concrete structures, and in Detroit's first automobile factories. With its resemblance to a multistory factory, his project is much closer to an industrial register than to the towers of Manhattan or Chicago, which then represented the ideal of the business edifice. When Mies further developed the theme of the corporate office building (for example with the Verseidag Administration Building in Krefeld in 1937–38), he again appealed to a structure (in this case steel) resembling those of American factories, now of the 1930s.[11] The language he established in preparing his campus study for the Illinois Institute of Technology (IIT), begun in 1939—a great arrangement, industrial in both its conception and its modes of real-ization—also demonstrated his interest in such buildings, particularly those constructed by Albert Kahn Associates.[12] Mies's interest in Kahn's factories appears clearly in his Concert Hall Project of 1942: in the photocollage for the project, the photograph used to signify the great metal envelope within which the walls of the hall were to be arranged shows the trellis of girders in the Assembly Building of the Glenn Martin bomber factory, built by Kahn in Middle River, Maryland, in 1937.[13] The Concert Hall, like the contemporary Museum for a Small City Project, may be seen as inaugurating Mies's American production; it may also be seen as the final step in a relationship with American industrial architecture that he began twenty years earlier.

But the "new economy" praised by Rathenau in a famous book was not limited to industrial production;[14] it integrated the organizational sphere, for which the metropolis was the stage. Mies's thinking on this point cannot be reduced to the question of the skyscraper or the factory, it must be related to Germany's intense debate, in the first third of the twentieth century, on the *Großstadt* ("metropolis" in the German conception), its reason for being, and its structure. Mies was certainly aware of this debate, and his interest in the rationale of capitalism—a rationale later manifest in his American projects—was not dissociable from the urban frame-work in which the new social relations were inscribed. Massimo Cacciari has underscored the extent to which the metropolis could be thought of as *the* mode of

3. The Brooklyn Bridge and Lower Manhattan. From Erich Mendelsohn, *Amerika* (Berlin: Rudolf Mosse, 1926)

4. Albert Kahn Associates. Continental Motors Company factory, Detroit. 1912. From Walter Gropius, "*Die Entwicklung moderner Industriebaukunst,*" in *Die Kunst in Industrie und Handel: Jahrbuch des Deutschen Werkbundes 1913* (Jena: Eugen Diederichs, 1913)

existence for a capitalist society, and this relationship between organization and space seems to underlie Mies's ideas about the city.[15]

Given the intensity of the German debate about the city, Mies's reticence about embarking on a large-scale discussion of the subject himself is worth noting. With the big exception of his plan for the Weissenhof Housing Colony, Stuttgart, of 1925–27, he did not practice urban planning and did not study neighborhood maps.[16] Moreover, none of his few texts on the subject can be seen as addressing urbanism alone. Yet his projects and theoretical positions have at the very least a latent urban dimension. This has scarcely been addressed in most analyses of his architecture, which have considered the buildings but not the spaces in which they are inscribed, although they in some way internalize urban situations.

It is true that interpreting Mies's remarks on the urban condition is a delicate matter. These remarks bring together considerations relating both to the city as physical form, as in the Latin *urbs*, and to the city as social space, as in the Latin *civitas*. Saint Augustine, an author Mies often cited, uses the latter term in *The City of God*, a book written to emphasize the survival of a Christian *civitas* despite the barbarians' sacking of Rome.

Mies's ideas on the city are also inscribed in two distinct sets of circumstances. The first involves the growth of Germany's cities between the late nineteenth century and World War I, a growth that was comparable only to the cities of America in the same period and that provoked the methodological leap of allowing the constitution of urbanism as a discipline.[17] In order to master what they called the *Stadterweiterung*, the expansion of the cities that they were codifying in their manuals, German planners invented zoning, which was quickly taken up by their American colleagues. In turn they borrowed the park system from the United States. At the same time, the very notion of the metropolis became the center of nascent bodies of sociology and cultural critique. The second set of circumstances corresponded mainly to the period between the two world wars, when reforms that had been outlined before 1914 were carried out. This period was marked by vast construction programs and by the emergence of regional planning

and highway infrastructures. Americanism took on a new configuration, in which the interest in ways of governing cities and in solutions to the problems of automobile traffic was transparently clear.

Mies had encountered these issues in his personal history. In 1905 he had left Aachen, which had had a glorious past but was by this time a second-tier provincial town, to pursue his ambitions in the professional and intellectual circles of the capital. His awareness of urban transformation in Germany, which he witnessed at both ends of the spectrum of the country's cities, appears when he makes an accounting of the process of urbanization, using an epic mode, in a lecture of 1926:

The unified German empire achieved world power status. International traffic and international trade determine life from now on. Metropolises of enormous proportions develop. The speed of development permits no reflection.

One builds street upon street in endless sequence. Industry experiences unexampled expansion. A new technology arises with unforeseen possibilities. Bold constructions never seen before are invented. Here, too, one knows no limits.

Traffic takes on immense dimensions and interferes in the organism of our cities with fierce brutality.

Gigantic industrial complexes arise, yes, entire industrial cities [figs. 5, 6].[18]

By 1928, when he delivered the lecture "The Preconditions of Architectural Work" (which he illustrated with images of the New York skyline and streets), Mies had expanded his thoughts to an almost global dimension, affirming that the "world shrinks more and more." The problematic he imagined had changed as well, insofar as it was no longer traffic or industry that he saw as the motor guiding urban transformation, but the economy in its entirety:

Traffic serves economy. Economy becomes the great distributor, interferes in all domains, forces man into its service.

Economy begins to rule. Everything stands in the service of use. Profitability becomes law. Technology forces economic attitudes, transforms material into power, quantity into quality. The most effective use of power is consciously brought about.[19]

Here Mies was echoing ideas on the inexorable development of the metropolis that dated back to the Berlin of the years before World War I, emanating not only from architects such as Behrens, Möhring, and

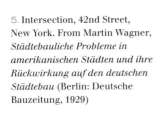

5. Intersection, 42nd Street, New York. From Martin Wagner, *Städtebauliche Probleme in amerikanischen Städten und ihre Rückwirkung auf den deutschen Städtebau* (Berlin: Deutsche Bauzeitung, 1929)

6. Park Avenue, New York. From Walter Curt Behrendt, *Städtebau und Wohnungswesen in den Vereinigten Staaten: Bericht über eine Studienreise* (Berlin: Guido Hackebeil AG, 1927)

August Endell but from intellectuals such as Georg Simmel, Werner Sombart, and Karl Scheffler.[20] Fritz Neumeyer has underscored the importance for Mies of Scheffler's remarks on the "heroic monumentality" of iron-framed construction,[21] but Scheffler's *Architektur der Großstadt* (Architecture of the metropolis, 1913) also proposed interpretations of the metropolis to which the architect's analyses are strangely similar.

In its ideal form, Scheffler wrote, the metropolis must "contain the familial economy as much as that of the city, correspond perfectly to modern demands, and be a point of crystallization of interests oriented toward an international economy." Not content with simply making observations, he advocated a "city structured logically" and dominated by skyscrapers, with a surrounding area of large housing blocks, "necessary compromise," and "residential neighborhoods linked to the city by a rapid urban railway." Internal specialization and internalization are the characteristic features of the metropolis, which for Scheffler may be the only place "where the struggle for a new architecture may be waged in all its components."[22] Mies's practice itself embodied this split between the dense center, for which he designed the Friedrichstrasse Skyscraper (1921) and the Reichsbank (1933) projects, and the residential periphery to the west, site of the single-family houses that were his first actual buildings.

Expressionism. In praising the "crystalline forms" of great modern enterprise and the "beauty of labor," which the culture of Weimar would bring to the forefront, he also anticipates both the ironic critique of Dada and the stance, too grave to be totally serious, of Mies and the group around the magazine *G*.

Through his glass skyscrapers, the first of them developed for the Friedrichstrasse competition, Mies became attached to the realization of the "rationally constructed city" proposed by Scheffler.[25] As in American downtowns, and in opposition to the theories of Bruno Taut, the city center as Scheffler imagined it was not made up of edifices reconstituting a sense of community but by the tall, anonymous offices of the large corporation.[26] From this point of view, Mies's decision to make the beehive the emblem of his project—the name he chose to identify his submission to the competition, in which the identities of the architects were to be unknown to the judges, was *Wabe*, "Honeycomb"— had nothing innocent about it, but evoked the walls of glass used in beehives by beekeepers.[27] It must not be forgotten that when Beaux-Arts students in Paris were invited to produce a study for a skyscraper in 1892, the program was styled as a "commercial beehive."[28] Mies's next project, the Glass Skyscraper, presented at the *Grosse Berliner Kunstausstellung* of 1923 in the form of a translucent model contrasting with a row of Berlin houses in modeling clay, could have illustrated Rathenau's criticism in the *Berliner Morgenpost* of the buildings current in 1912: "These bastard office and residential buildings, whose fourth floor overflows with windows in a sudden fit, are difficult to treat architectonically. By contrast, the tower, which American cities offer us as an example, effectively allows new solutions that satisfy all needs of air and light."[29]

A collective reflection now emerged on the skyscraper, with the new images echoing Szafranski's drawing.[30] Writing in 1920, Ludwig Hilberseimer and Udo Rukser emphasized the vertical articulation of Ernest Graham's Equitable Building (fig. 7), whose narrow courtyards anticipated the canyons of Mies's Friedrichstrasse project. They also evoked the "reinterpretation of windows" introduced by American architecture in its games of repetition.[31] To the most

Another basic discourse on the new urban spaces is Endell's slightly earlier book *Die Schönheit der grossen Stadt* (The beauty of the great city, 1908). Mies no doubt read the passage on the Friedrichstrasse train station and "the play of light on large glass panes," which may have led to his skyscraper of glass.[23] Endell takes on a Zarathustra-like tone in condemning the depravity of the metropolis, but he knows enough to recognize that "the metropolis . . . is a marvel of beauty and poetry to anyone who is willing to look, a fairy tale, brighter, more colorful, more diverse than anything ever invented by a poet, a home, a mother who daily bestows new happiness and great abundance over her children."[24] In enumerating these myriad beauties, Endell heralds the aesthetics of both Futurism and

7. Ernest Graham. Equitable Building, New York. 1915. From Erich Mendelsohn, *Amerika* (Berlin: Rudolf Mosse, 1926)

skeptical critics of the modern radicals, such as Werner Hegemann, the salvation of Mies's project was its "calm and regular repetition of an idea, even perhaps a false one, which can be formally assured and much more effective artistically than the chaotic confusion" that he saw in the projects of de Stijl, whose "formlessness" he denounced.[32]

The city planner Martin Mächler saw in this type of building the "economic center" of a living and working community.[33] The question was discussed in the general press by critics like Siegfried Kracauer, who denounced the "ugliness of New York"; in his eyes the skyscraper incorporated "that same spirit of materialism and capitalist exploitation." The realization of the projects proposed in various competitions of the time would depend not only on the "creative strength of our architects but also on the social conscience, the sense of community, of our entire population."[34]

Mies had an original position. He did not figure among the thirty-seven German participants in the Chicago Tribune competition, and did not endorse all of the projects for a vertical city, even when the debate on the skyscraper resumed under more favorable economic conditions at the end of the 1920s.[35] But his awareness of the changing configurations of the American debate is not in doubt.[36] At the same time, contrasting the Voisin plan, which Le Corbusier worked out in 1925 for Paris, with the German problematic, he essentially reproached the Paris architect (also criticized by other German authors) for dealing only with "the formal problem of the metropolis" (fig. 8):

He is of the opinion that the city of the future cannot do without skyscrapers, rather they appear to him an appropriate means to control increasing traffic congestion. . . .

In continuation of the work of [Baron] Haussmann, Le Corbusier suggested rebuilding the antiquated medieval quarters of Paris.

Here, too, he suggests the skyscrapers.

The plans of Le Corbusier can only be understood from the Parisian point of view.

Paris is, on account of its historical development, a city of representation.[37]

The critique was original, insofar as what most observers of the Voisin plan criticized was precisely the

absence of a link with historical Parisian identity. It is as though Mies saw Le Corbusier's approach as a manifestation of *Zivilisation* to which one had to contrast *Kultur*—as a limited vision in the form of *urbs*, when what actually had to be addressed was the fashioning of a *civitas*.[38] Rather than proposing a definite project, Mies seems to plead in the name of capitalism in its entirety, in order to introduce the notion of regulating it. Unlike his friend Hilberseimer, he managed to avoid formulating a project to "correct" the general structure of Berlin, no doubt because he recognized the value of the city as a fixed social center. On the national scale, on the other hand, he deplored the absence of foresight, underscoring the interest of the Siedlungsverband Ruhrkohlengebiet's recent experience of regional planning:[39]

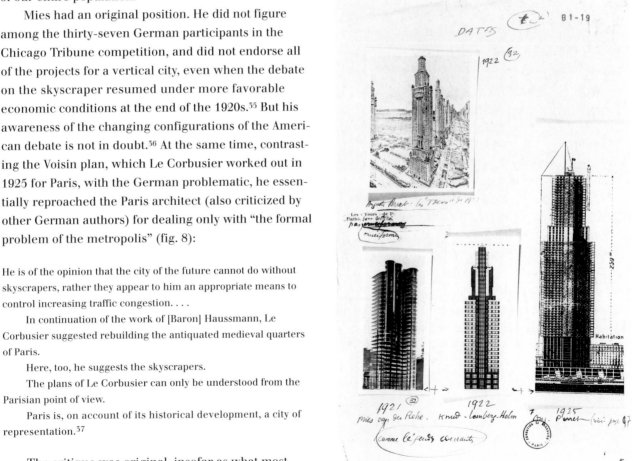

8. Le Corbusier. Layout for the *Almanach d'architecture moderne.* 1925. Page shows Mies's Glass Skyscraper, Knut Lonberg-Holm's Chicago Tribune competition entry, and two designs by Auguste Perret

That this lack of planning will in the short or long run stifle the economic and industrial development, yes, stop it altogether, gradually seems to be sinking in. Sociological considerations are gaining influence in city planning. The value of the siting theory [*Standorttheorie*] in urban planning has begun to be recognized. Industry must be housed where it finds the most advantageous conditions. . . . With the creation of the Ruhr Settlement Association, 325 city administrations were united under one urban planning concept. This offered the opportunity to establish a unified economic plan, independent of individual administrative districts. . . . Thus traffic installations do not determine but follow a specifically planned development, or to say it in other words, traffic planning follows economic development.[40]

The alternative to the urbanism of representation illustrated by the Voisin plan was a process that did not place form at the forefront. Mies detected such a process in Taut's work as a city planner in Magdeburg, where he devised a plan with nothing "fantastic or arbitrary" about it, for it was "designed in response to the landscape, the traffic, and with respect for the people that have to live and work there." For Mies, "this plan has obtained its significant and characteristic form just because form was not striven for."[41] It is precisely because of the "dominance of economic power over us" that a principle of planning can be established that "will lead to an organic form [*Organische Gestalt*] for our cities."[42]

This "organic Gestalt," heralding a "free unfolding" of urban centers, echoes the idea of an "organic" economy that Rathenau had called for before he was assassinated, in 1922. Articulated with the concept of the *Stadtlandschaft* or city-country, the idea would gain ground in the urbanist work of Rudolf Schwarz, a member of Romano Guardini's Catholic Quickborn movement, with which Mies was in sympathy—he would maintain a friendly correspondence with Schwarz until 1945. Schwarz would propose his own conception of an urbanism infused with spiritual thought in his work *Von der Bebauung der Erde* (On the building of the world, 1949).[43] In his 1928 essay "*Großstadt als Tatsache und Aufgabe*" (The metropolis as fact and program) he criticizes Germany's official urbanism and the "unimaginative tedium of optimistic rationalism," and posits the metropolis as the paradigmatic site of the conflict between "form" and "life."[44] Ultimately, didn't

the "reign of technology," which Schwarz analyzed and whose arrival Mies announced in his "Preconditions of Architectural Work," call for, to use the words of his manifesto of 1924, a sort of large-scale "will of the epoch" as represented in space?[45]

The posing of the question of the metropolis in "organic" terms led Mies to unexpected solutions, such as the first, flexible, overall plan for the Weissenhof Housing Colony, dominated by a "city crown" on the modest scale of the neighborhood and made up of residential buildings. Here Mies made sure "to avoid everything schematic and rule out everything that could constitute a restriction to free work processes."[46] But it was not until 1937, and in the United States itself, that he encountered a discourse that nourished his economic credo, when Wright presented his Broadacre City project to the German architect as a sort of "organic capitalism" (fig. 9).[47]

9. Frank Lloyd Wright and the Taliesin Fellowship. Broadacre City. 1935. Model: painted wood, cardboard, and paper, 12'8" x 12'8" (386 x 386 cm). The Frank Lloyd Wright Foundation

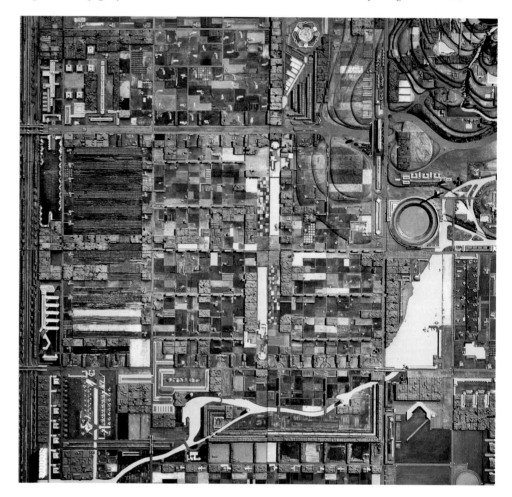

10. Chicago's North Side. From Martin Wagner, *Städtebauliche Probleme in amerikanischen Städten und ihre Rückwirkung auf den deutschen Städtebau* (Berlin: Deutsche Bauzeitung, 1929)

imagine a horizontal landscape of inhabitable layers very different not only from the dense cities but also from the model neighborhoods of Weimar Germany. Mies's interest in a landscape of diffuse urban areas became clear in 1944, when he lent his support to the theories formulated by Hilberseimer in *The New City*.[49]

Mies first visited America in 1937, theoretically to work on a project for a house for Stanley Resor (a trustee of The Museum of Modern Art) in Jackson Hole, Wyoming. On seeing the great landscape of the Teton Range, he recycled ideas laid out in sketches of 1934 for a "Glass House on a Hillside" and finally took the measure of the infinite horizons he had hinted at in the Brick Country House Project of 1924. But it is also possible to see this project, which put a large visual frame around the region's sprawling mountains, as calling to mind Karl May's children's books at the turn of the century, describing the adventures of the American Indian Winnetou.[50] The Resor project from this point of view would be but an acting out, the condensation of a latent vision of a house set in wide open spaces.[51] Mies's precise attention to a natural landscape that may have evoked the reveries of the young Ludwig contrasts strongly with his apparent indifference to the American cities he visited after 1938 (fig. 10). The reality of the South Side of Chicago, where he produced his study for the IIT campus, was indeed rather bleak next to the idealized visions of an America where economy and reason would coincide. If the construction of housing blocks defined by urban rationality in Chicago or Toronto allowed him to find a remedy for this disappointment, Mies's quasi-mutism on the American metropolis contrasts with his attention to it in the 1920s, and suggests the divide between attention at a distance and the concrete experience of an America that has ceased to be imaginary.

In the 1930s, Mies disengaged himself from the vertical-city model, and his more organic orientation led him to become interested in such other matters as the spatial definition of highways, a program that had been discussed since the early 1920s. He wrote on the question of landscape in the columns of the house publication of the Hafraba company, which had determined to build a Hamburg-Frankfurt-Basel highway years before the Nazi program of 1933.[48] Still rather mysterious in their genesis and their sequence (see Terence Riley, "From Bauhaus to Court-House," in the present volume), the court-houses of the 1930s allow one to

Notes

In the notes that follow, certain frequently cited books are referred to by abbreviated titles only. They are: Arthur Drexler, ed., *The Mies van der Rohe Archive. Part I: 1910–1937* (New York and London: Garland Publishing, Inc., 1986), 4 vols., numbered vols. 1–4; Franz Schulze, ed., *The Mies van der Rohe Archive. Part 1: 1910–1937, Supplementary Drawings in Two Volumes* (New York and London: Garland Publishing, Inc., 1990), 2 vols., numbered vols. 5 and 6; Fritz Neumeyer, *The Artless Word: Mies van der Rohe on the Building Art*, Eng. trans. Mark Jarzombek (Cambridge: The MIT Press, 1991; first published as *Mies van der Rohe. Das kunstlose Wort. Gedanken zur Baukunst* [Berlin: Wolf Jobst Siedler, 1986]); Schulze in association with the Mies van der Rohe Archive of The Museum of Modern Art, *Mies van der Rohe: A Critical Biography* (Chicago and London: The University of Chicago Press, 1985); and Wolf Tegethoff, *Mies van der Rohe: The Villas and Country Houses*, Eng. trans. Russell M. Stockman (New York: The Museum of Modern Art, 1985; first published as *Mies van der Rohe: Die Villen und Landhausprojekte* [Essen: R. Bacht, 1981]).

Terence Riley, "Making History: Mies van der Rohe and The Museum of Modern Art," pp. 10–23

1. By 1947 Mies had prepared various articles and public lectures on his work and architectural thinking, but never a book. (A collection of his writings appears in English translation in Fritz Neumeyer, *The Artless Word*.) After his completion of the Riehl House, in 1907, individual projects of his work were covered in journals and magazines, but rarely at any length. Short essays on him had appeared in *Cahiers d'Art* (Paris) and *Kunstblatt* (Berlin), and his work had been featured in Gustav Adolf Platz, *Die Baukunst der neuesten Zeit* (Berlin: Propyläen-Verlag, 1926); Philip Johnson cites the expanded second edition of this book, from 1930, as his introduction to Mies's work. The first essay on Mies in English was Johnson's "Ludwig Miës van der Rohe," in Henry-Russell Hitchcock, Jr., Johnson, and Lewis Mumford, *Modern Architecture: International Exhibition*, exh. cat. (New York: The Museum of Modern Art, 1932), the publication for the Museum's exhibition of the same title, popularly known as the "International Style" exhibition. Also released as a trade publication under the title *Modern Architects* (New York: The Museum of Modern Art and W. W. Norton, 1932), the exhibition publication is frequently confused with Hitchcock and Johnson, *The International Style: Architecture since 1922* (New York: W. W. Norton, 1932, reprint eds. 1966, 1995), also published at the time of the exhibition.
2. Johnson, *Mies van der Rohe*, exh. cat. (New York: The Museum of Modern Art, 1947).
3. Ibid., p. 49. While Johnson's citation wedded the aphorism to Mies, the architect himself recalled in later years that its author was Peter Behrens.
4. The 1947 edition was expanded and reprinted in 1953, and again in 1978 with an epilogue, "Thirty Years After," that recorded a conversation between Johnson, Arthur Drexler, and Ludwig Glaeser. The German translation is Stuttgart: Verlag Gerd Hatje, 1956, trans. Elke Kaspar; the Spanish, Buenos Aires: Editorial Victor Lerú, 1960, trans. Nicoletta Ottelenghi.
5. Mies, "On the Theme: Exhibitions," *Die Form* 3, no. 4 (1928), trans. in Neumeyer, *The Artless Word*, p. 121.
6. Ada Louise Huxtable, label copy for *Mies van der Rohe* exhibition, n.d. [1947]. Archives of the Department of Architecture and Design, The Museum of Modern Art, New York. Huxtable worked closely with Johnson in composing the texts and labels that appeared in the exhibition; interview with the author, December 14, 2000.
7. In 1937, acting on Mies's behalf, Lilly Reich closed his office and transferred his drawings to her studio. When the Allies began bombing Berlin, she moved the drawings again, to a farmhouse owned by the parents of his ex-student and employee Eduard Ludwig, in what would become East Germany. In 1943 Reich's studio was destroyed in an air raid. Johnson's book credits her with helping assemble material for the exhibition; presumably she furnished photographic material from Germany.
8. Huxtable, "Memo to Miss Newmeyer from Mrs. Huxtable re: Mies van der Rohe exhibition," July 25, 1947. Archives of the Department of Architecture and Design, The Museum of Modern Art. The author does not know the identity of Miss Newmeyer.
9. Herbert Matter further enhanced the exhibition's apparent relationship with the Museum for a Small City Project by manipulating the negative to eliminate lighting fixtures and air ducts, so that the photograph, like Mies's collages, shows a perfectly flat ceiling. Compare Matter's photograph in the frontispiece to the present essay with fig. 3.
10. Johnson and Edgar Kaufmann, jr., lent their Mies-designed furniture to the exhibition.
11. The plan for the exhibition (fig. 2) shows a mural entitled "Illinois Institute of Technology." No such mural, however, appears in any installation photograph.
12. As we have seen, Mies might have been unable to retrieve his original drawings from Germany even had he wanted to. Nonetheless, early on he showed an interest in reproducible methods of presenting his work. While he made collages for the Bismarck Monument Project, the Friedrichstrasse Skyscraper Project, the S. Adam Department Store Project, the Bank and Office Building Project, the Urban Design Proposal for Alexanderplatz, and the Friedrichstrasse Office Building Project, all except the first of these survive only in photographs, suggesting that Mies may have considered the collages secondary to their photographic reproductions.
13. Baptized Maria Ludwig Michael Mies, the architect was known as Ludwig Mies until he was thirty-five. His *nom d'artiste* sounded more distinctive than his family name, and the use of the umlaut changed the pronunciation, which was homonymous with the adjective *mies*, meaning "seedy" or "poor." While Mies's estrangement from his family does not elicit sympathy, it may appear at least somewhat predictable when you consider that none of his three siblings married, with the exception of a sister who married at the age of fifty. See Franz Schulze, *A Critical Biography*, for other biographical details.
14. A studio assistant, Sergius Ruegenberg, later recounted Mies's directions to discard the material (see Neumeyer, *The Artless Word*, p. 170). While the decision seems dramatic in retrospect, it should not be overinterpreted. Mies retained photographs of all the built works, and the decision to remove the drawings is less important than his previous decision to no longer publish or present the material.
15. It is interesting to compare Mies's attitude to his early work with that of his peers. Le Corbusier, who otherwise documented his work assiduously in his *Oeuvre complète*, declined to publish the earliest villas he designed in La-Chaux-de-Fonds, commencing his own history with the more ideological project for the Maison Dom-ino of 1914–15. Frank Lloyd Wright, on the other hand, retained every project he ever designed, although he altered the dates (as he did that of his own birth) in later years so that some projects appeared to have been designed earlier than they were.
16. Mies reportedly received the commission for the Werner House because the Werners liked the Perls House, which is on the adjoining site. Given the differences in the houses, historians have often wondered about the circumstances of the commission. It may be that the Werners were aware of the earlier scheme for the Perls House and based their decision on that, rather than on the executed design.
17. In 1919 in Berlin, when Walter Gropius organized the *Ausstellung für unbekannte Architekten* (Exhibition of unknown architects) under the auspices of the Arbeitsrat für Kunst, Mies submitted the Kröller-Müller Villa Project to Gropius, who rejected it.
18. Johnson, *Mies van der Rohe*, p. 162.
19. Huxtable, label copy for *Mies van der Rohe*.
20. See my essay "From Bauhaus to Court-House," in the present volume.
21. George Danforth, letter to the author, December 4, 2000.
22. Johnson, *Mies van der Rohe*, p. 9. Johnson's account creates the impression that Mies obtained a classic liberal arts education. In fact Mies spent a scant two years at the Cathedral School; most of his education was in trade schools. Nor is there any reason to believe that he ever took any philosophy courses, much less studied Augustine or Thomas Aquinas, neither of whom had any particular connection to Aachen. It is unclear whether Johnson was aware of this at the time. See Schulze, *A Critical Biography*, pp. 13–14.
23. Ibid., p. 14.
24. Paul Westheim, "Entwicklung eines Architekten," *Das Kunstblatt* 11, no. 2 (February 1927): 55–62.
25. Johnson, *Mies van der Rohe*, p. 10.
26. Ibid., p. 20. The house Johnson identifies as the Kempner House was published by Westheim under the name Haus K., in "Entwicklung eines Architekten," p. 55, and dated to 1919. The very different design for the Kempner House that was actually built dates from 1922.
27. Johnson refers to (but does not name) the somewhat ponderously neoclassical Mosler House, which indeed might not be precisely "Romantic" but is definitely traditional, in ibid., p. 35.
28. Ibid., p. 22.
29. Ibid., p. 34.
30. Johnson's essay accompanying the "International Style" exhibition had mentioned only three of the five projects—the Friedrichstrasse Skyscraper, the Concrete Office Building, and the Brick Country House—and only the last was illustrated. The Friedrichstrasse Skyscraper, moreover, received hardly any notice, except to underscore its suspect connections to Expressionist architecture. See Johnson and Hitchcock, *Modern Architecture: International Exhibition*, p. 114.
31. Johnson, *Mies van der Rohe*, p. 35.
32. Ibid., p. 96. The term "court-house" is hyphenated in this and subsequent editions of Johnson's book, but later authors, including Drexler, dropped the hyphen.
33. Mies, letter to Stefano Desideri, January 29, 1962. Archives, Canadian Centre for Architecture, Montreal.
34. Professor Christian Wolsdorff of the Bauhaus-Archiv, Berlin, provided me with the information regarding the absence of the term from documents related to the Bauhaus. The term *Flachbau mit Wohnhof* appears on three of the projects completed by Ludwig, one of Mies's first students, who later worked in Mies's office. There are photographs of these projects in the Mies van der Rohe Archive at The Museum of Modern Art. It might be noted that Ludwig Hilberseimer, Mies's longtime colleague at both the Bauhaus and IIT, is rather terse on the subject of the court-house in his book on Mies, devoting no more than one sentence to it and illustrating it with the same project that Mies reworked from the Hubbe Court-House Studies of 1934–35. See Hilberseimer, *Ludwig Mies van der Rohe* (Chicago: Paul Theobald and Co., 1956), pp. 62, 75.
35. See my essay "From Bauhaus to Court-House."
36. Drawings separately catalogued as a Glass House on a Hillside and a House on a Terrace in the Mies van der Rohe Archive appear to be all part of the same exercise. While the principal scheme, illustrated by Johnson, was indeed developed in the mid-1930s, the drawings he selected may have been drawn later, in the United States.
37. Johnson, *Mies van der Rohe*, p. 98.
38. Ibid., p. 164.
39. Ibid.
40. Hilberseimer, *Ludwig Mies van der Rohe*, p. [200].
41. Johnson, *Mies van der Rohe*, p. 34.
42. Ibid., p. 10.
43. Ibid., p. 162.
44. Ibid., p. 140.
45. Ibid., pp. 137, 138.

46. Written two years after the end of World War II, Johnson's text may also be read as an attempt to associate Mies with pre-modern German values of craft and order, rather than with the Germany of the immediate past.
47. Drexler, *Mies van der Rohe* (New York: George Braziller, 1960), p. 20.
48. Ibid., p. 23.
49. Ibid., p. 24. Perhaps Drexler would have expanded on this view (which is only sketched out in his 1960 monograph) in the book he planned to accompany the exhibition of 1986. But although he completed the layout of the plate section for that book, he did not finish the text before his death, in 1987.
50. Huxtable, label copy for *Mies van der Rohe*. The text was not used, as the Promontory Apartments were withdrawn from the exhibition.
51. Mies, lecture, dated 1926, trans. in Neumeyer, *The Artless Word*, p. 252.
52. Thomas Mann, letter from Arosa, Switzerland, to Lavinia Mazzucchetti, March 13, 1933, in *Letters of Thomas Mann 1889–1955*, selected and trans. Richard and Clara Winston, 1970 (reprint ed. Berkeley and Los Angeles: University of California Press, 1990), p. 168.
53. Johnson, *Mies van der Rohe*, p. 26. In Johnson and Hitchcock's "Historical Note," *Modern Architecture: International Exhibition*, p. 20, they refer to Expressionist architecture as having "indulged in arbitrary curves, zigzags and fantastic decoration."
54. Mies, "Thank You Speech on the Voice of America on the Occasion of His Seventy-Fifth Birthday, 1961," trans. in Neumeyer, *The Artless Word*, p. 333.

Vittorio Magnago Lampugnani, "Berlin Modernism and the Architecture of the Metropolis," pp. 34–65

1. "Wettbewerb um einen Grundplan für die Bebauung von Gross-Berlin," *Der Baumeister* 7, no. 2 (1908): 18b. See also Albert Hofmann, "Gross-Berlin, sein Verhältnis zur modernen Großstadtbewegung und der Wettbewerb zur Erlangung eines Grundplanes für die städtebauliche Entwicklung Berlins und seiner Vororte im zwanzigsten Jahrhundert," *Deutsche Bauzeitung* 27 (April 2, 1910): 198. See also *Deutsche Bauzeitung* 25 (March 26, 1910): 169–76; 26 (March 30, 1910): 181–88; 27 (April 2, 1910): 197–200; 29 (April 9, 1910): 213–16; 31 (April 16, 1910): 233–36; 35 (April 30, 1910): 261–63; 37 (May 7, 1910): 281–87; 40 (May 18, 1910): 311; and 42 (May 25, 1910): 325–28.
2. Hermann Jansen entry in "Wettbewerb Gross-Berlin 1910: Die preisgekrönten Entwürfe mit Erläuterungsberichten" (Berlin, 1911), p. 8. Quoted in Wolfgang Sonne, "Ideas for a Metropolis: The Competition for Greater Berlin 1910," in Thorsten Scheer, Josef Paul Kleihues, and Paul Kahlfeldt, *City of Architecture—Architecture of the City: Berlin 1900–2000*, exh. cat. (Berlin: Nicolai Verlag, 2000), p. 70.
3. Camillo Sitte, *Der Städte-Bau nach seinen künstlerischen Grundsätzen* (Vienna: Verlag von Carl Graeser, 1889).
4. Rudolf Eberstadt, Bruno Möhring, and Richard Petersen entry in "Wettbewerb Gross-Berlin," pp. 3, 26.
5. Möhring, "Die neue Großstadt," *Die Bauwelt* 1, no. 14 (1910): 17.
6. Ferdinand Tönnies, *Gemeinschaft und Gesellschaft* (Leipzig, 1887, reprint ed. as *Gemeinschaft und Gesellschaft: Grundbegriffe der reinen Soziologie*, Berlin: Curtius, 1912).
7. Georg Simmel, "Die Großstädte und das Geistesleben," in *Die Großstadt: Vorträge und Aufsätze zur Städteausstellung. Jahrbuch der Gehe-Stiftung zu Dresden*, ed. Th. Petermann (Dresden, 1903), 10:185–206.
8. Ibid., p. 188.
9. Ibid., p. 204.
10. Karl Scheffler, "Ein Weg zum Stil," *Berliner Architekturwelt* 5 (1903): 293.
11. Ibid., p. 295.
12. Scheffler, *Die Architektur der Großstadt* (Berlin: Bruno Cassirer, 1913), pp. 33–34.
13. Ibid., p. 37.
14. Ibid., p. 130.
15. Ibid., p. 138.
16. Hendrik Petrus Berlage, "Bouwkunst en Impressionisme," *Architectura* 2 (1894), no. 22, pp. 93–95; no. 23, pp. 98–100; no. 24, pp. 105–6; no. 25, pp. 109–10. Gustave Kahn, *L'Esthétique de la rue* (Paris, 1901). Emil Magne, *L'Esthétique des villes* (Paris, 1908), p. 83. Daniel Hudson Burnham, "A City of the Future under a Democratic Government," *Town Planning Conference, London, October 10–15, 1910, Transactions* (London: Royal Institute of British Architects, 1911), pp. 368–78. And Otto Wagner, *Die Großstadt: Eine Studie über diese* (Vienna: Anton Schroll, 1911), p. 3.
17. Max Berg, "Der neue Geist im Städtebau auf der grossen Berliner Kunstausstellung," *Stadtbaukunst alter und neuer Zeit* 8, no. 3 (June 20, 1927): 44.
18. Ibid.
19. Kaiser Wilhelm II, speech at the opening of the street, 1901. The painter Max Liebermann is said to have remarked that the Siegesallee's "derailment in taste he could only bear with dark glasses."
20. See "Das Danziger Hochhaus: Eine 'Germanisierung' des Wolkenkratzers," *Vossische Zeitung* 40 (October 7, 1921), second insert, "Umschau in Technik und Wirtschaft."
21. *Berlins dritte Dimension*, ed. Alfred Dambitsch (Berlin: [Ullstein & Co.], n.d. [1912]), p. 9.
22. Otto Rappold, *Der Bau der Wolkenkratzer: Kurze Darstellung auf Grund einer Studienreise für Ingenieure und Architekten* (Munich and Berlin, 1913).
23. Hugh Ferriss, *The Metropolis of Tomorrow* (New York, 1929, reprint ed. Princeton: Princeton Architectural Press, 1986).
24. Walter Riezler, "Revolution und Baukunst," in *Mitteilungen des deutschen Werkbundes* no. 1 (May 1919): 18–20, reprinted in *Arbeitsrat für Kunst: Berlin 1918–1921*, exh. cat. (Berlin: Akademie der Künste, 1980), p. 96. Mies had submitted an entry to the *Ausstellung für unbekannte Architekten*, but had been rejected.
25. Paul Wittig, *Über die ausnahmsweise Zulassung einzelner Turmhäuser in Berlin* (Berlin, 1918), p. 14.
26. H. M., "Der erste Wolkenkratzer in Europa?," *Baugewerbs-Zeitung* 51/52 (1920): 188.
27. Berg, "Der Bau von Geschäftshochhäusern in Breslau zur Linderung der Wohnungsnot," *Stadtbaukunst alter und neuer Zeit* 7 (1920): 99–104, and 8 (1920): 116–18; reproduced with a slightly altered conclusion as "Der Bau von Geschäfts-Hochhäusern in den Großstädten als Mittel zur Linderung der Wohnungsnot, mit Beispielen für Breslau," *Ostdeutsche Bau-Zeitung* 18, no. 63 (August 7, 1920): 273–77.
28. Möhring, "Über die Vorzüge der Turmhäuser und die Voraussetzungen, unter denen sie in Berlin gebaut werden können," *Stadtbaukunst alter und neuer Zeit 22* (1920): 353–57; 23 (1920): 370–76; 24 (1920): 383–91; cited: 23 (1920): 371.
29. Otto Kohtz, *Büro-Turmhäuser in Berlin* (Berlin, 1921).
30. Wording from the inscription on the plan.
31. Kohtz, "Das Reichshaus am Königsplatz in Berlin. Ein Vorschlag zur Verringerung der Wohnungsnot und der Arbeitslosigkeit," *Stadtbaukunst alter und neuer Zeit* 16 (1920): 241–45. Also published in expanded form under the same title by Verlag Der Zirkel, Berlin, 1920.
32. Le Corbusier, "curiosité?—non: anomalie!," *L'Esprit nouveau* 9 (June 1921): 1017.
33. Mies, n.t., *Frühlicht* 1, no. 4 (1922): 124, Eng. trans. Fritz Neumeyer, *The Artless Word*, p. 240.
34. Scheffler, *Die Architektur der Großstadt*, p. 294.
35. Mies, n.t., *Frühlicht* 1, no. 4 (1922):124, Eng. trans. Neumeyer, *The Artless Word*, p. 240.
36. Mies, "Bürohaus," *G: Material zur elementaren Gestaltung* no. 1 (July 1923): [3], Eng. trans. Neumeyer, *The Artless Word*, pp. 241–42.
37. Peter Behrens, "Brief an die *Berliner Morgenpost*," 1912. Quoted in Fritz Hoeber, *Peter Behrens* (Munich, 1913), pp. 226–27.
38. Walter Curt Behrendt, *Die einheitliche Blockfront als Raumelement im Stadtbau* (Berlin, 1911).
39. Ludwig Hilberseimer, "Vom städtebaulichen Problem der Großstadt," *Sozialistische Monatshefte* 29, vol. 60, no. 6 (June 19, 1923): 352–53.
40. Ibid., p. 355.
41. Le Corbusier, *Urbanisme*, Collection de *L'Esprit nouveau* (Paris: Les Éditions G. Crès & Cie, 1925).
42. Hilberseimer, "Vom städtebaulichen Problem der Großstadt," p. 357, note 17; see also [Le Corbusier], *La Charte d'Athènes*, 1933 (Paris: Plon, 1943).
43. Hilberseimer, "Großstadtarchitektur," *Der Sturm* 15, no. 4 (1924): 188–89 (reprint ed. Nendeln: Kraus, 1970), pp. 188–89.
44. Hilberseimer, *Großstadtbauten* (Hannover: Aposs-Verlag, 1925), and *Großstadtarchitektur* (Die Baubücher 3) (Stuttgart: Verlag Julius Hoffmann, 1927, reprint ed. Stuttgart: Verlag Julius Hoffmann, 1978).
45. Hilberseimer, "Das Hochhaus," *Das Kunstblatt* 6, no. 12 (December 1922): 525–31.
46. Hilberseimer, *Großstadtbauten*, p. 170; "Schema einer Hochhausstadt," *G* no. 4 (March 1926): 8; "Über die Typisierung des Mietshauses," *Die Form: Zeitschrift für gestaltende Arbeit* 1, no. 15 (1926): 338–40; and *Großstadtarchitektur*, especially pp. 17–21.
47. Hilberseimer, *Entfaltung einer Planungsidee* (Bauwelt Fundamente 6) (Berlin, Frankfurt am Main, and Vienna: Ullstein Verlag, 1963), p. 22.
48. Scheffler, *Die Architektur der Großstadt*, pp. 33–34.
49. Hilberseimer, "Die Wohnung als Gebrauchsgegenstand," in *Bau und Wohnung: Die Bauten der Weissenhofsiedlung in Stuttgart errichtet 1927 nach Vorschlägen des Deutschen Werkbundes im Auftrag der Stadt Stuttgart und im Rahmen der Werkbund-ausstellung "Die Wohnung"* (Stuttgart: Akademischer Verlag Dr. F. Wedekind & Co. for the Deutscher Werkbund, 1927), pp. 69–71. Reprint ed. Stuttgart: Karl Krämer Verlag, 1992.
50. "Bericht über die am 29.5.1926 in Berlin abgehaltene Tagung der Architekten-Vereinigung 'Der Ring,'" reprinted in Peter Pfankuch, ed., *Hans Scharoun: Bauten, Entwürfe, Texte. Schriftenreihe der Akademie der Künste* (Berlin: Mann Verlag, 1974), 10:59.
51. Bruno Taut, *Bauen: Der neue Wohnbau* (Berlin and Leipzig: Klinkhardt & Biermann, for the architects' association The Ring, 1927), n.p.
52. Peter Bruckmann and Karl Lautenschlager, "Vorläufiger Plan zur Durchführung der Werkbund-Ausstellung Die Wohnung. Stuttgart," sent from the Württemberg chapter of the Deutscher Werkbund to Mies, June 27, 1925. The Mies van der Rohe Archive, The Museum of Modern Art, New York.
53. Gustaf Stotz, letter to Mies, September 24, 1925. The Mies van der Rohe Archive.
54. Hugo Häring, letter to Gustaf Stotz, September 26, 1925. The Mies van der Rohe Archive.
55. Württemberg chapter of the Deutscher Werkbund, letter to Stadtschultheissamt, October 8, 1925. Stadtarchiv Stuttgart. See also Karin Kirsch, *Die Weissenhofsiedlung: Werkbund-Ausstellung "Die Wohnung." Stuttgart 1927* (Stuttgart: Deutsche Verlags-Anstalt, 1987), p. 54.
56. Paul Bonatz, in *Schwäbischer Merkur*, May 5, 1926, and Paul Schmitthenner, in *Süddeutsche Zeitung* 13, no. 203, evening edition, May 5, 1926, quoted in Kirsch, *Die Weissenhofsiedlung*, p. 48.
57. Bonatz, in ibid.
58. Schmitthenner, in ibid.
59. Bonatz, in ibid.
60. Richard Döcker, letter to Mies, May 18, 1926. The Mies van der Rohe Archive.
61. Mies, letter to Döcker, May 27, 1926. The Mies van der Rohe Archive.
62. Notes of the Bauabteilung des Gemeinderats, July 24, 1926, §2213. Stadtarchiv Stuttgart.
63. Notes of the Bauabteilung des Gemeinderats, October 1, 1926, §2213. Stadtarchiv Stuttgart.
64. Heinrich Tessenow, letter to Mies, September 16, 1926. The Mies van der Rohe Archive.
65. "Werkbundausstellung Die Wohnung Stuttgart 1927," memorandum of the Deutscher Werkbund, Stuttgart, 1926.
66. Mies, "Eröffnungsrede zur Werkbund-Ausstellung Die Wohnung," *Stein, Holz, Eisen. Wochenschrift für moderne Bauwirtschaft und Baugestaltung* 41, no. 109, special issue 3 (August 11, 1927): 9; also in *Werkbund-Ausstellung "Die Wohnung"*, exh. cat. (Stuttgart, 1927).
67. Martin Wagner, *Das sanitäre Grün der Städte: Ein Beitrag zur Freiflächentheorie*, Ph.D. dissertation (Berlin: Carl Heymanns Verlag, 1915).
68. Berlage, "Bouwkunst en Impressionisme."
69. Eugène Hénard, *Études sur les transformations de Paris* (Paris, 1903–9). The concept appears in the first volume: *Projet de prolongement de la rue de Rennes avec pont en X sur la Seine* (Paris: Librairie Centrale d'Architecture, 1903), quoted in Hénard, *Études sur les transformations de Paris, et autres écrits sur l'urbanisme*, ed. Jean-Louis Cohen (Paris: Éditions l'Équerre, 1982), p. 19.
70. Magne, *L'Esthétique des villes*.
71. Behrens, "Kunst und Technik," *Elektrotechnische Zeitschrift* 22 (June 2, 1910): 554.
72. Behrens, "Einfluss von Zeit- und Raumausnutzung auf moderne Formentwicklung," *Jahrbuch des Deutschen Werkbundes 1914* (Jena, 1914), p. 9.
73. Filippo Tommaso Marinetti, "Manifeste du Futurisme," *Le Figaro*, February 20, 1909, p. 1.
74. Robert Musil, *Der Mann ohne Eigenschaften*, 1930–42 (reprint ed. Hamburg: Rowohlt Verlag, 1957), p. 9.
75. Martin Wagner, *Wirtschaftlicher Städtebau* (Stuttgart: Verlag Julius Hoffmann, 1951), p. 139.
76. Erich Mendelsohn, "Die internationale Übereinstimmung des neuen Baugedankens oder Dynamik und Funktion," 1923, lecture, published in *Erich Mendelsohn. Das Gesamtschaffen des Architekten. Skizzen. Entwürfe. Bauten* (Berlin: Rudolf Mosse Buchverlag, 1930), p. 28.
77. Martin Wagner, "Das Formproblem eines Weltstadtplatzes," *Das neue Berlin* 2 (1929): 33–38.
78. Martin Wagner, "Zur kommenden Umbildung Berlins: Notwendigkeiten einer planmässigen Führung," *Die Bauwelt* 18, no. 29 (1927): 707–9.
79. Martin Wagner, "Die städtebaulichen Probleme der Großstadt," lecture in the series "Berlin," Berlin, March 18, 1929, quoted in Ludovica Scarpa, *Martin Wagner und Berlin: Architektur und Städtebau in der Weimarer Republik* (Braunschweig and Wiesbaden: Vieweg & Sohn, 1986), p. 13, note 13.
80. Alfred Döblin, *Berlin Alexanderplatz: Die Geschichte von Franz Biberkopf* (Berlin: S. Fischer Verlag, 1929), Eng. trans. as *Berlin Alexanderplatz: The Story of Franz Biberkopf*, trans. Eugene Jolas, A Frederick Ungar Book (reprint ed. New York: Continuum, 1999), p. 220. The novel was serialized in the *Frankfurter Zeitung* from September 8 to October 11, 1929.
81. August Endell, *Die Schönheit der grossen Stadt* (Stuttgart, 1908).
82. Döblin, *Berlin Alexanderplatz*, pp. 219–20.
83. Martin Wagner, "Das Formproblem eines Weltstadtplatzes," p. 33.
84. Ibid., p. 37.
85. Hilberseimer, n.t., *Das neue Berlin* 2 (1929): 39–40.
86. Marcel Breuer, "Verkehrsarchitektur—ein Vorschlag zur Neuordnung des Potsdamer Platzes," *Das neue Berlin* 7 (1929): 136.
87. Ibid., p. 141.
88. Häring, "Die Sonderausstellung städtebaulicher Projekte Gross-Berlins in der Grossen Berliner Kunstausstellung, veranstaltet von der Architek-

ten-Vereinigung 'Der Ring,'" *Stadtbaukunst alter und neuer Zeit* 8, no. 3 (June 20, 1927): 50–53.
89. Hilberseimer, "Reichstagerweiterungen und Platz der Republik," *Die Form* 5, no. 13 (1930): 337.
90. Martin Kiessling, "Der Reichstagswettbewerb," *Das neue Berlin* 12 (1929): 242.
91. Ibid., p. 243.
92. Werner Hegemann, "Turmhaus am Reichstag?!," *Wasmuths Monatshefte für Baukunst* 45, no. 3 (1930): 97–104.
93. Heinrich Mendelssohn, "Zum Platz der Republik," *Das neue Berlin* 7 (1929): 143.
94. Häring, "Herrn Heinrich Mendelssohn zur Erwiderung," *Das neue Berlin* 7 (1929): 146.
95. Fritz Höger, "Kunst und Volkstum," *Deutsche Technik*, October 1933, p. 33.
96. "Vorstellung der prämierten Entwürfe mit den Gutachten des Preisgerichts," *Die Baugilde* 15 (1933): 713.
97. Ibid., p. 719.

Barry Bergdoll, "The Nature of Mies's Space," pp. 66–105

In developing the ideas presented here—in Columbia University seminars on Mies's work conducted with Terence Riley at The Museum of Modern Art, and on research trips to Berlin generously supported by the Getty Grant Program—I appreciated my conversations with Dr. Christiane Kruse, who made her unpublished dissertation available to me, and Professor Mirka Beneš, of Harvard University, who has developed a parallel set of concerns.

1. The exhibition *Modern Architecture: International Exhibition*, organized by Henry-Russell Hitchcock, Jr., and Philip Johnson, was accompanied by a catalogue of the same name (New York: The Museum of Modern Art, 1932). The show is widely known as the "International Style" exhibition, and that same year, Hitchcock and Johnson published a separate book, *The International Style: Architecture since 1922* (New York: W. W. Norton, 1932, reprint eds. 1966, 1995). The same reworked plan of the Tugendhat House appeared in the second edition of F. R. S. Yorke's widely consulted book *The Modern House* (London: The Architectural Press, 1935), p. 116.
2. These changes have gone without comment in the Mies literature. Indeed Mies's involvement with garden design has hardly been addressed, although insights into his view of landscape are to be gleaned from José A. Sosa Díaz-Saavedra, *Contextualismo y abstracción: Interrelaciones entre suelo, paisaje y arquitectura* (Las Palmas: Universidad de Las Palmas de Gran Canaria, 1995), pp. 115 ff. Observations on landscape are also at the heart of Wolf Tegethoff's *The Villas and Country Houses*, but Tegethoff largely overlooks Mies's pre-World War I work—which at the time of his writing was in the German Democratic Republic, and largely inaccessible to West Germans—and omits mention of Mies's involvement in the garden reform movement.
3. Mies, speech to the Deutscher Werkbund, 1932, in Fritz Neumeyer, *The Artless Word*, p. 312. The inaccuracies of the plans were only partly corrected by photographs—the trellis is clearly visible in the view of the garden facade chosen to illustrate *The International Style*—and by the model of the Tugendhat House that was prepared under Mies's supervision in Berlin, which includes foundation planting along the base of the building and plants in the conservatory, but omits the furniture and trellis from the upper, rooftop terrace.
4. There is some disagreement over when Mies discarded old drawings; perhaps it happened on several occasions. In his *Critical Biography*, Franz Schulze mentions 1924 (p. 332, note 1), while Neumeyer, in *The Artless Word*, p. 170, gives a date in 1926, derived from Sergius Ruegenberg. The latter may be the more credible, since Ruegenberg only began working for Mies in 1925.
5. Johnson, *Mies van der Rohe*, exh. cat.(New York: The Museum of Modern Art, 1947), p. 60.
6. Hitchcock and Johnson had pointed out the importance of Karl Friedrich Schinkel for Mies in their earliest writings on him—see, for instance, their *Modern Architecture: International Exhibition*, exh. cat. (New York: The Museum of Modern Art, 1932), p. 112—and the theme would later become a leitmotiv of Johnson's interpretations. See Johnson, *Mies van der Rohe*, p. 12, and his "Schinkel and Mies," 1961, in *Program, Columbia University School of Architecture*, Spring 1962, pp. 14–34, and reprinted in *Writings: Philip Johnson*, ed. Robert A. M. Stern (New York: Oxford University Press, 1979), pp. 164–81. But in all of this Schinkel was seen as influential in his expression of structure and his involvement with classical order, not in his interest in nature.
7. See Jean-Louis Cohen, *Mies van der Rohe* (London: E & FN Spon, 1996), p. 13; Schulze, *A Critical Biography*, pp. 23–30; Renate Petras, "Drei Arbeiten Mies van der Rohes in Potsdam-Babelsberg," *Deutsche Architektur* 23, no. 2 (February 1974): 120–21; Arnold Schink, *Mies van der Rohe: Beiträge zur ästhetischen Entwicklung der Wohnarchitektur* (Stuttgart: Karl Krämer Verlag, 1990), pp. 38–46; Verena von Beckerath, "Mies-van-der-Rohe Komplex (2)—Spuren," *Arch+* 95 (August 1988): 20–21; "Hilferuf für Mies van der Rohes Erstlingswerk," *Deutsches Architektenblatt* 27 (October 1995): 1877; and Gunnar Porikys, "Das 'Klösterli': Ein Gesamtkunstwerk in der Babelsberger Spitzweggasse," *Potsdamer Neueste Nachrichten*, March 11, 1999, p. 10.
8. See Hermann Muthesius, *Das englische Haus: Entwicklung, Bedingungen, Anlage, Aufbau, Einrichtung und Innenraum*, 3 vols. (Berlin: E. Wasmuth, 1904–5).
9. Mies, "Mies Speaks: I Do Not Design Buildings. I Develop Buildings," *Architectural Review* 144 (December 1968): 451.
10. Paul Mebes, *Um 1800: Architektur und Handwerk im letzten Jahrhundert ihrer traditionellen Entwicklung* (Munich: F. Bruckmann, 1908). Unless otherwise noted, or from Neumeyer's *Artless Word*, translations from the German in this essay are by the author.
11. See, e.g., *Sommer- und Ferienhäuser aus dem Wettbewerb der Woche*, 10th and 11th supplement, new series (Berlin: Druck und Verlag August Scherl, 1907). The competition featured here had taken place in 1906 and was published in May and September of 1907, the year of the Riehl House. The following year another competition yielded similar results; see *Hausgärten, Skizzen und Entwürfe aus dem Wettbewerb der Woche* (Berlin: Druck und Verlag August Scherl, 1908). Houses that share garden and house walls are to be found in virtually all of the model-house books of the period; see, for instance, Gerold E. Beetz, *Das eigene Heim und sein Garten, unter besonderer Berücksichtigung der Verhältnisse unseres Mittelstandes* (Wiesbaden: Westdeutsche Verlagsgesellschaft, 1909), p. 43. On the relationship between the Riehl House and Peter Behrens's Crematorium at Hagen, see Neumeyer, *The Artless Word*, p. 52, and "Space for Reflection: Block versus Pavilion," in Schulze, ed., *Mies van der Rohe: Critical Essays* (New York: The Museum of Modern Art, 1989), p. 158; and Cohen, *Mies van der Rohe*, p. 13.
12. See Barry Bergdoll, *Karl Friedrich Schinkel: An Architecture for Prussia* (New York: Rizzoli International, 1994), chapter 3.
13. Muthesius, *Landhaus und Garten*, 2nd rev. and expanded ed. (Munich: F. Bruckmann, 1910), p. L, plates 50–51. Given this promotion of the design, it is curious that as late as 1952 Hitchcock could maintain, "I have never seen Mies's first house of 1907 nor even a picture of it." Hitchcock, "The Evolution of Wright, Mies, and Le Corbusier," *Perspecta* 1 (Summer 1952): 13.
14. See Muthesius, *Das englische Haus*, 1:210 ff.
15. Victor Zobel, *Über Garten und Gartengestaltung* (Munich, 1905), quoted in Gisela Moeller, *Peter Behrens in Düsseldorf: Die Jahre von 1903 bis 1907* (Weinheim: VCH, 1991), p. 313. Muthesius echoed this critique in *Das englische Haus*, 1:218, and again in *Landhaus und Garten*, p. xii. On Joseph Maria Olbrich and the architectonic garden see, most recently, Birgit Wahmann, "Gärten der Mathildenhöhe," in *Mathildenhöhe Darmstadt 100 Jahre Planen und Bauen für die Stadtkrone 1899–1999* (Darmstadt: Häusser, 1999), 1:66–79.
16. Muthesius, *Das englische Haus*, 1:218.
17. Muthesius, *Landhaus und Garten*, 1st ed. (Munich: F. Bruckmann, 1907), p. xxv.
18. Paul Schultze-Naumburg, *Kulturarbeiten*, vol. 2, *Gärten*, 3rd ed. (Munich: Georg D. W. Callwey im Kunstwart-Verlag, 1909). See also Norbert Borrmann, *Paul Schultze-Naumburg 1869–1949: Maler, Publizist, Architekt, vom Kulturreformer der Jahrhundertwende zum Kulturpolitiker im Dritten Reich* (Essen: R. Bacht, 1989), pp. 25–60.
19. See Moeller, *Peter Behrens in Düsseldorf*, pp. 341–69, and *Düsseldorfer Gartenlust*, exh. cat. (Düsseldorf: Düsseldorf Stadtmuseum, 1987), pp. 183–87.
20. Muthesius, *Landhaus und Garten*, p. xxv.
21. Muthesius, *Das englische Haus*, 2:83.
22. Anna Fischer-Dückelmann, *Die Frau als Hausärztin: Ein ärtzliches Nachschlagbuch der Gesundheitspflege und Heilkunde in der Familie mit besondere Berücksichtigung der Frauen- und Kinderkrankheiten, Geburtshilfe und Kinderpflege*, 2nd rev. ed. (Stuttgart: Süddeutscher Verlags Institut, n.d. [c. 1905]), p. 165.
23. This diagram appears in Muthesius, *Landhaus und Garten*, 1907, p. xxiii.
24. Muthesius, *Landhaus und Garten*, p. xxv.
25. Neumeyer, *The Artless Word*, pp. 38 ff. See also Neumeyer, "Mies's First Project: Revisiting the Atmosphere at Klösterli," in the present volume.
26. Muthesius, *Das englische Haus*, 2:96. Mies owned a copy of *Häuser und Gärten* (Berlin: E. Wasmuth, 1912), the German translation of Mackay Hugh Baillie Scott's book *Houses and Gardens* (London, 1906).
27. See family photographs from the 1930s in the collection of Thomas Ukert, Hamburg.
28. Alois Riehl, *Introduction to the Theory of Science and Metaphysics*, trans. Arthur Fairbanks (London: K. Paul, Trench, Trubner & Co., 1894), pp. 16–17.
29. Walter Freiherr von Engelhardt, *Kultur und Natur in der Gartenkunst* (Stuttgart: Strecker & Schoder, 1910), p. 73.
30. See Bergdoll, *Schinkel*, esp. chapter 3, pp. 134 ff.
31. See Neumeyer, "Mies's First Project: Revisiting the Atmosphere at Klösterli." I am grateful to Franz and Margit Kleber for making available their photographic copy of the guest book.
32. See Eva Foerster and Gerhard Rostin, eds., *Ein Garten der Errinerung: Sieben Kapitel von und über Karl Foerster* (Berlin: Buchverlag Union, 1982, 3rd rev. ed. 1992), esp. pp. 48–49. See also Mathias Iven, ed., *3 x Foerster, Beiträge zu Leben und Werk von Wilhelm Foerster, Friedrich Wilhelm Foerster und Karl Foerster* (Milow: Shibri Verlag, 1995).
33. Karl Foerster, *Winterharte Blütenstauden und Sträucher der Neuzeit: Ein Handbuch für Gärtner und Gärtenfreunde* (Leipzig: J. J. Weber, 1911). The book continued to second and third editions in 1917 and 1924. The 1911 edition includes at least five photographs of the Riehl garden and possibly more, since many images include no architecture and are therefore hard to identify. All but one of these photographs were eliminated from the later editions.
34. Behrens, "Der moderne Garten," *Berliner Tageblatt* 40, no. 291 (June 10, 1911, reprint ed. Berlin: Pückler Gesellschaft, 1981), p. 9.
35. See Günter Mader, *Gartenkunst des 20. Jahrhunderts: Garten- und Landschaftsarchitektur in Deutschland* (Stuttgart: Deutsche Verlags-Anstalt, 1999), pp. 80–83.
36. Behrens, "Der moderne Garten," p. 8.
37. Ibid., p. 9.
38. See Arthur Drexler, ed., *The Mies van der Rohe Archive*, 1:6–29; Schulze, *A Critical Biography*, pp. 53–57; Neumeyer, *The Artless Word*, p. 78; and Schink, *Mies van der Rohe*, pp. 47–58. Schink's argument that the house cannot be firmly attributed to Mies seems contradicted by contemporary references to his authorship, notably Paul Westheim, "Das Haus eines Sammlers: Die Sammlung Eduard Fuchs, Zehlendorf," *Das Kunstblatt* 10 (March 1926): 108.
39. Hugo Perls's assertion to this effect, in his autobiography, *"Warum ist Camilla schön?"* (1962), is quoted by Dietrich von Beulwitz, the architect who restored the house in the late 1970s, in "The Perls House by Ludwig Mies van der Rohe," *Architectural Design* 53 (1983): 63–71, esp. p. 67.
40. The plan is unsigned, and is apparently not in Mies's hand, but comparison to other works signed by Mies, including the Riehl House and later the Eichstaedt House, makes its authorship clear. It survived, interestingly enough, in the papers of the Werner family, clients of Mies's for a later house on an adjacent site, and is now in the collection of the Bauhaus-Archiv, Berlin. The garden plan discussed in relationship to the Perls House in Annette Ciré's recent "'Hinter der Weltstadt': Städtebau und Architektur der Landhauskolonie und Gartenstädte in den Berliner Vororten vor 1914," in Thorsten Scheer, Josef Paul Kleihues, and Paul Kahlfeldt, eds., *Stadt der Architektur—Architektur der Stadt: Berlin 1900–2000*, exh. cat. (Berlin: Nicolai Verlag, 2000), p. 55, fig. 50, is a plan of the garden as it was reworked, presumably by Mies, in 1927, in conjunction with the extension to the house that Mies designed for Eduard Fuchs.
41. See Freiherr von Wolzogen, *Aus Schinkels Nachlass* (Berlin: Verlag der königlichen geheimen Oberhofbuchdruckerei, 1862–64), 2:207, and Bergdoll, *Schinkel*, p. 86.
42. Behrens, "Der moderne Garten," p. 8.
43. See H. Allen Brooks, *Le Corbusier's Formative Years* (Chicago: at the University Press, 1997), pp. 241–43. On the Wiegand House see Wolfram Hoepfner and Neumeyer, *Das Haus Wiegand von Peter Behrens in Berlin-Dahlem* (Mainz: von Zabern, 1979).
44. Christiane Kruse, "Haus Werner: Ein ungeliebtes Frühwerk Mies van der Rohes," *Zeitschrift für Kunstgeschichte* 56 (1993): 555, note 6. See also Drexler, ed., *The Mies van der Rohe Archive*, 1:34–39, and Schulze, ed., *The Mies van der Rohe Archive: Supplementary Drawings*, 5:7–8.
45. There are family photographs documenting the Werner House in the Bauhaus-Archiv, Berlin.
46. Behrens, "Der moderne Garten," p. 9.
47. This idea was first suggested to me by Fernando Quesada. On Adolphe Appia see Marco De Michelis, "Gesamtkunstwerk Hellerau," in Werner Durth, ed., *Entwurf zur Moderne. Hellerau: Stand Ort Bestimmung* (Stuttgart: Deutsche Verlags Anstalt, 1996), pp. 33 ff, and Richard C. Beacham, De Michelis, Martin Dreier, et al., *Adolphe Appia ou le renouveau de l'esthétique théâtrale: Dessins et esquisses de décors* (Lausanne: Éditions Payot, 1992).
48. See, e.g., Johannes van der Wolk, *De Kröllers en hun architecten*, exh. cat. (Otterlo: Rijksmuseum Kröller-Müller, 1992). On that exhibition see Sergio Polano, "Rose-Shaped, like an Open Hand. Helene Kröller-Müller's House," *Rassegna* 15 (December 1993): 18–47, and Polano, "I Kröller e i loro architetti. Spiritus et Materia Unum," *Domus*, January 1993, pp. 48–53. See also Rem Koolhaas, "The House That Mies Made," *ANY* 1 (March–April 1994): 14–15, and Koolhaas, *SMLXL* (New York: Monacelli, 1994).

49. Westheim, "Schinkel und die Gegenwart," *Der Baumeister* 11 (January 1913): B83.
50. Mies, "A Tribute to Frank Lloyd Wright," *College Art Journal* 6, no. 1 (Autumn 1946): 42.
51. Schinkel, quoted in Goerd Peschken, *Karl Friedrich Schinkel: Das architektonische Lehrbuch* (Munich: Deutscher Kunstverlag, 1979), p. 19, and in Bergdoll, *Schinkel*, p. 114.
52. See "Ein Landhaus in Neu-Babelsberg," *Innen-Dekoration* 31 (1920): 182–98; Drexler, ed., *The Mies van der Rohe Archive*, 1:40–44; and the report on the restoration of the house prepared by Winfried Brenne, in the Mies van der Rohe Archive, The Museum of Modern Art, New York.
53. See Elizabeth Urbig, letter to Jörg Limberg, December 9, 1990, in Brenne's restoration report. The garden was denatured in 1961, when the Berlin Wall was constructed across it. (The Griebnitzsee marked the boundary between East and West Germany.)
54. See Schulze, *A Critical Biography*, p. 77.
55. Urbig, letter to Limberg, in Brenne's restoration report.
56. On the Gilly/Schinkel revival see Neumeyer, "Eine neue Welt entschleiert sich, von Friedrich Gilly zu Mies van der Rohe," in *Friedrich Gilly 1772–1800 und die Privatgesellschaft junger Architekten* (Berlin: Verlag Willmuth Arenhövel, 1984), pp. 41–64, and my forthcoming article "Mies and Schinkel: Nature and Consciousness in the Modern House," in S. M. Peik, ed., *Karl Friedrich Schinkel: Aspekte seines Werks* (Stuttgart: Axel Menges, 2001).
57. These drawings are in the Stadtarchiv, Potsdam; two of them are published in Schink, *Mies van der Rohe*, p. 73, figs. 46 and 47.
58. A drawing for the terraces at the Urbig House was long thought to pertain to the Wolf House, and was published as a Wolf House drawing in Drexler, ed., *The Mies van der Rohe Archive*, 2:121, no. 30.76; it was Lars Scharnholz who first correctly identified it. The pedestal is absent from this drawing, making it possible that both statue and pedestal were added after Mies's initial design. In fact the gardens were laid out only after Mies had left the project, on being inducted into the army. To my knowledge, the statue's popularity in the period has yet to be studied: it was also used, for instance, in the gardens of the Darmstadt artists' colony, around 1901.
59. See Meier Gräfe, memorandum for Mrs. Kröller, November 1912. The Kröller-Müller file, the Mies van der Rohe Archive.
60. Mies, letter to Walter Dexel, 1924. Box 1, File D, Early Correspondence, 1921–40, Mies van der Rohe Papers, Manuscript Division, Library of Congress, Washington, D.C.
61. For property that Mies tried to acquire in Potsdam in those very years; see Tegethoff, *The Villas and Country Houses*, pp. 33–34.
62. Mies, "Bauen," *G: Material zur elementaren Gestaltung* no. 2 (September 1923): 1. Eng. trans. from Neumeyer, *The Artless Word*, p. 243.
63. Mies, "Office Building," *G* no. 1 (July 1923): 3. Eng. trans. from Neumeyer, *The Artless Word*, p. 241.
64. Mies, letter to Walter Jackstein, November 14, 1923. Box 1, File J, Early Correspondence, Mies van der Rohe Papers, Library of Congress. See also Neumeyer, *The Artless Word*, p. 108.
65. Mies, "Was wäre Beton, was Stahl, ohne Spiegelglas?," prospectus for the Verein Deutscher Spiegelglas-Fabriken (Union of German plate glass manufacturers), unpublished, March 13, 1933. Mies van der Rohe Papers, Library of Congress. Eng. trans. modified from Neumeyer, *The Artless Word*, p. 314.
66. Curiously, however, there is no interior study for the Concrete Country House, nor even any evidence that a floor plan ever existed.
67. See Tegethoff, *The Villas and Country Houses*, p. 33.
68. On Wright's impact on Mies see Eva-Maria Amberger, *Sergius Ruegenberg, Architekt zwischen Mies van der Rohe und Hans Scharoun* (Berlin: Berlinische Galerie, 2000), esp. pp. 33–34.
69. See Kenneth Frampton, "Modernism and Tradition in the Work of Mies van der Rohe," in John Zukowsky, ed., *Mies Reconsidered: His Career, Legacy and Disciples*, exh. cat. (Chicago: The Art Institute of Chicago, 1986), pp. 35–53.
70. As Tegethoff notes in *The Villas and Country Houses*, p. 37, the elevation and the plan do not fully correspond, and both surviving copies of the plan, that at The Museum of Modern Art and that at the Mannheim Kunsthalle, are prints cut down from an originally larger sheet.
71. Tegethoff, "On the Development of the Conception of Space in the Works of Mies van der Rohe," *Daidalos* 13 (September 15, 1984): 116.
72. Westheim, "Mies van der Rohe: Entwicklung eines Architekten," *Das Kunstblatt* 11, no. 2 (February 1927): 57–58.
73. Ibid.
74. When Mies instructed Ruegenberg to discard unneeded drawings sometime in the mid-1920s, he held on to the construction detail for the Kempner House *Blumenfenster*.
75. Christine and Bärbel Wolf, daughters of Erich Wolf, in an interview conducted on February 20, 1999, for Scharnholz, to whom I am grateful for making available a transcript.
76. Before commissioning Robert Mallet-Stevens and Gabriel Guévrékian to develop his garden, the Comte de Noailles first contacted Mies, in 1924. See Dorothée Imbert, *The Modernist Garden in France* (New Haven: Yale University Press, 1993), p. 130 and p. 233, note 30.
77. On Farkas Molnár see Mader, *Gartenkunst des 20. Jahrhunderts*, pp. 86–87; on the Dresden exhibition see Kruse, "Garten, Natur und Landschaftsprospekt: Zur ästhetischen Inszenierung des Aussenraums in den Landhausanlagen Mies van der Rohes," unpublished dissertation, Kunsthistorisches Institut der Freien Universität Berlin, 1994, pp. 48 ff.
78. On *Gestaltung* see Detlef Mertins, Introduction, in Walter Curt Behrendt, *The Victory of the New Building Style* (Santa Monica: The Getty Center for the History of Art and the Humanities, 2000), pp. 46–52.
79. The Krefeld houses are among the best documented of all of Mies's projects. In addition to Tegethoff, *The Villas and Country Houses*, pp. 60–63, and Schulze, *A Critical Biography*, pp. 144–46, see Julian Heynen, *Ein Ort für Kunst/A Place for Art: Ludwig Mies van der Rohe Haus Lange–Haus Esters* (Krefeld: Krefelder Kunstmuseum, 1995), and Edward Ford, *The Details of Modern Architecture* (Cambridge, Mass.: The MIT Press, 1990), pp. 267 ff. On the gardens see the unpublished report by A. Spelberg, "Gartdenkmalpflegerische Bearbeitung der Gärten Haus Lange/Haus Esters," Krefeld, September 1992. I thank Heynen for contributing this document to the Mies van der Rohe Archive.
80. On Siegfried Ebeling's *Der Raum als Membran* see Neumeyer, *The Artless Word*, pp. 171 ff.
81. See Spelberg, "Gartdenkmalpflegerische Bearbeitung der Gärten Haus Lange/Haus Esters."
82. The effect is even more pronounced in family photographs included in Kruse, "Garten, Natur und Landschaftsprospekt," 2:figs. 143–48.
83. Mies, "Lecture," June 19, 1924. Ms. in collection of Dirk Lohan, here quoted from Neumeyer, *The Artless Word*, p. 250.
84. Mies, notebook, 1927–28, in ibid., p. 288.
85. Mies, "The Preconditions of Architectural Work," 1928, in ibid., p. 301.
86. Mies quoting Romano Guardini, notebook, 1927 or 1928, in ibid., p. 89.
87. Ibid., p. 281. A slightly different translation is offered in Guardini, *Letters from Lake Como: Explorations in Technology and the Human Race*, trans. Geoffrey W. Bromiley (Grand Rapids, Mich.: William B. Eerdmans Publishing Company, 1994), p. 10.
88. Neumeyer, *The Artless Word*, pp. 210–13.
89. See, e.g., José Quetglas, "Fear of Glass: The Barcelona Pavilion," and the response to this essay by K. Michael Hays, both in Beatriz Colomina, ed., *Architectureproduction, Revisions* 2 (New York: Princeton Architectural Press, 1988): 152–79 and 240–43 respectively; Robin Evans, "Mies van der Rohe's Paradoxical Symmetries," *AA Files* 19 (Spring 1990): 56–68, reprinted in Evans, *Translations from Drawing to Building and Other Essays* (Cambridge, Mass.: The MIT Press, 1997), pp. 233–77; and Caroline Constant, "The Barcelona Pavilion as Landscape Garden: Modernity and the Picturesque," *AA Files* 20 (1990): 47–54.
90. Walter Genzmer, "Der Deutsche Reichspavilion auf der Internationalen Ausstellung Barcelona," *Die Baugilde* 11 (October 25, 1929): 1654–57, quoted in Tegethoff, *The Villas and Country Houses*, p. 69.
91. Raymond McGrath, *Twentieth Century Houses* (London: Faber & Faber, 1934), p. 168.
92. See Tegethoff, *The Villas and Country Houses*, p. 75.
93. See Père Joan Ravetllat, "The Barcelona Pavilion: The Walls Came First," *Sites* 15 (1986): 36–43.
94. See Amberger, *Sergius Ruegenberg*, p. 35. There is a copy of Ruegenberg's memoir, "Mies van der Rohe, Entwürfe und Bauten von 1908 bis 1939," in the collection of the Berlinische Galerie, BG-AS 3.80.
95. The planters are visible in period photography, notably several aerial views of the fairgrounds, where they appear to be embedded in the top of the wall, and in a later model in the collection of The Museum of Modern Art, where they are shown as attached to the outside face of the wall.
96. See Neumeyer, *The Artless Word*, p. 284.
97. Guardini, quoted in ibid., p. 287 and p. 289, note 62.
98. See Daniela Hammer-Tugendhat and Tegethoff, eds., *Ludwig Mies van der Rohe: The Tugendhat House* (Vienna and New York: Springer, 2000), p. 6.
99. Ibid., p. 31.
100. Grete Tugendhat, "On the Construction of the Tugendhat House," lecture of January 17, 1969, reprinted and trans. in ibid., p. 5.
101. Ibid., translation adapted by author, p. 6.
102. See Tegethoff, *Im Brennpunkt der Moderne: Mies van der Rohe und das Haus Tugendhat in Brünn* (Munich: HypoVereinsbank, 1998).
103. Little is recorded of the career of Grete Müller-Roder, who is known principally because her office stamp appears on a Tugendhat drawing (2.189) in the Mies van der Rohe Archive. Kruse discusses her involvement in the Tugendhat House in "Garten, Natur und Landschaftsprospekt."
104. A young weeping willow has been planted in the most recent garden restoration.
105. Hammer-Tugendhat and Tegethoff, eds., *The Tugendhat House*, p. 19.
106. These are reproduced in ibid.
107. Mies, "The Preconditions of Architectural Work," p. 301.
108. The texts are discussed and the Tugendhats' responses are reprinted in Hammer-Tugendhat and Tegethoff, eds., *The Tugendhat House*, pp. 29–39.
109. Roger Ginsburger and Walter Rizler, "Zweckhaftigkeit und geistige Haltung," *Die Form* 10 (October 1931): 431–37, and quoted and trans. in ibid., pp. 29–30.
110. Grete Tugendhat, *Die Form* 11 (November 15, 1931): 431–37, reprinted in Hammer-Tugendhat and Tegethoff, eds., *The Tugendhat House*, p. 35.
111. Ludwig Hilberseimer, in *Die Form* 6 (June 1931): 438.
112. Grete Tugendhat, *Die Form* 11 (November 15, 1931): 431–37; reprinted in Hammer-Tugendhat and Tegethoff, eds., *The Tugendhat House*, p. 35.
113. Any statement on the first appearance of a specific drawing technique must remain speculative, given the number of Mies's drawings from before 1926 that were discarded. Beginning with the Tugendhat House, one is struck by the sheer number of drawings in Mies's designs, so that the relatively small number for the earlier projects may suggest a significant body of missing sketches.
114. See Randall Ott, "The Horizonal Symmetry of Mies van der Rohe," *Dimensions* 7 (Spring 1993): 113–31.
115. "Programm für den Neubau eines Einfamilienhauses auf dem Grundstück Berlin-Wannsee, Grosse Seestrasse 2–4," 1932. Folder 9, Later German Projects, the Mies van der Rohe Archive.
116. Guardini, *Letters from Lake Como*, pp. 14–15.
117. See Amberger, *Sergius Ruegenberg*, esp. p. 35. The rose-onyx wall in the Tugendhat House is of course also such a wall.
118. Karl Lemke, letter to Mies, April 27, 1932. The Mies van der Rohe Archive. On the Lemke House see Paolo Berdini, "Una piccola casa di Mies," *Casabella* 48, no. 506 (1984): 37–39; Volker Welter, "Landhaus Lemke in Berlin-Hohenschönhausen," *Die Bauwelt* 82 (March 28, 1991): 536; and Wita Noack, *Landhaus Lemke, Mies van der Rohe Haus*, brochure (Berlin: Bezirksamt Hohenschönhausen, Abteilung Jugend, Familie und Kultur, Mies van der Rohe Haus, 1995).
119. On the *Bornimer Kreis* see Mader, *Gartenkunst des 20. Jahrhunderts*, pp. 102–4, and Kruse, "Garten, Natur und Landschaftsprospekt," pp. 82 ff. See also Grit Hottenträger, "New Flowers—New Gardens: Residential Gardens Designed by Karl Foerster, Hermann Mattern, and Herta Hammerbacher (1928–c. 1943)," *Journal of Garden History* 12, no. 3 (July–September 1992): 207–27.
120. This is how Müller-Roder characterized Mies's approach to landscape, according to František Kalivoda, unpublished conversation with Makreta Müllerova of the Arboretum of the School for Rural Economy, Brno, April 1, 1969, quoted in Kruse, "Garten, Natur und Landschaftsprospekt," 1:75.
121. Mies, "Haus H. Magdeburg," *Die Schildgenossen* 14, no. 6 (1935): 514–15. Eng. trans. from Neumeyer, *The Artless Word*, p. 314. The ms. of this text and Mies's letter about it are in the Early Correspondence 1921–40 folder, Mies van der Rohe Papers, Library of Congress.
122. Schwarz, quoted in Neumeyer, *The Artless Word*, pp. 164–65.
123. William H. Jordy seems to be the only writer to realize the connection of the Hubbe design with Schinkel. In a review of the 1986 Mies exhibition at The Museum of Modern Art, he notes, "What the Hubbe House really does is to invoke, in new ways, Schinkel's country villas in Potsdam. It provides a wonderful play between classical equilibrium and asymmetrical layout, between a continuous sense of architectural movement (as of a light breeze moving through the house) and restful balance, between building and nature. This is pure Schinkel." Jordy, "The Return of Mies van der Rohe," *The New Criterion* 4, no. 9 (May 1986): 54.
124. Behrens, "Der moderne Garten," p. 8.
125. Behrens, quoted in Jordy, "The Return of Mies van der Rohe," p. 51.

Detlef Mertins, "Architectures of Becoming: Mies van der Rohe and the Avant-Garde," pp. 106–33

1. The artists and architects included in the *Ausstellung für unbekannte Architekten* were Fidus, Hermann Finsterlin, Jefim Golyscheff, Wenzil Hablik, O. Herzog, César Klein, Gerhard Marcks, Moritz Melzer, Johannes Molzahn, Arnold Topp, and

Oskar Treichel. Statements by Walter Gropius, Bruno Taut, and Adolf Behne were published in the accompanying leaflet (Berlin: Arbeitsrat für Kunst, 1919), Eng. trans. Michael Bullock as "Gropius/Taut/Behne: New Ideas on Architecture," in Ulrich Conrads, ed., *Programs and Manifestoes on 20th-Century Architecture* (Cambridge, Mass.: The MIT Press, 1970), pp. 46–48.
2. Gropius, in ibid. Taut expressed similar thoughts in the leaflet.
3. According to Mies, in an interview with Conrads and Horst Eifler in Berlin in 1966, recorded on the album *Mies in Berlin* (Bauwelt Archiv 1). There is a translation of the transcript, titled "German Record 1966, Berlin," in Box 62, Interviews, Mies van der Rohe Papers, Library of Congress, Washington, D.C. Mies's rejection by Gropius was noted by Sandra Honey in her "Mies in Germany," in Frank Russell, ed., *Mies van der Rohe: European Works* (London: Academy Editions, and New York: St. Martin's Press, 1986), p. 16.
4. Kurt Gerstenberg, *Der Cicerone*, 1919, pp. 255–57.
5. Behne, "Werkstattbesuche: Jefim Golyscheff," *Der Cicerone* 11, no. 22 (1919): 722–26.
6. Behne, *Die Wiederkehr der Kunst* (Leipzig: Kurt Wolff, 1919), p. 38.
7. Behne also admired Paul Klee, Franz Stuckenberg, Carl Mense, and Topp.
8. The Crystal Chain correspondence, initiated by Bruno Taut with a group of likeminded artists and architects, dates from November 24, 1919, to December 24, 1920. Taut's *Alpine Architektur* and *Die Stadtkrone* were published in 1919, his *Auflösung der Städte* and *Weltbaumeister* the following year.
9. See László Moholy-Nagy, *Von Material zu Architektur* (Munich: Albert Langen, 1929), Eng. trans. Daphne M. Hoffman and enlarged as *The New Vision* (New York: George Wittenborn, 1947).
10. Gropius, "Glasbau," *Die Bauzeitung* 23 (1926): 20, 159–62, reprinted in Hartmut Probst and Christian Schädlich, eds., *Walter Gropius*, vol. 3, *Ausgewählte Schriften* (Berlin: Ernst & Sohn, 1988), pp. 103–6.
11. Theo van Doesburg, "Vernieuwingspogingen der Ooostenrijksche en Duitsche architectuur," *Het Bouwbedrijf* 2, no. 6 (June 1925): 225–27, Eng. trans. Charlotte I. Loeb and Arthur L. Loeb as "The Significance of Glass: Toward Transparent Structures," in *Theo van Doesburg on European Architecture: Complete Essays from Het Bouwbedrijf 1924–31* (Basel: Birckhäuser, 1990), pp. 63–69.
12. Van Doesburg, quoted in A. Elzas, "Theo van Doesburg," *De 8 en Opbouw* 6, 1935, p. 174, Eng. trans. Nancy J. Troy, *The de Stijl Environment* (Cambridge, Mass.: The MIT Press, 1983), p. 106.
13. Paul Scheerbart's book *Glasarchitektur* (Glass architecture, 1914) was included in an exhibition of books accompanying a lecture of Mies's at the Staatliche Kunstgewerbeschule Bremen in 1925. Mies approved the selection of books; see his correspondence with Emilie Bosse of the Staatliche Kunstgewerbeschule Bremen, November 6, 1925–February 1, 1926, together with the book list itself: Box 1, File K, Mies van der Rohe Papers, Library of Congress.
14. The exhibition was not of course the sole reason for the changes in Mies's life, but it may certainly have contributed to his feeling that a change was needed. Gene Summers has recalled that when asked how he had made the leap from neoclassical houses to the skyscraper projects, Mies replied that "he had lots of time when he was in the army to think. He had just gotten back to Berlin where so many things were happening in the arts. I am not sure that these were the exact words, but that was the meaning: he said, 'I knew that I had to get on with it. I had to make this change.'" See Fritz Neumeyer, ed., *Ludwig Mies van der Rohe: Hochhaus am Bahnhof Friedrichstrasse. Dokumentation des Mies-van-der-Rohe-Symposium in der Neuen Nationalgalerie, Berlin* (Tübingen and Berlin: Wasmuth, 1993), p. 46.
15. Before World War I, Mies had socialized with the artistic circle of his future wife, Ada Bruhn, in Hellerau, Dresden. Bruhn was studying rhythmic movement with Emile Jaques-Dalcroze and was friends with Mary Wigman, who became a leading modern dancer, and Erna Hoffmann, later the wife of Hans Prinzhorn, whose psychoanalytic approach to the art of the insane would come to interest Mies. In 1915, Mies became friends with the sculptor Wilhelm Lehmbruck. See Franz Schulze, *A Critical Biography*, pp. 70–71 and 80–81.
16. The *Zehnerring*—later just the *Ring*—emerged out of meetings hosted by Mies and Hugo Häring in 1923 and 1924, when Häring was sharing Mies's studio. Initially an informal group of architects, in 1926 it expanded its membership in the hopes of achieving greater influence.
17. Mies, "On Form in Architecture," *Die Form* 2, no. 2 (1927): 59, Eng. trans. in Neumeyer, *The Artless Word*, p. 257.
18. See the Mies biography in the "Biographien" section of Helga Kliemann, *Die Novembergruppe* (Berlin: Gebruder Mann Verlag, 1969), n.p.
19. See, for instance, Mies, letter to Peter Behrens, May 1, 1924. Box 1, File N, Mies van der Rohe Papers, Library of Congress.
20. See Schulze, *A Critical Biography*, p. 104. The first use of the new name appears to have been by Max Berg in *Die Bauwelt* of May 1922. Mies continued to use the umlaut in Miës in the 1930s, and his name appears as such in a few American publications. Mies formed an affinity for Dutch architecture during his stay in the Netherlands in 1912 to work on the Kröller-Müller Villa Project.
21. Richard Huelsenbeck, "What Did Expressionism Want?," in Huelsenbeck, ed., *Dada Almanac*, trans. Malcolm Green (London: Atlas Press, 1993), p. 44.
22. Huelsenbeck, "Der neue Mensch," *Neue Jugend* 1 (1917): 2.
23. Huelsenbeck, "What Did Expressionism Want?," p. 44.
24. "Reversal of values, changes in point of view, name, and concept, result in the other view, the next faith. Dada, court jester in this kingdom, plays ball with paradoxes and makes the atmosphere free and easy." Oskar Schlemmer, "Manifesto for the First Bauhaus Exhibition, 1923," leaflet, Eng. trans. in Conrads, ed., *Programs and Manifestoes*, pp. 69–70.
25. See Timothy O. Benson, *Raoul Hausmann and Berlin Dada* (Ann Arbor: UMI Research Press, 1987), p. 23.
26. Ibid., p. 57. Hausmann understood seeing as an enchanted process, symbolically and magically grasping, condensing, and fixing humanity's relations to and perceptions of the world.
27. Carl Einstein, *Negerplastik* (Leipzig: Verlag der weissen Bücher, 1915), p. xxi, Eng. trans. in ibid., p. 39.
28. For an account of Club Dada as a "Scheerbart society" see Hanne Bergius, ed., *Das Lachen Dadas: Die Berliner Dadaisten und ihre Aktionen* (Giessen: Anabas Verlag, 1989), pp. 42–47. Much of the misunderstanding of Scheerbart's reception among artists in this period stems from the ambiguity of "Expressionism" as an art-historical category. Paul Fechner's book *Der Expressionismus* (Munich: R. Piper, 1914) brought the term into use to designate a broad array of modern painting, distinguished only from Cubism and Futurism. Thus, when Herwath Walden called Scheerbart "the first Expressionist" ("Paul Scheerbart," *Der Sturm* 6 [1915]: 96), he established an interpretation that was unaffected by the subsequent formation of Berlin Dada and its claim to the poet's legacy.
29. On Ludwig Hilberseimer see Richard Pommer, *In the Shadow of Mies: Ludwig Hilberseimer, Architect, Educator, and Urban Planner* (Chicago: The Art Institute of Chicago, 1988), p. 54.
30. Hilberseimer, "Paul Scheerbart und die Architekten," *Das Kunstblatt* 3, no. 9 (September 1919): 271–74.
31. In 1929, Hilberseimer reiterated his rationalist interpretation of Scheerbart's vision and claimed that the poet had anticipated the widespread use of glass in building. See his "Glas Architektur," *Die Form* 4, no. 19 (October 1929): 521–22, a review of Arthur Korn's *Glas im Bau und als Gebrauchsgegenstand* of 1926 and Konrad Werner Schultze's *Glas in der Architektur der Gegenwart* of 1929.
32. Hausmann, "Présentismus," in *Raoul Hausmann: Texte bis 1933*, ed. Michael Erlhoff (Munich: Texte + Kritik, 1982), 2:23–26. Author's translation.
33. Hausmann, "Lob des Konventionellen," in ibid., p. 49.
34. See Hausmann, Hans Arp, Ivan Puni, and Moholy-Nagy, "Aufruf zur elementaren Kunst," *De Stijl* 4, no. 10 (October 1921): 156. Eng. trans. as "Manifesto of Elemental Art" in Krisztina Passuth, *Moholy-Nagy* (London: Thames & Hudson, 1985), p. 286.
35. Richter suggests that the meeting occurred after his "Präludium" (1919–20) but before he finished his first film, in 1921.
36. During one eleven-day visit to Berlin, van Doesburg met Taut, Gropius, Fréd Forbát, Hausmann, Hannah Höch, and Kurt Schwitters. See Bernd Finkeldey, "Hans Richter and the Constructivist International," in Stephen C. Foster, ed., *Hans Richter: Activism, Modernism, and the Avant-Garde* (Cambridge, Mass.: The MIT Press, 1998), pp. 96–99.
37. Reproduced in Paul Westheim, "Mies van der Rohe: Entwicklung eines Architekten," *Das Kunstblatt* 11, no. 2 (February 1927): 55.
38. See for instance J. J. P. Oud's warehouse in Purmerend (1918), published in *De Stijl* 3, no. 11 (November 1920), or his Kallenbach House (1921). For van Doesburg's course at Weimar see Evert van Straaten, *Theo van Doesburg: Painter and Architect* (The Hague: SDU Publishers, 1988), pp. 105–7.
39. Westheim, "Entwicklung eines Architekten," p. 55.
40. Richter, *Köpfe und Hinterköpfe* (Zurich: Der Arche, 1967), p. 70. Author's translation.
41. The ideal of the *Gesamtkunstwerk* was initially formulated by Richard Wagner in relation to opera, in his essay "Kunstwerk der Zukunft" of 1850–51. Taken up in design culture around 1900, it was reiterated by Gropius in the early years of the Bauhaus. See Harald Szeemann, *Der Hang zum Gesamtkunstwerk*, exh. cat. (Zurich: Kunsthaus Zürich and Verlag Sauerländer, 1983).
42. Richter, *Köpfe und Hinterköpfe*, p. 69.
43. Mies, n.t., *Frühlicht* 1, no. 4 (1922): 122–24, Eng. trans. in Neumeyer, *The Artless Word*, p. 240.
44. Ibid.
45. In this Mies followed writers such as August Endell, *Die Schönheit der Großstadt* (Stuttgart: Strecker & Schröder, 1908), and Alfred Gotthold Meyer, *Eisenbauten* (Esslingen: Paul Neff, 1907).
46. Sergius Ruegenberg worked for Mies from 1925 until 1927 (and again from the end of 1928 to 1931). It has accordingly been assumed that his sketch must date from 1925, but he himself dates it to 1924. Dietrich Neumann has dated it 1923–24, but provides no supporting evidence. See Eva-Maria Amberger, *Sergius Ruegenberg, Architekt zwischen Mies van der Rohe und Hans Scharoun*, exh. cat. (Berlin: Berlinische Galerie, 2000), pp. 33–39 and 220–21, and Neumann, "Three Early Projects by Mies van der Rohe," *Perspecta* 27 (1992): 97.
47. This is certainly implied in the classic monographs by Philip Johnson, Hilberseimer, and Peter Carter, as well as by the Mies retrospective at The Museum of Modern Art, New York, in 1947. Summers also recalls that in 1965, Mies asked him to work on the charcoal drawing of the Friedrichstrasse Skyscraper Project "to darken the blacks and to lighten the reflections." While Summers did not alter the drawing, he says, this incident does speak to the extent that the drawing and project remained important to Mies. See Neumeyer, ed., *Hochhaus am Bahnhof Friedrichstrasse*, p. 45.
48. See Marco De Michelis, "Modernity and Reform: Heinrich Tessenow and the Institut Dalcroze at Hellerau," *Perspecta* 26 (1990): 143–70.
49. Gropius, *Internationale Architektur*, Bauhaus Bücher (Passau: Passavia Druckerei, 1925), p. 49. Mies's perspective of the Concrete Office Building Project also appears here.
50. See Troy, *The de Stijl Environment*, pp. 200–201.
51. See van Doesburg, letter to Mies, 28 July, 1923. Correspondence 1-V, Mies van der Rohe Papers, Library of Congress.
52. Mies, letter to van Doesburg, August 27, 1923, in ibid.
53. In Mies, letter to van Doesburg, September 10, 1923, Mies records sending the two photographs of the skyscraper model; in Mies, letter to van Doesburg, October 8, 1923, he records the other items sent. Both in ibid.
54. See van Doesburg and Cornelis van Eesteren, "Vers une construction collective," *De Stijl* 6, nos. 6–7 (June/July 1924): 89–92.
55. See Dawn Ades, *Photomontage* (London: Thames & Hudson, 1986), p. 104.
56. Hans Prinzhorn, letter to Mies, and Richter, untitled, *G: Material zur elementaren Gestaltung* no. 3 (June 1924): n.p.
57. Eng. trans. in Neumeyer, *The Artless Word*, p. 242.
58. Lissitzky, "Proun," *De Stijl* 5, no. 6 (June 1923). In German. Eng. trans. as "Proun. Not world visions, BUT—world reality, 1920," in Sophie Lissitzky-Küppers, *El Lissitzky: Life-Letters-Texts* (London: Thames & Hudson, 1968), pp. 347–48.
59. Raoul H. Francé, "Die sieben technischen Grundformen der Natur," *Das Kunstblatt* 7, no. 1 (January 1923): 5–11. The article is excerpted from Francé, *Die Pflanze als Erfinder* (Stuttgart: Kosmos, 1920), Eng. trans. as *Plants as Inventors* (Stuttgart: Jung & Son, 1923).
60. See Lissitzky-Küppers, *El Lissitzky: Life-Letters-Texts*, pp. 45–46.
61. See Oliver Árpád István Botar, *Prolegomena to the Study of Biomorphic Modernism: Biocentrism, László Moholy-Nagy's "New Vision" and Ernó Kállai's Bioromantik*, Ph.D. dissertation, University of Toronto, 1998.
62. See Schulze, *A Critical Biography*, pp. 17–18.
63. I am indebted to Botar, *Prolegomena*, p. 189, for this summary of vitalist concepts.
64. In addition to the journals discussed here, the curvilinear skyscraper was also shown in the radically *sachlich*, antiaesthetic journal *ABC* (nos. 3–4, p. 4) in 1925. The year before, *ABC* had published four images with captions, most likely by Lissitzky, in a way that bears on the link between Mies's Glass Skyscraper Project and the biotechnics of Francé. Entitled "Gestalten-Form," the images included a photographic enlargement of a plant stem as demonstrative of a structure resistant to wind, as well as a photograph of the steel frame of a Baltimore high-rise building under construction. Mies's skyscraper, which proposed to clad such a structural cage in glass sheets, may by implication be understood here as analogous with the plant stem.
65. See Mies, "Inaugural Address as Director at Armour Institute of Technology," in Neumeyer, *The Artless Word*, pp. 316–17: "In its simplest form architecture is entirely rooted in practical considerations, but it can reach up through all degrees of value to the highest realm of spiritual existence, into the realm of the sensuously apprehendable, and into the sphere of pure art."
66. Alfred H. Barr, Jr., *Cubism and Abstract Art*, exh. cat. (New York: The Museum of Modern Art, 1936), p. 157.
67. See Henry-Russell Hitchcock, Jr., *Painting toward Architecture* (New York: Duell, Sloan and Pearce, 1948), p. 34, and Hellmuth Sting, *Der Kubismus*

und seine Einwirkung auf die Wegbereiter der Modernen Architektur, Ph.D. dissertation, Rheinisch-Westfälischen Technischen Hochschule Aachen, 1965. The comparison has in recent years been questioned and the references extended to include constructivists Lissitzky and Richter; see Jean-Louis Cohen, *Mies van der Rohe* (London: E & FN Spon, 1996), pp. 36–37, and Bruno Reichlin, "Mies' Raumgestaltung: Vermutung zu einer Genealogie und Inspirationsquellen," *Das Haus Tugendhat: Ludwig Mies van der Rohe. Brünn 1930*, exh. cat. (Vienna: Anton Pustet, 1999), pp. 53–62.

68. Johnson, "House at New Canaan, Connecticut," *Architectural Review*, September 1950, pp. 152–59.
69. In 1923, van Doesburg revised these illustrations for basic elements to a matrix of colored rectangles for painting and one of his Counter Construction works for architecture, retaining the earlier prisms only for sculpture. See van Doesburg, *Grundbegriffe der neuen gestaltenden Kunst*, Bauhaus Bücher (Frankfurt am Main: Oehmsdruck, 1925, reprint ed. Mainz: Florian Kupferberg, 1966), plates 1–3.
70. In his Design for a Refreshment Building (1922), van Doesburg himself interpreted the basic blocks of architecture not in an urban ensemble but in a single aggregative building composition. See van Straaten, *Theo van Doesburg*, p. 104.
71. Although Mies's personal library in Chicago did not include Camillo Sitte's *Der Städte-Bau nach seinen künstlerischen Grundsätzen* (*City Planning according to Artistic Principles*, 1889), it did include A. E. Brinkmann's modernist revision, *Platz und Monument* (Berlin: E. Wasmuth, 1912), and the German translation of Raymond Unwin's Sittesque treatise on garden city design, *Grundlagen des Städtebaues: Eine Anleitung zum entwerfen stadtebaulicher Anlagen* (Berlin: O. Baumgartel, 1922).
72. For Sitte's proto-"de Stijl" plan see George R. Collins and Christiane Crasemann Collins, *Camillo Sitte: The Birth of Modern City Planning* (New York: Rizzoli, 1986), with a translation of *City Planning according to Artistic Principles*, fig. 109, "Modified Rectangular Layout of City Blocks."
73. See van Doesburg, "Abstracte Filmbeelding," *De Stijl* 4, no. 5 (May 1921): 71–75, and "Licht-en Tijdbeelding (Film)," *De Stijl* 6, no. 5 (May 1923): 58–62 (two scroll works by Gräff were also included in the later issue), and Richter, "Prinzipielles zur Beweungskunst," *De Stijl* 4, no. 7 (July 1921): 109–12, "Film," *De Stijl* 5, no. 6 (June 1922): 91–92, and "Film," *De Stijl* 6, no. 5 (May 1923): 65–66. Van Doesburg continued to be concerned with film and published the follow-up article "Film a abstrakce, Film und Abstraktion" in *Fronta* (Brno), 1927, pp. 109–10, and the summary statement "Film als reine Gestaltung," *Die Form* 4, no. 10 (1929): 241–48.
74. See Linda Dalrymple Henderson, *The Fourth Dimension and Non-Euclidean Geometry in Modern Art* (Princeton: at the University Press, 1983).
75. Richter, "Film," *De Stijl* 6, no. 5 (May 1923): 65–66.
76. On van Doesburg's relationship with Oud and de Boer, see Troy, *The de Stijl Environment*, p. 91.
77. See Yve-Alain Bois, *Painting as Model* (Cambridge, Mass.: The MIT Press, 1990), p. 106.
78. Troy, *The de Stijl Environment*, pp. 112–13. Troy cites van Doesburg, "Tot een beeldende architectuur," *De Stijl* 6, nos. 6–7 (1924): 81. On van Doesburg and the fourth dimension see Joost Baljeu, "The Fourth Dimension in Neoplasticism," *Form* 9 (1969): 6–14, and Henderson, *The Fourth Dimension*, pp. 300–338.
79. Richter, "Film," *De Stijl* 6, no. 5 (May 1923): 65–66.
80. Gilles Deleuze, *Cinema 1: The Movement-Image*, trans. Hugh Tomlinson and Barbara Habberjam (Minneapolis: University of Minnesota Press, 1986), pp. 54–55. The distinction between Richter's rhythmic and Sergei Eisenstein's dialectical conceptions of montage is apt despite the close personal and professional relationship between the two men, described in Marion von Hofacker, "Richter's Films and the Role of the Radical Artist, 1927–1941," in Foster, ed., *Hans Richter*, pp. 143–47. See also Estera Milman, "Hans Richter in America: Traditional Avant-Garde Values/Shifting Sociopolitical Realities," and von Hofacker, "Chronology," in the same volume, pp. 163–66 and 260 respectively.
81. Lissitzky's Proun series and accompanying text are featured in *De Stijl* 6, no. 5 (May 1923), pp. 58–62.
82. Mies's strategy with respect to color is more comparable to that of the architect Oud than to that of the painter van Doesburg. Oud had in fact parted company with van Doesburg over color: where van Doesburg wanted to dematerialize Oud's volumes by applying color to their surfaces, Oud preferred to maintain the integrity of his volumes and to achieve color affects through the properties of the materials themselves.
83. Mies, letter to Richard Döcker, May 27, 1926. 12.1.B, the Mies van der Rohe Archive, The Museum of Modern Art, New York.
84. Richter, "Der neue Baumeister," *Qualität* 4, nos. 1–2 (January–February 1925): 3–9. Richter's comment appears in the caption for fig. 7.
85. The cover of the issue showed a Man Ray photogram titled *New Landscape*.
86. The event, called "Der Absolute Film," was held on May 3, 1925, at the UFA Filmpalast, Berlin. It featured Ludwig Hirschfeld-Mack's *Reflektorische Farbenspiele*, Richter's *Film ist Rhythmus*, Eggeling's *Symphonie Diagonal*, Walther Ruttmann's *Opus 2, 3, and 4*, Fernand Léger's and Dudley Murphy's *Ballet mécanique*, and René Clair's and Francis Picabia's *Entr'acte*. See Foster, ed., *Hans Richter*, p. 260. Mies's involvement in the financing for the screening of Léger's film is suggested in an undated letter from George Anteil, addressed "Dear Friend," in Box 1, Correspondence File W, Mies van der Rohe Papers, Library of Congress.
87. Henri Bergson, *Evolution créatrice*, 1911, Eng. trans. Arthur Mitchell as *Creative Evolution* (Mineola, NY: Dover, 1998), pp. 304–8 and 329.
88. Lissitzky, "Nasci," Eng. trans. in Lissitzky-Küppers, *El Lissitzky*, p. 351.
89. The canonical experimental projects were defined by Johnson as the two glass skyscrapers, the Concrete Office Building, the Concrete Country House, and the Brick Country House. See Johnson, *Mies van der Rohe*, exh. cat. (New York: The Museum of Modern Art, 1947), pp. 21–34.
90. See Wolf Tegethoff, *The Villas and Country Houses*, pp. 66–68. See also Richter, *Orchestration der Farbe*, 1923, serigraph, reproduced in Foster, ed., *Hans Richter*, color plate opposite p. 149.
91. The photograph, by Jan Kamman, shows Brinkmann and van der Vlugt's van Nelle factory, Rotterdam.
92. Moholy-Nagy, *Von Material zu Architektur*, p. 236.
93. Häring refers to film as "light architecture" in *G* nos. 5–6 (April 1926). Hilberseimer applies the same phrase to Mies's Glass Skyscraper Project in *G* no. 4 (March 1926).
94. See Walter Benjamin, "Surrealism: The Last Snapshot of the European Intelligentsia," *Selected Writings*, vol. 2, *1927–1934* (Cambridge, Mass., and London: Harvard University Press, 1999), pp. 207–21.
95. Tristan Tzara, "Die Photographie von der Kehrseite, 1922," trans. Benjamin, *G* no. 3 (June 1924): n.p.
96. Richter, *Filmgegner von Heute, Filmfreunde von Morgen* (Berlin: Verlag Hermann Reckendorf, 1929), p. 89.
97. Ibid., p. 93.
98. See note 16, and De Michelis, "Modernity and Reform."
99. Van Doesburg presented this idea frequently in lectures and published an early version of it in the philosophical journal *Het Tijdschrift voor Wijsbegeerte* in 1919. It also appears in his book *Grundbegriffe der neuen gestaltenden Kunst*, of 1925.
100. Clair, "Rhythmus," *G* nos. 5–6 (April 1926): n.p.
101. Siegfried Ebeling, *Der Raum als Membran* (Dessau: C. Dünnhaupt, 1926), p. 3. Mies's copy of this book is heavily annotated. See Neumeyer, *The Artless Word*, pp. 171 ff.
102. See Michael Blackwood's film *Mies* (1987).
103. See John Peter, untitled typescript of interview with Mies, New York, 1955, p. 4. Box 62, Interviews with Mies van der Rohe, Mies van der Rohe Papers, Library of Congress.
104. Mies, letter to S. Adam firm, July 2, 1928. Later German Projects, Folder 1, the Mies van der Rohe Archive. See also Neumeyer, *The Artless Word*, p. 303.
105. Lissitzky, "Nasci," Eng. trans. in Lissitzky-Küppers, *El Lissitzky*, p. 351.
106. Bergson, *Creative Evolution*, p. 128.
107. Ibid., pp. 128–29. Mies's copy of this book is in the Mies van der Rohe Collection, Special Collections Room, of the main library of the University of Illinois Chicago Circle.

Wolf Tegethoff, "Catching the Spirit: Mies's Early Work and the Impact of the 'Prussian Style,'" pp. 134–51

1. On Mies's youth and background see Franz Schulze, *A Critical Biography*. Wolf Tegethoff, "Ludwig Mies van der Rohe," in Wolfgang Ribbe and Wolfgang Schäche, eds., *Baumeister, Architekten, Stadtplaner: Biographien zur baulichen Entwicklung Berlins* (Berlin: Stapp Verlag, 1987), pp. 467–88, gives some additional information.
2. Peter Ruhnau, *Das Frankenberger Viertel in Aachen* (Cologne: Rheinland-Verlag, 1976), p. 46.
3. "Das neue Rathaus in Rixdorf bei Berlin," *Deutsche Bauzeitung* 43 (1909): 621–22, 637–38, 673–74.
4. See Sonja Günther, *Bruno Paul, 1874–1968* (Berlin: Gebr. Mann Verlag, 1992), and Alfred Ziffer, ed., *Bruno Paul: Deutsche Raumkunst und Architektur zwischen Jugendstil und Moderne* (Munich: Klinckhardt & Biermann, 1992).
5. See Fritz Neumeyer, *The Artless Word*, pp. 36–50, and Neumeyer, "Space for Reflection: Block versus Pavilion," in Schulze, ed., *Mies van der Rohe: Critical Essays* (New York: The Museum of Modern Art, 1989), pp. 148–71, in particular pp. 150–57. On the circle of Alois Riehl see Neumeyer, "Mies's First Project: Revisiting the Atmosphere at Klösterli," in the present volume.
6. L. Deubner, "German Architecture and Decoration," *The Studio Year Book of Decorative Art* (London: The Studio, 1911), pp. 147–56, in particular p. 150, fig. p. 178; "Architekt Ludwig Mies: Villa des Herrn Geheime Regierungsrat Prof. Dr. Riehl in Neu-Babelsberg," *Moderne Bauformen* 9 (1910): 42–48; and Anton Jaumann, "Vom künstlerischen Nachwuchs," *Innen-Dekoration* 21 (1910): 265–72.
7. See Rudolf Fahrner, ed., *Paul Thiersch: Leben und Werk* (Berlin: Gebr. Mann Verlag, 1970), p. 27.
8. See Fritz Hoeber, *Peter Behrens* (Munich: G. Müller u. E. Rentsch, 1913); Tilmann Buddensieg and Henning Rogge, *Industriekultur: Peter Behrens und die AEG, 1907–1914* (Berlin: Gebr. Mann Verlag, 1979); and Stanford Anderson, *Peter Behrens and a New Architecture for the Twentieth Century* (Cambridge, Mass.: The MIT Press, 2000).
9. The date was probably May or June 1911, since according to a police document of October 23, 1937, Mies was listed as a resident of Aachen from June 1910 to May 1911. Mies van der Rohe Papers, Manuscript Division, Library of Congress, Washington, D.C.
10. See Anderson, *Peter Behrens*, p. 300, note 25.
11. See note 9.
12. The competition was covered in virtually all of the German newspapers and in the professional press. The present account is based on articles in vols. 43–45 (1909–11) of the *Deutsche Bauzeitung*. See also Max Dessoir and Hermann Muthesius, *Das Bismarck-Nationaldenkmal: Eine Erörterung des Wettbewerbes* (Jena: E. Diederichs Verlag, 1912), and Max Schmid, ed., *Hundert Entwürfe aus dem Wettbewerb für das Bismarck-National-Denkmal auf der Elisenhöhe bei Bingerbrück-Bingen, hrsg. im Auftrag der Denkmal-Ausschüsse* (Düsseldorf, 1911). The latter may be termed the official publication of the competition; fig. 77 shows entry no. 216, titled *Deutschlands Dank* (Germany's gratitude), and names L[udwig] and E[wald] Mies as authors.
13. For the enduring impact of the Orianda project on Mies's oeuvre see Tegethoff, "Orianda–Berlin: Das Vorbild Schinkel im Werk Mies van der Rohes," *Zeitschrift des Deutschen Vereins für Kunstwissenschaft* 38 (1981): 174–84.
14. [Arthur] Moeller van den Bruck, *Der Preussische Stil* (Munich: Piper & Co. Verlag, 1916), quoted from the revised edition of 1922, pp. 144–45.
15. See Neumeyer, "Aus Freude an Schinkel: Das Haus Perls in Berlin-Zehlendorf von Ludwig Mies van der Rohe," in Günther and Dietrich Worbs, eds., *Architektur-Experimente in Berlin und anderswo* (Berlin: Konopka, 1989), pp. 172–81.
16. 26.8, the Mies van der Rohe Archive, The Museum of Modern Art, New York.
17. 26.33, the Mies van der Rohe Archive.
18. See Neumeyer, "Aus Freude an Schinkel," p. 177.
19. See Schulze, *A Critical Biography*, pp. 58–64, and Johannes van der Wolk, *De Kröllers en hun architecten* (Otterlo: Rijksmuseum Kröller-Müller, 1992), pp. 17–19, 45–46.
20. Salomon van Deventer, letter to Helene Kröller-Müller, August 29, 1911. Original in the possession of Mary van Deventer, German transcript in the Mies van der Rohe Archive.
21. Hoeber, *Peter Behrens*, pp. 200–202, figs. 230–34, and van der Wolk, *De Kröllers*, pp. 14–17, 41–44.
22. Unlike the drawing illustrated in Philip Johnson, *Mies van der Rohe*, exh. cat. (New York: The Museum of Modern Art, 1947), p. 13, where the gallery wing is indeed completely closed, a photograph of the model shows a colonnade on the side facing the courtyard; see the illustrations in van der Wolk, *De Kröllers*, pp. 45–46.
23. With the exception of a rough sketch that Mies drew from memory for his Bauhaus students in around 1930, no floor plan survives. See plate 22, and van der Wolk, *De Kröllers*, p. 46. The sketch is discussed in Schulze, *A Critical Biography*, pp. 61–62.
24. Kröller-Müller, letter to H. P. Bremmer, June 28, 1910, quoted in van Deventer, *Aus Liebe zur Kunst: Das Museum Kröller-Müller* (Cologne: Dumont Schauberg, 1958), p. 51.
25. Kröller-Müller, letter to van Deventer, March 18, 1911, quoted in ibid., p. 53. Mies later stated that he always needed to have a wall at his back; personal communication from Sergius Ruegenberg to the author.
26. Bremmer, quoted in van Deventer, *Aus Liebe zur Kunst*, pp. 70–71. See also Mies's letters to Kröller-Müller of March 13 and April 2, 1913, in the files of the Kröller-Müller Museum, Otterlo.
27. Julius Meier-Graefe, letter to Mies, November 13, 1912. The Mies van der Rohe Archive. Quoted in part in Schulze, *A Critical Biography*, pp. 62–63.
28. Mies, in conversation with Horst Eifler and Ulrich Conrads in October 1964, recorded for RIAS, Berlin, on the record album *Mies in Berlin* (Bauwelt Archiv I, 1966). Whether Mies was referring to Behrens's mock-up, his own, or both in his discussion of the rails is not altogether clear.
29. Mies, letters to Kröller-Müller, March 13 and April 2, 1913.
30. See Schulze, *A Critical Biography*, pp. 70–82 and 94–96. The date of Mies's emigration is sometimes given as 1937; in fact he spent the last part of

that year in the United States, then returned to Germany for four months before emigrating permanently in 1938.

31. See Arnold Schink, *Mies van der Rohe: Beiträge zur ästhetischen Entwicklung der Wohnarchitektur* (Stuttgart: Karl Krämer, 1990), pp. 59–68, and Christiane Kruse, "Haus Werner: Ein ungeliebtes Frühwerk Mies van der Rohes," *Zeitschrift für Kunstgeschichte* 56 (1993): 554–63.
32. This may also have been why, according to Dirk Lohan, Mies did not waste a glance on the Werner House when he visited the neighboring Perls House in 1965; see Schulze, *A Critical Biography*, p. 72.
33. The other one, the obscure Haus an der Heerstrasse of Mies's personal job-list, has recently been identified as the Johann Warnholz House of 1914–15 (destroyed in 1959). See Markus Jager's article "Das Haus Warnholz von Mies van der Rohe (1914–15)," forthcoming in *Zeitschrift für Kunstgeschichte* in 2001.
34. See Schulze, *A Critical Biography*, pp. 80–82.
35. See Renate Petras, "Drei Arbeiten Mies van der Rohes in Potsdam-Babelsberg," *Deutsche Architektur* 23 (1974): 120–21.
36. See *Die Bauwelt* 49 (1958): 1152, and also Hans Vollmer, ed., *Allgemeines Lexikon der bildenden Künstler des XX. Jahrhunderts* (Leipzig: VEB E. A. Seemann, 1961), 5:77.
37. Petras, "Drei Arbeiten Mies van der Rohes in Potsdam-Babelsberg," p. 121.
38. On the restoration see Jager, "Winfried Brenne: Restaurierung Haus Urbig von Ludwig Mies van der Rohe, Potsdam-Neubabelsberg," *DAM* [Deutsches Architekturmuseum, Frankfurt] *Architektur Jahrbuch/Architecture Annual*, 1996, pp. 32–37.
39. This reveals a major deviation from the application drawings of June 1915 (published in Schink, *Beiträge zur ästhetischen Entwicklung der Wohnarchitektur*, pp. 73–74), which show pilasters on all four sides of the building, with double pilasters accentuating the entrance bay and the three center bays on the lake front.
40. For two contemporary photographs of the kitchen see Alexander Koch, ed., *Handbuch neuzeitlicher Wohnungskultur*, vol. 7, *Speise-Zimmer und Küchen* (Darmstadt: Koch, 1920), pp. 176, 177; the illustration on p. 174 shows the pantry of another, still unidentified early Mies building.
41. On Mies's early familiarity with the Wasmuth portfolio see his "Tribute to Frank Lloyd Wright," 1940, *College Art Journal* 6, no. 1 (Autumn 1946): 41–42.
42. See my analysis in Daniela Hammer-Tugendhat and Tegethoff, eds., *Ludwig Mies van der Rohe: The Tugendhat House* (Vienna and New York: Springer, 2000), pp. 73 ff.
43. See Barbara Miller Lane, *Architecture and Politics in Germany, 1918–1945* (Cambridge, Mass.: The MIT Press, 1968).
44. Johnson, *Mies van der Rohe.*
45. Paul Westheim, "Mies van der Rohe: Entwicklung eines Architekten," *Das Kunstblatt* 11, no. 2 (1927): 55–62.

Fritz Neumeyer, "Mies's First Project: Revisiting the Atmosphere at Klösterli," pp. 309–17

1. Fritz Neumeyer, *The Artless Word*, p. 40. Alois Riehl was buried in the cemetery at Klein-Glienicke, near Karl Friedrich Schinkel's palace and its glorious park. The Riehl family grave, plot 122, no longer exists.
2. On May 14, 1925, the firm of Köstner and Gottschalk, Berlin-Wannsee, sent Mies the estimate for a "monument consisting of a base 1.85, 0.45, 0.40, a main stone 1.80, 0.40, 1.00, and an enclosure 2.60 deep, 3.00 wide." As stones "suitable for vines" they suggested Kirchhiem limestone, German travertine, or Krensheim limestone. On June 15, 1925, there followed by messenger "2 samples of travertine with painted letters and the request for a decision on which colors to use." Early Projects #4, the Mies van der Rohe Archive, The Museum of Modern Art, New York.
3. Sofie Riehl, postcard to Mies, June 4, 1925. Early Projects #4, the Mies van der Rohe Archive.
4. Sofie Riehl, postcard to Mies, n.d. Early Projects #4, the Mies van der Rohe Archive. Sofie Riehl died on September 23, 1928.
5. The directory *Wer ist's: Zeitgenossenlexikon* (Leipzig: Hermann A. L. Degener, 1908) lists the Riehls at Von der Heydstrasse 11. The 1914 edition shows them at Kaiserallee 15, the 1922 and 1928 editions at Victoria-Luise Platz 12.
6. Mies, "Inaugural Address as Director of Architecture at Armour Institute of Technology," 1938, in Neumeyer, *The Artless Word*, p. 317.
7. On philosophy at the University of Berlin, see Volker Gerhardt, Reinhart Mehring, and Jana Rindert, *Berliner Geist: Eine Geschichte der Berliner Universitätsphilosophie bis 1946* (Berlin: Akademie Verlag, 1999).
8. Mies, "Baukunst unserer Zeit," Foreword, in Werner Blaser, *Mies van der Rohe: Die Kunst der Struktur* (Zürich and Stuttgart: Birkhäuser, 1965); and Carl Siegel, *Alois Riehl: Ein Beitrag zur Geschichte des Neukantianismus*, Festschrift der Universität Graz (Graz: Leuschner & Lubensky, 1932), p. 4.
9. I would like to thank Frau Ivonne Reyer for lending me the guest book for study, and for permission to publish parts of it.
10. See note 33 below.
11. See Heinrich Wölfflin, letter to his parents, Berlin, March 27, 1908: "Another visitor who gave me great pleasure was Peter Behrens (known for modern applied art): he was recently appointed artistic director at the Allgemeine Elektricitätsgesellschaft here and out of sheer sympathy for my kind of art history wishes to give students two weekly drawing lessons relating to the material of my lecture." In Joseph Gantner, ed., *Heinrich Wölfflin 1864–1945: Autobiographie, Tagebücher und Briefe* (Basel and Stuttgart: Schwabe & Co. AG, 1984), p. 226.
12. Mies, in an interview with Ulrich Conrads and Horst Eifler, recorded on the album *Mies in Berlin* (Bauwelt Archiv 1, 1966).
13. See Wölfflin, letters and diary entries 1905–11, in Gantner, ed., *Heinrich Wölfflin 1864–1945*, pp. 218–63. See also Neumeyer, *The Artless Word*, pp. 51 ff.
14. Mies van der Rohe library, Special Collections Department, University Library, University of Illinois, Chicago. Needless to say, Wölfflin's *Renaissance und Barock* and *Kunstgeschichtliche Grundbegriffe* were also among Mies's books.
15. Alois Riehl, *Friedrich Nietzsche: Der Künstler und der Denker. Ein Essay* (Stuttgart, 1897). The only earlier monographs were Rudolf Steiner, *Friedrich Nietzsche: Ein Kämpfer gegen seine Zeit* (Weimar, 1895), and Lou Andreas-Salomé, *Friedrich Nietzsche in seinen Werken* (Vienna, 1894).
16. Siegel, *Alois Riehl*, p. 6.
17. Ibid., p. 49.
18. Ibid., pp. 13, 18, 49.
19. Riehl, "Bemerkungen zum Problem der Form in der Dichtkunst," 1897, in Riehl, *Philosophische Studien aus vier Jahrzehnten* (Leipzig: Quelle & Meyer, 1925), p. 283.
20. Alois Riehl, "Der Beruf der Philosophie in der Gegenwart," lecture at Princeton University, October 20, 1913, in ibid., p. 305. The lecture appears in English as "The Vocation of Philosophy at the Present Day" in *Lectures in Connection with the Dedication of the Graduate College of Princeton University in October 1913, by Émile Boutroux, Alois Riehl, A. D. Godley, Arthur Shipley* (Princeton and London, 1914), pp. 45–63; see esp. p. 47.
21. See Richard Frank Krummel, *Nietzsche und der deutsche Geist* (Berlin and New York: Walter de Gruyter, 1998), 2:161.
22. See Siegel, *Alois Riehl*, p. 145.
23. Erich Jaensch, "Zum Gedächtnis von Alois Riehl. Gedanken über den Mann und das Werk, über das Fortwirken und die Zukunftsaussichten des realistischen Kritizismus," in *Kant-Studien* 30 (1925): vii, referring to a letter by Riehl.
24. Ibid. See also Heinrich Maier, "Alois Riehl: Gedächtnisrede, gehalten am 24. Januar 1925," *Kant-Studien* 31 (1926): 563–79.
25. Eduard Spranger, "Kurze Selbstdarstellungen," 1961, in H. Walter Bähr and Hans Wenke, eds., *Eduard Spranger: Sein Werk und sein Leben* (Heidelberg: Quelle & Meyer, 1964), p. 16.
26. See Mies van der Rohe library, University of Illinois. Mies also owned Spranger's *Gedanken zu Daseinsgestaltung* (1954).
27. Siegel, *Alois Riehl*, p. 18.
28. Anton Jaumann, "Vom künstlerischen Nachwuchs," *Innen-Dekoration* 21 (July 1910): 266.
29. See Siegel, *Alois Riehl*, p. 159.
30. Adolf Hildebrand, *Das Problem der Form* (Strassburg, 1893, 3rd ed. 1918), pp. ix, viii.
31. "Bemerkungen zum Problem der Form in der Dichtkunst," pp. 219 ff. On Riehl's engagement with Hildebrand see also Oskar Walzel, *Wechselseitige Erhellung der Künste: Ein Beitrag zur Würdigung kunstgeschichtlicher Begriffe* (Berlin, 1917), pp. 58 ff.
32. Mies owned Hildebrand's *Gesammelte Aufsätze* (Strasbourg, 1909) and Conrad Fiedler's *Schriften über Kunst*, ed. H. Marbach (Leipzig, 1896). See Mies van der Rohe library, University of Illinois.
33. Klösterli guest book, entry for January 6, 1912. The poem later implies that Mies found his "treasure" in the garden of the Riehl House, apparently at the bidding of the same "kind fairy": "But by moonlight / And with the singing of nightingales, / Something pressed the architect / To follow the rose-lined path. / And among the thorns and hedges / He came upon the treasure / And he led it out of the rosebeds / Back into the Klösterli. / Softly the clever fairy / Whispered to the lord of the cloister / 'The nightingale's sweet song / Ensures a happy marriage!'"
34. Siegel, *Alois Riehl*, p. 18.
35. Mies, Bruhn's designated "cavalier," heads the list of participants in the dance on March 5, 1912.
36. Gustav Schmoller, Klösterli guest book, June 6, 1911; Hans Delbrück and Walther Rathenau, Klösterli guest book, presumably May 1914.
37. Leo Frobenius, Klösterli guest book, July 5, 1913. For Mies's love of *Das unbekannte Afrika* see Neumeyer, *The Artless Word*, p. 129.
38. Peter and Petra Behrens, Klösterli guest book, July 17, 1911.
39. See Siegel, *Alois Riehl*, p. 16.
40. An entry in the guest book describes the first such meeting, in May 1910: "In memory of the philosophical evening on the birthday of Herr Bruhn, celebrated with a spring storm. Featured speaker: Hans Lindau. Official members: Eduard Spranger, Wolfgang Bruhn. Absent member: Herr von Gossler. Following the official presentation the accustomed philosophical discussion failed to develop. But all present were infused with an ancient idea, a desire to—'bring back all things.' Ada, member extraordinary (by fiat), without teaching assignment, but with (profound) substance."
The philologist Lindau, whose eloquent "Festrede" apparently gave the evening an unusual turn, was intimately familiar with the philosophy of August Schmarsow, perhaps the most important representative of late-nineteenth-century space-oriented architectural theory. See Lindau, "August Schmarsow," *Nord und Süd: Eine deutsche Monatsschrift* 31, no. 122 (1907): 173–82. (I am grateful to my doctoral candidate Y. Kim for this reference.) Lindau also used Schmarsow's aesthetic theories in his fiction, for example his *Abenden in Versailles* (1903), a practice in which he may have been inspired by Riehl's application of Hildebrand's theory to poetry.
41. Klösterli guest book, July 1923: seminar on Spinoza's ethics; winter 1923–24: seminar on Nietzsche; summer 1924: seminar on Kant.
42. A Fritz Burger, for example, charmingly signed the guest book on July 31, 1910, with "sincere thanks for lovely hours in Klösterli." The entry continued, "View is splendid, garden is superb, everything delightful. Hans Burger Bella Burger." It is unclear whether this was the Fritz Burger who had qualified for university teaching with his *Vitruv und die Renaissance*, had just published *Die Villen des Palladio: Ein Beitrag zur Entwicklungsgeschichte des Renaissancearchitektur* (Leipzig, 1909), and was among the small group of art historians who championed the art of the early twentieth century. It is perhaps no coincidence that Burger's was the only book on Palladio in Mies's library.
43. "Architekt Ludwig Mies: Villa des Herrn Geheimer Regierungsrat Prof. Dr. Riehl in Neu-Babelsberg," *Moderne Bauformen* 9 (1910): 20–24; Hermann Muthesius, *Landhaus und Garten*, 2nd rev. and expanded ed. (Munich: F. Bruckmann, 1910), p. L, plates 50–51.
44. Karl Foerster, *Winterharte Blütenstauden und Sträucher der Neuzeit* (Leipzig: J. J. Weber, 1911), plates after pp. 16, 32, 112, 212, 240. The cover picture also appears in large format inside the book, p. 213, with a slight change of props. The latter photograph is also in Foerster, *Vom Blütengarten der Zukunft* (Berlin, 1917), p. 133.
45. Klösterli guest book, June 6, 1911.
46. Ibid., November 26, 1911; author unknown.
47. Aristotle, *Über die Seele*, trans. Adolf Lasson (Jena, 1924). Mies's copy is now in the possession of Dirk Lohan, Chicago.
48. Klösterli guest book, May 4, 1914.
49. See *Kongress für Ästhetik und Allgemeine Kunstwissenschaft, Berlin 7–9 Oktober 1913. Bericht hrsg. vom Ortsausschuss* (Stuttgart, 1914), p. 3.
50. See Max Dessoir and Muthesius, *Das Bismarck Nationaldenkmal, eine Erörterung des Wettbewerbes. Mit aktenmässigen Anlagen* (Jena, 1912).
51. See Dessoir, *Buch der Erinnerung* (Stuttgart: Enke, 1946, 2nd ed. 1947), esp. pp. 176 ff.
52. Erich Mendelsohn, letter to Luise Mendelsohn, July 16, 1919, in the archive of Mendelsohn's letters at the Getty Center for the History of Art and the Humanities, Santa Monica. Mendelsohn's "striking thesis" on garden design can only be guessed at; it may well have called for a garden arranged in terms of the house's architecture near the house, then farther away making a gradual transition to a more natural plan. At the time of Mendelsohn's visit, Alois Riehl was away on a trip.
53. "For the first time together in the Klösterli! With most heartfelt thanks, Dora Dammholz and Werner Jaeger, August 2, 1912." Klösterli guest book.
54. Spranger, *Der gegenwärtige Stand der Geisteswissenschaften und die Schule*, 1921 (2nd ed. Leipzig and Berlin: Teubner, 1925), p. 7.
55. On Jaeger see William M. Calder, "Werner Jaeger," in *Berlinische Lebensbilder: Geisteswissenschaftler*, ed. Michael Erbe (Berlin, 1989), pp. 343–63, and Johannes Irmscher, "Werner Jaeger zum 100. Geburtstag," in *Sitzungsberichte der Akademie der Wissenschaften der DDR*, 1990, pp. 3–7.
56. Werner Jaeger, *Paideia: The Ideals of Greek Culture*, vol. 1: *Archaic Greece. The Mind of Athens* (Oxford: at the University Press, 1945). Now owned by Dirk Lohan, Chicago.
57. Mies, "Baukunst unserer Zeit."
58. Mies van der Rohe library, University of Illinois; and Neumeyer, *The Artless Word*, p. 203. Jaeger started the journal *Die Antike* in 1925 and edited it as a quarterly until 1936. The first three issues for 1928, containing Jaeger's Plato essay, are among

Mies's books, as is another publication of Jaeger's, "Die geistige Gegenwart der Antike" (1929), which appeared independently in *Die Antike* in 1929.
59. Spranger, "Kurze Selbstdarstellungen," p. 15.

Jan Maruhn, "Building for Art: Mies van der Rohe as the Architect for Art Collectors," pp. 318–23

1. Georg Hollberger, ed., *Expressionismus und Exil: Die Sammlung Ludwig und Rosi Fischer*, exh. cat. (Frankfurt am Main: Jüdisches Museum, 1990).
2. Henrike Junge, ed., *Avantgarde und Publikum: Mäzenatentum in Berlin* (Cologne, Weimar, and Vienna: Böhlau, 1992). See also Thomas W. Gaehtgens und Martin Schieder, eds., *Mäzenatisches Handeln: Studien zur Kultur des Bürgersinns in der Gesellschaft. Festschrift für Günter Braun zum 70. Geburtstag* (Berlin: Fannei & Walz, 1998); Günter and Waldtraut Braun, eds., *Mäzenatentum in Berlin: Bürgersinn und kulturelle Kompetenz unter sich verändernden Bedingungen* (Berlin and New York: de Gruyter, 1993); and Manuel Frey, *Macht und Moral des Schenkens: Staat und bürgerliche Mäzene vom späten 18. Jahrhundert bis zur Gegenwart* (Berlin: Fannei & Walz, 1999).
3. Nina Senger, *"Die Kunst der Lebenden" in der Sammlung Hermann Lange in Krefeld: Qualität als Sammlungsprinzip*, master's thesis, Freie Universität Berlin, 1993.
4. See Jonathan Petropoulos, *Art as Politics in the Third Reich* (Chapel Hill and London: University of North Carolina Press, 1996, German trans. as *Kunstraub und Sammelwahn: Kunst und Politik im Dritten Reich* [Berlin: Propyläen, 1999]).
5. See Jan Thomas Köhler, Jan Maruhn, and Senger, eds., *Berliner Lebenswelten der zwanziger Jahre: Bilder einer untergegangenen Kultur. Photographiert von Marta Huth*, exh. cat. (Berlin: Bauhaus-Archiv, 1996).
6. Even in the Tugendhat House (1928–30), an incunabulum of the modernist dwelling, Grete Tugendhat had no desk in her room: see Daniela Hammer-Tugendhat, "Leben im Haus Tugendhat," in Hammer-Tugendhat and Wolf Tegethoff, eds., *Ludwig Mies van der Rohe: Das Haus Tugendhat* (Vienna: Springer, 1998), p. 23.
7. See Franz Schulze, *A Critical Biography*, p. 313.
8. Hugo Perls, *"Warum ist Kamilla schön?": Von Kunst, Künstlern und Kunsthandel* (Munich: List, 1962), pp. 18–19.
9. For example the Neuhaus House (1907). See Julius Posener, *Berlin auf dem Wege zu einer neuen Architektur: Das Zeitalter Wilhelms II* (Munich: Prestel, 1995), p. 138.
10. Perls, *"Warum ist Kamilla schön?"*, p. 18.
11. Peter Blake, "Interview with Mies van der Rohe," in Blake, *Four Great Makers of Architecture* (New York, 1963), p. 50; see also Schulze, *A Critical Biography*, p. 56.
12. See ibid., p. 57, fig. 34.
13. See ibid., p. 66.
14. Ibid., p. 70.
15. See Sepp-Gustav Gröschel, "Glienicke und die Antike," *Schloss Glienicke*, exh. cat. (Berlin: Staatliche Schlösser und Gärten, 1987), pp. 243–67.
16. No contemporary floor plan survives, but Mies apparently reconstructed one from memory around 1930, in an unpublished drawing (plate 22) previously in the Library of Congress and now in the Mies van der Rohe Archive, The Museum of Modern Art, New York. I am grateful to Christian Wolsdorff for information on this drawing, on which Schulze's description in *A Critical Biography*, pp. 61–62, is also based.
17. Julius Meier-Graefe, letter to Mies, November 13, 1912, Eng. trans. in ibid., pp. 62–63.
18. Comparable in modern architecture are only Walter Gropius's Meisterhäuser in Dessau (1926), Le Corbusier's buildings for the Weissenhof Housing Colony in Stuttgart (1927), and Le Corbusier's double houses in Paris (La Roche/Jeanneret, 1923–25, and Lipschitz/Miestschaninoff, 1924).
19. See Maruhn and Senger, "Hermann Lange: Förderer der Moderne," in Julian Heynen, *Ludwig Mies van der Rohe. Haus Lange—Haus Esters. Ein Ort für die Kunst* (Stuttgart: Hatje, 1995), pp. 14–19; also Maruhn, *Bauherr der Moderne: Der Krefelder Seidenfabrikant Hermann Lange und sein Architekt Ludwig Mies van der Rohe (1926–1938)*, master's thesis, Freie Universität Berlin, 1996.
20. Carl and Hermann Lange, letter to Friedrich Deneken, July 19, 1901. Archiv des Kaiser-Wilhelm-Museums Krefeld, Akte VII, 3, p. 24.
21. See Senger, *"Die Kunst der Lebenden"*. On the collection's anthropocentric bent see Josef Esters, "Trauerrede für Hermann Lange am 20.12.1942," *Wir im Werk* 50 (December 1942): n.p.
22. Deutscher Werkbund, membership list from 1920, Werkbund-Archiv, Berlin; on Hermann Lange as a founding member of the *Verein der Freunde* (Society of friends) of the National Gallery, see Zentralarchiv der Staatlichen Museen zu Berlin—Preussischer Kulturbesitz, I/NG, Sep. 2a; on the history of the society see Andrea Meyer, *In guter Gesellschaft. Der Verein der Freunde der Nationalgalerie Berlin von 1929 bis heute* (Berlin: Fannei & Walz, 1998).
23. Theo van Doesburg, letter to Cornelis van Eesteren, March 17, 1925, in Evert van Straaten, ed., *Theo van Doesburg: Painter and Architect*, exh. cat. (Rotterdam: Museum Boymans-van-Beuningen, 1988), p. 171.
24. Ibid., p. 108.
25. Walter Cohen, "Haus Lange in Krefeld," *Museum der Gegenwart* 1 (1930–31): 164.
26. Van Doesburg also wrote for the journal *G: Material zur elementaren Gestaltung*, on which Mies collaborated with El Lissitzky and Hans Richter.
27. See van Straaten, *Theo van Doesburg 1883–1931: Een Documentaire op de Basis van Materiaal uit de Schenking van Moorsel* (The Hague: Staatsuitgeverij, 1983), p. 127.
28. Van Doesburg, letter to van Eesteren, March 17, 1925, in van Straaten, ed., *Theo van Doesburg: Painter and Architect*, p. 171.
29. I am indebted to Wolsdorff for this information.
30. Mies recalled thirty years later, "I wanted to use much more glass in [the Lange] house, but the client wouldn't have it. I had problems. They were very nice people. We became good friends. He was president of the silk industry in Germany, and that caused him worry. He drank a great deal of wine and such. That's what was behind it." Interview with H. T. Cadbury-Brown, 1959, quoted in Schulze, *Mies van der Rohe: Leben und Werk* (Berlin: Ernst & Sohn, 1986), p. 152.
31. Henry-Russell Hitchcock, Jr., and Philip Johnson, *Modern Architecture: International Exhibition*, exh. cat. (New York: The Museum of Modern Art, 1932), pp. 7, 119; and Hitchcock and Johnson, *The International Style: Architecture since 1922* (New York: W. W. Norton & Co., Inc., 1932), p. 185.
32. Cohen, "Haus Lange in Krefeld."
33. Hermann Lange already had a large house, and his children were already grown. After 1930 he spent most of his time in Berlin. See Maruhn, *Bauherr der Moderne*, pp. 7–13, 46–56.
34. Senger, *"Die Kunst der Lebenden"*, pp. 112–13.
35. In a remodeling of the house after World II, the wall between the central hall and the dining room was removed, so that on entering the hall one looks directly into the garden rather than at the art. In this respect the present layout is the opposite of the original. See Cohen, "Haus Lange in Krefeld," pp. 160–61.
36. Senger, *"Die Kunst der Lebenden"*, p. 112–13.
37. Cohen, "Haus Lange in Krefeld," pp. 163–64.
38. Ibid., p. 161. A family photograph shows Mies's dining table with wooden chairs covered in pigskin.
39. Stadtarchiv Krefeld, B30, 57, Reg. 1236.
40. See Karl Otto Lüffgens, "Die Verseidag-Bauten von Ludwig Mies van der Rohe 1933–37," *Die Heimat* 48, no. 12 (1977): 57–61.
41. See Jan Thomas Köhler and Maruhn, "Der Wettbewerb der BVG 1929," *Der Schrei nach dem Turmhaus: Der Ideenwettbewerb Hochhaus am Bahnhof Friedrichstrasse Berlin 1921/22*, exh. cat. (Berlin: Bauhaus-Archiv, 1988), pp. 167–83.
42. Paul Ortwin Rave, letter to Countess Sophie Arnim, October 16, 1930. Zentralarchiv der Staatlichen Museen zu Berlin, I/NG, Sep. 2c 830.
43. Unsigned page of notes in ibid. Like Hermann Lange, Erich Wolf was a founding member of the *Verein der Freunde* of the National Gallery. See Zentralarchiv der Staatlichen Museen zu Berlin, I/NG, Sep. 2a.
44. In photographs published shortly after the structure was completed, the foundations for the addition already appear. See Hitchcock, *Modern Architecture: Romanticism and Reintegration* (New York: Payson & Clarke, 1929), no. 39.
45. Rave, letter to Arnim.
46. For an undated floor plan of the Wolf House see Arthur Drexler, ed., *The Mies van der Rohe Archive* 1:131, no. 30.14.
47. Family photographs have recently come to light, however. The "Haus Wolf" research project of the Brandenburgische Technische Universität Cottbus, directed by Lars Scharnholz, has been investigating the construction history of the house; see the Website www.iba-fuerst-pueckler-land.de/wolf-house-project.
48. Perls, *"Warum ist Kamilla schön?"*, p. 65.
49. Eduard Fuchs, *Illustrierte Sittengeschichte vom Mittelalter bis zur Gegenwart* (Munich: Albert Langen, 1909–12). On Fuchs see Walter Benjamin, "Eduard Fuchs, der Sammler und der Historiker," *Zeitschrift für Sozialforschung* 6 (1937): 346–99.
50. Paul Westheim, "Das Haus eines Sammlers: Die Sammlung Eduard Fuchs, Zehlendorf," *Das Kunstblatt* 10 (March 1926): 106–13.
51. Ulrich Weitz, *Eduard Fuchs: Salonkultur und Proletariat* (Stuttgart: Stöffler & Schütz, 1991), p. 333.
52. Westheim, "Das Haus eines Sammlers," pp. 108–9.
53. Schulze, *A Critical Biography*, pp. 124–25.
54. Westheim, "Das Haus eines Sammlers," p. 110.
55. See Tegethoff, *The Villas and Country Houses*, pp. 99–104.
56. Ibid., p. 99.
57. Tegethoff's comment about a slot planned in the floor, through which paintings could be lowered for storage in the basement, and the German *Saal* indicated in the plan support the idea that this was to be an working *and* exhibition space. See ibid., p. 102.
58. Karin von Maur, *Oskar Schlemmer. Monographie* (Munich: Prestel, 1979), p. 89.
59. Karl Nierendorf, letter to Otto Dix, January 30, 1933. Germanisches Nationalmuseum Nürnberg, Archiv für Bildende Kunst.
60. *Gedächtnisausstellung Emil Nolde*, exh. cat. (Hamburg: Kunstverein Hamburg, 1957), no. 140.
61. See Drexler, ed., *The Mies van der Rohe Archive* 3:98, no. 27.33.
62. Henke House Addition, the Mies van der Rohe Archive.
63. Erich Henke, letters to Mies, May 26, September 13, and October 21, 1930; Mies, letter to Henke, July 21 and September 16, 1930; in ibid.
64. I am grateful to the Lange family for this information.
65. Tegethoff, *The Villas and Country Houses*, fig. 18.7.
66. Drexler conjectures that the project stalled in 1933 because Mies refused to accept the building inspectors' demand that he hide the flat-roofed building behind an earthen wall, but this is unlikely given both Mies's strained financial situation at the time and the influence of the Lange family. See ibid., p. 123.
67. See Katharina Schmidt and Harwig Fischer, eds., *Ein Haus für den Kubismus: Die Sammlung Raoul La Roche* (Ostfildern-Ruit: Hatje, 1998).
68. See Schulze, *A Critical Biography*, p. 80–81.
69. See Tegethoff, *The Villas and Country Houses*, p. 80 and p. 83, note 61, where this concept is discussed in relation to the German Pavilion, Barcelona. See also Dietrich Schubert, *Die Kunst Lehmbrucks* (Worms: Werner, 1981), pp. 178–79.
70. On the Tugendhat House see, e.g., Hammer-Tugendhat and Tegethoff, eds., *Das Haus Tugendhat*; Tegethoff, *Im Brennpunkt der Moderne: Mies van der Rohe und das Haus Tugendhat in Brünn* (Munich: HypoVereinsbank, 1998); and Adolph Stiller, ed., *Das Haus Tugendhat: Ludwig Mies van der Rohe, Brünn 1930* (Salzburg: Pustet, 1999).
71. Or 280 square meters. See Tegethoff, "Das Haus Tugendhat: Ein Schlüsselwerk der Moderne in Brünn," in Hammer-Tugendhat and Tegethoff, eds., *Das Haus Tugendhat*, p. 37.
72. The sculpture is now in the Moravska Galerie, Brno. See Hammer-Tugendhat and Tegethoff, eds., *Das Haus Tugendhat*, p. 174, fig. 14. It would be interesting to know whether the Tugendhats already owned the sculpture or were urged to buy it by the architect. Hermann Lange possessed a cast of the same sculpture. See Senger, *"Die Kunst der Lebenden"*, p. 125.
73. See Cohen, "Haus Lange in Krefeld."
74. Mies, letter to Henke, July 21, 1930. Henke House Addition, the Mies van der Rohe Archive.
75. Mies, letter to Hermann Lange, December 5, 1928: "In the discussion on November 29 . . . it was determined: that the picture slot would be 25 cm wide and at least three meters long." General Correspondence 1920s, in ibid.
76. See Walter, "Haus Lange in Krefeld," p. 160. The Henke House was to have "simple illumination" from above in the form of P-H lamps (as the Fuchs annex to the Perls House apparently did); see Henke, letter to Mies, July 17, 1930, and Mies, letter to Henke, July 21, 1930, in Henke House Addition, Mies van der Rohe Archive.
77. On the Nolde House skylight see Tegethoff, *The Villas and Country Houses*, p. 102.
78. See Drexler, ed., *The Mies van der Rohe Archive* 1:19, no. 26.23.

Andres Lepik, "Mies and Photomontage, 1910–38," pp. 324–29

1. See Franz Schulze, *A Critical Biography*, pp. 14, 15.
2. He himself said that it was the drawings he submitted in response to a classified ad that allowed him to move to Berlin. See ibid., p. 18.
3. Arthur Drexler, ed., *The Mies van der Rohe Archive*, 1:xv.
4. See Fritz Neumeyer, *The Artless Word*, p. 170.
5. I use the term "montage" for all of Mies's presentations combining drawing and photography, although it would often be more correct to speak of drawings inserted into photographs. Unlike collage, which aims to rupture pictorial unity, montage preserves a unified pictorial form.
6. See Winfried Nerdinger, *Die Architekturzeichnung: Vom barocken Idealplan zur Axonometrie* (Munich: Prestel, 1986), pp. 142–43 and note 6.
7. Mies may have come across the montage technique early on, in his father's workshop; see Rolf Sachsse, *Bild und Bau: Zur Nutzung technischer Medien beim Entwerfen von Architektur* (Braunschweig and Wiesbaden: Vieweg, 1997), p. 148.
8. In this case the photograph was not necessarily taken at the spot in question.
9. Another photomontage of the Bismarck Monument with a more distant view has been lost, but is documented by a photograph; see Drexler, ed., *The Mies van der Rohe Archive*, 1:3.
10. See *Walter Gropius*, exh. cat. (Berlin: Bauhaus-Archiv, 1985), p. 216, W6.
11. Mies could also have seen an effective

combination of realized and unrealized designs in Karl Friedrich Schinkel's *Sammlung architektonischer Entwürfe*. See Sachsse, *Bild und Bau*, p. 26. The same combination appears in Schinkel's Orianda publication, which Mies owned.

12. See Neumeyer, *The Artless Word*, p. 21.
13. See Florian Zimmermann, ed., *Der Schrei nach dem Turmhaus: Der Ideenwettbewerb Hochhaus am Bahnhof Friedrichstrasse Berlin 1921–22* (Berlin: Bauhaus-Archiv, 1988), p. 106, and Christian Wolsdorff, entry for cat. no. 268 in Magdalena Droste and Jeanine Fiedler, eds., *Experiment Bauhaus: Das Bauhaus-Archiv (West) zu Gast im Bauhaus Dessau*, exh. cat. (Berlin: Kupfergraben, 1988), p. 316.
14. Drexler, ed., *The Mies van der Rohe Archive*, 1:xx.
15. *G: Material zur elementaren Gestaltung* no. 3 (June 1924): n.p. [13].
16. See, for example, Paul Westheim, "Mies van der Rohe: Entwicklung eines Architekten," *Das Kunstblatt* 11, no. 2 (February 1927): 58 right.
17. *Frühlicht* 1, no. 4 (1922): 124.
18. Another montage, now lost, showing the Friedrichstrasse Skyscraper from the south (p. 43, fig. 13), explores an extreme contrast between drawing and photograph—apparently an experiment that was abandoned. A charcoal drawing was probably a study for it; see Drexler, ed., *The Mies van der Rohe Archive*, 1:no. 20.3. See the juxtaposition in Zimmermann, *Der Schrei nach dem Turmhaus*, p. 108.
19. "'One so rarely requires of men the impossible' (Goethe)." Bruno Taut, *Alpine Architektur* (Hagen: Folkwang-Verlag, 1919), p. 10.
20. *Frühlicht* 1, no. 4 (1922): 122. See also Drexler, ed., *The Mies van der Rohe Archive*, 1:62: "The Archive has several photographs showing the glass model placed outside the window of Mies's office." In a photograph of the *Internationale Architektur* exhibition at the Bauhaus, Weimar, in 1923, the models of the Glass Skyscraper and of the Concrete Office Building stand next to each other (p. 120, fig. 16).
21. In *G* the signature is replaced by the initials "M.v.d.R."
22. See Detlef Mertins, "Architectures of Becoming: Mies van der Rohe and the Avant-Garde," in the present volume, and particularly its frontispiece, p. 106. On Mies and Hannah Höch see the many references to him, extending to 1964, in *Hannah Höch: Eine Lebenscollage*, 6 vols. (Berlin: Stiftung Archiv der Akademie der Künste, 1989).
23. See Sachsse, *Bild und Bau*, p. 149.
24. "Whereas previously huge amounts of time, devotion, and effort had been expended on the painting of a body, a hat, a shadow, etc., we need only pick up a pair of scissors and cut out from paintings and photographs the things we can use." Wieland Herzfelde, in Karl Rifa, ed., *Dada Berlin: Texte, Manifeste, Aktionen* (Stuttgart: Reclam, 1977), p. 118.
25. See Hanno-Walter Kruft, *Geschichte der Architekturtheorie* (Munich: Beck, 1985), pp. 429–30.
26. Heinrich Klotz, ed., *Mies van der Rohe: Vorbild und Vermächtnis* (Frankfurt am Main: Deutsches Architekturmuseum, 1986), pp. 114–16, cat. nos. 17, 19, 21a, 22b, 23a.
27. Drexler, ed., *The Mies van der Rohe Archive*, 3: nos. 19.66, 19.67, and Schulze, ed., *The Mies van der Rohe Archive: Supplementary Drawings*, 6:5, no. 19.52.
28. Here Mies may have been thinking of Schinkel's *Sammlung architektonischer Entwürfe*, which features similar ways of depicting interior spaces.
29. I am grateful to Terence Riley for suggesting this possibility.
30. See Neil Levine, "'The Significance of Facts': Mies's Collages Up Close and Personal," *Assemblage* 37 (1998): 70–110.
31. To say that "Mies's medium was montage," as Sachsse does, nevertheless goes too far; see Sachsse, *Bild und Bau*, p. 147.
32. See Klotz, ed., *Vorbild und Vermächtnis*, cat. nos. 108, 109, 122. Many of the montages associated with Mies's later projects may have been produced by his staff and students.
33. See the frequently reproduced montage of 1978 by Stanley Tigerman, in which Mies's Crown Hall in Chicago is seen sinking into the sea like the *Titanic*. Reproduced in Neumeyer, *The Artless Word*, p. xvi.
34. For example the montage *Pool Enclosure for Rod Stewart, Ascot*, from 1972. Also Hans Hollein and others.
35. In the exhibition of his work at the New National Gallery, Berlin (that is, in the building that was Mies's last major project), in the summer of 2000, Renzo Piano actually placed a reproduction of Mies's montage next to his view of his own building.
36. Notwithstanding Francesco Dal Co's argument that "It is no accident . . . that chance plays a dominant role in his collages." See Dal Co, "Einzigartigkeit: Mies van der Rohes philosophisch-kultureller Hintergrund," in Klotz, ed., *Vorbild und Vermächtnis*, p. 72.

Terence Riley, "From Bauhaus to Court-House," pp. 330–37

1. Ada Louise Huxtable, label copy for *Mies van der Rohe* exhibition, The Museum of Modern Art, 1947. The Museum of Modern Art Archives. The project has been referred to by more than one name; Huxtable's wall label read "Project: Three Houses"; the exhibition publication used the phrase "Project: Group of Court-Houses" —see Philip C. Johnson, *Mies van der Rohe*, exh. cat. (New York: The Museum of Modern Art, 1947), p. 105; and more recently Wolf Tegethoff, in *The Villas and Country Houses*, 19.9–11, uses the name "Group of three Court-Houses."
2. Johnson, *Mies van der Rohe*, p. 96. In that this description might apply to a great number of structures dating back as early as Roman times, "Mies's 'court-house' scheme of 1931" should be understood as the first manifestation of Mies's interest in exploring a building type with both direct and indirect precedents.
3. In the Preface, Johnson notes, "All the buildings and projects which Mies considers in any way important are illustrated in this volume." Ibid., p. 7. From this statement it is clear that Mies had a good deal of influence—precisely how much we cannot say—over the selection of projects and hence the essential elements of the narrative.
4. Johnson hyphenated the term "court-house," as I do here; his successor in the Museum's Department of Architecture and Design, Arthur Drexler, dropped the hyphen in subsequent Museum publications, as has become the common usage.
5. Johnson, *Mies van der Rohe*, German trans. (Stuttgart: Verlag Gerd Hatje, 1956), p. 96.
6. Howard Dearstyne, "Mies van der Rohe's Teaching at the Bauhaus in Dessau," in Eckhard Neumann, ed., *Bauhaus and Bauhaus People* (New York: Van Nostrand Reinhold, 1993), p. 225. Dearstyne says that one of Eduard Ludwig's court-houses was published in "'Wingler's book"; see Hans M. Wingler, *The Bauhaus* (Cambridge, Mass.: The MIT Press, 1978), p. 541.
7. My thanks to Dr. Christian Wolsdorff of the Bauhaus-Archiv for reviewing relevant documents for me in this regard.
8. In addition to Johnson, the ex-Bauhaus student John Barney Rodgers served as a translator for Mies in his early years in America. Rodgers was not involved with either the exhibition or the catalogue, but he, too, may have suggested the term "court-house" as a translation of *Flachbau mit Wohnhof*.
9. Johnson, *Mies van der Rohe*, pp. 97, 99–101.
10. According to George Danforth, letter to the author, December 4, 2000, Mies drew in the vines and other freehand details on these drawings. In 1938, the Illinois Institute of Technology (IIT) was called the Armour Institute of Technology.
11. A similar plan and elevation, apparently drawn by the same hand, does exist in the Mies van der Rohe Archive at The Museum of Modern Art, New York, but is catalogued there as a student project.
12. Tegethoff notes the use of Strathmore board, in American twenty-by-thirty-inch format. *The Villas and Country Houses*, p. 124.
13. Johnson, *Mies van der Rohe*, pp.102–3.
14. Mies, letter to Desideri.
15. The reproductions Mies retained, now in the Mies van der Rohe Archive, do not show all of his Bauhaus students' works. It is reasonable to assume they represent his own selection.
16. Ludwig Hilberseimer, on the other hand, who had been hired by Hannes Meyer, Mies's predecessor as the director of the Bauhaus, taught housing as part of a course on urban planning.
17. Hermann Blomeier, Wilhelm Heyeroff, Edgar Hecht, and Hubert Döllner.
18. Dearstyne, "Mies van der Rohe's Teaching at the Bauhaus," p. 225.
19. Ludwig to some degree personifies the notion that Mies's teaching was intermingled with his architectural practice. One of Mies's most talented students, Ludwig joined his office on graduating. With Lilly Reich, he watched over Mies's affairs after the architect left for the United States.
20. Mies, letter to Desideri.
21. During the Allied bombardment of Berlin, Reich and Ludwig removed Mies's and Reich's drawings from the city, leaving them with Ludwig's parents in what would later become East Germany. These drawings eventually came to Mies in Chicago, but not until 1964. They were transferred to The Museum of Modern Art in 1968. The drawings for the Hubbe Court-House Studies, then, which would have greatly assisted in the identification of the court-house sketches, were unavailable at the time of Johnson's exhibition. Even after they arrived at the Museum, their relationship to the individual sketch plans was not noted. Drexler, who edited the first four volumes of the catalogue of the Archive, believed some of the sketch plans for the court-houses to be alternate designs for the Hubbe House. Tegethoff was the first to note their relationship, in *The Villas and Country Houses*, p. 124.
22. Mies appears to be referring to this in his 1962 letter to Desideri: "During the thirties we made some plans for court houses of various sizes, some with one court, others with two or three courts."
23. Most of the students only drew one plan, but slight extensions of the lines of the outer walls indicate that the house was to be produced in series.
24. Johnson, *Mies van der Rohe*, p. 96.
25. Unlike Mies's original Hubbe Court-House Studies, the "Miesian" court-houses by Johnson, Anderson Todd of Houston, and others were freestanding. Y. C. Wong of Chicago and others designed court-houses in series, but the more widely published freestanding projects came to be understood as the model.
26. Many of the drawings in the cache were given to The Museum of Modern Art after the exhibition of 1947, and can be identified by examination of the accession dates of the drawings in the Museum's collection. He apparently had with him at IIT drawings from the Mountain House Studies, the Gericke, Ulrich Lange, and Hubbe houses, and the Hubbe Court-House Studies. The photographs of his Bauhaus students' work are also now in the Museum's Archive.
27. Elaine Hochman, *Architects of Fortune: Mies van der Rohe and the Third Reich* (New York: Weidenfeld and Nicolson, 1989), p. 216.
28. Dearstyne, "Mies van der Rohe's Teaching at the Bauhaus," p. 224. The luxuriousness of Mies's Tugendhat House was noted by others besides his critics. In 1930, Johnson wrote of the house, "It has cost so far nearly a million marks so it ought to be good. The main room . . . is twenty-seven meters long and the wall is entirely of glass as is one of the side walls at least ten meters long. The steel posts are clad in chrome, an onyx wall separates the library from the main living room, and a curved wall of some exotic wood makes the dining niche." Johnson, letter to J. J. P. Oud, September 17, 1930. The Mies van der Rohe Archive.
29. Like Mies's Bauhaus curriculum, Mackay Hugh Baillie Scott's book *Houses and Gardens: Arts and Crafts Interiors*, 1906 (reprint ed. Woodbridge, Suffolk: Antique Collector's Club, 1995), exclusively addressed the problem of the house, from grand country houses to modest row houses. Mies owned a German-language edition of the book.
30. Ibid., p. 130.
31. The *Flachbau mit Wohnhof* might appear an inevitable result of such a project, but it was not based on a readily available model. As Wolsdorff points out, the Berlin building code forbade the use of perimeter masonry walls to separate one house from the next.
32. Mies, "The New Time," speech delivered late June, 1930, published in *Die Form* 7, no. 10 (1932): 306. Reprinted in Fritz Neumeyer, *The Artless Word*, p. 309.
33. Hannes Meyer, "Bauen," *Bauhaus—Zeitschrift für Gestaltung* 2, no. 2 (1928): 12–13, Eng. trans. Michael Bullock in Ulrich Conrads, ed., *Programs and Manifestoes on 20th-Century Architecture* (Cambridge, Mass.: The MIT Press, 1970), p. 120.

Wallis Miller, "Mies and Exhibitions," pp. 338–49

1. Richard Pommer, "Mies van der Rohe and the Political Ideology of the Modern Movement in Architecture," in Franz Schulze, ed., *Mies van der Rohe: Critical Essays* (New York: The Museum of Modern Art, 1989), pp. 100, 103.
2. Philip Johnson, "In Berlin: Comment on Building Exposition," *New York Times*, August 9, 1931. Reprinted in Johnson, *Writings* (New York: Oxford University Press, 1979), p. 49.
3. Ausstellungs-, Messe- und Fremdenverkehrs-Amt der Stadt Berlin, *Deutsche Bauausstellung Berlin 1931, Amtlicher Katalog und Führer* (Berlin: Bauwelt-Verlag/Ullsteinhaus, 1931), pp. 160–77.
4. Völkers, "Die Halle II der Deutschen Bauausstellung," *Stein Holz Eisen* no. 14 (1931): 261.
5. Like Mies, Walter Gropius designed both the context and the content of the exhibit. He also designed a series of rooms within *Die Wohnung unserer Zeit*—the same rooms he had exhibited in the Werkbund exhibition in Paris the year before. Unlike Mies's work, these rooms made no concession to the exhibition context, but appeared as rooms lifted from an actual building—and thus not as "exhibition architecture" at all.
6. Matilda McQuaid, *Lilly Reich: Designer and Architect*, exh. cat. (New York: The Museum of Modern Art, 1996), p. 21. McQuaid is discussing the 1926 exhibition *Von der Faser zum Gewebe* (From fiber to textile).
7. The sponsor of the linoleum section, the Deutsche Linoleum Werke, saw the exhibit as a model for studying color and its effects. See *Die Wohnung*, supplement to *Stuttgarter Neues Tageblatt*, no. 2 (July 30, 1927), quoted in Karin Kirsch, *The Weissenhofsiedlung*, 1987 (Eng. trans. New York: Rizzoli, 1989), p. 29. Linoleum was of great interest to the Berlin avant-garde architects in the Ring.
8. Elsa Herzog, "Die Berlinerin in Mode!," *Berliner Nachtausgabe*, September 21, 1927. The interior of the exhibition hall was designed by Emil Pirchan and Ernst Friedmann. See also McQuaid, *Lilly*

Reich, p. 25, and Sonja Günther, *Lilly Reich 1885–1947* (Stuttgart: Deutsche Verlags-Anstalt, 1988), p. 23.

9. See, for example, McQuaid, *Lilly Reich*, p. 25, and Schulze, *A Critical Biography*, p. 143.
10. Associating this flexibility with a floating quality, McQuaid compares the Velvet and Silk Café to the Glass Room and the German Pavilion. McQuaid, *Lilly Reich*, p. 25.
11. See, e.g., "Weltausstellung 1929," *Frankfurter Zeitung* 73, no. 410.
12. See McQuaid, *Lilly Reich*, p. 26, and Günther, *Lilly Reich 1885–1947*, p. 25.
13. Visitors who had entered Hall I of the German Building Exhibition passed into Hall II, which contained *Die Wohnung unserer Zeit*, via an escalator and bridge leading to the balcony occupied by Reich's *Materialienschau*. From there they descended to the rest of the architecture exhibit. The exhibits were numbered to reflect this sequence: exhibits 1 (marble) to 24 (furniture, glass) were on the balcony; exhibits 25 (Gropius's Apartment House) to 48 (Mies's Exhibition House) were on the main floor. A stair at one end of the hall and a ramp at the other led from the balcony down to *Die Wohnung unserer Zeit*. Drawings indicate that Mies designed both the ramp and the stairs, replacing stairs along the sides of the building as the primary circulation routes. See Arthur Drexler, ed., *The Mies van der Rohe Archive* 3:207, No. 25.191, and 210–12, nos. 25.6, 25.7, and 25.8. Also, although Mies used displays to hide them, entries from the outside led directly to the main floor and the model houses, allowing one to ignore the official sequence completely. I have found no records of any decision regarding the numbering or sequence of the exhibits; all of my conclusions have been drawn from the visual evidence. See plans accompanying *Deutsche Bauausstellung Berlin 1931*.
14. Describing Reich's house, Günther writes that "Lilly Reich relied much too much on a ready-made building that she divided in rooms after the fact." *Lilly Reich 1885–1947*, p. 36.
15. The public reception of the *Materialienschau* was generally in keeping with the perspective on materials that Reich tried to create with her displays: one reviewer learned from them that "color and the happiness derived from it were important for an apartment." "Die Deutsche Bauausstellung," *Berliner Illustrierte Woche* 13, no. 24 (1931): 12–13.
16. Many journals used the same descriptions and photographs to describe the show; only an introductory commentary distinguished one article from another. See, for example, "Die Wohnung unserer Zeit," *Innen-Dekoration* 42 (July 1931): 250–81; "'Die Wohnung unserer Zeit' auf der Deutschen Bauausstellung Berlin 1931," *Moderne Bauformen* 30, no. 7 (July 1931): 329–47; and Wilhelm Lotz, "Die Halle II auf der Bauausstellung," *Die Form* 6, no. 7 (July 15, 1931): 241–49.
17. Most of these curtains—a sheer curtain to the exterior, and a dark one behind it—were placed next to fixed glass walls, transforming perception of the boundary without physically altering it. In two places the curtains even distinguished the interior from the exterior of the house on their own. At one end of the house—in the dining room—Mies placed a curtain inside a retractable window. At the other, the curtain closed a gap in the center of the exterior glass wall, at once joining the two bedrooms while separating them from the world outside.
18. Johnson, "The Berlin Building Exposition of 1931," *T-Square* 2, no. 1 (January 1932): 18.
19. Mies and Reich jointly designed the mining exhibit, set in an exhibition hall housing industrial exhibits; it was probably Reich alone who designed a ceramic, glass, and porcelain section in a gallery above the same space. See Günther, *Lilly Reich 1885–1947*, p. 38, and McQuaid, *Lilly Reich*, p. 33.
20. See Claire Zimmerman, "Mies van der Rohe, Political Ideology, and the Free Plan," unpublished manuscript (2000).
21. The plans, in any case, were realized not by Mies and Reich but by the Nazi architect Ernst Sagebiel, who was probably assigned the project by Hermann Göring. Sagebiel adopted nearly all of Mies's and Reich's plans, with modifications—for example, he cut the nine-meter-long S-shaped glass wall they had designed into three parts and draped fabric over it. See McQuaid, *Lilly Reich*, p. 39.
22. Sigfried Giedion, *Space, Time and Architecture*, 1941 (reprint ed. Cambridge, Mass.: Harvard University Press, 1982), p. 591.
23. Eduard Foertsch, "Die Weltausstellung in Barcelona," *Vossische Zeitung* (June 1929); Dr. Richard von Kühlmann, "Blick von Barcelona auf Deutschland," *Berliner Tageblatt* (December 1, 1929, morning edition).
24. My colleague Yusuke Obuchi confirmed these observations on his recent visit to the reconstructed pavilion.
25. As Robin Evans and Juan Pablo Bonta have pointed out, the irony in this observation is that while the pavilion was almost immediately destroyed, and relatively little was written about it when it was standing, a proliferation of criticism by people who had never seen it redefined it as a masterpiece of architecture. See Evans, "Mies van der Rohe's Paradoxical Symmetries," *Translations from Drawing to Building and Other Essays* (London: A. A. Publications, 1997), p. 234, and Bonta, *Architecture and Its Interpretation* (New York: Rizzoli, 1979), pp. 134, 135, 146, 217.
26. The building was 15 meters high by 20 meters on each side (c. 49 feet high by 65 feet). Willy Lesser, "Der Deutsche Anteil an der Weltausstellung in Barcelona," *Technische Rundschau* no. 30 (1929).
27. Fritz Neumeyer, *The Artless Word*, p. 226.
28. Mies, interview with Dirk Lohan, 1968, in the Mies van der Rohe Archive, The Museum of Modern Art, New York, and quoted in Schulze, *A Critical Biography*, pp. 15–16. Mies carried on at large or full-scale in his Chicago office: "He has required wooden models of the details of supports and their connections to be built in his studio to a scale of 1:1." Giedion, *Space, Time and Architecture*, p. 616.
29. Remarking on the size of the drawings, Schulze implies that Mies was trying to emulate a full-scale building: "His own presentation pieces were huge—one of his later Novembergruppe drawings measures more than nine feet—not least because the structures they depicted were usually meant to be exhibited rather than built. Paper architecture was still the rule of the day, the economy being what it was; thus architects had only other architects, and other artists, to talk to." Schulze, *A Critical Biography*, p. 104.
30. Walter Lehwess, "Architekturschau im Moabiter Ausstellungspalast," *Stadtbaukunst: Alter und Neuer Zeit* 2, no. 7 (1921): 107.
31. In John Zukowsky, ed., *Mies Reconsidered* (Chicago: The Art Institute of Chicago, and New York: Rizzoli Publications, 1986), p. 6, the photograph is credited to William Leftwick.
32. According to the competition brief (a copy of which is in the Mies van der Rohe Archive), the architects were asked to submit drawings at 1:200, a model at 1:500, and a site plan at 1:1000. Zimmerman, in "Mies van der Rohe, Political Ideology, and the Free Plan," argues that the building was to be 110 meters per side; in a drawing at a scale of 1:200, one side of the main building would have been about 21 inches.
33. See Pommer and Christian Otto, *Weissenhof 1927 and the Modern Movement in Architecture* (Chicago: at the University Press, 1991), p. 37.
34. See ibid., pp. 19, 27, and the exhibition program statement "Wohnung der Neuzeit," 1925, in the Mies van der Rohe Archive.
35. "After first arguing that the exhibition would show the lower and middle classes new methods for rational housing, . . . [Deputy Mayor Sigloch] and his advisers were caught short by the lavishnesss of Mies's design. In response they quickly changed their tune to ask that the design be approved because, in Sigloch's half-hearted words, 'something entirely new will be attempted, departing from tradition, so that one ought not to refrain from furthering it, difficult though that may seem at first.'" Pommer and Otto, *Weissenhof 1927*, p. 28, and p. 194, notes 3–5.
36. *Werkbundausstellung "Die Wohnung" Stuttgart 1927* (November 1926), p. 3. In the copy of this program in the Mies van der Rohe Archive, this sentence is underlined, perhaps by Mies.
37. Max Taut, letter to Mies, July 5, 1927. The Mies van der Rohe Archive.
38. Mies, letter to Gustaf Stotz, December 28, 1926. The Mies van der Rohe Archive.
39. Mies, in *Die Form* 2, no. 9 (1927): 257, trans. in Pommer and Otto, *Weissenhof 1927*, p. 60, and p. 215, note 63.
40. Mies, "Die Wohnung unserer Zeit," *Die Baugilde* 13, no. 9 (May 10, 1931): 691.
41. Beatriz Colomina, "Mies Not," *Columbia Documents of Architecture and Theory* 5 (December 1996): 94.
42. Wolf Tegethoff, "From Obscurity to Maturity: Mies van der Rohe's Breakthrough to Modernism," in Schulze, ed., *Critical Essays*, p. 65.
43. Evans, "Mies van der Rohe's Paradoxical Asymmetries," p. 248.
44. Mies, Foreword to *Bau und Wohnung* (Stuttgart: Deutsche Werkbund, 1927), p. 7, quoted in Neumeyer, *The Artless Word*, p. 156.
45. See, e.g., Mies, "Industrial Building," *G: Material zur elementaren Gestaltung* no. 3 (June 1924): 8–13, trans. in Neumeyer, *The Artless Word*, p. 248.
46. Neumeyer, *The Artless Word*, p. 159.
47. Mies, "On the Theme: Exhibitions," *Die Form* 3, no. 4 (1928):121, trans. in ibid., p. 304.
48. Mies, notebook (possibly from 1927), in ibid., p. 274. Translation partially mine. On the transformation of Mies's position, its philosophical origins, and its architectural implications, see Neumeyer, *The Artless Word*, pp. 146–61, 171–93, 195–213.
49. Lotz, "Die Halle II auf der Bauausstellung," p. 247.
50. Mies, "Die neue Zeit," *Die Form* 5, no. 15 (August 1, 1930): 406, trans. in Neumeyer, *The Artless Word*, p. 309.
51. Mies, letter to Stotz, September 11, 1925, quoted in Tegethoff, "From Obscurity to Maturity," p. 68.
52. Mies, letter to Gropius, April 6, 1927. The Mies van der Rohe Archive.
53. Tegethoff, "From Obscurity to Maturity," p. 70, and Pommer and Otto, *Weissenhof 1927*, p. 33.
54. The apartments are referred to in this way in the drawings. In the official guide the descriptions were neutralized to "Apartment for a Man," "Apartment for a Lady," "Apartment for Two Ladies," "Apartment for a Married Couple," and "Apartment with an Office." *Deutsche Bauausstellung Berlin 1931*, p. 166.
55. Credit for the design of the building was given to Vorhoelzer, Wiederanders, and Schmidt, of Munich, but a comparison of photographs of the exhibit with drawings in the Mies van der Rohe Archive shows that Mies did most of the design work for it. The contribution of the Munich firm to the overall building design was minimal and was based on Mies's and Reich's proposals.
56. *Deutsche Bauausstellung Berlin 1931*, p. 166. The conservative journal *Deutsche Bauhütte* was immediately suspicious of the Boarding House: "The people, who paid a high rent for handsome accommodations, found themselves degraded to hotel occupants, who had too much control over each other's private lives." "Kritische Spaziergänge durch die Berliner Bauausstellung," *Deutsche Bauhütte* 35, no. 16 (August 5, 1931): 236.
57. See Barbara Kirshenblatt-Gimblett, "Objects of Ethnography," *Exhibiting Cultures: The Poetics and Politics of Museum Display*, ed. Ivan Karp and Steven D. Lavine (Washington, D.C.: Smithsonian Institution Press, 1991), pp. 386–443.
58. Colomina, "Mies Not," p. 93.
59. There are large elevation drawings of the Esters House (1928–30) that measure 20 1/2 x 80 3/4 inches (no. 3.260, for example, in Drexler, ed., *The Mies van der Rohe Archive*, 2:46). These, however, are not rendered.

Rosemarie Haag Bletter, "Mies and Dark Transparency," pp. 350–57

I am greatly indebted to Mary McLeod for her invaluable advice. I also want to thank my graduate students Poyin Auyeung, Marianne Eggler-Gerozissis, and Claire Zimmerman for their assistance with research.

1. See, e.g., José Quetglas, "Fear of Glass: The Barcelona Pavilion," in Joan Ockman, ed., Beatriz Colomina, guest ed., *Architectureproduction* (New York: Princeton Architectural Press, 1988), pp. 122–51. According to Quetglas, the title of his essay (a revised version of which appears as "Loss of Synthesis: Mies's Pavilion" in K. Michael Hays, ed., *Architecture Theory since 1968* [Cambridge, Mass.: The MIT Press, 1998], pp. 384–91) is based on a short story by Paul Scheerbart. On larger issues of modernism as "haunted by a myth of transparency" and "dark space," see Anthony Vidler, *The Architectural Uncanny* (Cambridge, Mass.: The MIT Press, 1992), pp. 217 ff., 167 ff., and *Warped Space* (Cambridge, Mass.: The MIT Press, 2000), pp. 2–3. See also Mark Jarzombek, *The Psychologizing of Modernity* (New York and Cambridge: Cambridge University Press, 2000).
2. On Dada and Expressionism see Rose-Carol Washton Long, ed., *German Expressionism: Documents from the End of the Wilhelmine Empire to the Rise of National Socialism* (New York: G. K. Hall/Macmillan, 1993), pp. 262 ff.
3. Ibid., pp. 290 ff. On the changing meaning of *Neue Sachlichkeit* in art and architecture during the 1920s see Rosemarie Haag Bletter, "Introduction," *Adolf Behne: The Modern Functional Building* (Santa Monica: Getty Research Institute for the History of Art and the Humanities, 1996), pp. 49 ff.
4. See Bletter, "Paul Scheerbart and Expressionist Architecture," *Via* 8 (1986): 126–33; Bletter, "Paul Scheerbart's Architectural Fantasies," *Journal of the Society of Architectural Historians* 34 (May 1975): 83–97; and Bletter, "Paul Scheerbarts Architekturphantasien," in Achim Wendschuh, ed., *Bruno Taut 1880–1938*, exh. cat. (Berlin: Akademie der Künste, 1980), pp. 86–94. All of these are based on a chapter in Bletter, "Bruno Taut and Paul Scheerbart: Some Aspects of German Expressionist Architecture," Ph.D. dissertation, Columbia University, 1973.
5. See Hans Richter, *Dada: Art and Anti-Art* (London: Thames & Hudson, 1965), p. 120. See also Susan Babilon, "Hugo Ball and the Development of Sound Poetry," Ph.D. dissertation, City University of New York Graduate Center, 1999.
6. See Detlef Mertins, "The Enticing and Threatening Face of Prehistory: Walter Benjamin and the Utopia of Glass," *Assemblage* 29 (April 1996): 6–23.
7. On Expressionism and anarchism see Long, "Occultism, Anarchism, and Abstraction: Kandinsky's Art of the Future," *Art Journal* 46 (Spring 1987): 38–45.
8. Scheerbart, *Glasarchitektur* (Berlin: Verlag Der Sturm, 1914, reprint ed. Munich: Rogner & Bernhard, 1971). See also Dennis Sharp, ed., *Glass Architecture by Paul Scheerbart and Alpine Architecture by Bruno Taut*, trans. James Palmes and Shirley Palmer (New York: Praeger, 1972). Reyner Banham was the first historian to point out

Scheerbart's importance for modern architectural history, in "The Glass Paradise," *Architectural Review* 125 (February 1959): 87–89. However, he interprets him within a scientific, progressivist context.

9. See Bletter, "The Interpretation of the Glass Dream: Expressionist Architecture and the History of the Crystal Metaphor," *Journal of the Society of Architectural Historians* 40 (March 1981): 20–43. Separate elements of this ongoing iconography are discussed in Paul Frankl, *The Gothic: Literary Sources and Interpretations through Eight Centuries* (Princeton: at the University Press, 1960), and F. P. Bargebuhr, *The Alhambra: A Cycle of Studies on the Eleventh Century in Moorish Spain* (Berlin: de Gruyter, 1968).
10. See Louis Ginzberg, *The Legends of the Jews* (Philadelphia: Jewish Publication Society of America, 1913, 1941, twelfth impression 1987), IV:145, and VI (1928, 1956, ninth impression 1987), p. 289.
11. See Bargebuhr, "The Alhambra Palace of the Eleventh Century," *Journal of the Warburg and Courtauld Institutes*, XIX (1956): 229.
12. Ibid., pp. 257–58, note 116.
13. Sheba's Arabic name, Bilqis, may be related to the Hebrew word for "concubine" (see Ginzberg, *The Legends of the Jews*, VI:289). Solomon's appropriation of her powers also suggests the desire to incorporate the wealth and power of the historical region of Sheba.
14. Frankl, *The Gothic*, p. 173.
15. Ibid., pp. 177–79.
16. Ibid., pp. 173, 194. The early glass/crystal iconography will reappear in a Renaissance work, Francesco Colonna's *Hypnerotomachia Poliphili* (1499), in which the dreaming Poliphilo fears falling into a "black abyss" when he sees Venus sitting in a fountain in the middle of a black obsidian floor. See Linda Fierz-David, *The Dream of Poliphilo*, trans. M. Hottinger (New York: Pantheon, 1950). For a contemporary novelistic interpretation see Alberto Perez-Gomez, *Polyphilo or the Dark Forest Revisited: An Erotic Epiphany of Architecture* (Cambridge, Mass.: The MIT Press, 1992). Hieronymus Bosch's *Garden of Earthly Delights* (c. 1510–15) associates an imagery of glass and water with lust. Comparable references appear in Celtic folk tales; see Flavia Anderson, *The Ancient Secret: In Search of the Holy Grail* (London: Gollancz, 1953), Chapter XII, "The Sea of Glass."
17. See, for example, Mircea Eliade, *The Forge and the Crucible*, trans. S. Corrin (New York: Harper, 1962), and G. F. Hartlaub, *Alchemisten und Rosenkreuzer* (Willsbach and Heidelberg: Scherer, 1947). The Rosicrucians also used the crystal as a symbol.
18. See Bletter, "The Interpretation of the Glass Dream," p. 29, notes 39–41.
19. Friedrich Nietzsche, *Thus Spake Zarathustra*, trans. T. Common (New York: Macmillan, 1916), pp. 95, 117, 163.
20. See, for example, *Selected Works of Alfred Jarry*, ed. Roger Shattuck and S. W. Taylor (New York: Grove, 1965), p. 236. Paul Klee also identified the crystal with the brain and with images of the self; see Bletter, "The Interpretation of the Glass Dream," p. 31, note 53.
21. Stanford Anderson, *Peter Behrens and a New Architecture for the Twentieth Century* (Cambridge, Mass.: The MIT Press, 2000), p. 29 and chapter 2, "Behrens's Changing Concept of Life as Art," pp. 27–44. The poet Richard Dehmel, in residence at the Darmstadt artists' colony, was a close friend of Scheerbart's.
22. See Frederic J. Schwartz, *The Werkbund: Design Theory and Mass Culture before the First World War* (New Haven: Yale University Press, 1996).
23. Scheerbart had written aphorisms for the Glass House, such as "Light seeks to penetrate the whole cosmos / And is alive in crystal," and "Colored Glass / Destroys Hatred." Some of these were inscribed on a concrete band under the dome. See Sharp, ed., *Glass Architecture*, p. 14, and Angelika Thiekötter et al., *Kritallisationen, Splitterungen: Bruno Tauts Glashaus* (Basel: Birkhäuser, 1993).
24. Adolf Behne, "Gedanken über Kunst und Zweck dem Glashause gewidmet," *Kunstgewerbeblatt N.S.* XXVII (October 1913): 4.
25. Taut led the Arbeitsrat from 1918 until February 1919, when Walter Gropius took it over. Through this contact the glass/crystal iconography became incorporated in the opening manifesto of the Bauhaus, in April 1919; see Manfred Schlösser, ed., *Arbeitsrat für Kunst: Berlin 1918–1921*, exh. cat. (Berlin: Akademie der Künste, 1980). The Gläserne Kette was organized by Taut in late 1919. See Iain Boyd Whyte, ed. and trans., *The Crystal Chain Letters* (Cambridge, Mass.: The MIT Press, 1985).
26. Taut, *Die Auflösung der Städte* (Hagen: Folkwang Verlag, 1920), title page. This and Taut's other utopian books are fully reproduced with (sometimes inadequate) English translations in F. Borsi and G. K. König, *Architettura dell'Espressionismo* (Genoa: Vitali e Ghianda, 1967).
27. See Bletter, "Global Earthworks," *Art Journal* 42 (Fall 1982): 222–25.
28. See Eckhard Herrel, "Farbe in der Architektur der Moderne," in Vittorio Magnago Lampugnani and Romana Schneider, eds., *Moderne Architektur in Deutschland 1900 bis 1950: Expressionismus und Neue Sachlichkeit* (Stuttgart: Hatje, 1994), pp. 98–113.
29. Mies, n.t., *Frühlicht* 1, no. 4 (Summer 1922): 122–24, reprinted in Ulrich Conrads, ed., *Bruno Taut, Frühlicht 1920–1922* (Berlin: Ullstein, 1963), pp. 212–14. Mies's text is translated in Fritz Neumeyer, *The Artless Word*, p. 240. On these projects see Jean-Louis Cohen, *Mies van der Rohe* (London: E & FN Spon, 1996), pp. 23–29.
30. Franz Schulze, *A Critical Biography*, p. 104.
31. Mies, n.t., Eng. trans. in Neumeyer, *The Artless Word*, p. 240.
32. See Quetglas, "Fear of Glass," p. 144. Quetglas also discusses this effect in Mies's and Lilly Reich's Glass Room (1927), p. 130. Barry Bergdoll has pointed out to me that the intended internal lighting effect was not carried out in the German Pavilion because the required cut in the roof was never made.
33. Siegfried Kracauer, quoted in Janet Ward Lungstrum, "The Display Window: Designs and Desires of Weimar Consumerism," *New German Critique* 76 (Winter 1999): 128.
34. This point was suggested by Terence Riley.
35. Wolf Tegethoff, *The Villas and Country Houses*, p. 81.
36. See Neumeyer, *The Artless Word*, chapter 5, section 3, "Space for the Unfolding of the Spirit," pp. 171–93.
37. Karl Ernst Osthaus, "Das Schaufenster," *Jahrbuch des Deutschen Werkbundes* (1913), pp. 59–69. On the spiritualization of corporate imagery see Schwartz, *The Werkbund*.
38. Lungstrum, "The Display Window," p. 126. Lungstrum is mistaken, incidentally, in grouping Scheerbart with the orthodox modernists; citing only his *Glasarchitektur*, she is apparently unaware of his ironic mode. She also compares one of Taut's Expressionist proposals for glass architecture with the exhibitionism of Weimar store windows, without differentiating between a utopian project and an actual window display. Ibid., pp. 126–27.
39. See Claude Schnaidt, *Hannes Meyer: Bauten, Projekte und Schriften* (London: Tiranti, 1965), p. 23. See also Mary McLeod, "Architecture and Politics in the Reagan Era: From Postmodernism to Deconstruction," *Assemblage* 8 (February 1989): 23–59, reprinted in Hays, ed., *Architecture Theory since 1968*, esp. pp. 682–84.
40. Hays, *Modernism and the Posthumanist Subject: The Architecture of Hannes Meyer and Ludwig Hilberseimer* (Cambridge, Mass.: The MIT Press, 1992). Critiquing Hays's position, McLeod and Ockman see Meyer's supposed "antiformalism" as an "extreme formal rigorism," and regard the categorization of architects into "humanists" and "posthumanists" as a confusing back-formation; see their "Some Comments on Reproduction with Reference to Colomina and Hays," *Architecturereproduction*, pp. 223–31. See also Alan Colquhoun, "Response to Michael Hays," in ibid., pp. 213–16.
41. Winfried Nerdinger, "Anstössiges Rot," *Hannes Meyer: Architekt, Urbanist, Lehrer 1889–1954* (Berlin: Bauhaus-Archiv, 1989), pp. 14, 24.
42. Mertins, "The Enticing and Threatening Face of Prehistory."
43. Benjamin, "Erfahrung und Armut," 1933, quoted in Jacques Derrida, "An Exchange between Jacques Derrida and Peter Eisenman," *Assemblage* 12 (August 1990): 9. Mertins writes that Benjamin was influenced by Sigfried Giedion's *Bauen in Frankreich* of 1928, which he interpreted as "materialist history." "The Enticing and Threatening Face of Prehistory," p. 8.
44. Ernst Bloch, *Der Geist der Utopie* (Munich: Duncker und Humblot, 1918). See also Wayne Hudson, *The Marxist Philosophy of Ernst Bloch* (New York: St. Martin's Press, 1982).
45. Whyte, for example, describes Taut as essentially conservative, but ends his examination with the architect's utopian work; see his *Bruno Taut and the Architecture of Activism* (Cambridge: at the University Press, 1982). Magdalena Bushart, in *Der Geist der Gotik und die expressionistische Kunst* (Munich: S. Schreiber, 1990), sees Behne as an opportunist because he changed his political opinions during the 1920s. Addressing Bloch's and Georg Lukács's debate on Expressionism, Hays ignores its politicized context and treats Lukács's theory of realism uncritically for its contemporary applicability (*Modernism and the Posthumanist Subject*, pp. 48–53). On the other hand, Manfredo Tafuri and Francesco Dal Co see in the Expressionist utopias an attempt to recover "prebourgeois values." See their *Modern Architecture*, trans. Robert Erich Wolf (New York: Abrams, 1979), p. 129.
46. Regine Prange, "Das kristallene Sinnbild," in Lampugnani and Schneider, eds., *Moderne Architektur in Deutschland*, pp. 69–97. This essay, of impressively wide cultural range, is an abbreviated version of Prange's *Das Kristalline als Kunstsymbol: Bruno Taut und Paul Klee* (Hildesheim: Georg Olms, 1991).
47. On the history of the USPD and the KPD see Bletter, *Adolf Behne*, pp. 6–8, and A. J. Ryder, *Twentieth-Century Germany: From Bismarck to Brandt* (New York: Columbia University Press, 1973), p. 171. The mainstream Social Democrats (SPD) were part of the establishment of the Weimar Republic, and were more responsible for its fate than was the USPD. In this context it is interesting to note that Eduard Fuchs, who commissioned Mies to design the Monument to the November Revolution (1926), was the manager of the SPD paper *Vorwärts* (Cohen, *Mies van der Rohe*, p. 42).
48. Long writes, "It is ironic that while the right wing views Expressionism and other avant-garde movements as leading to communism, the extreme left viewed Expressionism as leading to fascism." In "Scholarship: Past, Present, and Future Directions," *German Expressionist Prints and Drawings*, exh. cat. (Los Angeles: Los Angeles County Museum of Art, and Munich: Prestel, 1989), p. 187.
49. See Fredric Jameson, ed., *Aesthetics and Politics*, trans. Ronald Taylor (London: NLB, 1977). See also Long, "The Left and the Debate over Expressionism in the Thirties," in Long, ed., *German Expressionism*, pp. 312–27. For a comparative look at social theories of the period see David Frisby, "Social Theory, the Metropolis, and Expressionism," in Timothy O. Benson, *Expressionist Utopias: Paradise, Metropolis, Architectural Fantasy*, exh. cat. (Los Angeles: Los Angeles County Museum of Art, 1993), pp. 88–111.
50. See Jameson, ed., *Aesthetics and Politics*, pp. 68, 70 ff.
51. Some critics, Mertins among them, have proposed Dadaist collage as a politically stronger statement than Expressionism. This judgment is largely based on the work of the Dada artist John Heartfield, who was also a Communist; but it must be remembered that Communist Party functionaries criticized photocollage as a "fashionable bourgeois game," incapable of the "simple great facts" available to the proletarian photographer. See Christopher Phillips, ed., *Photography in the Modern Era*, exh. cat. (New York: Metropolitan Museum of Art and Aperture, 1989), pp. 128–30.
52. John Baldacchino, *Post-Marxist Marxism. Questioning the Answer: Difference and Realism after Lukács and Adorno* (Brookfield: Avebury, 1996), p. 98.
53. Georg Simmel, "The Future of Our Culture," in Dal Co, *Figures of Architecture and Thought: German Architecture Culture 1880–1920*, trans. Donald Flanell Friedman (New York: Rizzoli, 1990), pp. 303, 307.
54. See also Frisby, "Social Theory, the Metropolis, and Expressionism," pp. 99–100.
55. See Richard Pommer, "Mies van der Rohe and the Political Ideology of the Modern Movement in Architecture," in Schulze, ed., *Mies van der Rohe: Critical Essays* (New York: The Museum of Modern Art, 1989), pp. 96–145. See also Bletter, "Proclamation of the Creators of Culture, 1934: Mies and the Nazis," *Assemblage* 2 (February 1987): 44–45. Elaine S. Hochman, in *Architects of Fortune: Mies van der Rohe and the Third Reich* (New York: Weidenfeld & Nicolson, 1989), does not prove her thesis that Mies was a member of the National Socialist party.
56. Paulette Singley, "Living in a Glass Prism: The Female Figure in Mies van der Rohe's Domestic Architecture," *Critical Matrix* 6, no. 2 (1992): 47–57; and Quetglas, "Fear of Glass," p. 143. Singley is reductive, however, in categorizing glass as masculine and opaque materials as feminine; glass contained feminine allusions as well. Mies's role in the placement of the sculpture in the Glass Room is unclear, since he collaborated on the design with Lilly Reich. Massimo Cacciari, in "Eupalinos or Architecture," trans. Stephen Sartarelli, *Oppositions* 21 (Summer 1980): 106–13, sees the extensive use of glass in Mies's work as "the concrete negation of dwelling" (113). Reprinted in Hays, ed., *Architecture Theory since 1968*, 394–406.
57. Lungstrum, "The Display Window," p. 126.
58. Derrida, "An Exchange between Jacques Derrida and Peter Eisenman," p. 9. See also Thomas Keenan, "Windows of Vulnerability," in Bruce Robbins, ed., *The Phantom Public Sphere* (Minneapolis: University of Minnesota Press, 1993), p. 133.
59. Colin Rowe and Robert Slutzky, "Transparency: Literal and Phenomenal," *Perspecta* 8 (1963), reprinted in *The Mathematics of the Ideal Villa and Other Essays* (Cambridge, Mass.: The MIT Press, 1976), pp. 159–83. See also my critique: Bletter , "Opaque Transparency," *Oppositions* 13 (1978): 121–26.
60. See Terence Riley, *Light Construction*, exh. cat. (New York: The Museum of Modern Art, 1995).
61. See Bletter, "Global Earthworks," pp. 222–25.
62. These were exhibited in the Siah Armajani exhibition at the Senior & Shopmaker Gallery, New York, November 9, 2000–January 6, 2001. Armajani told me that he had been familiar with my essay "The Interpretation of the Glass Dream" since the 1980s and readily admits having been influenced by it (discussion, November 9, 2000, and Senior & Shopmaker publicity release). See also Ministerio de Educación y Cultura, *Siah Armajani*, exh. cat.

(Madrid: Museo Nacional Centro de Arte Reina Sofía, 1999).

63. Robert Smithson, in "The Crystal Land," *Harper's Bazaar* no. 3054 (May 1966): 72–73, suggests an interest in the geological formations of crystals and offers an early instance of his concern with ordinary sites outside the gallery, but in later essays he points more directly to the materialist nature of his theme—see, e.g., *Robert Smithson: The Collected Writings*, ed. Jack Flam (Berkeley: University of California Press, 1996).
64. See Benjamin, "The Work of Art in the Age of Mechanical Reproduction," in *Illuminations*, ed. Hannah Arendt (New York: Schocken, 1969), pp. 233–37. Benjamin most likely appropriated the idea for his essay from Behne's earlier "Das reproduktive Zeitalter," *Marsyas* 3 (November/December 1917): 219–26. See Arnd Bohm, "Artful Reproduction: Benjamin's Appropriation of Adolf Behne's 'Das reproduktive Zeitalter' in the Kunstwerk-Essay," *The Germanic Review* 68, no. 4 (1993): 146–55.
65. Wolfgang Schivelbusch, *Licht, Schein und Wahn* (Berlin: Ernst & Sohn, 1992), quoted in Lungstrum, "The Display Window," p. 127.
66. Konrad Werner Schulze, *Glas in der Architektur der Gegenwart* (Stuttgart: Zaugg, 1929).
67. See Lungstrum, "The Display Window," pp. 126–27, citing Michel Foucault on Jean-Jacques Rousseau's and Jeremy Bentham's "dream of a transparent society, visible and legible in each of its parts, the dream of there no longer existing any zones of darkness." See Foucault, "The Eye of Power," in Colin Gordon, ed., *Power/Knowledge: Selected Interviews and Other Writings, 1972–1977* (Brighton: Harvester Press, 1980), p. 152.

Jean-Louis Cohen, "German Desires of America: Mies's Urban Visions," pp. 362–71

1. Alfred Dambitsch, ed., *Berlins dritte Dimension* (Berlin: Ullstein, 1912). Kurt Szafranski produced many posters, sometimes under the pseudonym "Söderström." He would eventually become the director of the Ullstein press, and in that role his trajectory would cross Mies's in 1925, when he was annoyed about the delay of an article for *Die Bauwelt*: See Fritz Neumeyer, *The Artless Word*, p. 346.
2. Walther Rathenau, in *Berlins dritte Dimension*, p. 20.
3. Bruno Möhring, in ibid., p. 12. On Möhring, an extremely important architect in Berlin's debate on urbanism, see Ines Wagemann, *Der Architekt Bruno Möhring 1863–1929* (Witterschlick: M. Wehle, 1992).
4. Peter Behrens, in *Berlins dritte Dimension*, pp. 10–11. Behrens would develop these positions in other texts: see Francesco Passanti, "Le Corbusier et le gratte-ciel: aux origines du plan Voisin," in Jean-Louis Cohen and Hubert Damisch, eds., *Américanisme et modernité: L'Idéal américain dans l'architecture* (Paris: Flammarion/École des Hautes Études et Sciences Sociales, 1993), pp. 171–89.
5. Behrens, in *Berlins dritte Dimension*.
6. There was a large popular German literature on Chicago. On the question of urbanism, Werner Hegemann wrote a book on D. Burnham's and E. Bennett's plan for the city: *Der Neue Bebauungsplan für Chicago* (Berlin: Ernst Wasmuth, 1911). Mies could also have read H. P. Berlage's account of his visit to Chicago: Berlage, "Neuere amerikanische Architektur," *Schweizerische Bauzeitung* 60 (1912), September 14, pp. 148–50, and September 21, pp. 165–67.
7. On *Amerikanismus* in Germany see Miles David Samson, *German-American Dialogues and the Modern Movement before the Design Migration 1910–1933* (Cambridge, Mass.: Harvard University Press, 1988). On the general purview of Americanism see Cohen and Damisch, eds., *Américanisme et modernité*, and Cohen, *Scenes of the World to Come: European Architecture and the American Challenge 1893–1960* (Paris: Flammarion, 1995).
8. I am indebted to Detlef Mertins for information arising from the books Mies owned. But this information must clearly remain partial: the possession of a book does not mean it was read, just as the absence of a book does not mean it was ignored. Only underscored passages, markings, and annotations can vouch for the book's actual assimilation.
9. See Reyner Banham, *A Concrete Atlantis: U.S. Industrial Buildings and European Modern Architecture 1900–1925* (Cambridge, Mass.: The MIT Press, 1986).
10. Walter Gropius, "Die Entwicklung moderner Industriebaukunst," in *Die Kunst in Industrie und Handel: Jahrbuch des Deutschen Werkbundes 1913* (Jena: Eugen Diederichs, 1913), pp. 17–22.
11. For this project, and also later for the Illinois Institute of Technology, Mies seems to have studied models, plans, and facades published by Werner Lindner. See Karl Otto Lüfkens, "Die Verseidag-Bauten von Mies van der Rohe (1933 bis 1937), ein Dokument der Architektur des XX. Jahrhunderts," *Die Heimat* 48 (December 1977): 57–61, and Wolf Tegethoff, "Industriearchitektur und Neues Bauen, Mies van der Rohes Verseidag-Fabrik in Krefeld," *Archithese* no. 13 (May–June 1983): 33–38.
12. This explicit interest was reported by Myron Goldsmith. See William H. Jordy, *American Buildings and Their Architects* (Garden City, N.Y.: Anchor Press, 1976), 4:224. In a general way, American industrial buildings, outside specialist periodicals such as *Der Industriebau* (published from 1910 to 1931), are presented in thematic analyses by traditionalist architects: see Lindner and Georg Steinmetz, *Die Ingenieurbauten in ihrer guten Gestaltung* (Berlin: Wasmuth, 1923), and Lindner, *Bauten der Technik, ihre Form und Wirkung: Werkanlagen* (Berlin: Wasmuth, 1927).
13. On Kahn see George Nelson, *Industrial Architecture of Albert Kahn, Inc.* (New York: Architectural Book Publishing Co., 1939), Grant Hildebrand, *Designing for Industry: The Architecture of Albert Kahn* (Cambridge, Mass.: The MIT Press, 1974), and Federico Bucci, *Albert Kahn: Architect of Ford* (New York: Princeton Architectural Press, 1993).
14. Walther Rathenau, *Die neue Wirtschaft* (Berlin: S. Fischer, 1918).
15. Massimo Cacciari, *Metropolis: Saggi sulla grande città di Sombart, Endell, Scheffler e Simmel* (Rome: Officina, 1973).
16. On Weissenhof see Christian Otto and Richard Pommer, *Weissenhof 1927 and the Modern Movement in Architecture* (Chicago: at the University Press, 1991), and Mertins, Introduction, in Walter Curt Behrendt, *The Victory of the New Building Style* (Los Angeles: Getty Research Institute for the History of Art and the Humanities, 2000).
17. See Brian Ladd, *Urban Planning and Civic Order in Germany, 1860–1914* (Cambridge, Mass.: Harvard University Press, 1990).
18. Mies, lecture, dated March 17, 1926, in Neumeyer, *The Artless Word*, p. 254.
19. Mies, "The Preconditions of Architectural Work," lecture, delivered February 1928, in ibid., p. 300.
20. See Francesco Dal Co, ed., *Figures of Architecture and Thought: German Architectural Culture 1880–1920* (New York: Rizzoli, 1990).
21. Karl Scheffler, *Moderne Baukunst* (Berlin: Julius Bard, 1907), quoted in Neumeyer, *The Artless Word*, p. 113.
22. Karl Scheffler, *Die Architektur der Großstadt* (Berlin: Bruno Cassirer, 1913).
23. See Neumeyer, *The Artless Word*, pp. 181–83.
24. August Endell, *Die Schönheit der grossen Stadt* (Stuttgart: Strecker & Schroeder, 1908). Endell's writings are republished in Endell, *Vom Sehen, Texte 1896–1925*, ed. Helge David (Basel and Berlin: Birkhäuser, 1995).
25. Neumeyer, "Architektur als mythisches Bild: Anmerkungen zur imaginären Realität des gläsernen Hochhauses am Bahnhof-Friedrichstrasse," in Neumeyer, ed., *Ludwig Mies van der Rohe: Hochhaus am Bahnhof Friedrichstrasse. Dokumentation des Mies-van-der-Rohe-Symposiums in der Neuen Nationalgalerie* (Berlin: E. Wasmuth, 1993), pp. 9–29.
26. On German responses to the skyscraper program see Florian Zimmermann, ed., *Der Schrei nach dem Turmhaus: Der Ideenwettbewerb Hochhaus am Bahnhof Friedrichstrasse Berlin 1921–1922* (Berlin: Argon-Verlag, 1988), Rainer Stommer, *Hochhaus, der Beginn in Deutschland* (Marburg: Jonas, 1990), and Dietrich Neumann, *"Die Wolkenkratzer kommen!" Deutsche Hochhäuser der zwanziger Jahre, Debatten, Projekte, Bauten* (Braunschweig and Wiesbaden: Vieweg, 1990).
27. See the subtle remarks on this theme in Juan Antonio Ramírez, *The Beehive Metaphor from Gaudí to Le Corbusier* (London: Reaktion Books, 2000), pp. 92–97.
28. U. A., "École des Beaux-Arts: Concours du 'Prix des Américains,'" *La Construction moderne*, February 13, 1892, pp. 219–21.
29. Rathenau, in *Berlins dritte Dimension*, pp. 20–21.
30. See Julius Klinger's lithograph *Tabu* (1919), in Neumeyer, ed., *Hochhaus am Bahnhof Friedrichstrasse*, p. 14.
31. Ludwig Hilberseimer and Udo Rukser, "Amerikanische Architektur," *Kunst und Künstler* 18 (1920): 541–42. Graham's building was well-known in Germany; see "Der neue Equitable-Bau in New York: das grösste Gebäude der Welt," *Die Bauwelt* 4, no. 17 (1914): 27–28.
32. Hegemann, text adjoining an article by Theo van Doesburg, "Die neue Architektur und ihre Folgen," *Wasmuths Monatshefte für Baukunst* 9, no. 12 (1925): 509. That same year, in the journal he edited, Hegemann published an article by Fiske Kimball celebrating the victory of classicism in the United States: Kimball, "Alte und neue Baukunst in Amerika: Der Sieg des jungen Klassizismus über den Funktionalismus der Neunziger Jahre," *Wasmuths Monatshefte für Baukunst* 9, no. 6 (1925): 225–39.
33. Martin Mächler, "Zum Problem des Wolkenkratzers," *Wasmuths Monatshefte für Baukunst* 5 (1920–21): 191–205, 260–73.
34. Siegfried Kracauer, "Über Turmhäuser," *Frankfurter Zeitung*, March 2, 1921, in Neumann, *"Die Wolkenkratzer kommen!"*, p. 11.
35. See the responses by Martin Wagner, Hegemann, and Heinrich Mendelssohn to the question *"Soll Berlin Wolkenkratzer bauen?"* (Should Berlin build skyscrapers?), *Wasmuths Monatshefte für Baukunst* 12, no. 6 (1928): 286–89.
36. In particular, Mies owned two basic books on America published in Germany: Lewis Mumford, *Vom Blockhaus zum Wolkenkratzer: Eine Studie über amerikanische Architektur und Zivilisation* (Berlin: Bruno Cassirer Verlag, 1925, a translation of Mumford's *Sticks and Stones*, 1924), and Wagner, *Städtebauliche Probleme in amerikanischen Städten und ihre Rückwirkung auf den deutschen Städtebau* (Berlin: Deutsche Bauzeitung, 1929).
37. Mies, lecture, March 17, 1926, in Neumeyer, *The Artless Word*, p. 255. Mies owned a copy of the German translation of Le Corbusier's *Urbanisme: Städtebau* (Berlin and Leipzig: Deutsche Verlags-Anstalt, 1929).
38. On this question the Munich architect and theoretician Herman Sörgel wrote, "America has no culture, to be sure, but we have no civilization." Sörgel, "Amerika," *Baukunst* 1, no. 12 (1925): 323.
39. The Siedlungsverband Ruhrkohlengebiet, created by Robert Schmidt after World War I, provided the first European experience of regional planning.
40. Mies, lecture, March 17, 1926, in Neumeyer, *The Artless Word*, pp. 255–56. Mies's interest in the relationship between traffic and the city can be assumed from some of the books in his library, such as Hegemann's *Städtebau nach den Ergebnissen der Allgemeinen Städtebau-Ausstellung in Berlin* (Berlin: E. Wasmuth, 1911–13), and Hans Ludwig Sierk's *Wirtschaftlicher Städtebau und angewandte kommunale Verkehrswissenschaft* (Dresden: Kaden, 1926) and *Grundriss der sicheren, reichen, ruhigen Stadt* (Dresden: Kaden, 1929).
41. Mies, lecture, June 19, 1924, in Neumeyer, *The Artless Word*, p. 250. Despite these positive remarks, in 1925 Mies would refuse to take up Taut's position in Magdeburg.
42. Mies, lecture, March 17, 1926, in Neumeyer, *The Artless Word*, p. 256.
43. Rudolf Schwarz, *Von der Bebauung der Erde* (Heidelberg: Lambert Schneider Verlag, 1949). On Schwarz's urbanist thought see Panos Mantziaras, *La Ville-Paysage: Rudolf Schwarz et la dissolution des villes* (Saint-Denis: Université de Paris 8, 2000) (Ph.D. dissertation).
44. Schwarz, "Großstadt als Tatsache und Aufgabe," *Die Schildgenossen* 8, no. 4 (1927): 301–7.
45. Mies, "Baukunst und Zeitwille," in Neumeyer, *The Artless Word*, pp. 245–47.
46. Mies, in Neumeyer, *The Artless Word*, p. 259.
47. Frank Lloyd Wright, "Mr. Wright Talks on Broadacre City to Ludwig Mies van der Rohe," *Taliesin* 1 (October 1940): 10–18.
48. Mies, "Autobahnen als baukünstlerisches Problem," *Die Autobahn* 5, no. 10 (1932): 1, in Neumeyer, *The Artless Word*, p. 313. On the history of Germany's highway program see Rainer Stommer, ed., *Reichsautobahn—Pyramiden des Dritten Reiches: Analysen zur Ästhetik eines unbewältigten Mythos* (Marburg: Jonas, 1982), and Martin Kornrumpf, *HaFraBa e.V. Deutsche Autobahnplanung 1926–1934* (Bonn and Bad Godesberg: Kirschbaum Verlag, 1990).
49. Mies, introduction to Hilberseimer, *The New City: Principles of Planning* (Chicago: Paul Theobald, 1944).
50. The adventurer and writer Karl May published his first account of the adventures of the Winnetou Indians in 1878; a Winnetou trilogy followed in 1893; and a fourth volume followed in 1910, after May's delayed trip to America in 1908.
51. Tegethoff, *The Villas and Country Houses*, pp. 127–28.

Selected Bibliography

The fundamental resources for research on Mies remain the architectural archive that he left to The Museum of Modern Art, New York; his correspondence, in the Manuscripts Division of the Library of Congress, Washington, D.C.; and his library, in the Library of the University of Illinois at Chicago.

Archival and Bibliographical Source Books

Drexler, Arthur, ed. (vols. 1–4), and Franz Schulze, ed. (vols. 5–20). *The Mies van der Rohe Archive.* New York: Garland, 1986–92. 20 volumes.

Glaeser, Ludwig. *Ludwig Mies van der Rohe: Drawings in the Collection of The Museum of Modern Art.* New York: The Museum of Modern Art, 1969.

Harmon, Robert B. *Ludwig Mies van der Rohe, Master Architect: A Selected Bibliography.* Monticello: Vance, 1979.

Spaeth, David A. *Ludwig Mies van der Rohe: An Annotated Bibliography and Chronology.* New York: Garland, 1979.

Dahle, Terje Nils, ed. *Architects: Ludwig Mies van der Rohe.* Bibliography no. 57. Stuttgart: ICONDA, 1987, 2nd ed. 1990.

Books

Achilles, Rolf, Kevin Harrington, and Charlotte Myhrum, eds. *Mies van der Rohe: Architect as Educator.* Chicago: Illinois Institute of Technology, 1986.

Amberger, Eva-Maria. *Sergius Ruegenberg, Architekt zwischen Mies van der Rohe und Hans Scharoun.* Berlin: Berlinische Galerie, 2000.

Blake, Peter. *The Master Builders.* New York: Knopf, 1960, reprint. ed. W. W. Norton, 1996. The Mies section reprinted as *Mies van der Rohe, Architecture and Structure.* Harmondsworth: Pelican, 1960.

Blaser, Werner. *Mies van der Rohe.* Zurich: Verlag für Architektur, 1965.

———. *Mies van der Rohe: The Art of Structure.* New York: Praeger, 1965.

———. *West Meets East: Mies van der Rohe.* Basel and Boston: Birkhäuser, 1996.

Bonta, Juan Pablos. *Anatomia de la interpretación en arquitectura, resena semiotica de la critica del pabellón de Barcelona de Mies van der Rohe.* Barcelona: Gili, 1975.

Carter, Peter. *Mies van der Rohe at Work.* New York: Praeger, 1974. Paperback ed. London and New York: Phaidon, 1999.

Cohen, Jean-Louis. *Mies van der Rohe.* Paris: Hazan, 1994. Eng. trans. London: E & FN Spon, 1996.

Dal Co, Francesco. *Figures of Architecture and Thought: German Architecture Culture 1880–1920.* New York: Rizzoli, 1990.

Dearstyne, Howard. *Inside the Bauhaus.* New York: Rizzoli, 1986.

Drexler, Arthur. *Ludwig Mies van der Rohe.* New York: Braziller, 1960.

Erfurth, Helmut. *Ludwig Mies van der Rohe: Die Trinkhalle, seine einziger Bau in Dessau.* Dessau: Anhaltische Verlagsges, 1995.

Four Great Makers of Modern Architecture: Gropius, Le Corbusier, Mies van der Rohe and Wright. New York: Trustees of Columbia University, 1963. Reprint ed. New York: Da Capo Press, 1970.

Hammer-Tugendhat, Daniela, and Wolf Tegethoff, eds. *Ludwig Mies van der Rohe: Das Haus Tugendhat.* Vienna: Springer, 1998. Eng. trans. New York: Springer, 2000.

Heynen, Julian. *Ein Ort für Kunst/A Place for Art: Ludwig Mies van der Rohe Hause Lange—Hause Esters.* Krefeld: Krefelder Kunstmuseen, 1995.

Hilberseimer, Ludwig. *Mies van der Rohe.* Chicago: P. Theobald, 1956. Rev. eds. New York, 1965 and 1972.

Hochman, Elaine S. *Architects of Fortune: Mies van der Rohe and the Third Reich.* New York: Weidenfeld & Nicolson, 1989.

Honey, Sandra, ed. *Mies van der Rohe: European Works.* London: Academy Editions, 1986.

Johnson, Philip. *Mies van der Rohe.* New York: The Museum of Modern Art, 1947. Rev. ed. 1953, 3rd ed. 1978.

Kirsch, Karin. *Briefe zur Weissenhofsiedlung.* Stuttgart: Deutsche Verlags-Anstalt, 1997.

——— *Die Weissenhofsiedlung, Werkbund-Ausstellung "Die Wohnung"— Stuttgart 1927.* Stuttgart: Deutsche Verlags-Anstalt, 1987. Eng. trans. New York: Rizzoli, 1989.

Mertins, Detlef, ed. *The Presence of Mies.* New York: Princeton Architectural Press, 1994.

Neue Nationalgalerie Berlin, Dreissig Jahre. Berlin: Neue Nationalgalerie, 1998.

Neumeyer, Fritz. *The Artless Word: Mies van der Rohe on the Building Art.* Cambridge, Mass.: The MIT Press, 1991.

Neumeyer, Fritz, ed. *Ludwig Mies van der Rohe: Hochhaus am Bahnhof Friedrichstrasse: Dokumentation des Mies-van-der-Rohe-Symposiums in der Neuen Nationalgalerie, Berlin.* Berlin: Wasmuth, 1993.

Pommer, Richard, and Christian F. Otto. *Weissenhof 1927 and the Modern Movement in Architecture.* Chicago: at the University Press, 1991.

Quetglas, José. *Der gläserne Schrecken: Imágenes del Pabellón de Alemania.* Montreal: Section b, 1991.

Schink, Arnold. *Mies van der Rohe: Beiträge zur ästhetischen Entwicklung der Wohnarchitektur.* Stuttgart: Karl Krämer Verlag, 1990.

Schulze, Franz. *Mies van der Rohe: A Critical Biography.* Chicago and London: The University of Chicago Press, 1985.

———, ed. *Mies van der Rohe: Critical Essays.* New York: The Museum of Modern Art, 1989.

Solà-Morales, Ignasi de, Christian Cirici, and Fernando Ramos. *Mies van der Rohe—Barcelona Pavilon.* Barcelona: Gili, 1993.

Spaeth, David A. *Mies van der Rohe.* New York: Rizzoli, 1985.

Speyer, James. *Ludwig Mies van der Rohe.* Chicago: The Art Institute of Chicago, 1968.

Stiller, Adolf, ed. *Das Haus Tugendhat: Ludwig Mies van der Rohe, Brünn, 1930.* Salzburg: Pustet, 1999.

Tegethoff, Wolf. *Im Brennpunkt der Moderne: Mies van der Rohe und das Haus Tugendhat in Brünn.* Munich: HypoVereinsbank, 1998.

——— *Mies van der Rohe: The Villas and Country*

Houses. New York: The Museum of Modern Art, 1985.

Van der Wolk, Johannes. *De Kroellers en hun architecten.* Otterlo: Rijksmuseum Kröller-Müller, 1992.

Vegesack, Alexander von, and Matthias Kries, eds. *Mies van der Rohe: Architecture and Design in Stuttgart, Barcelona, Brno.* Weil-am-Rhein: Vitra Design Museum/Skira, 1998.

Wachter, Gabriela, ed. *Mies van der Rohes Neue Nationalgalerie in Berlin/Mies van der Rohe's New National Gallery in Berlin.* Berlin: Vice Versa Verlag, 1995.

Wolsdorff, Christian, ed. *Der vorbildliche Architekt: Mies van der Rohes Architekturunterricht 1930–1958 am Bauhaus und in Chicago.* Berlin: Bauhaus-Archiv, 1986.

Zimmerman, Florian, ed. *Der Schrei nach dem Turmhaus: Der Ideen wettbewerb Hochhaus am Bahnhof Friedrichstrasse Berlin 1921/22.* Berlin: Bauhaus-Archiv, 1988.

Zukowsky, John, ed. *Mies Reconsidered: His Career, Legacy, and Disciples.* Chicago: The Art Institute of Chicago, 1986.

Articles

This bibliography does not include most of the articles published on Mies in professional periodicals during his lifetime; for this see Spaeth's Annotated Bibliography and Chronology.

Berckenhagen, Ekhardt. "Mies van der Rohe und Ruegenberg: Ein Skizzenbuch." *Jahrbuch Preussischer Kulturbesitz* 10 (1972): 275–80.

Berdini, Paolo. "Una piccola casa di Mies: La teoria applicata." *Casabella* 48 (October 1984): 37–39.

Boyken, Immo. "Ludwig Mies van der Rohe and Egon Eiermann: The Dictate of Order." *Journal of the Society of Architectural Historians* 49 (June 1990): 42–46.

Brown, W. Gordon. "Form as the Object of Experience: Georg Simmel's Influence on Mies van der Rohe." *Journal of Architectural Education* 43 (Winter 1990): 42–46.

Buddensieg, Tilmann. "Mies und Messel. Zu einem fehlden Kapital in der frühen Biographie von Mies van der Rohe." In Christian Beutler, Peter-Klauss Schuster, and Martin Warnke, eds. *Kunst im 1800 und die Folgen, Werner Hofmann zu Ehren.* Munich: Prestel Verlag, 1988, pp. 346–51.

Cacciari, Massimo. "Mies's Classics." *RES* 16 (1988): 9–16.

Colomina, Beatriz. "Mies not." *Columbia Documents of Architecture and Theory* 5 (1996): 75–101.

Constant, Caroline. "The Barcelona Pavilion as Landscape Garden: Modernity and the Picturesque." *AA Files* 20 (1990): 47–54.

Evans, Robin. "Mies van der Rohe's Paradoxical Symmetries." *AA Files* 19 (Spring 1990): 56–68.

Forster, Kurt. "Four Unpublished Drawings by Mies van der Rohe: A Commentary." *RES* 16 (1988): 5–8.

Hays, K. Michael. "Critical Architecture: Between Culture and Form." *Perspecta* 21 (1984): 14–29.

Heuser, Mechtild. "La Finestra sul Cortile. Behrens e

Houses. New York: The Museum of Modern Art, 1985.

Mies van der Rohe: AEG Turbinenhalle, Berlino 1908–09." *Casabella* 651–52 (December 1997–January 1998): 14–25.

Honey, Sandra. "Mies at the Bauhaus." *Architectural Association Quarterly* 10, no. 1 (1978): 51–59.

———. "Who and What Inspired Mies van der Rohe in Germany." *Architectural Design* 49, nos 3–4 (1979): 99–102.

Kleinman, Kent, and Leslie van Duzer. "Eisen und Mörtel: Anmerkungen zu Haus Lange und Haus Esters." *Bauwelt* 91, no. 41 (November 3, 2000): 16–19.

Kruse, Christiane. "Haus Werner: ein ungeliebtes Fruhwerk Mies van der Rohes." *Zeitschrift für Kunstgeschichte* 56 (1993): 554–63.

Levine, Neil. "'The Significance of Facts': Mies's Collages Up Close and Personal." *Assemblage* 37 (1998): 70–101.

Miller, Wallis. "Schinkel and the Politics of German Memory: The Life of the Neue Wache in Berlin." In Scott Denham, Irene Kacandes, and Jonathan Petropoulous, eds. *A User's Guide to German Cultural Studies.* Ann Arbor: The University of Michigan Press, 1997, pp. 228–56.

Nelson, George. "Architects of Europe Today—Mies van der Rohe." *Pencil Points* 16 (September 1935): 453–60.

Neumann, Dietrich. "Three Early Designs by Mies van der Rohe." *Perspecta* 27 (1992): 76–97.

Neumeyer, Fritz. "Giedion og Mies van der Rohe: Et paradoks i modernismens historiografi/A Paradox in the Historiography of Modernism." *Skala* 28 (1993): 50–57. In Dutch as "Giedion en Mies van der Rohe: een paradox in de historiografie van het Moderne." *Archis* no. 4 (April 1992): 47–51.

———. "Schinkel im Zeilenbau: Mies van der Rohe's Siedlung an der Afrikanischen Strasse in Berlin-Wedding." In Andreas Beyer, Vittorio Lampugnani, and Gunter Schwikhart, eds. *Hülle und Fülle, Festschrift für Tilman Buddensieg.* Alfter: VDG, 1993, pp. 415–31.

Ott, Randall. "The Horizonal Symmetry of Mies van der Rohe." *Dimensions* 7 (Spring 1993): 112–31.

Quetglas, José. "Fear of Glass." In Beatriz Colomina and K. Michael Hays, eds. *Architectureproduction.* Princeton: Princeton Architectural Press, 1988.

Struck, Anette. "Stationen der Planung und des Bauens Ludwig Mies van der Rohe." *Architektur Jahrbuch/Architecture Annual 1994.* Munich and New York: Prestel, 1994, pp. 192–98.

Tegethoff, Wolf. "On the Development of the Concept of Space in the Works of Mies van der Rohe." *Daidalos* 13 (September 15, 1984): 114–23.

———. "Orianda–Berlin: das Vorbild Schinkels im Werk Mies van der Rohes." *Zeitschrift des Deutschen Vereins für Kunstwissenschaft* 38 (1981): 174–84.

———. "Weissenhof 1927: der Sieg des neuen Baustils." *Jahrbuch des Zentralinstituts für Kunstgeschichte* 3 (1987): 195–228.

Westheim, Paul. "Mies van der Rohe: Entwicklung eines Architekten." *Das Kunstblatt* 11, no. 2 (February 1927): 55–62.

Zervos, Christian. "Mies van der Rohe." *Cahiers d'art* 3 (1928): 35–38.

Index

Acknowledgments

A good deal of the inspiration for this exhibition and publication was provided by the revelatory experience of visiting the 1986 reconstruction of Mies's German Pavilion in Barcelona. We would like to note our deep gratitude to Ignasi de Solà-Morales, who died in March of this year, for his role in bringing the masterpiece of Mies's European career back to life.

Throughout the planning of this exhibition and publication, Phyllis Lambert, Francesco Dal Co, George Danforth, Jacques Herzog, Lluís Hortet, Jeffrey Kipnis, Josef Paul Kleihues, Dirk Lohan, and Lord Peter Palumbo provided advice of lasting value. Rosemarie Haag Bletter, Jean-Louis Cohen, K. Michael Hays, Detlef Mertins, Fritz Neumeyer, and Wolf Tegethoff contributed substantially to the intellectual development of the project.

We had always hoped that the exhibition would travel, and the advice and assistance of a number of people who would play a key role in realizing this important goal were critical: Wolf-Dieter Dube, Peter-Klaus Schuster, and Andres Lepik of the Staatliche Museen Zu Berlin–Preussischer Kulturbesitz; and Luis Monreal and Imma Casas of the Fundación La Caixa, Barcelona.

For over twenty years, Knoll, Inc., has supported the activities of the Mies van der Rohe Archive. This exhibition and publication could not have been organized without the ongoing scholarly research and organization of the 19,000 drawings in the archive, all of which is sustained through Knoll's commitment to The Museum of Modern Art and its activities. The initial research for *Mies in Berlin* was undertaken in a two-year symposium conducted as a joint initiative of The Museum of Modern Art and Columbia University, and generously funded by the Getty Grant Program. *Mies in Berlin* was generously supported by UBS PaineWebber, the Lily Auchincloss Foundation, Inc., Peter Norton of the Norton Family Foundation, and Tishman Speyer Properties. We also thank Elise Jaffe and Jeffrey Brown, Mrs. Frances Lewis, Sarah Peter, and The Government of The Federal Republic, Germany, for their additional assistance.

Various scholars, including Eva-Maria Amberger, Vittorio Magnago Lampugnani, Andres Lepik, Jan Maruhn, Wallis Miller, and Christian Wolsdorff, participated in the seminar and devoted time to other aspects of the project. In New York and during research trips in Germany, Pierre Adler, Mirka Beneš, Tilmann Buddensieg, Kai Gutschow, Matilda McQuaid, Stanislaus von Moos, James S. Russell, and Laurie Stein shared valuable insights and research resources with the seminar participants.

The work of other scholars also proved an invaluable resource: Ludwig Glaeser, Philip Johnson, Karin Kirsch, Christiane Kruse, and Franz Schulze may be unaware of the extent to which we relied on their work, but should be acknowledged anyway. The texts of Wolf Tegethoff and Fritz Neumeyer must also be cited in this regard.

The students of Columbia University and the Graduate Center of the City University of New York who participated in the seminar enthusiastically took up the challenge of exploring with us a new perspective on Mies's work before 1938: Benjamin Aranda, Kimberly Elman, Felix Finkernagel, Leslie Fitzpatrick, Judith Gieseler, Victoria Koppel, Casey Mack, Miriam Torres Marcos, Sjoukje van der Meulen, Ken Oshima, Eeve-Liisa Pelkonen, Fernando Quesada, Christian Rattemeyer, and Nader Vossoughian. A number of students made subsequent contributions that enriched the project: Josef Asteinza, Paul Galvez, Lucy M. Maulsby, and Amanda Reeser. Marianne Eggler-Gerozissis and Claire Zimmerman not only provided scholarly contributions but gave extensively of their logistical and linguistic skills on our research trips.

A number of people made invaluable resources of themselves by responding to our requests for documents and information, helping us with securing loans, and assisting in other ways: Guus Bakker, Julian Heynen, Dietrich Neumann, Christian Otto, Lars Scharnholz, Adrian Sudhalter, Johannes van der Wolk, Kent Kleinmann, and Leslie Van Duzer.

Our research in Europe and the United States was made immeasurably more effective by the advice and assistance of colleagues at numerous institutions: Cammie MacAtee and Elsbeth Cowell, Canadian Centre for Architecture, Montreal; Donna Robertson, Illinois Institute of Technology, Chicago; Elke Blauert, Kunstbibliothek, Berlin; Jochen Kronjäger, Kunsthalle Mannheim; Monika Bartsch and Barbara Schaeche, Landesarchiv Berlin; Ford Peatross, the Library of Congress, Washington, D.C.; Heinz Poker, Staatarchiv Stuttgart; Hardt-Waltherr Hämer and Margret Kentgens-Craig, Stiftung Bauhaus Dessau; and Manfred Reuther, Stiftung Seebüll Ada und Emil Nolde, Neukirchen. Other individuals provided assistance and gave generously of their knowledge during our research trips: Marianne Förster, Marianne Giwolies, Mechtild Heuser, Pawel Konieczny, Rudiger Krisch, Manfred Ludewig, Lutz Materne, Ilona Petrick, Ralf Pfeiffer,

Gunnar Porikys, Francesca Rogier, Klaus Rupprecht, Sabine Sander, and Adrianna Tyrek; Evelin Richter, City of Guben; Zenon Turowski and Bogusław Jaskøwski, City of Gubin; and Heinz-Josef Vogt, City of Krefeld.

Special thanks are due to the heirs of Mies's clients who have been so helpful with their personal knowledge: A. F. Gericke-Urbig, Daniela Hammer-Tugendhat, Wolfgang Henke, Nikolas and Ellen Dyvik Henke, Isa Jeromin, Alfred Krech, Christina Lange-Castenow, Bill Resor, Stan Resor, Jr., Mr. and Mrs. Sever Severain, Sever Severain, Jr., the Familie Thelosen-Urbig, Renate Werner, Goetz Wolf, Christine Wolf, and Baerbel Wolf. We would like to also acknowledge the current custodians and owners of Mies's buildings who made the sites accessible to us and to the heirs of the former owners: Christina Geiseler, Hans Jörg Duvigneau, Beatriz Kindler, and Christina Panhoff, Gemeinnützige Siedlungs- und Wohnungsbaugesellschaft, Berlin; Thomas Kramberg and Reinhard Wegener, Heilpädagogisches Theurapeutikum, Berlin-Zehlendorf; Joachim Heitmann, Heike Hönsch, Heide Katzschmann, and Volker Döhne, Kunstmuseum der Stadt Krefeld; Lluís Hortet and Diane Grey, Mies van der Rohe Foundation, Barcelona; Wita Noack, Mies van der Rohe Haus, Hohenschönhausen; Jiri Vanek and Helena Vilímková, Muzeum Mesta, Brno; Angela Schnieder, Neue Nationalgalerie, Berlin; Friedrich-Wilhelm Pape, Oberlinhaus, Neubabelsberg; Mr. and Mrs. Edmund Pattberg, Lillemor Speckmann, Dieter Jung, and Helmut Reinhäckel, Verseidag GMBH, Krefeld; and Konrad Wolf. Special mention should be made of the kindness and hospitable efforts of Franz and Margit Kleber, who have enthusiastically undertaken their stewardship of the Riehl House.

A number of design professionals, architects, engineers, and others who have spent considerable time working with Mies's extant structures undertook specific tasks at our request. We are very grateful to Horst Krainhöfer, Ingenieurbüro Dipl.-H. Krainhöfer, Cottbus; Thomas Piecha, Messen und Zeichnen, Berlin; Ivan Reimann and Thomas Müller, Müller Reimann Architekten, Berlin; and Tomasz Plocharz, Heribert Sutter,

Winfried Brenne, and Ulrich Borgert, Winfried Brenne Architekten, Berlin.

Exhibitions of this scale would be impossible without the extraordinary generosity of the institutions—their directors and staff—and individuals who make their holdings available for loan. We would like to acknowledge Pauline W. Kruseman and Corine de Jong, Amsterdams Historisch Museum/Beurs van Berlage; John Zukowsky and Martha Thorne, The Art Institute of Chicago; Christian Wolsdorff, Bauhaus-Archiv; Eva-Maria Amberger, Berlinische Galerie; Renate Klingbeil, Bezirksamt Mitte von Berlin; Jurgen Reiser, Bezirksamt Steglitz-Zehlendorf von Berlin; Phyllis Lambert and Marie-Agnès Benoit, Canadian Centre for Architecture, Montreal; Elaine Lustig Cohen; Marc Dessauce; Inge Wolf, Deutsches Architekturmuseum, Frankfurt; Wim de Wit and Irene Lotspeich-Phillips, Getty Research Institute, Santa Monica; Joachim C. Heitmann; Rik Vos and Hannie Straver, Instituut Collectie Nederland, Amsterdam; E. J. van Straaten and Atty Heijting, Kröller-Müller Museum, Otterlo; Sigrid Achenbach, Kupferstichkabinett, Schinkel Archiv, Berlin; Andreas Matschenz, Landesarchiv Berlin; Bernd Evers, Kunstbibliothek Berlin; Manfred Fath, Kunsthalle Mannheim; Edwin Lachnit and Barbara von der Heiden-Kopf, Museum Moderner Kunst Stiftung Ludwig, Vienna; Dieter Radicke, Plansammlung der Universitätsbibliothek der TU Berlin; Max Protetch, Max Protetch Gallery, New York; Thomas Ruff; Roland Müller, Stadtarchiv Stuttgart; Jörg Limberg and Andreas Kalesse, Stadtverwaltung Potsdam; Gudrun Schmidt, Heartfield Archive, Stiftung Archiv der Akademie der Künste, Berlin; Albrecht Werwigk; and T. Paul and Margaret Fox Young. I would also like to thank my colleagues at The Museum of Modern Art for lending material out of their respective collections: Peter Galassi, Department of Photography; Deborah Wye, Department of Prints and Illustrated Books; Gary Garrels, Department of Drawings; and Milan Hughston, Library.

A number of people were commissioned to produce elements of the exhibition. Thomas Ruff's spectacular photographic portraits of Mies's work are a wonderful contribution, for

which we are very grateful. Kay Fingerle traveled to each of Mies's extant European works and produced a remarkable series of fresh new views of seemingly well-known buildings. Mark Jones, Barbara Jones, and Omei Eaglerider of Environ Modelmakers, Tempe, Arizona; Ed Howard and Sean Young of Ed Howard Architectural Models, Toledo, Ohio; and Kathleen Seafirth, Richard Sturgeon, and Derek Conde recast a dozen projects, mostly known through drawings or photographs, in three dimensions. John Bennett and Gustavo Bonevardi, Proun Space Studio, directed the work of a number of students from New York's Parsons School of Design—Peter Clark, Jessica Fein, Sarah Ludington, Jason Sean, and Francisco Simmons—to create digital models of several projects, further enhancing our understanding of the relationship between interior and exterior in those key works. Mary Bright designed the curtains, so reminiscent of the work of Lilly Reich, for the video theater and "Silk Cyber-Café," and Kathryn Biddinger contributed her expertise in metalworking for their installation, as well as for other elements in the exhibition. Amanda Reeser produced floor plans of certain projects for which clear documents were not available.

The staff of The Museum of Modern Art devoted enormous effort to ensuring that the exhibition and publication were of the highest quality, reflecting the high priority given to the project, and to all the efforts of the Department of Architecture and Design, by the director of the Museum, Glenn D. Lowry. We would like to express our gratitude to Karl Buchberg and Narelle Jarry (Conservation), Tom Griesel, Paige Knight, Jacek Marczewski, and John Wronn (Imaging Services), Peter Perez, Polly Lai, Cynthia Kramer, John Martin, and Bill Ashley (Exhibition Design and Production), and Susan Palamara (Registrar) for their treatment, documentation, safe handling, and protection of the works. The physical appearance of the exhibition was greatly enhanced by the work of Jerry Neuner and Mark Steigelman (Exhibition Design and Production), as well as by Burns Magruder, Ed Pusz, and Claire Corey (Graphics).

Rebecca Stokes, Monika Dillon, and Michael Margitich (Development) have taken as much care to see that we have the funds to organize the show as Maria DeMarco, Jennifer Russell, and Beatrice Kernan (Exhibitions), and Nancy Adelson and Stephen Clark (General Counsel), have in seeing that we do so on time, on budget, and in an appropriate fashion.

While exhibitions are public events, many are the ways in which the public learns and benefits from them. We in turn have greatly benefited from the efforts of Josiana Bianchi and Patterson Sims (Education), Maggie Lederer and Astrida Valigorsky (New Media), and K Mita (Information Services). Daniela Carboneri and Mary Lou Strahlendorff (Communications), Caroline Baumann (Membership), and Peter Foley and Beth Wildstein (Sales and Marketing) have also greatly assisted us in reaching the largest audience. No exhibition would be complete without an opening, and for that we are grateful to Anne Davy and Ethel Shein (Special Events). There are, of course, many others whose efforts are invaluable to an exhibition like this, including Mikki Carpenter (Imaging Services) and Katherine Krupp and Bonnie Mackay (Sales and Marketing).

As *Mies in Berlin* is being exhibited simultaneously with the exhibition *Mies in America*, we would like to acknowledge the efforts of our colleagues at the Whitney Museum of American Art, New York. Among other collaborative efforts, the preparations for a symposium to be held at Columbia University, with Michael Hays acting as convener, need to be cited. We thank Bernard Tschumi, Dean of the Graduate School of Architecture, Preservation, and Planning, for his hospitality in this regard.

The most long-lasting means of communicating the message of the exhibition is of course the catalogue. Michael Maegraith, the Museum's publisher, has taken a great personal interest in this book, as has his excellent staff. Tony Drobinski's design of the structure of the book makes a complicated series of texts and images accessible in a memorable way. Gina Rossi has executed that design flawlessly and her cover design is nothing short of beautiful. Marc Sapir has followed the book through every stage with an eye on all aspects of its production, and his work on press has ensured its excellent quality. Essays in French and in German were translated by Jeanine Herman and Russell Stockman respectively. We would especially like to express our gratitude to David Frankel, the book's editor, who has with unrivaled exactitude found the right word, its correct spelling, and its most appropriate use. His imprint is evident on every page.

On a day-to-day basis, we have worked for months and in some cases years with a core group of assistants. Each has contributed in a singular way and we are very grateful for their peerless efforts. Throughout the long process of assembling the exhibition, Kate Howe has researched and recorded critical information, documents, and images. Luisa Lorch has assisted in every aspect of the production of the exhibition, anticipating problems and carefully monitoring the complex tasks that are so crucial to transforming a plan into reality. Working directly with archival material, Claire Zimmerman has researched and organized the construction of new material for the exhibition—models, drawings, and digital productions—and has served as staff translator. Finally, Curbie Oestreich has inestimably lightened our burdens by effectively serving as an alter ego in solving countless logistical, institutional, and diplomatic crises before we even heard about them.

—*Terence Riley and Barry Bergdoll*

Photograph Credits

Photographs of works of art reproduced in this volume have been provided in most cases by the owners or custodians of the works, identified in the captions. Individual works of art appearing herein may be protected by copyright in the United States of America or elsewhere, and may thus not be reproduced in any form without the permission of the copyright owners. The following copyright and/or other photograph credits appear at the request of the artists, their heirs or representatives, and/or owners of the works.

Amsterdams Historische Museum: plates 11, 12.
Archigram Archives: p. 329, fig. 12.
The Art Institute of Chicago © 2000. All rights reserved: p. 49, figs. 19, 21; p. 51, fig. 23; p. 335, fig. 14; plate 180.
Photograph courtesy The Art Institute of Chicago. All rights reserved: p. 47, figs. 14, 15; p. 48, figs. 16, 17; p. 49, fig. 20; p. 52, fig. 24.
The Art Institute of Chicago, Hilberseimer Collection. Photograph copyright A. Gross, Illustrationsverlag, Berlin: p. 52, fig. 25.
Artists Rights Society (ARS), New York/ADAGP, Paris/FLC, © 2001: p. 49, fig. 18; p. 23, fig. 17.
Courtesy Baerbel, Christine, and Goetz Wolf: plates 5, 32.
Bauhaus-Archiv, Berlin: p. 43, fig. 13; p. 75, fig. 13; p. 77, fig. 17; p. 79, fig. 21; p. 85, fig. 27; p. 146, fig. 14; p. 326, fig. 4; p. 331, fig. 3; p. 332, fig. 6; plates 27, 28, 31, 33, 45, 49–54.
Thedor Born, Bauhaus-Archiv, Berlin: plate 29.
Carl Rogge, Bauhaus-Archiv Berlin: plate 30.
Barry Bergdoll: p. 73, fig. 10; p. 150, fig. 18.
Berlinische Galerie. Artists Rights Society (ARS), New York/VG Bild-Kunst, Bonn, © 2001: p. 92, fig. 36; p. 96, fig. 40; p. 119, fig. 15; p. 145, fig. 13.
Berlinische Galerie Landesmuseum fur Moderne Kunst Photographie und Architektur: p. 106, frontispiece.
Markus Hawlik, photograph courtesy the Berlinische Galerie, Berlin: p. 36, fig. 1.
Bezirksamt, Zehlendorf: p. 17, fig. 9; p. 77, fig. 16; plate 15.
Bildarchiv Foto Marburg: p. 138, fig. 3.
Bildarchiv Preussischer Kulturbesitz: p. 112, fig. 5.
Centre Canadien d'Architecture/Canadian Centre for Architecture, Montreal: p. 127, figs. 26, 27; p. 364, fig. 2; plates 68–71, 185, 186, 265, 292, 293, 299.
Photograph: Hedrich-Blessing. Courtesy The Chicago Historical Society: p. 21, fig. 14.
Marc Dachy Archives: p. 113, fig. 6.
Deutsche Architektur Museum: plate 284.
Courtesy Erbengemeinschaft Bankier Urbig (Franz Urbig Trust): p. 81, figs. 22–25; p. 148, fig. 16; plates 38, 41, 43.
M. G. Esch, GSW: plate 88.
Ezra Stoller, ESTO: p. 335, fig. 15.
ETSAB Barcelona: p. 93, fig. 37.
Kay Fingerle: p. 20, fig. 12; p. 76, fig. 14; p. 94, fig. 38; p. 150, fig. 19.
Ute Frank: p. 319, fig. 1.
Skot Weidemann, © 1994, 2001, The Frank Lloyd Wright Foundation, Scottsdale, AZ: p. 370, fig. 9.
Getty Research Institute, Los Angeles: p. 69, fig. 5; p. 70, fig. 6; p. 134, frontispiece; plates 279, 281.
Courtesy Daniela Hammer-Tugendhat: p. 97, fig. 42;

p. 99, fig. 46.
David Hirsch: p. 359, figs. 2, 3; p. 360, figs. 5, 6; p. 361, figs. 8–10.
Hochschule für Architektur und Bauwesen, Weimar: p. 120, fig. 16.
Instituut Collectie Nederland/Netherlands Institute for Cultural Heritage, Rijswijk: p. 120, fig. 17.
Craig Konyk: p. 344, fig. 14.
Balthazar Korab: p. 359, fig. 4.
Kunstbibliothek, Berlin: p. 57, figs. 27, 28; p. 60, fig. 32.
Dietmar Katz, Kunstbibliothek, Berlin: p. 66, frontispiece; plates 142–44, 150, 171, 173, 176.
Kunstmuseum im Ehrenhof, Düsseldorf: p. 50, fig. 22.
Reinhard Sacewski, 1999/144/405, Kupferstichkabinett, Staatliche Museen zu Berlin, Bildarchiv Preussischer Kulturbesitz: foldout, front, and p. 138, fig. 2; p. 139, fig. 4.
Landesarchiv, Berlin: foldout, map; p. 34, frontispiece.
Landesbildstelle, Berlin: p. 60, fig. 31.
Erich Lessing, Vienna: p. 73, fig. 9; p. 77, fig. 15.
Detlef Mertins: p. 152, fig. 32.
The Museum of Modern Art, New York: p. 16, figs. 7, 8; p. 82, fig. 26; p. 87, fig. 30; p. 89, fig. 33; p. 122, fig. 20; p. 326, figs. 3, 5; p. 328, fig. 8; p. 341, fig. 9; p. 360, fig. 7; p. 369, fig. 8; plates 19, 58, 61, 62, 79, 82, 85, 87, 95, 147, 245, 247, 248.
The Museum of Modern Art, New York, Imaging Studios Staff—Tom Griesel, Paige Knight, Jacek Marczewski, John Wronn: p. 68, fig. 4; p. 98, fig. 45; p. 96, fig. 41; p. 98, fig. 43; p. 101, fig. 48; p. 104, fig. 51; p. 105, fig. 52; p. 321, fig. 6; p. 322, fig. 8; p. 324, fig. 1; plates 9, 12–14, 22, 46–48, 55–57, 59, 60, 63, 64, 72–74, 76–78, 83, 90, 92–94, 96, 99, 100, 101, 105, 108, 110, 111, 117, 119, 120, 122, 127–29, 133, 134, 141, 152, 157, 160, 162, 166, 175, 177, 181–84, 187–89, 192–206, 208–20, 226–44, 246, 249–64, 266–78, 280, 282, 283, 285–91, 294–98, 300–326.
Photograph: Berliner Bild Bericht, Berlin. The Museum of Modern Art, New York: plates 86, 112, 113, 145, 148, 149, 221, 222, 224.
Courtesy Department of Prints, The Museum of Modern Art, New York: p. 122, fig. 19.
Photograph: Atelier Rudolph Desandalo, Brno. The Museum of Modern Art, New York: plates 158, 164, 168, 169.
Charles Eames, The Museum of Modern Art, New York: p. 13, fig. 3.
Tom Griesel, The Museum of Modern Art, New York: p. 68, figs. 1, 2; p. 70, fig. 7; p. 87, fig. 31; p. 109, fig. 4; p. 118, fig 14; p. 121, fig. 18; p. 123, fig. 21; p. 124, fig. 22; p. 125, figs. 23, 24; p. 327, fig. 6; p. 358, fig. 1.
Photograph: Bill Hedrich, Hedrich-Blessing. The Museum of Modern Art, New York: p. 20, fig. 13.
Photograph: Hedrich-Blessing. The Museum of Modern Art, New York: p. 12, fig. 1; p. 14, fig. 4; p. 15, fig. 6; p. 23, fig. 16; p. 332, fig. 5; plates 10, 39, 42, 106.
Kate Keller, The Museum of Modern Art, New York: p. 68, fig. 1.
Photograph: Emil Leitner. The Museum of Modern Art, New York: plate 223.
Photograph: Dr. Lossen and Co. The Museum of Modern Art, New York: plates 102, 104.
Herbert Matter, The Museum of Modern Art, New York: p. 10, frontispiece.

James Matthews, The Museum of Modern Art, New York: p. 327, fig. 7.
Rolf Petersen, The Museum of Modern Art, New York: p. 12, fig. 2; p. 14, fig. 5; p. 20, fig. 11; p. 329, fig. 11; p. 330, fig. 1; p. 331, figs. 2, 4; p. 362, frontispiece.
Photograph: Arthur Köster, Photowerkstett für Architektur. The Museum of Modern Art, New York: plates 81, 107.
Photograph: Curt Rehbein. The Museum of Modern Art, New York: plate 225.
Photograph: William & Meyer Co., Chicago. The Museum of Modern Art, New York: p. 309, fig. 1; plates 2, 4, 6.
The Museum of Modern Art, The Mies van der Rohe Archive, New York: p. 137, fig. 1; p. 311, fig. 4; p. 332, fig. 7; p. 333, figs. 8–10; p. 354, figs. 11–13; p. 337, fig. 16; p. 339, figs. 1–3; p. 340, figs. 4–6; p. 341, figs. 7, 8, 10; p. 342, figs. 11, 12; p. 343, fig. 13; p. 345, figs. 15, 16; p. 337, fig. 17; p. 346, fig. 17; p. 353, figs. 5, 6; p. 354, fig. 8; plates 11, 91.
Pierre Adler, The Museum of Modern Art, the Mies van der Rohe Archive, New York: p. 86, fig. 29; p. 90, fig. 34; p. 95, fig. 39; p. 102, fig. 49; p. 103, fig. 50; p. 140, fig. 5; p. 140, fig. 6; p. 322, fig. 7; p. 325, fig. 2; p. 328, figs. 9, 10.
Schector Lee, The Museum of Modern Art, the Mies van der Rohe Archive, New York: p. 98, fig. 44; p. 320, fig. 4.
Nederlands Architectuurinstituut/Netherlands Architecture Institute, Rotterdam: p. 126, fig. 25.
Netherland Office for the Arts, The Hague: p. 115, fig. 9.
Fritz Neumeyer: p. 310, figs. 2, 3; p. 314, figs. 5–7.
Plansammlung der Technische Universität Berlin: p. 36, fig. 2; p. 37, fig. 5; p. 39, fig. 6; p. 41, figs. 10, 11.
Marthe Prevot Collection, Limoges. © 2001 Artists Rights Society (ARS), New York/ADAGP, Paris: p. 114, fig. 8.
Sammlung Siegfried Cremer/Hamburger Kunsthalle: p. 108, fig. 2.
Staatliche Museen zu Berlin, Preussischer Kulturbesitz: p. 99, fig. 47; p. 116, fig. 10.
Staatsbibliothek zu Berlin, Preussischer Kulturbesitz: p. 40, fig. 7; p. 364, fig. 1.
Stadtarchiv Krefeld: p. 91, fig. 35.
Städtische Kunsthalle, Mannheim: plate 65.
Stadtverwaltung, Potsdam: plates 40, 66, 67.
Stichting Kröller-Müller Museum Otterlo, The Netherlands: p. 141, fig. 8; p. 142, figs. 9, 10; plates 25–26.
Stiftung Archiv der Akademie der Künste, Berlin-Sammlung Baukunst: p. 58, fig. 29; p. 61, fig. 33.
Stiftung für die Photographie Kunsthaus Zürich: p. 57, fig. 26.
Stiftung Preussische Schlösser und Gärten, Berlin-Brandenburg: p. 75, fig. 12.
Courtesy Albrecht Werwigk: plates 135–40.
Walker Art Center, Minneapolis: p. 357, fig. 9.